# THE LIABILITY OF THE HOLDING COMPANY
# FOR THE DEBTS OF ITS INSOLVENT SUBSIDIARIES

*This study is dedicated*
*to my Mum and Dad*
*for their love and support*

# The Liability of the Holding Company for the Debts of its Insolvent Subsidiaries

ANDREW MUSCAT
LL.D., LL.M. (Lond.), M.Litt. (Oxon.), Ph.D. (Lond.).

## Dartmouth

Aldershot • Brookfield USA • Singapore • Sydney

Published by
Dartmouth Publishing Company Limited
Gower House
Croft Road
Aldershot
Hants GU11 3HR
England

Dartmouth Publishing Company
Old Post Road
Brookfield
Vermont 05036
USA

**British Library Cataloguing in Publication Data**
Muscat, Andrew
   The liability of the holding company for the debts of its insolvent subsidiaries
   1.Holding companies - Law and legislation - England  2.Business failures -
   Law and legislation - England  3.Liability (Law) - England
   I.Title
   344.2'0678

**Library of Congress Cataloging-in-Publication Data**
Muscat, Andrew.
      The liability of the holding company for the debts of its
   insolvent subsidiaries / Andrew Muscat.
         p.    cm.
      Revision of the author's thesis (Ph.D.–University of London, 1994).
      Includes bibliographical references and index.
       ISBN 1-85521-844-5 (hb)
      1. Holding companies–Great Britain. 2. Subsidiary corporations-
   -Great Britain. 3. Corporate debt–Law and legislation–Great
   Britain. 4. Disregard of corporate entity–Great Britain.
   I. Title
   KD2112.M87    1996
   346.41'0668–dc20
   [344.106668]                                              96-20667
                                                                   CIP

ISBN 1-85521 844 5

Printed in Great Britain by Antony Rowe Ltd, Chippenham, Wiltshire

# Foreword

Dr. Muscat's book is based on his Ph.D. thesis submitted to the University of London. The thesis was commended by its distinguished examiners as making a significant and original contribution to existing literature on the problems for creditors posed by the corporate group phenomenon. I respectfully agree.

The author identifies four types of behaviour practised by corporate groups which may prejudice the interests of external creditors or otherwise constitute an abuse of the corporate form: the subservient subsidiary; the inadequately financed subsidiary; the fragmented economic enterprise; and the use of misleading group persona techniques.

Each one of these situations is examined in the light of the relevant principles of English law and of underlying policy considerations. Crucial to the discussion are two related principles of English company law. First, that a company is a juridical entity separate from its shareholders. Secondly, that shareholders are not liable for the debts of their company. The author argues that English law, bound as it is to the entity principle, sometimes condones unacceptable corporate behaviour.

Dr. Muscat submits some radical proposals for reform. The basic thrust of his reform proposals is that in a number of well-defined circumstances "entity law" should give way to an "enterprise" analysis and holding company or group liability be imposed in respect of the debts of insolvent subsidiaries.

Dr. Muscat's book takes account of material available as at 1st May 1995. However, the problems examined in the book continue to occupy the Courts in England. During May 1996, English judges added two further decisions to the jurisprudence on the subject: see *Re H and others* [1996] 2 All E.R. 391 (C.A.) and *Re Polly Peck International plc* [1996] 2 All E.R. 433.

The tension between legal form and economic substance is likely to continue. The book refers to an enormously wide range of primary and secondary sources from the United Kingdom and the United States in particular. It will therefore be of real value to academics and practitioners in the fields of company law and financial law both in the United Kingdom and overseas.

*Gray's Inn*
*London*

*Michael Crystal QC*
*June 1996*

# Acknowledgements

This study is a revised and updated version of my Ph.D. thesis submitted to the University of London in 1994. It was undertaken under the supervision of Harry Rajak, then Senior Lecturer and Director of the Insolvency Research Unit, School of Law, King's College, London, and now Professor of Law at the University of Sussex. To him goes my profound gratitude for his invaluable and expert guidance in supervising the thesis. I could always rely on his time to discuss any aspect of my work and profited from his stimulating comments. His constant encouragement was in itself a source of inspiration.

My thanks also go to my Ph.D. examiners, Professor Len Sealy (S J Berwin Professor of Corporate Law at Gonville and Caius College, Cambridge) and Fiona Macmillan Patfield (Senior Research Fellow in Company and Commercial Law at the Institute of Advanced Legal Studies, University of London) for encouraging me to have the work published.

Finally, I owe much to my wife Louise, and to my children Matthew and Kelly, for their boundless patience and unconditional support throughout my work.

*Andrew Muscat*

---

The author is donating the royalties from the sale of this book to the Malta Down Syndrome Association.

# Table of Contents

*Foreword*                                                                    v
*Acknowledgements*                                                          vii
*Table of Cases*                                                            xxi
*Table of Statutes*                                                         xli


## Chapter 1: Introduction

1.  The corporate group - not a recent phenomenon                            1
2.  Proliferation, growth and power of corporate groups                      3
    2.1.  The corporate group : the typical form of business organisation    3
    2.2.  Widespread transnational character                                 4
    2.3.  Immensity of corporate group activity                              5
    2.4.  Diversity of corporate group activity                              6
    2.5.  Power of corporate groups                                          7
3.  Incredibly complex structures                                            8
4.  Evolution of corporate groups - advantages of corporate group
    organisation                                                            10
    4.1.  Limited liability                                                  11
    4.2.  Tax relief                                                         12
    4.3.  Other benefits                                                     13
5.  Diversity in size                                                        15
6.  Various issues raised by the group phenomenon                            15
    6.1.  A host of complex problems                                         15
    6.2.  Various legal issues                                               16
          6.2.1.  Competition policy and regulation                         16
          6.2.2.  Taxation                                                   17
          6.2.3.  Minority shareholders                                      17
          6.2.4.  Creditor protection                                        18
          6.2.5.  Accountability of directors                                19
          6.2.6.  Employee representation and disclosure of information      19
    6.3.  Heightened complexity in transnational groups                      22
7.  Various interests in the corporate group arrangement                     25
8.  Current law ill-suited to deal with the various issues and conflicting
    interests                                                               27
9.  Desirability of a comprehensive system governing corporate groups        28
10. The principal issue - liability towards creditors                        29

11. Separate juridical personality and limited liability - major obstacles to
    inter-corporate liability                                              30
12. Purpose and scope of work - methodology                                32
    12.1. Purpose and scope of work                                        32
    12.2. The methodology adopted                                          32
13. Relevance of different types of creditors                              33
14. The role of the policy of limited liability                            34
15. Reforms long called for                                                35
16. Disregard of entity for the benefit of the holding company            39
17. Reasons for lack of progress                                           40
18. American law for comparative purposes                                  42
    18.1. Benefit of comparative law generally                             43
    18.2. Relevance of American law                                        43
        18.2.1. Broadly similar cultural, social and political heritage and
                similar level of economic development                      44
        18.2.2. Common underlying conceptual substratum                    44
        18.2.3. Advanced economy                                           45
        18.2.4. Extensive judicial and academic investigations             45
        18.2.5. Similar accounting systems                                 46

## Chapter 2:   The Corporate Group - Risks of Abuse and Unfairness in Certain Behavioural Practices

1.  Introduction                                                           47
2.  Need to study behavioural aspects of corporate group activity          48
3.  What does the investigation reveal?                                    48
4.  Control of corporate groups                                            49
    4.1.  Latent control                                                   49
    4.2.  Factual control                                                  50
    4.3.  Autonomous, co-ordinated and dominated subsidiaries              51
        4.3.1.   Autonomous subsidiaries                                   52
        4.3.2.   Co-ordinated subsidiaries                                 55
        4.3.3.   Dominated subsidiaries                                    57
5.  Domination alone not necessarily abusive or unfair                     61
6.  Issues falling outside the purview of this study                       63
7.  The four categories of abuse or unfairness                             64
8.  The subservient subsidiary situation                                   65
    8.1.  Group profit maximisation                                        65
        8.1.1.   Transfer pricing                                          68
        8.1.2.   Diversion of corporate opportunities                     73
        8.1.3.   Manipulation of assets                                    76

|  |  |
|---|---|
| 8.1.3.1. Commingling of assets | 76 |
| 8.1.3.2. Shuttling of funds and other assets | 77 |
| 8.1.3.3. Draining of assets | 78 |
| 8.1.4. Financial support of group | 79 |
| 8.1.5. Operation of the subsidiary without a profit motive | 81 |
| 8.2. The sham or shell subsidiaries | 82 |
| 8.3. The subservient subsidiary situation - concluding remarks | 83 |
| 9. Inadequate financial structure | 84 |
| 9.1. Success depends on adequate financing | 84 |
| 9.2. Equity and debt - different risks | 84 |
| 9.3. Unfairness in certain financial structures | 85 |
| 9.3.1. The inadequately financed subsidiary | 86 |
| 9.3.2. Holding company competing as creditor | 87 |
| 9.4. Creditor-proof devices | 88 |
| 9.4.1. The loan-cum-mortgage device | 88 |
| 9.4.2. The lease device | 89 |
| 9.5. Creditor-proof devices compounded by "milking" | 90 |
| 9.6. Assumption of risk by creditors | 91 |
| 9.7. Inadequate financial structure results in dependence | 92 |
| 10. Integrated economic enterprise situation | 92 |
| 10.1. Vertical integration | 93 |
| 10.2. Horizontal integration | 93 |
| 10.3. Is integration inequitable? | 93 |
| 10.4. Abusive economic integration | 94 |
| 11. The group persona situation | 95 |
| 12. The potential for abuse or unfairness - concluding remarks | 97 |
| 12.1. Greater likelihood of abuse in the smaller groups | 97 |
| 12.2. Both domestic and transnational groups affected | 98 |
| 12.3. Abuse not necessarily widespread | 98 |
| 12.4. Lack of scientific precision should not bar reform | 101 |

# Chapter 3: The Relevance of Ordinary Principles to the Question of Inter-Corporate Liability

|  |  |
|---|---|
| 1. Introduction | 102 |
| 2. The relationship between separate juridical personality and limited liability | 103 |
| 3. Judicial and statutory inroads | 107 |
| 3.1. Adherence to traditional notions in English law | 107 |
| 3.2. Liberal approach adopted by American courts | 112 |
| 4. Direct holding company liability | 118 |

4.1.  Agency                                                          119
4.2.  Holding company's liability in tort                             125
        4.2.1.  Preliminary                                           125
        4.2.2.  Torts of agent                                        125
        4.2.3.  Assumption of duty                                    125
        4.2.4.  Joint torts                                           127
        4.2.5.  Fraud                                                 129
        4.2.6.  Inducing breach of contract                           129
        4.2.7.  Principal-servant relationship                        130
        4.2.8.  Ordinary tort situations often viewed as instrumentality
                cases                                                 130
4.3.  Vicarious performance                                          130
4.4.  Guarantees                                                     131
4.5.  Inducing contractor's reliance                                132
4.6.  Estoppel                                                      133
4.7.  Fraudulent transfers                                         133
4.8.  Action by liquidator of insolvent subsidiary                 134
4.9.  The "through carriage" cases                                 135
4.10. Conclusion                                                   138

# Chapter 4: Policy Objectives and the Corporate Group

1.  Broad guiding principles                                         139
        1.1.  Preliminary                                            139
        1.2.  Law and social and economic problems                  139
        1.3.  Objectives of company and insolvency law              141
        1.4.  Corporate responsibility                              144
        1.5.  Certainty and predictability vs justice and flexibility  146
        1.6.  Taking account of policies underlying other areas of law  148
        1.7.  Implementation of reform proposals - the need for statutory reform  148
        1.8.  International uniformity                               151
        1.9.  Conflicting policy considerations                     152
2.  The role of limited liability within corporate groups - the need for a
    re-assessment                                                   153
        2.1.  Limited liability and economic development            153
        2.2.  The need for a re-assessment                          154
3.  Historical sequence : limited liability before the advent of corporate
    groups                                                          155
        3.1.  The English position                                  155
        3.2.  The American position                                 158
4.  Socio-economic analysis of limited liability                   161

4.1.   Introduction                                                             161
4.2.   The arguments for limited liability                                      162
       4.2.1.   Creates an incentive to invest - increase in the level of
                economic activity                                              163
       4.2.2.   Encourages socially desirable high-risk projects               167
       4.2.3.   Permits the functioning of an efficient capital market         169
       4.2.4.   Enables the promotion of large projects                        170
       4.2.5.   Diminishes agency and social costs - spreads risks
                efficiently                                                     171
       4.2.6.   Encourages diversified portfolios                              173
       4.2.7.   Reduces costs of contracting around liability                  174
       4.2.8.   Avoids litigation and bankruptcy costs                         174
       4.2.9.   Socio-economic analysis - conclusion                          175
5.  The relevance of different types of creditors                             176
    5.1.   The meaning and role of credit                                      176
    5.2.   Credit in the corporate world                                       176
    5.3.   Existence of "non-consensual" creditors                             177
    5.4.   Corporate liability in tort ignored in the nineteenth century
           debate                                                              178
    5.5.   Limited liability and tort objectives                               180
    5.6.   Parameters of voluntary/involuntary creditors' distinction          182
           5.6.1.   Trade creditors                                            182
           5.6.2.   Involuntary claims arising out of contractual
                    relationships                                              183
           5.6.3.   Employees                                                  184
           5.6.4.   Unsophisticated creditors generally                       185
           5.6.5.   Resources and opportunity to bargain                      186
    5.7.   Relevance of the voluntary/involuntary creditor distinction to the
           holding company liability question                                 187
           5.7.1.   Different standards required                              187
           5.7.2.   The distinction in the subservient subsidiary situation   188
           5.7.3.   The distinction in the under-capitalised subsidiary       188
           5.7.4.   The distinction in the integrated economic enterprise
                    situation                                                  190
           5.7.5.   The distinction in the group persona situation            190
    5.8.   The judicial approach to the voluntary/involuntary creditor
           distinction                                                         191
6.  Limited liability and corporate groups - some concluding remarks          193
7.  Distinction between the holding-subsidiary relationship and the
    one-man company                                                           194
    7.1.   The nature of the distinction                                      194
    7.2.   The distinction in case-law                                        195

8.  Conceptual unity to the reform proposals                          197
    8.1.  The privilege of incorporation                             197
    8.2.  Powers in trust                                            199


## Chapter 5:  The Subservient Subsidiary Situation

1.  Introduction                                                     200
2.  Existing remedies                                                201
    2.1.  Introduction                                               201
    2.2.  Holding company liability in tort                          202
    2.3.  Liability based on agency principles                       203
    2.4.  Fraudulent trading                                         205
          2.4.1.  Introduction                                       205
          2.4.2.  Could a holding company qualify as a person who is
                  knowingly a party to the carrying on of the business?   208
          2.4.3.  Does the implementation of subservient practices signify
                  an intent to defraud creditors?                    209
    2.5.  Wrongful trading                                           211
          2.5.1.  The origin of the remedy                           211
          2.5.2.  The essential features of wrongful trading         211
          2.5.3   Could a holding company qualify as a "shadow
                  director"?                                         213
          2.5.4.  Could the holding company in a subservient subsidiary
                  company situation be held liable for wrongful trading?   217
    2.6.  Adjustment of prior transactions                           218
          2.6.1.  Introduction                                       218
          2.6.2.  Transactions at an undervalue                      220
          2.6.3.  Preferences                                        224
          2.6.4.  Cross-stream and upstream guarantees               226
          2.6.5.  Inadequacy of the statutory provisions             234
    2.7.  Common law duties of directors towards creditors           239
          2.7.1.  Introduction                                       239
          2.7.2.  Directors' fiduciary duties in the group context   240
                  2.7.2.1.  Lack of precise definitions              246
                  2.7.2.2.  Dicta often *obiter*                     247
                  2.7.2.3.  Doctrine perhaps stunted by legislative
                            developments                             249
          2.7.3.  Can a holding company qualify as a director for the
                  purposes of directors' duties towards creditors?   249
          2.7.4.  Inadequacy of doctrine as a remedy in the subservient
                  subsidiary situation                               252

2.8. Lifting the veil jurisprudence 254
   2.8.1. The weakness of English law 254
   2.8.2 The position in American law 256
      2.8.2.1. The " instrumentality" doctrine 256
         2.8.2.1.1. Excessive control 259
         2.8.2.1.2. Improper purpose 261
         2.8.2.1.3. Injury or injustice to the plaintiff 263
      2.8.2.2. Difficulties with the instrumentality doctrine 263
2.9. The doctrine of *ultra vires* 266
2.10. Misfeasance proceedings under section 212 of the Insolvency
    Act 1986 273
3. Special cases of subservient practices 275
   3.1. Diversion of corporate opportunities 275
      3.1.1. The nature of the abuse 275
      3.1.2. The doctrine of corporate opportunities 276
      3.1.3. The doctrine in holding-subsidiary situations 280
         3.1.3.1 The doctrine and common directorships 281
         3.1.3.2. The doctrine and holding company liability 284
      3.1.4. The doctrine and creditor protection 288
   3.2. Commingling of assets 290
      3.2.1. The nature of the abuse 290
      3.2.2. Is a remedy available? 292
4. Extra-legal and indirect checks on subservient practices 293
   4.1. Business and managerial expediency 293
   4.2. Presence of minority shareholders 294
   4.3. Transfer pricing regulation 295
5. Inadequacy of existing remedies 296
6. Proposal for reform 298
   6.1. The essence of the reform proposal 298
   6.2. Details of the reform proposal 300
      6.2.1. Meaning of subservience 300
      6.2.2. Subservience must be customary or habitual 300
      6.2.3. A *gestalt* approach 300
      6.2.4. An overall view 301
      6.2.5. Recovery conditional upon the subsidiary's
         insolvent liquidation 301
      6.2.6. Liability to be by way of contribution to the assets
         of the subsidiary 302
      6.2.7. Voluntary and involuntary creditors 303
      6.2.8. Courts to exercise discretion in determining extent
         of liability 303
      6.2.9. Liability to be complementary to existing remedies 305

# Chapter 6:  The Undercapitalised Subsidiary Situation

1. Introduction                                                                                  306
   1.1. Different definitions of capital                                                          306
   1.2. The need for adequate financing - different forms of financing                           309
2. Flexibility in capital structure - resulting unfairness                                       311
   2.1. Introduction                                                                             311
   2.2. The inadequately financed subsidiary                                                     312
   2.3. Holding company competing as creditor                                                    316
   2.4. Creditor-proof subsidiaries                                                              320
        2.4.1.  The loan-cum-mortgage device                                                     321
        2.4.2.  The lease device                                                                 322
   2.5. Creditor-proof devices compounded by "milking" - keeping the
        subsidiary "dry"                                                                         324
   2.6. Heightened risk of subservience in an inadequately financed
        subsidiary                                                                               324
3. Existing remedies and inadequacy thereof                                                      325
   3.1. Introduction                                                                             325
   3.2. Lack of statutory minimum capital requirements                                           325
   3.3. Fraudulent trading                                                                       332
   3.4. Wrongful trading                                                                         336
   3.5. Common law duties of directors towards creditors                                         340
   3.6. Disqualification of directors                                                            341
   3.7. The doctrine of capital maintenance                                                      344
   3.8. Lifting the veil jurisprudence                                                           346
        3.8.1.  The position in English law                                                      346
        3.8.2.  The position in American law                                                     348
                3.8.2.1. Introduction                                                            348
                3.8.2.2. Undercapitalisation and the instrumentality
                         doctrine                                                                348
                3.8.2.3. Undercapitalisation and the doctrine of
                         subordination                                                           355
        3.8.3.  Inconsistency and imprecision in American position                               360
4. Proposal for reform                                                                           363
   4.1. Statement of principle                                                                   363
   4.2. Various aspects of the proposal                                                          364
        4.2.1.  Requirement of insolvency                                                        364
        4.2.2.  Complementary remedies                                                           365
        4.2.3.  Measuring adequate capitalisation                                                365
                4.2.3.1. Adequate financing                                                      366
                4.2.3.2. "Risk" capital                                                          368
                         (i)  Reasonable expectation of payment                                  375

(ii) Debt-equity ratio 375
(iii) Use made of the loan 378
(iv) Terms of the loan and nomenclature 378
(v) Proportionality of advances with equity holdings 379
(vi) Whether outsiders would make such advances 380
(vii) Borrowing and earnings history 381
(viii) Motive of the parties 381
4.2.3.3. Concluding remarks on adequate financing and "risk" capital 382
4.2.4. The voluntary-involuntary creditor distinction 383
4.2.5. Is the provision of an adequate financial structure a continuing obligation? 385
4.2.6. Intrusive domination - a *sine qua non* condition? 386
4.2.7. Is a causal link necessary? 387
4.2.8. The problem of shareholder-guaranteed loans 388
4.2.9. Duty owed to the subsidiary and not directly to creditors 389
4.2.10. Extent of contribution or subordination in court's discretion 389

# Chapter 7: The Integrated Economic Enterprise Situation

1. Types of economic integration 391
   1.1. Introduction 391
   1.2. Vertical integration 391
   1.3. Horizontal integration 393
   1.4. Various combinations possible 394
2. Should economic integration lead to enterprise liability? 394
   2.1. Arguments for enterprise liability 394
   2.2. Enterprise liability unwarranted 397
3. Abusive economic integration 399
4. Limited legal recognition of the group as an economic unit 401
   4.1. Position under English law 401
       4.1.1. Economic integration generally 401
       4.1.2. Abusive economic integration 404
   4.2. Position under American law 406
       4.2.1. Economic integration generally 406
       4.2.2. Abusive economic integration 411
5. Abusive economic integration - proposal for reform 413

5.1. Statement of principle - holding company or group liability    413
5.2. Voluntary and involuntary creditors    414
5.3. Other aspects of the reform proposal    415


# Chapter 8: The Group Persona Situation

1. Introduction    416
  1.1. The means of promoting a group persona    416
  1.2. The nature of the abuse    417
  1.3. Should a group persona strategy lead to liability?    421
2. Group persona and existing remedies    423
  2.1. Position under English law    423
    2.1.1. Liability as a contracting party    423
    2.1.2. Misrepresentation    423
    2.1.3. Sections 216 and 217 Insolvency Act 1986    425
  2.2. Position under American law    426
    2.2.1. Liability as a contracting party    426
    2.2.2. Group persona sometimes actionable *per se*    426
    2.2.3. A factor in the piercing the veil jurisprudence    427
    2.2.4. A factor in the bankruptcy cases    430
    2.2.5. Impact in the area of product liability    431
3. Proposal for reform    433
  3.1. Holding company liability    433
  3.2. Voluntary and involuntary creditors    434
  3.3. Substantive consolidation    435
  3.4. Other aspects of the reform proposal    435
  3.5. Identifying the proper defendant    436


# Chapter 9: Common Issues

1. Introduction    437
2. The meaning of "holding company" and "group of companies" for purposes of reform proposals    437
  2.1. The need for definitions    437
  2.2. Current definitions of the holding-subsidiary relationship    437
  2.3. Definition for the purposes of this study    441
  2.4. Definition of a "group of companies"    442
  2.5. Should liability be on the immediate holding company or on the ultimate holding company?    443
  2.6. Qualification as a holding company - only the threshold question    444
3. Irrelevant factors to the question of holding company liability    444

3.1. One hundred per cent share ownership    444
3.2. Incorporation by the holding company    445
3.3. Domination and unified management    446
3.4. Common directors    447
3.5. Lack of compliance with corporate formalities    447
3.6. The size of the group    448
3.7. Public and private companies    449
4. Should a floating charge attach to the sums recovered from the holding company?    450
5. Liability in respect of an "acquired" company    453
6. Insolvency of holding company and of various affiliates    456
7. Substantive consolidation    458
7.1. The remedy of substantive consolidation in American law    458
7.2. The role of substantive consolidation in the reform proposals    460
8. Liability in respect of partly owned subsidiaries    462
9. Liability of affiliated companies in the absence of a holding company    464

## Chapter 10: Conclusion

1. Various recommendations for reform made over a number of years    466
2. Effect on other areas of the law    470
3. Call for an international and comprehensive system governing corporate groups    471
4. Possible objections to the reform proposals    472
4.1. Objections to the proposals as a whole    472
4.1.1. "Bailing out"    472
4.1.2. "Flighting of capital"    475
4.1.3. Creditors of the holding company adversely affected    478
4.1.4. Fear of frequent insolvencies    479
4.1.5. Elaborate schemes to avoid liability    479
4.2. Specific objections to an "adequate capitalisation" rule    480
4.2.1. Courts lack requisite expertise    481
4.2.2. Holding company would not advance funds to enable the subsidiary to weather the storm    482
5. Concluding thought    483
*Bibliography of Works Cited*    484
*Index*    513

# Table of Cases

A

A.P. Smith Mfg. Co. v. Barlow, 98 A. 2d 581 (N.J. 1953) .................................... 26
Abbey Glen Property Corp. v. Stumborg (1976) 65 D.L.R. (3d) 235 ................. 242
Abbott Redmont Thinlite Corp. v. Redmont 475 F.2d 85 (2d Cir. 1973) ............ 277
Abraham v. Lake Forest, Inc. 377 So. 2d 465 (La. Ct. App. 1980) .................349, 354
Adams v. Cape Industries plc [1990] BCLC 479 (C.A.) .................. 14, 22, 31, 42, 82
............................................................................ 108, 110, 111, 112, 113
...............................................................................120, 123, 255, 391, 393
.................................................................................401, 402, 403, 405, 474
Adams v. R [1995] 2 BCLC 17 (P.C.) ...................................................... 58, 63
Advocat v. Nexus Industries, Inc. 497 F. Supp. 328 (D. Del. 1980).................... 448
Affiliated Research, Inc. v. United States 351 F.2d 646 (Ct. Cl. 1965).. 369, 376, 380
Aiglon Ltd. and L'Aiglon S.A. v. Gau Shan Co. Ltd. [1993] 1 Lloyd's Rep.
    164 ................................................................................ 78, 109, 134
Albazero, The [1977] A.C. 774 (C.A.), reversed [1977] A.C. 774 (H.L.) ........ 37, 39
................................................................................................... 109
Alexander Dispos-Haul Sys., Inc., Re 36 Bankr. 612 (Bankr. D. Or. 1983)......... 233
Allegheny Airlines, Inc. v. United States 504 F.2d 104 (7th Cir. 1974), cert.
    denied, 421 U.S. 978 (1975)........................................................ 407
Allright Texas, Inc. v. Simons 501 S.W.2d 145 (Tex. Civ. App. 1973) ........... 93, 393
............................................................................................ 406, 416
Am. Circular Loom Co. v. Wilson 84 N.E. 133 (1908)..................................... 276
American Commercial Lines, Inc. v. Ostertag, 582 S.W.2d 51 (Ky. App.
    1979)................................................................................. 115
American Pioneer Life Ins. Co. v. Sandlin 470 So. 2d 657 (Ala. 1985).............. 447
American Trading & Production Corp. v. Fischbach & Moore, Inc. 311
    F.Supp. 412 (N.D. Ill. 1970) .................................................. 59, 407
Amsted Industries, Inc. v. Pollak Industries, Inc. 382 N.E.2d 393 (Ill. App.
    1978)...............................................................................196, 350
Anderson v. Abbott 321 U.S. 349 (1944)................................... 114, 350, 361
Anglo Eastern Bulkships Ltd. v. Ameron, Inc. 556 F. Supp. 1198 (S.D.N.Y.
    1982)................................................................................ 126
Anglo-Austrian Printing and Publishing Union, Re [1985] 2 Ch. 891 ................ 451
ANZ Executors and Trustee Co. Ltd. v. Qintex Ltd. (1990) 2 ACSR 307 .......... 81
Arlington Park Jockey Club v. Sauber 262 F.2d 902 (7th Cir. 1959) .............379, 380
Arnold v. Phillips 117 F.2d 497 (5th Cir. 1941), cert. denied, 313 U.S. 583
    (1941) ................................................................... 359, 361, 378, 381
Ashbury Railway Carriage and Iron Co. Ltd. v. Riche (1875) LR 7 HL 653 ....... 267

Asiatic Banking Corporation, Re (1869) L.R. 4 Ch. 252; .................................... 1
Asiatic Electric Co. Pty. Ltd., Re (1970) 92 W.N. (N.S.W.) 361 ........................ 451
Associated Vendors, Inc. v. Oakland Meat Co. 26 Cal. Rptr. 806 (1963) ........... 115
Atchison, T. & S.F.R. Co. v. Cochran 23 P. 151 (Kan. 1890)............................. 409
Atlantic Coast Line R. Co. v. Riverside Mills 219 U.S. 186 (1911).................... 137
Atlas Maritime Co. S.A. v. Avalon Maritime Ltd. ("The Coral Rose") (No. 1)
    [1991] 1 Lloyd's Rep. 563 (C.A.) .................................37, 87, 111 120,123, 403
Atlas Maritime Co. S.A. v. Avalon Maritime Ltd. ("The Coral Rose") [1990]
    2 Lloyd's Rep. 258 ............................................................................ 82
Atlas Maritime Co. S.A. v. Avalon Maritime Ltd. (No. 3) [1991] 1 W.L.R.
    917 (C.A.) ..............................................    58, 108, 402,403, 472
Attorney General v. Great Eastern Railway Co. (1880) 5 App. Cas. 473............. 267
Augustus Barnett & Son Ltd., Re [1986] BCLC 170 ........... 37, 208, 214, 333, 474
Austin Village, Inc. v. United States 432 F.2d 741 (6th Cir. 1970) ..................... 380
Austinsuite Furniture Ltd., Re [1992] BCLC 1047 .................................338, 342
Automoritz Del Golfo De California S.A. v. Resnick 306 P.2d 1 (1957)........350, 352
Avco Delta Corporation Canada Ltd. v. United States 540 F.2d 258 (7th Cir.
    1976) *cert. denied*, 429 U.S. 1040 (1977) ...................................... 258
Aveling Barford Ltd. v. Perion Ltd. 5 BCC 677 (1989) .................................... 134

## B

B. Johnson & Co. (Builders) Ltd., Re [1955] Ch. 634 ......................................... 451
B.P. Exploration (Libya) Co. Ltd. v. Hunt (No. 2) [1979] 1 W.L.R. 783 ............. 317
Baker Motor Vehicle Co. v. Hunter 238 Fed. 894 (C.C.A. 2d 1916) ..............357, 368
Baker v. Caravan Moving Corp. 561 F.Supp. 337 (N.D. Ill. 1983).................. 80, 392
Bank of Scotland v. Wright [1991] BCLC 244 ................................................. 80, 131
Bank of Tokyo Ltd. v. Karoon [1987] 1 A.C. 45 (C.A.)................................. 92, 403
Bank voor Handel en Scheepvaart N.V. v. Slatford [1953] 1 Q.B. 248
    (C.A.) ...................................................................................123, 124
Barlow v. Budge 127 F.2d 440 (8th Cir.), *cert. denied*, 317 U.S. 647 (1942) ...... 482
Barned's Banking Company, ex p. The Contract Corporation, Re (1867) L.R.
    3 Ch. 105; ................................................................................... 1, 156
Barr & Creelman Mill & Plumbing Supply Co. v. Zoller 109 F.2d 924 (2d Cir.
    1940)............................................................................................... 224
Bartle v. Home Owners Cooperative, Inc. 127 N.E.2d 832 (App. N.Y. 1955)..... 352
Bathory v. Procter & Gamble Distributing Co. 306 F.2d 22 (6th Cir. 1962)........ 393
Bauer v. Commissioner 748 F.2d 1365 (9th Cir. 1984) .......................... 375, 376, 381
Beal v. Chase 31 Mich. 490 (1875)................................................................. 112
Beaver Pipe Tools, Inc. v. Carey 240 F.2d 843 (6th Cir. 1957)......................376, 379
Bell Houses Ltd. v. City Wall Properties Ltd. [1966] 1 Q.B. 207 reversed
    [1966] 2 Q.B. 656 (C.A.)............................................................... 268

Bell Oil & Gas Co. v. Allied Chemical Corp. 431 S.W.2d 336 (Tex. 1968) ...192, 354

Bendix Home Systems, Inc. v. Hurston Enterprises, Inc. 566 F.2d 1039 (5th
 Cir. 1978)............................................................................................................ 407

Berkey v. Third Avenue Railway Co. 155 N.E. 58 (1926)............. 111, 113, 116, 121
 ........................................................................ 137, 352, 393, 408, 428

Bird, Re (ex parte Hill) (1883) 23 Ch.D. 695 C.A. ............................................. 224

Black & Decker Mfg. Co. v. Union Trust Co. 4 N.E.2d 929 (1936).................... 431

Black & White, Inc. v. Love 367 S.W.2d 427 (Ark. 1963) ................................ 411

Blaustein v. Pan American Petroleum & Transport Co. 56 N.E. 2d 705 (N.Y.
 1944)................................................................................................ 74, 280

Bonee v. L. & M. Construction Chemicals 518 F. Supp. 375 (M.D. Tenn.
 1981)...........................................................................................................181, 265

Boulting v. Association of Cinematograph, Television and Allied Technicians
 [1963] 2 Q.B. 606 (C.A.)............................................................................. 240

Boyum v. Johnson 127 F.2d 491 (8th Cir. 1942)................................................ 378

Braddy v. Randolph 352 F.2d 80 (4th Cir. 1965) ............................................. 358

Brady v. Brady [1988] BCLC 20 (C.A.) ...................... 243, 244, 245, 246, 247, 249

Brake & Electric Sales Corp. v. United States 287 F.2d 426 (1st Cir. 1961)........ 376

Branding Iron Steak House, Re 536 F.2d 299 (9th Cir. 1976)............. 358, 368, 377

Bristol and Exeter Ry. Co. v. Collins (1859) 7 H.L.C. 194 ................................ 135

British & Commonwealth Holdings plc, Re (No 3) [1992] BCLC 322................ 356

British Motor Trade Association v. Salvadori [1949] Ch. 556............................ 129

British Thomson-Houston Co. Ltd. v. Sterling Accessories, Ltd. [1924] 2
 Ch.33...................................................................................................... 120

British Waggon Co. v. Lea (1880) 5 Q.B.D. 149 ............................................. 131

Broderip v. Salomon [1895] 2 Ch. 323 (C.A.) ........................................... 157, 183

Brown v. Cork [1985] BCLC 363 .................................................................... 80

Bruce v. Knox 180 F. Supp. 907 (D. Minn. 1960)............................................. 375

Brunner Air Compressor Corp., Re 287 F. Supp. 256 (N.D.N.Y.
 1968)................................................................................ 359, 366, 377

Bugle Press Ltd., Re [1961] 1 Ch. 270 (C.A.).................................................. 64

Burg v. Horn 380 F.2d 897 (2d Cir. 1967)....................................................... 277

Byerlite Corp. v. Williams 286 F.2d 285 (6th Cir. 1960)............................376, 379

## C

Califf v. Coca Cola Co. 326 F. Supp. 540 (N.D. Ill. 1971)............................ 433

Camburn Petroleum Products Ltd., Re [1980] 1 W.L.R. 86 ............................ 331

Canadian Aero Service Ltd. v. O'Malley (1974) 40 D.L.R. (3d) 371 .............276, 279

Cannon Manufacturing Corp. v. Cudahy Packing Co. 267 U.S. 333 (1925)........ 57

Caple v. Raynel Campers, Inc. 526 P.2d 334 (Nev. 1974)................................. 261

Carl Zeiss Stiftung v. V.E.B. Carl Zeiss, Jena 298 F. Supp. 1309 (S.D.N.Y. 1969)..................................................................................................408, 448
Carlesimo v. Schwebel 197 P.2d 167 (Cal. 1948) .............................................. 350
Centmont Corp. v. Marsch 68 F.2d 460 (C.C.A. 1st 1933), *cert. denied* 291 U.S. 680 (1934) ...................................................................................... 360
Charterbridge Corp. Ltd. v. Lloyds Bank Ltd. [1970] Ch. 62 .................. 17, 66, 80
.................................................................................................. 240, 241, 270
Chartmore Ltd., Re [1990] BCLC 673............................................... 312, 342
Chemical Bank New York Trust Co. v. Kheel 369 F.2d 845 (2d Cir. 1966)
................................................................................. 77, 81, 291, 293, 430
Chesapeake Stone Co. v. Holbrook 181 S.W. 953 (1916)................................ 82
Chestnut Hill T. Co. v. Rutter 4 Sergeant & Rawle 6 (Penn. March, 1818) ......... 179
Chicago, Milwaukee & St. Paul Railway Co. v. Minneapolis Civic & Commerce Association 247 U.S. 490 (1918)........................................114, 257
Chohan v. Saggar [1992] BCC 306 ...................................................... 219
City Investment Centres Ltd., Re [1992] BCLC 956............................... 342
City of Warrensburg v. RCA Corp. 550 F. Supp. 1364 (1982)........................... 129
Cladrose Ltd., Re [1990] BCLC 204................................................... 316
Clark v. Workman (1920) 1 I.R. 107 ...................................................... 240
Clayton Brokerage Co. of St. Louis v. Teleswitcher Corp. 418 F. Supp. 83 (E.D. Mo. 1976), *aff'd*, 555 F.2d 1349, 562 F.2d 1137 (8th Cir. 1977)..122, 349
Codomo v. Emanuel 91 So. 2d 653 (Fla. 1956) ...................................... 262
Commercial Solvents Corporation v. E.C. Commission [1974] 1 C.M.L.R. 309 ................................................................................ 16, 50, 401, 402
Commissioner of Inland Revenue v. Sansom [1921] 2 K.B. 492 ...................... 119
Commonwealth Light & Power Co., Re 141 F.2d 734 (7th Cir.), *appeal dismissed*, 322 U.S. 766 (1944)................................................................ 457
Commonwealth v. Blue-Hill Turnpike Corp. 5 Mass. 420 (1809)...................... 106
Company, Re A (No 005009 of 1987), ex parte Copp [1989] BCLC 13 ............ 214
Company, Re A (No. 001418 of 1988) [1991] BCLC 197............................206, 334
Company, Re A (No. 002470 of 1988), ex parte Nicholas [1991] BCLC 480..... 288
Company, Re A (No. 00477 of 1986) [1986] BCLC 376............................... 140
Company, Re A [1985] BCLC 333 (C.A.) ......................................... 9, 111
Connectitcut Co. v. New York, N. H. & H.R. Co. 107 A. 646 (1919)............257, 260
Connelly v. Uniroyal, Inc. 370 N.E.2d 1189 (Ill. App. 1977) *rev'd 389* N.E.2d 155 (Sup. Ct. 1979) ...................................................... 432
Conry v. Baltimore & O.R. Co. 112 F. Supp. 252 (W.D. Pa. 1953) .............137, 429
Consolidated Rock Products Corp. v. DuBois 312 U.S. 510 (1941)........... 293, 445
Consolidated Sun Ray, Inc. v. Oppenstein 355 F.2d 801 (8th Cir. 1964) ........... 262
Continental Vending Machine Corp., Re 517 F.2d 997 (2d. Cir. 1975), *cert. denied sub. nom* James Talcott, Inc. v. Wharton 424 U.S. 913 (1976) .................................................................................407, 460

Cook v. Deeks [1916] 1 A.C. 554 (P.C.) ............................................... 276
Cooper Ex p., Zucco, Re (1875) L.R. 10 Ch. App. 510 ...................................... 450
Copperweld Corporation v. Independence Tube Corporation 104 S. Ct. 2731
    (1984) ........................ 16
Cornford v. Carlton Bank, Limited [(1899] 1 Q.B. 392 ...................................... 179
Costan v. Manila Electric Co. 24 F.2d 383 (2d Cir. 1928) .............. 59, 195, 392, 446
Costello v. Fazio 256 F.2d 903 (9th Cir. 1958) ...................................... 358, 368, 481
Cotman v. Brougham [1918] A.C. 514 ............................... 268
Coventry and Dixon's Case (1880) 14 Ch. D. 660 (C.A) ...................................... 274
Creasey v. Breachwood Motors Ltd. [1992] BCC 638 ................... 78, 108, 111, 393
Cromwell Corp. Ltd. v. Soframa Immobilier (NZ) Ltd. (1992) 6 N.Z.C.L.C.
    67,997 (C.A.) ...................................... 58
Cutts, Re [1956] 1 W.L.R. 728 (C.A.) ............................... 224
Cuyana Realty Company v. United States 382 F.2d 298 (Ct. Cl. 1967) .............. 310

D

D.C. Thomson & Co. Ltd. v. Deakin [1952] 1 Ch. 646 ............................... 129
D.H.N. Food Distributors Ltd. v. Tower Hamlets L.B.C. [1976] 1 W.L.R. 852
    (C.A.) ........................ 31, 39, 50, 110, 392
D.L. Auld Co. v. Park Electrochemical Corp. 553 F. Supp. 804 (E.D.N.Y.
    1982) ........................ 349, 428
Dania Jai-Alai Palace, Inc. v. Sykes 425 So.2d 594 (Fla. Dis. Ct. App. 1983),
    *rev'd*, 450 So.2d 1114 (Fla 1984) ...................................... 430
Daniels v. Daniels [1978] Ch. 406 ............................... 288
Dare To Be Great, Inc. v. Commonwealth ex rel. Hancock 511 S.W.2d 224
    (Ky. 1974) ...................................... 427
Darling Stores Corp. v. Young Realty Co. 121 F.2d 112 (8th Cir.), *cert.*
    *denied*, 314 U.S. 658 (1941) ...................................... 122, 417
David J. Greene & Co. v. Dunhill International, Inc. 249 A.2d 427 (Del. Ch.
    1968) ........................ 74, 285
Davis v. Alexander 269 U.S. 114 (1925) ...................... 135, 136, 137, 259
Davis v. United States Elec. Power and Light Co. 25 A. 982 (1893) ................... 160
De La Vergne Refrigerating Machine Co. v. German Savings Institution 175
    U.S. 40 (1899) ...................................... 2
DeWitt Truck Brokers v. W. Ray Flemming Fruit Co. 540 F.2d 681 (4th Cir.
    1976) ........................ 260, 349, 354
Distillers Co. (Bio-Chemicals) Ltd. v. Thompson [1971] 1 All E.R. 694 ............ 121
Dixie Coal Min. & Mfg. Co. v. Williams 128 So. 799 (Ala. 1930) ..................... 354
Dollar Cleansers and Dyers, Inc. v. MacGregor 161 A. 159 (1932) ................... 177
DRW Property Co., Re 54 B.R. 489 (Bankr. N.D. Tex. 1985) ......................... 458
Dudley v. Smith 504 F.2d 979 (5th Cir. 1974) ............................... 115, 447

Duffy v. Treide 75 F.2d 17 (C.C.A. 4th 1935).................................................... 357
Dunlop Pneumatic Tyre Company, Limited v. David Moseley & Sons,
    Limited [1904] 1 Ch. 164, [1904] 1 Ch. 612 (C.A.)................................... 127
Dunn Appraisal Co. v. Honeywell Information Systems, Inc. 687 F.2d 877
    (6th Cir. 1982)............................................................................................. 427
Durfee v. Durfee & Canning, Inc. 80 N.E.2d 522 (Mass. 1948) ....................... 278
Durham v. Southern Railway Co. 256 F. Supp. 879 (W.D. Va. 1966)................. 55

E

E.B. Tractors Ltd., Re [1987] PCC 313 .............................................................. 206
Eagle Air, Inc. v. Corroon & Black/Dawson & Co. 648 P.2d 1000 (Alaska
    1982).............................................................................................................. 79
East Anglian Railway Co. v. Eastern Counties Railway Co. (1851) 11 CB 775... 267
Eastern Air Lines, Inc. v. Gulf Oil Corp. 415 F.Supp. 429 (1975)................. 66, 70
Eastern Counties Railway Co. v. Broom (1851) 6 Ex. 314 ................................. 179
Ebbw Vale Urban District Council v. South Wales Traffic Area Licensing
    Authority [1951] 2 K.B. 366, [1951] 1 All E.R. 806 (C.A.)................... 30, 121
Ebrahimi v. Westbourne Galleries Ltd. [1973] A.C. 360 (H.L.)......................... 140
Edgar v. Fred Jones Lincoln-Mercury of Oklahoma City, Inc. 524 F.2d 162
    (10th Cir. 1975)............................................................................................ 393
Edmunds v. Brown and Tillard (1668) 1 Lev. 237 ............................................. 104
Edwards Co., Inc. v. Monogram Industries, Inc. 730 F.2d 977 (5th. Cir.
    1984).................................................................................................... 192, 349
Edwards v. Newland & Co. [1950] 2 K.B. 534 .................................................. 131
Ellzey v. Fyr-Pruf, Inc. 376 So.2d 1328 (Miss. 1979)....................................... 278
Equity Corp. v. Milton 221 A.2d 494 (Del. 1966) ............................................ 278
Erickson v. Minnesota and Ontario Power Co. 158 N.W. 979 (1916)............ 88, 119
    ................................................................................................................321, 324
Esal Commodities, Re [1993] BCLC 872 ........................................................... 452
Estate of Mixon v. United States 464 F.2d 394 (5th Cir. 1972)....................378, 379
Etic Ltd., Re [1928] Ch. 861 .............................................................................. 451
European Society Arbitration Acts, Re (1878) 8 Ch. App. 679 ........................... 1
Eurostem Maritime Ltd., Re [1987] PCC 190..................................................... 250
Evans Temple Church of God in Christ and Communication Center, Re, Inc.
    55 B.R. 976 (Bankr. N.D. Ohio 1986) ...................................................... 462
Evans v. Brunner, Mond & Co. Ltd. [1921] 1 Ch. 359....................................... 26
Exchange Bank of Macon v. Macon Construction Co. 25 S.E. 326 (Geo.
    1895)........................................................................................ 30, 198, 406
Exchange Banking Co., Flitcroft's Case Re (1882) 21 Ch. D. 519 (C.A.) .......... 344

F

F.G. (Films) Ltd., Re [1953] 1 W.L.R. 483 .............................................. 82, 123, 346

Farmers Warehouse of Pelham, Inc. v. Collins 137 S.E.2d 619 (1964)............... 196

Fett Roofing & Sheet Metal Co., Re 438 F. Supp. 726 (E.D. Va. 1977), aff'd,
   605 F.2d 1201 (4th Cir. 1979)......................................................359, 376

Feucht v. Real Silk Hosiery Mills, Inc. (1938) 12 N.E. 2d 1019 (Ind. App.)....... 39

Fidenas AG v. Honeywell, Inc. 501 F. Supp. 1029 (S.D.N.Y. 1980)...... 56, 122, 264
   ...............................................................................................258, 407

Fin Hay Realty Co. v. United States 398 F.2d 694 (3d. Cir. 1968)..................... 378

Firestone Tyre and Rubber Co. Ltd. v. Lewellin [1957] 1 All E.R. 561 (H.L.) 58, 204

Fish v. East 114 F.2d 177 (10th Cir. 1940)......................................115, 258

Fisser v. International Bank 282 F.2d 231 (2nd Cir. 1960)............................258, 352

Flora Mir Candy Corp., Re 432 F.2d 1060 (2d Cir. 1970) ............................458, 460

Florida Industrial Commission v. Schwob Co. (1943) 14 So. 2d 666, 153 Fla.
   356 .................................................................................................. 39

FMC Finance Corp. v. Murphree 632 F.2d 413 (5th Cir. 1980)....... 97, 416, 422, 427

Food Fair, Inc., Re 10 Bankr. 123 (Bankr. S.D.N.Y. 1981)............................... 430

Francis O. Day Co. v. Shapiro 267 F.2d 669 (1959) ..................................... 361

Friedman v. Snelling 389 F. Supp. 684 (D. Mass. 1975)................................. 392

G

Gannett Co. v. Larry 221 F.2d 269 (2d Cir. 1955)......................................... 82

Garden City Co. v. Burden 186 F.2d 651 (10th Cir. 1951)......................... 92, 324

Garnac Grain Co., Inc. v. H.M.F. Faure & Fairclough Ltd. [1968] A.C. 1130 ..... 120

Garrett v. Southern Railway Co. 173 F.Supp. 915 (E.D. Tenn. 1959), aff'd,
   278 F.2d. 424 (6th Cir.), *cert. denied*, 364 U.S. 833 (1960) ..................... 55, 56
   .......................................................................................... 107, 114, 407

Gartner v. Snyder 607 F.2d 582 (2d Cir. 1979) ......................................... 353

Geletucha v. 222 Delaware Corp. 7 A.D.2d 315, 182 N.Y.S.2d 893 (4th Dept.
   1959)............................................................................................. 393, 406

Gentry v. Credit Plan Corp. 528 S.W.2d 571 (Tex. 1975)............................... 192

Gentry v. Credit Plan Corporation of Houston 528 S.W.2d 571 (Tex.
   1975)............................................................................................349, 354

George Fischer (Great Britain) Ltd. v. Multi Construction Ltd., Dexion Ltd.
   (third party) [1995] 1 BCLC 260 (C.A.)............................................ 393

Gilbert v. Commissioner 248 F.2d 399 (2d Cir. 1957) ............................... 375, 378

Gilford Motor Co. Ltd. v. Horne [1933] 1 Ch. 935 (C.A.).....................64, 255, 405

Glazer v. Commission on Ethics for Public Employees 431 So. 2d 752 (La.
   1983)............................................................................................... 266

Gledhill v. Fisher & Co. 262 N.W. 371 (1935) ...................................................... 154
Glenn v. Wagner 313 S.E.2d 832 (N.C. Ct. App. 1984).............. 392, 395, 410, 412
Gooding Amusement Co. v. Commissioner 236 F.2d 159 (6th Cir. 1956) .......... 376
Gordon & Breach Science Publishers Ltd., Re [1995] 2 BCLC 189.................... 70
Gramaphones and Typewriters Ltd. v. Stanley [1908] 2 K.B. 89 ..............49, 119, 120
Gray's Inn Construction Co. Ltd., Re [1980] 1 W.L.R. 711 (C.A.).................... 303
Great Eastern Railway v. Turner (1872) L.R. 8 Ch. 149 ................................. 1
Grove v. Flavel (1986) 11 A.C.L.R. 161 ................................................ 245
Gulf C. & S.F. Ry. Co. v. Cities Service Co. 281 Fed. 214 (D. Del. 1922) ......... 129
Gulfco Inv. Corp., Re 593 F.2d 921 (10th Cir. 1979)................................. 458
Guth v. Loft, Inc. 5 A.2d 503 (Del. Sup. Ct. 1939)...................... 75, 276, 278

# H

Handlos v. Litton Industries, Inc. 326 F.Supp. 965 (E.D. Wis. 1971) ................. 428
Hanson Southwest Corp. v. Dal-Mac Construction Co. 554 S.W.2d 712 (Tex.
    Civ. App. 1977)................................................................192, 428
Hanson v. Bradley 10 N.E.2d 259 (1937) ............................................. 192
Harold Holdsworth & Co. (Wakefield) Ltd. v. Caddies [1955] 1 W.L.R. 352
    (H.L.) ................................................39, 49, 50, 108, 110, 401, 402
Harris v. Curtis 87 Cal. Rptr. 614 (App. 1970)............................ 349, 352, 353
Hayes v. Sanitary & Improvement District No. 194, 244 N.W.2d 505 (Neb.
    1976)....................................................................... 448
Hayhurst v. Boyd 300 P. 895 (1931) ................................................ 196
Henderson v. Rounds & Porter Lumber Co. 99 F.Supp. 376 (W.D. Ark. 1951)... 81
    ..........................................................................262, 445, 463
Henry Browne & Son, Ltd. v. Smith [1964] 2 Ll. L.R. 476 ........................... 312
Hertz International, Ltd. v. Richardson 317 So.2d 824 (Fla. Dist. Ct. App.
    1975)..................................................................... 420, 429
Holbrook, Cabot & Rollins Corp. v. Perkins 147 F. 166 (1st Cir.
    1906)................................................................. 81, 90, 324
Holland v. Joy Candy Manufacturing Corp. 145 N.E.2d 101 (Ill. App. 1957)..... 323
Home Loans Fund (NZ) Limited (unreported, M589/78, High Court,
    Christchurch, 7 December 1982................................................ 299
Horsley & Weight Ltd., Re [1982] 3 All E.R. 1045
    (C.A.)................................................ 241, 245, 246, 247, 267
Houston-American Life Ins. Co. v. Tate 358 S.W. 2d 645 (Tex. Civ. App.
    1962)....................................................................... 392
Hunter v. Baker Motor Vehicle Co. 225 Fed. 1006 (N.D.N.Y. 1915) ................. 114
Hydrodam (Corby) Ltd., Re [1994] 2 BCLC 180 ........................... 213, 215, 250

I

Imperial Chemical Industries and others v. E.C. Commission [1972] C.M.L.R. 557 ............... 16
Indian Lake Estates, Inc., Re 448 F.2d 574 (5th Cir. 1971) (35:1) ............... 376
Industrial Development Consultants Ltd. v. Cooley[1972] 1 W.L.R. 443 ............ 279
Industrial Equity Ltd. v. Blackburn (1977) 137 C.L.R. 567, 52 A.L.J.R. 89 ........ 107
Inland Gas Corp., Re 187 F.2d 813 (6th Cir. 1951) ............................ 457
Intel Corporation v. General Instrument Corporation [1991] R.P.C. 235 ............ 127
International Telephone & Tel. Corp. v. Holton 247 F.2d 178 (4th Cir. 1957) ..... 359
Interstate Stores, Inc., Re 15 Collier Bankr. Cas. 634 (Bankr. S.D.N.Y. 1978). 8, 407
Interstate Tel. Co. v. Baltimore & O. Tel. Co. 51 F. 49 (D. Md. 1892), *aff'd* Baltimore and O. Tel. Co. v. Interstate Tel. Co. 54 F. 50 (C.C.A. 4th 1893) ...................... 133
Irving Trust Co. v. Deutsch 73 F.2d 121 (2d. Cir. 1934), *cert. denied*, 294 U.S. 708 (1935) ............... 278
Island Export Finance Ltd. v. Umunna [1986] BCLC 460 ............... 280

J

J.H. Rayner Ltd. v. Dept of Trade and Industry [1989] 3 W.L.R. 969; [1990] BCLC 102 (H.L.) ...................... 103, 476
J.W. Williams Co. v. Leong Sue Ah Quin 186 P. 401 (1919) ............... 196
Jackson v. General Electric Co. 514 P.2d 1170 (Alaska 1973) ............ 56
Japan Petroleum Co. (Nigeria) Ltd. v. Ashland Oil, Inc. 456 F.Supp. 831 (D.Del. 1978) ...................... 56, 428
Jefferson Pilot Broadcasting Co. v. Hilary & Hogan, Inc. 617 F.2d 133 (5th Cir. 1980) ...................... 441
Jeffree v. National Companies & Securities Commission (1989) 15 A.C.L.R. 217 ...................... 249
John Kelley Co. v. Commissioner 326 U.S. 521 (1946) ............... 376, 379
Johnson v. Kinchen 160 So. 2d 296 (La. App. 1964) ............... 153
Jones v. Commissioner 357 F.2d 644 (6th Cir. 1966) ............... 379
Jones v. H.F. Ahmanson & Co. 460 P.2d 464 (1969) ............... 66
Jones v. Lipman [1962] 1 All E.R. 442 ............... 64, 255, 405
Joseph R. Foard Co. v. State of Maryland 219 F. 827 (4th Cir. 1914) ....... 81, 90, 195 ...................... 324, 393, 406
J-R Grain Co. V. FAC, Inc. 627 F.2d 129 (8th Cir. 1980) ............... 481

K

Kamens v. Summit Stainless, Inc. 586 F. Supp. 324 (E.D. Pa. 1984) ............ 266
Kaplan v. Fenton 278 A.2d 834 (Del. 1971) ............... 278

Kasel v. Remington Arms Co. 101 Cal. Rptr. 314 (App. 1972) ........................... 431
Kashfi v. Phibro-Salomon, Inc. 628 F. Supp. 727 (S.D.N.Y. 1986)................. 407
Kent v. Courage and Co. Ltd. (Croft v. Same) (1890) 55 J.P. 264...................... 179
Kentucky Wagon Mfg. Co., Re 3 F. Supp. 958 (W.D. Ky. 1932)........................ 132
Kentucky Wagon Mfg. Co., Re 71 F.2d 802 (C.C.A. 6th Cir. 1934)...... 132, 196, 357
Kingston Dry Dock Co. v. Lake Champlain Transp. Co. 31 F.2d 265 (2d Cir.
    1929)............................................................................................................... 120
Kinsela v. Russell Kinsela Pty. Ltd. (1986) 10 A.C.L.R. 395...................26, 239, 244
    ........................................................................................................... 245, 246
Klein v. Tabatchnick 610 F. 2d 1043 (2d Cir. 1979) ........................................... 228
Kleinwort Benson Ltd. v. Malaysia Mining Corporation Berhad [1989] 1
    W.L.R. 379 (C.A.)............................................................................................ 132
Kohn v. American Metal Climax, Inc. 322 F.Supp. 1331 (E.D. Pa. 1971).......... 438
Kuwait Asia Bank EC v. National Mutual Life Nominees Ltd. [1990] BCLC
    868 (P.C.)....................................................................................... 240, 243, 251


L


L & M Realty Corp. v. Leo 249 F.2d 668 (4th Cir. 1957) ...............................375, 379
L.B. Holliday & Co. Ltd., Re [1986] BCLC 227 .................................................. 355
La Bourgogne [1899] P. 1 ..................................................................................... 120
Laborers Clean-Up Contract Administration Trust Fund v. Uriarte Clean-Up
    Service, Inc. 736 F.2d 516 (9th Cir. 1984)............................. 196, 313, 354, 406
Lalandia, The [1933] P. 56 .................................................................................... 120
Lane, Re 742 F.2d 1311, 1315 (11th Cir. 1984) ................................................... 379
Lawson (HM Inspector of Taxes) v. Johnson Matthey PLC (*Financial Times*,
    19th April 1991) .............................................................................................. 473
Leather's Best, Inc. v. S.S. Mormaclynx 451 F. 2d 800 (2d Cir. 1971)................ 131
Lee v. Lee's Air Farming Ltd. [1961] A.C. 12 (P.C.) ........................................... 120
Leeward Petroleum, Ltd. v. Mene Grande Oil Co. 415 F. Supp. 158 (D. Del.
    1976)................................................................................................................. 129
Lehigh Valley R. Co. v. Delachesa 145 F. 617 (2d. Cir. 1906)........................... 408
Lehigh Valley R. Co. v. Dupont 128 F. 840 (2d Cir. 1904) ...........................135, 136
    ............................................................................................... 404, 408, 429
Levien v. Sinclair Oil Corp. 261 A.2d 911 (Del. Ch. 1969)....................... 282, 285
Lewellyn, Re 26 Bankr. 246 (Bankr. S.D. Iowa 1982)...................................... 430
Liflans Corp. v. United States 390 F.2d 965 (Ct. Cl. 1968)....................375, 376
Lindgren v. L. & P. Estates Ltd. [1968] Ch. 572 (C.A.) ............................. 241, 242
Linn & Lane Timber Co. v. United States 236 U.S. 574 (1915)........................ 112
Littlewoods Mail Order Stores, Ltd. v. McGregor [1969] 3 All E.R. 855
    (C.A.).............................................................................................................. 347
Loewer's Gambrinus Brewery Co., Re 167 F.2d 318 (2d Cir. 1948)...... 85, 87, 317

Lo-Line Electric Motors Ltd., Re [1988] BCLC 698 ............................... 250, 342
Long v. McGlon 263 F. Supp. 96 (D.S.C. 1967) ...................................... 293
Lonrho Ltd. v. Shell Petroleum Co. Ltd. [1980] 2 W.L.R. 367 (C.A.), *aff'd*
   [1980] 1 W.L.R. 627 (H.L.) ...................................26, 30, 103, 107, 240
Louis K. Liggett Co. v. J. M. Lee 288 U.S. 517 (1932) ........................... 2, 7, 159
Louisville & N. R. Co. v. Carter 10 S.W. 2d. 1064 (Ky. Ct. App. 1927)............. 137
Louisville & Nashville R.R. Co. v. Howard 15 Ky. L. Rep. 25 (1893) ............... 137
Louisville & Nasville R. Co. v. Commonwealth of Kentucky 161 U.S. 677
   (1896) ................................................................................... 2, 159
Louisville Banking Co. v. Eisenman 21 S.W. 531 (1893) ..................................... 160
Lowendahl v. Baltimore & O. Ry. 247 A.D. 144, *aff'd*, 6 N.E. 2d 56 (1936)...... 258
   .................................................................................................. 410
Lucey Mfg. Corp. v. Oil City Iron Works 131 So. 57 (La. Ct. App. 1930) .......... 430
Luckenbach S.S. Co. v. W.R. Grace & Co. 267 F. 676 (4th Cir.
   1920)................................................................................ 196, 323, 349
Luckett v. Bethlehem Steel Corp. 618 F.2d 1373 (10th Cir. 1980)...................... 55
Lumber, Inc., Re 124 F. Supp. 302 (D. Or. 1954) .....................................366, 368

M

Mader's Store for Men, Inc., Re 254 N.W.2d 171 (Wis. 1977)........... 354, 367, 382
Mandel v. Scanlon 426 F. Supp. 519 (W.D. Pa. 1977) ...................................... 228
Mangan v. Terminal Transportation System, Inc. 284 N.Y.S. 183 (Sup. Ct.
   1935), *aff'd per curiam*, 247 A.D. 853 (3d Dept. 1936) .....................399, 411
   ..................................................................................................416, 428
Manley, Inc. et al. v. Fallis (1977) 38 C.P.R. (2d) 74, 2 B.L.R. 277...................... 40
Marr v. Postal Union Life Ins. Co. 105 P.2d 649 (1940) ..................................... 266
Marsch v. Southern New England R. Corp. 120 N.E. 120 (Mass. 1918) ............. 360
Matter of the Ohio Corrugating Company 70 B.R. 920 (B. Ct. N.D. Ohio
   1987)........................................................................................... 231
Maund v. Monmouthshire Canal Co. (1842) 4 Man. & G. 452............................ 179
Maxwell Communications Corp plc, Re (No 2) [1994] BCLC 1 ......................... 356
Mayfair Property Co., Re [1898] 2 Ch. 28........................................................... 307
MC Bacon Ltd., Re [1990] BCLC 324 ....................................................... 220, 224
McCandless v. Furlaud 296 U.S. 140 (1935) ...................................................... 289
McCarthy v. Ference 58 A.2d 49 (1948).............................................................. 59
McDermid v. Nash Dredging & Reclamation Co. Ltd. [1987] A.C. 906 ............. 131
McGill v. Grand Trunk Ry. (1892) 19 O.A.R. 245................................................ 135
Merchandise Transport Ltd. v. British Transport Commission [1962] 2 Q.B.
   173 ...................................................................................... 401, 402
Mercury Bay Co-Operative Dairy Co. Ltd. v. Lilley [1946] N.Z.L.R. 766,
   *aff'd* [1947] N.Z.L.R. 632 ........................................................... 26

Merriman v. Standard Grocery Co. 242 N.E.2d 128 (Ind. App. Ct. 1968)........... 421

Mersey Docks and Harbour Board v. Coggins and Griffiths [1947] A.C. 1 ........ 130

Miles v. American Telephone and Telegraph Co. 703 F.2d 193 (5th Cir. 1983) .. 394

............................................................................................................................ 445

Miller v. Miller 222 N.W.2d 71 (Minn. 1974)..................................................... 278

Minifie v. Rowley 202 P. 673 (1921) ................................................................. 113

Minton v. Cavaney 364 P.2d 473 (Cal. App. 1961)............................. 350, 351, 352

............................................................................................................ 353, 354, 360

Mississippi River Grain Elevator, Inc. v. Bartlett & Co. 659 F.2d 1314 (5th
    Cir. 1981)................................................................................................... 406

Mitchell v. Lea Lumber Co. 86 Pac. 405 (1906)..................................................... 133

Mobil Oil Corp. v. Commissioner of Taxes of Vermont 445 U.S. 425 (1980) .... 409

Mobile Steel Co., Re 563 F.2d 692 (5th Cir. 1977)............... 313, 354, 358, 377, 481

Molnlycke A.B. v. Procter & Gamble Ltd. [1992] 1 W.L.R. 1112 (C.A.)............ 127

Moorgate Metals Ltd., Re [1995] 1 BCLC 503...................................................... 250

Morton-Norwich Products, Inc. v. Intercen Ltd. [1978] R.P.C. 501 ..................... 127

Mueller v. Seaboard Commercial Corp. 73 A.2d 905 (1950)............................... 125

Mull v. Colt Co. 31 F.R.D. 154 (S.D.N.Y. 1962)............... 95, 112, 115, 122, 191, 353

............................................................................................. 354, 400, 411, 412, 427

Mullaney, Wells & Company v. Savage 402 N.E.2d 574 (Ill. 1980).................... 276

Multinational Gas and Petrochemical Co. v. Multinational Gas and
    Petrochemical Services [1983] 1 Ch. 258, [1983] 3 W.L.R. 492 (C.A.)    25, 36
............................................................................................. 121, 244, 245, 246

Muschamp v. Lancaster and Preston Junction Ry. (1841) 8 M & W 421 ............ 135

My Bread Baking Co. v. Cumberland Farms, Inc. 233 N.E.2d 748 (Mass.
    1968)................................................................................................. 427, 428

Myers v. Irwin 2 Serg. & Rawle 367 (Pa. 1816) ................................................. 106

Myrick v. Michigan Cent. R.R. 107 U.S. 102 (1883)............................................ 135

## N

Nassau Lens Co. v. Commissioner 308 F.2d 39 (2d Cir. 1962).................... 369, 379

National Marine Service, Inc. v. C.J. Thibodeaux & Co. 501 F.2d 940 (5th
    Cir. 1974)................................................................................................... 354

Nelsen, Re 24 B.R. 701 (Bankr. D. Or. 1982)....................................................... 228

Nelson v. International Paint Co., Inc. 734 F.2d 1084 (5th Cir. 1984) ........ 55, 428

............................................................................................................ 432, 447

New York Credit Men's Adjustment Bureau, Inc. v. Weiss 110 N.E.2d 397
    (1953) ..................................................................................................... 289

New Zealand Shipping Co. Ltd. v. A.M. Satterthwaite & Co. Ltd. ("The
    Eurymedon") [1975] A.C. 154 (P.C.)........................................................ 393

Nicholas v. Soundcraft Electronics Ltd. [1993] BCLC 360 ............................... 242

Nichols v. Thomas 4 Mass. 232 (1808)............................................................. 106
Nicholson v. Permakraft (N.Z.) Ltd. [1985] 1 N.Z.L.R. 242.................. 154, 178, 241
.......................................................................................... 243, 246, 248
Northern Ill. Gas Co. v. Total Energy Leasing Corp. 502 F.Supp. 412 (N.D.
    Ill. 1980) ................................................................................ 65, 263, 312
Northern Natural Gas Co. of Omaha v. Superior Court 134 Cal. Rptr. 850
    (1976) ......................................................................................... 122

O

Obre v. Alban Tractor Co. 179 A.2d 861 (1962)....................................185, 379
Ohio Edison Co. v. Warner Coal Corp. 72 N.E.2d 487 (App. Ohio 1946)........... 361
Ollag Construction Equipment Corp., Re 578 F.2d 904 (2d Cir. 1978) .............. 233
Oriental Investment Co. v. Barclay 25 Tex. Civ. App. 543, 64 S.W. 80 (1901)... 90
.......................................................................................... 323, 324
Orlando Executive Park, Inc. v. P.D.R. 402 So.2d 442 (Fla. Dis. Ct. App.
    1981)......................................................................................... 427, 430
Ostego Waxed Paper Co., Re 14 F. Supp. 15, 16 (W.D. Mich. 1935)................. 357
Overstreet v. Southern Railway Co.  371 F.2d 411 (5th Cir. 1967), *cert.
    denied*, 387 U.S. 912 (1967)............................................................... 410
Owl Fumigating Corp. v. California Cyanide Co. 24 F. 2d 718 (D. Del. 1928) ... 259
.......................................................................................... 428

P

Pacific Can Co. v. Hewes 95 F.2d 42 (9th Cir. 1938).................................. 120, 121
Palmer v. Ring 99 N.Y. Supp. 290 (1906) .............................................. 30
Park Gate Waggon Works Co., Re (1881) 17 Ch. D. 234 (C.A.) ......................... 451
Parker v. Bell Asbestos Mines, Ltd. 607 F. Supp. 1397 (E.D. Pa. 1985) ............. 262
Patrick & Lyon Ltd., Re [1933] Ch. 786 ...................................................... 206, 334
Pauley Petroleum, Inc. v. Continental Oil Co. 239 A.2d 629 (Del. 1969)........... 262
Penick v. Frank E. Basil, Inc. 579 F.Supp. 160 (D.D.C. 1984) ................. 53, 56, 407
Pennsylvania R.R. v. Anoka Nat. Bank 108 F. 482 (8th Cir. 1901)............. 137, 408
Pennsylvania Railroad Co. v. Jones 155 U.S. 333 (1894)..................... 161, 394, 408
People v. Michigan Bell Telephone Co. 224 N.W. 438 (1929) ......................... 122
Pepper v. Litton 308 U.S. 295 (1939) .................................... 117, 238, 289, 355
Pepsi-Cola Metropolitan Bottling Company, Inc. v. Checkers, Inc. 754 F.2d
    10 (1st Cir. 1985)................................................................ 196, 447, 292
Percival v. Wright [1902] 2 Ch. 421................................................................. 243
Peterick v. State of Washington 589 P.2d 251 (Wash. App. 1979)..................... 113
Piedmont Print Works, Inc. v. Receivers of People's State Bank 68 F.2d 110
    (4th Cir. 1934)............................................................................... 431

Pierson v. Jones 625 P.2d 1085 (1981)................................................................ 362
Pioneer Concrete Services Ltd. v. Yelnah Pty. Ltd. (1986) 11 ACLR 108 ......404, 405
Plantation Patterns, Inc. v. Commissioner 462 F.2d 712 (5th Cir. 1972), *cert.*
     *denied*, 409 U.S. 1076 (1972)..............................................................378, 389
Platt v. Bradner Co. 230 P. 633 (1924)............................................................ 122
Pocatello Coca-Cola Bottling Co. v. United States 139 F. Supp. 912 (D. Idaho
     1956)....................................................................................................... 376, 379
Produce Marketing Consortium Ltd. (No. 2), Re [1989] BCLC 520 .......... 211, 212
     .................................................................................................................. 216,451
Professional Investors Life Insurance Co. v. Roussel 445 F. Supp. 687 (D.
     Kan. 1978) ............................................................................................... 258
Puamier v. Barge BT 1793, 395 F. Supp. 1019 (E.D. Va. 1974)....................... 256
Purpoint Ltd., Re [1991] BCLC 491 ............................................. 211, 217, 338, 339

## Q

Queen v. Waverley Construction Co. Ltd. 30 D.L.R. 3d 224 (1972)................... 265

## R

R. v. Birmingham and Gloucester Railway Co. (1842) 3 Q.B. 223..................... 179
R. v. Grantham [1984] BCLC 270 (C.A.) ................................................... 206, 207
R. v. Great North of England Railway Co. (1846) 9 Q.B. 315 ......................... 179
R. v. Kemp [1988] QB 645 (C.A.) ................................................................207, 336
Radio and Television Broadcast Technicians Local Union v. Broadcast
     Service of Mobile, Inc. 380 U.S. 255 (1965)............................................ 409
Radio-Craft Co. v. Westinghouse Electric & Mfg. Co. 7 F.2d 432 (3d Cir.
     1925)....................................................................................................... 122
Rainham Chemical Works, Ltd. v. Belvedere Fish Guano Co. Ltd. [1921] 2
     A.C. 465.................................................................................................. 163
Refco, Inc. v. Farm Production Association, Inc. 844 F.2d 525 (8th Cir. 1988)... 349
Regal (Hastings) Ltd. v. Gulliver [1967] 2 A.C. 134...................................... 279
Rego Crescent Corp. 23 Bankr. 958 (Bank. E.D.N.Y. 1982)............................. 359
Reliable Manufacturing Corp., Re 703 F.2d 996 (7th Cir. 1983) ...................272, 273
Revlon, Inc. v. Cripps & Lee Ltd. [1980] F.S.R. 85 (C.A.)...... 13, 50, 55, 58, 59, 66
     ................................................................................. 108, 394, 402, 416, 417
Ring v. Sutton (1980) 5 A.C.L.R. 546 (C.A. N.S.W.) ................................... 79, 245
Roberta, The (1937) 58 Ll.L.R. 159...................................................... 31, 108, 196
Roberts v. Coventry Corporation [1947] 1 All E.R. 308 .................................. 196
Robinson v. Chase Maintenance Corp. 190 N.Y.S.2d 773 (Sup. Ct.
     1959)................................................................................... 95, 400, 411, 412

Rolled Steel Products (Holdings) Ltd. v. British Steel Corporation [1986] Ch. 246 (C.A.) .................................................................................. 267, 269, 270

Rounds & Porter Lumber Co. v. Burns 225 S.W.2d 1 (1949) .......................... 81

Rowan v. United States 219 F.2d 51 (5th Cir. 1955) .................................... 376

Roy v. Chesapeake and O.R. Co. 57 S.E. 39 (1907) .................................... 135

Rubin v. Manufacturers Hanover Trust Company 661 f. 2d 979 (2d Cir. 1981) .. 227
.................................................................................................... 231

Rur. Mun. of Assiniboia v. Suburban Rapid Transit Co. [1931] 2 D.L.R. 862, 39 Man. L.R. 402 *sub. nom.* Re Suburban Rapid Transit Co., Winnipeg Electric Co. and Rural Municipality of Assiniboia (C.A.) ..................... 30, 107

Ryde Holdings Ltd. v. Sorenson [1988] 2 NZLR 157 .................................... 12

## S

Saccharin Corporation, Limited v. Chemische Fabrik A.G. [1911] 2 K.B. 516 (C.A.) ....................................................................................... 120

Sagebrush Sales Co. v. Strauss 605 S.W.2d 857 (Tex. 1980) ......................... 416

Salmon v. Hamborough Co.(1671) 1 Ch. Cas. 204 (H.L.) ............................ 105

Salomon v. A. Salomon and Co. Ltd. [1897] A.C. 22 (H.L.) ...... 11, 30, 35, 103, 121
.............................................................................. 149, 157, 177,321

Sampsell v. Imperial Paper & Color Corp. 313 U.S. 215 (1941) ..................... 355

Sarflax Ltd., Re [1979] 2 W.L.R. 202 ...................................................... 210

Sarkes Tarzian, Inc. v. United States 240 F.2d 467 (7th Cir. 1957) ................. 382

Schildberg Rock Products Co. v. Brooks 140 N.W.2d 132 (Iowa 1966) ............ 278

Schlamowitz v. Pinehurst, Inc. 229 F.Supp. 278 (1964) ................................ 83

Schlecht v. Equitable Builders, Inc. 535 P.2d 86 (Or. 1975) ..................... 80,263

Schmid v. Roehm GmbH 544 F. Supp. 272 (D. Kan. 1982) ...................... 115, 408

Schouls v. Canadian Meat Processing Corp et al. (1983) 147 D.L.R. (3d) 81 ..... 40

Schreiber v. Bryan 396 A.2d 512 (Del. Ch. 1978) ............................ 75, 278, 283

Scottish Co-Operative Wholesale Society Ltd. v. Meyer [1959] A.C. 324 (H.L.) ......................................................................... 40, 108, 217
.............................................................. 240, 242, 283, 287, 401

Securitibank Ltd. (No. 2), Re [11978] 2 NZLR 136 ..................................... 402

Segan Construction Corporation v. Nor-West Builders, Inc. 274 F. Supp. 691 (D. Conn. 1967) ............................................................................ 352

Selangor United Rubber Estates Ltd. v. Cradock (No. 3) [1968] 1 W.L.R. 1555 ........................................................................................ 240

Service Iron Foundry, Inc. v. M.A. Bell Co. 588 P.2d 463 (Kan. App. 1978) ...... 352

Sharp v. Jackson [1899] A.C. 419 H.C. ................................................... 224

Shlensky v. Wrigley, 237 N.E. 2d 776 (Ill. App. Ct. 1968) ............................. 26

Sinclair Oil Corp. v. Levien 280 A.2d 717 (Del. 1971) .................. 74, 79, 286, 287

Sisco-Hamilton Co. v. Lennon 240 F.2d 68 (7th Cir. 1957) ........................... 410

Slappey Drive Industrial Park v. United States 561 F.2d 572 (5th Cir. 1977)...... 310
Small v. Williams 313 F.2d 39 (4th Cir. 1963).................................................... 482
Smith & Fawcett Ltd., Re [1942] 1 All E.R. 542 (C.A.) ...................................... 247
Smith Kline & French Laboratories Ltd. v. Bloch [1983] 2 All E.R. 72 ............. 121
Smith, Stone & Knight Ltd. v. Birmingham Corporation [1939] 4 All E.R.
    116 ................................................................................ 39, 122, 123, 196
Snider Bros., Inc., Re 18 B.R. 230 (Bankr. D. Mass. 1982)....................... 393, 459
Soanes v. Baltimore & O. R. Co., Inc. 89 F.R.D. 430 (E.D.N.Y. 1981) .............. 410
Solar International Shipping Agency, Inc. v. Eastern Proteins Export, Inc. 778
    F.2d 922 (2d Cir. 1985).................................................................... 83
Southard & Co. Ltd., Re [1979] 1 W.L.R. 1198 (C.A.)........................... 37, 89, 321
Southern Pacific Co. v. Bogert 250 U.S. 483 (1919) ................................. 250, 284
Southern Ry. Co. v. Crosby 201 F.2d 878 (4th Cir. 1953).................................. 137
Soverio v. Franklin National Bank of Long Island 328 F.2d 446 (2d Cir. 1964).. 293
    ................................................................................ 416, 430, 460
Spear v. Grant 16 Mass. 9 (1819)........................................................... 106
Specht v. Missouri Pac. R. Co. 191 N.W. 905 (1923) ....................................... 137
St. Michael Uranium Mines Ltd. v. Rayrock Mines Ltd. (1958) 15 D.L.R.
    (2d) 609 ...................................................................................... 306, 308
St. Paul Fire & Marine Insurance Co. v. Arkla Chemical Corp. 435 F.2d 857
    (8th Cir. 1971)................................................................................ 410
Stanford Services Ltd., Re [1987] BCLC 607.............................................. 182, 342
State ex rel. Sorensen v. Weston Bank (1933) 251 N.W. 164 (Neb. 1933) .......... 40
States v. Jon-T Chemicals, Inc. 768 F.2d 686 (5th Cir. 1985), *cert. denied*,
    106 S. Ct. 1194 (1986)...................................................................... 447
Steven v. Roscoe Turner Aeronautical Corp. 324 F.2d 157 (7th Cir. 1963)...... 59, 114
    ................................................................................ 263, 256, 258, 349, 360
Stinnett's Pontiac Service, Inc. v. Commissioner 730 F.2d 634 (11th Cir.
    1984)....................................................................................... 379, 380
Stone v. Cleveland, C.C. & St. L. Ry. Co. 95 N.E. 816 (1911) .................... 137, 409
Stone v. Eacho 127 F.2d 284 *reh'g denied*, 128 F.2d 16 (4th Cir.), *cert.
    denied*, 317 U.S. 635 (1942)................................................................ 430
Stone v. Marshall Oil Co. 57 Atl. 183 (1904) ......................................... 76, 291
Stotter v. Arimaru Holdings Ltd. [1994] 2 N.Z.L.R. 655 (C.A.)........................ 356
Sun Properties, Inc. v. United States 220 F.2d 171 (5th Cir. 1955).................... 376
Sweet v. Watson's Nursery 92 P.2d 812 (1939)....................................... 293

## T

T.E. Mercer Trucking Co., Re 16 B.R. 176 (Bankr. N.D. Tex. 1981) .................. 458
T.S.B. Private Bank International S.A. v. Chabra [1992] 1 W.L.R. 231............ 9, 109
Tasbian Ltd., Re (No. 3) [1991] BCLC 792 ............................................. 250

Taylor v. Chichester and Midhurst Railway Co. (1867) LR 2 Exch 356 .............. 267

Taylor v. Standard Gas & Electric Corporation 306 U.S. 307 (1939) ....... 65, 79, 113
.................................................................................... 238, 357, 358, 381, 445

Telefest, Inc. v. VU-TV, Inc. 591 F. Supp. 1368 (D.N.J. 1984).................... 231, 233

Teller v. Clear Service Co. 173 N.Y.S. 2d 183 (Sup. Ct. 1958).............. 353, 399, 400
................................................................................................................ 411, 412

Texas Farm Bureau v. United States 725 F.2d 307 (5th Cir. 1984), *cert.
denied*, 469 U.S. 1106 (1985)....................................................... 378, 382

Texas Industries, Inc. v. Dupuy & Dupuy Developers, Inc., 227 So. 2d 265
(La. Ct. App. 1969)................................................................................. 350

Texas Industries, Inc. v. Lucas 634 S.W.2d 748 (Tex. Ct. App. 1982)...........349, 416

The Motel Co. v. Commissioner 340 F.2d 445 (2d Cir. 1965) ........................... 376

Theodora Holding Corp. v. Henderson 257 A. 2d 398 (Del. Ch. 1969).............. 26

Thorne v. Silverleaf [1994] 1 BCLC 637 (C.A.)................................................. 425

Tigrett v. Pointer 580 S.W.2d 375 (Tex. Civ. App. 1979) .......... 349, 352, 377, 394

Townsend v. Haworth (1875) 48 L.J.Ch. 770..................................................... 127

Trans World Airlines, Inc. v. Summa Corp. 374 A.2d 5 (Del. Ch. 1977)............. 286

Transystems, Inc., Re 569 F.2d 1364 (5th Cir. 1978)......................................... 375

Trent v. Atlantic City Electric Co. 334 F.2d 847 (3d Cir. 1964)......................... 59

Trevor v. Whitworth (1877) 12 App. Cas. 409 (H.L.)............................... 332, 345

Trimble Co., Re 479 F.2d 103 (3d Cir. 1973)..................................................... 380

Tri-State Developers, Inc. v. Moore 343 S.W.2d 812 (App. Ky. 1961)............... 330

Tunstall v. Steigmann [1962] 2. Q.B. 593 ................................................... 40, 255

TWA, Inc. v. Summa Corp. 374 A.2d 5 (1977)................................................... 287

U

Unilever plc v. Gillette (U.K.) Ltd. [1989] R.P.C. 583 (C.A.)...................... 127, 128

Union Sulphur Co. v. Freeport Texas Co. 251 Fed. 634 (D. Del. 1918) .............. 129

United Rubber, Cork, Linoleum & Plastic Workers of America, AFL-CIO v.
Great American Industries, Inc. 479 F. Supp. 216 (S.D.N.Y. 1979) ........... 354

United States v. Reserve Mining Co. 380 F.Supp. 11 (D. Minn. 1974)
*modified*, 514 F.2d 492 (8th Cir. 1975)........................................... 393

United States of America v. Gleneagles Investment Co., Inc. 565 F. Supp. 556
(1983), *aff'd sub nom.* United States of America v. Tabor Court Realty
Corp. 803 F. 2d 1288 (3rd Cir. 1986, *cert. denied* McClellan Realty Co.
v. United States 107 S.Ct. 3229 (1987)........................................... 227

United States v. Firestone Tire & Rubber Co. 518 F. Supp. 1021 (N.D. Ohio
1981)....................................................................................... 265

United States v. Healthwin-Midtown Convalescent Hospital and
Rehabilitation Center, Inc. 511 F. Supp. 416 (C.D. Cal. 1981)................... 362

United States v. Hoyt 53 F.(2d) 881 (S.D.N.Y. 1931) ....................................... 113

United States v. Jon-T Chemicals, Inc. 768 F.2d 686 (5th Cir. 1985), *cert.*
*denied*, 106 S. Ct. 1194 (1986) ..................................................... 114, 349, 445
United States v. Lehigh Valley R.R. Co. 220 U.S. 257 (1911) .................... 112, 257
United States v. Milwaukee Refrigerator Transit Co. 142 F.2d. 247 (C.C.E.D.
Wis. 1905) ................................................................................... 64, 103, 112
United States v. Reading Co. 253 U.S. 26 (1920) ................................................ 257
United States v. Reserve Mining Co. 380 F. Supp. 11, 28 (D. Minn. 1971),
*modified on other grounds*, 514 F.2d 492 (8th Cir. 1975) ........................... 82
United States v. West 299 F. Supp. 661 (D. Del. 1969) ...................................... 228
United States v. Wood 366 F. Supp. 1074 (1973), *rev'd* 505 F.2d 1400
(C.C.P.A. 1974) ....................................................................................... 259

## V

Vaughn v. Chrysler Corp. 442 F.2d 619 (10th Cir.), *cert. denied*, 404 U.S. 857
(1971) ............................................................................................... 397, 431
Vecco Const. Indus., Inc., Re 4 B.R. 407 (Bankr. E.D. Va. 1980) ................... 3, 12
...................................................................................................... 407, 458

## W

Walker v. Wimborne and others (1976) 50 A.L.J.R. 446 ........... 77, 78, 81, 239, 248
Walkovszky v. Carlton 223 N.E.2d 6 (1966) ..................... 95, 195, 352, 400, 429
Wallace v. Tusla Yellow Cab Taxi & Baggage Co. 61 P.2d 645 (Okl. 1936) ....... 354
Wallersteiner v. Moir (No. 1) [1974] 3 All E.R. 217 (C.A.) ......................... 123, 124
Warshaw v. Calhoun 221 A.2d 487 (Del. 1966) .......................................... 282, 284
Watertown Paper Co., Re 169 F. 252 (2d Cir. 1909) ............... 114, 257, 357, 392
Watson v. The Ambergate, Nottingham and Boston Ry. Co. (1851) 15 Jur
448, Cox M & H 495 ................................................................................. 135
Weinberger v. UOP, Inc. 457 A.2d 701 (Del. Supr. 1983) ................................. 281
Weisser v. Mursam Shoe Corp. 127 F.2d 344 (2d Cir. 1942) ....................... 77, 354
West Mercia Safetywear Ltd. v. Dodd [1988] BCLC 250 (C.A.) ................ 243, 244
...................................................................................................... 246, 249
Wheeler v. Superior Mortgage Co. 17 Cal. Rptr. 291 (1961) ...................... 350, 352
White and Osmond (Parkstone) Ltd., Re (unreported, 30 June 1960 Ch.D)
...................................................................................................... 206, 334
White v. G.W. Marquardt & Sons 74 N.W. 930 (1898) .................................... 160
White v. Winchester Land Development Corp. 584 S.W.2d 56 (Ky. App.
1979) ...................................................................................................... 177
Wichita Falls & N.W. Ry. Co. v. Puckett, 157 P. 112 (1916) ........................... 137
Wilby v. West Cornwall Railway Co. (1858) 2 H & N 703 ............................... 135
Willem Van Driel, The Sr. 252 F. 35 (4th Cir. 1918) ............................... 57, 195

William C. Leitch Brothers Limited, Re [1932] 2 Ch. 71 ............ 206, 333
William Cory & Son Ltd. v. Dorman Long & Co. Ltd. [1936] 2 All E.R. 386
    (C.A.) ................................................................................ 57, 119, 121
William Thomas & Co. Limited, Re [1915] 1 Ch. 325 ...................... 1
Willmott v. London Celluloid Co. [1886] 31 Ch. D. 425 ................... 450
Winkworth v. Edward Baron Development Co. Ltd. [1987] 1 All E.R. 114
    (H.L.) ............................................................................ 243, 248, 249
Wood v. Dummer 30 Fed. Cas. 435 (C.C.D. Me. 1824) ..................... 106
Woolfson v. Strathclyde Regional Council (1978) S.L.T. 159 (H.L. Sc.) ........ 31
    .............................................................. 109, 110, 255, 402, 404
Worldwide Carriers Ltd. v. Aris Steamship Co. 301 F.Supp. 64 (S.D.N.Y.
    1968) .................................................... 79, 258, 292, 406

Y

Yagerphone Limited, Re [1935] Ch. 392 .................... 450, 452
Yarborough v. The Bank of England (1812) 16 East 6 ........................ 179

Z

Zaist v. Olson 227 A.2d 552 (Conn. 1967) ............... 114, 115, 258, 262, 264
Zidell v. Zidell 560 P.2d 1091 (1977) ................................... 278
Zubik v. Zubik 384 F.2d 267 (3d Cir. 1967), *cert. denied*, 390 U.S. 988
    (1968) ............................................................... 196, 265

# Table of Statutes

**United Kingdom**

Bankruptcy Act 1914
  s. 44(1) .................................................................................................. 224
Building Societies Act 1986
  ss. 7-9 ................................................................................................... 326
  s. 22(1) .................................................................................................. 118
Chartered Companies Act 1837 ............................................................... 155
Companies Act 1862
  s. 165 .................................................................................................... 274
Companies Act 1928
  s. 75 ...................................................................................................... 205
Companies Act 1929
  s. 275 ............................................................................................. 205, 333
Companies Act 1948
  s. 150 .................................................................................................... 112
  s. 152(1) ................................................................................................. 20
  s. 165(b) ........................................................................... 58, 207, 241, 284
  s. 332 ........................................................................................ 205, 207, 334
  Sched. 8 para. 17-22 ............................................................................. 20
Companies Act 1980 ............................................................. 330, 419, 468
  s. 3(2) .................................................................................................... 328
  s. 85(1) .................................................................................................. 328
Companies Act 1985
  s. 2(5)(a) ............................................................................................... 307
  s. 11 ........................................................................... 84, 312, 326, 328
  s. 23 ........................................................................................................ 27
  s. 35 ...................................................................................................... 268
  s. 35(1) ........................................................................................... 268, 269
  s. 35(2) ........................................................................................... 268, 270
  s. 35(3) .................................................................................................. 269
  s. 35A .............................................................................................. 270, 271
  s. 35B .................................................................................................... 268
  ss. 43-45 ............................................................................................... 326
  s. 101 .................................................................................................... 326
  s. 113(2)(a) ........................................................................................... 140
  s. 117 .................................................................................................... 326
  s. 117(8) ............................................................................................... 326
  s. 120 .................................................................................................... 307

ss. 135-141 ............................................................................................. 345
s. 142(1) ......................................................................................... 332, 386
ss. 143-150 ............................................................................................. 345
s. 151 ..................................................................................................... 248
s. 153 .............................................................................................. 27, 248
ss. 151-158 ............................................................................................. 345
s. 159(1) ................................................................................................. 310
s. 221 ..................................................................................................... 216
s. 221(1) ................................................................................................. 291
s. 221(2)(b) ............................................................................................ 291
s. 221(6) ................................................................................................. 292
ss. 221-262A ............................................................................................ 20
ss. 227-232 .............................................................................................. 27
s. 258 ................................................................................... 50, 439, 440
s. 258(2)(a),(b),(d) ................................................................................ 439
s. 259 ..................................................................................................... 439
s. 260(1) ................................................................................................. 440
s. 263 .............................................................................................. 79, 345
s. 264 ....................................................................................... 17, 79, 141
s. 264(1) ................................................................................................... 80
s. 309 ....................................................................................................... 26
s. 310 ..................................................................................................... 251
s. 318(1)(c) ............................................................................................. 27
s. 319 ............................................................................................. 438, 442
s. 319(1) ................................................................................................... 27
s. 320(1) ................................................................................................... 27
s. 321 ....................................................................................................... 27
ss. 322-342 ............................................................................................ 438
s. 323(3) ................................................................................................... 27
s. 324 .............................................................................................. 17, 27
s. 330 ....................................................................................................... 27
s. 346 ....................................................................................................... 27
s. 382 ..................................................................................................... 216
s. 433 ....................................................................................................... 27
s. 458 .............................................................................................. 64, 207
s. 459 ..................................................................................................... 140
s. 461 ..................................................................................................... 304
s. 630 ..................................................................................................... 205
s. 719 ....................................................................................................... 26
s. 727 ..................................................................................................... 304
s. 736A ................................................................................................... 438
s. 736B ................................................................................................... 439

s. 737(1) .................................................................................................. 307
s. 741(1) .................................................................................................. 250
s. 741(2) ......................................................................................... 251, 343
s.736 ....................................................................................................... 438
Sched. 4-6 ......................................................................................... 20, 27
Sched. 10A ............................................................................................ 439
Sched. 10A para. (4) ...................................................................... 50, 440
Companies Act 1989
s. 21(1) ................................................................................................... 439
s. 22 ....................................................................................................... 440
s. 108 ..................................................................................................... 269
s. 108(1) ................................................................................................. 268
s. 109 ....................................................................................................... 22
s. 144 ..................................................................................................... 439
s. 144(1) ................................................................................................. 438
Schedule 9 ............................................................................................. 439
Companies Clauses Consolidation Act 1845 ....................................... 155
Companies (Winding-up) Act 1890
s. 10 ....................................................................................................... 451
Company Directors Disqualification Act 1986
s. 1(1)(a) ................................................................................................ 343
s. 1(1)(d) ................................................................................................ 343
s. 2 ................................................................................................. 341, 342
s. 3 ................................................................................................. 341, 342
s. 4 ................................................................................................. 341, 342
s. 5 ................................................................................................. 341, 343
s. 6 ................................................................................................. 302, 343
s. 7(1)(b) ................................................................................................ 343
ss. 6-9 .................................................................................................... 341
s. 10(1) ................................................................................................... 343
ss. 10-12 ................................................................................................ 341
s. 15(1)(a) .............................................................................................. 344
s. 15(3)(a) .............................................................................................. 344
s. 16(2) ................................................................................................... 342
s. 22(4) ........................................................................................... 250, 343
s. 22(5) ................................................................................................... 343
Employers' Liability (Compulsory Insurance) Act 1969
s. 1 ......................................................................................................... 185
European Communities Act 1972
s. 9(1) ..................................................................................................... 268
Finance Act 1967
s. 20 ....................................................................................................... 112

Finance Act 1995
  s. 87.................................................................................................. 371
Financial Services Act 1986
  Sched. 1 para. 18.............................................................................. 27
Income and Corporation Taxes Act 1988
  s. 74(j)........................................................................................... 183
  s. 209(2)(da)(i)................................................................................ 371
  s. 209(2)(da)(ii).............................................................................. 371
  s. 209(2)(e)(iv), (v) ........................................................................ 371
  s. 218(1) ......................................................................................... 438
  s. 229(1) ......................................................................................... 438
  s. 413(3)(b) ..................................................................................... 438
  s. 402-413 ....................................................................................... 12
  s. 770.............................................................................................. 71
  s. 773(4) .......................................................................................... 71
  s. 838.............................................................................................. 438
  s. 839(5) .......................................................................................... 438
Insolvency Act 1985
  s. 12(9)............................................................................................ 341
  s. 15(1)-(5) ...................................................................................... 341
  s. 15(7)............................................................................................ 341
  Sched. 9 para. 4............................................................................... 341
Insolvency Act 1986
  s. 8(1)............................................................................................. 302
  s. 74(2)(f)........................................................................................ 355
  s. 107.......................................................................................... 303, 355
  s. 112(2) .......................................................................................... 304
  s. 122(1)(f)....................................................................................... 386
  s. 122(1)(g) .................................................................................. 140, 148
  s. 123........................................................................... 223, 302, 386
  s. 126(1) .......................................................................................... 304
  s. 130(2) .......................................................................................... 304
  s. 183(2)(c)...................................................................................... 304
  s. 187............................................................................................... 26
  s. 207............................................................................................... 206
  s. 212(1) .......................................................................................... 273
  s. 213........................................................................................... 332, 365
  s. 213(1) .......................................................................................... 208
  s. 213 (2) ..................................................................................... 304, 335
  s. 214.............................31, 134, 148, 206, 211, 212, 339, 365, 386, 451
  s. 214(4) .......................................................................................... 212

s. 214(5) ............................................................................................... 216
s. 214(7) ................................................................................................. 31
s. 215(4) ............................................................................... 88, 337, 355
s. 216 .................................................................................................... 425
s. 217 .................................................................................................... 425
s. 238 ............................................................... 219, 220, 223, 365
s. 238(3) ............................................................................................... 220
s. 238(4)(b) .......................................................................................... 220
s. 238(4)(b) .......................................................................................... 228
s. 238(5) ............................................................................................... 220
s. 238(5)(a) .......................................................................................... 233
s. 238(5)(b) .......................................................................................... 223
s. 239 ............................................................ 210, 219, 224, 365, 383
s. 239(4) ....................................................................................... 224, 237
s. 239(5) ............................................................................................... 224
s. 239(6) ....................................................................................... 225, 237
s. 240(1)(a) ................................................................................... 220, 224
s. 240(1)(b) .......................................................................................... 224
s. 240(2) ................................................................... 220, 221, 223, 235
s. 244 .................................................................................................... 219
s. 245 .................................................................................................... 219
s. 245(4) ............................................................................................... 302
s. 249 ............................................................................................ 221, 224
s. 250 ............................................................................................ 221, 224
s. 251 ............................................................ 31, 213, 214, 251, 343
s. 423 ............................................................................................ 134, 219
s. 424 .................................................................................................... 134
s. 425 .................................................................................................... 134
s. 435 ............................................................................................ 221, 224
s. 435(6) ................................................................................................. 27
Insurance Companies Act 1982
s. 32 ...................................................................................................... 326
Joint Stock Companies Act 1844 ..................................................... 155
s. 3 ........................................................................................................ 155
Joint Stock Companies Act 1856 ........................................ 156, 157, 328
s. 67 ...................................................................................................... 332
Joint Stock Companies Winding-up Act 1848 ........................... 155, 163
s. 3 ........................................................................................................ 155
s. 84 ...................................................................................................... 163
Limited Liability Act 1855 ......................................................... 155, 156
s. 13 .............................................................................................. 332, 386

**United States**

Act of May Session, 1818, ch. 8, 1818 Conn. Pub. Acts 305 ................................ 159
ABA-ALI Model Business Corporation Act
   s. 52 ........................................................................................................ 291
Act of Feb. 23, 1830, ch. 53, para. 8, 1830 Mass. Acts 325, 329 ......................... 159
Act of Feb. 5, 1823 ch. 221 para. 1, 1823 Me. Laws 929 .................................... 159
Act of May 15, 1851, Mass. Acts and Resolves 1849-1851, c. 133, p. 633 ........... 159
Act of June Session, 1847, R.I. Acts and Resolves 30 ......................................... 159
Arkansas State Ann. 1980
   s. 64-502(G) ........................................................................................... 329
Bankruptcy Act
   s. 67d ..................................................................................................... 221
Bankruptcy Code
   s. 7 ......................................................................................................... 226
   s. 101(2) ................................................................................................. 226
   s. 101(30)(B), (E) .................................................................................. 226
   s. 502(c) ................................................................................................. 230
   s. 510(c) ......................................................................................... 355, 357
   s. 547 ............................................................................................. 219, 225
   s. 547(b)(3) ............................................................................................ 225
   s. 547(b)(4)(A) ....................................................................................... 225
   s. 547(b)(4)(B) ....................................................................................... 226
   s. 547(b)(5) ............................................................................................ 225
   s. 547(f) ................................................................................................. 225
   s. 548 ...................................................................................... 134, 219, 227
   s. 548(a)(1) ...................................................................................... 222, 226
   s. 548(a)(2)(A) ...................................................................................... 222
   s. 548(a)(2)(B)(i) .............................................................................. 222, 235
   s. 548(a)(2)(B)(ii) .................................................................................. 222
   s. 548(a)(2)(B)(iii) ................................................................................. 222
   s. 726 ..................................................................................................... 317
California Corporations Code
   s. 202(d)(e) ............................................................................................ 308
   s. 25154 ................................................................................................. 351
Corpus Juris Secundum Vol. 100
   s. 351(1) ................................................................................................. 185
Florida Limited Liability Company Act 1982 ....................................................... 478
Georgia Code Ann. 1977
   ss. 22-802(a)(8) ..................................................................................... 329
Internal Revenue Code
   s. 11(a) .................................................................................................. 373

s. 163(a) ............................................................................................ 373
ss. 165(f)-(g) .................................................................................... 373
s. 166 ..................................................................................... 183, 373
s. 301 ................................................................................................ 373
s. 302 ................................................................................................ 373
s. 316 ................................................................................................ 373
s. 385 ................................................................................................ 373
s. 482 ....................................................................................... 71, 296
ss. 1211-1212 ................................................................................... 373
Interstate Commerce 1887 ................................................................. 137
Model Business Corporation Act ........................................................ 26
s. 3.02(7) ........................................................................................... 273
s. 3.04 ................................................................................................ 272
s. 54 para. 3.03(7) ............................................................................. 329
New Jersey Acts, 40th Gen. Assembly, 2d sitting, 1816 ....................... 159
New York. Act of Mar. 22, 1811, ch. 67
s. 7, 1811 N.Y. Laws 111 ................................................................... 159
Oklahoma Business Corporation Act 1951
s. 18-1.15 .......................................................................................... 329
Public Laws of New Jersey, c. 269, p. 385 (1888) ........................... 1, 160
Tax Reform Act 1969, Pub. L. No. 91-172, Title IV
s. 415(a), 83 Stat. 613 ....................................................................... 373
Texas Business Corporation Act
s. 3.02(7) ........................................................................................... 329
Uniform Fraudulent Conveyance Act ........................................ 134, 219
s. 1 ..................................................................................................... 222
s. 2 ..................................................................................................... 223
s. 2(1) ................................................................................................. 230
s. 3 ............................................................................................ 223, 228
s. 4 .............................................................................. 222, 226, 235
s. 5 .............................................................................................. 222, 235
s. 6 ..................................................................................................... 222
s. 7 ..................................................................................................... 222
Uniform Fraudulent Transfer Act ....................................................... 227

## New Zealand

Companies Amendment Act 1980
s. 30 ....................................................................... 293, 299, 414
New Zealand Companies Act 1955
s. 315A .............................................................................................. 299
s. 315B ................................................................... 293, 299, 414

s. 315C ................................................................................ 293, 299, 414
New Zealand Companies Act 1993
    s. 2(3) ................................................................................... 299
    s. 271(1)(a) ........................................................................... 299
    s. 271(1)(b) ................................................................. 293, 414, 458
    s. 272(1) ............................................................................... 304
    s. 272(2) ................................................. 293, 304, 414, 458, 461

**European Union**

Directive 83/349
    Art. 1 ................................................................................... 439
Directive 89/299 O.J. L124/89 on the own funds of credit institutions ................. 325
Directive 89/647, O.J. L386/89 on a solvency ratio for credit institutions ............ 326
Directive 91/633, O.J. L339/91 ............................................................. 325
Directive 92/16, O.J. L75/92 ............................................................... 326
Regulation No. 2137/85 ..................................................................... 107
Second Company Law Directive on Company Law Harmonisation ................. 328
Seventh Company Law Directive (83/349/EEC) .......................................... 20
Works Council Directive (94/45/EC) ....................................................... 20

**Other Jurisdictions**

Gibraltar Companies (Taxation and Concessions) Ordinance 1983
    Art. 3(a) ................................................................................ 14
International Business Corporations Act of Antigua and Barbuda
    Art. 3(1) ................................................................................ 14

# 1 Introduction

## 1. THE CORPORATE GROUP - NOT A RECENT PHENOMENON

To dwell upon the problems raised by corporate groups is to lament deep-rooted deficiencies of English law. In order to appreciate this concern, a brief historical excursion into the development of corporate groups is essential.

The corporate group is by no means a late 20th century phenomenon. Indeed, at least as early as the mid-19th century in England, and some decades later in the United States, the creation of a holding-subsidiary company relationship - which is of course at the heart of the corporate group arrangement - was already possible. In England, the power of a company to acquire and own shares in another company (thus making possible the holding subsidiary relationship) has never been expressly provided for in any of the general incorporation statutes. It was however generally accepted, even in the mid-19th century, that such power could be specified in the Memorandum of Association and that such power was contrary neither to the common law nor to the applicable companies legislation.[1] Where neither express nor implied authority could be found in the Memorandum, it was considered *ultra vires* to acquire the shares of another company.[2] In the United States (where the powers of a corporation were largely specified by general incorporation statutes, and not, as in England, by the Memorandum) corporate groups emerged after state corporation laws authorised corporations generally to acquire and own shares in other corporations. This process started in the state of New Jersey in 1888[3] and gradually spread to other states by the early part of the 20th century.[4] Prior to such general

---

[1] *Vide In re Barned's Banking Company, ex p. The Contract Corporation* (1867) L.R. 3 Ch. 105; *In re Asiatic Banking Corporation* (1869) L.R. 4 Ch. 252; *Thring's Law and Practice of Joint Stock and Other Companies* (4th ed., edited by G.A.R. Fitzgerald, 1880) p. 35.

[2] *Vide In re William Thomas & Co. Limited* [1915] 1 Ch. 325. Cf. *In re European Society Arbitration Acts* (1878) 8 Ch. App. 679; *Great Eastern Railway v. Turner* (1872) L.R. 8 Ch. 149.

[3] Public Laws of New Jersey, c. 269, p. 385 (1888).

[4] *Vide* Elvin R. Latty, *Subsidiaries and Affiliated Corporations : A Study in Stockholders' Liability* (1936) p. iv; Phillip I. Blumberg, *The Law of Corporate Groups - Substantive Law* (1987) (hereinafter cited as "Blumberg, *Substantive Law*") pp. 55-60; William

authorisations, specific statutes or charters granted to a limited number of corporations the right to own shares of other corporations. Without such specific or general authorisation, it had been settled law in the United States that it was *ultra vires* or unlawful for a corporation to acquire shares in another corporation.[1]

Notwithstanding that the holding-subsidiary relationship was in principle allowed during the 19th century, it was not until the early days of the 20th century that commercial enterprises gradually started to develop and mutate into corporate groups.[2] And following the Second World War, the world has witnessed an explosive proliferation of corporate groups, even of transnational corporate groups.[3] Indeed, corporate groups have, over the last three decades at least, become a familiar every-day feature of the commercial scene. Business is increasingly being conducted by what are often complex organisations consisting of several companies collectively undertaking a common business enterprise.

Yet although the corporate group has for some time been the predominant form of doing business, the underlying conceptual and regulatory framework is still deeply rooted in the traditional model of the "single-company" business prevalent in the 19th century. As we approach the dawn of a new century, English law has barely begun to grapple with the unique problems raised by the corporate group phenomenon.[4] In particular, it has ignored the fundamental problem (with which this study is primarily concerned) of holding company liability for the debts of insolvent subsidiaries.

Were corporate groups to play a minor part in contemporary society, then the group phenomenon might hardly deserve deep inquiry. Yet, as will

---

*Cont.*

Randall Compton, "Early History of Stock Ownership by Corporations" 9 Geo. Wash. L.R. 125 (1940).

[1] *Louisville & N.R.R. Co.* v. *Commonwealth Kentucky* 161 U.S. 677 (1896); *De La Vergne Refrigerating Machine Co.* v. *German Savings Institution* 175 U.S. 40 (1899); *Louis K. Liggett Co.* v. *J.M. Lee* 288 U.S. 517, 556 (1932). *Vide* William M. Fletcher, *Cyclopedia of the Law of Private Corporations* (1917) Vol. II, paras. 1117-1118, pp. 2067-2071.

[2] *Vide* Robert Ian Tricker, *Corporate Governance* (1984) pp. 39-40.

[3] *Vide* Tom Hadden, "Inside Corporate Groups" 12 International Journal of the Sociology of Law 271 (1984) p. 271; M.A. Eisenberg, "Megasubsidiaries : The Effect of Corporate Structure on Corporate Control" 84 Harv. L.R. 1577 (1971) p. 1577; David K. Eitmann and Arthur I. Stonehill, *Multinational Business Finance* (2nd ed. 1979) p.1; Peter Hertner and Geoffrey Jones (ed.), *Multinationals : Theory and History* (1986) Ch. 1. *Vide* also *post* pp. 3 *et seq.*

[4] *Vide post* pp. 27-28.

presently be shown, corporate groups are playing an increasingly significant role in the modern world. As a result, problems stemming from the group phenomenon become magnified, meriting serious consideration.

## 2. PROLIFERATION, GROWTH AND POWER OF CORPORATE GROUPS

As the following pages will demonstrate, the proliferation, growth and power of corporate groups make the group phenomenon truly impressive.

### 2.1. The corporate group : the typical form of business organisation

The stark reality of the business enterprise in contemporary society is no longer the "single-company" organisation. Rather, the typical form of business organisation is the complex corporate group[1] composed of interrelated corporate components operating under a "parent entity's corporate umbrella".[2] Nor is the use of the corporate group structure limited to the large business enterprises. Even with medium sized and smaller enterprises, it has become common for the business to be divided amongst a number of companies each constituting a separate legal unit. Only in the case of the smallest private business enterprise is the single independent company the typical form of organisation.[3]

The phenomenon of corporate group activity is certainly not unique to the United Kingdom. On the contrary, it is evident that the corporate group has become a familiar characteristic of commercial life throughout the developed world.[4]

---

[1] Cf. Blumberg, *Substantive Law* p. xxxi.

[2] *In re Vecco Const. Indus., Inc.* 4 B.R. 407, 409 (Bankr. E.D. Va. 1980).

[3] Tom Hadden, *The Control of Corporate Groups* (1983) p. 1; N.C. Sargent, "Corporate Groups and the Corporate Veil in Canada : a penetrating look at Parent - Subsidiary relations in the modern Corporate Enterprise" 17 Manitoba L.J. 156 (1988) pp. 159-160. Cf. Gerry Weiss, "The Collapse of a Single Company in the Group" in R.M. Goode (ed.), *Group Trading and the Lending Banker* (1988) p. 89.

[4] N.C. Sargent, "Beyond the legal entity doctrine : Parent - Subsidiary relations under the West German Konzernrecht" 10 Can. Bus. L.J. 327 p. 327; Klaus J. Hopt, "Legal Elements and Policy Decisions in Regulating Groups of Companies" in Clive M. Schmitthoff and Frank Wooldridge (ed.), *Groups of Companies* (1991) p. 81. (Hopt's contribution is hereinafter cited as "Hopt, Regulating Groups").

## 2.2. Widespread transnational character

The proliferation of corporate groups is by no means confined to the domestic arena. Today's business world is replete with immensely powerful corporate groups whose operations span the entire globe.[1] Indeed it is in the form of the transnational organisation that the corporate group achieves its most complex and problematic form, with enterprises often multiplying into intricate networks of foreign and local subsidiaries and affiliates which could number in the hundreds world-wide.

Transnational corporate groups have been around for quite some time.[2] But it was only following the Second World War that the spectacular rise in the growth and proliferation of transnational corporate groups has occurred.[3] In Europe, post-war growth has been largely attributed to the recovery of the various European economies, greater political stability, the return of European currencies to convertibility and the creation of the European Community.[4] World-wide, the spread of transnational corporate groups can be credited to a number of factors including advances in technology, improvement in communications and transportation, a relatively free trading and investment environment and the ease with which assets are able to move across national boundaries. All these factors combine to facilitate the

---

[1] Cf. Blumberg, *Substantive Law* p. xxxii; Christopher Tugendhat, *The Multinationals* (1971) p. 24. The transnational character of corporate groups is largely limited to large and medium sized organisations.

[2] *Vide* generally, Hertner and Jones (ed.), *op. cit.* Hertner and Jones' work deals with the transnational corporation generally and not specifically with transnational corporate groups. Clearly, however, transnational organisations have been operating through groups since the early days of the 20th century. *Vide* Lawrence G. Franko, *The European Multinationals* (1976), Ch. 1; Mira Wilkins, "Modern European Economic History and the Multinationals", [1977] Journal of European Economic History 575; John M. Stopford, "The Origins of British-Based Multinational Manufacturing Enterprises" Business History Review, Vol. XLVIII 303 (1974); Mira Wilkins, *The Emergence of Multinational Enterprise: American Business Abroad from the Colonial Era to 1914* (1970); Mira Wilkins, *The Maturing of Multinational Enterprise: American Business Abroad from 1914 to 1970* (1974) Chs. 1 and 2.

[3] *Vide* Clive M. Schmitthoff, "Multinationals in Court" [1972] J.B.L. 103 p. 103; J.H. Farrar et al., Company Law (3rd ed. 1991) (hereinafter cited as "Farrar") p. 725; Hopt, *Regulating Groups*, p. v.

[4] *Vide* Joan Edelman Spero, *The Politics of International Economic Relations* (4th ed. 1990) p. 113.

"globalisation of production".[1] Undoubtedly, the end of the Cold War and the emergence of new market economies in Eastern Europe and the Far East is also accelerating the trend.

Recently published statistics on transnational corporations bear witness to the extensive proliferation of corporate groups in the international arena.[2] By the early 1990s there were over 37,000 transnational corporations with over 170,000 foreign affiliates.[3] And the number of transnational corporations has been steadily increasing. For example, those that are based in 14 major developed home countries "have more than tripled during the past two decades, from slightly more than 7,000 in 1969 ... to nearly 24,000 in 1990".[4] The universe of transnational corporations is indeed large, diverse, dynamic, and flourishing.

## 2.3. Immensity of corporate group activity

The sheer number of corporate groups and the multitude of subsidiaries comprised therein is certainly noteworthy; yet it is the size and the extent of the business activity collectively undertaken by such organisations that is really striking.[5] Recent estimates, for example, calculate that about one third of the world's private sector productive assets are under the common governance of transnational corporations.[6] The growing influence of transnational corporations can be noticed in the increase in the stock of

---

[1] *Vide* John H. Dunning, *Multinational Enterprises and the Global Economy* (1993) Ch. V.

[2] *Vide* generally, United Nation Conference on Trade and Development (UNCTAD), World Investment Report 1993, Transnational Corporations and Integrated International Production, ref. ST/CTC/156 (1993) (hereinafter cited as "World Investment Report 1993"); "Multinationals take lead as world economic force" *Financial Times*, 21st July 1993.

[3] World Investment Report 1993 pp. 19, 22.

[4] *Ibid.* p. 19.

[5] Cf. Edward S. Herman, *Corporate Control, Corporate Power* (1981) p. 1; Harry G. Henn and John R. Alexander, *Laws of Corporations and other Business Enterprises* (3rd ed. 1983) pp. 5-6. The figures given by Herman and by Henn and Alexander do not distinguish between corporate groups and "one-company" organisations. However, it is clear that practically all the large and even medium sized enterprises operate through the group structure (*vide* Tom Hadden, *The Control of Corporate Groups* (1983) p. 1; Tricker, *op. cit.* pp. 54-55) and the figures can for practical purposes be taken as being applicable to corporate groups.

[6] World Investment Report 1993 p. 1.

foreign direct investment : since the early 1980's annual foreign direct investment flows have grown rapidly[1] so that by 1992, the global stock of foreign direct investment had reached approximately US$ 2 trillion, which generated about US$ 5.5 trillion in sales by foreign affiliates.[2] And the indications are that in the future corporate groups will continue to handle a growing proportion of world trade.[3]

## 2.4. Diversity of corporate group activity

Corporate groups are now to be found in virtually all sectors of domestic and international economies.[4] Moreover, there is a marked tendency for diversification even *within* groups of companies, with groups expanding into production processes, markets, products and services outside the scope of their original business activity.[5] Such diversification - horizontally into new product lines, vertically in upstream or downstream processes, or conglomerate diversification into new business sectors - effectively commenced with the acquisition strategies of the 1960's.[6] More recently

[1] These declined marginally in 1991 and, based on preliminary data, again in 1992. The decline is probably attributable to the economic recession in the major developed countries. World Investment Report 1993 p. 13.

[2] World Investment Report 1993 p. 1. The transnational corporation is in certain respects highly concentrated. For example, approximately 1 per cent of parent transnational corporations own one half of the foreign direct investment stock or total affiliate assets. In 1990, the largest 100 transnational corporations ranked by the size of the foreign assets accounted for about US$ 3.2 trillion in global assets and for about one third of the world-wide outward stock of foreign direct investment. (World Investment Report pp. 22-24). *Vide*, for a somewhat earlier assessment of the influence of transnational corporations, Tugendhat, *op. cit.* pp. 106 *et seq.* Concentration of economic power is evident (probably to a greater degree) even in domestic markets. In the United Kingdom the top 100 quoted companies account for well over half the turnover, profit and capital employed of the entire top 1000 quoted companies. The top 10 alone account for 28% of turnover, 47% of profit and 25% of capital employed of the top 1000 quoted companies. Tricker, *op. cit.* p. 47.

[3] Cf. Michael Z. Brooke and H. Lee Remmers, *The Strategy of Multinational Enterprise* (1978) p. 241.

[4] Cf. M.A. Eisenberg, *The Structure of the Corporation : A Legal Analysis* (1976) p. 277; World Investment Report 1993 Table I.10. pp. 26-27.

[5] *Vide* J.M. Stopford et al., *Managing the Multinational Enterprise* (1972) p. 5; Tricker, *op. cit.* p. 52; Charles Wilson, *Unilever 1945-1965 - Challenge and Response in the Post-War Industrial Revolution* (1968) p. 132.

[6] Tricker, *op. cit.* p. 52.

there has been a tendency amongst corporate groups to divest subsidiaries and rationalise their product and market strategies. The extent of diversification, however, remains high.[1]

## 2.5. Power of corporate groups

The proliferation, size, growth and diversity of corporate groups combine to make the emergence of the group phenomenon one of the most dramatic developments of recent decades.[2] And their significance is not merely economic or industrial. Corporate groups have become dominant institutions in the modern world, profoundly affecting the role of governments in national domestic economies and even the relationship between states.[3]

In every age, power has been founded upon the dominant interests of the time. Over 60 years ago, Justice Brandeis had asserted that corporations "have become an institution ... which has brought such concentration of economic power that so-called private corporations are sometimes able to dominate the State."[4] Justice Brandeis may have slightly overstated the case for his times. Today, however, his statement would more closely reflect the truth. Indeed, there can be little doubt that nowadays corporate groups - though not quite so powerful as to actually dominate the state - do sometimes compete on practically equal terms therewith. Sometimes, corporate groups rival the state in the influence they exert on society. Often they effectively outrun the state in the efficiency of their organisation. On the domestic level, powerful corporate groups are perhaps reminiscent of the feudal system.[5] And where corporate groups are transnational in character,

---

[1] Tricker, *op. cit.* p. 52.

[2] *Vide*, in this regard, the prophetic analysis and intuition of Berle and Means in their monumental work, *The Modern Corporation and Private Property*, published in 1932 (rev. ed. 1968). Writing generally about the corporation, whilst at the same time recognising the impact of corporate groups, Berle and Means stated : "We are examining this institution probably before it has reached its zenith. Spectacular as its rise has been, every indication seems to be that the system will move forward to proportions which would stagger the imagination today." *Ibid.* at p. 3.

[3] *Vide* Tugendhat, *op. cit.* pp. 1, 106. In terms of Gross National Product, a transnational like General Motors would rank fourteenth in the world if it were a state. *Vide* Farrar, p. 728.

[4] *Louis K. Liggett Co.* v. *Lee* 288 U.S. 517 (1933) at p. 565.

[5] Cf. Henn and Alexander, *op. cit.* p. 5.

they "sometimes represent a latter-day vestige of a former colonial regime".[1] There appears to be the need for international regulation. States (individually or collectively) may seek to regulate the power of corporate groups. Groups, as they steadily gain power, may succeed in resisting any such erosion of their power. Given however the interests at stake and the inherent power possessed by the state, it is unlikely that the future will see corporate groups actually displacing the state as the dominant force in social organisation.[2]

## 3. INCREDIBLY COMPLEX STRUCTURES

The prevalence of the group form of business organisation is far removed from the original corporate concept envisaged by our forefathers. The sharp departure from the conventional model (which, as we shall see, remains the focus of English law) is evidently creating difficulties[3] - difficulties which are often compounded by the incredible complexity of many corporate groups. It is not just a question of the holding company spawning a large number of subsidiaries, sometimes literally hundreds of them.[4] The real problem arises where, rather like "models of chemical molecules",[5] corporate groups evolve into intricate networks of sub-holding companies, operating subsidiaries, sub-subsidiaries and services companies - many held at various levels of sub-subsidiaries in the group structural hierarchy.[6] Nor is such structural complexity restricted to the large transnational groups.

---

[1] Farrar, pp. 728-729.

[2] Cf. Detlev F. Vagts, "The Multinational Enterprise : A New Challenge for Transnational Law" 83 Harv. L.R. 739 (1970). For a contrary view, *vide* Berle and Means, *op. cit.* p. 313.

[3] *Vide post* pp. 15-24.

[4] *Vide* Blumberg, *Substantive Law* p. xxxi; N.C. Sargent, "Beyond the legal entity doctrine: Parent - Subsidiary relations under the West German Konzernrecht" 10 Can. Bus. L.J. 327 p. 327.

[5] T.W. Cashel, "Groups of Companies - Some US Aspects" in Clive M. Schmitthoff and Frank Wooldridge (ed.), *Groups of Companies* (1991) at p. 21.

[6] *Vide* Tom Hadden, "Inside Corporate Groups" 12 Int. J. of Soc. of Law 271 (1984) p. 273; Farrar, p. 46; *In re Interstate Stores, Inc.* 15 Collier Bankr. Cas. 634, 640-641 (Bankr. S.D.N.Y. 1978); Tricker, *op. cit.* pp. 2, 16. Tricker's study shows that in 1984 the top 50 UK corporate groups had over 10,000 subsidiaries. The average was 230 companies in each group, with a range from 5 (Sainsburys) to 858 (British Petroleum). Even companies in the 451-500 ranking had an average of 25 subsidiaries each, with a range from 2 to 74. *Ibid.* p. 55.

Medium sized and even small enterprises can involve structures and inter-relationships so intricate and sophisticated that it may be practically impossible to disentangle the corporate web.[1]

Difficulties associated with corporate group structures are further exacerbated by the device of "pyramiding". This essentially involves the holding of a majority of the shares of one company which in turn holds a majority of the shares of another - a "process which can be repeated a number of times".[2] In this way, an "interest equal to slightly more than a quarter or an eighth or a sixteenth or even a smaller proportion of the ultimate property to be controlled is ... legally entrenched."[3] The owner perched at the apex of such a pyramid could have complete control of the entire group even though his ownership interest may be less than one per cent of the whole group.[4] Pyramiding plainly magnifies the problems faced by the subsidiaries' external shareholders.[5]

Corporate groups also portray considerable flexibility in the organisation structure adopted for operational purposes, for taking management decisions

---

[1] *Vide* e.g., *Re a Company* [1985] BCLC 333 (C.A.); *T.S.B. Private Bank International S.A.* v. *Chabra* [1992] 1 W.L.R. 231.

[2] Berle and Means, *op. cit.* p. 69. This type of pyramiding is not to be confused with "pyramid" companies supposedly structured in a way to generate money-for-nothing for their investors. Pyramid company schemes operate by recruiting new subscribers in order to provide the money required to pay off existing investors. The schemes are inherently flawed because of their constant need to "breed". Indeed, they eventually require the involvement of an infinite number of investors. Pyramid schemes appear to be a feature of the newly emerging capitalist economies, such as Russia and Rumania. A similar type of scheme is "pyramid selling" which involves selling goods or services through a trading scheme which operates on more than one level. Pyramid selling companies have also sprouted in developed economies, such as the United Kingdom and Japan. *Vide* generally "Alchemy turns to dust under DTI spell" *Financial Times*, 5th August 1994; "DTI pulls another company into pyramid selling probe" *Financial Times*, 6th-7th August 1994; "Japanese investors hit by the curse of the pyramids" *Financial Times*, 10th August 1994; Rinita Sarker, "Pyramid selling" 16 The Company Lawyer 278 (1995).

[3] Berle and Means, *op. cit.* p. 69.

[4] *Ibid.* p. 69. "Fantastic corporate pyramids" were constructed in the 1920's in the United States, particularly but not exclusively, in the public utility sector. Pyramiding in the latter sector was statutorily controlled by the Public Utility Holding Company Act of 1935. There is little direct legal control in other sectors. Pyramiding has apparently declined, though it has by no means disappeared. *Vide* M.A. Eisenberg, *The Structure of the Corporation : A Legal Analysis* (1976) p. 311. No empirical study of the use of pyramiding in the United Kingdom appears to have ever been conducted.

[5] *Vide* M.A. Eisenberg, *The Structure of the Corporation : A Legal Analysis* (1976) p. 312.

and for measuring performance.[1] This flexibility, however, may result in a divergence between the legal structure and the organisational structure of the group.[2] Problems naturally tend to follow.

It is the complexity of corporate groups - no less than their sheer size or scale of operations - which makes their power so elusive and so formidable a challenge to the rule of law and to the world economic and political order.[3]

## 4. EVOLUTION OF CORPORATE GROUPS - ADVANTAGES OF CORPORATE GROUP ORGANISATION

Rather than evolving as single units, business enterprises often mutate into corporate groups.[4] This tendency increases as the scale of the business enlarges.

The addition of a new member to the corporate group family usually takes place either by "adoption" or by "birth". The "adoption" process is generally the result of corporate concentration[5] involving the acquisition of a substantial participation by one company in the equity of another established and independent company. An example of the "adoption" process is a successful take-over bid.[6] The "birth" method is usually far more

[1] *Vide* Tricker, *op. cit.* p. 3. Sometimes, companies within a corporate group may use a "division" - an organisational unit that behaves like a subsidiary in all respects but that has no separate legal existence. Such a "quasi-subsidiary" division would have a full complement of officers and sales, production and other functional departments. It would often have some form of supervisory body, akin to a board of directors of a subsidiary. Sometimes the division is even allowed to "declare dividends". *Vide* Robert W. Murphy, "Corporate Divisions vs Subsidiaries" 34 Harv. Bus. Rev. 83 (1956) pp. 84-85.

[2] Tom Hadden, *The Control of Corporate Groups* (1983) p. vii.

[3] Cf. Adolf A. Berle, "Subsidiary corporations and credit manipulation" 41 Harv. L.R. 874 (1928) p. 874; C. Wilfred Jenks, "Multinational Entities in the Law of Nations" in Wolfgang Friedmann et al (ed.), Transnational Law in a Changing Society, *Essays in Honor of Philip C. Jessup* (1972) p. 80.

[4] *Vide* Robert W. Murphy, "Corporate Divisions vs Subsidiaries" 34 Harv. Bus. Rev. 83 (1956).

[5] *Vide* N.C. Sargent, "Corporate Groups and the Corporate Veil in Canada : a penetrating look at Parent-Subsidiary relations in the modern Corporate Enterprise" 17 Manitoba L.J. 156 (1988) p. 160.

[6] Cf. P. Derom, "The EEC Approach to Groups of Companies" 16 Va J. Int. L. 565 (1976) p. 569; M.A. Eisenberg, "Megasubsidiaries : The Effect of Corporate Structure on Corporate Control" 84 Harv. L.R. 1577 (1971) p. 1585; Tom Hadden, *The Control of Corporate Groups* (1983) p. 10.

straightforward : a company is specifically incorporated as a subsidiary. This may result from a process of internal expansion or reorganisation of an existing corporate enterprise.[1]

The instincts of self-preservation, survival and material enhancement are as strong in business enterprises as they are in human beings.[2] An enterprise will, quite understandably, act in accordance with those instincts. The transformation of a business enterprise into a number of related but separate legal units is often a manifestation of such instincts. For by such transformation, the enterprise may stand to gain certain benefits.[3] The benefits are varied and can range from the legal and fiscal to the operational and commercial. The principal advantages of the organisation of an enterprise into a number of legal units will be examined in the next few pages.

## 4.1. Limited liability

Individual traders usually have the benefit of limited liability in mind when incorporating their business[4] - just as the legendary Mr. Salomon did when incorporating his ill-fated business over a hundred years ago.[5] Undeniably, the primary advantage of incorporating a subsidiary as a medium for the conduct of a commercial or industrial activity lies in the same notion of limited liability : the insulation of the holding company from the debts of the subsidiary. The organisation of a business activity through a separate subsidiary will effectively reduce the risks of insolvency for the enterprise represented by the group. Limited liability is particularly attractive where the

---

[1] N.C. Sargent, "Corporate Groups and the Corporate Veil in Canada : a penetrating look at Parent-Subsidiary relations in the modern Corporate Enterprise" 17 Manitoba L.J. 156 (1988) p. 160; Adolf A. Berle, "The Theory of Enterprise Entity" 47 Colum. L.R. 343 (1947) p. 343; Farrar, pp. 537-538.

[2] John Campbell, "Hong Kong Companies on the Bermuda Trail" International Corporate Law, March 1991, p. 20.

[3] *Vide* Henry W. Ballantine, *Ballantine on Corporations*, s. 135 at pp. 309-310 (Rev. ed. 1946); Henn and Alexander, *op. cit.* p. 56; Jonathan M. Landers, "A Unified Approach to Parent, Subsidiary, and Affiliate Questions in Bankruptcy" 42 Univ. of Chicago L.R. 589 (1975) p. 589; Tricker, *op. cit.* pp. 55-56.

[4] John W. Salmond, *Jurisprudence* (12th ed. P.J. Fitzgerald, 1966) p. 319. Bernard F. Cataldo, "Limited Liability with One-Man Companies and Subsidiary Corporations" 18 Law and Contemporary Problems 473 (1953) p. 474.

[5] *Vide Salomon* v. *A. Salomon and Co. Ltd.* [1897] A.C. 22 (H.L.).

enterprise is to embark upon some new high-risk venture.[1] With the benefit of limited liability, group management is more willing to undertake operations it would otherwise have deemed too risky.[2] Profits can be pursued but the exposure to liability controlled. Limited liability is clearly a significant investment incentive.

## 4.2. Tax relief

As a general rule of course, the law views each company within a group as a legal entity distinct from other companies in the group. A strict application of this principle in the context of taxation would clearly have considerable disadvantages as losses in one company would not be available for deduction from the profits of other companies in the group. As an exception to the rule of separate personality, tax legislation in the United Kingdom - as indeed in many other countries - does however afford to groups a special tax treatment by which profits and losses in particular subsidiaries can to some extent be set-off against each other.[3] The special tax treatment afforded to groups does not in itself constitute an incentive to split an enterprise into legally separate but related units. The group tax relief provisions do however help to preserve the tax *status quo* of the enterprise where a group structure is employed.

The group structure also allows considerable flexibility (and even manipulation) in the tax planning of transnational groups. It may be group policy to arrange and value transfers of assets and services in such a way as to concentrate group profit in the jurisdiction affording the most favourable

---

[1] Martin Wolff, "Nature of Legal Persons" 54 L.Q.R. 494 (1988) pp. 503-504; R.S. Nathan, "Controlling the Puppeteers : Reform of Parent-Subsidiary laws in New Zealand" 3 Canterbury L.R. 1 (1986) p. 1.

[2] P. Derom, "The EEC Approach to Groups of Companies" 16 Va J. Int. L. 565 (1976) p. 571.

[3] *Vide* generally ss. 402-413 of the Income and Corporation Taxes Act 1988; Stephen W. Mayson and Susan Blake, *Mayson on Revenue Law* (13th ed. 1992-1993) Ch. 33; Michael B. Squires, *Tax Planning for Groups of Companies* (2nd ed. 1990) Ch. 3; Blumberg, *Substantive Law* p. xxxiii; Robert W. Murphy, "Corporate Divisions vs Subsidiaries" 34 Harv. Bus. Rev. 83 (1956) pp. 88-89. Cf. *In re Vecco Const. Indus., Inc.*, 4 B.R. 407, 409 (Bankr. E. D. Va. 1980). Sometimes elaborate schemes are created, involving the incorporation of subsidiary or affiliated companies, to benefit from tax relief provisions. *Vide* e.g., *Ryde Holdings Ltd.* v. *Sorenson* [1988] 2 NZLR 157.

tax treatment.[1] This in turn has led states, both at national and international levels, to implement measures aimed at controlling abuses in tax planning schemes by transnational groups.[2]

## 4.3. Other benefits

Other "miscellaneous" but equally significant benefits can sometimes be gained from the organisation of an enterprise into separate legal units. These can be listed as follows :

(1) Economic efficiencies sometimes militate in favour of the group structure. As a business grows, inefficiency creeps in because of organisational rigidity, problems of co-ordinating and stabilising objectives, and the allocation of resources. No enterprise can expand indefinitely without suffering inefficiencies at some level. The use of the corporate group structure can minimise these inefficiencies and maximise the benefits of decentralisation.[3]

(2) Flexibility is another important advantage of the group structure. The legal structure may be tailored in such a manner as to "minimize legal or regulatory control over the group's activities, while still allowing strategic control to be exercised over investment, marketing or internal group financial decisions affecting the group as a whole."[4]

(3) The group structure may also enable the enterprise to operate with greater administrative and accounting convenience.[5]

---

[1] R.S. Nathan, "Controlling the Puppeteers : Reform of Parent-Subsidiary laws in New Zealand" 3 Canterbury L.R. 1 (1986) p. 6.

[2] *Vide post* Chapter II pp. 70-73.

[3] *Vide* P. Derom, "The EEC Approach to Groups of Companies" 16 Va J. Int. L. 565 (1976) pp. 570-571; Karl Hofstetter, "Parent Responsibility for Subsidiary Corporations Evaluating European Trends" 39 I.C.L.Q. 576 (1990) p. 576. Cf. also *Revlon, Inc.* v. *Cripps & Lee Ltd.* [1980] F.S.R. 85 (C.A.) at p. 110 per Templeman L.J.

[4] N.C. Sargent, "Corporate Groups and the Corporate Veil in Canada : a penetrating look at Parent-Subsidiary relations in the modern Corporate Enterprise" 17 Manitoba L.J. 156 (1988) at p. 160.

[5] *Vide* Henn and Alexander, *op. cit.* p. 56; Tom Hadden, *Company Law and Capitalism* (2nd ed. 1977) p. 389. Cf. Robert W. Murphy, "Corporate Divisions vs Subsidiaries" 34 Harv. Bus. Rev. 83 (1956) pp. 90-92.

(4) Especially where foreign investment is concerned, the enterprise may gain added advantages from incorporating a separate company rather than opening up a branch.[1] Advantages may include avoiding the applicability to the enterprise of the laws of the foreign state and avoiding the service of process and litigation in the courts of such state.[2] In some instances, the use of a separate legal unit as an investment vehicle in a foreign state is obligatory by the law of such foreign state.[3]

(5) Sometimes, the organisation of a particular line of business as a separate legal unit will have the advantage, if the need arises, of facilitating the sale of that particular line. It is considerably easier to dispose of one of the companies in a group rather than to negotiate the sale of a line of business operated as a division.[4]

(6) There may also be reasons for retaining a newly acquired company as a separate legal unit. One reason may be to maintain and utilise the goodwill, highly publicised corporate name or separate marketing policies of the previously independent company.[5]

(7) Finally, it may occasionally be useful to keep in existence even a dormant or a redundant operating subsidiary despite the running expenses involved. One reason may relate to the strong desire amongst executives to retain or

---

[1] *Vide* Confederation of British Industry, Responsibility for the Liabilities of Group Companies - Memorandum by the Confederation of British Industry, October 1980 (hereinafter cited as "CBI Memorandum (1980)") p. 3; Blumberg, *Substantive Law* p. xxxiii.

[2] Bernard F. Cataldo, "Limited Liability with One-Man Companies and Subsidiary Corporations" 18 Law and Contemporary Problems 473 (1953) p. 487; Ballantine, *op. cit.* s. 135 p. 309. Cf. *Adams* v. *Cape Industries plc* [1990] BCLC 479 (C.A.).

[3] Many tax havens, for example, require the incorporation of a separate company under their own domestic law as a condition to the granting of fiscal and other benefits. *Vide*, for example, Art. 3(a) of the Companies (Taxation and Concessions) Ordinance of 1983 of Gibraltar; Art. 3(1) of the International Business Corporations Act (Act No. 28 of 1982) of Antigua and Barbuda.

[4] *Vide* Martin Wolff, "On the Nature of Legal Persons" 54 L.Q.R. 494 (1938) pp. 503-504; P. Derom, "The EEC Approach to Groups of Companies" 16 Va J. Int. L. 565 (1976) p. 571.

[5] Ballantine, *op. cit.* s. 135 p. 309; CBI Memorandum (1980) p. 3; Martin Wolff, "On the Nature of Legal Persons" 54 L.Q.R. 494 (1938) pp. 503-504.

gain the status of a director. This desire can be fulfilled "by leaving lower level corporate subsidiaries in existence even if they are functionally redundant."[1] Again, dormant companies may be maintained in existence to be used as and when the need for the creation of a legal unit within the group arises.[2]

## 5. DIVERSITY IN SIZE

Corporate groups are not invariably the huge, monstrous organisations they are sometimes made out to be. Nor do they consist merely of the headline makers - be they famed, such as the ICIs and the Royal Dutch Shells, or not so famed, such as the Maxwell Corporations, the Polly Pecks or the BCCIs. Rather, corporate groups can have widely varying dimensions : from having just one beneficial shareholder to literally thousands, from comprising just two companies to several hundreds, and from owning hardly any assets to billions of pounds worth.

Undoubtedly, the majority of groups embody medium sized and smaller enterprises. And as we shall see, it is usually the medium sized and the smaller, lesser known, non-listed enterprises that accentuate the problem of insolvent subsidiaries that lies at the heart of this work.[3] Large groups, dependent as they often are on their corporate group image would be rather reluctant to abandon an insolvent subsidiary to the dogs. Indeed, the level of concern with preserving the group corporate image tends to decline as the scale of the enterprise diminishes. The smaller the enterprise the lower is the incentive to bail out a sinking subsidiary.[4]

## 6. VARIOUS ISSUES RAISED BY THE GROUP PHENOMENON

### 6.1. A host of complex problems

The holding-subsidiary company relationship and, more broadly, the corporate group phenomenon raise a host of complex, often inter-related

---

[1] Tom Hadden, *The Control of Corporate Groups* (1983) p. 10.

[2] *Ibid.* p. 10.

[3] *Vide post* Chapter II pp. 97-98.

[4] On the subject of bailing out *vide* further *post* Chapter X pp. 472-475.

problems : problems of a political, sociological, environmental, economic, accounting, financial management and of course, of a legal, nature. All of these problems are further complicated by the transnational character of many enterprises.

## 6.2. Various legal issues

The legal problems are themselves multi-faceted and, in common with many legal issues, typically involve various interest groups with conflicting expectations, interests and claims. The legal problems are receiving varying degrees of institutional, academic and judicial attention.

Much of the difficulty originates from superimposing the unique features of group corporate activity and organisation onto a legal system still broadly tailored on the conventional "single company" model.

The legal problems raised by corporate groups can be broadly classified under a number of headings.

### 6.2.1. Competition policy and regulation

The principal question in competition policy and regulation is whether a holding company and its subsidiaries should, for the purposes of competition regulation, constitute a single economic enterprise in which they would be deemed, for example, incapable of conspiring with one another. Though the law is not yet settled, the trend in the law of both the European Union and the United States appears to be in favour of the recognition of the notion of the group enterprise - at least where the subsidiary's lack of autonomy *vis-à-vis* its market behaviour reflects the economic unity of the holding and subsidiary companies.[1]

---

[1] *Imperial Chemical Industries and others* v. *E.C. Commission* [1972] C.M.L.R. 557; *Commercial Solvents Corporation* v. *E.C. Commission* [1974] 1 C.M.L.R. 309; *Copperweld Corporation* v. *Independence Tube Corporation* 104 S. Ct. 2731 (1984). *Vide* further Note, "Efficacy of the Corporate Entity in evasion of statutes" 26 Iowa L.R. 350 (1941); Clive M. Schmitthoff, "The Wholly Owned and Controlled Subsidiary" [1978] J.B.L. 218 pp. 223-224; H.D. McCoy, "United States Parent Corporation - European Subsidiary Relationship under the European Anti-trust regulations" 3 Virginia Journal of International Law 46 (1963); Joseph P. Griffin, "The Power of Host Countries over the Multinational : Lifting the Veil in the European Economic Community and the United States" 6 Law and Policy in International Business 375 (1974) pp. 402-404; Note, "Parent and Subsidiary - subsidiary as instrumentality of parent when used to carry

## 6.2.2. Taxation

Taxation is another area where group activity requires specific consideration. As already noted,[1] this area is now largely regulated by detailed legislation which basically affords to groups favourable treatment by allowing losses and profits in particular subsidiaries to be set off. The problem here is that groups may attempt to manipulate their inter-corporate dealings to gain benefits beyond those envisaged by legislation. National and international regulation attempt to control such abuse.[2]

### 6.2.3 Minority shareholders

At law, the position of a minority shareholder in a subsidiary company should be no different from that of a minority shareholder in the single independent company. Yet in practice a minority shareholder in a subsidiary company is potentially at greater risk. Clearly, the interests of the holding company differ from those of minority shareholders. The holding company is concerned primarily with maximising the profits of the whole group as a single economic enterprise. The minority shareholder is interested in increasing the return on his investment. Integrated group management structures and intra-group lending heightens the risk that directors will put the interests of the group before those of the company they are supposed to represent. Conflict situations are therefore inevitable.

Where oppressive conduct is patently obvious, a remedy at law should certainly exist.[3] Problems however arise where no practicable remedy is available or where the enforcement of a remedy by the minority shareholder

---

*Cont.*
on unfair trade practices" 5 Vanderbilt L.R. 637 (1952); John Huddleston, "Can Subsidiaries be Purchasers from their Parents under the Robinson-Patman Act? A Plea for a Consistent Approach" 63 Wash. L.R. 957 (1988) pp. 957-958, 964-965; David Aronofsky, "Piercing the Transnational Corporate Veil : Trends, Developments and the Need for Widespread Adoption of Enterprise Analysis" 10 N.C.J. Int'l L. & Com. Reg. 31 (1985) pp. 70-71; Dimitris Avgitidis, *Groups of Companies : The Liability of the Parent Company for the Debts of Its Subsidiary*, Ph.D. thesis, University of London (1993) pp. 127-132.

[1] *Supra* pp. 12-13.

[2] *Vide post* Chapter II pp. 70-73.

[3] *Vide* C.A. 1985, s. 459; *Scottish Co-Operative Wholesale Society Ltd.* v. *Meyer* [1959] A.C. 324. Cf. *Charterbridge Corp. Ltd.* v. *Lloyds Bank Ltd.* [1970] Ch. 62.

proves difficult in practice.[1] Frequently, it is difficult for minority shareholders to establish with precision the mischief complained of. Corporate groups are not required to disclose full details of all inter-corporate transactions and a shareholder is not entitled to obtain information on any suspect transaction or set of transactions. Admittedly, if judicial proceedings are instituted discovery may be obtained, but costs act as a sufficient deterrent to any but the most determined or convinced minority shareholder.[2] The law on the subject is clearly unsatisfactory.

### 6.2.4. Creditor protection

One of the fundamental problems raised by corporate group activity is the question of inter-corporate liability towards the external creditors of companies within the group.[3] Are there, or should there be, any circumstances in which a corporate member of a group is or should be held answerable to the creditors of its holding, subsidiary or affiliated companies? This problem, which till today remains broadly unresolved, constitutes in effect the central issue of this work.

---

[1] *Vide* generally R.S. Nathan, "Controlling the Puppeteers : Reform of Parent-Subsidiary laws in New Zealand" 3 Canterbury L.R. 1 (1986) pp. 8-13; T.W. Walde, "Parent Subsidiary Relations in the integrated corporate system : a comparison of American and German law." 9 Journal of International Law and Economics 455 (1974); Neil C. Sargent, "Corporate Groups and the Corporate Veil in Canada : a penetrating look at Parent-Subsidiary relations in the modern Corporate Enterprise" 17 Manitoba L.J. 156 (1988) pp. 168-175; D.D. Prentice, "Groups of Companies : The English Experience" in Klaus J. Hopt (ed.), *Groups of Companies in Europe* (1982) pp. 112-126; Tom Hadden, *The Control of Corporate Groups* (1983), Ch. 5; Robert Drury and Peter G. Xuereb (ed.), *European Company Laws : A Comparative Approach* (1991) pp. 113-125; Tom Hadden, *Company Law and Capitalism* (2nd ed. 1977) p. 396; E. Merrick Dodd, "Liability of a Holding Company for obtaining for itself property needed by a subsidiary : the Blanstein case" 58 Harv. L.R. 125 (1944); M.A. Eisenberg, "Megasubsidiaries : The Effect of Corporate Structure on Corporate Control" 84 Harv. L.R. 1577 (1971) pp. 1613-1617; Lawrence P. Kessel, "Trends in the Approach to the Corporate Entity Problem in Civil Litigation" 41 Georgtown L.J. 525 (1953) pp. 534-541.

[2] Tom Hadden, *The Control of Corporate Groups* (1983) p. 32.

[3] The expression "external creditors" is used in this work to mean creditors of a subsidiary excluding creditors who are also members of the corporate group.

## 6.2.5. Accountability of directors

Another special area of concern in the context of corporate groups relates to the accountability of the directors of the various companies within the group, especially with respect to the power of the holding company to dictate the affairs of its subsidiaries.[1] This issue is also closely linked to the questions of minority rights and creditor protection identified above. Two problems can be highlighted : (i) to what extent can the directors of a subsidiary be held liable towards minority shareholders for breach of duties by complying with the holding company's instructions?; and (ii) in what circumstances, if any, will directors of a subsidiary be liable towards creditors of the subsidiary for acting in the interests of some other company within the group (or in the interests of the group as an economic unit) rather than in the interests of their subsidiary? The latter question, being related to the issue of creditor protection, will be discussed in the course of this work.[2]

## 6.2.6. Employee representation and disclosure of information

The last 25 years or so have witnessed occasional heated debate on the question of the involvement of employees in corporate governance.[3] In the United Kingdom, the debate was originally kindled by the Bullock Report.[4] Since then, the Report has largely been ignored but attention has shifted to the European Union Draft Fifth Directive on Employee Participation and the Company Structure[5]. The Draft, which has not yet been adopted, has undergone numerous revisions over the years.[6]

---

[1] *Vide* D.D. Prentice, "Groups of Companies : The English Experience" in Klaus J. Hopt (ed.), *Groups of Companies in Europe* (1982) pp. 126-128. (Prentice's contribution is hereinafter cited as "Prentice, The English Experience").

[2] *Vide post* Chapter V pp. 239-254.

[3] Cf. Keir, *op. cit.* pp. 46-47.

[4] The Bullock Report, Report of the Committee of Inquiry on Industrial Democracy, (1977) Cmnd. 6706 (hereinafter cited as the "Bullock Report").

[5] 26 OJ, No. C 240/2-240/38 9th September 1983.

[6] On the Draft Fifth Directive generally, *vide* Mark Clough, "Trying to Make the Fifth Directive Palatable" 3 The Company Lawyer 109 (1982); Janet Dine, "The Draft Fifth EEC Directive on Company Law" 10 The Company Lawyer 10 (1989); A.J. Boyle, "Draft Fifth Directive : Implications for Directors' Duties, Board Structure and Employee Participation" 13 The Company Lawyer 6 (1992); Janet Dine, *Company Law* (2nd ed. 1994) pp. 320-327.

Corporate groups pose special problems with regard to employee representation.[1] Assuming that the notion of employee participation in corporate governance is broadly acceptable in principle, should employee representatives of a subsidiary be entitled to sit on the board of the subsidiary, on the board of the holding company or possibly on both boards? If employee representatives sit on the board of the subsidiary, it may be more difficult to achieve long term and coherent strategic planning for the whole group. If representation takes place at holding company level, the interests of the subsidiary may have to be subsumed to those of the group as a whole, with consequent conflicting situations. Participation at both levels may resolve the conflict, but would probably burden the group with too unwieldy a structure.

One of the underlying themes in company law concerns the disclosure of information relating to companies. English law has for some time now recognised the interests of shareholders and creditors in having information made available on the financial state of corporate groups and their constituent members.[2] A recent significant development in the European Union has been the adoption, in September 1994, of the Works Council Directive.[3] This Directive is not binding on the United Kingdom which had opted out of the social chapter of the 1991 Maastricht Treaty. The Directive lays down requirements for informing and consulting employees in all undertakings, or groups of undertakings, which operate in more than one member State and employ more than 1000 employees within the Union, including at least 150 employees in each of at least two different Member States.[4] Such undertakings, or groups of

---

[1] *Vide* Tom Hadden, *The Control of Corporate Groups* (1983) pp. 40-44.

[2] The notion of group accounts was introduced by the Companies Act 1948 (*vide* s. 152(1) and Sched. 8 paras. 17-22). Other provisions were subsequently introduced, most recently by the C.A. 1989 which implemented the Seventh Company Law Directive (83/349/EEC, OJ 1983 L 193/1) on group accounts. The relevant provisions are now contained in ss. 221-262A and Sched. 4-6 of the Companies Act 1985 (this Act is hereinafter cited as "C.A. 1985"). On the Seventh Directive *vide* Welf Muller, "Group Accounts under the Proposed Seventh EEC Directive : A Practitioner's View" in Klaus J. Hopt (ed.), *Groups of Companies in Europe* (1982) p. 175.

[3] Council Directive 94/45/EC of the 22 September 1994 OJ No. L. 254/64.

[4] Articles 1 and 2. For a thorough analysis of the history of employee participation in the European Union *vide* Peter Cressey, "Employee Participation" in Michael Gold (ed.), *The Social Dimension - Employment Policy in the European Community* (1993) at pp. 85-104.

undertakings,[1] must set up a European Works Council which will serve as the channel for informing and consulting employees.[2]

Considerable criticism had been levelled, within the United Kingdom, at the proposals for informing and consulting employees in transnational companies. The Department of Employment and the Department of Trade and Industry, for example, had considered that the compulsory implementation of community-wide legislation would contribute nothing to the establishment of a common market in goods and services, but would serve primarily to increase costs, damage the competitive position of industry, disrupt existing industrial relations and do nothing to stem the rising tide of unemployment.[3] The Departments did however favour a voluntary adoption of the principles of information disclosure and consultation. Within the United Kingdom, the whole subject of disclosure and consultation, together with the deeper question of the desirability or otherwise of compulsory rules in this area, remain the subject of considerable debate.[4]

[1] A "group of undertakings" is defined as "a controlling undertaking and its controlling undertakings" (Article 2(1)(b)) and a "controlling undertaking" is defined as "an undertaking which can exercise a dominant influence over another undertaking ("the controlled undertaking") by virtue, for example, of ownership, financial participation or the rules which govern it." (Article 3(1)).

[2] The Directive replaces the now defunct Vredeling Directive OJ No. C217/3, 12th August 1983. Article 4 of the draft Vredeling Directive had imposed strict disclosure obligations on the parent undertaking if it proposes to take a decision which is liable to have serious consequences for the interests of the employees of the subsidiaries. The draft Vredeling Directive had been criticised for its rigidity and unsatisfactory drafting and also for the confusion expected to be associated with its implementation. *Vide* Editorial, "Amendments to the Fifth Draft Directive and to Vredeling" [1983] J.B.L. 456; Editorial, "Vredeling" [1984] J.B.L. 103; Editorial, "Further comments on the Draft Fifth Directive and Vredeling" [1984] J.B.L. 100; Tom Hadden, *The Control of Corporate Groups* (1983) p. 44; James Keir, "Legal Problems in the Management of a Group of Companies" in Clive M. Schmitthoff and Frank Wooldridge (ed.), *Groups of Companies* (1991) p. 47.

[3] Vide "Draft European Communities Directive on Procedures for Informing and Consulting Employees - A Consultative Document" published jointly by the Department of Employment and the Department of Trade and Industry (November, 1993) pp. 1-10, 39-52.

[4] *Vide* "Big companies hasten to set up EU works councils" *Financial Times*, 20th February 1995.

## 6.3. Heightened complexity in transnational groups

The complexity of the problems raised by the group phenomenon in a purely domestic context is undeniable. In a transnational dimension, not only is the complexity of such problems heightened, but other issues of a different nature arise.

Whenever a legal issue is cloaked with an international character, difficult questions associated with conflicts of laws - such as questions relating to applicable law, jurisdiction and the enforcement of judgments - may crop up. Legal issues involving transnational corporate groups are no exception.[1] Thus, a court seized of a dispute involving some component of a transnational group may have to decide whether to exercise subject matter jurisdiction and whether foreign or domestic law or some combination of the two should govern.[2] Should judgment be awarded against a member of the corporate group in a foreign territory, the question will arise whether such judgment is enforceable in the domestic courts.[3]

Conflict of laws problems may also be generated, for example, whenever matters of competition regulation and taxation are promoted to the international arena. Different competition and merger control systems and disparate systems of taxation create basic conflicts of interests and choice of law problems which can really only be solved by international conventions.[4]

Jurisdictional and enforcement problems arise because corporate groups do not easily fit into jurisdictional criteria geared to "turn of the century

---

[1] Karl Hofstetter, "Multinational Enterprise Parent Liability : Efficient Legal Regimes in a World Market Environment" 15 North Carolina J. of Int. Law and Comm. Reg. 299 (1990); Cynthia Day Wallace, *Legal Control of the Multinational Enterprise* (1982) p. 23.

[2] *Vide* David Aronofsky, "Piercing the Transnational Corporate Veil : Trends, Developments and the Need for Widespread Adoption of Enterprise Analysis", 10 N.C.J. Int'l L. & Com. Reg. 31 (1985) pp. 45-61; Hopt, Regulating Groups, p. 109.

[3] *Vide Adams v. Cape Industries plc* [1990] BCLC 479 (C.A.).

[4] *Vide* generally, World Investment Report 1993, p. 200. Re competition policy, *vide* Klaus J. Hopt (ed.), *Groups of Companies in Europe* (1982) p. vi; re taxation *vide* Model Double Taxation Agreement on Income and on Capital, Report of the OECD Committee on Fiscal Affairs (1977) pp. 7-15; David Aronofsky, "Piercing the Transnational Corporate Veil : Trends, Developments and the Need for Widespread Adoption of Enterprise Analysis", 10 N.C.J. Int'l L. & Com. Reg. 31 (1985) p. 61; Howard La Mont, "Multinational Enterprise, Transfer Pricing and the 482 Mess" 14 Columbia Journal of Transnational Law 383 (1975).

business conditions of branch offices and independent shipping agents".[1] The typical question is whether a holding company should be liable to suit in a country where a subsidiary is registered or is operating. Where the subsidiary operates like a branch office and can bind the holding company, jurisdiction will be extended over the holding company on the basis of agency, but not otherwise.[2] This however may be taking too narrow a view of the situation. At least in jurisdictional matters - where issues of substantive liability are not directly involved - it is arguable that the economic reality of the relationship between the holding and the subsidiary company, rather than a pure agency relationship, should be adopted as a test for the "presence" or "doing business" criteria of jurisdiction.[3]

Cross-border insolvencies foster complex conflict of laws issues. The variety, as between the legal systems, in the types of proceedings that may be initiated when a debtor is unable to pay its debts, the various localities in which assets and liabilities may be situated and the different rules of priority raise difficult problems even where only one company is concerned.[4] Where the cross-border insolvency involves a corporate group, the different attitudes evidenced by courts and governmental authorities regarding group trading and the varying levels of respect shown towards the entity principle in different countries combine to create virtually irreconcilable conflict situations. With the rapid expansion of cross-border mergers and acquisitions in the 1980s, the 1990's will probably witness a growing number of insolvencies with serious cross-border implications.[5] Substantial interests

---

[1] J.J. Fawcett, "Jurisdiction and Subsidiaries" [1985] J.B.L. 16 at p. 25.

[2] *Vide ibid.* p. 25; Latty, *op. cit.* p. 60.

[3] *Vide* Lawrence P. Kessel, "Trends in the Approach to the Corporate Entity Problem in Civil Litigation" 41 Georgtown L.J. 525 (1953) pp. 526-532; J.J. Fawcett, "Jurisdiction and Subsidiaries" [1985] J.B.L. 16 p. 25; John K. Rothpletz, "Ownership of a Subsidiary as a Basis for Jurisdiction" 20 New York University Intramural Law Review 127 (1965); Henry D. McCoy, "The United States Parent Corporation - European Subsidiary Relationship under the European Antitrust Regulations" 3 Virginia Journal of International Law 46 (1963) at p. 62; Cf. Note, "Piercing the Corporate Veil : the Alter Ego Doctrine under Federal Common Law" 95 Harv. L.R. 853 (1982).

[4] *Vide* UNCITRAL, Note by the Secretariat of the United Nations Commission on International Trade Law (UNCITRAL), ref. A/CN.9/378/Add.4, 23 June 1993, pp. 3-8; UNCITRAL, Note by the Secretariat of the United Nations Commission on International Trade Law (UNCITRAL), ref. A/CN.9/398, 31 May - 17 June 1994, pp. 2-3.

[5] Cf. Rupert M.A. Connell, "Chapter 11 - the United Kingdom Dimension" (1990) 6 Ins. L. & P. 90 at p. 90.

will therefore often be at stake. The need for international regulation by multilateral convention is patently obvious.[1]

Moreover, transnational corporate groups provoke issues that transcend the difficulties traditionally encountered by the lack of harmonisation in the laws of different legal systems. The rapid growth and proliferation of transnational groups has created problems for both home and host states *inter se* and in their relationship with the transnational groups.[2] Home countries have an interest to control transnational groups even extra-territorially in such areas as anti-trust enforcement, securities legislation, balance of payments control, tax policy and national security related export controls.[3] Host countries often fear that foreign transnational groups impinge upon their national sovereignty and ultimate industrial independence. Host countries are particularly wary of abuses or excesses in matters of tax avoidance, repatriation of profits and employment policies. Transnational groups on their part resist attempts at eroding their functionality, flexibility and power. The fundamental aims of control should be to deal appropriately - preferably by international convention - with any sources of conflict, to allay fears that transnational groups will infringe upon national sovereignty and to increase and consolidate the benefits of transnational groups whilst eliminating or at least decreasing the possibility of abuse.[4]

---

[1] Efforts are being made by the United Nations Commission on International Trade Law (UNCITRAL) to broaden the discussion on the feasibility of harmonised rules on international insolvencies. *Vide* Note by the Secretariat of the United Nations Commission on International Trade Law (UNCITRAL), ref. A/CN.9/378/Add.4, 23 June 1993; Note by the Secretariat of the United Nations Commission on International Trade Law (UNCITRAL), ref. A/CN.9/398, 31 May - 17 June 1994. New pan-European insolvency procedures should also be in place by the end of 1995. At the time of writing, the text of a new convention is nearing completion. The proposed provisions would require the courts in each member state to recognise one another's authority and insolvency proceedings. *Vide* "EU plans rules on bankruptcy" *Financial Times*, 21st April 1994.

[2] Clive M. Schmitthoff, "Multinationals in Court" [1972] J.B.L. 103 p. 104.

[3] *Vide* Joseph P. Griffin, "The Power of Host Countries over the Multinational : Lifting the Veil in the European Economic Community and the United States" 6 Law and Policy in International Business 375 (1974) p. 377. Cf. David Aronofsky, "Piercing the Transnational Corporate Veil : Trends, Developments and the Need for Widespread Adoption of Enterprise Analysis" 10 N.C.J. Int'l L. & Com. Reg. 31 (1985) p. 81.

[4] Cf. Wallace, *op. cit.* p. 22; Tom Hadden, *The Control of Corporate Groups* (1983) p. 24.

## 7. VARIOUS INTERESTS IN THE CORPORATE GROUP ARRANGEMENT

Corporate groups give rise to a multitude of complex legal issues primarily because of the wide range of competing interests typically presented by group activity. The identity and variety of these interests could be gleaned even from the foregoing review of the particular legal issues involved in the group activity.[1] Some of these interests can be qualified as insiders : the "enterprise" as an economic unit, the various companies within the group, the shareholders (including future shareholders), the financial investors, the management and the employees (including pensioners).[2] Other interests can be regarded as outsiders : creditors (including tort victims), consumers, the government, the public at large and - where the group is transnational in character - the home and host states and the international community.

Each interest group - insider or outsider - is affected by the conduct of the activities of the corporate group. In many respects, these interests are no different from those that would be asserted in a "one-company" enterprise. But the group structure and group method of doing business exert additional pressure on existing tensions between the various interest groups involved. And the onset of insolvency will rudely awaken any dormant interests and create further conflicts even *within* the interest groups themselves.[3]

Legal analysis strives to understand, explain and where possible reconcile or balance the often conflicting claims and expectations involved in the corporate group scenario. Even in the case of the traditional "single-company" enterprise situation, the major obstacle to any attempt at striking an equilibrium is that English law still adheres to the traditional view that the interests of a company are essentially the interests of the shareholders.[4] This

---

[1] A number of commentators have attempted to identify the various stakeholders in company law generally. *Vide* The Law Society, The Reform of Company Law - Memorandum of the Company Law Committee of the Law Society, July 1991 (hereinafter cited as "Law Society Memorandum (1991)") p. 3; Jean Paillusseau, "The Nature of the Company" in Drury and Xuereb (ed.), *op. cit.* pp. 25-26; Hopt, Regulating Groups, p. 88; Lord Wedderburn, "The Legal Development of Corporate Responsibility : For Whom Will Corporate Managers Be Trustees?" in Klaus J. Hopt and Gunther Teubner (ed.), *Corporate Governance and Directors' Liabilities* (1985) pp. 3-54.

[2] Cf. Tom Hadden, *The Control of Corporate Groups* (1983) p. 20.

[3] Cf. Fidelis Oditah, "Assets and the Treatment of Claims in Insolvency" 108 L.Q.R. 459 (1992) p. 459.

[4] *Vide Multinational Gas and Petrochemical Co.* v. *Multinational Gas and Petrochemical Services* [1983] 3 W.L.R. 492 (C.A.).

orthodox doctrine means that if the interests of say, consumers, the community at large, the environment and, as long as the company is solvent, the interests of the creditors are taken into account, they must relate in some way to the financial interests of the company itself.[1] The interests of the employees may appear to be taken into account,[2] though the employees seem to have no effective means of enforcing such interests.[3] In other jurisdictions, such as the United States, there is a noticeable departure from identifying the interests of the company with the financial interests of its shareholders towards a recognition that a company constitutes an enterprise in which many conflicting interests must be reconciled.[4] The orthodox stand adopted in English law means that the reconciliation of conflicting interests in complex corporate groups has become considerably more difficult.

Legal systems should seek to fairly balance the various interests involved. The enterprise - represented by the corporate group - can perhaps be viewed as the centre of these interests.[5] The protection of the enterprise and of its orbital interests is probably the best guarantee of the various interests concerned. Admittedly, there will be times when a certain degree of

---

[1] *Evans v. Brunner, Mond & Co. Ltd.* [1921] 1 Ch. 359; *Mercury Bay Co-Operative Dairy Co. Ltd. v. Lilley* [1946] N.Z.L.R. 766, *aff'd* [1947] N.Z.L.R. 632. Where the company is insolvent or nearing insolvency, the interests of the creditors should be considered. *Vide Lonrho Ltd. v. Shell Petroleum Co. Ltd.* [1980] 1 W.L.R. 627 (H.L.); *Kinsela v. Russell Kinsela Pty. Ltd.* (1986) 4 A.C.L.C. 215.

[2] s. 309 of the C.A. 1985. *Vide* also s. 719 of the C.A. 1985, (power of company to provide for employees on cessation or transfer of business) and s. 187 of the Insolvency Act 1986 (power to make over assets to employees). (The Insolvency Act 1986 is hereinafter cited as the "I.A. 1986".)

[3] Cf. L.C.B. Gower, *Principles of Modern Company Law* (5th ed. 1992) pp. 554-555. (This edition is hereinafter cited as "Gower").

[4] *Vide Shlensky v. Wrigley*, 237 N.E. 2d 776 (Ill. App. Ct. 1968); *A.P. Smith Mfg. Co. v. Barlow*, 98 A. 2d 581 (N.J. 1953); *Theodora Holding Corp. v. Henderson* 257 A. 2d 398 (Del. Ch. 1969). The trend in the United States is also noticeable in statutory reform. The Model Business Corporation Act of the American Bar Association was drafted to balance the interests of the public, corporations, shareholders and management, though in recent years the philosophies underlying the Act have become increasingly "permissive" or management oriented. *Vide* Model Business Corporation Act Annotated (3 vols.) (2nd ed. 1971, with 1973 and 1977 Supplements); Henn and Alexander, *op. cit.* pp. 200-201.

[5] Cf. Paillusseau, *op. cit.* pp. 25-26; L.S. Sealy "Directors' 'Wider' Responsibilities - Problems Conceptual, Practical and Procedural" 13 Monash U.L.R. 164 (1987) p. 174.

prioritisation of interests will be necessary.[1] But as long as the various interests involved in the group phenomenon are perceived as one inter-related and inter-dependent network, the equitable resolution of conflicts should not be a forlorn hope. A legal system that fails to readjust itself by recognising and reconciling the respective needs and expectations of conflicting interests in corporate organisation will, as the community's confidence in it is eroded, witness a gradual deterioration of its former influence and possibly fall into disrepute.[2]

## 8. CURRENT LAW ILL-SUITED TO DEAL WITH THE VARIOUS ISSUES AND CONFLICTING INTERESTS

The preceding discussion demonstrates that the corporate group structure and the group method of business activity raise a host of legal issues whose complexity is often compounded by the conflicting interests at stake and sometimes by the transnational dimension involved. Yet even though groups have been a familiar feature of economic life for a number of decades, the law remains, except for a few specific exceptions, largely oblivious to the group phenomenon.[3]

Nor is the law well suited to deal with the challenge of change. The problem is that current law was fashioned to meet and regulate mid-nineteenth century exigencies and modes of conducting business.[4] Yet in the

[1] Cf. Drury and Xuereb (ed.), *op. cit.* p. 14; Klaus J. Hopt, "Self-Dealing and the Use of Corporate Opportunity and Information : Regulating Directors' Conflicts of Interests" in Hopt and Teubner (ed.), *op. cit.* pp. 320-321.

[2] *Vide* the somewhat more apocalyptic statement in Adolf. A. Berle, "For whom Corporate Managers *are* Trustees: A Note" 45 Harv. L.R. 1365 (1932) at p. 1372.

[3] The principal exceptions are the prohibition of cross-shareholding (s. 23, C.A. 1985), the duty to disclose information for the shareholders and the public especially through group accounts (ss. 227-232 and Schedules 4-6, C.A. 1985), the provision against directors' unfair dealing with subsidiaries (ss. 318(1)(c), 319(1), 320(1), 323(3), 324 and 330, C.A. 1985). The C.A. 1985 also takes the corporate group into account in the regulation of financial assistance by a company for the acquisition of its own shares (ss. 151 and 153, C.A. 1985), in the regulation of substantial property transactions (s. 321, C.A. 1985), in the powers of inspectors during an investigation (s. 433, C.A. 1985), in the definition of "connected persons" (s. 346, C.A. 1985), in the definition of associated companies (s. 435(6), I.A. 1986) and in the exclusion from "investment business" (Sched. 1, para. 18 of the Financial Services Act 1986).

[4] This point is widely made. *Vide* e.g., Farrar, p. 538; R.S. Nathan, "Controlling the Puppeteers : Reform of Parent-Subsidiary laws in New Zealand" 3 Canterbury L.R. 1

meantime the practices and structure of modern enterprise have, in certain important respects, evolved along a fundamentally different track.[1] Current law appears fettered to the "single-company" enterprise model and when forced to deal with commercial reality the solutions it uses "have to be cobbled together in a somewhat makeshift fashion."[2] The legal concepts of entity law originating in the context of a simpler economic order and surviving in part through the doctrine of binding precedent can no longer properly cater for a world dominated by complex corporate groups. We can no longer discuss problems in terms of old ideas when the solution may well depend upon getting rid of such ideas and replacing them with concepts more in consonance with current thought and knowledge. A re-examination of the underlying conceptual framework is not only desirable, but inevitable.

## 9. DESIRABILITY OF A COMPREHENSIVE SYSTEM GOVERNING CORPORATE GROUPS

Given the wide ranging, complex and inter-related issues involved in group activity, it would be desirable if a comprehensive system of law governing all aspects of corporate groups were to be introduced. Realistically however,

---

*Cont.*

(1986) p.1; N.C. Sargent, "Beyond the legal entity doctrine : Parent-Subsidiary relations under the West German Konzernrecht" 10 Can. Bus. L.J. 327 p. 327; K.W. Wedderburn, "Multinationals and the Antiquities of Company Law" 47 M.L.R. 87 (1984) p. 92; Leonard Sealy, "A Company Law for Tomorrow's World" 2 Co. Law. 195 (1981) p. 195; David Milman, "The Courts and the Companies Acts : the Judicial contribution to Company Law" [1990] LMCLQ 402 p. 402 footnote 17; T. W. Walde, "Parent Subsidiary Relations in the integrated corporate system : a comparison of American and German law" 9 Journal of International Law and Economics 455 (1974) p. 456; Tom Hadden, *Company Law and Capitalism* (2nd ed. 1977) pp. 425 *et seq*; Fidelis Oditah, "Wrongful Trading" [1990] LMCLQ 205 p. 205; Mary Stokes, "The Problem of the Legitimacy of Corporate Managerial Power" in William Twining (ed.), *Legal Theory and Common Law* (1986) pp. 167-168; Clive M. Schmitthoff and Frank Wooldridge (ed.), *Groups of Companies* (1991) p. ix; The Cork Report, Report of the Review Committee, Insolvency Law and Practice, Cmnd. 8558 (1982) (hereinafter cited as "Cork Report") para. 1922, p. 434.

[1] *Vide* Tricker, *op. cit.* at pp. 2-3, 13, 16, 23-24; Drury and Xuereb (ed.), *op. cit.* p. 11.

[2] Prentice, The English Experience, p. 128.

the chances of any such comprehensive reform - at least in the near future - appear nought.[1]

Certainly, however, many of the issues involved merit continuing study. The issues have to be clearly identified, the underlying policies examined, present law critically analysed and proposals for reform at both the domestic and the international level put forward and vigorously debated.

It is of course beyond the scope of this work to ponder upon all the legal issues and conflicting interests involved in the group phenomenon. To attempt to do so in a manner which would do justice to the subject would necessitate a multi-volumed effort. The proliferation, complexity and power of corporate groups together with the various issues and interests inherent in such phenomenon have been noted in order to throw into relief the one issue - that of holding company liability for the debts of insolvent subsidiaries - with which this work is primarily concerned. It is hoped that this study will constitute a modest contribution to a vast and complex area of the law.

## 10. THE PRINCIPAL ISSUE - LIABILITY TOWARDS CREDITORS

This study dwells broadly upon the issue of inter-corporate liability towards the external creditors of insolvent companies within a corporate group. The principal problem, stated in a somewhat over-simplified form, is the liability of a holding company for the debts of its insolvent subsidiaries. Allied questions, requiring only peripheral treatment, include : (i) the liability of a company towards creditors of an insolvent affiliated company; (ii) the liability of a subsidiary for the debts of its insolvent holding company and (iii) the position in the event of the insolvency of the whole group.

The work is therefore concerned with two opposing interest groups that play centre stage in the multi-corporate organisation : on the one hand there is the corporate group with its component members (that is the holding company and the various subsidiaries); on the other hand there are the creditors of the various members of the group. Internal conflicts also arise *within* each interest group. Thus, the interests of the group as a whole or the interests of one member may not be the same as those of another member.

---

[1] Apart from Germany, Brazil appears to be the only country to have enacted a distinct and fairly complete body of rules governing corporate groups. The enactment of a comprehensive system for groups has also been under consideration in France for a number of years. *Vide* Frank Wooldridge, "The Treatment of Groups of Companies in Germany and Brazil" in John Adams (ed.), *Essays for Clive Schmitthoff* (1983) p. 155.

And the interests of one creditor or class of creditors may not be the same as those of another creditor or class of creditors.

It must be recognised that the problem of inter-corporate liability is linked to some of the other issues involved in group activity which were identified earlier.[1] The claims of creditors, for instance, may compete with those of minority shareholders and of employees in the group. Similarly, any discussion on the rights of creditors will necessarily involve a consideration of the accountability of directors. The subject of creditor protection cannot be dealt with in an airtight compartmentalised manner.

## 11.  SEPARATE JURIDICAL PERSONALITY AND LIMITED LIABILITY - MAJOR OBSTACLES TO INTER-CORPORATE LIABILITY

The twin concepts of separate personality and limited liability feature whenever a company has been incorporated, whether the shares are held by individuals or by corporate members. The same concepts naturally arise also in the holding-subsidiary arrangement.[2] And it makes no difference if the shares are all substantially held by one shareholder.[3] A holding company is a member of the subsidiary, both are distinct entities at law[4] and the liability of the holding company is limited to its capital investment.[5] It follows that the holding company is, *qua* holding company, not liable for the debts of its subsidiary. Of course, a creditor of a subsidiary may, with regard to the same subject matter, also be a creditor of the holding company. But this will arise

---

[1]  *Supra* pp. 16-21.

[2]  *Lonrho Ltd.* v. *Shell Petroleum Co. Ltd.* [1980] 1 W.L.R. 627 (H.L.); *Rur. Mun. of Assiniboia* v. *Suburban Rapid Transit Co.* [1931] 2 D.L.R. 862, 39 Man. L.R. 402 *sub. nom. Re Suburban Rapid Transit Co., Winnipeg Electric Co. and Rural Municipality of Assiniboia* (C.A.); *Exchange Bank of Macon* v. *Macon Construction Co.* 25 S.E. 326 (Geo. 1895).

[3]  *Salomon* v. *A. Salomon and Co. Ltd.* [1897] A.C. 22 (H.L.); *Palmer* v. *Ring* 99 N.Y. Supp. 290 (1906).

[4]  *Ebbw Vale Urban District Company* v. *South Wales Traffic Area Licensing Authority* [1951] 2 K.B. 366, 370, [1951] 1 All E.R. 806, 808 (C.A.).

[5]  *Vide* R.S. Nathan, "Controlling the Puppeteers : Reform of Parent-Subsidiary laws in New Zealand" 3 Canterbury L.R. 1 (1986) p. 14; N.C. Sargent, "Corporate Groups and the Corporate Veil in Canada : a penetrating look at Parent-Subsidiary relations in the modern Corporate Enterprise" 17 Manitoba L.J. 156 (1988) pp. 175-176; R.M. Goode (ed.), *Group Trading and the Lending Banker* (1988) p. xvii; Robert. R. Pennington, *Company Law* (6th ed. 1990) pp. 37-38.

only because of some specific cause of action imposing a direct rather than "vicarious" liability on the holding company. Typical examples of direct liability are a guarantee by the holding company and a tort committed jointly by the holding company and its subsidiary.[1]

Equally clear is the principle that whilst a group may in economic reality constitute one enterprise, at law it has no separate existence. There is no separate "group personality".[2] And because there is no group personality, there can at law be neither group assets nor group liabilities.

The principles of separate personality and limited liability stand virtually unassailable in their bedrock foundations in English law. Admittedly, there are some ill-defined inroads - statutory and judicial - eroding at the foundations. But the process has been long and idle and the effect superficial. In the judicial sphere, efforts at carving out broad exceptions to the separate juridical personality rule in the context of corporate groups[3] were soon neutralised.[4] It is of course impossible to predict with any degree of accuracy how the courts will react in the future, but the outlook appears bleak.[5] In the statutory field, the only step forward has been the introduction of liability for "wrongful trading"[6] which, though not purposely directed at the holding-subsidiary relationship, would certainly encompass a holding company if such company qualifies as a "shadow" director.[7] The potentially profound implications of this statutory inroad in the context of group trading have not perhaps been widely appreciated.[8]

It will have been observed that many of the legal problems relating to corporate group activity (such as employee representation, disclosure and jurisdictional issues) do not actually involve a question of substantive

---

[1] Direct holding company liability is discussed *post*, in Chapter III.

[2] Robert Pennington, "Personal and real security for group lending" in R.M. Goode (ed.), *Group Trading and the Lending Banker* (1988) p. 52.

[3] *D.H.N. Food Distributors Ltd.* v. *Tower Hamlets L.B.C.* [1976] 1 W.L.R. 852 (C.A.). Cf. *The Roberta* 58 Ll.L.R. 159 (1937).

[4] *Woolfson* v. *Strathclyde Regional Council* 1978 S.L.T. 159 (H.L. Sc.); *Adams* v. *Cape Industries plc* [1990] BCLC 479 (C.A.). *Vide* Gower, pp. 126-132.

[5] *Vide* Gower, p. 132. Cf. by contrast the rather more hopeful commentary in the late 1970s and early 1980s, e.g., Prentice, The English Experience, at p. 101.

[6] I.A. 1986, s. 214.

[7] *Vide* I.A. 1986, ss. 214(7) and 251. *Vide* further *post* Chapter V pp. 213-217.

[8] *Vide* however D.D. Prentice, "Group Indebtedness" in Clive M. Schmitthoff and Frank Wooldridge (ed.), *Groups of Companies* (1991) pp. 77-79 (Prentice's contribution is hereinafter referred to as "Prentice, Group Indebtedness"); Gower, pp. 113-114.

liability. In such cases, only the principle of separate juridical personality is likely to be at issue. Limited liability plays no role. Where however an issue of substantive liability - such as holding company liability for the debts of its insolvent subsidiaries - is involved, the additional hurdle of limited liability must be surmounted or by-passed. Given the deep-seated commitment to the policy of limited liability, it is surmised that legal recognition of the reality of the group will probably come about earlier in those situations where issues of liability are not involved than in those situations where such issues are at stake.

## 12.  PURPOSE AND SCOPE OF WORK - METHODOLOGY

### 12.1. Purpose and scope of work

The central thesis of this work is that entity law is no longer entirely suitable to deal with the liability question in the corporate group context and that in certain well-defined situations entity law should give way to an enterprise analysis.

The main thrust of the study is essentially two-pronged :

(i) to challenge as outmoded and inadequate the virtual dogma of English law that a holding company is not answerable for the debts of its insolvent subsidiaries; and

(ii) to put forward a number of somewhat radical recommendations for reform in this area of the law.

### 12.2. The methodology adopted

The central theme of the work will be developed broadly on the following lines :

(i) In the first place, it will be demonstrated that inherent in the holding-subsidiary relationship is the potential for abusive or unfair behavioural practices that could prejudicially affect the interests of the external creditors of the group. Separate and distinct types of mischief, requiring different treatment, are discernible amongst the abusive or unfair practices. For this reason, such practices will need to be categorised.

(ii) In the second place, the underlying broad policy considerations in this area of the law will be identified and assessed.

(iii) In the third place, the abusive or unfair practices will be examined in the light both of the obtaining principles of English law and of the underlying broad policy considerations. The inadequacy of existing remedies, especially with regard to certain types of creditors, will be exposed. It will be shown that English law, bound as it is hand and foot to the entity principle, is locked away from the real world with the result that unacceptable corporate behaviour is sometimes condoned.

(iv) Finally, the study will, after weighing the various arguments for and against a change in the law, conclude that reform is called for and proceed to submit some radical proposals for reform. The basic thrust of the reform proposals will be that in certain well-defined circumstances liability should be imposed on the holding company for the debts of its insolvent subsidiaries.

## 13. RELEVANCE OF DIFFERENT TYPES OF CREDITORS

Each component member of the corporate group has its own exclusive orbit of creditors. Creditors also constitute one of the interest groups revolving around the corporate group as a whole. Conflicts between one creditor interest group and the other are bound to arise. Conflicting tensions surface even *within* each creditor interest group. Such conflicts arise from differences in the nature of the various claims and expectations pursued by creditors. Moreover, creditor interest groups also compete with other types of interest groups.

Now whereas some of the reform proposals to be made in this work benefit all creditors indiscriminately, other proposals depend on a distinction that should be drawn between different types of creditors. A distinction will in the first place be made between contract and tort creditors. The distinction is relevant to the observation often made in defence of the principle of limited liability that creditors know or should know they are dealing with a limited liability company, that they therefore assume the relative risks and that they should not complain in the event that the company declines into insolvency.[1] This argument of course clearly overlooks the position of tort creditors who *ex hypothesis* can *not* know that they are dealing with a company. But the contract-tort dichotomy is not the only distinction that should be drawn. For the *caveat* creditor argument also collapses when applied to certain contract creditors, such as consumers, employees and pensioners. Such creditors - though admittedly contract creditors - may lack the sophistication, resources or the opportunity to even recognise (let alone assess) the risk being taken when concluding a transaction with a company.[2] In this work it will be argued that such contract creditors should in certain cases qualify as "involuntary" creditors and benefit from the proposals to be made that a holding company should, in certain specified situations, be saddled with liability towards the involuntary creditors of an insolvent subsidiary.

## 14.  THE ROLE OF THE POLICY OF LIMITED LIABILITY

It is self-evident that any protection to be afforded to external creditors by the imposition of inter-corporate liability will impinge upon the principle of limited liability. It is equally clear that limited liability is widely acknowledged not only as a fundamental - even hallowed - tenet of company law, but also as an essential element of the economic order.[3] Certainly, no proper investigation into the question of inter-corporate liability can be conducted *in vacuo* without due consideration being given to the effect that the introduction of new remedies may have on the principle of limited liability and its role in the contemporary commercial world. The question of inter-corporate liability in fact necessarily involves economic considerations of some complexity, without which this study would not be complete. This indeed is one subject where law and economics cross paths. Here law and economics examine the same material from two different functional yet complementary standpoints. Clearly, the problem of group inter-corporate liability cannot be solved in the widest possible social terms if it is submitted to purely legal or economic analysis.[4] Basic economic analysis will therefore

---

[1]  *Vide post* Chapter IV p. 177.

[2]  *Vide* further *post* Chapter IV, pp. 182-186.

[3]  *Vide post* Chapter IV pp. 153-154.

[4]  Cf. C.A. Cooke, *Corporation, Trust and Company - An Essay in Legal History* (1950) pp. 12-13. Reflecting the significance of the company in the economy, much of the scholarly literature provoked by company law reform is the work of economists rather

feature in the discussion on limited liability, though it must be said that this work does not purport to adopt a multi-disciplinary approach.

One other point ought to be made at this stage. The proposals for reform set out in this study will admittedly encroach on the principle of limited liability. But this work will not be proposing the adoption of holding company liability as a blanket solution. The principle of limited liability will not only survive the reform proposals, but will continue to be recognised as a fundamental - though less sacred - tenet of company law.

## 15. REFORMS LONG CALLED FOR

The problem of inter-corporate liability which lies at the heart of this work is not a newly emergent strain of corporate virus. Nor has this study discovered it. Calls for reform in this area have in fact been made for a number of years. The attacks have originated largely from academic, judicial and law reform quarters.

Probably the earliest sortie came exactly half a century ago from Kahn-Freund. Whilst discussing the corporate entity concept in the so-called "one-man company" situation - a situation broadly analogous to the wholly-owned subsidiary - Kahn-Freund dismissed as "calamitous"[1] the decision of the House of Lords in *Salomon* v. *A. Salomon and Co. Ltd.*[2] There was in his view a "complete failure of the courts to mitigate ... the rigidities of the 'folklore' of corporate entity in favour of the legitimate interests of the company's creditors".[3] He also toyed with the idea of protecting outside creditors by a general clause under which persons with a controlling interest in a company should be liable for its debts.[4]

Almost forty years after Kahn-Freund's criticism, Schmitthoff, in a series of articles in the Journal of Business Law, observed that English law had not yet begun to grapple with the legal problems raised by the wholly owned

---

*Cont.*

than lawyers. Cf. Sian Elias, "Company Law in the 1990s" in J.H. Farrar (ed.), *Contemporary Issues in Company Law* (1987) p. 6.

[1] O. Kahn-Freund, "Some Reflections on Company Law Reform" 7 M.L.R. 54 (1944) at p. 54.

[2] [1897] A.C. 22 (H.L.).

[3] *Ibid.* at p. 55.

[4] *Ibid.* at p. 57.

subsidiary and the controlled company.[1] He labelled the holding company liability question as "one of the great unresolved problems of modern times"[2] and proposed that the holding company should always be liable for the debts of its wholly owned insolvent subsidiaries.[3]

Around the same time, Wedderburn, in a note on *Multinational Gas and Petrochemical Co.* v. *Multinational Gas and Petrochemical Services*[4] called for statute to break corporate veils and "make parent corporations, in stated circumstances, liable for some at least of the debts and liabilities of the subsidiaries".[5]

More recently - following the 1986 reforms in insolvency law which arguably ameliorated the lot of external creditors in a group context - Goode lamented that "[a]s the years pass the deficiencies of English law in the treatment of group trading become even more apparent both in relation to accounting requirements and in relation to liability for debts incurred by members of the group".[6] Goode also expressed the hope that the European Union Draft Ninth Directive may provide the impetus for change.[7] And Prentice, also writing after the 1986 reforms, stated that "[i]n many respects the state of English company law on the liability of a parent company for the debts of its subsidiary is far from satisfactory ...".[8]

Pot-shots have also occasionally been taken by the judiciary. In *Re*

---

[1] Clive M. Schmitthoff, "The Wholly Owned and Controlled Subsidiary" [1978] J.B.L. 218 at p. 229.

[2] Clive M. Schmitthoff, "Banco Ambrosiano and modern company law" [1982] J.B.L. 361 at p. 363. *Vide* also Clive M. Schmitthoff, "Multinationals and the antiquity of company law" [1984] J.B.L. 194 pp. 194-195.

[3] Clive M. Schmitthoff, "Lifting the Corporate Veil" [1980] J.B.L. 156 p. 160.

[4] [1983] 3 W.L.R. 492 (C.A.).

[5] K.W. Wedderburn, "Multinationals and the Antiquities of Company Law" 47 M.L.R. 87 (1984) at p. 90. *Vide* also Tom Hadden, *The Control of Corporate Groups* (1983) p. viii; Frank Wooldridge, *Groups of Companies - The Law and Practice in Britain, France and Germany* (1981) p. 112; Tricker, *op. cit.* p. 5; Michael Whincup, "'Inequitable Incorporation' - the Abuse of a Privilege" 2 Co. Law. 158 (1981) at p. 166. Cf. P.S. Atiyah, "Thoughts on Company Law Philosophy" 8 Lawyer 15 (1965) pp. 18-19 who even queried the soundness of limited liability as a general principle.

[6] R.M. Goode (ed.), *Group Trading and the Lending Banker* (1988) at p. xxvii.

[7] *Ibid.* at p. xxvii. On the Draft Ninth Directive *vide post* Chapter X pp. 466-467.

[8] D.D. Prentice, "Fraudulent Trading : Parent Company's Liability for the Debts of its Subsidiary" 103 L.Q.R. 11 (1987) p. 14.

*Southard & Co. Ltd.*[1] Templeman L.J., referring to the insulation that a holding company enjoys from the debts of its insolvent subsidiaries, observed that "English company law possesses some curious features which may generate curious results".[2] And in *The Albazero*[3] Roskill L.J. stated that "[m]odern commerce is hampered ... by too rigid an adherence to the basic principle ... that all companies within a group are separate legal entities. Where the group is in truth the party interested and injured, the law should not be too astute not to recognise the realities of the position ...".[4] More recently, Staughton L.J. noted in *Atlas Maritime Co. S.A.* v. *Avalon Maritime. Ltd. ("The Coral Rose")*[5] that "[t]he creation ... of a subsidiary company with minimal liability, which will operate with the parent's funds and on the parent's directions but not expose the parent to liability, *may not seem the most honest way of trading*".[6]

A number of salvos have also been launched from constituted bodies and from law reform agencies. In 1979, the Consultative Committee of Accountancy Bodies proposed that a holding company should be regarded as guaranteeing the debts of group companies unless it publicly declares otherwise.[7] This proposal was however somewhat tempered in a later report,

---

[1] [1979] 1 W.L.R. 1198 (C.A.).

[2] *Ibid.* at p. 1208.

[3] [1977] A.C. 774 (C.A.), reversed [1977] A.C. 774 (H.L.).

[4] [1977] A.C. 774 at p. 821.

[5] [1991] 1 Lloyd's Rep. 563 (C.A.).

[6] *Ibid.* at p. 571. (emphasis added). In *Re Augustus Barnett & Son Ltd.* [1986] BCLC 170, Hoffmann J. observed : "The circumstances in which parent companies should be liable for the debts of their subsidiaries is a matter of considerable public importance and debate. It may be that the law on this subject is inadequate." *Ibid.* at p. 173. Hoffmann J. however declined to express a definite opinion, rightly noting that to do so would require a wide investigation of the issues of public policy and that such an exercise could not be attempted in the case before him which concerned an interlocutory application to strike out a pleading. *Ibid.* p. 173.

[7] Consultative Committee of Accountancy Bodies, External Liabilities of Groups of Companies - Memorandum submitted in September 1979 to the Companies Division of the Department of Trade and to the Insolvency Law Review Committee of the Department of Trade on behalf of the Consultative Committee of Accountancy Bodies (hereinafter cited as "CCAB Memorandum (1979)"), para. 16-20. These proposals met with considerable opposition. *Vide* The Law Society, External Liabilities of Groups of Companies - Memorandum by the Standing Committee on Company Law of the Law Society, January 1981 (hereinafter cited as the "Law Society Memorandum (1981)"), para. 3.01-3.05 and 7.01; CBI Memorandum (1980), pp. 3-4.

published in 1981, that had taken into account responses to the earlier report.[1]

During the same period, the Cork Committee, whilst recognising "the enormous complexities" of the subject stated that "the matter [of holding company liability] is of such importance and of such gravity that there should be the widest possible review of the different considerations, with a view to the introduction of reforming legislation within the foreseeable future."[2] The Committee stressed that such revision "be undertaken as a matter of urgency",[3] but because its terms of reference were limited to insolvency law and because "the ramifications of group trading spread throughout company law",[4] it chose not to delve deeply into the matter and consequently refrained from making any specific recommendations.[5]

Regrettably, the judicial, academic and institutional volleys, though often eloquently stated, have been too sporadic. Moreover, they have inevitably lacked the concerted thrust necessary to penetrate the heavily fortified and thickly armoured battlements surrounding those within whose power it is to bring about fundamental change.[6]

---

[1] Consultative Committee of Accountancy Bodies, External Liabilities of Groups of Companies - Memorandum submitted in January 1981 to the Companies Division of the Department of Trade and to the Insolvency Law Review Committee of the Department of Trade on behalf of the Consultative Committee of Accountancy Bodies (hereinafter cited as "CCAB Memorandum (1981)"), para. 14.

[2] The Cork Report, para. 1939, p. 437; para. 1952, p. 439. In 1959, the Jenkins Report (Report of the Company Law Reform Committee, Cmnd. 1749 (1962)) (hereinafter cited as the "Jenkins Report") recorded Board of Trade evidence on "the dangers of abuse through the incorporation with limited liability of very small undercapitalised businesses". *Ibid.* para. 20, p. 5.

[3] *Ibid.* para. 1952, p. 439.

[4] *Ibid.* para. 1951, p. 439.

[5] The Cork Committee did however recommend that any intercompany indebtedness which appears to represent the long-term capital structure of a subsidiary should be subordination to the claims of external creditors. *Vide* the Cork Report, para. 1963, pp. 441-442. The recommendation has never been implemented. More recently, a leader in the *Financial Times* suggested that courts could be given a "wider equitable right to disregard the separate legal status of subsidiaries in specific circumstances." *Vide* "Make them liable" *Financial Times*, 5th January 1995.

[6] When the Bill which eventually became the Companies Act 1980 was being debated in Parliament, Mr. Stanley Clinton Davis moved amendments both at the Committee stage and the Report stage in the House of Commons aimed at imposing holding company liability for the debts of subsidiaries under certain conditions. A vigorous debate followed, but the Government did not support the amendments. Nevertheless, it was

## 16. DISREGARD OF ENTITY FOR THE BENEFIT OF THE HOLDING COMPANY

It is indeed ironic that despite the number of calls for the recognition of some form of group liability, most inroads to the entity principle in the context of corporate groups have actually benefited the group rather than worked against it. In taxation for example, the corporate group can gain immensely from certain group relief provisions.[1] And in the judicial field, cases such as *Smith, Stone & Knight Ltd.* v. *Birmingham Corporation,*[2] *Harold Holdsworth & Co. (Wakefield) Ltd.* v. *Caddies,*[3] *D.H.N. Food Distributors Ltd.* v. *Tower Hamlets L.B.C.*[4] and *The Albazero*[5] have tempered the strict rigidity of the entity approach for the undoubted benefit of the holding company.

This judicial approach is in sharp contrast to that adopted in the United States. American courts in fact broadly refuse to countenance any lifting of the veil *in favour* of the holding company - only third persons are allowed to invoke the doctrine.[6] The logical justification is that a holding company,

*Cont.*

recognised by a number of speakers, including government members, that the law as it stood was not wholly satisfactory. *Vide* Parliamentary Debates, Standing Committee A, Session 1979-1980 Vol. I, 11th December 1979 cols. 715-729; Parliamentary Debates (Hansard) 5th Series Vol. 979 (House of Commons) 26th February 1980, cols. 1249 -1272. Government speakers noted however that a comprehensive review of the law relating to insolvency was then being conducted by the Cork Committee and that it would be both premature and inappropriate to pass new legislation piecemeal in advance of that Committee's Report. *Vide* Mr. Reginald Eyre's statement in Parliamentary Debates (Hansard) 5th Series Vol. 979 (House of Commons) 26th February 1980, at cols. 1265-1266, and that of Mr. Cecil Parkinson in Parliamentary Debates, Standing Committee A, Session 1979-1980 Vol. I, 11th December 1979 at col. 725.

[1] *Vide supra* pp. 12-13.

[2] [1939] 4 All E.R. 116.

[3] [1955] 1 W.L.R. 352 (H.L.)

[4] [1976] 1 W.L.R. 852 (C.A.).

[5] [1977] A.C. 774 (C.A.), reversed [1977] A.C. 774 (H.L.). *Vide* especially the judgments of Roskill and Ormrod L.JJ. in the Court of Appeal [1977] A.C. 774 at p. 821 and p. 824 respectively. The House of Lords reversed the decision of the Court of Appeal on another point.

[6] *Feucht* v. *Real Silk Hosiery Mills, Inc.* 12 N.E. 2d 1019 (Ind. App. 1938). Cf. *Florida Industrial Commission* v. *Schwob Co.* 14 So. 2d 666, 153 Fla. 356 (1943); *State ex rel.*

having voluntarily incorporated its subsidiary, should not then set the machinery of the law to undo what it had itself done merely because the subsidiary device becomes disadvantageous. If the group, for fiscal or other beneficial business reasons, chooses to maintain separate legal personalities it should not later seek to cast aside the veil of incorporation because it no longer suits it. *Qui sentit commodum sentire debet et onus.*[1]

## 17.  REASONS FOR LACK OF PROGRESS

Given the numerous calls for reform made over the years, what is it, then, that accounts for the dismal failure to achieve any progress? Several considerations feature.

On a broad level, the subject of company law reform as such has never really been high on the parliamentary agenda. Company law does not arouse keen political interest. It is no vote-catcher.[2]

On a similarly broad level, there is also a systematic failure to take a long

---

*Cont.*

*Sorensen* v. *Weston Bank* 251 N.W. 164 (Neb. 1933). The same judicial reluctance to lift the veil at the request of the incorporator is evident in Canada. *Vide Manley, Inc. et al.* v. *Fallis* (1977) 38 C.P.R. (2d) 74, 2 B.L.R. 277; *Schouls* v. *Canadian Meat Processing Corp et al.* (1983) 147 D.L.R. (3d) 81.

[1] Cf. Note, "Set-off of Subsidiary's Claims against Parent's Indebtedness" 5 Univ. of Chic. L.R. 682 (1938) p. 683; Note, "Disregarding the Separate Entity" 8 Univ. of Cinn. L.R. 348 (1934); Allan G. Gimbel, "Piercing the Corporate Veil" 4 Univ. of Florida L.R. 352 (1951) p. 356; Thomas V. Harris, "Washington's Doctrine of Corporate Disregard" 56 Washington L.R. 253 (1981) p. 256; Note, 78 Univ. of Pennsylvania L.R. 908-9 (1930); Note, "Right of parent corporation to set off deposit of subsidiary against parent's indebtedness to insolvent bank" 21 Minnesota L.R. 851 (1937) p. 851; Henn and Alexander, *op. cit.* p. 357; Blumberg, *Substantive Law* pp. 330-335. The same reasoning was adopted by Ormerod L.J. in the one-man (or, to be precise, the one-woman) company case of *Tunstall* v. *Steigmann* [1962] 2. Q.B. 593. At p. 601 his Lordship, with the concurrence of Danckwerts L.J. (at p. 607) stated - with reference to an incorporator who was pleading the lifting of the veil in her favour - that "[s]he cannot say that ... that she is entitled to take the benefit of any advantages that the formation of a company gave to her, without at the same time accepting the liabilities arising therefrom". Cf. Henry E. Markson, "Corporate Unveiling : Judicial Attitudes" 123 Solicitors' Journal 831, p. 832; F.G. Rixon, "Lifting the Veil between Holding and Subsidiary Companies" 102 L.Q.R. 415 (1986) p. 423.

[2] *Vide* in this regard the trenchant article by P.S. Atiyah, "Thoughts on Company Law Philosophy" 8 Lawyer 15 (1965) p. 15.

term view of company law. There is no attempt to construct a theory of what the rules of company law are for. Indeed there is a propensity to avoid theoretical discussion altogether. Amendments continue to be made on an *ad hoc* piecemeal basis with the result that company legislation is bedevilled by detail.[1] This state of affairs diminishes the chances of any serious and broad discussion taking place - at Parliamentary level at least - on issues of such fundamental importance as that of group liability.

More specifically, it is evident that the subject of holding company liabilities is fraught with "enormous complexities"[2] involving legal, economic and political considerations of profound significance. To take only the legal implications, any proposal for reform for the introduction of some rule of holding company liability must consider several related questions such as : should liability only arise on insolvency? Should the liability of the holding company be direct to the creditors of the subsidiary or should it be by way of a contribution to the assets of the subsidiary? Should liability be joint and several or should the assets of the subsidiary first be discussed? Should the liability be unlimited, or should there be a threshold of liability? Should certain classes of creditors - say involuntary creditors - be treated preferentially to other classes of creditors? Should the holding company be able to exclude liability by contract or by some form of public notice? Should a distinction be made between wholly owned and partially owned subsidiaries? Should a distinction be made on the basis of size? Should liability be imposed on the holding company only or on the group as a whole? Should substantive consolidation ever be applied? Should liability depend on effective and actual control or should the mere potential for control be sufficient? Should undercapitalisation alone ground liability? Should the subordination of inter-corporate claims be a general rule independently of liability? Should presumptions of liability - rebuttable or otherwise - play a role? Should liability extend to subsidiaries acquired from third parties in respect of debts contracted prior to the acquisition?

---

[1] *Vide* The Law Society Memorandum (1991) p. 1; Note, "Is Company Law Still in a Muddle?" 12 Co. Law. 42 (1991).

[2] The Cork Report, para. 1939, p. 437. Arguing against the introduction of a new company law to deal with the liability of corporate groups, the Confederation of British Industry asserted, in 1980, that the question was "fraught with problems" to which it could not see "any satisfactory solution." *Vide* the CBI Memorandum (1980) para. 36 (iii), p. 12.

The above list - which is by no means exhaustive - illustrates the complexity of the whole subject. This complexity, combined with the other factors previously mentioned, naturally hinders the prospects for reform.[1]

One other consideration must not be overlooked. Any proposal advocating the introduction of some form of holding company liability would no doubt encounter very stiff opposition from the business community.[2] Such resistance, probably well organised and involving close parliamentary lobbying, would scuttle any but the most determined efforts at reform.

On the judicial plane, the rule of *stare decisis* and - in contrast to American courts - the persistently conservative attitude of the English courts in adjusting the entity principle to the growing complexities of today's world combine to dampen any hope for judicial reform.[3]

All told, the likelihood of substantial progress originating from within the United Kingdom in the foreseeable future must be judged remote. Reform, when it eventually comes, will be imported from mainland Europe bringing with it the inevitable difficulties - and benefits - associated with harmonisation.


## 18. AMERICAN LAW FOR COMPARATIVE PURPOSES

This work is primarily concerned with English law. Yet its scope is not limited to an analysis *de lege ferenda*. Rather, its focus will be on whether or not existing law adequately safeguards the legitimate interests of external creditors, and if not, on which avenues for reform should be advocated. The approach will therefore also be *de lege condenda*.

---

[1] In the European Union, the conceptual difficulties as well as the diversity of laws explain in part the failure of efforts to introduce group law harmonisation. *Vide* Hopt, Regulating Groups, p. 86.

[2] *Vide*, for example, the strong reaction of the Confederation of British Industry to the proposals made in 1979 by the Consultative Committee of Accountancy Bodies (noted *supra* pp. 37-38) and in 1979 and 1980 by Mr. Clinton Davis in the House of Commons (noted supra p. 38 footnote 6). *Vide* generally the CBI Memorandum (1980).

[3] *Vide*, for a recent illustration of judicial conservatism, the judgment of the Court of Appeal in *Adams* v. *Cape Industries plc* [1990] BCLC 479 (C.A.). The liberal approach of the American courts was already evident even at the turn of the century. Cf. I. Maurice Wormser, "Piercing the Veil of the Corporate Entity" 12 Colum. L.R. 496 (1912) at p. 518.

## 18.1. Benefit of comparative law generally

Although a comparative approach may in certain circumstances be inappropriate and can actually be misused,[1] there can be no doubt that the exercise to be conducted in this study should benefit immensely from the comparative method.

Comparative analysis is salutary on a number of levels.[2] In the first place, it provides a mechanism for discovering some of the matters that are sometimes taken for granted and hones the critical faculties to the sharper edge needed to more fully appreciate one's own system.[3]

Secondly, it introduces a different perspective and provides access and insight into possibly different solutions to the problem under consideration, enabling a more appropriate solution to be adopted.[4]

Thirdly, "cross-fertilisation", while improving "the strain" of the different breeds[5] promotes the mutual understanding essential for progress to the goal of international legal harmonisation.[6]

## 18.2. Relevance of American law

Since the work deals with one specific problem, a micro-comparative approach is evidently necessary.[7] And it is a prerequisite of such an approach that the systems to be compared be naturally or functionally comparable.[8] American law admirably satisfies this requirement.[9]

---

[1] *Vide* O. Kahn-Freund, "On Uses and Misuses of Comparative Law" 37 M.L.R. 1 (1974).

[2] *Vide* generally Konrad Zweigert and Hein Kotz, *Introduction to Comparative Law* (2nd rev. ed. 1992) Ch. II.

[3] *Vide* Drury and Xuereb (ed.), *op. cit.* p. 2.

[4] *Vide* Drury and Xuereb (ed.), *op. cit.* p. 2; Jay Lawrence Westbrook, "A Comparison of Bankruptcy Reorganisation in the US with the Administration Procedure in the U.K." 6 Ins. L. & P. 86 (1990) p.90.

[5] L.C.B. Gower, "Some contrasts between British and American Corporation Law" 69 Harv. L.R. 1369 (1956) at p. 1402.

[6] Cf. Jay Lawrence Westbrook, "A Comparison of Bankruptcy Reorganisation in the US with the Administration Procedure in the U.K." 6 Ins. L. & P. 86 (1990) p. 90.

[7] *Vide* Zweigert and Kotz, *op. cit.* pp. 4-5; Cf. Drury and Xuereb (ed.), *op. cit.* p. 1.

[8] Drury and Xuereb (ed.), *op. cit.* pp. 2, 5; Zweigert and Kotz, *op. cit.* p. 31.

[9] In the United States, "corporation law" falls primarily within the competence of the individual states. Strictly speaking, therefore, one should not really talk of an "American" law of corporations. There are however discernible patterns or trends amongst the various states, which give at least a conceptual unity to the various jurisdictions. It is in this sense

Indeed a number of reasons justifies the choice of American law as a particularly appropriate comparative partner.[1] These reasons are discussed below.

### 18.2.1.  Broadly similar cultural, social and political heritage and similar level of economic development

The United States and the United Kingdom share not only a common language, but also a broadly similar cultural, social and political heritage[2] second only to the Commonwealth countries of Canada, Australia and New Zealand. Moreover, both the United States and the United Kingdom have reached similar levels of economic development. Comparative analysis is more likely to produce results if such a broad similarity is present.[3] Differences - including differences in commercial and business attitudes - certainly exist[4] but they are not so deep as to detract from the utility of pairing English law with American law for comparative purposes.

### 18.2.2. Common underlying conceptual substratum

Writing almost 40 years ago, Gower noted that there seemed to be a widespread feeling both in Britain and the United States that comparative company law had ceased to be fruitful because of the rapid and independent growth of case law and legislation in the two countries.[5] Gower went on to

*Cont.*

that one can refer to American corporation law. *Vide* generally Henn and Alexander, *op. cit.* pp. 23-36.

[1] Immense benefit would undoubtedly be derived from a study of the position in Germany where group regulation has been extensively and comprehensively discussed. Regrettably, the language barrier confronting the author puts a proper consideration of German law beyond contemplation.

[2] L.C.B. Gower, "Some contrasts between British and American Corporation Law" 69 Harv. L.R. 1369 (1956) at p. 1370.

[3] This is a basic theme developed by O. Kahn-Freund in "On Uses and Misuses of Comparative Law" 37 M.L.R. 1 (1974).

[4] Cf. Jay Lawrence Westbrook, "A Comparison of Bankruptcy Reorganisation in the US with the Administration Procedure in the U.K." 6 Ins. L. & P. 86 (1990) p. 87; "Towards a rescue culture" *Financial Times*, 5th October 1993.

[5] L.C.B. Gower, "Some contrasts between British and American Corporation Law" 69 Harv. L.R. 1369 (1956) at p. 1369.

demonstrate that that feeling was misguided.[1] A relatively long time has passed since Gower's observations were recorded. Over such period case law and legislation no doubt continued to develop in both countries along independent paths. But Gower's point is still as valid today as it was in 1956. Both legal systems continue to deal with broadly similar problems resulting from economic and social conditions which are largely the same. Both systems are based on the same general principles of law and equity derived from a common heritage.[2] Fundamental concepts of the common law, such as contract, agency, trust and tort are to a considerable extent co-terminous. And historically, basic concepts even of company law, such as corporate personality, and to a lesser extent, limited liability (which are themselves central to this work) evolved on broadly similar, though parallel, lines both in England and the United States.[3]

### 18.2.3. Advanced economy

The United States has this century dominated the world economy. It has, in economic terms at least, been the most powerful nation, commanding - mostly through corporate groups - vast trading, financial and industrial resources.[4]

It is not surprising therefore that American "corporation law" has come face to face with, and tackled, the problems inherent in corporate group activity.

### 18.2.4. Extensive judicial and academic investigations

The United States, with its wealth of experience in corporate matters and with a strong tradition in the study of corporate issues, offers a multitude of judgments as well as extensive and scholarly literature on all aspects of corporate law, including the question of inter-corporate liability.[5]

---

[1] *Ibid.* pp. 1370 *et seq.*

[2] *Ibid.* p. 1370.

[3] *Vide* also Farrar, p. 726.

[4] *Vide* Tugendhat, *op. cit.* pp. 39, 56; World Investment Report 1993, Ch. I.

[5] Cf. T.W. Walde, "Parent Subsidiary Relations in the integrated corporate system : a comparison of American and German law" 9 Journal of International Law and Economics 455 (1974) p. 455; L.C.B. Gower, "Some contrasts between British and American Corporation Law" 69 Harv. L.R. 1369 (1956) p. 1400.

### 18.2.5. Similar accounting systems

Despite some significant differences, Britain and the United States share broadly similar corporate accounting systems.[1] This factor is relevant to this study in that some of the analysis and reform proposals, especially with regard to undercapitalisation, involve accountancy concepts.

---

[1]  *Vide* M.R. Matthews and M.H.B. Perera, *Accounting Theory and Development* (1991) Chs. 1 and 2. The principal differences in accounting practices between the two countries are identified in Coopers & Lybrand, *Accounting Comparisons - UK/USA* (1990).

# 2 The Corporate Group - Risks of Abuse and Unfairness in Certain Behavioural Practices

## 1. INTRODUCTION

Business enterprises often mutate into complex corporate groups. This transformation usually occurs because of certain attendant benefits either to the corporate group generally or to one or more of the separate components within the group. The principal advantage, no doubt, is the insulation of the various legal units in the enterprise from the liability incurred by any one of the other legal units within such enterprise. Other advantages, such as group tax relief, economic efficiency, flexibility and administrative and accountancy convenience, may further entice the enterprise to evolve into what is often a complex structure of legally separate but functionally inter-related and inter-dependent units.[1]

It is also arguable that the organisation of commercial enterprises into corporate groups may be of benefit even to the other interests concerned in such groups. External creditors and employees, for instance, may gain from the increased strength that may be derived by the organisation of the enterprise into a corporate group. Besides, external creditors of successful legal units within the group sometimes benefit from the insulation of such units from the liabilities of an insolvent affiliate. This latter advantage, however, could only arise where the extent of the deficit of the insolvent legal unit is so large that it would threaten the solvency of the successful legal units. Be that as it may, it is submitted that the possible advantages gained by creditors from the group set-up pale into insignificance when compared to the advantages enjoyed by the enterprise itself from such a set-up.

In any case, it is certain that the organisation of an enterprise into a corporate group brings with it increased risks of abuse and unfairness to the various interests affected by the group. Financial investors, for example, may have little knowledge and even less control over the way their capital is

---

[1] *Vide supra* Chapter I pp. 11-15.

being employed in the corporate group.[1] Minority shareholders are in a notoriously insecure position and the practical difficulty of proving fraud or oppression together with the high costs of litigation deters all but the most determined or convinced of shareholders from seeking redress in court.[2] Nor is any protection afforded to employees of subsidiaries which are closed down in the greater overall interests of the corporate group. And in an international context, transnational corporations, with their inherent ability to move funds, products, personnel and technology around the globe, have the potential to evade many of the policies of individual states in which they operate.[3]

Although the risks encountered by the aforementioned interests should not be overlooked, this work is primarily concerned with the particular risks of abuse and unfairness faced by external creditors of corporate groups and with whether English law adequately remedies such abuse or unfairness.

## 2. NEED TO STUDY BEHAVIOURAL ASPECTS OF CORPORATE GROUP ACTIVITY

In order to assess whether or not English law is satisfactory, it is essential in the first place to explore the behavioural practices of corporate groups. This will facilitate the identification of any abuses or unfair situations confronting external creditors. It is only then that English law can fairly be subjected to the test. The law cannot be examined in a factual vacuum.

## 3. WHAT DOES THE INVESTIGATION REVEAL?

The study of the structure, behaviour and activities of corporate groups reveals a number of significant features about the group phenomenon generally.

Certainly, such a study exposes the proliferation, complexity, expanding growth, dimensional variety and awesome power of corporate group activity. These features clearly raise the question of control both at the domestic and the international level. The study of the group phenomenon also

---

[1] Tom Hadden, *The Control of Corporate Groups* (1983) p. 2.

[2] *Vide supra* pp. 17-18.

[3] Stopford et al., *op. cit.* pp. 3-4.

demonstrates that the *de facto* structure of an enterprise conducted through a corporate group cannot be ascertained by merely examining its legal form. Indeed, the legal structure is often not an accurate reflection of the true distribution of management and control functions.[1] In other words, there is often a mismatch between the corporate structure and the underlying business reality.[2] This feature raises a difficult issue of corporate governance: if the legal structure does not accurately mirror the management reality, why should the legal framework be adopted as the basis for control?[3]

Of more direct concern to this work, however, the study of the group phenomenon also reveals that group corporate organisation and inter-corporate behavioural practices can sometimes prejudice external creditors and constitute, on a broader level, an abuse of the privilege of incorporation.

## 4. CONTROL OF CORPORATE GROUPS

Before identifying, classifying and examining the abusive and unfair practices, it is desirable to highlight the backdrop of control in which these practices occur. An appreciation of the operating context within which these practices occur will facilitate an understanding of the problems and the solutions thereto.

### 4.1. Latent control

Firstly, a distinction must be drawn between latent control and the factual exercise of such control. Inherent in virtually every holding-subsidiary relationship is a latent control.[4] And the holding company does not only have

---

[1] Cf. Wallace, *op. cit.* pp. 17-18.

[2] *Vide* Tricker, *op. cit.* p. 64.

[3] *Vide* Tricker, *op. cit.* p. 69 and Ch. 6.

[4] *Vide* the speeches in *Harold Holdsworth & Co. (Wakefield) Ltd.* v. *Caddies* [1955] 1 W.L.R. 352 (H.L.) especially at p. 358 (per Viscount Kilmuir L.C. and at p. 367 (per Lord Reid); *vide* also the observations of Rodgers A-JA in *Briggs* v. *James Hardie & Co Pty. Ltd.* 16 NSWLR 549 (1989) at p. 577. Cf. *Gramaphones and Typewriters Ltd.* v. *Stanley* [1908] 2 K.B. 89 at pp. 95-96. Contractually, the holding company may allow limits on its control. For example, the holding company may through a shareholders' agreement or in the Articles of Association bind itself to share control with minority shareholders. Similarly, in a takeover bid the acquiring company may, in an effort to placate the regulatory authorities or the management of the target company, agree not to interfere with the existing management of the target company.

the potential to exercise control, but also to exercise it to a considerable degree.[1]

Formally, a holding company can exercise control over its subsidiaries through its appointees on the boards of the subsidiaries. Holding companies generally ensure that such latent power is easily and effectively exercisable at any time. Articles of Association of subsidiaries are drafted in such a way that directors could be appointed and removed at will without the need to convene a general meeting or to get tied up with time-consuming formalities.[2] In the unlikely event of the board of a subsidiary refusing to comply with the wishes of the holding company,[3] it would only be necessary to remove the recalcitrant directors and replace them with more co-operative appointees in order to effectively implement the decision of the holding company.[4]

### 4.2. Factual control

In practice, of course, control is not exercised through such a formal arrangement. Nor can the *de facto* chain of command be determined merely by an examination of the legal structure.[5] There is in fact often a considerable divergence between the legal structure and the management structure within corporate groups.[6] The traditional *loci* of power can shift

---

[1] *Vide Revlon, Inc.* v. *Cripps & Lee Ltd.* [1980] F.S.R. 85 (C.A.) p. 107 (per Buckley L.J.); *Briggs* v. *James Hardie & Co Pty Ltd.* 16 NSWLR 549 (1989) at p. 577 (per Rodgers A-JA). Cf. *D.H.N. Food Distributors Ltd.* v. *Tower Hamlets L.B.C* [1976] 1 W.L.R. 852 (C.A.) p. 860 (per Lord Denning).

[2] *Vide* Tom Hadden, *The Control of Corporate Groups* (1983) p. 14.

[3] *Vide Commercial Solvents Corporation* v. *E.C. Commission* [1974] 1 C.M.L.R. 309 p. 321 (per Advocate-General Warner).

[4] Cf. Lord Reid's observations in *Harold Holdsworth & Co. (Wakefield) Ltd.* v. *Caddies* [1955] 1 W.L.R. 352 (H.L.) at p. 367.

[5] *Vide* Wallace, *op. cit.* p. 26. As a result of the implementation of certain optional tests in the European Community Seventh Directive, English law now formally recognises, for accounting purposes at least, that factual control alone - as opposed to legal control - can be a criterion for determining whether a parent-subsidiary undertaking relationship exists. *Vide* C.A. 1985, s. 258 and Sched. 10A para. (4). Cf.  Muller, *op. cit.* pp. 178-181; Hopt, Regulating Groups, pp. 92-93; *post* Chapter IX pp. 437-442.

[6] *Vide* Joseph P. Griffin, "The Power of Host Countries over the Multinational : Lifting the Veil in the European Economic Community and the United States" 6 Law and Policy in International Business 375 (1974) p. 380; Robert W. Murphy, "Corporate Divisions vs Subsidiaries" 34 Harv. Bus. Rev. 83 (1956) p. 90; World Investment Report 1993 p. 141;

dramatically. Indeed, control in a subsidiary is not usually exercised by its own board but by senior executives or management teams higher up in the group managerial hierarchy.[1]

### 4.3. Autonomous, co-ordinated and dominated subsidiaries

The degree of factual control exercised by holding companies over their subsidiaries can vary substantially. A subtle relationship is involved. Three broad levels of control are discernible. At one end of the spectrum, the holding company would allow a subsidiary to operate autonomously, exercising a good deal of initiative. Essentially, an investment relationship would then exist, with the holding company interested primarily in collecting dividends. At the other end, a subsidiary would be completely shackled by its holding company : the subsidiary would be managed as if it were an integral part of one large undertaking owned by the holding company. A subsidiary in the middle range of the spectrum would have a number of its internal operations integrated or co-ordinated on a collective arrangement with other affiliated companies. The rest of the spectrum is filled with subsidiaries over which varying degrees of control are exercised. The exact level of control is often difficult to determine.[2]

The variety in the degree of control is noticeable not only as between one corporate group and another,[3] but also within individual groups as between one company and another.[4] In a corporate group, for instance, a number of subsidiaries may be completely dominated by corporate headquarters,

*Cont.*
School of Industrial & Business Studies, Industrial Research Unit, University of Warwick, "The Control of Industrial Relations in Large Companies : An Initial Analysis of the Second Company Level Industrial Relations Survey" (Warwick Papers in Industrial Relations, Paper no. 45, December 1993) pp. 5-14; Michael Goold, Andrew Campbell and Marcus Alexander, *Corporate-Level Strategy* (1994) pp. 398-410.

[1] *Vide* T.H. White, *Power or Pawns : Boards of Directors in Canadian Corporations* (1978) p. 51; R.M. Goode (ed.), *Group Trading and the Lending Banker* (1988) p. xviii; Tom Hadden, *The Control of Corporate Groups* (1983) p. 15; Stopford et al., *op. cit.* p. 21; The Bullock Report, para. 12, p. 131.

[2] *Vide* William O. Douglas and Carrol M. Shanks, "Insulation from Liability through Subsidiary Corporations" 39 Yale L.J. 193 (1929) p. 202.

[3] *Vide* R. Blanpain, *The Badger Case and the OECD Guidelines on Multinational Enterprises* (1977) p. 16.

[4] *Vide* School of Industrial & Business Studies, Industrial Research Unit, University of Warwick, *op. cit.* pp. 5-14.

whereas other subsidiaries operate virtually at arm's length from the rest of the group.[1] Different degrees of control are sometimes detectable even within particular companies. An individual subsidiary, for example, may operate autonomously in certain matters (possibly to avoid tax problems) and may be subject to strict control in other matters (possibly to avoid anti-trust problems associated with intra-enterprise conspiracy).[2]

The three broad levels of control will now be examined further.

### 4.3.1. Autonomous subsidiaries

A relatively small number of subsidiaries are unmistakably autonomous.[3] These companies would be treated by the holding company as investments, or possibly even as customers. They would operate virtually at arm's length with the holding company and with the other affiliated companies within the group.

In these cases, the management team at headquarters may be expressly required - sometimes even in head office policy manuals - to have due regard to the autonomous character of the subsidiaries and to the notion that the position of the holding company is essentially that of a sole or majority shareholder with control to be effectively exercised only at general meetings of such subsidiaries.[4]

The characteristic of autonomy is more common amongst the conglomerates - that is, the highly diversified groups - than it is amongst the more closely integrated ones. Clearly, it is less practicable for the holding company to closely monitor and control subsidiaries operating in broadly separate and distinct lines of business than it is to monitor and control subsidiaries that are involved in highly integrated operations.

For equally obvious reasons, there is also a greater likelihood of autonomy amongst the partly-owned - as opposed to the wholly-owned -

---

[1] The Bullock Report, para. 12 p. 131.

[2] *Vide* Joseph P. Griffin, "The Power of Host Countries over the Multinational : Lifting the Veil in the European Economic Community and the United States" 6 Law and Policy in International Business 375 (1974) p. 381.

[3] Cf. Brooke and Remmers, *op. cit.* p.69; World Investment Report 1993 pp. 4-5. Groups appear to be increasingly decentralising authority from head office to their subsidiaries. *Vide* "The Schneider imbroglio" *Financial Times*, 6th June 1994.

[4] *Vide* Brooke and Remmers, *op. cit.* p. 58.

subsidiaries.[1] The presence of minority shareholders undoubtedly acts as a check on intrusive domination by the holding company over its partly-owned subsidiary. Wholly-owned subsidiaries, on the contrary, allow the holding company a high degree of that highly prized commodity : flexibility. For this reason, corporate groups attempt, wherever practicable, to buy out minority interests in the partly-owned subsidiaries.

Autonomy is also typical amongst joint-venture subsidiaries.[2] Such subsidiaries are actually intended to operate as autonomous entities and special provisions are included in the Articles of such subsidiaries, as well as in the relative joint venture agreements, to prevent the integration of the subsidiary into the management or financial orbit of either participating group.[3]

Particular considerations apply in the case of foreign subsidiaries of transnational corporate groups. These foreign subsidiaries are in a number of instances autonomously run.[4] Autonomy may be granted for a number of reasons. Initially, considerable autonomy is often afforded to newly incorporated subsidiaries in foreign countries. The management team appointed to run these "fledgling subsidiaries" are usually "allowed virtually unlimited powers of decision and action, at least at first" and the only practical link with headquarters is to remit dividends.[5] Sometimes, the foreign investment is small and not critical to the success of the group enterprise. They may even be regarded as "portfolio gambles" because the holding company may not be too sure of the viability of the new operation.[6]

---

[1] *Vide* Tugendhat, *op. cit.* pp. 130-131; Stopford et al., *op. cit.* p. 157. For a somewhat contrary analysis, *vide* Brooke and Remmers, *op. cit.* p. 79.

[2] E.g., *Penick v. Frank E. Basil, Inc.* 579 F.Supp. 160 (D.D.C. 1984). Cf. Stopford et al., *op. cit.* p. 166.

[3] Tom Hadden, *The Control of Corporate Groups* (1983) p. 36. For a "standard form" joint venture agreement providing for a joint management structure with deadlock provisions, together with an appropriate "standard form" of Articles of Association, *vide* Sir Peter Millett (ed.), *The Encyclopaedia of Forms and Precedents* (5th ed. 1990) Vol. 19 para. 1001-1039, pp. 241-265. There may be sound economic reasons for setting up joint-venture subsidiaries. *Vide* Stanley E. Boyle, "The Joint Subsidiary : An Economic Appraisal" 5 Antitrust Bulletin 303 (1960) pp. 303-304.

[4] Shell's and British Petroleum's subsidiaries in Rhodesia and South Africa were, in Lord Denning's view, autonomously managed. *Vide Lonrho Ltd.* v. *Shell Petroleum Co. Ltd.* [1980] 2 W.L.R. 367 (C.A.) at p. 374.

[5] Stopford et al., *op. cit.* p. 20.

[6] Stopford et al., *op. cit.* p. 20; cf. also Eitmann and Stonehill, *op. cit.* pp. 5-6; Joseph P. Griffin, "The Power of Host Countries over the Multinational : Lifting the Veil in the

Such subsidiaries will value their autonomy very highly and will strive to delay for as long as possible direct control by headquarters. Autonomy is sometimes transitory in nature. Especially where the subsidiary's operation grows rapidly and resources are accumulated, control from the holding company may creep in.[1] A few subsidiaries may succeed in retaining their independence, for example by developing a growing and profitable operation which is either self-financed or which utilises funds raised in the local market. Besides, a foreign subsidiary may retain a considerable degree of autonomy to enable the local management to comply with the laws and the policy of the host country.[2]

Decentralisation and diversification strategies (which appear to have been more fashionable in the 1960s and 1970s than in recent years)[3] will also result in a greater degree of autonomy being passed down to subsidiaries within the transnational corporate group. Lord Denning had accurately gauged the mood of the 1970s when he observed, in *Lonrho Ltd.* v. *Shell Petroleum Co. Ltd.*[4], that "the subsidiaries of multi-national companies have a great deal of autonomy".[5] More recently, however, the trend towards a return to "core businesses"[6], as well as the implementation of complex strategies pursued with deeper functional integration within corporate

---

*Cont.*
   European Economic Community and the United States" 6 Law and Policy in International Business 375 (1974) p. 378.

[1]  *Vide* Stopford et al., *op. cit.* pp. 20-21.

[2]  Cf. Clive M. Schmitthoff, "Lifting the Corporate Veil" [1980] J.B.L. 156; The Bingham Report, Foreign and Commonwealth Office, Report on the Supply of Petroleum and Petroleum Products to Rhodesia (1978) para. 14.9, pp. 219-220.

[3]  *Vide* Michael Goold, Andrew Campbell and Marcus Alexander, *Corporate-Level Strategy* (1994) pp. 50-51.

[4]  [1980] 2 W.L.R. 367 (C.A).

[5]  *Ibid.* at p. 374. A similar view was expressed by Mr. Nicholas Baker when addressing the House of Commons on the 11th December 1979 : "[I]t seems ... the fashion in companies now to decentralise and to give individual subsidiary companies much greater control over their own affairs and for them to be run as separate entities which, indeed, at law they are and also increasingly in terms of management". *Vide* Parliamentary Debates, Standing Committee A, Session 1979-1980 Vol. I, 11th December 1979 at cols. 721-722. The comment was made during the debate on the bill which eventually became the Companies Act, 1980.

[6]  *Vide* Michael Goold, Andrew Campbell and Marcus Alexander, *Corporate-Level Strategy* (1994) p. 50.

organisations,[1] are contributing to the exercise of a greater degree of control over subsidiaries.

### 4.3.2. Co-ordinated subsidiaries

The second broad level of control in the relationship between the holding and subsidiary companies refers to the co-ordinated subsidiaries. In this type of subsidiary, there is virtually no interference in the decision-making function of the subsidiary - the subsidiary enjoys almost complete freedom of action. The subsidiary would, however, in view of the gains to be realised, co-ordinate a number of its functions, activities and policies with the holding company or with other affiliated companies. Such arrangements, which generally necessitate comprehensive planning mechanisms, are naturally more common amongst the highly integrated groups than in the diversified groups.

The co-ordination can take place in various sectors : administration, technical services, information technology, personnel, marketing and production.

The subsidiary may, for example, lack a complete administrative infrastructure and relies on the holding company or some other affiliate company for administrative support for such matters as planning, co-ordination, budgetary control, reporting and book-keeping[2] and computer services.[3]

A co-ordinated subsidiary may also obtain assistance from other companies in the group in technical areas, such as research and development,[4] quality control, production techniques, health and safety and engineering services.[5]

---

[1] *Vide* World Investment Report 1993, Chapter VI. For a convincing appraisal of the situation in the early 1970s, *vide* Tugendhat, *op. cit.* pp. 11, 116. Tugendhat's analysis, though published in 1971 has clearly stood the test of time.

[2] *Vide* e.g., *Garrett* v. *Southern Railway Co.* 173 F.Supp. 915 (E.D. Tenn. 1959), *aff'd*, 278 F.2d. 424 (6th Cir.), *cert. denied*, 364 U.S. 833 (1960); *Durham* v. *Southern Railway Co.* 256 F. Supp. 879 (W.D. Va. 1966).

[3] Cf. Organisation for Economic Co-operation and Development (OECD), Report on Transfer Pricing and Multinational Enterprises - Three Taxation Issues (1984) (hereinafter cited as "OECD Report on Transfer Pricing (1984)") p. 73.

[4] *Vide* e.g., *Revlon, Inc.* v. *Cripps & Lee Ltd.* [1980] F.S.R. 85; *Nelson* v. *International Paint Co, Inc.* 734 F.2d 1084 (5th Cir. 1984).

[5] *Vide* e.g., *Luckett* v. *Bethlehem Steel Corp.* 618 F.2d 1373 (10th Cir. 1980).

Personnel matters is another sector where a co-ordinated subsidiary can benefit from the holding or affiliated companies. Services may be offered in respect of staff recruitment and training and in employee relations.[1] A programme of exchange and rotation of personnel as between the subsidiary and other companies in the group could also be implemented.[2]

Co-operation in purchasing, distribution and marketing strategies,[3] being clearly in the interests of most companies in integrated groups, is also common.

Co-ordinated subsidiaries also engage in cost-saving exercises by commonly procuring certain services from *outside* the group, such as common insurance coverage[4] and common personnel retirement, profit sharing or other benefit plans.

Typically, a highly integrated group might also offer centralised advisory services, such as a legal department,[5] a financial advisory department and even a medical services department.

The broad assortment of common services utilised by a co-ordinated subsidiary are often centralised in the holding company, although in many cases specific subsidiaries render particular services for the whole group or for regional or functional parts of it.[6]

In the normal course, a co-ordinated subsidiary benefiting from any such services would compensate the affiliate providing the services.[7] Various methods can be used for charging subsidiaries for costs incurred by the affiliate providing the service. One method is to directly charge for the individualised services. Another method involves indirect charging: the group may apportion and allocate costs to each of the affiliates either by requiring a contribution related to some broad aspect of the business of the affiliates concerned (such as turnover) or by the inclusion of a mark-up in

---

[1] *Vide* e.g., *Jackson* v. *General Electric Co.* 514 P.2d 1170 (Alaska 1973).

[2] *Vide* e.g., *Japan Petroleum Co. (Nigeria) Ltd.* v. *Ashland Oil, Inc.* 456 F.Supp. 831 (D.Del. 1978); *Penick* v. *Frank E. Basil, Inc.* 579 F.Supp. 160 (D.D.C. 1984).

[3] *Vide* e.g., *Fidenas AG* v. *Honeywell, Inc.* 501 F.Supp. 1029 (S.D.N.Y. 1980).

[4] *Vide* e.g., *Fidenas AG* v. *Honeywell, Inc.* 501 F.Supp. 1029 (S.D.N.Y. 1980).

[5] *Vide* e.g., *Garrett* v. *Southern Railway Co.* 173 F.Supp. 915 (E.D. Tenn. 1959), *aff'd*, 278 F.2d. 424 (6th Cir.), *cert. denied*, 364 U.S. 833 (1960).

[6] *Vide* OECD Report on Transfer Pricing (1984) p. 73.

[7] *Vide* e.g., *Jackson* v. *General Electric Co.* 514 P.2d 1170 (Alaska 1973); *Japan Petroleum Co. (Nigeria) Ltd.* v. *Ashland Oil, Inc.* 456 F.Supp. 831 (D.Del. 1978); *Penick* v. *Frank E. Basil, Inc.* 579 F.Supp. 160 (D.D.C. 1984)

the price of the products sold by the company providing the services.[1] Where no compensation is paid, tax problems are likely to rear their head, especially in the context of transnational corporations where an arm's length approach is generally expected by the revenue authorities.[2]

No doubt, as trade barriers fall, and as information and communication technology improves, the level of co-ordination between the various affiliates in a corporate group will continue to increase. Long gone are the days when trans-Atlantic and trans-European business trips took a number of days, and communications between companies were clumsily effected by letter, telegram or even twentieth century versions of the pony express. Today's revolutionary advances in technology can, in respect of several functional purposes, make two affiliates on opposite sides of the globe practically next-door neighbours.[3]

### 4.3.3. Dominated subsidiaries

In many instances, a subsidiary's management is closely controlled in respect of its decision-making power by the holding company. Often, holding companies regard their subsidiaries - in particular their wholly-owned subsidiaries - as mere tools to carry out group policy. The holding company is the brain and the nerve centre of the group. Its subsidiaries are the limbs, moving as directed by headquarters.[4] Subsidiaries work within a framework devised and effectively controlled by the holding company.[5] There is a shift

---

[1] *Vide* OECD Report on Transfer Pricing (1984) p. 84.

[2] *Ibid.* pp. 73-91.

[3] Totally interactive communication systems now make it possible for two parties literally thousands of miles apart to simultaneously exchange and display documents or other information and conduct face to face conferences. *Vide* "Telecommunications in Business" *Financial Times* Survey, 15th June 1994. The electronic linking of global operations cannot of course replace the need for true face-to-face contact. *Vide* "Does it matter where you are?" *The Economist*, 30th July 1994 (Vol. 332, no. 7874).

[4] E.g., *Cannon Manufacturing Corp.* v. *Cudahy Packing Co.* 267 U.S. 333 (1925); For an extreme case of domination, *vide The Willem Van Driel, Sr.* 252 F. 35 (4th Cir. 1918). Exceptionally, the holding company takes over complete management of the subsidiary. *Vide* e.g., *William Cory & Son Ltd.* v. *Dorman Long & Co. Ltd.* [1936] 2 All E.R. 386 (C.A.).

[5] *Vide* Tugendhat, *op. cit.* p. 11; World Investment Report 1993, Chs. V and VI.

in the real seat of power away from the subsidiaries. This is perhaps the most striking feature of the modern corporate group.[1]

Within a group of dominated subsidiaries, dominating control can be evident in a number of sectors. Financing is one such area.[2] Group management techniques are nowadays increasingly based on integrated financing. Ultimate control over the money movements and the allocation of resources, including the system of intra-group lending, is therefore typically retained by the holding company. Major investment decisions, in particular, are likely to be subject to central office control.[3] Similarly, the holding company would exercise considerable control over the distribution and pricing of the raw materials or products bought or sold by the subsidiaries.[4] Nor would a subsidiary generally be free to choose whether to manufacture a particular product or how and where its products are to be sold.[5] Such decisions would be taken higher up in the group managerial hierarchy.[6] The same goes for the allocation of projects as between the different affiliates. The company where the idea originated from may argue that it is best qualified to test it and market it. But nothing alters the reality that group headquarters will take the final decision.

In most corporate groups, domination is exercised through management links rather than through the subsidiary's board of directors.[7] The headquarters is able to integrate the subsidiary's management into the group managerial hierarchy. Senior managers in the subsidiary then report, and are accountable, directly to the central office or to the board of the holding company.[8] This management link is the china connector between the holding

---

[1]  *Vide* Eitmann and Stonehill, *op. cit.* p. 2.

[2]  E.g., *Atlas Maritime Co. S.A.* v. *Avalon Maritime Ltd. (No. 3* [1991] 4 All E.R. 783 (C.A.). *Vide* also Department of Trade, The Cornhill Consolidated Group Limited (In Liquidation), Investigation under Section 165(b) of Companies Act 1948, Report by David Calcutt, QC and John Whinney, FCA, (pub. HMSO 1980) para. 10.01 p. 293.

[3]  Tom Hadden, "Problems with integrated financing" in R.M. Goode (ed.), *Group Trading and the Lending Banker* (1988) p. 71. Cf. Tom Hadden, *The Control of Corporate Groups* (1983) pp. 17-18. *Vide* e.g., *Adams* v. *R* [1995] 2 BCLC 17 (P.C.). Cf. also *Cromwell Corp. Ltd.* v. *Soframa Immobilier (NZ) Ltd.* (1992) 6 N.Z.C.L.C. 67,997 (C.A.) at p. 68,011.

[4]  E.g., *Firestone Tyre and Rubber Co. Ltd.* v. *Lewellin* [1957] 1 All E.R. 561 (H.L.).

[5]  E.g., *Revlon, Inc.* v. *Cripps & Lee Ltd.* [1980] F.S.R. 85 (C.A.).

[6]  Cf. Tugendhat, *op. cit.* p. 112.

[7]  White, *op. cit.* p. 51. Cf. Stopford et al., *op. cit.* p. 21.

[8]  Cf. The Bullock Report, para. 12, p. 131.

and the subsidiary company. It sidesteps the subsidiary's board which is so often little more than a legally-ordained appendix.[1]

The holding-subsidiary line of command may also be reinforced when executives sit on several boards within the group and when the chairmen or managing directors of the subsidiaries sit on the board or management committee of the holding company. Occasionally, the directors and officers of both the holding and the subsidiary company are even identical.[2] These arrangements may be perceived by the group as ensuring that the policies and instructions originating from the holding company are effectively implemented by the various subsidiaries and efficiently co-ordinated by head office.

In the more complex groups - with various levels of sub-subsidiaries - there may be a considerable "organisational distance" between a subsidiary on one of the lower levels of the organisational structure and the top of the enterprise.[3] For such a subsidiary, its control link would probably not be directly with the ultimate holding company but with some regional or sectional headquarters, which would in its turn be answerable to head office or to the highest level within the group's hierarchy.[4] In such complex organisations, policy documents may set out the point in the organisation at which specific decisions could be taken. Sometimes, detailed manuals stipulate the standards and methods for each function. The force of a manual could vary from one subsidiary to another. It may be obligatory for one and be merely advisory for another.[5]

---

[1] *Vide* White, *op. cit.* pp. 46-51; Tricker, *op. cit.* p. 227. In some extreme cases the whole management of the subsidiary is bypassed, the subsidiary being virtually ignored by the holding company in all but name. *Vide Trent* v. *Atlantic City Electric Co.* 334 F.2d 847 (3d Cir. 1964); *McCarthy* v. *Ference* 58 A.2d 49 (1948); *Costan* v. *Manila Electric Co.* 24 F.2d 383 (2d Cir. 1928). The same situation arose in the Badger dispute, where neither Belgian subsidiary's board nor its general meeting actually functioned. *Vide*, Blanpain, *op. cit.* p. 69.

[2] E.g., *Revlon, Inc.* v. *Cripps & Lee Ltd.* [1980] F.S.R. 85 (C.A.); *Steven* v. *Roscoe Turner Aeronautical Corp.* 324 F.2d 157 (7th Cir. 1963); *American Trading & Pro. Corp.* v. *Fischbach & Moore, Inc.* 311 F.Supp. 412 (N.D. Ill. 1970).

[3] *Vide* e.g., the control structure of the Badger group as described in Blanpain, *op. cit.* p. 69. Cf. Brooke and Remmers, *op. cit.* p. 49.

[4] Sometimes there will also be a considerable degree of overlap between the various layers in the hierarchy. *Vide* the valuable analysis in Michael Goold, Andrew Campbell and Marcus Alexander, *Corporate-Level Strategy* (1994) at pp. 399-410.

[5] Brooke and Remmers, *op. cit.* pp. 56-57.

The dominating force of the holding company can hardly be resisted, although it has been observed that in transnational corporations there is a constant pull away from the centre by units at the periphery.[1] Given the ultimate latent power of the holding company as well as the inherent self-interest of human nature, it is of course very unlikely for a subsidiary's management team to actually revolt against any specific direction from headquarters. Even when they do arise, conflicts of this nature are rarely afforded any publicity. A major factor explaining such lack of publicity is possibly the desire of corporate executives to maintain confidentiality.[2] Disputes are expected to be resolved in private and will only arouse public comment if outside interests, such as employees or minority shareholders, are involved.[3]

Even where a subsidiary is dominated in the sense used in this section, the subsidiary would usually still have relatively extensive powers to operate in respect of day-to-day matters. It would, for example, negotiate and conclude many of its contracts, hire and fire staff, and deal with customers without referring back to head office. Corporate groups do not generally encourage yes-men.[4] Underneath the surface of day-to-day operations, however, the subsidiary would constantly remain subject to a considerable degree of control - albeit at a higher level. This appears to have been the arrangement, for example, in the case of Union Carbide's subsidiary in India when the dreadful pesticide disaster struck the town of Bhopal on the night of the 2nd-3rd December 1984. Union Carbide's corporate charter stated that the objectives of the corporation were to be "realised through management of a mix, or portfolio of businesses in selected areas" around the world and that the management system was designed "to provide centralised integrated corporate strategic planning, direction and control; and decentralised business strategic planning and operation implementation". The group's policy manuals distinguished between Category I policies (which provided

---

[1] *Vide* Stopford et al, *op. cit.* p. 3.

[2] Neil C. Sargent, "Corporate Groups and the Corporate Veil in Canada : a penetrating look at Parent-Subsidiary relations in the modern Corporate Enterprise" 17 Manitoba L.J. 156 (1988) p. 167.

[3] *Ibid.* p. 167. A notable exception to the shroud of secrecy usually surrounding internal conflicts of this nature was the dispute over the function of board of the US subsidiary of Olympia and York. The group's financial difficulties and the public's scrutiny of its affairs possibly explain the publicised flare-up. *Vide* "Head of US arm of O&Y threatens to resign" *Financial Times*, 7th June 1993.

[4] Cf. Tugendhat, *op. cit.* p. 102.

for worldwide directives and were issued by the Chairman of the Board and the Chief Executive Officer or the President and the Chief Operating Officer) and Category II policies (which were operational procedures derived from Category I policies). Both Categories of policies were issued to subsidiaries for adoption and implementation and the subsidiaries could not change the substance of any policy without authorisation from the holding company. Control over the subsidiaries was achieved through a matrix system of reporting that required subsidiaries to inform the head office of its activities and by the presence of the holding company's representatives on the subsidiaries' board.[1]

There are of course sound economic and commercial reasons why the decision-making process in several important areas is considered by the group to be the exclusive prerogative of headquarters. Efficient decision-making on the allocation of resources, financing of new projects, the purchasing and distribution of raw materials and finished products and the closure of unprofitable operations require a single, centralised and co-ordinated scheme. Nothing is probably more crucial to the group's success than the ability to pursue comprehensive co-ordinated strategies and to ensure that such strategies are effectively implemented at all levels of the group. Such comprehensive co-ordination raises the overall performance above the level that would be possible had each subsidiary to act autonomously.[2] This is not to say that the subsidiary's and the group's interest necessarily conflict. On the contrary, these interests often converge. Nevertheless, there are circumstances where the interests of individual subsidiaries will - if group profit maximisation is perceived as paramount - have to be sacrificed.[3]

## 5. DOMINATION ALONE NOT NECESSARILY ABUSIVE OR UNFAIR

It must be stressed that domination - even perhaps in the extreme form sometimes witnessed - does not *per se* involve abusive or unfair conduct exposing external creditors to increased dangers in their dealings with companies in the group. Domination is a power that is, almost by definition,

---

[1] *Vide* generally, P.T. Muchlinski, "The Bhopal Case : Controlling Ultrahazardous Industrial Activities undertaken by Foreign Investors" 50 M.L.R. 545 (1987).

[2] Cf. Stopford et al., *op. cit.* p. 21.

[3] *Vide post* pp. 65-82.

inherent in every holding company.[1] And in the normal course, the exercise of such latent power benefits the group (and often each individual unit therein) without prejudicing the interests of external creditors and without giving rise to any sign of unfairness. The holding company's possession and exercise of control should in principle be an acceptable norm. One hundred per cent share ownership, the overlapping or identity of directors and officers, the bypassing of the subsidiary's board of directors, the holding company's determination of and control over group policy and significant decisions - all these are factors which, even in combination, are not in themselves abusive or unfair.[2]

For the truth is, what difference does it make how much control is exercised? It would be remarkable if the law should say to an individual (or to a company) who intends to conduct a commercial operation through a company (or through a subsidiary) to be specifically set up for the purpose : "Go ahead and incorporate. Your liability will be limited as long as you do not exercise too much control over the company". Surely what the law ought to say is that the incorporator must not abuse of his position to control the company in a manner that would prejudice creditors or other interested parties.

There are however situations - usually, though not invariably, in the context of *dominated* subsidiaries - when behavioural practices within the group are objectionable either because they directly prejudice the lot of external creditors or because they give rise to unfairness on a broader level. It is with these behavioural practices that this work is primarily concerned.

Various types of potentially abusive or unfair practices in the group context can be identified. These include the commingling and shuttling of assets, transfer pricing policies, the circumvention of the management of the subsidiaries, the use of phantom subsidiaries, the diversion of corporate opportunities, the undertaking of operations through inadequately financed subsidiaries, the use of creditor-proof devices, the sub-division of one integrated business into various legal units and the use of a group persona image to mislead creditors. This list is merely indicative of the abuse or unfairness sometimes detectable in group behaviour.

---

[1] Cf. Clive M. Schmitthoff, "The Wholly Owned and the Controlled Subsidiary" [1978] J.B.L. 218, p. 222; *Briggs* v. *James Hardie & Co. Pty. Ltd.* 16 NSWLR 549 (1989) at p. 577.

[2] *Vide* further *post* Chapter IX pp. 444-446.

A close examination of the various abusive or unfair practices reveals that there are in fact four broadly distinct and separate categories into which these practices can be classified. The categorisation is essential because inherent differences in the abusive or unfair practices give rise to distinct issues meriting different remedial sanctions.

## 6. ISSUES FALLING OUTSIDE THE PURVIEW OF THIS STUDY

Before proceeding to identifying, classifying and analysing the various situations of abuse and unfairness, two matters have to be noted.

(1) Firstly, this work is not concerned with the incidence or control of fraud within corporate groups. Fraud occurs in every field of human activity. Corporate groups are no exception.[1] Indeed, given that fraudulent behaviour is more easily camouflaged in more complex organisations, it is surmised that the incidence especially of large scale fraud is relatively higher amongst corporate groups than it is amongst the single company enterprise.[2] It is perhaps arguable that there is a greater need for wider powers to be granted to investigating and prosecuting authorities in their fight against corporate fraud. From the private substantive law point of view, however, existing

---

[1] *Vide* e.g., Department of Trade, Report by R.A. Morritt QC and P.L. Ainger FCA into the affairs of Gilgate Holdings Ltd, Raybourne Group Ltd, Calomefern Ltd. and Desadean Properties Ltd, Investigation under Section 165(b) of the Companies Act 1948 (pub. HMSO 1981). The last four years have witnessed some headline-hitting fraudulent behaviour affecting considerably large enterprises : Bank of Credit and Commerce International (BCCI) (*vide* Maximillian J.B. Hall, "BCCI and the Lessons for Bank Supervisors" in Joseph J. Norton (ed.), *Banks : Fraud and Crime* (1994) pp. 120-125); Polly Peck International Company; the Maxwell Group (*vide* "Maxwell ruled a fraudster" *Financial Times*, 11th/12th December 1993); Ferranti International; the Levitt Group (*vide* "Levitt Group was 'riddled with fraud'" *Financial Times*, 12th November 1993, "Levitt trial ends with guilty plea" *Financial Times*, 24th November 1993); and LUI group (*vide* "LUI brokers diverted millions to Liechtenstein accounts" *Financial Times*, 24th September 1993); Bestwood Group (*vide* Department of Trade, Report by Gabriel Moss and John Venning into the affairs of Bestwood plc and Atlanta Fund Managers Limited, Investigation under Sections 432(2) and 442 of the Companies Act 1985; *Financial Times*, 21st January 1994). *Vide* also *Adams* v. *R* [1995] 2 BCLC 17 (P.C.).

[2] Fraud may of course be committed within one subsidiary without any involvement by the holding company. *Vide*, for example, "Fake Kidder trading profits date back to 1991" *Financial Times*, 20th April 1994.

remedies are probably adequate.[1] A discussion of the role of fraud in corporate groups is therefore beyond the scope of this work.

(2) In the second place, neither is this work concerned with the situation where a subsidiary company is specifically organised or utilised for some unlawful purpose, as for evading a statutory obligation, for committing or protecting a fraud or for circumventing some legal obligation. These acts speak for themselves. The remedies are there.[2] A discussion of such cases, which are numerous, is not necessary to this study.

## 7.  THE FOUR CATEGORIES OF ABUSE OR UNFAIRNESS

Four broad categories of behaviour are discernible which, *prima facie* at least, are prejudicial to the interests of external creditors.

They are the following :

(1) The first refers to those situations where the subsidiary acts not in its own interests as a separate unit, but - to its own detriment - in the interests either of the holding company, or of one or more affiliated companies within the group, or of the group as a whole. This type of subsidiary is referred to in this work as a "subservient subsidiary".[3]

(2) The second category comprises the situation where the subsidiary is organised with an inadequate or with a creditor-proof financial structure. This type of subsidiary is referred to as the "undercapitalised subsidiary".[4]

---

[1] Difficulties however are bound to crop up when secretive offshore jurisdictions are involved. The Maxwell empire saga highlighted these difficulties. *Vide* "Probe of Maxwell links urged by MPs" *Financial Times*, 3rd June 1992; "Investigators unravel more of Maxwell web" *Financial Times*, 2nd June 1992; "Maxwell millions hunt speeded up" *The Observer*, 14th June 1992.

[2] *Vide Gilford Motor Co. Ltd.* v. *Horne* [1933] 1 Ch. 935 (C.A.); *Jones* v. *Lipman* [1962] 1 All E.R. 442; *In Re Bugle Press Ltd.* [1961] 1 Ch. 270 (C.A.); *United States* v. *Milwaukee Refrigerator Transit Co.* 142 F.2d. 247, 255 (C.C.E.D. Wis. 1905). *Vide* also C.A. 1985, s. 458 and I.A. 1986, s. 213.

[3] *Vide post* pp. 65-84.

[4] *Vide post* pp. 84-92.

(3) The third category refers to the case where a single integrated economic enterprise is sub-divided into a number of separate legal units. This situation is referred to as the "integrated economic enterprise" situation.[1]

(4) The fourth category covers the situation where the group projects an image which may give the creditors of a subsidiary a false impression that they are dealing with the holding company (or with the group as a whole) or that the holding company (or the whole group) are backing the subsidiary in its commitments. This situation is referred to as the "group persona" situation.[2]

These types of situation will now be considered in turn.


## 8. THE SUBSERVIENT SUBSIDIARY SITUATION

As already noted, the subservient subsidiary situation arises where a subsidiary acts not in its own interests as a separate unit, but acts - to its detriment - in the wider interests of the holding company or of one or more affiliated companies within the group or even in the interests of the group as a whole. In essence, a subservient subsidiary is not allowed to act as an independent profit-centre.[3] Its business is not conducted "with an eye single to its own interests".[4] Its interests are expected to be sacrificed, or at least sidestepped, in the greater interest of the group enterprise which is seen as the profit centre. This state of affairs usually arises in the context of intrusive domination by the holding company.


### 8.1. Group profit maximisation

Undoubtedly, one of the salient features of group economic activity is that a policy of group profit maximisation is often pursued in which the interests of the individual constituent companies are subordinated to the interest of the

---

[1] *Vide post* pp. 92-95.

[2] *Vide post* pp. 95-97.

[3] E.g., *Northern Ill. Gas Co.* v. *Total Energy Leasing Corp.* 502 F.Supp. 412 (N.D. Ill. 1980). *Vide* also Department of Trade, The Cornhill Consolidated Group Limited (In Liquidation), Investigation under Section 165(b) of Companies Act 1948, Report by David Calcutt, QC and John Whinney, FCA, (pub. HMSO 1980) especially at para. 17.12 p. 295.

[4] *Taylor* v. *Standard Gas & Electric Co.* 306 U.S. 307 (1939) at p. 323.

group as a whole.[1] The subsidiary is perceived as a cog in the corporate wheel.

Conflicts between the interests of the holding company and those of a subsidiary are sometimes inevitable, especially in the transnational context. A decision to invest and expand for a higher rate of return and greater share of the market may make good financial sense for the subsidiary, while for the holding company seeking transferability of funds, such a policy may well be risky in a country where strict exchange control regulations apply.[2] Similarly, the subsidiary may see considerable potential in concluding a particular contract and yet head office may require the contract to be performed by an affiliate in some other country. Again, differences may arise, for example over tax policies. Certain tax incentives may seem favourable to a subsidiary, while the holding company, influenced by differing tax laws, finds no advantage in them.

Head office pursues a global group interest. This is achieved by implementing a number of policies which are dictated down to the subsidiaries at the various levels : pricing policies, tax policies, currency policies, dividends policies, investment policies, capital and profit repatriation policies, financing policies and so on. Whatever the policies,

---

[1] *Vide* the Cork Report para. 1926, pp. 434-435;   Jonathan M. Landers, "A Unified Approach to Parent, Subsidiary, and Affiliate Questions in Bankruptcy" 42 Univ. of Chicago L.R. 589 (1975) pp. 624-625; Brooke and Remmers, *op. cit.* p. 126; Wallace, *op. cit.* p. 26. Cf. Hugh Collins, "Ascription of Legal Responsibility to Groups in Complex Patterns of Economic Integration" 53 M.L.R. 731 (1990). The widespread policy of group profit maximisation is also recognised in the Explanatory Memorandum   to the Proposal for the European Union Seventh Directive : "The basic characteristic of such groups is that the management of the companies belonging to them is coordinated in such a way that they are managed on a central and unified basis by the dominant company or companies in the interest of the group as a whole". (1976 Bulletin of the E.C., Supplement 9/76 pp. 19-32, at p. 19). Cases also recognise the policy of group profit maximisation. *Vide* e.g., *Charterbridge Corp. Ltd.* v. *Lloyds Bank Ltd.* [1970] Ch. 62; *Revlon, Inc.* v. *Cripps & Lee Ltd.* [1980] F.S.R. 85 (C.A.) at p. 115 (per Templeman L.J.); *Eastern Air Lines, Inc.* v. *Gulf Oil Corp.* 415, 440 F.Supp. 429 (1975); *Jones* v. *H.F. Ahmanson & Co.* 460 P.2d 464, 474 (1969). In the latter judgment, at p. 474, the Court quoted with approval Gower's observation that a holding company may wish "to operate the subsidiary for the benefit of the group as a whole and not necessarily for the benefit of that particular subsidiary." The quotation was taken from L.C.B. Gower, *Principles of Modern Company Law* (2nd ed. 1957) at p. 561.

[2] *Vide* Thomas W. Walde, "Parent-Subsidiary Relations in the Integrated Corporate System: A Comparison of American and German Law" 9 Journal of International Law and Economics 455 (1974) p. 486.

they are set by headquarters and if necessary take precedence over the narrower interests of the individual subsidiaries.

The policy of group profit maximisation is recognised as a requirement of efficient management and rational optimisation. A group which allows its subsidiaries to pursue their own interests would therefore experience sub-optimal results.[1]

The activities of a subsidiary may therefore be less geared to meeting its own objectives than they are to achieving those of the group.[2] The subsidiary knows this. Its management knows this. And it is unlikely to raise much of an issue. The consoling factor is that subsidiaries "are judged not by their individual performance, but by the contribution they make to the group as a whole."[3] Accordingly, "a subsidiary which records a loss but whose operations prevents a rival from moving into one of its parent company's more profitable markets may be fulfilling a more valuable task than a subsidiary with a better financial record".[4] In a corporate group, profits are not the only measure of management performance in the subsidiaries. Often, pricing policies also distort the true profits of a subsidiary. Other more qualitative indices of performance are used.[5]

Although the overall goal is generally to achieve the best results for the group as a whole rather than for the individual subsidiaries, certain practical restraints - apart from any legal ones - sometimes impede the implementation of such a single-minded strategy by dominating holding companies. If, for example, corporate headquarters demands conduct which appears arbitrary or unreasonable, managerial disincentives may arise.[6] Head office would be concerned with maintaining "loyalty", "incentive" and "initiative" within the subsidiaries' management team in the long term and is usually prepared to accept a "less-than-optimum compromise ... to keep the principal members of the team in play."[7] On a transnational level, the group may occasionally be less intrusive and deliberately seek to further the direct interest of the foreign subsidiary in order to appease the host country. Moreover, as a group

---

[1] *Ibid.* p. 487.

[2] John H. Dunning, *Economic Analysis and the Multinational Enterprise* (1974) p. 364.

[3] Tugendhat, *op. cit.* p. 11.

[4] *Ibid.* p. 11.

[5] *Vide* Brooke and Remmers, *op. cit.* p. 118.

[6] Cf. Eitmann and Stonehill, *op. cit.* p. 406.

[7] Raymond Vernon, "The Role of U.S. Enterprises Abroad" 98 Daedalus 113 (1969) at pp. 115-116.

increases in size, the overhead costs associated with the management and information systems required to adequately control all the enterprise's activities become overwhelming and diseconomies of scale and complexity may threaten to outweigh the benefits of a group profit maximisation approach. Some groups may therefore choose to reduce the diseconomies of scale by pushing more and more responsibilities down to the subsidiaries foregoing at the same time the advantages of overall group control.[1]

The policy of group profit maximisation manifests itself in the implementation of various practices which may in fact be economically rational and consistent with good business practice but which may, at the same time, be detrimental both to the subservient subsidiary and to its creditors who bear the risks of enterprise-wide strategies which may result in the insolvency of particular affiliates.

These practices include various transfer pricing techniques, the diversion of corporate opportunities, the manipulation and commingling of assets, the subsidiary's financial support of the group, and the use of sham subsidiaries. The degree of subservience to the overall welfare of the group varies from one subsidiary to another and from one group to another. In some cases, the subservience need only be practised on an occasional basis. In other cases, the subservience becomes habitual. A closer examination of these subservient practices will illustrate the nature and mischief thereof.

### 8.1.1. Transfer pricing

Money moves within corporate groups in a number of ways : dividends; royalties; loans and other capital transfers; interest payments; and payments for goods, services and the use of intangibles. Transfer price manipulation is the practice of obscuring the actual cost of transactions as between affiliated companies. It therefore directly affects the money flow within the group and the profitability of particular subsidiaries. Although transfer pricing manipulations commonly involve the sale of goods, there are various other transactions - involving for example the provisions of services or know-how - in which the actual cost is distorted. A few examples will illustrate the point : a subsidiary may undertake to perform some works for an affiliated company for a fee less than what it would have charged had it been dealing with an independent party at arm's length; it may pay for services rendered

---

[1] Cf. Stopford et al., *op. cit.* pp. 172-174.

to it by an affiliate a higher amount than their real value; it may pay its holding company royalties that are in excess of their true value; it may lease or hire an asset from an affiliated company at a rent that is higher than the real rental value of the asset; or it may lease or hire an asset to an affiliated company for a rent below its real rental value. In all these cases the subsidiary either pays too much for what it receives or is paid too little for what it supplies. Equality of exchange has been jeopardised.

Pricing manipulation can be effected not just by artificially determining prices, but also by varying the actual and the declared quality or quantity of goods, services or know-how.[1] Transfer pricing may also involve juggling book-keeping entries.[2]

In the context of transnational groups, the manipulation of transfer pricing can, if handled with care and discretion,[3] serve a wide range of purposes.

Occasionally, transfer pricing directly benefits the particular subsidiary involved in the manipulation. By underpricing imports to a subsidiary, for example, the impact of customs duty will be minimised and the subsidiary may be able to engage in predatory pricing behaviour aimed at eliminating competitors in order to obtain or reinforce market dominance.[4]

Usually, however, the manipulation of transfer pricing serves to benefit the group at the expense of the subservient subsidiary. Transfer pricing, for instance, may be used to withdraw funds from subsidiaries by raising prices on goods and services sold by one affiliate to another.[5] Transnational groups may therefore use this method where exchange control restrictions impede the repatriation of earnings, royalties and interest payments or where there is

---

[1] *Vide* Law Reform Commission of Papua New Guinea, Transfer Pricing Manipulation Report no. 12, November 1981 p. 9.

[2] *Ibid.* pp. 9, 21.

[3] A group which varies its prices frequently and significantly is asking for trouble from the revenue and customs authorities in the countries where it operates. *Vide* Tugendhat, *op. cit.* p. 137.

[4] *Vide* C.R. Greenhill and E.O. Herbolzheimer, "Control of Transfer Prices in International Transactions : The Restrictive Business Practices Approach" in Robin Murray (ed.), *Multinationals beyond the Market - Intra-Firm Trade and the Control of Transfer Pricing* (1981) p. 185.

[5] Sidney M. Robbins and Robert B. Stobaugh, *Money in the Multinational Enterprise : A Study of Financial Policy* (1975) p. 91. Transfer pricing may also be used to finance a subsidiary by lowering prices of goods and services sold to the subsidiary by other affiliates in the group.

apprehension about a country's currency.[1] The ability to manipulate transfer prices enables the group to by-pass, at least temporarily, even more severe exchange control restrictions.[2]

Sometimes, groups may also engage in transfer pricing techniques to artificially deflate a subsidiary's profits in order to discourage investors from taking up their options to buy shares,[3] or to inhibit pressure from governments or customers to reduce prices, or to suppress claims for wages increases by trade unions.[4]

More often, transfer price manipulation is used in tax planning.[5] This can range from systematic tax avoidance, to ensuring that the same profits are not subject to double taxation, and to taking advantage of anomalies in bilateral tax treaties.[6] The methods used are in principle quite simple. Merchandise is sold at a low price to a subsidiary in a low tax country which re-exports the merchandise at a high price to a subsidiary where it is actually needed. The subsidiaries at the beginning and at the end of the chain may register losses, but these losses are offset by the high profits in the low tax country.[7] Alternatively, the group may direct the flow of goods and services through the various subsidiaries in such a way that the highest tax liabilities precipitate in the countries with the lowest tax rates.

In the eyes of the tax authorities, transfer pricing has long been recognised as offensive. Arbitrary profit-shifting through transfer pricing and other techniques has therefore been prohibited. Transfer pricing techniques are sometimes used in purely domestic transactions, but the practice is far more widespread in transnational enterprises.[8] Indeed, anti-transfer pricing provisions are particularly aimed at transnational corporate group

---

[1] *Ibid.* p. 92.

[2] *Vide* Tugendhat, *op. cit.* p. 137.

[3] Law Reform Commission of Papua New Guinea, Transfer Pricing Manipulation Report no. 12, November 1981 p. 10.

[4] *Vide* Tugendhat, *op. cit.* p. 139.

[5] *Vide* e.g., *Eastern Air Lines, Inc.* v. *Gulf Oil Corp.* 415 F.Supp. 429, 440 (1975). Cf. *Re Gordon & Breach Science Publishers Ltd.* [1995] 2 BCLC 189 at p. 200.

[6] *Vide* Richard E. Caves, *Multinational Enterprise and Economic Analysis* (1982) pp. 244-249. Cf. Tugendhat, *op. cit.* p. 138.

[7] Tugendhat, *op. cit.* p. 141.

[8] *Vide* Frank Wooldridge, *Groups of Companies - The Law and Practice in Britain, France and Germany* (1981) p. 83; Douglas A. Kahn, *Basic Corporate Taxation* (3rd ed. 1981) pp. 509-510.

transactions where the arbitrary allocation of profit is considered particularly reprehensible and certainly more difficult to control.[1]

The general rule in international tax regulation is that the profits of a company should be calculated on the assumption that the prices charged by such a company are at arm's length. This is the approach incorporated in the OECD Model Double Taxation Convention[2] and is generally accepted by the revenue authorities and transnational groups.[3]

Determining the arm's length price may prove difficult.[4] The comparable uncontrolled sales method, by which the transfer price is gauged by reference to comparable transactions between a buyer and a seller who are not associated enterprises, is of course the most accurate method in relation to goods. The problem is that in some cases such data is simply not available. In such cases recourse may be had to the resale price method,[5] the cost-plus method,[6] or some other equitable method.[7]

---

[1] *Vide* R.K. Ashton, *Anti-Avoidance Legislation* (1981) p. 138. Anti-avoidance provisions exist in s. 770 of the Income and Corporation Taxes Act 1988 to prevent artificial prices being placed on trading stock between associated companies unless both are resident in the United Kingdom. This provision is designed to protect the United Kingdom revenue authorities by ensuring that profits earned in the United Kingdom are not transferred to a foreign country by transfer pricing techniques. By s. 773(4) of the same Act, the provisions of s. 770 also apply, *mutatis mutandis*, to lettings and hirings of property, grants and transfers of rights, interests or licences and the giving of business facilities of whatever kind in the same way as it applies to sales. *Vide* further Mayson and Blake, *op. cit.* pp. 598-599. In the United States, transfer pricing is regulated by section 482 of the Internal Revenue Code (26 U.S.C. section 482). *Vide* further Kahn, *op. cit.* pp. 509-512; Howard La Mont, "Multinational Enterprise, Transfer Pricing and the 482 Mess" 14 Columbia Journal of Transnational Law 383 (1975) pp. 384-385.

[2] Model Double Taxation Convention on Income and on Capital, Report of the OECD Committee on Fiscal Affairs (1977), Art. 7(2). *Vide* also the commentary on Art. 7(2), *ibid.* at pp. 74-76.

[3] *Vide* Eitmann and Stonehill, *op. cit.* pp. 411-412. The arm's length approach has provoked considerable debate and is not universally accepted by economists. *Vide* Robin Murray (ed.), *op. cit.* p. 9.

[4] *Vide* Brooke and Remmers, *op. cit.* pp. 118-119. Cf. Joseph Flom, "Tangled skein of tax adjustments" *Financial Times*, 7th May 1992.

[5] The resale price method starts with the resale price of the goods which have been purchased from a related purchaser, with the arm's length price being arrived at by calculating an appropriate mark-up.

[6] In this method, the arm's length price is arrived at by starting with the cost of the goods and adding an appropriate mark-up.

[7] Cf. Organisation for Economic Co-operation and Development (OECD), Transfer Pricing and Multinational Enterprises (1979) (hereinafter cited as "OECD Report on Transfer

Despite the efforts of the tax authorities to control the negative effects of transfer pricing, abuse is still common. Recent evidence, for example, has indicated that many foreign owned United States companies are systematically under-allocating the portion of their worldwide income that should properly be attributable to sales and other activities in the United States.[1] The United States Internal Revenue Service is aggressively pursuing such abuses. And it may not be long before other governments follow the example set by the United States.[2]

Understandably, many groups are not particularly keen on manipulating transfer prices. The practice obviously tends to be disliked by the management of the subservient company and headquarters recognises the disincentive problems created by the related dissatisfaction and resentment.[3] Besides, transfer pricing, by artificially distorting profits, could also lead to inaccurate financial reports and statements, making for faulty strategic planning and performance assessment.[4] Moreover, groups are sometimes deterred by the power of the revenue authorities to strike down unrefined forms of manipulation. Finally, the increasing number of double taxation treaties has also made transfer pricing a far trickier tool to handle than some decades ago. It should be said however, that the control of transfer pricing remains difficult not only because of the existence of tax havens (which

---

*Cont.*
  Pricing (1979)") Ch. 1; OECD Report on Transfer Pricing (1984) pp. 11-14; Eitmann and Stonehill, *op. cit.* pp. 411-412.

[1] *Vide* Joseph Flom, "Tangled skein of tax adjustments", *Financial Times*, 7th May 1992; "US allows more flexible transfer pricing" *Financial Times*, 6th July 1994. Similarly, Japan's tax authorities have recently accused western companies of levying excessive royalty payments on their Japanese subsidiaries and associated companies and of charging too much for materials exported to such subsidiaries and associated companies. *Vide* "Foreign companies angered by Japanese tax increases" *Financial Times*, 16th May 1994.

[2] Joseph Flom, "Tangled skein of tax adjustments" *Financial Times*, 7th May 1992.

[3] Cf. Eitmann and Stonehill, *op. cit.* p. 406; Brooke and Remmers, *op. cit.* p. 119.

[4] This difficulty can be avoided by keeping two sets of records : one reflecting the true position (for internal consumption) and the other showing the manipulated result (for the authorities). Practical problems - and the risk of exposure - probably dissuade any but the most imprudent groups from keeping such double records. Cf. Brooke and Remmers, *op. cit.* p. 121.

drive a wedge between the host and the investing countries) but also because the necessary inter-state co-operation is often lacking.[1]

Still, where it does occur, the manipulation of transfer pricing does not prejudice solely the revenue authorities. Indeed, by reducing the net asset value of the subservient company[2] and therefore its resources, transfer pricing can weaken its financial backbone to the obvious detriment of its creditors.[3] The unfairness is all the more patent when it is realised that the subservient subsidiary is being enslaved for the benefit of its lord - the corporate group - which, when faced with difficulties, may well abandon its underling and rely on the exalted principles of separate juridical personality and limited liability.

### 8.1.2. Diversion of corporate opportunities

The management of a subsidiary is approached by a prospective customer inquiring whether the subsidiary can undertake a particular project. The subsidiary's management team, after looking into the feasibility of the project and concluding that it would be able to handle the project, advises headquarters of the project and of its conclusion. Rather than the congratulatory fax and the proverbial pat on the back it is expecting, the subsidiary's management team is informed by headquarters that the project should be performed by an affiliated company. The subsidiary has no option but to comply. A corporate opportunity which had been fairly presented to the subsidiary is diverted by the holding company, not because the subsidiary is unable to profitably and successfully complete the project but because its affiliate stands to gain some special advantage, perhaps some particular fiscal incentive. Subsequently, no other project comes the way of the subsidiary. Its order book dries up. Its work-force lies idle. Soon it may sink into insolvency and its creditors left to whistle for their money. Meanwhile, its affiliate has bloomed into prosperity.

---

[1] *Vide* Frances Stewart, "Taxation and the Control of Transfer Pricing" in Robin Murray (ed.), *op. cit.* pp. 182-183. *Vide* also Greenhill and Herbolzheimer, *op. cit.* pp. 192-193.

[2] Cf. R.J. Calnan, "Corporate Gifts and Creditors' Rights" 11 Co. Law. 91 (1990) p. 91.

[3] In *Re Gordon & Breach Science Publishers Limited,* Walker J. expressly acknowledged that transfer pricing may "operate to the prejudice of independent creditors". *Ibid.* at p. 200. Minority shareholders are no doubt also prejudiced by transfer pricing practices.

The above episode is not taken from a commercial fantasy book. It is a real-life - though probably not a common-place - situation.[1] Where the subsidiary which has been divested of its opportunity remains solvent, the issue will really be of concern only to the minority shareholders in the subsidiary.[2] Where however, as with the above example, the subsidiary decays into insolvency, the interests of its creditors assume paramount importance.

Difficult questions surface in the field of corporate opportunities. What exactly is meant by a corporate opportunity? On what basis does one determine who should be entitled to the opportunity? Adapting a definition from the American Law Institute's "Principles of Corporate Governance : Analysis and Recommendations" [3] a "corporate opportunity" may, for our purposes, be taken to mean any opportunity to engage in a business activity that is held out to the holding company as being within the scope of the business in which the subsidiary is engaged or may be reasonably expected to engage, and that is neither developed nor received by the holding company within the scope and regular course of its own activities.

A number of factors need to be taken into account in determining whether a corporate opportunity belongs to the subsidiary. Has an expectation been created that the subsidiary's existing or anticipated scope of operations will include the business activity or geographical area of operation under consideration? Even if this question is answered in the affirmative, other questions follow : was it contemplated that the subsidiary exclusively engage in the particular business activity or geographical area or was it expected that the holding or an affiliate company might also engage in such activity or

---

[1] Unfairness is probably common in the relationship between the holding and its subsidiaries. Cf. Andre' Tunc, "The Fiduciary Duties of a Dominant Shareholder" in Schmitthoff and Wooldridge (ed.), *Groups of Companies* (1991) pp. 4, 18. *Vide* also Tugendhat, *op. cit.* pp. 127-128; Blanpain, *op. cit.* p. 69. Probably, however, few cases involve both unfairness *and* insolvency.

[2] E.g., *Sinclair Oil Corp.* v. *Levien* 280 A.2d 717 (Del. 1971); *David J. Greene & Co.* v. *Dunhill International, Inc* 249 A.2d 427 (Del. Ch. 1968); *Blaustein* v. *Pan American Petroleum & Transport Co.* 56 N.E. 2d 705 (N.Y. 1944). *Vide* Victor Brudney and Robert Charles Clark, "A New Look at Corporate Opportunities" 94 Harv. L.R. 997 (1981) p. 1046. Cf. Karen McLaughlin, "Corporate Opportunity Doctrine in the Context of Parent-Subsidiary Relations" 8 Northern Kentucky L.R. 121 (1981); E. Merrick Dodd, "Liability of a Holding Company for Obtaining for Itself Property Needed by a Subsidiary : the *Blaustein* Case" 58 Harv. L.R. 125 (1944).

[3] Adopted and promulgated on the 13th May 1992 (hereinafter cited as the "ALI Principles of Corporate Governance") s. 5.12, pp. 349-350.

area? How did the holding company or affiliate gain access to the opportunity - was the opportunity developed by the holding or an affiliate within the scope and regular course of their own business activities? If it was, then the holding or affiliate company should have no duty to allow the subsidiary to take the opportunity unless it is an activity that was held out generally to the group as being within the subsidiary's area of business activity.[1] Even if, applying these tests, the opportunity is properly held to belong to the subsidiary, the financial or practical inability of the subsidiary to take advantage of the opportunity should enable the holding company to fairly divert the opportunity to itself or to another subsidiary.[2]

Closely integrated management structures and elaborate divisions of functions within many corporate groups will inevitably complicate the question of ownership of corporate opportunities. Opportunities may not come to a subsidiary as "individualized, identifiable, tangible expectancies".[3] Laying a claim to the opportunity may therefore well be problematic to the subsidiary. In a group implementing a group profit maximisation policy - where subsidiaries cease to operate as autonomous units - it may well happen that every opportunity will be an "expectancy" and "in the line of business activity" of the group as a whole, to be allocated as determined by headquarters in the overall interest of the group.

As a general rule, it may of course make sound *economic* sense to argue that the allocation of corporate opportunities should be determined on the basis of the promotion of efficiency and economic value and that the subsidiary with the higher potential of increased return should be allowed to develop the opportunity.[4] The interests of external creditors of a subsidiary may however be directly prejudiced by the diversion of a corporate opportunity properly belonging to it. Such prejudice will arise in the situation where a subsidiary would not have declined into insolvency had the opportunity not been diverted. Even where the insolvency of a subsidiary is not causally linked to the diversion of the corporate opportunity, it is at least

---

[1] *Vide* generally, ALI Principles of Corporate Governance, pp. 351-352.

[2] Cf. *Schreiber* v. *Bryan* 396 A.2d 512 (Del. Ch. 1978); *Guth* v. *Loft, Inc.* 5 A.2d 503, 514 (Sup. Ct. 1939). Lawrence P. Kessel, "Trends in the Approach to the Corporate Entity Problem in Civil Litigation" 41 Georgtown L.J. 525 (1953) pp. 539-540.

[3] *Vide* Thomas W. Walde, "Parent-Subsidiary Relations in the Integrated Corporate System: A Comparison of American and German Law" 9 Journal of International Law and Economics 455 (1974) p. 484.

[4] *Vide* Victor Brudney and Robert Charles Clark, "A New Look at Corporate Opportunities" 94 Harv. L.R. 997 (1981) p. 1050.

arguable that the forced submission of the subsidiary to the will of the group creates a corresponding obligation on the part of the holding company to shelter it from any ensuing blizzard.

The clue to an equitable solution may possibly lie either in the notion of adequate compensation for the loss of the corporate opportunity or in the extension of liability on the holding company in appropriate circumstances.[1]

### 8.1.3. Manipulation of assets

The manipulation of assets is an abusive practice that subservient subsidiaries are sometimes subjected to. Manipulation may assume three basic forms : the commingling of assets, the shuttling of assets, and the draining of assets.

### 8.1.3.1. Commingling of assets

Companies in a closely integrated group sometimes - perhaps unwittingly - commingle their assets. Two subsidiaries may, for example, conduct natural gas production from adjacent factories. They may intermix their gas supplies without keeping adequate records in such a way that the relative proportions are indeterminable.[2] Similarly, two subsidiaries engaged in the distribution of similar products may deposit their sales proceeds into a common account without keeping proper records of such sales or of their own stocks of products. As presently used, commingling refers to the confusion or intermingling of a subsidiary's assets - products or funds - combined with the failure to keep proper records. The failure to keep proper records is essential: indeed, an accounting separation can be maintained, notwithstanding physical intermingling.[3] If, in the first example, each subsidiary had kept account of the quantity of gas being intermingled, and if in the second example, each subsidiary held a record of the sales or stock, an accurate determination could be made of the relative proportions and there would be no commingling for the purposes of our analysis.

---

[1] *Vide post* Chapter V p. 290.

[2] A similar situation occurred in *Stone* v. *Marshall Oil Co.* 57 Atl. 183 (1904).

[3] *Vide* Latty, *op. cit.* p. 185.

Now it is trite law that, ordinarily, corporate creditors are to look to the corporate estate for payment. In a corporate group, each component company will have its own estate. It follows that there must be a sharp separation of one corporate estate from another.

The mischief with commingling of assets is self-evident. Commingling renders the identification of the assets available for the satisfaction of the subsidiary's debts difficult or even impossible.[1] Commingling is also suggestive of the lack of the subsidiary's financial integrity. Moreover, commingling heightens the risk that a subsidiary's assets may be utilised to satisfy the creditors of the holding or affiliated companies and would not therefore be available for the subsidiary's own creditors.

Even where the commingled assets can be traced and recovered, the conduct should probably still be viewed as abusive. The practice of commingling gives rise to a serious risk that the subsidiary's assets may be depleted or lost. The practice should be deterred by considering it as inherently abusive, even if it eventually transpires that the assets can somehow be identified and repossessed. Naturally, the problem is one of degree. If the commingling has been nominal and can be disentangled without undue difficulty, then improper conduct should not be attributed to the group.

### 8.1.3.2. Shuttling of funds and other assets

Groups sometimes transfer and re-transfer funds and other assets between one subsidiary and another to suit the convenience of one or more companies within the group.[2] These practices, which may be part of a group's integrated financial organisation,[3] are not *per se* improper.[4] Nevertheless, this type of conduct is undesirable because it increases the potential for the exploitation

---

[1] *Vide Chemical Bank N.Y. Trust Co.* v. *Kheel* 369 F.2d 845, 847 (2d Cir. 1966).

[2] E.g., *Atlas Maritime Co. S.A.* v. *Avalon Maritime Ltd. (No. 3* [1991] 4 All E.R. 783 (C.A.); *Weisser* v. *Mursam Shoe Corp.* 127 F.2d 344 (2d Cir. 1942); *Walker* v. *Wimborne and others* (1976) 50 A.L.J.R. 446; *Chemical Bank N.Y. Trust Co.* v. *Kheel* 369 F.2d 845 (2d Cir. 1966).

[3] Robbins and Stobaugh point out that inter-subsidiary loans are not extensively used because "it is difficult for headquarters to keep track of the intricate relationships that can materialize". *Vide* Robbins and Stobaugh, *op. cit.* p. 60.

[4] *Ibid.* pp. 13-15.

of creditors[1] and also because it evidences a lack of integrity in the subsidiary's supposedly autonomous status.[2]

### 8.1.3.3. Draining of assets

The draining of a subservient subsidiary's assets, or "asset-stripping",[3] can assume various forms. It can involve the transfer or the use of the subsidiary's corporate property or services without offsetting consideration. It can also include the payment by the subsidiary for services not received or the payment of excessive fees (for example by way of royalties or management fees) in relation to the value of services actually received.[4]

In extreme cases, the depletion or diminution of the assets impairs the subsidiary's ability to satisfy its commitments.[5] These are the patently wrongful ones. However, even where the draining of assets does not so seriously affect the subsidiary's solvency, the practice certainly reduces the net asset value of the subsidiary[6] and reflects the holding company's disregard of the seemingly independent status of the subsidiary.

The manipulation of a subsidiary's assets - whether by way of commingling, shuttling or draining - is unacceptable both because it indicates subservience on the part of the subsidiary in the overall interest of the group and also because it heightens the risk to the subsidiary's creditors.

---

[1] Tom Hadden, *The Control of Corporate Groups* (1983) p. 31. *Vide* e.g., *Creasey* v. *Breachwood Motors Ltd.* [1992] BCC 638.

[2] In *Walker* v. *Wimborne and others* (1976) 50 A.L.J.R. 446, Mason J. noted that the inability of one of the companies within the group concerned to pay a debt led to "a shortage of funds within the group ... and the adoption of a practice whereby funds were moved between the companies within the group to meet exigencies as they arose". *Ibid.* at p. 448.

[3] This is the term used by Hirst J. in *Aiglon Ltd. and L'Aiglon S.A.* v. *Gau Shan Co. Ltd.* [1993] 1 Lloyd's Rep. 164 at p. 170.

[4] *Vide* Frank Wooldridge, *Groups of Companies - The Law and Practice in Britain, France and Germany* (1981) p. 99; Hopt, Regulating Groups, pp. 105-106. *Vide* also *Aiglon Ltd. and L'Aiglon S.A.* v. *Gau Shan Co. Ltd.* [1993] 1 Lloyd's Rep. 164, especially the evidence referred to at pp. 167-168.

[5] *Vide Atlas Maritime Co. S.A.* v. *Avalon Maritime Ltd. (No. 3* [1991] 4 All E.R. 783 (C.A.); *Aiglon Ltd. and L'Aiglon S.A.* v. *Gau Shan Co. Ltd.* [1993] 1 Lloyd's Rep. 164.

[6] Cf. R.J. Calnan, "Corporate Gifts and Creditors' Rights" 11 Co. Law. 91 (1990) p. 91.

### 8.1.4. Financial support of group

As a rule, headquarters will attempt to structure the credit and financial arrangements within a group in such a way as to optimally exploit the creditworthiness of the stronger units. In the context of such a strategy, the subservient character of a subsidiary manifests itself in the financial support it affords to the group without any reciprocal corresponding benefit.

The financial support extended by the subsidiary could be in the form of loans made to the holding company or affiliated companies,[1] particularly if effected without interest or at below-market rates.[2] It could also involve the payments of debts due by the holding company or affiliated companies to third parties.[3]

Sometimes the financial support results from the pursuit by the group of a dividend policy which is optimum for the group but which is not in the interest of the subsidiary concerned.[4] Clearly, an optimal dividend policy generally involves striking the right balance between payout and growth.[5] Yet the group dividend policy may be influenced by the financial needs of other units within the group.[6] There are of course legal restraints on the amount of dividend that may be paid.[7] But what is legally permissible need not necessarily make commercial sense for the subsidiary. The holding company may - quite lawfully - cause the subsidiary to distribute dividends at a time when the subsidiary's financial condition is weak and the dividends

---

[1] E.g., *Eagle Air, Inc.* v. *Corroon & Black/Dawson & Co.* 648 P.2d 1000 (Alaska 1982). *Vide* also the Cork Report, para. 1926, p. 434; Tom Hadden, *The Control of Corporate Groups* (1983) pp. vii, 15-17.

[2] E.g., *Ring* v. *Sutton* (1980) 5 A.C.L.R. 546 (C.A. N.S.W.) (a case involving loans by a company to its principal shareholder and director at less than current commercial interest rates).

[3] E.g., *Worldwide Carriers, Ltd.* v. *Aris Steamship Co.* 301 F.Supp. 64 (S.D.N.Y. 1968).

[4] E.g., *Taylor v. Standard Gas & Elec. Co.* 306 U.S. 307 (1939); *Sinclair Oil Corp.* v. *Levien* 280 A.2d 717 (1971). Cf. the Cork Report, para. 1926, p. 435

[5] Richard A. Brealey and Stewart C. Myers, *Principles of Corporate Finance* (4th ed., 1991) Ch. 16; George E. Pinches, *Essentials of Financial Management* (4th. ed., 1992) Ch. 14.

[6] The dividend policy may also be determined by the fiscal position of the holding company. *Vide* Neil C. Sargent, "Corporate Groups and the Corporate Veil in Canada : a Penetrating Look at Parent-Subsidiary relations in the Modern Corporate Enterprise" 17 Manitoba L.J. 156 (1988) p. 170.

[7] *Vide* C.A. 1985, ss. 263-264 and 270.

would not otherwise have been paid. In such a case, the holding company is seeking to benefit itself notwithstanding the adverse affect on the subsidiary. Moreover, dividends may reduce the subsidiary's net worth[1] and therefore represent a potential threat to its creditors.[2]

More often, the creditworthiness of a subsidiary will be utilised to support borrowing by other weaker affiliates - either to reduce the cost of borrowing or to make the borrowing possible in the first place. Sometimes, a group financing package will be sought, enabling the various units to borrow jointly and severally.[3] A significant portion of the proceeds of group financing may then go to creditors of affiliated companies. The bank would rely primarily on the credit of the strongest subsidiary. The support extended by such a subsidiary would probably be in the form of guarantees given by it both in respect of its holding company obligations ("upstream guarantees")[4] and in respect of the affiliates' obligations ("cross-stream guarantees").[5] Moreover, it could involve the grant of real securities, such as the pledge of the subsidiary company's assets.[6]

The risks attached to the subsidiary's contingent liability on the guarantees[7] suggest the subservient function of the guarantor-subsidiary. The element of subservience is of course accentuated when, as in most cases, the subsidiary receives no fee or other payment for its guarantees.[8] Where the subsidiary has pledged its credit not for its own use but for the benefit of other units in the group and in addition receives no compensation, the

---

[1] *Vide* the discussion in Geoffrey Morse (ed.), *Charlesworth & Morse Company Law* (14th ed. 1991) pp. 626-633. By s. 264 (1) of the C.A. 1985, however, a *public* company may only make a distribution "(a) if at that time the amount of its net assets is not less than the aggregate of its called-up share capital and undistributable reserves and (b) if, and to the extent that, the distribution does not reduce the amount of those assets to less than that aggregate."

[2] *Vide* Phillip I. Blumberg, *The Law of Corporate Groups - Bankruptcy Law* (1985) (hereinafter referred to as "Blumberg, *Bankruptcy Law*") p. 114.

[3] *Vide* e.g., *Bank of Scotland* v. *Wright* [1991] BCLC 244.

[4] E.g., *Schlecht* v. *Equitable Builders, Inc* 535 P.2d 86 (1975).

[5] Cf. The Cork Report, para. 1926, p. 434; Cashel, *op. cit.* pp. 38-39. Inter-group guarantees are illustrated by *Charterbridge Corporation Ltd.* v. *Lloyds Bank Ltd.* [1970] Ch. 62 and *Brown* v. *Cork* [1985] BCLC 363.

[6] E.g., *Baker* v. *Caravan Moving Corp.* 561 F.Supp. 337 (N.D. Ill. 1983).

[7] *Vide* R.M. Goode, *Principles of Corporate Insolvency Law* (1990) pp. 147-148.

[8] *Vide* D.D. Prentice, "Some aspects of current British law" in R.M. Goode (ed.), *Group Trading and the Lending Banker* (1988) p. 84; (hereinafter cited as "Prentice, Aspects of British law"); Blumberg, *Bankruptcy Law* pp. 257-258.

subservience appears - at least *vis-a-vis* the subsidiary's external creditors - unacceptable. It is of course arguable that the guarantor-subsidiary's interests are in fact enhanced because the group's welfare is strengthened by the guarantee and that this constitutes in itself sufficient compensation.[1] Perhaps. But this argument offers little comfort to creditors later faced with an insolvent corporate debtor.

Where the subsidiary which is lending financial support to other units in the group is insolvent or nearing insolvency at the time the support is extended, creditors are obviously directly prejudiced.[2] Where the subsidiary is financially sound, creditors are not usually adversely affected. Nevertheless, even where the subsidiary *is* financially sound, creditors could in fact be prejudiced - say by an upstream or cross-stream guarantee which, if enforced by the bank, may well lead the subsidiary to financial distress, even insolvency.[3] In any case, the financial support given by a subsidiary will generally demonstrate the subservience of the subsidiary's interests to those of the group in line with a group profit maximisation policy.

### 8.1.5. Operation of the subsidiary without a profit motive

In what are probably rare cases, the holding company sometimes manipulates a subsidiary in such a way that the subsidiary is unable to earn a profit. In these cases, which are less likely to arise with wholly-owned subsidiaries than with partly-owned subsidiaries, the subsidiary's interests are completely submerged to those of the group.[4] The intention may be achieved by habitual siphoning of assets, transfer pricing techniques,[5] withholding of payments due to it and other similarly abusive practices.

---

[1] Cf. Prentice, Aspects of British law, p. 84; R.M. Goode, *Principles of Corporate Insolvency Law* (1990) p. 150.

[2] *Vide ANZ Executors and Trustee Co Ltd.* v. *Qintex Ltd.* (1990) 2 ACSR 307; *Walker* v. *Wimborne and others* (1976) 50 A.L.J.R. 446; *Chemical Bank N.Y. Trust Co.* v. *Kheel* 369 F.2d 845 (2d Cir. 1966).

[3] *Vide* Mason J's observations in *Walker* v. *Wimborne and others* (1976) 50 A.L.J.R. 446 at p. 449. Cf. Adolf A. Berle, "Subsidiary Corporations and credit Manipulation" 41 Harv. L.R. 874 (1928) p. 878.

[4] E.g., *Henderson* v. *Rounds & Porter Lumber Co.* 99 F.Supp. 376 (W.D. Ark. 1951); *Rounds & Porter Lumber Co.* v. *Burns* 225 S.W.2d 1 (1949). Both cases concerned a partly-owned subsidiary. *Vide* also *Holbrook, Cabot & Rollins Corp.* v. *Perkins* 147 F. 166 (1st Cir. 1906) (wholly-owned subsidiary).

[5] E.g., by taking out any profits as a management charge as in *Joseph R. Foard Co.* v. *State of Maryland* 219 F. 827 (4th Cir. 1914).

Such intention may also be evidenced by an arrangement whereby the subsidiary sells its products only to the holding company which simply reimburses the subsidiary for its production costs so that all of the "profits" are enjoyed by the holding company,[1] or where one company leases property from an affiliate at a rental so high that it would be impossible for it ever to make a profit.[2] The lack of a profit motive would also be evident where a previously profitable company is acquired and its product line changed to suit the new holding company's supply requirements even though the new product line cannot but operate at a loss.[3]

The operation of a subsidiary without a profit motive is patently offensive and prejudicial to the interests of creditors. It reflects an extreme form of subordination to the interests of the group and a total disregard of the interests of creditors.

## 8.2. The sham or shell subsidiaries

A somewhat unusual - though clearly abusive - situation occurs where the subsidiary is conceived merely as a sham or shell. This type of subservient subsidiary is distinguishable from the subservient subsidiary under a group profit maximisation policy in that in the latter type of situation, the subservient company actually functions within the group - it has a real, and not just a legal, existence. In the sham or shell situation, however, the subsidiary - though formally existing as a legal entity - lacks significant indicia of separate corporate existence.[4] Such a subsidiary would typically lack assets, have no employees and run no real business. It would not keep separate books of account, would have no separate bank accounts and hold no separate board or general meetings. Moreover, there may be a lack of physical separation between it and the holding company, evidenced by

---

[1] E.g., *United States v. Reserve Mining Co.* 380 F. Supp. 11, 28 (D. Minn. 1971), *modified on other grounds*, 514 F.2d 492 (8th Cir. 1975).

[2] E.g., *Chesapeake Stone Co. v. Holbrook* 181 S.W. 953, 956 (1916).

[3] E.g., *Gannett Co. v. Larry* 221 F.2d 269 (2d Cir. 1955).

[4] E.g., *Re F.G. (Films) Ltd.* [1953] 1 W.L.R. 483, [1953] 1 All E.R. 615. One of the subsidiaries involved in *Adams v. Cape Industries plc* [1990] BCLC 479 (C.A.) appears to have been a "sham" or a "shell". *Vide* the judgment of Slade L.J. [1990] BCLC 479 at p. 519. In *Atlas Maritime Co. S.A. v. Avalon Maritime Ltd. ("The Coral Rose")*[1990] 2 Lloyd's Rep. 258, Hobhouse J. considered the defendant subsidiary as a mere "nominee" having "nothing more than the barest legal existence independently of [its ultimate holding company]". *Ibid.* at p. 264. The Court of Appeal however credited the subsidiary with more than just a bare legal existence. *Vide* [1991] 1 Lloyd's Rep. 563.

common directors and common officers, common offices, and common telephone and fax numbers, if any. The subsidiary is quite literally a sham.[1] Apart from the fact that creditors may be fooled by the subsidiary's "paper" status and are therefore prejudiced thereby, the holding company's failure to maintain for its subsidiary a minimum level of real, as distinct from purely formal, existence should in itself deny to the holding company the right to plead, at its convenience, the subsidiary's separate existence.

### 8.3. The subservient subsidiary situation - concluding remarks

Some general remarks should be made at this stage regarding the subservient subsidiary situation.

First, there is a policy issue. Any observer will acknowledge the temptation for every holding company to deal with its subsidiaries at less than arm's length. Should not the holding company's power to use the subsidiary in the group's interest and to the detriment of the subsidiary attract a corresponding financial responsibility for the welfare of the subsidiary - and of its creditors - in the event that the subsidiary faces difficulties? Should not the exercise of the power to control the subsidiary's destiny involve commitment? Should not a holding company's management of the affairs of its subsidiary for its own benefit and at the expense of the subsidiary be viewed as *inequitable* mismanagement and constitute both a breach of its obligations towards the subsidiary (and its creditors) as well as a breach of the privilege of incorporation?

Secondly, a question of proof. It must be recognised that proving abuse or unfairness would, in many instances, be a difficult, if not impossible task. The intra-group activities of a subservient company - the transfer pricing manipulations, the shuttling and commingling of assets, the diversion of corporate opportunities and other such servile behaviour - are not outwardly manifested. Creditors are unlikely to even suspect, let alone prove, such practices. Indeed, even the experienced and specialised machinery of the modern revenue authorities is often unable to identify potentially abusive practices such as transfer pricing.[2] The obstacles facing creditors barely need highlighting. Any remedy to be afforded to creditors will certainly need to be

---

[1] E.g., *Schlamowitz* v. *Pinehurst, Inc.* 229 F.Supp. 278 (1964); *Solar International Shipping Agency, Inc.* v. *Eastern Proteins Export, Inc.* 778 F.2d 922 (2d Cir. 1985).

[2] Cf. Frank Wooldridge, *Groups of Companies - The Law and Practice in Britain, France and Germany* (1981) p. 83.

bolstered by granting to liquidators wider powers and duties to investigate the activities of the group involved and to pursue claims in the interests of the creditors.

## 9. INADEQUATE FINANCIAL STRUCTURE

### 9.1. Success depends on adequate financing

If a business venture is to stand any chance of success it requires adequate financing.[1] The simplest and most important source of finance is the shareholders' equity - in ordinary or preference shares - usually raised either by an issue of shares or by the capitalisation of retained earnings. Another important source of finance is debt.[2] Debtholders are generally entitled to a fixed regular payment of interest and eventually the final repayment of principal. It is widely recognised by economists that the inclusion of some debt in the financial structure is beneficial to the enterprise.[3]

### 9.2. Equity and debt - different risks

English law allows incorporators considerable flexibility as to the form of capital structure to be utilised for the company and, except for public companies, there is no minimum paid up capital requirement.[4] In particular, the debt-equity composition of the company's capital structure is left entirely to the discretion of the incorporators.

---

[1] *Vide* R.P. Brooker, "Company Law Reform : is unlimited liability likely to be effective?" 3 Solicitor Quarterly 239 (1964) p. 249.

[2] *Vide* Brealey and Myers, *op. cit.* p. 334.

[3] *Vide* Pinches, *op. cit.* Ch. 13.

[4] Public companies have to possess an issued capital of £50,000 of which at least one quarter and the whole of any premium has been paid up (C.A. 1985, ss. 11 and 118). The figure of £50,000 has been termed a "derisively small sum for guaranteeing economic viability". *Vide* Prentice, The English Experience, at p. 107. The £50,000 minimum limit is almost wholly irrelevant for our purposes as the vast majority of subsidiaries are private companies. The absence of a general statutory requirement for a minimum issued capital has often been criticised. *Vide* Paul Stock, "Case shows why *all* companies need a minimum paid up share capital" 1 Co. Law. 249 (1980); P.S. Atiyah, "Thoughts on Company Law Philosophy" 8 Lawyer 15 (1965). *Vide* further *post*, Chapter VI pp. 325-332.

This raises a fundamental issue. In any enterprise, both the shareholders and the creditors assume some risk of its failure. Their risks are however different. As Judge Learned Hand put it : "The shareholders stand to lose first, but in return they have all the winnings above the creditors' interest, if the venture is successful; on the other hand the creditors have only their interest, but they come first in distribution of the assets."[1]

This notion of risk gives rise to a cardinal question. If a shareholder who provides say minimal equity and substantial debt is allowed to prove in insolvency on a parity with other creditors in respect of his debt, the shareholder would be in a position of taking all the profits if the venture succeeds and yet expose himself only to a creditor's risk, if it fails. The unfairness to other creditors is evident. Every creditor "rightly assumes that his risk is measured by the collective claims of other creditors, and by creditors he understands those alone, who like him, have only a stipulated share in the profits."[2] To force a creditor to "divide the assets in insolvency with those who at their option have all along had power to take all the earnings, is to add to the risk which he accepted."[3] In these circumstances, it is at least arguable that any funds provided by the shareholder and intended as shareholder's investment should be subject to a shareholder's risk. The shareholder's investment should, independently of the label attached to it by the shareholder (that is equity or debt), be considered as equity capital to the extent reasonably required for the particular venture.

## 9.3. Unfairness in certain financial structures

Two principles should follow from the above analysis. In the first place, the entrepreneur should reasonably ensure that the venture is provided with sufficient financing to enable it to stand a fair chance of success. In the second place, the entrepreneur should himself risk as equity capital an adequate portion of his investment as genuinely reflects the capital needs of the venture.

Applying the present discussion to the holding-subsidiary set-up, it will be observed that two situations give rise to concern.

---

[1] *In re Loewer's Gambrinus Brewery Co.* 167 F.2d 318 (2d Cir. 1948) at p. 320.

[2] *Ibid.* at p. 320.

[3] *Ibid.* at p. 320.

### 9.3.1. The inadequately financed subsidiary

In the first situation, a holding company which decides to embark on a new project through the incorporation of a subsidiary fails to provide the subsidiary with the financing backbone that is reasonably required for the conduct of the business. The subsidiary may have at its disposal such trivial financing that it cannot stand on its own feet. Such a subsidiary would be doomed to failure. This situation is clearly reprehensible. The prejudice to creditors is self-evident. Surely, the holding company should have an obligation to provide the subsidiary with financing reasonable for its needs in the light of the business to be undertaken.[1]

Inadequately financed ventures can obviously feature whatever the organisational medium used. The enterprise need not necessarily be a subsidiary. Subsidiaries however appear to be at a higher risk of being inadequately financed, at least initially, than other companies. This is probably due to the expectation that the group's resources will be made available should the need arise.[2] In any case, the double insulation from liability enjoyed by the shareholders of the holding company justifies stricter adequate capitalisation requirements for subsidiary companies.

Difficult questions arise in discussing the issue of inadequate capitalisation. For the moment it is only necessary to highlight these questions. Primarily, how is adequate capitalisation to be measured? Must it not be related to the nature and magnitude of the corporate undertaking? Secondly, need the financing be provided by means of issued share capital? Should not adequate financing depend essentially on the total funds invested, whether by way of equity or debt? Thirdly, should the obligation to provide adequate capital be an on-going obligation? Or should initial adequate capitalisation be sufficient? Finally, what should the remedy be in the event that an inadequately capitalised subsidiary flounders? Should *unlimited* liability be imposed on the holding company or should liability be limited to the amount of adequate capitalisation? Certainly, these are all challenging questions involving profound policy issues. And yet, fair and workable solutions must be found. These problems and the solutions thereto are more appropriately debated in another part of this work.[3]

---

[1] *Vide* further *post* Chapter VI pp. 311-316.

[2] *Vide* Jonathan M. Landers, "Another Word on Parent, Subsidiaries and Affiliates in Bankruptcy" 43 Univ. of Chicago L.R. 527 (1976) p. 528.

[3] *Vide post*, Chapter VI.

### 9.3.2. Holding company competing as creditor

In many instances, a holding company sets up a subsidiary which is, in fact, adequately financed. The financing however may be almost totally debt financing emanating from the holding company itself. Sometimes, the lending appears to amount to the provision of capital on a more or less permanent basis.[1] There is in principle nothing objectionable in the holding company financing its subsidiary through both equity and debt. But if the subsidiary, despite adequate financing, becomes insolvent, the holding company may claim to be entitled - as creditor for the debt advances - to share in the proceeds with other creditors. In an insolvency scenario, the holding company's claim as creditor for all its debt advances may be unfair.[2] This is because on analysis it may be determined that part, or perhaps all, of the debt should more properly be characterised as an equity investment subject to a shareholder's risk. What counts is the substance. If the funds have been advanced without any reasonable expectation of payment and are as a matter of substantial economic reality risked on the success of the venture, they may not really be loans but capital.[3] If the holding company is allowed to prove on a parity with the other creditors for all its debt advances (including those which should more properly be characterised as equity), it would mean that the holding company can take all the winnings where the subsidiary is successful, and yet expose itself only to a creditor's risk, if it fails.[4] To condone this state of affairs would be unfair to creditors.[5] In the event of insolvency, the holding company's claim based on the portion of the financing which it chose to denominate as debt should pass the characterisation test before it is accorded a true debt status. If it fails the test, then the claim should arguably be subordinated to the claims of the

---

[1] *Vide* further *post* Chapter VI pp. 316-320.

[2] In *Atlas Maritime Co. S.A.* v. *Avalon Maritime Ltd. ("The Coral Rose")* [1991] 1 Lloyd's Rep. 563 (C.A.), Staughton L.J. stated that "[t]he creation ... of a subsidiary company with minimal liability, which will operate with the parent's funds and on the parent's directions but not expose the parent to liability, *may not seem the most honest way of trading*" (emphasis added). He noted moreover that the arrangement is "extremely common in the international shipping industry, and perhaps elsewhere". *Ibid.* p. 571.

[3] *Vide post* Chapter VI pp. 368-382.

[4] Cf. *In re Loewer's Gambrinus Brewery Co.* 167 F.2d 318, 320 (2d Cir. 1948).

[5] *Vide supra* pp. 84-85. Cf. CCAB Memorandum (1979) p. 4; CCAB Memorandum (1981) p.5.

other creditors and be paid only after such other claims have been paid in full.[1]

Difficult questions also arise in this type of situation. Again, it is only necessary at this stage to highlight the issues and to leave their discussion to a later part of this work.[2] The fundamental question will be the basis on which the categorisation into debt or equity should be made. Another question relates to the remedy : if an investment labelled by the holding company as debt is to be characterised by law as equity, should the remedy be merely the subordination of the relative claim or should it be disallowance? Finally, should special consideration be afforded to advances made by the holding company to a subsidiary in distress to enable it to weather the storm?

## 9.4. Creditor-proof devices

Sometimes, the problem of inadequate financing and the strategy of financing on a high debt-equity ratio assume a particularly obnoxious form through the use of certain "creditor-proof" devices. It is to these devices that the discussion now turns.

### 9.4.1. The loan-cum-mortgage device

The holding company's freedom to invest in the subsidiary by means of debt rather than equity can be combined with the taking of security rights over the debt. A subsidiary may be incorporated with a share capital of say ten shares of one pound each. The holding company would then lend the subsidiary the substantial funds it needs for its business and secure the loan on the assets of the subsidiary.[3] The net effect of this device, which is strangely allowed by

---

[1] A similar proposal was made in the Cork Report, para. 1963, pp. 441-442. Regrettably, the proposal was not implemented in the legislation that followed the Report. *Vide* also the somewhat unrefined proposal made by D.G. Rice in "One man" Company or one man "Company" [1964] J.B.L. 36 at p. 42. The courts do however now have the power to defer debts due from the company to persons found liable for fraudulent or wrongful trading in relation to it (I.A. 1986, s. 215(4)). The discussion on the characterisation of advances and the notion of subordination is developed *post*, Chapter VI pp. 363-383.

[2] *Vide post*, Chapter VI.

[3] *Vide* e.g., *Erickson* v. *Minnesota and Ontario Power Co.* 158 N.W. 979 (1916).

law,[1] and which was recognised by traders and abused of even in the nineteenth century,[2] is to enable the holding company to rank first in competition proceedings in respect of its advances should the subsidiary be wound up on the grounds of insolvency.[3] The mortgage effectively functions as a buffer against creditors' claims. One can only speculate on the number of times that this type of subsidiary has been incorporated on the counsel of professional advisers who then lay back in haughty self-satisfaction at the immunised wonder of their creation.

The device can be said to have received its judicial imprimatur by the monstrous decision of the House of Lords in *Salomon* v. *A. Salomon and Co. Ltd.*[4] In that case, Lord Herschell acknowledged that the issue of debentures as part of the purchase price was "certainly open to *great abuse*, and has often worked *great mischief*" but that as the law stood there was "certainly nothing unlawful in the creation of such debentures".[5] In a similar vein, Lord Macnaghten noted that "when there is a winding-up debenture-holders generally step in and sweep off everything; and *a great scandal it is*".[6] Judicial ingenuity - say by developing a notion of subordination - does not seem to have been too fashionable at the time. Meanwhile, the "great scandal" lives on and preparations are now in hand to celebrate the first centennial of its judicial recognition.

### 9.4.2. The lease device

As a general rule, a creditor's ultimate remedy against a company is to its property. If the company has no property, the creditor remains without a remedy. One ploy that has been used by holding companies to protect their investment in the subsidiaries from the creditors' claws is for the holding

---

[1] *Vide* Templeman L.J.'s comment in *Re Southard & Co. Ltd.* [1979] 1 W.L.R. 1198 (C.A.) at p. 1208.

[2] *Vide* Paddy Ireland, "The Triumph of the Company Legal Form, 1856-1914" in John Adams (ed.), *Essays for Clive Schmitthoff* (1983) p. 50.

[3] Unless of course other creditors enjoy prior-ranking claims *ex lege* or *ex contractu* as in the case of the contractual subordination of the holding company's security rights to a bank. On the validity of subordination agreements *vide post* Chapter VI p. 355 footnote 2.

[4] [1897] A.C. 22 (H.L.).

[5] *Ibid.* at p. 47 (emphasis added).

[6] *Ibid.* at p. 53 (emphasis added).

company to lease to the subsidiary all the property that may be needed in the conduct of its activities.[1] The lease may be on a fixed short- or long-term basis or it may be terminable either at the option of the lessor or on the happening of a specific event such as the winding up of the lessee. When the crunch comes, the property that had appeared as belonging to the subsidiary is, sometimes quite literally, snatched from its possession. This device is actually more pernicious to the creditors' interest than the "loan-cum-mortgage" stratagem. In the latter case there is at least the possibility that the value of the subsidiary's assets acquired by the loan is actually higher than the holding company's claims. In the lease device there will, in the event of the subsidiary's insolvency, almost certainly be nothing left for the creditors.

## 9.5. Creditor-proof devices compounded by "milking"

The repugnance of "loan and mortgage" and "lease" devices just described is sometimes compounded by the use of a scheme whereby the corporation cannot really make any profit and whereby the net income in the course of the subsidiary's activities is siphoned off as an operating charge of one sort or another.[2] The holding company may, for example, having leased to the subsidiary its property (say a hotel or restaurant) to be operated by the subsidiary in its (the subsidiary's) behalf, proceed to charge the subsidiary a rent that is either equal to the subsidiary's gross profit or that is so high as to ensure that the subsidiary cannot trade profitably.[3] Or a ship broking company may organise a subsidiary stevedoring company and keep its profits as a charge for managing its business.[4] Or the only asset belonging to a subsidiary may be an intangible asset - such as a construction contract - and the holding company, in return for the performance of the contract by the subsidiary, pays to the subsidiary a sum equal to the wages of the employees and the cost of the materials, plus a trifling percentage.[5]

In the pure creditor-proof devices there is at least a possibility that the subsidiary actually becomes profitable and its creditors paid. The combination of such devices with the "milking" of profits, however, not only

---

[1]  *Vide* e.g., *Oriental Investment Co.* v. *Barclay* 25 Tex. Civ. App. 543, 64 S.W. 80 (1901).

[2]  Latty, *op. cit.* p. 138.

[3]  *Vide Oriental Investment Co.* v. *Barclay* 64 S.W. 80 (1901).

[4]  *Vide* e.g., *Joseph R. Foard Co.* v. *State of Maryland* 219 F. 827 (4th Cir. 1914).

[5]  *Vide* e.g., *Holbrook, Cabot & Rollins Corp.* v. *Perkins* 147 F. 166 (1st Cir. 1906).

considerably limits the holding company's risk but it also virtually eliminates the creditors' chances of recovery. Further comment would surely be superfluous.

### 9.6. Assumption of risk by creditors

Whenever a subsidiary has an inadequate financial structure - be it inadequate financing, the use of excessive debt in relation to equity or the deployment of creditor-proof devices - creditors are bound to be prejudiced. From the purely theoretical point of view it may be argued that creditors are in a position to assess the risk and to protect themselves against any increased risk either by increasing the interest rate at which they extend credit or by seeking additional security or by requesting the holding company to subordinate its own claim.

This view, however, is wholly unrealistic. Are creditors really in a position to assess the risk? A sophisticated creditor, such as a financing institution, obviously is. But what about other creditors, such as trade creditors, consumers and employees. Certainly, they would usually have neither the opportunity nor the means to conduct an investigation.[1] Nor would they have the ability to interpret any findings without costly professional advice.[2] The argument that creditors assume the risk of a company's inadequate financial structure is also, to an extent, theoretically flawed. The argument in fact conveniently ignores the position of involuntary creditors - such as tort victims - who *ex hypothesis* are unable to perceive, let alone assess, the risk.[3]

The truth is that any argument justifying the legality of undercapitalised companies will have to rest on some ground other than the creditors' abilities to perceive the risk and to safeguard themselves against any increase in such risk. It may be that the justification lay in the promotion of trade through the attractive principle of limited liability. But is there no cost at which limited liability is to be acquired? Must the risks associated with the promotion of

---

[1] The situation would be different where the creditor knowingly contracted with a subsidiary of dubious credit.

[2] Again the position would be different where the creditor chose to proceed when his credit investigation of the subsidiary indicates financial weakness or fails to disclose its financial status.

[3] These issues are discussed further *post*, Chapter IV pp. 176-193.

new companies be transferred onto unsuspecting creditors endeavouring to earn their daily bread?[1]

## 9.7. Inadequate financial structure results in dependence

Apart from the fact that an inadequate financial structure is *per se* objectionable, it should be observed that such a financial structure may lead to an excessive dependence by the subsidiary on the holding company or some other component of the group.[2] An inadequate financial structure exacerbates the subsidiary's inability to function autonomously and casts doubt on the genuine separation of its conduct from that of the holding company.[3]

## 10.    INTEGRATED ECONOMIC ENTERPRISE SITUATION

One of the most striking features of corporate groups is the close co-ordination of the activities of the various legal units by means of centralised control. Subsidiaries, without necessarily being subservient, are generally directed from headquarters. Headquarters is the brain and nerve centre. The subsidiaries are the limbs.[4]

In a smaller number of groups, however, integration goes beyond centralised control and co-ordination of activities. In this smaller number of groups, the separate legal units conduct themselves as closely inter-related fragments of a single unitary business. Together they constitute a "firm". This of course is an economic concept, for the law does not, outwardly at least, purport to be concerned with economic units.[5]

Economic integration can be of two types : vertical or horizontal.

---

[1] These questions are analysed at length *post*, Chapter IV.

[2] Cf. Tom Hadden, *The Control of Corporate Groups* (1983) pp. 17-18.

[3] *Vide Garden City Co.* v. *Burden* 186 F.2d 651 (10th Cir. 1951).

[4] Tugendhat, *op. cit.* p. 4. *Vide supra* pp. 48-61.

[5] In *Bank of Tokyo Ltd.* v. *Karoon* [1987] 1 A.C. 45 (C.A.), Goff L.J. observed - in response to a suggestion by counsel that in the particular context the holding and subsidiary companies were, economically, one - that "... we are concerned not with economics but with law. The distinction between the two is, in law, fundamental and cannot here be bridged". *Ibid.* at p. 64.

## 10.1. Vertical integration

The essential characteristic of vertical integration is the group's dependence on the subsidiary for some particular industrial or commercial function. In the vertically integrated group, each subsidiary exercises a function that is crucial for the group enterprise - a function which, if not performed by the subsidiary, would have to be performed by some other unit in the group. In many cases the subsidiary serves only its holding company or some other affiliate within the group. In other cases it may also service third parties outside the group. A typical example of a vertically integrated group occurs where the research and development functions, the different stages of manufacture, and the activities of marketing, selling, distribution, transportation and financing are carried out by different subsidiaries, often in different countries around the globe.[1]

## 10.2. Horizontal integration

In horizontally integrated groups, each subsidiary conducts a business that is virtually identical to the business carried out by its affiliates. Hotel chains, retail stores, car park services, department stores, catering businesses and ship owning and ship chartering organisations, for example, typically comprise a number of subsidiaries each operating one hotel, one shop, one car park, one restaurant, one department store or one ship.[2] Usually, the subsidiaries would conduct the businesses from different localities.

## 10.3. Is integration inequitable?

Vertically integrated subsidiaries exist solely, or almost solely, to serve the operational functions of the group. The economic autonomy of the individual subsidiaries may be effectively destroyed. Economic autonomy may also be lacking in horizontal integration. Where subsidiaries are each involved in the conduct of a fragment of an economically integrated business, the insulation of the group's assets from liability appears hard to justify. Both in the public's perception, as well as in economic terms, integration means that the

---

[1] Cf. OECD Report on Transfer Pricing (1984) p. 13. Judgments provide several examples of vertical integration. *Vide post* Chapter VII pp. 391-393, where the technique of vertical integration is further illustrated.

[2] *Vide* e.g., *Allright Texas, Inc.* v. *Simons* 501 S.W.2d 145 (Tex. Civ. App. 1973).

same business is involved.[1] Insulation would appear especially hard to justify in certain situations, such as disasters involving substantial personal injuries or environmental claims.

It is submitted however that neither form of integration - vertical or horizontal - should be considered as *per se* objectionable. The truth is that mere economic integration - be it horizontal or vertical - does not necessarily result in unfairness or prejudice to creditors.[2] Other elements would be required for unfairness or prejudice to develop - such as subservience, inadequate capitalisation or the abuse of a group persona.[3] Such circumstances, however, would in themselves funnel the subsidiary into specific categories of abuse. Those circumstances, rather than economic integration, would constitute the mischief.

There is another, perhaps more fundamental, reason why economic integration should not spontaneously lead to overall group liability. As will be discussed in a later part of this work, the policy of limited liability, though much abused of, is still worthy of protection.[4] The economic benefits inherent in a system of limited liability outweigh the unfortunate consequences that occasionally result from its implementation. What is necessary is to adequately control and sanction the sometimes obvious abuses that the policy of limited liability is subjected to. The division of an enterprise - horizontally or vertically - is not in itself an abuse of this policy.

## 10.4. Abusive economic integration

There is however one form of economic integration which is clearly abusive. This occurs where the privilege of incorporation is manipulated to create what is effectively an absurd division of a single unitary enterprise into a host of separate legal compartments. Both vertical and horizontal methods of integration can be involved.

---

[1] *Vide* Blumberg, *Substantive Law* p. 691.

[2] *Vide contra*, Hugh Collins, "Ascription of Legal Responsibility to Groups in Complex Patterns of Economic Integration" 53 M.L.R. 731 (1990) at p. 734 where it is argued that injustice may be caused whenever two firms are economically integrated, despite the formal legal separation.

[3] For subservience and inadequate capitalisation *vide supra* pp. 69-83 and pp. 84-92 respectively. The group persona situation - where the component companies within the group are held out to the public as a single enterprise - is dealt with *post* pp. 95-97.

[4] *Vide post*, Chapter IV.

The use of this abusive device in the context of vertical integration will be illustrated first. An entrepreneur runs a tailoring business. In a crude attempt to reduce the enterprise's exposure virtually down to nought, he incorporates a holding company and a series of subsidiaries. The tailoring business will be conducted through the subsidiaries : one subsidiary to take the orders, one to purchase the raw materials, one to cut the drapery, one to sew the suits, one to iron the outfits, one to own the delivery van and so on. The holding company might take overall managerial charge of the enterprise.

Abusive horizontal integration can be illustrated by the taxi-cab situation. The owner of a fleet of taxicabs - again in an effort to insulate the assets of the enterprise from liability - would incorporate each taxicab as a separate subsidiary, wholly owned by a holding company. Naturally, each taxicab would be centrally managed by the holding company.[1]

In any of the above situations, the design is to jettison the particular subsidiary in the event of a major claim. But surely, there must be limits to the use of the privilege of incorporation. There must be some control on the extent to which a business enterprise can be divided into a number of legal units. After all, the social and economic needs of limited liability would already have been met when the law allowed the enterprise to be incorporated.[2]

## 11. THE GROUP PERSONA SITUATION

Evident in a number of groups is the use of a common public group persona. Through the use of a group persona, the various components within the corporate group are held out to the public as a single enterprise, as a unified persona.[3]

Various methods are employed to promote the group persona, including the adoption of a common group name, the use of common trade marks, trade names and logos, the implementation of integrated advertising campaigns, the promotion of a group slogan, the use of common letterheads,

---

[1] *Vide Mull* v. *Colt Co.* 31 F.R.D. 154 (S.D.N.Y. 1962); *Robinson* v. *Chase Maintenance Corp.* 190 N.Y.S.2d 773 (Sup. Ct. 1959). Cf. *Walkovszky* v. *Carlton* 223 N.E.2d 6 (1966).

[2] The underlying policy implications of limited liability are discussed *post* in Chapter IV.

[3] Similar remarks were made by Martin Stevens during the debate in the House of Commons on the Companies Bill in 1979. *Vide* Parliamentary Debates, Standing Committee A, Session 1979-1980 Vol. I, 11th December 1979 at col. 720.

and the depiction in the corporate literature of each company as part of one corporate whole.[1] Sometimes, there is a lack of identification of the separate subsidiaries or the adoption of similar names for the various legal units.[2]

The vice with the group persona situation lies in its strong propensity to mislead creditors dealing with a particular component into believing that they are actually doing business either with the group as a separate person or with the holding company. Occasionally, the creditor, while recognising the individuality of the subsidiary he is contracting with, is led to believe that the group or the holding company will financially support the subsidiary in the event it encounters financial problems. The uninitiated are particularly at risk.[3]

The difficulty of course is to determine whether the use of the aforementioned techniques to promote the group image is necessarily harmful and should therefore be controlled. One point is certain. To the layman, at least, even the distinction between a holding and a subsidiary company will sometimes be a slender one.[4] Where group persona techniques are used with tact, confusion will very easily result and the distinction may disappear altogether. The man on the Gatwick Express is often credited with too fine an appreciation of juridical niceties. Consumers, though nowadays far less gullible than in the days of the Clapham omnibus, can still be quite easily impressed by the marketing strategies implemented by a corporate group.[5] Frequently of course, the mists of confusion can be lifted on closer examination or deeper thought. Should consumers however be expected to examine the facts more closely or think more profoundly? Should the consumer have to grope through the mysteries of business technicalities entirely alien to him, especially when the intrigue originates from the group itself for its own promotional purposes?

Undoubtedly abusive are the situations where misrepresentation is involved. A group may engage in conduct that is likely to create in the creditor the reasonable expectation that he is extending credit to an economic entity larger than the subsidiary he actually contracted with and

---

[1] *Vide* further *post* Chapter VIII p. 416.

[2] *Vide* further *post* Chapter VIII p. 416.

[3] *Vide* generally *post* Chapter VII pp. 417-421, where these issues are discussed at some length.

[4] *Vide* further *post* Chapter VIII pp. 419-420.

[5] *Vide* further *post* Chapter VIII pp. 419-421.

the creditor reasonably relies - potentially to his detriment - on his understanding concerning who, or what, he was dealing with.[1]

A number of issues will need to be considered in the search for a solution to the group persona mischief. The first matter to be tackled will be whether existing remedies are entirely adequate. As will be demonstrated in a later part of this work, existing remedies are unfortunately not sufficiently adequate.[2] The second question to be tackled is the nature of the desired reform : should some form of group liability or holding company liability be introduced? Or is the remedy to be sought in consolidation of the assets of the various components of the group? Certainly, the precise circumstances when any such remedy will be imposed will also have to be established. In this connection, the nature and level of misrepresentation required for the imposition of a sanction will have to be determined. Also relevant will be the question whether consolidation or group or holding company liability should favour creditors generally or only the specific creditors misled by the misrepresentation. In other words, should the notion of reliance therefore feature in the application of a remedy? Clearly, complete consolidation may prove unfair to those creditors who specifically relied on the credit of a particular component. But should tort victims - who would not usually be able to plead reliance on the group persona notion - be denied relief? These and other related questions will be dealt with in a later part of this work in the context of proposals for reform.[3]

## 12. THE POTENTIAL FOR ABUSE OR UNFAIRNESS - CONCLUDING REMARKS

A number of concluding remarks need to be made concerning the potential for abuse or unfairness in the conduct of corporate groups.

### 12.1. Greater likelihood of abuse in the smaller groups

Clearly, the risks of abuse and unfairness particular to the group phenomenon do not feature merely in the larger corporate organisations. On the contrary, it is more likely for abuse or unfairness to occur in the context

---

[1] *Vide FMC Finance Corp.* v. *Murphree* 632 F.2d 413 (5th Cir. 1980).

[2] *Vide post*, Chapter VIII.

[3] *Vide post*, Chapter VIII.

of the smaller groups. A number of factors explain this. To begin with, the larger corporate groups are generally subject to stricter control by regulatory bodies and financing institutions. Besides, corporate management within the larger organisations generally tends to practise relatively higher standards of corporate behaviour. This may be partly due to the stricter controls to which such groups are subject, and partly due to the fact that top managerial personnel in such groups are often recruited from relatively more professional circles. Moreover, the larger groups, dependent as they are on the image they project to the public at large - often on a global scale - are much more averse to allowing abusive or unfair practices to tarnish their reputation and thereby lessen their market share.

## 12.2. Both domestic and transnational groups affected

It is self-evident that the questionable practices described in this chapter occur both in domestic corporate groups as well as in transnational groups. Given the difficulties inherent in the international control of corporate behaviour, it may at first sight appear that there exists a greater likelihood of abuse in the case of transnational groups. Other factors, however, tend to limit the risk of abusive behaviour on the part of transnational groups. Thus, transnational groups, in an effort to avoid upsetting host countries, probably exercise more caution in their activities than purely domestic firms. Besides, a foreign enterprise will almost certainly be under closer scrutiny and viewed with greater suspicion than its domestic counterpart. A foreign enterprise may also be expected by the host countries to adhere more closely to the rules of "good corporate citizenship".[1] Moreover, a host country can sometimes put considerable pressure to bear on transnational corporations to reverse the effects of abuses or excesses in their corporate behaviour.[2]

## 12.3. Abuse not necessarily widespread

It must also be stressed that the study of group structures and behavioural practices undertaken in this work does not set out to demonstrate whether or not the abusive and unfair practices are widespread. The work does not

---

[1] Cf. Wallace, *op. cit.* pp. xviii, 7.

[2] A notable illustration of such pressure is described in Blanpain, *op. cit.*

purport to log the readings of the sometimes blustery winds of the business world.

The prevalence or otherwise of abuse and unfairness in the context of corporate groups was however a controversial issue in the famous, if somewhat heated, Landers-Posner debate that took place in the pages of the University of Chicago Law Review in the mid-1970s.[1] Landers argued that creditors of a multi-corporate enterprise faced certain dangers not faced by creditors of a single corporation. These dangers include the lesser importance afforded to the adequate capitalisation of newly-formed subsidiaries, the increased chance of commingling and shuttling of assets, the likelihood of creditors being misled regarding the ownership of assets within the group, and the taking of corporate decisions with a view to overall return on investment rather than the profitability of a particular unit - with the concomitant danger that a subsidiary will not be operated as a separate profit-making centre with a realistic potential for profitability.[2] Landers' view was essentially that the abuses of limited liability in corporate groups was so prevalent as to warrant a rule dispensing with the need to prove that an abuse occurred.

Posner rejected Landers' thesis. He asserted that Landers had exaggerated the prevalence of abuses "by limiting his data source to reported bankruptcy cases".[3] He also argued that cases are not likely to constitute a representative sample of credit transactions generally. In his view, anyone who only reads the cases will leave with a mistaken impression that the usual purpose and effect of corporate affiliation is to mislead creditors.[4] Posner accepted that a corporate group can take measures that conceal or distort the relative profitability of the different legal units, but argued that corporate groups do not invariably or typically adopt such measures.[5] He submitted that such measures are costly because they reduce the information available

---

[1] Jonathan M. Landers opened the debate in "A Unified Approach to Parent, Subsidiary, and Affiliate Questions in Bankruptcy" 42 Univ. of Chicago L.R. 589 (1975). Judge R.A. Posner challenged Landers' views in "The Right of Creditors of Affiliated Corporations" 43 U. Chic. L. Rev. 499 (1976). Landers then had the last word in "Another Word on Parent, Subsidiaries and Affiliates in Bankruptcy" 43 Univ. of Chicago L.R. 527 (1976).

[2] *Vide* Jonathan M. Landers, "Another Word on Parent, Subsidiaries and Affiliates in Bankruptcy" 43 Univ. of Chicago L.R. 527 (1976) p. 528.

[3] Richard A. Posner, "The Right of Creditors of Affiliated Corporations" 43 U. Chic. L. Rev. 499 (1976) p. 524.

[4] *Ibid.* p. 524.

[5] *Ibid.* p. 513.

to the group about the efficiency with which the various units are being managed. For this reason, large groups typically treat their major divisions and subsidiaries as "profit centers" which are expected to conduct themselves as if they were independent units.[1] This behavioural pattern, according to Posner, manifests itself even when the activities of affiliated companies are closely related - that is, when they produce substitute or complimentary goods - and it is only in the exceptional case that maximising the profits of a group will involve different behaviour from what could be expected of independent firms.[2]

As already mentioned, the determination of the extent of abuse in corporate groups is beyond the scope of this work. The objects of this study are rather to prove the reality and the nature of the abusive and unfair practices, to measure the adequacy of existing law in this area and to then submit proposals for reform.

Certainly, the group structure performs legitimate functions and is in many cases legitimately used.[3] Groups are not inherently pernicious. However, abuses *do* undoubtedly occur.[4] An examination of the reported cases alone is sufficient to dispel any notion that abusive or unfair conduct is non-existent. And the number of such cases[5] is perhaps enough to indicate that the instances of abuse and unfairness are not as uncommon as Posner would have us believe.[6] The truth is that groups are neither all good nor all bad. Of course, the courts are only occasionally exposed to the sometimes stormy weather of group activity; and a climate cannot be accurately diagnosed from a specimen of captured raindrops. Such technical analysis is not however the object of this exercise.

---

[1] *Ibid.* p. 513.

[2] *Ibid.* pp. 513-514. Posner used the same arguments in R.A. Posner, *Economic Analysis of Law* (2nd ed. 1977) pp. 298-299.

[3] *Vide* Adolf A. Berle, "Subsidiary Corporations and Credit Manipulation" 41 Harv. L.R. 874 (1928) p. 892. For the transnational perspective, *vide* Rita M. Rodriguez and E. Eugene Carter, *International Financial Management* (1976) pp. 1-2; Wallace, *op. cit.* pp. 8.

[4] Cf. Prentice, The English Experience, p. 103.

[5] Cf. Tunc, *op. cit.* p. 18.

[6] Cf. also ALI Principles of Corporate Governance, Part V, Ch. 3.

## 12.4. Lack of scientific precision should not bar reform

Finally, it must be acknowledged that the labelling of a given set of circumstances as unfair or abusive will inevitably lack scientific precision. It may, for example, not always be easy to decide whether a subsidiary's behaviour identifies it as subservient. Nor would it be simple to establish whether a subsidiary's financial structure reveals inadequacy or whether the division of a unitary enterprise into a number of separate legal units constitutes an abuse of the privilege of incorporation. Nor would it be easy to assess whether the projection of a group image misled creditors into believing they were dealing with a single enterprise. The determination of these questions will sometimes have to involve the familiar difficulty of drawing a line - of finely balancing the interests of the various stakeholders involved in corporate groups. This realisation may be somewhat disheartening. But let it not discourage the effort at seeking a just solution to the problems raised. The alternative would be to trek along the well-trodden path of outdated dogma.

# 3 The Relevance of Ordinary Principles to the Question of Inter-Corporate Liability

## 1. INTRODUCTION

The potentially abusive and unfair situations identified in the preceding chapter need to be diagnosed under the dual spot-lights of existing law and relevant policy considerations. For it is only if existing law fails to measure up to desirable policy standards that recommendations for reform would be welcome.

It will of course have been observed that certain inherent differences distinguish the four types of abuse or unfairness, bringing into play distinct legal principles and also diverse policy considerations. Proper analysis demands that each type of abuse or unfairness be dealt with separately. This is the approach adopted in this work.[1]

It is however evident that a number of issues are common to all the categories of abuse or unfairness. Some of these common issues are best tackled prior to the specific discussion on the four categories. Other common issues then are more appropriately considered after the four categories have been separately analysed.[2]

This Chapter and the next will consider those common issues that are properly dealt with *prior* to the separate analysis of each of the four categories.

---

[1] *Vide post* Chapter V (Subservient Subsidiaries), Chapter VI (Undercapitalised Subsidiaries), Chapter VII (Integrated Economic Enterprise situation) and Chapter VIII (Group Persona situation).

[2] *Vide post* Chapter IX.

## 2. THE RELATIONSHIP BETWEEN SEPARATE JURIDICAL PERSONALITY AND LIMITED LIABILITY

The traditional view of the company in both the common and the civil law systems is firmly based on entity law - the notion that a company is endowed with a separate juridical personality, with its own rights and obligations, distinct from those of its shareholders.[1] The precise nature of the relationship between this principle and another equally elementary and fundamental principle of company law - that of limited liability - has given rise to conflicting views and considerable confusion. In fact, some commentators assert that limited liability is a necessary consequence of separate juridical personality,[2] while others argue that limited liability is not an essential characteristic of the corporation and that no historical basis exists for assuming that shareholders are immune from liability for corporate debts.[3] The truth, as so often happens in conflict situations, lies somewhere in between the two opposing positions.

---

[1] *Salomon* v. *A. Salomon and Co. Ltd.* [1897] A.C. 22 (H.L.); *United States* v. *Milwaukee Refrigerator Transit Co.* 142 Fed. 247 (C.C.E.D. Wis. 1905). A more recent affirmation of the doctrine appears in a forceful way in *Lonrho Ltd.* v. *Shell Petroleum Co. Ltd.* [1980] 2 W.L.R. 367 (C.A.), *aff'd* [1980] 1 W.L.R. 627 (H.L.). *Vide* also *J.H. Rayner (Mincing Lane) Ltd.* v. *Dept. of Trade and Industry* [1989] 3 W.L.R. 969 (H.L.). Academic writing on corporate personality is voluminous. *Vide* the extensive bibliography in R.W.M. Dias, *A Bibliography of Jurisprudence* (3rd ed. 1979) s. 12 (pp. 186-204). Much of the legal writing on corporate personality is of such philosophical flavour that it cannot be of much use to the lawyer or to the court when faced with real-life situations.

[2] Gower, for example, states that limited liability is "the most important advantage conferred by incorporation" and that "[i]t follows from the fact that a corporation is a separate person that its members are not as such liable for its debts". *Vide* Gower, at pp. 22 and 88. Gower's statement at p. 88 (which had also appeared in the 4th edition at p. 100) was quoted and relied upon by Kerr L.J. in *J.H. Rayner (Mincing Lane) Ltd.* v. *Dept. of Trade* [1989] Ch. 72 (C.A.) at p. 176. *Vide* also *J. H. Rayner Ltd.* v. *Dept of Trade and Industry* [1989] 3 W.L.R. 969 pp. 1008-1010; James Grant, *A Practical Treatise on the Law of Corporations* (1850) p. 5; Walter Horrowitz, "Historical Development of Company Law" 62 L.Q.R. 375 (1946) p. 375; Cathy S. Krendl and James R. Krendl, "Piercing the Corporate Veil : Focusing the Inquiry" 55 Denver L.J. 1 (1978) p. 1.

[3] Maurice Dix, "Adequate Risk Capital : The Consideration for the Benefits of Separate Incorporation" 53 N.W.U.L. Rev. 478 (1958) p. 478; Blumberg, *Substantive Law* p. 37; Arthur S. Dewing, *The Financial Policy of Corporations* (5th ed. 1953) Vol. I, pp. 14-15. Cf. Farrar, p. 81.

In English law, the notion of corporate personality owes its origins to medieval interpretations of Roman Law.[1] Roman law however had not designed separate personality to limit personal liability. The Romans conceived the corporation as an artificial person to take title to plunder acquired in conquest.[2]

Whatever the historical reasons for the genesis of separate juridical personality, it is clear that the notions of separate juridical personality and limited liability are closely intertwined. In the context of corporations, the essential attribute of separate personality is that the corporation is distinct from the members who compose it. A natural consequence of this attribute is that when the corporation contracts a debt, it will be regarded as the debt of the corporation - as a legal entity or artificial person - and not the debt of the individual members. Individual members cannot therefore be held liable towards the creditors of the corporation.[3] This relationship between juridical personality and "immunity" from liability was recognised very early in English law. Holdsworth notes that as early as the fifteenth century it was clear that an individual corporator was not personally liable for the debts of the *non-trading* corporation and that after some hesitation this conclusion was ultimately accepted - in the latter part of the seventeenth century - even with regard to *trading* corporations.[4] In 1765, Blackstone had stated that if anything be owing to a corporation, it is not owing to the individual members; nor do the individual members owe that which is owing by the corporation.[5] And a few years later, in 1784, the Attorney-General had confidently asserted that incorporation, whether by royal charter or by Act of Parliament, implied immunity from liability.[6]

---

[1] W.W. Buckland and Arnold D. McNair, *Roman Law and Common Law - A Comparison in Outline* (1952) p. 54.

[2] Maurice Dix, "Adequate Risk Capital : The Consideration for the Benefits of Separate Incorporation" 53 N.W.U.L. Rev. 478 (1958) p. 480.

[3] *Vide* Cooke, *op. cit.* (1950) p. 110; William M. Fletcher, *Cyclopedia of the Law of Private Corporations* (1917) Vol. I para. 22, pp. 43-46.

[4] W.S. Holdsworth, *A History of English Law*, Vol. VIII (1925) p. 203. *Vide* also *Edmunds v. Brown and Tillard* (1668) 1 Lev. 237. *Vide contra*, Oscar Handlin and Mary F. Handlin, "Origins of the American Business Corporation" 5 J. Econ. Hist. 1 (1945) where it is contended that the question of limited liability was still unsettled at the end of the eighteenth century. *Ibid.* p. 12.

[5] William Blackstone, *Commentaries on the Laws of England*, Vol. I, p. 472.

[6] Armand Budington DuBois, *The English Business Company after the Bubble Act, 1720-1800* (1938) pp. 95-96.

Yet however closely linked the two notions may be, it does not follow that limited liability is an inevitable consequence of separate personality. In other words, corporate personality does not necessarily exclude or limit the members' liability. The members may still be liable towards their own corporation and therefore indirectly liable for claims by creditors of the corporation. *Salmon* v. *Hamborough Co.*[1] is the early authority. In that case, members of a corporation were held liable for its debts even though it was a *de jure* corporation with a regularly issued and valid charter. The House of Lords imposed liability on the members for the plaintiff's loan to the corporation on the basis that the corporation had a right, which unpaid creditors could compel it to assert, to levy and collect assessments from the members for payment of the corporate debt. Members of a corporation were not however directly liable for the debts of the corporation. Their liability resulted from the exercise by the corporation of its right to make assessments upon its members. Yet creditors could have obtained an order requiring the corporation to make "leviations", that is to assess the members in such amount as may have been necessary to satisfy the corporate debt.[2] Moreover, the creditors could use the powers of the corporation and proceed directly against the members if the corporation refrained from taking action.[3] Strictly speaking, of course, this was not the same thing as shareholder liability for corporate debts. The crucial question was whether the power of the corporation to make assessments was an inherent power or whether it depended on an express provision in the charter. Although this question does not appear to have ever been judicially considered in the seventeenth and eighteenth centuries, it is evident that doubts had been raised on the extent of the power of corporations to make assessments.[4] In any case, a contractual device for limiting the members' exposure to liability was soon to be implemented : a provision would be included in the charter whereby the corporation's powers to make levies was excluded or limited. Limited liability could in effect be made the subject of an agreement between the

---

[1] (1671) 1 Ch. Cas. 204 (H.L.).

[2] Holdsworth, *op. cit.*, Vol. VIII (1925) p. 204.

[3] Holdsworth, *op. cit.*, Vol. VIII (1925) p. 204. For a different interpretation of *Salmon* v. *Hamborough Co. vide* Dafydd Jenkins, "Skinning the Pantomine Horse : Two Early Cases on Limited Liability" [1975] C.L.J. 309.

[4] *Vide* DuBois, *op. cit.* pp. 98-99.

members and the corporation. Indirectly therefore, the liability of the members eventually disappeared.[1]

The position in the United States is considerably clearer. In the early days of corporate organisation, some statutes did actually create corporations with express provision for unlimited liability.[2] During the same period, however, other statutes were silent on the question of liability. In the latter case, it was commonly accepted that the corporation alone was liable for its debts and that incorporation activated limited liability.[3] Though virtually no discussion on the question had taken place in the eighteenth century,[4] it was therefore clearly established, at least by the early nineteenth century, that limited liability was considered to be a natural consequence of incorporation.[5] In certain circumstances - such as in the case of banks and other financial institutions - statutes did sometimes authorise assessments to be levied from shareholders.[6] In the absence of such authorisation, however, it was clear that the corporation had no inherent power to raise assessments, and that except for any unpaid balance due on the shares held by them, the shareholders would have no additional liability either to the corporation or directly to the corporation's creditors for unpaid debts.[7]

The historical evolution of separate personality and limited liability demonstrates that separate personality was firmly established well before the adoption of limited liability as a general consequence of incorporation in the

---

[1] Holdsworth, *op. cit.*, Vol. VIII (1925) pp. 204-205.

[2] E. Merrick Dodd, "The Evolution of Limited Liability in American Industry : Massachusetts" 61 Harv. L.R. 1351 (1948) pp. 1352-1353, 1361-1365.

[3] *Nichols* v. *Thomas* 4 Mass. 232 (1808); *Commonwealth* v. *Blue-Hill Turnpike Corp.* 5 Mass. 420 (1809); *Myers* v. *Irwin* 2 Serg. & Rawle 367, 371-372 (Pa. 1816); *Spear* v. *Grant* 16 Mass. 9 (1819); *Wood* v. *Dummer* 30 Fed. Cas. 435, 436 (C.C.D. Me. 1824).

[4] E. Merrick Dodd, "The Evolution of Limited Liability in American Industry : Massachusetts" 61 Harv. L.R. 1351 (1948) p. 1356. *Vide* also Oscar Handlin and Mary F. Handlin, "Origins of the American Business Corporation" 5 J. Econ. Hist. 1 (1945) pp. 16-17.

[5] *Vide contra* Maurice Dix, "Adequate Risk Capital : The Consideration for the Benefits of Separate Incorporation" 53 N.W.U.L. Rev. 478 (1958) where it is asserted that shareholders were personally liable for corporate debts unless specifically exempted by legislation. *Ibid.* p. 480. Dix's analysis, however, is contradicted by the relevant case-law.

[6] William P. Hackney and Tracey G. Benson, "Shareholder Liability for Inadequate Capital" 43 Univ. of Pittsburgh L.R. 837 (1982) p. 848.

[7] *Vide* E. Merrick Dodd, "The Evolution of Limited Liability in American Industry : Massachusetts" 61 Harv. L.R. 1351 (1948) pp. 1359-1361.

19th century. It would indeed appear that the principle of limited liability arose in the wake of the widespread implementation of the doctrine of separate personality, rather than as a necessary outcome thereof.[1] Even today, of course, limited liability is not an inevitable consequence of juridical personality and there exist associations vested with juridical personality, the liability of whose members is unlimited.[2]

Irrespective of the historical link between the notion of corporate personality and limited liability, it is now trite law that a holding company is a juridical person separate and distinct from its subsidiaries.[3] The holding company is a member of its subsidiary and has its liability limited to the amount, if any, unpaid on the issued shares held by it in the subsidiary.[4] Each company within a group will have its own debtors and creditors. A creditor of a subsidiary will, as a general rule, have no remedy against the holding company. Nor, for that matter, will he have a remedy against any other affiliate within the group.

## 3. JUDICIAL AND STATUTORY INROADS

### 3.1. Adherence to traditional notions in English law

Notwithstanding the fundamental principle of separate personality, English law does, by way of exception, occasionally ignore the separate identity of the holding company and its subsidiary. Both legislative and statutory inroads have been made. These exceptions will be analysed in the next

---

[1] *Vide* Blumberg, *Substantive Law* pp. 7-8. Cf. Farrar, p. 81.

[2] The European Economic Interest Grouping (EEIG) is a modern example. From the date of its registration the EEIG shall be "a body corporate by the name contained in the contract" and its members are unlimitedly and jointly and severally liable for all its debts. (*Vide* Reg. 3 of the European Economic Interest Grouping Regulations, 1989, and Art. 24 of Sched. 1 incorporating the EC Council Regulation No. 2137/85 on the EEIG - SI 1989 no. 638).

[3] *Lonrho Ltd.* v. *Shell Petroleum Co. Ltd.* [1980] 1 W.L.R. 627 (H.L.); *Industrial Equity Ltd.* v. *Blackburn* (1977) 137 C.L.R. 567, 52 A.L.J.R. 89; *Rur. Mun. of Assiniboia* v. *Suburban Rapid Transit Co.* [1931] 2 D.L.R. 862, 39 Man. L.R. 402 sub. nom. *Re Suburban Rapid Transit Co., Winnipeg Electric Co. and Rural Municipality of Assiniboia* (C.A.); *Garrett* v. *Southern Railway Co.* 173 F.Supp. 915 (E.D. Tenn. 1959), *aff'd*, 278 F.2d. 424 (6th Cir.), *cert. denied*, 364 U.S. 833 (1960).

[4] *Vide* Robert. R. Pennington, *Company Law* (6th ed. 1990) pp. 37-38; R.M. Goode (ed.), *Group Trading and the Lending Banker* (1988) p. xvii.

Chapters when dealing with the specific categories of abuse and unfairness. At this stage, however, it is necessary to make some general observations.

Clearly, the courts will disregard the separate identity of the company and its shareholders when corporate personality is being blatantly used as a cloak for fraud or improper conduct[1] or where a company is a mere façade concealing the true facts.[2] The separate personality would also be disregarded by the courts where "the protection of public interests is of paramount importance, or where the company has been formed to evade obligations imposed by law".[3] These judicial exceptions apply generally, whether or not a holding-subsidiary relationship is involved.

Apart from the aforesaid exceptions, English courts have regrettably failed to remedy many of the abusive and unfair situations that can result from the holding-subsidiary relationship. The judicial attitude to the problems created by corporate groups has in fact been remarkably conservative. The courts do of course recognise the reality of the corporate group, but are prepared to give only very limited legal effect to that reality.[4] Recently, for example, the Court of Appeal acknowledged the reality of the holding-subsidiary relationship in *Atlas Maritime Co. S.A.* v. *Avalon Maritime Ltd. ("The Coral Rose") (No. 1)*[5] and in *Atlas Maritime Co. S.A.* v. *Avalon Maritime Ltd. (No. 3)*.[6] A Mareva injunction had been obtained restraining Avalon Maritime Ltd. ("Avalon") from disposing of its assets. Avalon's ultimate holding company was Marc Rich & Co. A.G. ("Marc Rich"). In the first case, Avalon sought an order varying the injunction to allow it to repay sums which it alleged were owing to Marc Rich on the basis of a pure debtor-creditor relationship.[7] The Court of Appeal refused to vary the order on the ground that the money sought to be repaid was in effect loan capital of Avalon rather than a trading debt incurred in the normal course of

---

[1] *Re a Company* [1985] BCLC 333 (C.A.); *Creasey* v. *Breachwood Motors Ltd.* [1992] BCC 638. *Vide* also Farrar, pp. 75-76.

[2] *Adams* v. *Cape Industries plc* [1990] BCLC 479 (C.A.).

[3] Robert. R. Pennington, *Company Law* (6th ed. 1990) p. 39.

[4] *Vide* e.g., *The Roberta* (1937) 58 Ll.L.R. 159; *Harold Holdsworth & Co. (Wakefield) Ltd.* v. *Caddies* [1955] 1 W.L.R. 352 (H.L.); *Scottish Co-Operative Wholesale Society Ltd.* v. *Meyer* [1959] A.C. 324; *Revlon, Inc.* v. *Cripps & Lee Ltd.* [1980] F.S.R. 85 (C.A.).

[5] [1991] 4 All E.R. 769.

[6] [1991] 4 All E.R. 783.

[7] Mareva injunctions may be varied to allow the defendant to pay normal trading debts out of frozen funds.

business. In the second case, the Court of Appeal also rejected an application by Avalon to vary the injunction to enable it to draw its legal expenses from the frozen assets. The Court took into account evidence that Avalon had never had any funds which it controlled independently of Marc Rich, that the solicitors did not really mind who paid them and that there was no suggestion that if Avalon were prevented from paying them, Marc Rich would refuse to do so. In both cases the Court of Appeal emphasised that in granting injunctive relief it was prepared to look behind the corporate veil to achieve justice. The Court of Appeal made it amply clear however that it was not prepared to treat Avalon's liabilities as the liabilities of its ultimate holding company.[1]

The conservative judicial attitude towards corporate groups is easily discernible from the elaborate judgment of the Court of Appeal in *Adams v. Cape Industries plc.*[2] Two aspects of the decision are worth noting. In the first place, the Court rejected the argument that the separate companies within a group could be treated as one economic unit. Only as an aid to the interpretation of a particular statute or document might the court have regard to the economic realities.[3] In the second place, the Court of Appeal acknowledged that "there is one well-recognised exception to the rule prohibiting the piercing of 'the corporate veil'"[4] and identified that exception as the case of "a mere façade concealing the true facts".[5] The

---

[1] In *Aiglon Ltd. and L'Aiglon S.A.* v. *Gau Shan Co. Ltd.* [1993] 1 Lloyd's Rep. 164, the court granted an injunction against a company in connection with a liability owed by its affiliate. In this case however there was evidence of transactions at an undervalue between the two companies. Similarly in *T.S.B. Private Bank International S.A.* v. *Chabra* [1992] 1 W.L.R. 231 an injunction was granted against a company in connection with a claim against its controlling shareholder. Mummery J. justified the injunction on three grounds : (1) uncertainty as to the beneficial ownership of immovable property registered in the name of the company; (2) that it was arguable that the company was the alter ego of the controlling shareholder; and (3) the risk of a dissipation of assets. *Ibid.* at pp. 238-240. Mummery J.'s observations on the alter ago aspect are made without analysis and without any apparent awareness of the profound implications such a holding could have on the question of liability. The observations on alter ego should therefore be restricted to the particular facts of the case and in particular to the fear of the dissipation of assets.

[2] [1990] BCLC 479. *Vide* also the earlier judgment of the House of Lords in *The Albazero* [1977] A.C. 774 reversing the judgment of the Court of Appeal [1977] A.C. 774.

[3] [1990] BCLC 479 at p. 512.

[4] [1990] BCLC 479 at p. 515.

[5] [1990] BCLC 479 at p. 515. The Court of Appeal was quoting from the speech of Lord Keith in *Woolfson* v. *Strathclyde Regional Council* 1978 S.L.T. 159 (H.L. Sc.) at p. 161.

difficulty of course is to determine exactly what will label a company as a "mere façade". Regrettably, the Court of Appeal declined to "attempt a comprehensive definition" of those principles which should guide the court in determining whether or not the arrangements of a corporate group involve a façade.[1] It would appear however that the motive behind the arrangement should be considered as a crucial factor and that only if some behaviour bordering on impropriety or wrongdoing is apparent could the arrangement qualify as a "façade". This requirement considerably restricts the type of situation where the separate corporate personality can be disregarded and renders the doctrine of veil piercing practically sterile. Certainly, almost none of the abusive and unfairness situations identified in Chapter II fall within the façade exception allowed by the judgment.

Some earlier judgments had not felt so hemmed in by the principle of separate personality. In *D.H.N. Food Distributors Ltd.* v. *Tower Hamlets L.B.C.*[2] Lord Denning had made a valiant - if somewhat inept[3] - effort at chiselling out a broad exception to the separate personality rule by calling for the recognition, in certain circumstances, of the group as an "economic unit". His efforts however were soon snuffed out.[4] In any case, of course, *D.H.N. Food Distributors* was not concerned with the imposition of holding

---

[1] [1990] BCLC 479 at p. 519.

[2] [1976] 1 W.L.R. 852 (C.A.).

[3] In support of his contention, Lord Denning quoted the following passage from Gower's Principles of Modern Company Law (3rd ed. 1969) at p. 216 : " ... there is evidence of a general tendency to ignore the separate legal entities of various companies within a group, and to look instead at the economic unity of the whole group". If read in its proper context however, Gower's statement can be seen to have been made as a "tentative" conclusion which "may, perhaps, be drawn". In an earlier passage, Gower had expressly noted that "the rule that a company is distinct from its members applies equally to the separate companies of a group". *Ibid.* p. 71. Lord Denning also relied upon the decision of the House of Lords in *Harold Holdsworth & Co. (Wakefield) Ltd.* v. *Caddies* [1955] 1 W.L.R. 352 which Lord Denning described as a "striking instance" of the "tendency to ignore the separate legal entities of various companies within a group". (*D.H.N. Food Distributors Ltd.* v. *Tower Hamlets L.B.C.* [1976] 1 W.L.R. 852 (C.A.) at p.860). A close reading of the speeches in *Harold Holdsworth & Co. (Wakefield) Ltd.* v. *Caddies* [1955] 1 W.L.R. 352 (H.L.) however reveals no hint that the separate personae of the companies in a group may be disregarded. The judgment, it is submitted, merely turned on the construction of the terms of appointment of the managing director of the holding company.

[4] *Vide Woolfson* v. *Strathclyde Regional Council* 1978 S.L.T. 159 (H.L. Sc.); *Adams* v. *Cape Industries plc* [1990] BCLC 479 (C.A.).

company liability for the debts of a subsidiary, but rather with the recognition of the reality of the group for the benefit of the holding company itself. The judgment is therefore clearly distinguishable, even if it were to be afforded any authority. Still, as recently as 1985, the Court of Appeal declared, in *Re A Company*,[1] that "the cases ... show that the court will use its powers to pierce the corporate veil if it is necessary to achieve justice irrespective of the legal efficacy of the corporate structure ...".[2] Such a wide view is however clearly inconsistent with the later judgment of the Court of Appeal in *Adams* v. *Cape Industries plc*[3] which unequivocally rejected the suggestion that the entity principle should be disregarded if to do so were necessary to serve the interests of justice.[4]

On the question of ignoring the separate juridical personality of the holding and its subsidiary companies, a distinction ought therefore to be drawn. On the one hand, there is evidence of a general willingness to "lift" or to "look behind" the corporate veil - that is, to have regard to the holding-subsidiary relationship for some legal purpose (other than to impose liability on the holding company). On the other hand, there is an almost total refusal to "pierce" the corporate veil - that is, to treat the liabilities of the subsidiary company as the liabilities of its holding company.[5] On matters of liability, the orthodox principle clearly prevails in the judicial mind.

---

[1] [1985] BCLC 333 (C.A.).

[2] [1985] BCLC 333 at pp. 337-338.

[3] [1990] BCLC 479 (C.A.).

[4] [1990] BCLC 479 p. 513. *Vide* however *Creasey* v. *Breachwood Motors Ltd.* [1992] BCC 638 where it was stated, at pp. 646-647 that "[t]he power of the court to lift the corporate veil ... is a strong power which can be exercised to achieve justice where its exercise is necessary for that purpose".

[5] The distinction between "looking behind" or "lifting" and "piercing" the corporate veil was noted by Staughton L.J. in *Atlas Maritime Co. S.A.* v. *Avalon Maritime Ltd. ("The Coral Rose") (No. 1)* [1991] 4 All E.R. 769 (C.A.) at p. 779 and by Lord Donaldson M.R. in *Atlas Maritime Co. S.A.* v. *Avalon Maritime Ltd. (No. 3* [1991] 4 All E.R. 783 (C.A.) at pp. 789-790. Metaphors abound in this area of law. In *Adams* v. *Cape Industries plc* [1990] BCLC 479 (C.A.) Slade L.J. uses the terms "piercing" (at p. 515), "look behind" (at p. 518) "pull aside" (at p. 518) and "tear away" (at p. 519). Around the same period, Ottolenghi had distinguished between four categories, in a progressive order: "peeping", "penetrating", "extending" and "ignoring" the veil. *Vide* S. Ottolenghi, "From Peeping Behind the Corporate Veil, to Ignoring it Completely" 53 M.L.R. 338 (1990). Great caution must of course be exercised in the use of such phrases for as Cardozo J. had warned in *Berkey* v. *Third Ave. Ry. Co.* 155 N.E. 58 (1926), "[m]etaphors in law are to be narrowly watched, for starting as devices to liberate thought, they end often by enslaving it". *Ibid.* at p. 61.

In contrast to the Bench, Parliament has been somewhat less reluctant to disregard corporate personality.[1] Even in matters of liability, Parliament has occasionally been prepared to "pierce" the veil. A significant development in this connection have been the introduction of liability for wrongful trading on directors and "shadow" directors.[2]

As will be demonstrated in the course of this study, the judicial and statutory inroads to the general principles of separate personality and limited liability are essentially too narrow and too ill-defined to remedy the situations of unfairness and abuse identified in Chapter II. The twin doctrines of separate juridical personality and limited liability stand as firmly cemented stumbling blocks in the way of any effort aimed at visiting the holding company with liability for the debts of its subsidiary.[3]

## 3.2. Liberal approach adopted by American courts

The judicial conservatism evident in England contrasts sharply with the liberal approach adopted by the courts in the United States. Although the general rule in the United States is that corporate personality will be respected, American courts will unquestionably disregard the fiction of the legal entity where the company is used to evade an existing obligation,[4] or to circumvent a statute or to modify the purpose for which the statute was enacted[5] or to "defeat public convenience, justify wrong, protect fraud, or defend crime".[6] But American courts go further. The entity principle will be

---

[1] Earlier legislative recognition of the corporate group came in the form of group tax relief (Finance Act 1967, s. 20) and the requirement of consolidated financial statements (Companies Act 1948, s. 150).

[2] *Vide* I.A. 1986, s. 214. A holding company may in certain circumstances qualify as a "shadow" director. *Vide post* Chapter V pp. 213-217.

[3] *Vide* also *The Albazero* [1977] A.C. 774 (C.A.) where Roskill L.J. noted that the principle that "each company in a group of companies ... is a separate legal entity possessed of separate legal rights and liabilities" is "now unchallengeable by judicial decision". *Ibid.* at p. 807. The cap on judicial inroads was firmly sealed by the Court of Appeal in *Adams* v. *Cape Industries plc* [1990] BCLC 479 (C.A.).

[4] *Beal* v. *Chase* 31 Mich. 490 (1875); *Mull* v. *Colt* Co 31 F.R.D. 154 (S.D.N.Y. 1962).

[5] *United States* v. *Lehigh Valley R.R. Co.* 220 U.S. 257 (1911).

[6] *United States* v. *Milwaukee Refrigerator Transit Co.* 142 F. 247 (C.C.E.D. Wis. 1905) per Sanborn J. at p. 255. *Vide* also *Linn & Lane Timber Co.* v. *United States* 236 U.S. 574 (1915); *Mull* v. *Colt Co.* 31 F.R.D. 154 (S.D.N.Y. 1962); I. Maurice Wormser, "Piercing the Veil of the Corporate Entity" 12 Colum. L.R. 496 (1912) p. 517.

disregarded when it is necessary to promote justice or to obviate inequitable results.[1] The American attitude differs palpably from the English position. An English court will not lift the veil merely because it considers that justice so requires.[2] The liberal approach adopted by American courts has profound implications in the context of corporate groups.

It is perhaps arguable that any rule which takes justice as its yardstick must be ill-conceived - both because of the difficulty in defining such a philosophical term and also because of the existence of differing perceptions as to what constitutes justice. It should of course be stressed that the notion of justice is not used in the American veil piercing cases as an "Open Sesame" technique in total disregard of legal principles. Yet American courts do tend to interpret and apply the law with a keen sense of what is necessary to achieve fairness between the parties.[3] Lifting the veil jurisprudence is applied in a variety of situations and the notion of justice can be viewed as the common factor linking those situations. The use of the notion of justice in the lifting of the veil cases at least has the merit of focusing attention on what ought to be an important objective of any legal system.[4]

Given that the doctrine in the United States is essentially equitable in character, the factual conditions under which entity may be disregarded in the holding-subsidiary relationship (or the analogous one-man company situation) will obviously vary with the circumstances of each case. Broadly stated, entity will be disregarded - and limited liability jettisoned - where to do so "is essential to the end that some accepted public policy may be defended or upheld".[5]

---

[1] *Minifie* v. *Rowley* 202 P. 673 (1921); *United States* v. *Hoyt* 53 F.(2d) 881 (S.D.N.Y. 1931); *Peterick* v. *State of Washington* 589 P.2d 251, 264 (Wash. App. 1979). *Vide* also Warner Fuller, "The Incorporated Individual : A Study of the One-Man Company" 51 Harv. L.R. 1373 (1938) pp. 1402-1403; William M. Fletcher, *Cyclopedia of the Law of Corporations* (rev. ed. 1990 and supp. 1993) Vol. I, s. 41.30 p. 662.

[2] *Adams* v. *Cape Industries plc* [1990] BCLC 479 (C.A.) p. 513. In the exercise of a discretion in relation to injunctive relief, the "eye of equity" will however "look behind the corporate veil in order to do justice". *Vide Atlas Maritime Co. S.A.* v. *Avalon Maritime Ltd. ("The Coral Rose") (No. 1)* [1991] 4 All E.R. 769 (C.A.) at p. 776 (per Neill L.J.).

[3] *Vide* I. Maurice Wormser, "Letter to the Editor" 5 Calif. L.R. 65 (1916) p. 67.

[4] *Vide* Warner Fuller, "The Incorporated Individual : A Study of the One-Man Company" 51 Harv. L.R. 1373 (1938) at p. 1403.

[5] *Berkey* v. *Third Ave. Ry. Co.* 155 N.E. 58 (1926) at p. 61 per Cardozo J. *Vide* also *Taylor* v. *Standard Gas & Elec. Co.* 306 U.S. 307 (1939).

Stated so broadly of course, the doctrine is unlikely to be of much use to the development of predictable criteria for solving real-life situations. Efforts have however been made at defining somewhat more precisely the parameters within which the doctrine will operate. A common formulation - the instrumentality test - provides that the corporate entity may be disregarded "in a case where a corporation is so organized and controlled, and its affairs are so conducted, as to make it merely an instrumentality or adjunct of another corporation".[1]

A reading of the American cases reveals that a wide variety of factors are taken into account in deciding whether to disregard the entity in the holding-subsidiary situation or in the one-man company situation. These factors include : the manipulation of assets, gross undercapitalisation, the failure to maintain proper records, the failure to comply with corporate formalities, direct intervention or participation by the holding company or the controlling shareholder in the management of the company as if it were a division of the holding company or the business of the controlling shareholder, and misrepresentation as to the financial stability or financial backing of the subsidiary or of the one-man company. Actual fraud need not be shown.[2]

The American position is not entirely satisfactory. The difficulty with the instrumentality test, for example, is that it does not provide a very accurate insight into the factors that are to be taken into account or the relative importance to be attached to them.[3] Yet despite often trenchant criticism of the instrumentality test by academic writers,[4] the test is still utilised by American courts both in cases imposing liability on the controlling shareholder[5] and in cases refusing to impose such liability.[6]

---

[1] *In re Watertown Paper Co.* 169 F. 252 (2d Cir. 1909) at p. 256. *Vide* also *Chicago, Milwaukee & St. Paul Railway Co.* v. *Minneapolis Civic & Commerce Association* 247 U.S. 490 (1918); *Hunter* v. *Baker Motor Vehicle Co.* 225 Fed. 1006 (N.D.N.Y. 1915). *Vide* further *post*, Chapter V pp. 256-263.

[2] *Anderson* v. *Abbott* 321 U.S. 349 (1943); *United States* v. *Jon-T Chemicals, Inc.* 768 F.2d 686 (5th Cir. 1985).

[3] *Vide* further *post*, Chapter V pp. 263-266.

[4] E.g., Latty, *op. cit.* pp. 156-163.

[5] E.g., *Zaist* v. *Olson* 227 A.2d 552 (1967).

[6] E.g., *Steven* v. *Roscoe Turner Aeronautical Corp.* 324 F.2d 157 (7th Cir. 1963); *Garrett* v. *Southern Railway Co.* 173 F.Supp. 915 (E.D. Tenn. 1959), *aff'd*, 278 F.2d. 424 (6th Cir.), *cert. denied*, 364 U.S. 833 (1960).

Another problem is that many of the piercing the veil judgments fail to articulate reasoned grounds of decision.[1] Moreover, it is impossible to determine from the judgments what relative weight, if at all, will be attached by the court to the various factors typically characterised as affecting the liability issue. Though "piercing" does not - as has occasionally been suggested - happen "freakishly",[2] judgments are not thoroughly consistent.[3] To take but a few examples : some cases consider undercapitalisation to be an important factor towards establishing liability on the controlling shareholder,[4] whereas others refuse to impose liability even in the face of gross undercapitalisation;[5] some cases hold that the failure to comply with corporate formalities is one of the factors making for liability,[6] while others virtually ignore the question of formalities.[7] Another difficulty presented by American judgments is that a veil piercing case will often enumerate a number of relevant *and* neutral factors to the point in issue.[8] Such indiscriminate mingling of relevant with irrelevant factors hinders proper analysis.

A number of courts and academic writers have attempted to put order into the maze of judgments that have been handed down.[9] A number of patterns

---

[1] *Vide* "Liability of a Corporation for Acts of a Subsidiary or Affiliate" 71 Harv. L.R. 1122 (1958) p. 1123. Cf. Latty, *op. cit.* p. 3.

[2] *Vide* Frank H. Easterbrook and Daniel R. Fischel, "Limited Liability and the Corporation" 52 Univ. of Chicago L.R. 89 (1985) at p. 89. Eastbrook and Fischel evidently over-licensed the metaphor when they stated that "[l]ike lightning, [piercing] is rare, severe and unprincipled". *Ibid.* p. 89.

[3] *Vide* C. E. Brooks's somewhat exaggerated statement in "Parent and Subsidiary, right of parent or subsidiary to share with other creditors in assets of associated corporation on the latter's insolvency" 37 Michigan L.R. 440 (1939) at p. 449 : "The corporate entity has been disregarded in many different situations, and the tests used by the Courts have been nearly as varied as the situations themselves".

[4] E.g., *Mull v. Colt Co.* 31 F.R.D. 154 (S.D.N.Y. 1962).

[5] E.g., *American Commercial Lines, Inc. v. Ostertag*, 582 S.W.2d 51 (Ky. App. 1979).

[6] E.g., *Dudley v. Smith* 504 F.2d 979 (5th Cir. 1974).

[7] *Vide* e.g., *Schmid v. Roehm GmbH* 544 F. Supp. 272, 276-277 (D. Kan. 1982). On the question of compliance with corporate formalities, *vide* further *post* Chapter IX pp. 447-448.

[8] E.g., *Associated Vendors, Inc. v. Oakland Meat Co.* 26 Cal. Rptr. 806, 813-816 (1963). *Vide* John F. Dobbyn, "A Practical Approach to Consistency in Veil Piercing Cases" 19 Kansas L.R. 185 (1971) p. 188.

[9] *Vide* e.g., *Fish v. East* 114 F.2d 177, 191 (10th Cir. 1940); *Zaist v. Olson* 227 A.2d 552 (1967); Powell, *Parent and Subsidiary Corporations* (1931); Latty, *op. cit.*; William O.

tending towards the imposition of liability on the holding company or controlling shareholder have in fact been identified and categorised. At least the subject is probably no longer shrouded in the "mists of metaphor".[1] The truth however is that only limited success has been achieved. A definitive doctrinal basis for such patterns - necessary for accurately predicting the outcome of a case - remains elusive.[2]

Clearly therefore, the doctrine of disregard of the entity as developed in the United States can only be formulated in the most general terms. To some this may signal a danger that the law is evolving in a manner which is haphazard and unprincipled - a danger which to a far lesser extent, may also be afflicting English veil-lifting jurisprudence : witness, for example, the divergent classifications of the judicial inroads to the entity principle attempted by Farrar,[3] Friedmann,[4] Gower,[5] Ottolenghi,[6] Palmer,[7] Pennington,[8] Schmitthoff[9] and Smith and Keenan.[10]

In all likelihood, the general (and somewhat inexact) terms in which the American doctrine is formulated is inevitable. The entity-disregard cases present so many variables in so many different settings that a precise set of principles may be impossible to state. Still it is the very generalisation in which the doctrine is formulated that gives it its strength and vigour. For in

*Cont.*
Douglas and Carrol M. Shanks, "Insulation from Liability through Subsidiary Corporations" 39 Yale L.J. 193 (1929) p. 218; Jonathan M. Landers, "A Unified Approach to Parent, Subsidiary, and Affiliate Questions in Bankruptcy" 42 Univ. of Chicago L.R. 589 (1975); Blumberg, *Substantive Law.*

[1] This is the phrase used by Cardozo, J. in *Berkey* v. *Third Ave. Ry. Co.* 155 N.E. 58 (1926) at p. 61 in assessing the problems relating to the holding-subsidiary relationship. Cardozo, J. was referring to the then widespread use of verbal characterisations and epithets such as "cloak", "creature", "dummy" and so on. For a comprehensive list of such phrases *vide post*, Chapter V p. 264 footnote 3.

[2] *Vide* Jonathan M. Landers, "A Unified Approach to Parent, Subsidiary, and Affiliate Questions in Bankruptcy" 42 Univ. of Chicago L.R. 589 (1975) p. 620.

[3] Farrar, pp. 73-79.

[4] W. Friedmann, *Legal Theory* (5th ed. 1967) p. 523.

[5] Gower, pp. 124-134.

[6] S. Ottolenghi, "From Peeping Behind the Corporate Veil to Ignoring it Completely" 53 M.L.R. 338 (1990) p. 340.

[7] *Palmer's Company Law* (25th ed. 1992) Vol. I, pp. 215-219.

[8] Robert. R. Pennington, *Company Law* (6th ed. 1990) pp. 46-52.

[9] Clive M. Schmitthoff, "Salomon in the Shadow" [1976] J.B.L. 305, p. 307.

[10] *Smith and Keenan's Company Law* (7th ed. 1987) pp. 19-20.

this field of law, generalisations allow the courts to employ the doctrine as a panacea for a bewildering variety of wrongs. The fundamental issue remains one of fairness.[1] And fairness, like justice - and indeed like the proverbial elephant - is easy to recognise but practically impossible to define in legal terms.

Of significant importance is the fact that despite the lack of a consistent doctrinal pattern, the American approach appears at once characterised by a far greater degree of flexibility and responsiveness to commercial realities than the English approach. Perhaps more fundamentally, an analysis of the holding-subsidiary cases (and of the veil piercing doctrine as a whole) reveals a profound contrast in the judicial attitudes of the two jurisdictions. English courts appear fettered - in part by Salomon's chains, but principally by an innate conservatism - to a strict entity vision of corporate affairs. The result, at least where liability issues are concerned, is that the notion of entity is sometimes exalted to a fetish with commercial reality and the interests of creditors being sacrificed in its name. By contrast, American courts view the principle of entity essentially as one of commercial convenience. It *will* be recognised and protected - but only as long as it does not conflict with the reality of the situation or with the demands of fairness.

Despite its shortcomings, American law remains particularly fruitful for comparative purposes. Because of the inherent flexibility of the entity-disregard doctrine as developed in the United States, American courts have encountered a myriad of situations involving the holding-subsidiary relationship. Typical fact situations giving rise to unfairness or abuse have been identified and their mischief exposed. Appropriate remedies have been sought and often found. All this exercise has been accompanied by a wide-ranging, continuing and often incisive analysis by academic writers. The American piercing the veil doctrine is not yet - nor perhaps ever will be - finally settled. This may be the inevitable consequence of the equitable basis of the doctrine. Nor should this fact necessarily be regrettable. Others of course may feel uneasy with what they perceive to be an unpredictable doctrine. Be that as it may, it must be stressed that the aim of this study is not to pass judgement on American law. Rather, it is to assess the adequacy or otherwise of English law and to suggest proposals for reform where inadequacy is located. In this context the American experience offers a fertile ground for the incubation of ideas. This work will not however be

---

[1] *Pepper* v. *Litton* 308 U.S. 295, 310-312 (1939).

advocating the wholesale grafting of the American approach onto English law.

Finally, it need hardly be mentioned that the American courts' exercise of the equitable jurisdiction to ignore the separate legal personality of a subsidiary and to saddle the holding company with its liabilities has neither created undue uncertainty nor discouraged group activity.[1]

## 4. DIRECT HOLDING COMPANY LIABILITY

Legal responsibility for the acts of a subsidiary company lies with the subsidiary itself. The holding company is not liable for the acts of its subsidiaries.[2] This rule flows naturally from the notion of separate juridical personality.

This study is primarily concerned with the question whether certain practices in the holding-subsidiary arrangement result, or should result, in holding company liability for the acts of the subsidiary. In a broad sense, therefore, this work seeks a "vicarious" basis for holding company liability.

It should be emphasised that there may be situations where the holding company is held liable for acts or transactions involving its subsidiaries on grounds entirely distinct from that sought in this work. In such cases, however, liability rests on an independent basis - the fact of a holding-subsidiary relationship being largely irrelevant to the imposition of liability. Unfortunately, however, many of the judgments in these situations speak of disregarding the corporate entity and appear to proceed on the basis that the holding-subsidiary relationship itself justifies the imposition of liability. On closer analysis, however, it will be realised that liability does not involve piercing the veil techniques at all. Liability is incurred directly by the holding company on the basis of general principles of law. Because of their tendency to confuse the discussion on holding company liability, these cases must be identified and their true rationale highlighted.

---

[1] *Vide* the Cork Report, para. 1937, p. 436.

[2] Specific legislation does however impose a form of holding company liability in certain sectors of the economy. A notable example is s. 22(1) of the Building Societies Act 1986 which imposes upon building societies an obligation to discharge the liabilities of their subsidiaries in so far as such subsidiaries are unable to discharge them out of their own assets.

## 4.1. Agency

In its strict sense, agency requires that (i) the agent be acting for the principal, not for itself; (ii) the agent be under the control of the principal; and (iii) both the principal and the agent have consented to the relationship.[1] The agent's authority to act on behalf of the principal may arise in three ways : (i) express; (ii) implied; or (iii) apparent.[2]

Naturally, a company can act as an agent. It can carry on business as an agent for any individual or company,[3] including its own members.[4] It follows that a subsidiary company can act as an agent even for its holding company.[5] The holding company may for example, by express or implied contract, actually appoint the subsidiary as an agent to sell the holding company's products.[6] In any such case, the subsidiary would be acting on the holding company's behalf when concluding transactions with third parties. Sales contracts, for example, would legally be entered into, and be binding, between the holding company and the third party purchasers. The holding company would be liable for the subsidiary's obligations incurred within the scope of the agency. And in the normal course, the subsidiary, *qua* agent, would not be liable on such contracts. Moreover, if the contract claim arises where the agency was not disclosed, the doctrine of election would require the plaintiff, on ascertaining the existence of the agency, to elect which of the two companies to hold responsible.[7] If the claim sounds in tort, both companies may be liable. Where, for example, the purchaser acquired the product in reliance on false representations made by the subsidiary acting

---

[1] *Vide Bowstead on Agency* (15th ed. 1985) Art. 1, p. 1; American Law Institute, Restatement (Second) of Agency (1958) para. 1.

[2] Bowstead, *op. cit.* Art. 1, p. 1; American Law Institute, Restatement (Second) of Agency (1958) paras. 26, 27.

[3] *Vide Erickson v. Minnesota and Ontario Power Co.* 158 N.W. 979, 981 (1916).

[4] *Gramaphones and Typewriters Ltd. v. Stanley* [1908] 2 K.B. 89, 95-96; *Commissioner of Inland Revenue v. Sansom* [1921] 2 K.B. 492, 503. *Vide* also O. Kahn-Freund, "Corporate Entity" 3 M.L.R. 226 (1940) p. 227; Murray A. Pickering, "The Company as a Separate Legal Entity" 31 M.L.R. 481 (1968) p. 490; Clive M. Schmitthoff, "Salomon in the Shadow" [1976] J.B.L. 305 p. 307.

[5] Conversely, the holding company may also act as an agent for its subsidiary. *Vide* e.g., *William Cory & Son Ltd. v. Dorman Long & Co. Ltd.* [1936] 2 All E.R. 386 (C.A.).

[6] Agency may also result from ratification and by the application of the doctrine of estoppel.

[7] *Vide* G.H.L. Fridman, *The Law of Agency* (6th ed. 1990) pp. 237-238; American Law Institute, Restatement (Second) of Agency (1958) paras. 209-210A, 337.

within the scope of its authority, both companies would be liable in an action of deceit.[1]

The existence or otherwise of agency depends on whether the proprietary, contractual or other rights in question are being exercised on behalf of the holding company. Fundamental to the agency relationship is the consent of the principal and the agent thereto.[2] On these questions the court may have to examine both the subsidiary's ability to bind the holding company[3] as well as the degree of control exercised by the holding company over the subsidiary.[4] But whether or not the subsidiary is acting as an agent clearly does not depend on the existence of an independent mind to control the company.[5] And as important as the ability to bind the holding company is the actual behaviour of the subsidiary. For example, does the subsidiary enter into contracts on its own behalf or as agent of the holding company? Ultimately, it is a question of fact whether a subsidiary is acting on behalf of the holding company or on its own behalf.[6]

Where a true agency does exist, it is of course incorrect to speak of "lifting the veil" or of "disregarding entity". In the true agency cases, the defendant holding company would simply be liable, *qua* principal, for the act of its agent, the subsidiary. True agency confirms, rather than refutes, the separate personality of the holding and subsidiary companies.

Undoubtedly, the typical holding-subsidiary relationship differs considerably from the common law agency situation. For although a true agency relationship can be easily visualised as a theoretical situation, it is very unlikely to arise in practice.[7] Indeed there appear to be only very few

---

[1] *Vide* Fridman, *op. cit.* pp. 286, 300. American Law Institute, Restatement (Second) of Agency (1958) paras. 257, 343.

[2] *Vide Garnac Grain Co., Inc.* v. *H.M.F. Faure & Fairclough Ltd.* [1968] A.C. 1130, especially at p. 1137 (per Lord Pearson) and *Atlas Maritime Co. S.A.* v. *Avalon Maritime Ltd. ("The Coral Rose")* [1991] 4 All E.R. 769 (C.A.) at p. 774 (per Neill L.J.).

[3] *Vide Saccharin Corporation Limited* v. *Chemische Fabrik A.G.* [1911] 2 K.B. 516 (C.A.) p. 525; *Adams* v. *Cape Industries plc* [1990] BCLC 479 (C.A.).

[4] Cf. *La Bourgogne* [1899] P. 1 pp. 13, 17-18. Cf. also J.J. Fawcett, "Jurisdiction and Subsidiaries" [1985] J.B.L. 16 p. 17.

[5] Cf. *Lee* v. *Lee's Air Farming Ltd.* [1961] A.C. 12 (P.C.).

[6] *Vide The Lalandia* [1933] P. 56, especially at pp. 66-67; *Gramaphones and Typewriters Ltd.* v. *Stanley* [1908] 2 K.B. 89, 96; *British Thomson-Houston Co., Ltd.* v. *Sterling Accessories Ltd.* [1924] 2 Ch. 33, 38; *Pacific Can Co.* v. *Hewes* 95 F.2d 42, 46 (9th Cir. 1938).

[7] *Vide Kingston Dry Dock Co.* v. *Lake Champlain Transp. Co.* 31 F.2d 265, 267 (2d Cir. 1929). Cases where, typically, the subsidiary acted on its own behalf and not on behalf of

cases which have been decided on common law agency principles.[1] A true agency relationship between holding and subsidiary companies is rare because one of the main reasons for incorporating a subsidiary is precisely the avoidance or limitation of liability as a principal.[2]

Unquestionably, control through the ownership of shares does not establish an agency relationship.[3] If an agency relationship had to be inferred from the control inherent in any holding-subsidiary relationship, the holding company would be liable in all cases for the obligations of its subsidiary. Nor should agency be inferred where a subsidiary is dominated in its affairs by the holding company. Even in such cases, the subsidiary would generally still be acting on its own behalf.[4] Nor should the existence of complete control over the subsidiary of itself establish the subsidiary as the agent of its holding company.[5] And despite some eloquent dicta to the contrary,[6] it is also submitted that common law agency should not necessarily be inferred even if the holding company is especially intrusive in its dominion over the subsidiary. Where the extent of dominion and interference over the subsidiary is particularly acute, the correct analysis may be to consider the

---

*Cont.*
    its holding company include *Distillers Co. (Bio-Chemicals) Ltd.* v. *Thompson* [1971] 1 All E.R. 694 and *Smith Kline & French Laboratories Ltd.* v. *Bloch* [1983] 2 All E.R. 72, 77.

[1] An example is *Pacific Can Co.* v. *Hewes* 95 F.2d 42 (9th Cir. 1938).

[2] *Vide* Staughton L.J.'s observations in *Atlas Maritime Co. S.A.* v. *Avalon Maritime Ltd.* *("The Coral Rose") (No. 1)* [1991] 4 All E.R. 769 (C.A.) p. 779. *Vide* also Denise L. Speer, "Piercing the Corporate Veil in Maryland: An Analysis and Suggested Approach" 14 U. of Baltimore L.R. 311 (1985) p. 314. In *Multinational Gas and Petrochemical Co.* v. *Multinational Gas and Petrochemical Services* [1983] 1 Ch. 258, [1983] 3 W.L.R. 492 (C.A.) three multinational oil companies, on the advice of tax counsel, set up two wholly owned subsidiaries (one registered in Liberia and the other in England). An agency agreement was then entered between the two subsidiaries, with the English subsidiary acting as an agent for its principal, the Liberian subsidiary. The limited liability of the three multinational companies was not of course affected.

[3] *Salomon* v. *A. Salomon and Co. Ltd.* [1897] A.C. 22 (H.L.); *Atlas Maritime Co. S.A.* v. *Avalon Maritime Ltd. ("The Coral Rose")* [1991] 4 All E.R. 769 (C.A.); *Kingston Dry Dock Co.* v. *Lake Champlain Transp. Co.* 31 F.2d 265, 267 (2d Cir. 1929).

[4] Cf. Rene A. Brassard, "Parent and Subsidiary" 22 Boston Univ. L.R. 127 (1942) p. 129.

[5] *Vide William Cory & Son Ltd.* v. *Dorman Long & Co. Ltd.* [1936] 2 All E.R. 386 (C.A.); *Ebbw Vale Urban District Council* v. *South Wales Traffic Area Licensing Authority* [1951] 2 K.B. 366, [1951] 1 All E.R. 806 (C.A.).

[6] *Vide* e.g., *Berkey* v. *Third Ave. Ry. Co.* 155 N.E. 58, 61 (1926). *Vide* also Blumberg, *Substantive Law* p. 125.

holding company as having itself become the actor in the transaction. But in such an event, the holding company would be acting directly rather than through the agency of the subsidiary.

Regrettably, the notion of "agency" has been misused in several cases. Indeed, the terms "agency" and "agent" have often been loosely employed by the courts as one of the many familiar metaphors in the lifting of the veil cases.[1] This use of agency unfortunately appears to reflect a basic misunderstanding of the common law notion. A typical approach would be something like this. The court would have decided to lift the veil by reason of some factors being in fact unrelated to a consensual common law agency. Instead of rationalising its decision, the court would merely present the conclusion and describe the subsidiary as the "agent" of the holding company. The "agency" label would often be used together with other quasi-meaningless phrases such as "tool", "puppet", "dummy", "alter ego" or "instrumentality". In such cases, the courts would view the holding and subsidiary companies as one entity and not - as is implied in a true agency situation - two separate entities one of which is the principal and the other the agent.[2]

Much of the criticism in this regard can be levelled at American judgments[3] in which "agency" is often confusingly employed as a synonym for the "instrumentality" rule.[4] English courts, by contrast, have been generally far more cautious with their diction in the lifting of the veil cases - with the admirable result that the confusion reigning in numerous American

---

[1] *Vide* e.g., *Smith, Stone & Knight Ltd.* v. *Birmingham Corporation* [1939] 4 All E.R. 116; *Mull* v. *Colt Co.* 31 F.R.D. 154, 162-163 (S.D.N.Y. 1962); *Fidenas AG* v. *Honeywell, Inc.* 501 F.Supp. 1029, 1037 (S.D.N.Y. 1980); *People* v. *Michigan Bell Telephone Co.* 224 N.W. 438, 440 (1929).

[2] The difference between a true agency situation and the alter ego or instrumentality situation is neatly drawn in *Northern Natural Gas Co. of Omaha* v. *Superior Court* 134 Cal. Rptr. 850, 857 (1976).

[3] *Vide* e.g., *Clayton Brokerage Co. of St. Louis* v. *Telswitcher Corp.* 418 F. Supp. 83, 86 (E.D. Mo. 1976), *aff'd*, 555 F.2d 1349, 562 F.2d 1137 (8th Cir. 1977); *Fidenas AG* v. *Honeywell, Inc.* 501 F.Supp. 1029 (S.D.N.Y. 1980); *Darling Stores Corp.* v. *Young Realty Co.* 121 F.2d 112, 116 (8th Cir. 1941); *Radio-Craft Co.* v. *Westinghouse Electric & Mfg. Co.* 7 F.2d 432, 435 (3d Cir. 1925); *Platt* v. *Bradner Co.* 230 P. 633, 635 (1924).

[4] J. Penn Carolan, "Disregarding the Corporate Fiction in Florida: the Need for Specifics" 27 Univ. of Florida L.R. 175 (1974) p. 183; Henry W. Ballantine, "Separate Entity of Parent and Subsidiary Corporations" 14 Calif. L. Rev. 12 (1925) p. 18. On the instrumentality rule, *vide post* Chapter V, pp. 256-263.

judgments does not afflict English law. In *Adams* v. *Cape Industries plc*,[1] for example, the Court of Appeal tackled the "agency argument" with commendable clarity.[2] In determining whether a particular subsidiary was to be regarded as an agent of an affiliate or of its holding company, the Court of Appeal started by acknowledging that the various companies were different entities at law[3] and then proceeded to examine the subsidiary's actual functions within the group. It found that the subsidiary's services were of great assistance to its affiliate and holding company in arranging their sales. Their inter-relationship was seen to be very close. Nevertheless, the Court of Appeal found that the subsidiary had no general authority to bind the affiliate or holding company to any contractual obligation. Nor was there any evidence that the subsidiary (with or without prior authority) ever effected any transaction in such manner that the affiliate or the holding company thereby became subject to contractual obligations to any person.[4] The agency argument was, quite rightly, rejected.[5]

Odd exceptions in English law - where the agency notion is loosely used - are *Smith, Stone & Knight Ltd.* v. *Birmingham Corporation*,[6] *Re F.G. (Films) Ltd.*,[7] and *Wallersteiner* v. *Moir*.[8] In *Smith, Stone and Knight*, Atkinson J. outlined six criteria for the determination of the question whether a

---

[1] [1990] BCLC 479 (C.A.).

[2] *Vide* also *Bank voor Handel en Scheepvaart N.V.* v. *Slatford* [1953] 1 Q.B. 248 (C.A.).

[3] *Adams* v. *Cape Industries plc* [1990] BCLC 479 (C.A.) at p. 520.

[4] *Ibid.* at p. 522.

[5] A correct approach to the agency concept was also taken by the Court of Appeal in *Atlas Maritime Co. S.A.* v. *Avalon Maritime Ltd. ("The Coral Rose")*[1991] 4 All E.R. 769 where the Court of Appeal, contrary to the views expressed by the court of first instance, refused to infer an agency relationship between a subsidiary and its ultimate holding company. The judgment of the court of first instance is reported at [1990] 2 Lloyd's Rep. 258.

[6] [1939] 4 All E.R. 116.

[7] [1953] 1. W.L.R. 483.

[8] [1974] 3 All E.R. 217 (C.A.). Writing in 1990, Ottolenghi stated that "[i]f the case is one of firm and intensive ties of management and decision making, and the subsidiary is wholly owned by the holding company, the courts tend to regard them as one going concern, generally by attributing to them a 'constructive' agency relationship." S. Ottolenghi, "From Peeping Behind the Corporate Veil to Ignoring it Completely" 53 M.L.R. 338 (1990) at p. 352. Even though made before the judgment of the Court of Appeal in *Adams* v. *Cape Industries plc* [1990] BCLC 479, Ottolenghi's statement was far too sweeping. Except in the revenue cases, the courts had only rarely adopted the agency construction. *Vide post* Chapter V p. 204 footnote 2.

subsidiary could be considered as the agent of its holding company. The first related to the ownership of profits; the other five to various aspects of control of and by management. The latter five criteria are simply descriptive of the form of control commonly found in the holding-subsidiary set-up. The categorisation however ignores the requirements of true agency and therefore provides an unsatisfactory - indeed an incorrect - basis for determining the existence of the relationship. It should also be noted that none of the decisions referred to by Atkinson J. appear to support the test he purported to establish. In any case, his judgment is clearly inconsistent with other authority such as *Salomon* v. *A. Salomon and Co. Ltd.*[1] and *Bank voor Handel en Scheepvaart N.V.* v. *Slatford*.[2]

*Re F.G. (Films) Ltd.* also involves a loose and incorrect use of the term "agent". The question was whether a particular film was "made" by the *de facto* English subsidiary of an American company.[3] The decision could have rested on the interpretation of the word "made" in the applicable statute. But Vaisey J. went further and - without analysis - stated that the subsidiary was a "nominee of and agent" for the holding company. Clearly, however, the terms were merely being used in a descriptive non-technical manner.

*Wallersteiner* v. *Moir (No. 1)* illustrates the danger of juggling with metaphors in a legal context. Lord Denning first described the companies controlled by Dr. Wallersteiner as his "puppets". Dr. Wallersteiner "controlled their every movement. Each danced to his bidding. He pulled the strings".[4] Then, casually but deliberately, Lord Denning switched to legal language and, without any analysis, stated that the companies were "... his agents to do as he commanded. He was the principal behind them".[5] Again, the problem with *Wallersteiner* on the agency issue is that the evidence was not tested against the strict requirements of agency. Agency appears to have been inferred merely from intrusive control. The "sham" or "façade" route would have been more appropriate.[6]

The misuse of the terms "agent" and "agency" in several American, and fewer English, judgments unquestionably confounds the real issues at stake

---

[1] [1897] A.C. 22 (H.L.).

[2] [1953] 1 Q.B. 248 (C.A.).

[3] The majority shares in the English company were registered in the name of the President of the American company.

[4] *Wallersteiner* v. *Moir (No. 1)* [1974] 3 All E.R. 217 (C.A.) at p. 238.

[5] *Ibid.* at p. 238.

[6] On the sham or façade exception, *vide post* Chapter V pp. 254-255.

and stymies constructive analysis. If courts ignore the technicalities of the law of agency - or what is worse bend them beyond recognition to suit the conclusion intended to be reached - then the concept will lose its meaning and function in the holding-subsidiary situation. It becomes suspect.

## 4.2. Holding company's liability in tort

### 4.2.1. Preliminary

A vital question addressed in this work is whether there can be peculiar aspects of the holding-subsidiary relationship which result - or which ought to result - in holding company liability for the torts of the subsidiary.

For the moment however it is essential to note that there can be instances where the holding company is held liable in tort - on ordinary principles of law - for acts involving the subsidiary's operations. In other words, liability can attach to the holding company on a basis independent of the existence of a holding-subsidiary relationship. To avoid the risk of confusion creeping in at a later stage, it is now proposed to outline the more common situations where holding company tort liability is predicated on "ordinary" principles.

### 4.2.2. Torts of agent

Under the law of agency, the principal may be liable for the torts of its agent committed within the scope of his authority, actual or apparent.[1] As already noted, a subsidiary company may actually serve as an agent of its holding company.[2] In such a case, the holding company would be liable for the torts of the subsidiary committed within the subsidiary's authority.[3]

### 4.2.3. Assumption of duty

Another type of situation where direct tort liability may be imposed on a holding company for operations carried out by the subsidiary occurs where - by reason of the nature of the inter-relationship between the holding

---

[1] *Vide* Bowstead *op. cit.* Art. 97, pp. 389-397; Fridman, *op. cit.* p. 286; American Law Institute, Restatement (Second) of Agency (1958) para. 251; Warren A. Seavey, *Handbook of the Law of Agency* (1964) pp. 161-168.

[2] *Supra* p. 119.

[3] *Vide Mueller* v. *Seaboard Commercial Corp.* 73 A.2d 905 (1950).

company, the subsidiary company and third parties (such as employees or consumers) - the holding company has assumed certain duties directly towards such third parties. This type of scenario may arise in the context of dominating control by the holding company. As we have already seen,[1] holding companies exercise varying degrees of control over the affairs of the subsidiary. Occasionally, it may happen that the nature and level of the control exercised by the holding company is such that the holding company becomes the actor in the particular transaction or activity. In such an event it is likely that the holding company's actions would give rise to a duty of care towards third parties (probably consumers and employees) dealing with the subsidiary. Direct liability would result from a breach of such duty.[2] In all likelihood, this form of direct liability would arise in the context of safety policies and practices. The holding company may have directly participated in devising, implementing and supervising certain safety features for its subsidiaries. In such a situation the holding company can be taken to have assumed a duty towards, say, the subsidiaries' employees with regard to the maintenance of a safe workplace. The negligent performance of such a duty - even if voluntarily assumed - should attract liability.

A holding company's own negligent conduct may of course also directly result in injuries to persons dealing with its subsidiaries. The holding company may, for example, have carried out product testing procedures for goods manufactured by the subsidiary. The holding company would be held liable in the event that it was aware of, or should have been aware of, deficiencies in the testing procedures and failed to rectify them with resulting injuries to purchasers.[3] The liability would be direct and would result from traditional common law principles without reference to piercing the veil techniques.[4]

---

[1] *Supra* Chapter II pp. 49-61.

[2] The third party may also of course have an actionable claim in tort against the subsidiary.

[3] *Anglo Eastern Bulkships, Ltd.* v. *Ameron*, Inc. 556 F. Supp. 1198, 1202-1203 (S.D.N.Y. 1982).

[4] In the debate following the Bhopal disaster, it was suggested that a direct action in tort be instituted against Union Carbide. Union Carbide was the holding company of Union Carbide of India Ltd. which produced the deadly pesticide. *Vide* P.T. Muchlinski, "The Bhopal Case : Controlling Ultrahazardous Industrial Activities undertaken by Foreign Investors" 50 M.L.R. 545 (1987) p. 567.

### 4.2.4. Joint torts

A holding company can of course also be jointly liable with its subsidiary for the tortious acts of the subsidiary. This situation is more likely to arise where the holding company is directly involved in the activities of the subsidiary or where the holding company is particularly intrusive in the affairs of the subsidiary.

The concept of joint tortfeasors has recently been considered in the context of patent infringements. For a long time there was a distinction between "procuring" and "facilitating" an infringement of a patent. A person who merely facilitated, but did not procure, the infringement was not considered a joint tortfeasor with the infringer.[1] More recently, however, the notion has developed that parties will be regarded as joint tortfeasors if on the facts they have a common design to market articles which in fact infringe patent rights.[2]

The notion of common design was adopted by the Court of Appeal in *Unilever plc* v. *Gillette (UK) Ltd.*,[3] involving an action by Unilever plc against Gillette (UK) Limited for patent infringement. The allegation was that Gillette (UK) Limited ("the subsidiary") had imported the infringing product manufactured by its American holding company. In order to obtain discovery of certain documents in the possession of the holding company, Unilever plc sought to join the holding company in the action against the subsidiary on the basis that it was a knowing party to the infringement. The Court of Appeal held that there existed at least an arguable basis for inferring a common design between the holding and subsidiary companies with a view to marketing the allegedly infringing product. The Court of Appeal noted that if this common design was proved the holding company could be liable to the plaintiff as a "joint tortfeasor" with the subsidiary. Accordingly, the plaintiff was granted leave to join the holding company in the action. The Unilever approach was subsequently followed in *Intel Corporation* v. *General Instrument Corporation*[4] where the court indicated

---

[1] *Townsend* v. *Haworth* (1875) 48 L.J.Ch. 770; *Dunlop Pneumatic Tyre Company Limited* v. *David Moseley & Sons Limited* [1904] 1 Ch. 164, [1904] 1 Ch. 612 (C.A.).

[2] *Morton-Norwich Products, Inc.* v. *Intercen Ltd.* [1978] R.P.C. 501. *Vide* Dillon L.J.'s survey of these developments in *Molnlycke A.B.* v. *Procter & Gamble Ltd.* [1992] 1 W.L.R. 1112 (C.A.) at p. 1118.

[3] [1989] R.P.C. 583. (C.A.).

[4] [1991] R.P.C. 235.

that the law on joint torts in the case of patent infringement was the same whether a common design was alleged to exist between individuals or between members of a corporate group. Significantly, the court observed that mere capacity to control would not establish a common design. The crucial factor was the extent of the control actually exercised.

Now although the concept of common design has been developed and applied in the patent infringement cases, there appears to be no reason to restrict the concept to such cases. Inherent in the concept of common design is the joint participation or concerted action by two parties in the tort of infringement.[1] Such joint participation can arise in any tort situation. The question is whether such common design or joint participation will be readily inferred in the holding-subsidiary cases. Certainly, latent control will not be sufficient. Nor, it is submitted, should the exercise of the level of control typical in an integrated group lead to an inference of a joint participation in the tort committed by the subsidiary. Only the intrusive exercise of control by the holding company or its direct participation in the tort should qualify the holding company as a joint tortfeasor in the case, say, of an action in tort for negligence. Evidence of a common design appears to be more readily available in the patent infringement cases simply because the acquisition by the subsidiary from its holding company of the infringing articles for sale to third parties provides an automatic and obvious link to the holding company's involvement.

A holding company may of course even be directly and solely liable for the infringement of a patent even though the infringement may have appeared to be the act of the subsidiary. Thus, a holding company has been held liable where it employed personnel to build and construct a manufacturing plant in which, to the knowledge of the holding company, infringing acts were to be committed by the subsidiary in violation of the

---

[1] In *Unilever plc* v. *Gillette (UK) Ltd.* [1989] R.P.C. 583 (C.A.) Mustill L.J. made it absolutely clear that the phrase "common design" was to be construed as a statutory term. In this regard he stated : "I use the words 'common design' because they are readily to hand, but there are other expressions in the cases, such as 'concerted action' or 'agreed on common action' which will serve just as well. ... They all convey the same idea. This idea does not, as it seems to me, call for any finding that the secondary party has explicitly mapped out a plan with the primary offender. Their tacit agreement will be sufficient. Nor, as it seems to me, is there any need for a common design to infringe. It is enough if the parties combine to secure the doing of acts which in the event prove to be infringements." *Ibid.* at p. 609.

plaintiff's patent rights.[1] The infringing acts were considered to be committed by the holding company.[2]

### 4.2.5. Fraud

The holding company's participation in any fraud involving or committed by its subsidiary will clearly result in the imposition of liability on the holding company.[3] Liability for fraud is perhaps too obvious to merit analysis. In any case, fraud is outside the scope of the present inquiry.[4]

### 4.2.6. Inducing breach of contract

Apart from the more obvious negligence, patent and "fraud" cases just considered, there are other instances where a holding company may be a direct participant in the tort. The holding company may, for example, be held liable in tort for inducing the subsidiary to breach a contract with the plaintiff.[5] Clearly, an intention on the part of the holding company to injure the plaintiff need not be established in claims for inducing a breach of contract.[6] Evidence of knowing involvement by the holding company will however be essential.[7] But again, the mere existence of the holding-subsidiary relationship will not be sufficient to visit the holding company with liability. It is the exercise of the latent power of control to the extent of a direct interference in the internal decision-making function of the subsidiary which will make the holding company the actor in the tort. Liability is direct not vicarious. It is the act of the holding company that is in issue.

---

[1] *Union Sulphur Co.* v. *Freeport Texas Co.* 251 Fed. 634, 661 (D. Del. 1918).

[2] *Ibid.* p. 662.

[3] *Vide* I.A. 1986, s. 213. Cf. *Re a Company* [1985] BCLC 333 (C.A.). *Vide* also *supra* p. 108.

[4] *Vide supra* Chapter II pp. 63-64.

[5] *Gulf C. & S. F. Ry. Co.* v. *Cities Service Co.* 281 Fed. 214, 215 (D. Del. 1922). Cf. *City of Warrensburg* v. *RCA Corp.* 550 F. Supp. 1364, 1380 (1982); *Leeward Petroleum Ltd.* v. *Mene Grande Oil Co.* 415 F. Supp. 158, 164 (D. Del. 1976). *Vide* American Law Institute, Restatement (Second) of Torts (1965) para. 766 (1965).

[6] *D.C. Thomson & Co. Ltd.* v. *Deakin* [1952] 1 Ch. 646.

[7] *Vide British Motor Trade Association* v. *Salvadori* [1949] Ch. 556.

### 4.2.7. Principal-servant relationship

It is also possible to envisage a situation - at least in theory - where the holding company is considered to be the principal in a principal-servant relationship with the subsidiary qualifying as the servant. It is of course unlikely in practice for a subsidiary to qualify as a servant in this technical sense as long as it exercises any degree of control over its employees. The criteria of a principal-servant relationship would only be satisfied in the rare case where the holding company directs not simply the day-to-day affairs but also goes so far as to direct all aspects of its operations, including the activities of the employees.[1] In this unusual type of situation the holding company would be directly liable for the subsidiary's torts under principal-servant common law principles.

### 4.2.8. Ordinary tort situations often viewed as instrumentality cases

It should finally be observed that many American judgments which are cited as illustrative of entity disregard are also intelligible - and possibly more so - on familiar principles of tort law. In other words, the holding company would be liable in tort even if no holding-subsidiary relationship were involved. The plaintiff's contention - often accepted by the court - has frequently been that since the holding company so controlled and dominated the subsidiary as to make it a mere instrumentality, the two companies were really one and the holding company therefore becomes an actor in, and liable for, any resultant tort. The plain fact might have been however that the holding company was itself directly responsible for its own tort. The holding company's involvement could well have been analysed without recourse to the entity doctrine and its disregard.[2]

### 4.3. Vicarious performance

In general, a contract may be performed vicariously unless the contracting party expressly or impliedly undertakes to perform it personally or by his

---

[1] *Vide* Blumberg, *Substantive Law* p. 307; P.T. Muchlinski, "The Bhopal Case : Controlling Ultrahazardous Industrial Activities undertaken by Foreign Investors" 50 M.L.R. 545 (1987) p. 568. Cf. *Mersey Docks and Harbour Board* v. *Coggins and Griffiths* [1947] A.C. 1.

[2] *Vide* Latty, *op. cit.* p. 82.

own servants or agents.[1] Naturally, where the holding company enters into a contract with a third party and the contract is "personal", in the sense that such party relies on the skill and judgement of the holding company, the latter must perform personally - the duty is non-delegable.[2] And as a general rule, a contracting party is liable for the acts of his sub-contractors to whom he has delegated performance of his obligations. Clearly therefore the holding company will be liable for the negligent performance by its subsidiary of any obligation undertaken by it (the holding company) but performed vicariously by the subsidiary. If the holding company, for example, is in the position of a bailee it will be liable for the tort of a subsidiary if the subsidiary had been appointed as a sub-bailee without the consent of the creditor.[3] Liability here arises from traditional common law principles.

## 4.4. Guarantees

A straightforward situation where liability attaches to the holding company on general principles of law rather than on any particular aspect of the holding-subsidiary relationship is the case of a guarantee granted by a holding company in favour of the creditors of its subsidiary. Often the guarantee is given to the group's bankers in the context of an "interavailable" facility opened in favour of the various components in the group.[4]

Legal issues do of course feature in holding company guarantees. Did the holding company have the necessary capacity to give the guarantee?[5] Could

---

[1] *British Waggon Co.* v. *Lea* (1880) 5 Q.B.D. 149.

[2] *Vide* G.H. Treitel, *The Law of Contract* (8th ed. 1991) p. 657; Hugh Collins, "Ascription of Legal Responsibility to Groups in Complex Patterns of Economic Integration" 53 M.L.R. 731 (1990) p. 735. Cf. also *McDermid* v. *Nash Dredging & Reclamation Co. Ltd.* [1987] A.C. 906 where, on the basis of a breach of a non-delegable duty to its employee to provide a safe system of work, a subsidiary was held liable for the negligence of an employee of its holding company.

[3] Cf. *Edwards* v. *Newland & Co.* [1950] 2 K.B. 534; *Leather's Best, Inc.* v. *S.S. Mormaclynx* 451 F. 2d 800 (2d Cir. 1971). *Vide* N.E. Palmer, *Bailment* (2nd ed. 1991) pp. 989-995, 1270-1275, 1346.

[4] *Vide* e.g., *Bank of Scotland* v. *Wright* [1991] BCLC 244. *Vide* also John Davies and Jonathan Goodlife, "Parent liability for subsidiaries - The right move for effective redress" 4 Practical Law for Companies 17 (1993) pp. 17-19.

[5] *Vide* Prentice, Aspects of British law, pp. 81-82; Blumberg, *Bankruptcy Law* Ch. 6.

the guarantee be challenged on the ground that the directors of the holding company were not acting in good faith and in the interests thereof?[1] Under what circumstances, if any, is the guarantee voidable as a transaction at an undervalue?[2] What if the undertaking is in the form of a "letter of comfort" - is the holding company legally bound?[3] These questions, however stimulating they may be, fall outside the scope of this discussion. The point here is that holding company guarantees represent a special and direct form of liability. It is the holding company's own contractual liability that is involved. The underlying holding-subsidiary relationship is basically irrelevant.

### 4.5. Inducing contractor's reliance

A type of situation broadly analogous to the guarantee case is where the circumstances clearly indicate that the plaintiff's contract is with the subsidiary, but the holding company represents that it would be responsible on the contract. The holding company may have represented that the subsidiary is essentially the same as the holding company or that the holding company is "behind it" or that the subsidiary is actually operating the business in the holding company's name.[4] The contractor then relies on such statements. Such statements can of course be taken as representations of responsibility and liability imposed on the holding company accordingly.[5] But decisions imposing liability for such representations cannot be interpreted as establishing a rule of holding company liability in terms of the

---

[1] Prentice, Aspects of British law, pp. 82-83.

[2] *Vide* R.M. Goode, *Principles of Corporate Insolvency Law* (1990) pp. 146-151; Prentice, Aspects of British law, p. 84; Blumberg, *Bankruptcy Law* Ch. 9.

[3] English law would appear to be to the effect that there is no liability unless there is a formal guarantee. *Vide Kleinwort Benson Ltd.* v. *Malaysia Mining Corporation Berhad* [1989] 1 W.L.R. 379 (C.A.); E.P. Ellinger, "Letters of comfort" [1989] J.B.L. 259. On "letters of comfort" in the context of groups *vide* Frank Wooldridge, *Groups of Companies - The Law and Practice in Britain, France and Germany* (1981) p. 107; Clive M. Schmitthoff, "Lifting the Corporate Veil" [1980] J.B.L. 156 p. 161; John Davies and Jonathan Goodlife, "Parent liability for subsidiaries - The right move for effective redress" 4 Practical Law for Companies 17 (1993) pp. 19-20; Robbins and Stobaugh, *op. cit.* p. 68.

[4] Latty, *op. cit.* p. 94.

[5] *Vide In re Kentucky Wagon Mfg. Co.* 3 F. Supp. 958, 967 (W.D. Ky. 1932); *In re Kentucky Wagon Mfg. Co.* 71 F.2d 802 (C.C.A. 6th 1934).

functional or structural peculiarities of the holding-subsidiary relationship. The holding company's liability is directly predicated on its own representations.[1] Again the holding company is liable for its own acts.

### 4.6. Estoppel

Another form of liability that may attach to a holding company independently of the peculiar features of the holding-subsidiary relationship stems from the doctrine of estoppel. A cause of action in tort may have arisen against a subsidiary company but the claimant wrongly believes that the holding company is responsible. In negotiations between the plaintiff and personnel from the holding company (during which the claimant's misapprehension becomes evident) the holding company discusses and attempts to bargain on the claim as if it would be the appropriate defendant in the action. The holding company should be estopped from denying it was the real tortfeasor.[2]

### 4.7. Fraudulent transfers

Cases involving the transfer of the assets of a subsidiary in fraud of its creditors are also explicable in terms of general principles of law, even though at times they may contain considerable language about disregarding the corporate status.[3] One extreme form is for the subsidiary to transfer all or nearly all its property to a newly organised subsidiary whose shares are in the first place issued to the transferring subsidiary (as a consideration for the transfer) and are then distributed to the holding company. Such a transaction and other less severe forms of fraudulent transfer involve familiar principles

---

[1] This type of liability cannot be extended to a tort situation where the doctrine of reliance does not apply.

[2] Cf. *Mitchell* v. *Lea Lumber Co.* 86 Pac. 405, 406 (1906). *Vide* further Latty, *op. cit.* pp. 98-99.

[3] E.g., *Interstate Tel. Co.* v. *Baltimore & O. Tel. Co.* 51 F. 49 (D. Md. 1892), *aff'd Baltimore and O. Tel. Co.* v. *Interstate Tel. Co.* 54 F. 50 (C.C.A. 4th 1893). Fraudulent transfer analysis was, correctly, applied by the Circuit Court of Appeals. *Vide* also Robert L. McWilliams, "Limitations of the Theory of Corporate Entity in California" 4 Calif. L.R. 465 (1916) p. 474; William O. Douglas and Carrol M. Shanks, "Insulation from Liability through Subsidiary Corporations" 39 Yale L.J. 193 (1929) pp. 211-212; Latty, *op. cit.* pp. 68-70.

of the law of fraudulent transfers mostly resulting from statute.[1] Fraudulent transfer cases are largely irrelevant to the liability problem raised by corporate groups and discussed in this work.

## 4.8. Action by liquidator of insolvent subsidiary

Assuming that the particular circumstances do not support the imposition of direct holding company liability in contract or in tort as discussed in the preceding pages, it may still be possible for creditors of an insolvent subsidiary to indirectly obtain some redress by yet another method which does not involve the disregarding of the separate personality of the holding company. Given that the holding and subsidiary companies are different legal entities, it is possible that in the inter-relationship between the two companies, the holding company has breached duties - contractual or otherwise - which it owed to the subsidiary. In such an eventuality, the subsidiary's liquidator should be able to seek recovery from the holding company.[2] Moreover, if property has been transferred to the holding company at an undervalue or as a preference the liquidator (or the administrator) may seek recovery under the Insolvency Act 1986.[3] The liquidator (or the administrator) may also seek recovery on the common law basis that a particular transfer was equivalent to an unlawful distribution.[4] Any monies recovered would of course inflate the fund available to the subsidiary's creditors.[5]

---

[1] I.A. 1986, ss. 423-425. *Vide Aiglon Ltd. and L'Aiglon S.A.* v. *Gau Shan Co. Ltd.* [1993] 1 Lloyd's Rep. 164. On English law, *vide* generally Ian F. Fletcher, *The Law of Insolvency* (1990) pp. 216-218, 516; R.M. Goode, *Principles of Corporate Insolvency Law* (1990) pp. 193-194. U.S. statutory law is found primarily in s. 548 of the Bankruptcy Code (11 U.S.C. (1982)) and the Uniform Fraudulent Conveyance Act (7A U.L.A. 161). On American law, *vide* generally Blumberg, *Bankruptcy Law* Ch. 7.

[2] The liquidator may also have an action against the holding company for wrongful trading based on s. 214 of the I.A. 1986. This action however is more properly characterised as one involving a "piercing" of the corporate veil. Holding company liability for wrongful trading is dealt with *post*, Chapter V pp. 211-218.

[3] *Vide* ss. 238, 239 and 423.

[4] *Aveling Barford Ltd.* v. *Perion Ltd.* 5 BCC 677 (1989).

[5] This method of recovery was recommended against Union Carbide in the aftermath to the Bhopal tragedy. *Vide* Jay Lawrence Westbrook, "Theories of Parent Company Liability and the Prospects for an International Settlement" 20 Texas Int. L.J. 321 (1985) p. 328.

## 4.9. The "through carriage" cases

A number of cases - involving holding and subsidiary companies in "through carriage" operations - must be distinguished from all other holding-subsidiary cases. "Through carriage" arises where goods or passengers are transported by more than one carrier, that is in several stages.[1] Where the first carrier does not expressly assume responsibility for carriage to final destination, there are two broad views as to the liability of such carrier for goods or passengers received beyond his own stage. Under the "English rule" the first carrier is, at common law, liable for loss or damage occurring even during the carriage by the successive carrier.[2] Under the "American rule" (adopted by the courts of several States and by the Federal Courts) the liability of the first carrier is, at common law, limited to his stage, and the mere acceptance of goods or passengers destined to points beyond his stage does not operate to extend his liability. His liability in fact terminates when he has delivered the goods or passenger to the next succeeding carrier.[3]

In several American cases, the first carrier and the second carrier were actually holding and subsidiary companies in economically integrated enterprises.[4] These cases indeed constituted a major arena for the assertion

---

[1] A. A. Mocatta *et al.* (ed.), *Scrutton On Charterparties and Bills of Lading* (19th ed. 1984) p. 377; Halsbury's Laws of England (4th ed., reissue, 1993) Vol. 5(1) para. 536, p. 425. On "through carriage" generally *vide* Andrew Muscat, *The Liability of Carriers engaged in Through Carriage and Combined Transport of Goods* (M.Litt. thesis, Oxford University, 1983).

[2] *Muschamp* v. *Lancaster and Preston Junction Ry.* (1841) 8 M & W 421; *Watson* v. *The Ambergate, Nottingham and Boston Ry. Co.* (1851) 15 Jur 448, Cox M & H 495; *Bristol and Exeter Ry. Co.* v. *Collins* (1859) 7 H.L.C. 194; *Wilby* v. *West Cornwall Railway Co.* (1858) 2 H & N 703. The doctrine also prevails in Canada. *Vide McGill* v. *Grand Trunk Ry.* (1892) 19 O.A.R. 245.

[3] *Roy* v. *Chesapeake and O.R. Co.* 57 S.E. 39 (1907); *Myrick* v. *Michigan Cent. R.R.* 107 U.S. 102 (1883). *Vide* William F. Elliott, *A Treatise on the Law of Bailments and Carriers* (1914) s. 264, p. 287.

[4] E.g., *Davis* v. *Alexander* 269 U.S. 114 (1925); *Lehigh Valley R. Co.* v. *Dupont* 128 F. 840 (2d Cir. 1904). This particular feature is not present in any of the English "through carriage" cases. Historically, the U.S. railroad systems emerged from individual railroad companies which were geographically interconnected. Railroads soon outgrew their intrastate origins and developed into inter-state systems. Rather than combining into larger companies, however, the original railroad companies retained their corporate individuality and became components within corporate groups. Separate corporate existence for these components was retained in view of outstanding franchises, leases, and local tax and political considerations. *Vide* Blumberg, *Substantive Law* pp. 231-232.

of inter-corporate vicarious liability. And despite the American rule limiting the first carrier's liability to his stage, it was held, in a number of the cases, that the holding company was responsible for the injuries or damages caused by the negligence of the subsidiary company. At first blush, of course, this approach is indicative of a general rule that the holding company is responsible for the acts of its subsidiaries. One of the leading cases is *Davis* v. *Alexander*[1] in which cattle was shipped from a point on the holding company's road and over the road of the subsidiary. The plaintiff recovered against the holding company for injuries sustained by the cattle during their carriage over the subsidiary's road. The Court declared that where "one railroad company actually controls another and operates both as a single system, the dominant company will be liable for injuries due to the negligence of the subsidiary".[2] Liability on the railroad holding company was also imposed in *Lehigh Valley R. Co.* v. *Dupont*[3] where the deceased had bought a ticket from the holding company for carriage over the lines of both the holding and its subsidiary company.

Prima facie, therefore, the railroad "through carriage" cases appear to support a general rule of holding company liability for the negligence of subsidiary companies. Closer analysis however dispels any such principle. To take the *Lehigh Valley* case first. In that case, the Lehigh Valley Railroad group operated as a single system. The Court based liability on the theory that this integration indicated a joint operation resulting in a partnership.[4] System operation led to the imposition of liability. Perhaps more significantly, the ticket acquired by the deceased from the holding company "evinced a contract for through carriage" and did not mention the subsidiary.[5] The *Lehigh Valley* judgment, though sparse on the factual details, can in fact easily be explained on the basis that the holding company was *contractually* bound in respect of the various stages of the carriage.

The *Davis* judgment, too, stressed system operation and concluded that where "one railroad company actually controls another and operates both as a single system, the dominant company will be liable for the injuries due to

---

[1] 269 U.S. 114 (1925).

[2] *Ibid.* at p. 117.

[3] 128 F. 840 (2d Cir. 1904).

[4] *Lehigh Valley R. Co.* v. *Dupont* 128 F. 840, 845-846 (2d Cir. 1904).

[5] *Ibid.* at p. 846. Notwithstanding the "American" rule that the first carrier is not responsible beyond his stage, it is of course always possible for the first carrier to assume responsibility for the overall carriage.

the negligence of the subsidiary company."[1] A number of other judgments around the time also relied on system analysis,[2] though a few state decisions expressly refused - on the basis of entity law - to impose railroad holding company liability.[3]

The earlier railroad cases should, it is submitted, be viewed in the context of the particular characteristics of the relationship between the consignor (or passenger) and the first and successive carriers : the difficulty of the injured party in recovering damages from successive carriers and the ease with which connecting carriers could settle inter-carrier claims.[4] These policy considerations had indeed led to the introduction of the Carmack Amendment[5] to the Interstate Commerce Act of 1887[6] which imposed liability on the first carrier for loss of or damage to goods caused by him or any successive carrier.[7]

In any case, it soon became clear that the system analysis proposed in *Davis* v. *Alexander* was not to be followed. In *Berkey* v. *Third Avenue Railway Co.*[8] the New York Court of Appeals expressly rejected the general applicability of the system doctrine and restricted *Davis* v. *Alexander* to its facts.[9] And apart from some exceptions,[10] later railway cases relied on the lifting the veil approach rather than the single system analysis.[11] System integration was deemed insufficient for the imposition of liability. Other more traditional veil piercing factors were required. More importantly, it is clear that, except in the taxi-cab business, system analysis never really exerted any influence in any field of group corporate activity.[12] The dicta of

---

[1] *Davis* v. *Alexander* 269 U.S. 114 (1925) at p. 117.

[2] E.g., *Pennsylvania R.R.* v. *Anoka Nat. Bank* 108 F. 482 (8th Cir. 1901); *Wichita Falls & N.W. Ry. Co.* v. *Puckett* 157 P. 112 (1916); *Specht* v. *Missouri Pac. R. Co.* 191 N.W. 905, 907 (1923).

[3] E.g., *Louisville & Nashville R.R. Co.* v. *Howard* 15 Ky. L. Rep. 25 (1893); *Stone* v. *Cleveland* C.C. & St. L. Ry. Co. 95 N.E. 816 (1911).

[4] *Vide Atlantic Coast Line R. Co.* v. *Riverside Mills* 219 U.S. 186, 200-201 (1911).

[5] 49 U.S.C. s. 20 (11).

[6] 49 U.S.C.

[7] The rule is now contained in 49 U.S.C. s. 11707(d)(2)(A).

[8] 155 N.E. 58 (1926).

[9] *Ibid.* pp. 60-61.

[10] E.g., *Conry* v. *Baltimore & O.R. Co.* 112 F. Supp. 252, 255 (W.D. Pa. 1953); *Southern Ry. Co.* v. *Crosby* 201 F.2d 878, 882-883 (4th Cir. 1953).

[11] E.g., *Louisville & N.R. Co.* v. *Carter* 10 S.W. 2d. 1064 (Ky. Ct. App. 1927).

[12] *Vide* further *post* Chapter VII pp. 408-410.

the earlier connecting carrier cases should therefore be treated with caution and should not be extended to all types of claims involving subsidiaries.

## 4.10. Conclusion

From the foregoing discussion it is evident that holding company liability can often be explained in terms of relatively straightforward and familiar principles of law independently of the underlying holding-subsidiary relationship. Subsequent chapters will however reveal that those familiar principles of law are patently inadequate to effectively remedy the type of abuses and unfairness identified in Chapter II. And if no other rules of law can be invoked to curb the mischief, new principles must be conceived to perform that role.

# 4 Policy Objectives and the Corporate Group

## 1. BROAD GUIDING PRINCIPLES

### 1.1. Preliminary

One's perception of the adequacy or otherwise of existing law in any given field of legal activity and of the nature of any reform that may be deemed necessary or desirable in that regard is conditioned by a number of underlying notions that shape one's outlook to legal analysis generally and to the field of activity in particular.

Before proceeding, in the next chapters, to a closer examination of holding company liability, it would be useful - for a better understanding of the analysis to be conducted - for the author's views on basic underlying issues to be defined. This exercise will involve : (i) a consideration of the relevant guiding principles and policy objectives; (ii) an identification of different types of creditors and the need for such a distinction; (iii) an evaluation of the broad arguments for and against a change in the law, including a socio-economic analysis of the principle of limited liability in the context of corporate groups; (iv) a discussion of the distinction between the holding-subsidiary arrangement and the one-man company; and (v) a search for a conceptual unity to the reform proposals.

The basic guiding principles and policy objectives should be dealt with first.

### 1.2. Law and social and economic problems

The primary aim of law should be to bring order and justice into the community. To do so, law cannot be thought about only in abstract and formal terms. Law has to take into account social and economic considerations and it must play its part in solving any related problems that may arise. Legal theory cannot be divorced from social and economic issues. In dealing with corporate groups, therefore, the law has to consider not merely the abstract or formal notions, but also the social and economic realities - realities which should shape the development of the law. Take the concept of juridical personality that is so central to the debate on corporate groups. There must be nothing absolute about it. The concept has to yield to the realities of life where social or economic considerations no longer justify its rigid application.

The notions of justice and fairness, which should lie at the heart of any legal system, are hardly capable of definition. Nor is it necessary to attempt a definition. It perhaps suffices to state broadly that, in the commercial context at least, justice and fairness demand both the supremacy of substance over the form or colour of things - of reason over quibbles and quillets - as well as the provision of adequate remedies for losses or injuries caused by others. The truth is that ordinary people readily recognise injustice or unfairness. No doubt, the same can be said for judges and law-makers. Even company and insolvency statutes expressly acknowledge - but do not define - the notions of justice and fairness and provide for remedies where the principles are flouted.[1] Witness, for example, the test of "unfairly prejudicial" conduct in the context of shareholders' remedies in section 459 of the Companies Act 1985, the "just and equitable" ground of winding up in section 122(1)(g) of the Insolvency Act 1986 and the court's power to grant relief under section 113(2)(a) of the Companies Act 1985 where it is "just and equitable" to do so.[2] The use of terms like "unfairly" and "just and equitable" enable the courts to have regard to wider equitable considerations.[3]

Terms such as "justice" and "fairness" may initially sound somewhat anachronistic in a commercial law context. But quite apart from the continuing use of such terms by statute, commercial morality is becoming increasingly topical and determinative of corporate behaviour in the contemporary business world. Higher standards of ethical conduct towards employees and the community at large are being seen as targets to be achieved by a small, though growing, number of corporate organisations.

---

[1] There has however been some criticism of the failure to provide "terms of reference" where a statute provides for a test based on "justice" or "fairness". *Vide* Leonard Sealy, "A Company Law for Tomorrow's World" 2 Co. Law. 195 (1981) p. 199.

[2] The court's power is exercisable in connection with the liability of subsequent holders of shares allotted for an inadequate consideration.

[3] *Vide Ebrahimi* v. *Westbourne Galleries Ltd.* [1973] A.C. 360 (H.L.) at p. 379 per Lord Wilberforce; *Re a Company (No. 00477 of 1986)* [1986] BCLC 376 at p. 378 per Hoffmann J.

The gap between commercial morality and the law has to be closed. New and higher standards of law become imperative in response to the demands by the community for higher standards of just and fair dealing. And if the courts are unable to narrow the gap - either because of the constraining effects of precedent or out-moded statutory provisions or because of an innate conservatism - then the legislator must move in.

Care of course must be taken not to allow sentiment to blur analysis. Otherwise sentiment becomes an enemy. But analysis cannot be too clinical. Reason cannot sit in judgment if it is totally oblivious to the dictates of feelings. A right balance must be struck. This can only be achieved by carefully identifying and weighing against each other all relevant considerations.

Apart from the dominant theme of justice and fairness, there are of course more specific policy considerations that have to be taken into account in assessing the adequacy of existing law in the particular field of inquiry. The next sections of this chapter will deal with these policy considerations.

## 1.3. Objectives of company and insolvency law

The question of creditor protection in the context of corporate groups involves issues both of company law and of insolvency law. The principal objectives of these interrelated fields of law need to be highlighted.

The main objectives underpinning company law must be to encourage and facilitate commercial and industrial activity and to promote investment, thereby contributing to sound economic expansion.[1] Indeed, company law should be viewed more as an enabling rather than as a regulatory system : company law should allow entrepreneurs to utilise the corporate mechanism to organise and conduct their businesses to the maximum possible advantage.[2] Limited liability is unquestionably the key element of the

---

[1] Very little debate seems to have taken place in England on the objectives of company law. Notable exceptions include Sian Elias, "Company Law in the 1990s" in J.H. Farrar (ed.), *Contemporary Issues in Company Law* (1987) pp. 5-6; Leonard Sealy, "A Company Law for Tomorrow's World" 2 Co. Law. 195 (1981); The Law Society Memorandum (1991) pp. 3-4. An earlier contribution was P.S. Atiyah, "Thoughts on Company Law Philosophy" 8 Lawyer 15 (1965).

[2] Unfortunately company law is actually becoming more and more regulatory. The sheer length of the C.A. 1985 and related primary and subsidiary legislation has made the subject virtually unmanageable. Ironically, there has been much talk of "deregulation", especially in so far as private companies are concerned. *Vide* e.g., White Paper, Lifting

corporate mechanism. The policy aspects of limited liability merit separate analysis and are considered in a later section of this Chapter.[1]

Enterprise, to be sure, is encouraged not merely by the corporate mechanism and its inherent advantages. To a greater or lesser extent, several other factors play a part : the overall economic climate, domestic and international; interest rates; tax and other fiscal incentives; a balanced competition regulatory system and so on. Company law is only a partner in making business work better.

Whilst serving its principal objective of promoting investment and enterprise, however, company law must also define and balance the often conflicting interests of the various stakeholders in corporate activity : the investors *vis-a-vis* the management; the majority shareholders *vis-a-vis* the minority; the interests of creditors *vis-a-vis* the limited liability enjoyed by shareholders. Nor should the wider public interest - often in conflict with the interest of the company itself - be overlooked. A guiding principle must be the attainment of acceptable standards. Low ethical standards can bring individuals, organisations and entire markets into disrepute.[2] This leads to the dilemma faced by company law : to protect legitimate interests by raising standards without at the same time dampening investment and enterprise; to control without interfering. Regulation to prevent abuse and malpractice should also be commensurate with the risk involved. Otherwise the social and economic benefits of the corporate form will be impaired. Resolving the dilemma is, admittedly, no easy task. But a clear definition of objectives, after open and serious debate, will go a long way towards finding and formulating balanced and acceptable solutions.

---

*Cont.*

the Burden, Cmnd. 9571, July 1985 pp. 7, 24. In 1993, deregulation was promised by Neil Hamilton, then Corporate Affairs Minister, in a speech to the Institute of Company Accountants. (*Vide* Palmer's In Company, Issue 10/93, October 20, 1993, p. 1.). More recently, Mr. Hamilton signalled that the Law Commission would be considering measures aimed at helping the growth of small business. The two principal measures are the simplification of the C.A. 1985 and the creation of a new organisation along the lines of an incorporated partnership. (*Vide* "UK company law faces widespread reform" *Financial Times*, 7th April 1994). Precious little however is being achieved by way of action.

[1] *Vide post* pp. 161-176.

[2] *Vide* the comments made by the Director of Public Prosecutions, Mrs. Barbara Mills, as reported in "DPP chief suggests safeguards for companies" *Financial Times*, 29th April 1992.

Businesses do not always succeed and flourish. Sometimes they fail. On failure, the interests of some of the stakeholders in the business - creditors in particular - take on a heightened significance. Corporate insolvency law raises its own objectives. These objectives diverge considerably from the objectives of company law, reflecting the shift from the policy of encouragement of enterprise and investment in company law to one of salvage and equitable distribution in corporate insolvency.[1] Corporate insolvency in fact involves a variety of related objectives : to salvage, if possible, the business in the interests of employees, creditors, investors and the community at large; where salvage fails, to protect as far as possible the remaining value of the business in the interests of the creditors; to ensure a fair and equitable distribution of the estate amongst the creditors (who it must be remembered may suffer a catastrophe themselves); to consider whether creditors can demand that shareholders or management contribute to the estate of the company; to investigate the causes of failure; and to sanction any culpable conduct in the management of the company.

Given that company law and insolvency law view the same corporate mechanism from inherently different perspectives, it is understandable that their respective objectives diverge in many important respects. It must not be forgotten, however, that to a considerable extent the two subjects necessarily affect the same interests - investors, employees, creditors, and the wider public interest - though admittedly with a shift in emphasis away from the investors (in company law) towards creditors (in insolvency law). Nor must it be overlooked that a rule regulating one stage of a company's existence (its incorporation and operation as a going concern) may reverberate at a later stage of the company's existence (its insolvent liquidation). Take the position of creditors and the rule of limited liability. The interests of creditors of course are taken into account both by company law and by insolvency law. But the rule of limited liability, a rule conceived to further the objectives of company law, will actually affect the interests of creditors only when insolvency law enters the scene. At that stage, the reality of limited liability rises, phoenix-like, out of the ashes of business failure. It would be facetious to discuss the interests of creditors in corporate insolvency without questioning that fundamental rule of company law. Insolvency law must not take company law for granted.

---

[1] *Vide* generally R.M. Goode, *Principles of Corporate Insolvency Law* (1990) pp. 5-9; The Cork Report, paras. 191-204, pp. 53-56; Farrar, pp. 651-652.

## 1.4. Corporate responsibility

Corporate conduct cannot be viewed in the vacuum of company law. Social, economic and perhaps even moral factors need to be taken into account. To an extent, the legal system has recognised this. Indeed, corporate conduct is regulated by laws that go well beyond company law itself : employment law, consumer law, pension law, financial services law, industrial law and tax law. All combine to control the activities and power of companies in a variety of ways. This is salutary and commendable. Every legal system must place an effective restraint on power and ensure that power attracts a corresponding responsibility.

The pursuit of social responsibility involves, to be sure, an ambiguity; perhaps even a contradiction. For in the present stage of the development of the law, the interests of the company are still seen primarily as the interests of the shareholders. Creditors are taken into account only if insolvency is approaching or has actually befallen the company. Employees receive some protection and a lot of lip service. And the interests of the local community and of society at large may be incompatible with the interests of the company, unless some benefit can be shown to derive from pursuing such interests. The current legal position is moreover complemented by what is perhaps a more fundamental consideration : the pressures, external and internal, on management to increase and maintain profitability. Non-profit-making ideals are difficult to supplant onto the traditional profit-making function of corporate management.

Yet the drive for higher standards of corporate behaviour must go on. Ideally, companies should perform not merely a profit-making function. They have a social function to serve as well.[1] The mind of the corporate organisation has already been developed. Is it not time now for the heart and soul to be touched?[2]

The choice is not simply, as has been suggested,[3] between a system based on individual ownership of property and one where such notion disappears. It must be remembered that corporate business is permitted and encouraged

---

[1] *Vide contra* R.A. Posner, *Economic Analysis of Law* (2nd ed. 1977) pp. 310-313.

[2] Cf. the comments made by the Chairman of the Co-operative Bank (Mr. Terry Thomas) as reported in "Dixons' £1m to aid study into ethics of business" *Financial Times*, 31st July 1992.

[3] Adolf. A. Berle, "For whom Corporate Managers *are* Trustees : A Note" 45 Harv. L.R. 1365 (1932) p. 1368.

by law both because of its service to the community as well as because it is a source of profit to its owners.[1] Indeed, not only can the profit-making and social functions co-exist; to an extent, the social function can be viewed as complementary to the profit making function. In fact, an effort by corporate organisations to take into account wider social responsibilities will in the long run probably increase the profitability of the organisations. Such organisations create a favourable image with potential customers, turning social and moral concerns to competitive advantage. Motivation within the company may also be improved, leading to increased productivity.[2]

Nor is the notion of corporate social responsibility any longer a pious hope, a student's dream.[3] English business schools and academic writers are at last beginning to take the subject seriously, years after their American counterparts.[4] More significantly, it is increasingly - though cautiously -

---

[1] William H. Husband and James C. Dockeray, *Modern Corporation Finance* (1947) p. 211-222. Cf. E. Merrick Dodd Jr., "For whom are Corporate Managers Trustees?" 45 Harv. L.R. 1145 (1932) p. 1149.

[2] *Vide* "Ethics and worse" *Financial Times*, 31st July 1992; Letter from Mr. Alastair Bruce to the Editor, *Financial Times*, 14th September 1993; Herman, *op. cit.* pp. 255-256.

[3] When the debate on social responsibility opened in the United States in the early 1930's, Berle was evidently sceptical of any significant developments taking place. He also feared that developments unchecked by legal balances would be "unsafe". He conceded however - somewhat apocalyptically - that without a readjustment in favour of a broader social responsibility, "the corporate system will involve itself in successive cataclysms perhaps leading to its ultimate downfall". *Vide* Adolf. A. Berle, "For whom Corporate Managers *are* Trustees: A Note" 45 Harv. L.R. 1365 (1932) p. 1372. More recently, scepticism - mingled with a good dose of cynicism - was evident in Samuel Brittan's address to the British Association. "How economics is linked to ethics" *Financial Times*, 2nd September 1993. Mr. Brittan's views on the legitimacy of corporate social responsibility generated some enthusiastic debate. *Vide* "Letters to the Editor" *Financial Times*, 14th September 1993.

[4] *Vide* "Dixons' £1m to aid study into ethics of business" *Financial Times*, 31st July 1992; "Ethics and worse" *Financial Times*, 31st July 1992. Significant early American contributions include E. Merrick Dodd Jr., "For whom are Corporate Managers Trustees?" 45 Harv. L.R. 1145 (1932); Adolf. A. Berle, "For whom Corporate Managers *are* Trustees: A Note" 45 Harv. L.R. 1365 (1932); Sigmund Timberg, "Corporate Fiction - Logical, Social and International Implications" 46 Colum. L.R. 533 (1946). The last twenty years or so have witnessed a renewed and vigorous debate between economists and moral philosophers that had been interrupted during the heyday of positivist methodology in both disciplines. *Vide* generally Daniel M. Hausman and Michael S. McPherson, "Taking Ethics Seriously : Economics and Contemporary Moral Philosophy" 31 J. of Econ. Lit. 671 (1993).

being recognised by corporate organisations themselves.[1] Again, English organisations lag behind their parallels across the Atlantic.[2]

The recognition by companies of social responsibilities is not necessarily inbred. To an extent it is a response to pressure from shareholders to be seen to be ethical; in part it follows the demands of public opinion; and in part it may be linked to the notion of keeping up with peer competition. Corporate social responsibility is primarily reactive rather than proactive. It would of course be preferable if social responsibility were to be assumed voluntarily by corporate organisations.[3] For if enterprise were to share the public's perceptions of social responsibility, then higher standards will be achieved and maintained. The enforcement of legal rules tends to be less effective where the rules do not find the approval in the hearts and minds of the majority of organisations subject thereto. But where business fails to live up to acceptable standards, the compulsion of the law should be invoked.[4]

## 1.5. Certainty and predictability vs justice and flexibility

Certainty is a virtue to be sought in any field of law. In commercial law, it is lifeblood.[5] For in the regulation of business activities, certainty and its offspring - predictability - enable investors and entrepreneurs to organise their affairs, to engage in long-term corporate planning, and to assess relative risks.[6] Certainty is also desirable to minimise the waste of time and money involved in attempting to resolve nebulous rules through litigation or other

---

[1] *Vide* The Bullock Report p. 20; "Ethics and worse" *Financial Times*, 31st July 1992. For the historical development of the notion of corporate responsibility, *vide* Herman, *op. cit.* pp. 251-255.

[2] *Vide* "Time comes to mind corporate Ps and Qs" *Financial Times*, 8th May 1992. Significant also is the express recognition by the American Law Institute that even "if corporate profit and shareholder gain are not thereby enhanced, the corporation" may "take into account ethical considerations" and "devote a reasonable amount of resources to public welfare, humanitarian, educational, and philanthropic purposes." *Vide* s. 2.01 of the ALI Principles of Corporate Governance.

[3] Posner argues that in neither a competitive nor a monopolistic market is it realistic to expect much voluntary effort to subordinate profit maximisation to social responsibility. R.A. Posner, *Economic Analysis of Law* (2nd ed. 1977) pp. 312-313.

[4] On the inefficacy of voluntary codes of conduct, *vide post* Chapter X p. 475 footnote 1.

[5] *Vide* 0. Kahn-Freund, "Some Reflections on Company Law Reform" 7 M.L.R. 54 (1944) at p. 56.

[6] Cf. J.R. Macey and G.P. Miller, "Towards an Interest-Group Theory of Delaware Corporate Law" 65 Tex. L. Rev. 469 (1987) p. 484.

dispute-resolving mechanisms.[1] Moreover, certainty is desirable also from the national interest point of view as it helps to secure London's status as an international financial centre.[2] In an ideal world, legal certainty would have no exception.

Uncertainty may originate from a number of causes. Sometimes, it is a sign of careless or overly complex legislative drafting. Or it may be a result of a haphazard development in case-law. These situations - in theory avoidable - are at least remediable. Another type of uncertainty stems from the nature of the activity (or abuse) being regulated. Some activities are inherently incapable of strict and precise regulation. Flexibility and latitude in interpretation have to be introduced. Otherwise, justice and fairness would have to be sacrificed in the interests of legal certainty. Between the two, surely, justice and fairness ought to prevail. Certainty is not the primary end which the law seeks to attain.

The tension between flexibility (as a tool of justice and fairness) and predictability (as the consequence of certainty) is well illustrated by the lifting of the veil cases discussed in the course of this work. The lifting of the veil jurisprudence also serves to contrast the attitude of English courts with their American peers. The problem is that in this area of hazy equities and multivaried situations, it is impossible to establish an *a priori* test - except one that will be undesirably rigid and mechanical. The choice is effectively between flexibility - with a loss of predictability - and certainty - at the expense of justice. American courts, in their pursuit of justice, generally favour flexibility. English courts, in their passion for predictability, prefer certainty.[3]

In the formulation of any reform proposals in company and insolvency law a right balance has to be struck. Certainty - in the form of clear and simple rules - should be a basic goal. Its benefits are self-evident. But certainty should not be so highly prized as to lead to the introduction of rigid rules that may fail to adequately control abusive conduct. Where the activity to be regulated is somewhat amorphous or involves different degrees of culpability, then flexibility and discretion should be built into the rule. Broadly-worded statutory provisions will leave ample room for the desired

[1] *Vide* the Law Society Memorandum (1991) p. 3.

[2] The problem of uncertainty said to be threatening London's future as an international financial centre is behind the setting up of the Financial Law Panel on the recommendation of the Bank of England's Legal Risks Review Committee. *Vide* "Keeping ahead of the game" *Financial Times*, 21st September 1993.

[3] *Vide* the discussion *supra* Chapter III pp. 107-118.

judicial flexibility. The attainment of just and reasonable results based upon an individual analysis of the unique issue before the court is preferable to the loss of some of the certainty that results from the application of rigid rules. The adoption of a flexible approach, of course, is not unknown in English company and insolvency legislation. Notable examples include the "just and equitable" ground of winding up[1] and the discretion available to the court in ordering a director or shadow director to make a contribution for wrongful trading.[2]

### 1.6. Taking account of policies underlying other areas of law

No field of law can be viewed as a self-contained unit. In assessing the adequacy of existing law in any particular area and the desirability of reform thereto, it is essential to take account not merely of the direct and specific objectives underlying the particular area, but to search for and to take account of any policies which though properly "belonging" to other areas of law may yet affect, or be affected by, the particular area under consideration. The same approach must be taken in the study of company and insolvency law. Take the principle of limited liability. In assessing its validity in contemporary society, regard must be had not just to the underlying objectives of company and insolvency law, but also to the objectives underlying, say, the law of contract and the law of torts and the broader issue of the equitable allocation of losses.

### 1.7. Implementation of reform proposals - the need for statutory reform

Keeping dynamic areas of the law updated with society's requirements is, admittedly, no easy task. Characteristically, the law will lag behind. To an extent, of course, this is inevitable. But narrowing the time-lag in the implementation of necessary or desirable reforms will contribute towards a fairer and more effective legal system.

Almost certainly, reform in the field of law with which this work is concerned has to be by way of legislation. Legislative reform, after appropriate study, should have the advantages of certainty and breadth of application over any judicial attempt at law-making. In any case, the reforms

---

[1] I.A. 1986 s. 122(1)(g).

[2] I.A. 1986 s. 214(1).

required to update company law both with commercial reality and with the modern notion of fairness are so radical and technical that the courts - even if they had to have the will to free themselves of the fetters of *Salomon*[1] - are clearly ill-adapted for the task.

American law presents a different picture. As this study will show, American courts - free from the bonds of the strict Salomon doctrine and far more liberal in their approach - have achieved remarkable progress in the law of corporate groups. The result is that there is far less need for statutory reform in American law than in English law. Some American commentators have even argued that legislation would be of little help in solving problems associated with corporate personality. It is said that such problems are "not susceptible of any rule of thumb" and that to codify the law "would create the very strait-laced rigidity that the courts are trying to overcome in dealing with the legal fiction of separate corporate entity."[2] While it is true that the circumstances in which the corporate veil ought to be pierced are so varied that no statute can realistically list them all out, it is submitted that American law would - given its lack of uniformity[3] - benefit immensely if statute were at least to identify specific instances where the veil ought to be pierced, leaving others to be determined by the courts.

Although the case for statutory reform, at least in English law, is now unanswerable, it must be recognised that the Parliamentary process - which unfortunately does not allow much time for reforms which are low on the political agenda - is not particularly suited to producing or debating detailed

---

[1] *Salomon v. A. Salomon and Co. Ltd.* [1897] A.C. 22 (H.L.).

[2] Abner M. Israel, "The Legal Fiction of Corporate Entity and Modern Law" 3 Georgia Bar Journal 46 (1940) at p. 55. *Vide* also C.E. Brooks, "Parent and Subsidiary, Right of Parent or Subsidiary to Share with Other Creditors in Assets of Associated Corporation on the Latter's Insolvency" 37 Michigan L.R. 440 (1939) p. 448; Albert C. Heller, "Corporate Entity" 9 Wisconsin L.R. 286 (1934) p. 289. Cf. James R. Gillespie, "The Thin Corporate Line: Loss of Limited Liability Protection" 45 North Dakota L. R. 363 (1968) p. 405. Writing in 1937, Latty argued that courts "should be free, for some time at least, to call proper halts to limited liability, guided by their own common sense." He then added : "Gradually, a line of demarcation will be delineated by successive decisions. This is a field of law that is growing; it is proper that its growth be natural and along lines that best adjust the conflicting interests. Let codes come in the adult, rather than in the adolescent, stage." Elvin R. Latty, "Corporation Statutes as the Answer to Parent-Subsidiary Liability" 35 Michigan L.R. 794 (1937) p. 798. As we shall see in the course of this work, American law has developed very much as Latty had predicted. The codes, however, have not yet come. Almost six decades after Latty's observations, American law is probably still in the adolescent stage.

[3] *Vide post* Chapter V pp. 259-266.

legislation in the company law field.[1]    There must therefore be a more effective mechanism for keeping the law under constant review. In company law this means that a *permanent* law review and reform agency should be set up to monitor developments and recommend appropriate changes. For too long, the identification of problems has occurred on an ad hoc basis, often resulting in piecemeal reforms.[2] This contrasts sharply with the position in the United States where company law is the subject of constant scrutiny by the American Bar Association and the American Law Institute.[3]

Hope may not yet be lost. In November 1992, the Department of Trade and Industry announced it would be looking at selected areas of company law as part of a "rolling programme of reform" in this area.[4] It is assumed that part of the exercise will be to avoid the fragmented approach - only in part due to the need to implement the European Union Directives - that has characterised company law reform over the last forty years. To avoid such fragmentation, it will be necessary to define from the outset the guiding spirit and specific objectives of company law. Of paramount importance is the need for a coherent and co-ordinated strategy in both the analytical and the drafting stage. If, as it appears likely, different working parties are to be engaged on different areas of the law, great care must be taken to ensure that

---

[1] *Vide* the trenchant criticism by the Law Society in this regard. The Law Society Memorandum (1991) pp. 7-11. The Law Society also offered some valuable suggestions for improvement. *Ibid.* pp. 15-16. Commentators appear to be generally contemptuous of the manner in which Parliament handles the passage of important company and insolvency legislation. *Vide* e.g., L.C.B. Gower, "Reforming Company Law" 14 L. Teach. 111 (1980); Leonard Sealy, "A Company Law for Tomorrow's World" 2 Co. Law. 195 (1981) p. 196; David Milman, "Insolvency Act 1986 : how not to legislate" 7 Co. Law. 178 (1986); David Milman, "The Courts and the Companies Acts : the Judicial Contribution to Company Law" [1990] LMCLQ 402 p. 415.

[2] *Vide* The Law Society Memorandum (1991) p. 5.

[3] *Vide* e.g., the monumental effort of the American Law Institute's Principles of Corporate Governance and Structure : Analysis and Recommendations (adopted and promulgated on the 13th May 1992). Cf. also the comments of the Law Society in the Law Society Memorandum (1991) pp. 22-23.

[4] Palmer's In Company, Issue 10/93, October 20, 1993, pp. 1-2. A Department of Trade and Industry publication - "Companies in 1993-4" - contains a brief report on progress achieved in some areas of company law where reform is being considered. Consultation documents on registration of company charges and directors' duties are expected in the near future. The Department of Trade and Industry is also expected to respond to the Law Commission on ways to further deregulate small private companies. *Vide* Palmer's In Company, Issue 10/94, November 16, 1994.

the desired unison is achieved. Finally, an effort should be made to improve the technical quality of the drafting of company legislation.[1]

Once recommendations for reform have been made, it is essential that they be implemented without delay.[2] The impetus for reform will otherwise be lost.

### 1.8. International uniformity

Given that corporate groups are increasingly operating across international boundaries, considerable benefits would obviously be derived from the unification or harmonisation of municipal laws - not just of company laws but of laws generally.[3] Unification or, at least, harmonisation would enable companies to initiate and perform transnational activities without the uncertainties of potentially conflicting laws. Harmonisation would create a stable environment for long-term planning which is so highly prized by corporate organisations. In contrast to several other areas of law, success in company law harmonisation has unfortunately been limited to regional areas only, such as the European Union and the Nordic Council.[4] The reasons for this lack of progress probably include the complexity of company legislation, the close link of company law with the political interests and the economic and fiscal structure of each country,[5] and the low priority afforded

---

[1] Cf. the criticism in this regard by the Law Society, The Law Society Memorandum (1991) pp. 1-2.

[2] In March 1993 the Law Commission complained that the government failure to implement its proposals for reform, particularly in the area of property law, was costing millions of pounds in unnecessary legal costs and fees. More than half of the 40-plus reports of the Commission since 1984 have not been implemented. *Vide* "High cost of failure to carry out reforms" *Financial Times*, 16th March 1993.

[3] For a very useful contribution on the utility of harmonisation in commercial law and on the various methods of achieving such harmonisation, *vide* Roy Goode, "Reflections on the Harmonisation of Commercial Law" in [1991] Vol. I Uniform Law Review 54 (pub. International Institute for the Unification of Private Law).

[4] *Vide* Eric Stein, *Harmonisation of European Company Laws - National Reform and Transnational Coordination* (1971) pp. 70-73.

[5] Agreement on the "European Company" statute, which has been mooted for over two decades is being continuously postponed. The proposal has indeed met with considerable opposition. Britain, for example, has objected to the proposals for employee participation at board level.

to the subject on the international agenda.[1] Similar difficulties hamper progress in the achievement of uniformity and harmonisation in insolvency law.[2]

In seeking solutions to problems in company law and insolvency law, the field of vision should not be narrowed down to the domestic arena. Corporate organisations have become so transnational in character that legal systems - at least in a regional context - can no longer remain insular. Solutions should as far as possible be made compatible with regional norms of conduct and remedies. The sacrifice of domestic rules in the interest of greater international or regional uniformity should not be ruled out.

International or at least regional harmonisation is clearly desirable, perhaps even necessary in respect of any rule imposing additional liability on a holding company. For in an age of increasing cross-border activity, it would not be easy, without international uniformity and the extra-territorial enforcement of judgments, to implement any such rule.

English company law is of course being continuously influenced, and in certain aspects perhaps even dominated, by the legal systems of other member states of the European Union. Yet if more resources were to be allocated to the study of company law, it may not be too late for Britain to take a reforming lead in an area where to hold back may mean eventual submission to disadvantageous regulation.

## 1.9. Conflicting policy considerations

The purpose of the preceding pages has been to highlight those fundamental principles which - in this author's view - should guide the search for appropriate solutions to the situations of abuse and unfairness identified in this work. The search is not a straightforward one. The major difficulty is that the analysis is often beset by conflicting policy considerations : the conflict between the encouragement of enterprise through the principle of limited liability and the protection of the interests of creditors; the conflict

---

[1] For a general assessment of the difficulties inherent in achieving international uniformity in company law *vide* Stein, *op. cit.* Ch. 3.

[2] For a recent review of issues in cross-border insolvencies and initiatives toward uniformity and harmonisation in insolvency law *vide* UNCITRAL, Note by the Secretariat of the United Nations Commission on International Trade Law, ref. A/CN.9/378/Add.4, 23 June 1993. *Vide* also Ian F. Fletcher, *The Law of Insolvency* (1990) Ch. 30.

between corporate social responsibility and the profit-making function; the conflict between justice and certainty; the conflict between the policies of company law and those of other areas, such as contract law and tort law. The solution does not lie simply in adopting one objective to the exclusion of the other. For none of the conflicting situations are decidedly one-sided. Optimally, a balance has to be struck. Yet overall priorities have to be recognised. Occasionally hard choices have to be made.

## 2. THE ROLE OF LIMITED LIABILITY WITHIN CORPORATE GROUPS - THE NEED FOR A RE-ASSESSMENT

### 2.1. Limited liability and economic development

Limited liability has been considered to be of momentous significance to the expansion of the manufacturing and trading potential of the Western world and ultimately to world prosperity. Its merits have been hailed in all corners of the earth. On the basis of limited liability, "large undertakings are rested, vast enterprises are launched, and huge sums of capital attracted."[1] Limited liability has been termed "the greatest single discovery of modern times"[2] and "by far the most effective legal invention ... made in the nineteenth century."[3] Limited liability has been indirectly credited with providing employment, creating the sales of goods and adding to economic and financial growth, stability and prosperity.[4] The social and economic order is arranged accordingly.[5] There is a deep-seated commitment to the principle.

---

[1] *Anderson* v. *Abbott* 321 U.S. 349 (1943) at p. 362 per Douglas J.

[2] Nicholas Murray Butler, President of Columbia University, quoted in William M. Fletcher, *Cyclopedia of the Law of Private Corporations* (1917) Vol. I, para. 21, p. 43.

[3] President Eliot of Harvard, quoted in William W. Cook, "'Watered Stock' - Commissions - 'Blue Sky Laws' - Stock Without Par Value" 19 Mich. L.R. 583 (1921) p. 583, n. 4. In 1926 the Economist had stated that "[t]he economic historian of the future may assign to the nameless inventor of the principle of limited liability ... a place of honour with Watt and Stephenson and of the pioneers of the Industrial Revolution". *The Economist*, 18th December 1926 (Vol. CIII p. 1053).

[4] *Johnson* v. *Kinchen* 160 So. 2d 296, 299 (La. App. 1964).

[5] *Vide* William O. Douglas and Carrol M. Shanks, "Insulation from Liability through Subsidiary Corporations" 39 Yale L.J. 193 (1929) p. 193.

This view has persisted over the years and has been embraced by the judiciary, by law reform bodies, by economists and by academic writers.[1]

## 2.2. The need for a re-assessment

Yet despite the tenacious grip held by limited liability on the law and on current thinking, it is submitted that - at least in the context of corporate groups - the principle is due for a critical re-examination. Indeed, such re-assessment has been due for a number of decades. It will in fact be demonstrated that the underlying considerations that have historically and economically supported the principle of limited liability in the context of the single-company enterprise do not justify - and have never in fact justified - the blanket extension of the principle to the corporate group context.

The next section will examine the historical relationship between limited liability and the use of the holding-subsidiary company set-up. It will be shown that limited liability was introduced before the holding-subsidiary relationship effectively came into use and that at a later stage it was automatically extended to the holding company apparently without any awareness - and certainly without any debate - of the radically different considerations involved. A later section will then examine the underlying policy considerations (mostly of an economic nature) on which limited liability has rested. It will be asserted that the policies and advantages which support limited liability as a general principle do not necessarily extend to the corporate group context. Finally, it will be argued that both historical and economic considerations justify the dilution of limited liability in the context of corporate groups at least with regard to "involuntary" creditors.

---

[1] *Vide* e.g., the Report of the Company Law Amendment Committee 1925-1926 (the Greene Report), Cmd. 2657 (1926) paras. 6 and 9, p. 4; *Gledhill* v. *Fisher & Co.* 262 N.W. 371, 373-374 (1935); Lord Wilberforce, "Law and Economics" Presidential Address to the Holdsworth Club on the 25th February 1966, published by the Holdsworth Club of the University of Birmingham in 1966); James W. Hurst, *The Legitimacy of the Business Corporation in the Law of the United States, 1780-1970* (1970) p. 26; Richard A. Posner, "The Right of Creditors of Affiliated Corporations" 43 U. Chic. L. Rev. 499 (1976); Michael Whincup, "'Inequitable Incorporation' - the Abuse of a Privilege" 2 Co. Law. 158 (1981) p. 158; William P. Hackney and Tracey G. Benson, "Shareholder Liability for Inadequate Capital" 43 Univ. of Pittsburgh L.R. 837 (1982) p. 41; Juan M. Dobson, "'Lifting the Veil' in Four Countries : The Law of Argentina, England, France and the United States" 35 I.C.L.Q. 839 (1986) p. 852; *Nicholson* v. *Permakraft (NZ) Ltd.* [1985] 1 NZLR 252 p. 250.

## 3. HISTORICAL SEQUENCE : LIMITED LIABILITY BEFORE THE ADVENT OF CORPORATE GROUPS

### 3.1. The English position

General limited liability was introduced in England in 1855[1] after decades of heated debate.[2] It is clear from the arguments that were put forward by both sides to the struggle that the introduction of limited liability reflected a conscious decision based exclusively on socio-economic considerations. The legal notion of the separate juridical personality of the company - which arguably begets limited liability[3] - played no role in the debate.

Whether the holding-subsidiary arrangement was considered possible at the time is somewhat uncertain. To be sure, the legality of corporate membership was already beyond question. The Companies Clauses Consolidation Act of 1845,[4] for example, provided in its interpretation section that "shareholder" in that Act should include a corporation.[5] Similarly, both the Joint Stock Companies Act of 1844[6] and the Joint Stock Companies Winding-up Act of 1848[7] contained an interpretation clause which expressly provided that the word "person" throughout the Acts should include bodies politic or corporate, whether sole or aggregate.[8] Besides, the Chartered Companies Act of 1837[9] expressly provided that the Crown could grant a charter to a trading corporation the shareholders in which may themselves be corporate bodies, and whose liability under that charter may be limited.[10] And writing in 1850, Grant[11] stated that the members of a corporation "may be natural persons ... or natural persons joined with a

---

[1] By the Limited Liability Act 1855 (18 & 19 Vict., c. 133).

[2] For the historical background to the introduction of limited liability, *vide* H.A. Shannon, "The Coming of General Limited Liability" (1931-1932) 11 Economic History 267.

[3] *Vide supra* Chapter III pp. 103-107.

[4] 8 & 9 Vict. c. 16.

[5] *Ibid.* s. 3.

[6] 7 & 8 Vict. c. 110.

[7] 11 & 12 Vict. c. 45.

[8] *Vide* Joint Stock Companies Act 1844, s. 3 and Joint Stock Companies Winding-up Act 1848, s. 3.

[9] 7 Will. 4 & 1 Vict. c. 73.

[10] *Ibid.* ss. 3 and 4.

[11] James Grant, *A Practical Treatise on the Law of Corporations* (1850).

corporation or corporations aggregate or sole ... or the members may consist wholly of corporate persons".[1]

The aforesaid authorities however stand only in support of the legality of the corporate shareholder. They do not support the proposition that the entire or majority shareholding could be concentrated in the hands of *one* corporate shareholder. What is clear is that during the decades preceding the enactment of the Limited Liability Act, 1855, it was most unlikely that the use of a holding-subsidiary arrangement was actually contemplated. The underlying spirit of joint stock companies had always been to bring together a *number* of bona fide investors. And so it was at the time that the Limited Liability Bill was debated and enacted. Indeed, incorporation with limited liability was deliberately withheld from partnerships and individual proprietorships and in the House of Lords an amendment was introduced to the Limited Liability Bill limiting the company legal form to associations of 25 or more.[2] Robert Lowe, who introduced the Joint Stock Companies Bill (which was to incorporate the provision of the Limited Liability Act 1855 on limited liability) expressly rejected the extension of the company form to small partnerships and sole traders.[3] To Lowe, the requirement of the Joint Stock Companies Bill of at least seven members meant precisely that : seven members.[4] One-man joint stock companies were simply out of the question.[5] On this view, of course, the holding-subsidiary set-up would have been impossible.

---

[1] *Ibid.* p. 5. A few years later, in *Re Barned's Banking Co.* ((1867) L.R. 3 Ch. 105) Lord Cairns L.J. acknowledged that although it was "at first sight beyond the province of one trading corporation to become a shareholder in another" there was "no reason at common law .. why one body corporate should not become a member of another corporate body". *Ibid.* at pp. 112-113. *Vide* also Henry Thring, *The Law and Practice of Joint Stock and Other Companies* (5th ed. 1889) p. 40.

[2] A year later however the Joint Stock Companies Act of 1856 (19 & 20 Vict. c. 47) brought the minimum number of members down to seven. *Vide* further, Ireland, *op. cit.* p. 33.

[3] Parliamentary Debates (Hansard) 3rd Series Vol. CXL, 1st February 1856, at cols. 111-113.

[4] *Vide* Parliamentary Debates (Hansard) 3rd Series Vol. CXL, 1st February 1856, col. 110. For a commentary on the passage of the Joint Stock Companies Bill through Parliament, *vide* Ireland, *op. cit.* pp. 33-35.

[5] That this was the legislative intent has never really been seriously doubted. *Vide* L.C.B. Gower, "Some contrasts between British and American Corporation Law" 69 Harv. L.R. 1369 (1956) p. 1373; Note, 13 L.Q.R. 6 (1897) pp. 6-7.

Yet even during the committee stage some doubt had been expressed as to the exact meaning of the requirement of seven members. Indeed, the idea of using "dummy" shareholders was already planted. Alexander Hastie - who was opposed to the concept of limited liability - stated that limited liability would be subject to abuse where a trader formed a company of seven, consisting of himself and six others who might even be his servants to whom he gave a single share.[1] To this concern, Collier retorted that the Bill was not intended to apply to smaller associations and to ordinary partnerships.[2] But not too long after the enactment of the Joint Stock Companies Act 1856, Hastie's vision of one member and six puppets started to be seen in practice. In fact, some legal counsel actually began to advise, perhaps even encourage, the use of the one-man joint stock company.[3] And the practice of the one-man company soon became widespread. Writing in 1895, Palmer remarked that over the previous thirty years or so, "the most eminent counsel and the most eminent solicitors have repeatedly advised their clients" that all that was required "to insure limited liability was that there should be seven members ..." and that "it was immaterial what was the extent of their holding, and whether they were or were not trustees for others".[4] A year later, *Salomon* v. *A. Salomon and Co. Ltd.*[5] conclusively validated the practice of the one-man company.

---

[1] *Vide* Parliamentary Debates (Hansard) 3rd Series Vol. CXLII, 26th May 1856, at col. 643.

[2] Parliamentary Debates (Hansard) 3rd Series Vol. CXLII, 26th May 1856, at col. 645. Lowe had expressed a similar view when he introduced the Bill. *Vide* Parliamentary Debates (Hansard) 3rd Series Vol. CXL, 1st February 1856, cols. 110-113.

[3] E.g., Edward W. Cox, *The New Law and Practice of Joint Stock Companies with and without Limited Liability* (3rd ed. 1856) pp. iii, xviii-xix. During the same period however, other textwriters (such as Henry Thring who, significantly, had drafted the original Bill) still maintained that the Act of 1856 could not be adopted by small partnerships or sole traders. *Vide* Henry Thring, *The Joint Stock Companies Act 1856* (1856) pp. 26-27. *Vide* further Ireland, *op. cit.* pp. 35-38.

[4] Francis B. Palmer, *Company Precedents* (6th ed. 1895) Part I, p. 461. On the same point however, a note in the Law Quarterly Review of 1897 remarks that on the question of the validity of one trader and six dummies the decision of the House of Lords in *Salomon* v. *A. Salomon and Co. Ltd.* [1897] A.C. 22 (H.L.) would not have been possible thirty or even twenty years earlier. Note, 13 L.Q.R. 6 (1897) pp. 6-7. And in *Broderip* v. *Salomon* [1895] 2 Ch. 323 (C.A.) Lindley L.J. stated that "one-man companies ... were unheard of until a comparatively recent period, but have become very common of late years". *Ibid.* p. 336.

[5] [1897] A.C. 22 (H.L.).

Given that the principle of corporate membership had already been accepted, *Salomon's case*, in expressly validating the extension of the company legal form to the one-man company situation, must be taken to have implicitly validated the concentration of a company's shares in the hands of a single corporate member and therefore the holding-subsidiary relationship.

Whatever may be the historical sequence between the coming of limited liability, the recognition of corporate shareholders and the use of the holding-subsidiary arrangement, one matter is clear : that in none of the legislative inquiries, debates or commentaries on limited liability was the notion of the corporate shareholder ever raised.[1] And yet, without any apparent awareness - let alone discussion - of the profoundly different considerations, limited liability was automatically extended from the individual investor (who was clearly the intended beneficiary of the principle) to the corporate member and then on to the holding company. The creation of two or more strata of insulation from liability appears to have come about fortuitously.

## 3.2. The American position

The historical sequence of events is considerably clearer in the United States. Pressure for the introduction of general limited liability came from industrialists in the early part of the nineteenth century as industry continued its rapid expansion. Various states soon succumbed to the pressure and to the

---

[1] Over a number of years, limited liability provoked lengthy and heated debate both in and outside of Parliament. Legislative inquiries included H. Bellenden Ker, Report on the Law of Partnerships, (1837) B.P.P., Vol. XLIV no. 399; Report of the Select Committee on Joint Stock Companies, (1843) B.P.P., Vol. XI no. 215; Report of the Select Committee on Investments for the Savings of the Middle and Working Classes, (1850) B.P.P., Vol. XIX no. 508; Report of the Select Committee on the Law of Partnership, (1851) B.P.P., Vol. XVIII no. 509; First Report, Royal Mercantile Law Commission, (1854) B.P.P. Vol. XXVII no. 1791. Outside of Parliament, limited liability was discussed by lawyers (*vide*, the Report of the Committee on the Law of Partnership of the Law Society for Promoting the Amendment of the Law" in 10 Law Review 123 (1849), businessmen (*vide* e.g., the Memorandum of the Committee of Merchants and Traders for the Amendment of the Law of Debtor and Creditor - Appendix to the First Report, Royal Mercantile Law Commission, (1854) B.P.P. Vol. XXVII no. 1791. pp. 191-194), the Press (*vide* e.g., *The Times*, 17th April 1854; *The Economist*, 1st July 1854, Vol. XII pp. 698-700; *The Times*, 25th July 1855), and social reformers (*vide* e.g., "Partnerships with Limited Liability" LX Westminister Review 375 (1853), "The Limited Liability Act of 1855" LXV Westminister Review 34 (1856).

political clout of the industrialists.[1] New Hampshire in 1816,[2] Connecticut in 1818,[3] Maine in 1823[4] and Massachusetts in 1830[5] enacted statutes providing for limited liability for manufacturing companies. New York enacted a general manufacturing corporation act as early as 1811 and imposed a shareholders' double liability on dissolution : a liability to pay, if needed for the benefit of the company's creditors, an amount equal to the par value of their shares even if those shares had been issued as fully paid up.[6] New Jersey enacted a similar statute in 1816.[7] Last to yield to the movement for limited liability was Rhode Island, which enacted legislation in 1847.[8] In the United States, therefore, general limited liability had emerged well before its introduction in English law.

During the entire period during which the notion of limited liability was being discussed and introduced in the United States, corporate ownership of shares in another corporation was however strictly prohibited. Some states expressly outlawed intercorporate shareholding in their general incorporation statutes.[9] In other states, the prohibition was considered to be a matter of common law.[10] Although powers of share-ownership were

---

[1] *Vide* Blumberg, *Substantive Law* p. 33.

[2] A general limited liability statute was actually passed in 1837 (N. H. Laws 1837, c. 322, p. 297), but New Hampshire had been accepting limited liability in virtually all charters since 1816. *Vide* E. Merrick Dodd, "The Evolution of Limited Liability in American Industry : Massachusetts" 61 Harv. L.R. 1351 (1948) pp. 1375-1376.

[3] Act of May Session, 1818, ch. 8, 1818 Conn. Pub. Acts 305.

[4] Act of Feb. 5, 1823, ch. 221 para. 1, 1823 Me. Laws 929.

[5] Act of Feb. 23, 1830, ch. 53, para. 8, 1830 Mass. Acts 325, 329. Special incorporation was still required but it was freely granted. Self-incorporation was provided for in 1851 (Act of May 15, 1851, Mass. Acts & Resolves 1849-1851, c. 133, p. 633). *Vide* E. Merrick Dodd, "The Evolution of Limited Liability in American Industry : Massachusetts" 61 Harv. L.R. 1351 (1948) pp. 1373-1375.

[6] New York. Act of Mar. 22, 1811, ch. 67, 1811 N.Y. Laws 111.

[7] N.J. Acts, 40th Gen. Assembly, 2d sitting, 1816.

[8] Act of June Session, 1847, R.I. Acts and Resolves 30.

[9] E.g., New York. Act of Mar. 22, 1811, ch. 67, s. 7, 1811 N.Y. Laws 111.

[10] *Vide Louisville & Nasville R. Co.* v. *Commonwealth of Kentucky* 161 U.S. 677 (1896) at p. 698; *Louis K. Liggett Co.* v. *Lee* 288 U.S. 517 (1933) at 556. *Vide* further W.T. Walker, "Some Comments on the Liability of a Parent Corporation for the Torts or Contracts of its Subsidiary" 18 Ohio State Bar Association Report 198 (1945) p. 199; William B. Hale, "Holding Companies in Illinois Law" 7 Illinois L.R. 529 (1913) pp. 529-530; Charles Scott Sykes, "Corporate Control through Holding Companies" 3 Mississippi L.J. 151 (1930). Iowa and Maryland appear to have been the only states

sometimes given in special corporate charters at least as early as 1832,[1] it was not until the last few years of the nineteenth century that states, after an increase in the demand for the privilege of corporate shareholding, started authorising corporations generally to acquire and own shares in other corporations, thus making the privilege uniform and applicable to all without favour. New Jersey - which was always eager to attract capital by its liberal policies[2] - was the first to introduce the principle in 1888.[3] Other states eventually followed suit.[4] Significantly for our purposes, it appears that the original pressure to allow corporate shareholding derived not from a desire to obtain limited liability but from the wish of large enterprises to expand their empires through shareholding in other, usually competitive, corporations.[5] Eventually, although one-man corporations were not specifically authorised by statute,[6] American courts - like their counterparts across the Atlantic - sanctified the one-man corporation.[7]

---

*Cont.*

allowing corporate shareholders in the absence of express authorisation by statute or charter. *Vide White* v. *G.W. Marquardt & Sons* 74 N.W. 930 (1898); *Davis* v. *United States Elec. Power and Light Co.* 25 A. 982, 984 (1893). There was however nothing to stop the trust concept being used as a device to avoid the effects of the restriction. Trustees could own controlling shareholdings in several companies and perform a function now served by holding companies. It was against this use of the trust that anti-trust legislation was originally directed. *Vide* D.J. Hayton, The Law of Trusts (1989) pp. 2-3.

[1]  *Vide* William Randall Compton, "Early History of Stock Ownership by Corporations" 9 George Washington L.R. 125 (1940); William P. Hackney and Tracey G. Benson, "Shareholder Liability for Inadequate Capital" 43 Univ. of Pittsburgh L.R. 837 (1982) p. 871; Blumberg, *Substantive Law* p. 57.

[2]  William Randall Compton, "Early History of Stock Ownership by Corporations". 9 George Washington L.R. 125 (1940) p. 132.

[3]  Public Laws of New Jersey, c. 269, 385 (1888).

[4]  *Vide* further Blumberg, *Substantive Law* pp. 59.

[5]  Jonathan M. Landers, "A Unified Approach to Parent, Subsidiary, and Affiliate Questions in Bankruptcy" 42 Univ. of Chicago L.R. 589 (1975) p. 619.

[6]  Indeed the internal evidence of the incorporation statutes indicated that a number of bona fide investors was contemplated.

[7]  *Louisville Banking Co.* v. *Eisenman* 21 S.W. 531, 532 (1893); *Vide* I. Maurice Wormser, "Piercing the Veil of the Corporate Entity" 12 Colum. L.R. 496 (1912) p. 515; Warner Fuller, "The Incorporated Individual : A Study of the One-Man Company" 51 Harv. L.R. 1373 (1938) p. 1374; Bernard F. Cataldo, "Limited Liability with One-Man Companies and Subsidiary Corporations" 18 Law and Contemporary Problems 473 (1953) pp. 474-475.

In the United States, therefore, corporate membership and the use of the holding-subsidiary arrangement arose several decades after the adoption of general limited liability. Yet the prevalence of the entity doctrine ensured that the holding and subsidiary companies were deemed to have separate personalities.[1] The corporate shareholder was perceived as no different from the individual shareholder. The principle of limited liability - which, many years previously had been introduced in favour of individual investors - was unwittingly extended to the corporate shareholder and therefore to the holding company. The historical record shows that limited liability was never specifically intended to insulate the holding company from the liability of its subsidiaries. Multiplicity of artificial personalities, with layer upon layer of liability-tight compartments, is far from the original conception of the corporation.[2]

## 4. SOCIO-ECONOMIC ANALYSIS OF LIMITED LIABILITY

### 4.1. Introduction

Throughout the history of company law, various reasons of a socio-economic nature have been put forward in support of the principle of limited liability. At least in England, the arguments of the early proponents of limited liability were carefully set out and remarkably refined.[3] In the United States the origins of limited liability are rather obscure and the debate surrounding its introduction does not appear to have been particularly

---

[1] *Pennsylvania Railroad Co.* v. *Jones* 155 U.S. 333 (1894).

[2] Cf. Adolf A. Berle, "The Theory of Enterprise Entity" 47 Colum. L.R. 343 (1947) p. 344.

[3] *Vide* the discussion in the following pages. In his first edition of *Company Law and Capitalism* (1972) Tom Hadden had somewhat inaccurately observed that the corporate form of organisation had not been subjected to serious analysis by the founding fathers of economics. *Ibid.* at p. 19. This statement was omitted from the second edition (1977). The truth of course is that notions of the corporate form and of limited liability were, for practically three decades, the subject of continuing and refined debate involving substantial contributions from the leading economists of the time. *Vide* generally, Christine E. Amsler, Robin L. Bartlett and Craig J. Bolton, "Thoughts of some British economists on early limited liability and corporate legislation" 13 Hist. Pol. Econ. 774 (1981).

profound.[1] In recent times, however, limited liability has attracted some vigorous debate in the United States, especially from the economic perspective.[2] With the arguments surrounding limited liability becoming even more sophisticated, limited liability is now justified on grounds which were, without doubt, beyond the contemplation of the legislator at the time of the introduction of limited liability. There is of course no grievance with that - a rule originally introduced for one set of reasons does not lose its import, if, with the passage of time, additional or other reasons justify its retention. It is submitted, however, that while the reasons which have been asserted in support of limited liability are rational and persuasive insofar as individual investors are concerned, the same reasons are either irrelevant or apply with considerably less force in the context of the holding-subsidiary arrangement.

## 4.2. The arguments for limited liability

Historically, the debate on the socio-economic advantages or disadvantages of limited liability proceeded on the underlying assumption that the investor who was to be protected by limited liability was an individual. The notion of corporate shareholders or of holding-subsidiary relationship simply did not feature in the debate. The question that now requires analysis is whether the socio-economic reasons that have supported limited liability apply *per equipollens* to the corporate group phenomenon. Naturally, the fact that limited liability was originally premised on the individual investor scenario does not automatically negate its validity in the context of corporate groups. The socio-economic advantages of limited liability generally must be identified and their cogency tested in the context of the holding-subsidiary arrangement. This exercise will be conducted in the following pages.

---

[1] *Vide* Jonathan M. Landers, "A Unified Approach to Parent, Subsidiary, and Affiliate Questions in Bankruptcy" 42 Univ. of Chicago L.R. 589 (1975) p. 617. E. Merrick Dodd, "The Evolution of Limited Liability in American Industry : Massachusetts" 61 Harv. L.R. 1351 (1948).

[2] *Vide* the material referred to in the following pages.

### 4.2.1. Creates an incentive to invest - increase in the level of economic activity

Most individual investors are - in economic terms - risk averse, especially where a large part of their assets is concerned.[1] In the absence of a rule limiting liability, the investor would be risking his entire assets : creditors of an insolvent company may seek to recover any outstanding balance from him.[2] Risk averse persons would not therefore invest in projects that may be socially desirable but risky.

The traditional justification for limiting the liability of shareholders to the capital they have invested in the company is indeed that full exposure to the risk of business failure will discourage shareholders from investing. Limited liability, by contrast, encourages "enterprise and adventure".[3] It serves as a significant investment incentive.

Unlimited liability is a particularly strong deterrent in the cases where the investor cannot effectively participate in the management of the company - as in the case of a company with widely-held shares.[4] Unlimited liability exposes the shareholder to risks that derive from a system of decision-making over which he exercises no control and from which he might be far

[1] Richard A. Posner, "The Right of Creditors of Affiliated Corporations" 43 U. Chic. L. Rev. 499 (1976) p. 502. An individual is risk averse if he prefers the certain equivalent of an expected value to a chance of a higher return - the certainty of receiving one pound to a ten per cent chance of receiving ten pounds. *Ibid.* p. 502, n. 8.

[2] Until the Joint-Stock Companies Winding-up Act of 1848 (11th & 12th Vict. c. 45) investment in joint stock companies by the less-wealthy classes was often protected by a *de facto* limitation of liability. Although each shareholder was legally responsible for all the company's debts, creditors would typically reach the assets of the wealthier shareholders. Given that shareholders who were made to pay the company's creditors had no right of recourse against other shareholders, the less wealthy shareholders often escaped any further liability. Section 84 of the Joint-Stock Companies Winding-up Act of 1848, however, provided for the appointment of a Master to supervise the liquidation of companies with powers to distribute the debts of the company in any manner he deemed appropriate. Often, the Master would distribute the debts proportionately amongst the shareholders and thereby the limitation of liability in practice applicable to the less-wealthy shareholders was removed. *Vide* J.M. Ludlow's evidence in the minutes to the Report of the Select Committee on Investments for the Savings of the Middle and Working Classes, (1850) B.P.P., Vol. XIX no. 508, Appendix, p. 5, Q. 35.

[3] *Rainham Chemical Works Ltd.* v. *Belvedere Fish Guano Co. Ltd.* [1921] 2 A.C. 465, per Buckmaster L.C. *ibid.* at p. 475.

[4] Management is not of course a function of capital investors. *Vide* Henry G. Manne, " Our Two Corporation System : Law and Economics" 53 Virginia L.R. 259 (1967) p. 261.

removed.[1] The absence of control justifies limited liability. Otherwise, investment will be further suppressed.

Even in the early days of the debate of limited liability,[2] the investment incentive function was perceived as desirable both on an individual social level as well as on a national economic level.[3] On a social level, it is evident that by the 1840's England had developed a thriving middle class, and for the first time, the working class was earning more than a subsistence wage.[4] It was    acknowledged    that    limited    liability    would    encourage    "those

---

[1] In medieval Europe it was found that men would often decline to adventure in business transactions unless they could limit their liability, especially where they had no direct control over its management. *Vide* Max Radin, "The Endless Problem of Corporate Personality" 32 Colum. L.R. 643 (1932) p. 654. In the debate on limited liability in England, this deterrent characteristic of unlimited liability was highlighted as early as 1825 by John Austin. *Vide* "Joint Stock Companies", Parliamentary History and Review, 1825 Part II, 709 p. 711. A similar observation was made by John Duncan in evidence submitted to the Select Committee on Joint Stock Companies, 1843. *Vide* Report of the Select Committee on Joint Stock Companies, (1843) B.P.P. Vol. XI no. 215, Minutes of Evidence, p. 167, Q. 2072. It was again emphasised ten years later in the final exchanges before the introduction of limited liability in 1855. *Vide* First Report, Royal Mercantile Law Commission, (1854) B.P.P. Vol. XXVII no. 1791, Appendix p. 76. Cf. also *The Economist*, 13th February 1858 (Vol. XVI pp. 166-167).

[2] Limited liability for joint stock companies had been suggested as early as 1825 in the House of Commons. *Vide* Hudson Gurney's intervention during the debate on the Joint-Stock Companies Bill in Parliamentary Debates (Hansard) New Series Vol. XII, 29th March 1856, at col. 1284.

[3] One of the earliest proponents of limited liability in England was William Clay. Addressing the House of Commons in 1836, he blamed the unprecedented expansion of credit at the time to the absence of limited liability. He argued that "by rendering all the shareholders individually responsible, you afford the most dangerous facility in obtaining credit" with the banks "feeling no necessity to limit the accommodation they afford from want of funds". Parliamentary Debates (Hansard) 3rd Series Vol. XXXIII, 12th May 1836, at col. 844. The link between unlimited liability and excessive credit had already been identified in the United States some five years previously. *Vide* E. Merrick Dodd, "The Evolution of Limited Liability in American Industry : Massachusetts" 61 Harv. L.R. 1351 (1948) p. 1370. Clay's arguments were reiterated almost twenty years later by John Stuart Mill. In Mill's view, the supposed tendency of limited partnerships to stimulate undue credit was "a charge which may be brought, far more truly, against the principle of unlimited liability." *Vide* First Report, Royal Mercantile Law Commission, (1854) B.P.P. Vol. XXVII no. 1791, Appendix p. 237.

[4] Henry N. Butler, "General Incorporation in Nineteenth Century England : Interaction of Common Law and Legislative Processes" 6 International Review of Law and Economics 169 (1986) p. 178.

unaccustomed to business" to employ their savings more productively[1] and would provide "secure investments for the savings of the poor and middle classes".[2] Limited liability would prove to be "an instrument of immense latent capacities for elevating the condition of the whole labouring class to a higher grade, both of material comfort and of intellectual and moral cultivation, than they have yet attained"[3] and would give the "humbler classes" an additional interest in the welfare of the country.[4]

On the economic level it was argued that a regime of unlimited liability was retarding or diminishing the productiveness of national capital and that much capital which was being lent on foreign loans could be employed in the national economy.[5] It was also urged that limited liability would promote the alliance of science and ability with capital.[6]

---

[1] *Vide* the observations made by Nassau Senior in H. Bellenden Ker, Report on the Law of Partnerships, (1837) B.P.P., Vol. XLIV no. 399, Appendix p. 64. *Vide* also Viscount Palmerston's speech during the Committee stage of the Limited Liability Bill 1855. *Vide* Parliamentary Debates (Hansard) 3rd Series Vol. CXXXIX, 26th July 1855, at col. 1390.

[2] *Vide* Christine E. Amsler, Robin L. Bartlett and Craig J. Bolton, "Thoughts of some British economists on early limited liability and corporate legislation" 13 Hist. Pol. Econ. 774 (1981) p. 775.

[3] John Lalor, *Money and Morals : A Book for the Times* (1852) p. 203. In giving evidence before the Select Committee on Investments for the Savings of the Middle and Working Classes in 1850, John Stuart Mill declared that "the great value of a limitation of responsibility, as relates to the working classes, would not be so much to facilitate the investment of their savings, not so much to enable the poor to lend to those who are rich, as to enable the rich to lend to those who are poor". *Vide* Report of the Select Committee on Investments for the Savings of the Middle and Working Classes, (1850) B.P.P., Vol. XIX no. 508, Minutes of Evidence, p. 78, Q. 847. *Vide* also Report of the Select Committee on the Law of Partnership, (1851) B.P.P., Vol. XVIII no. 509 pp. vi-vii; "Limited Liability in Partnership" 9 Law Review 74 (1848-1849); Article V.1 XCV Edinburgh Review 405 (1852) p. 408. In 1852, Richard Cobden stated in the House of Commons that "he was for giving to the working classes the fullest opportunity of trying experiments for themselves." *Vide* Parliamentary Debates (Hansard) 3rd Series Vol. CXIX, 17th February 1852, at col. 680.

[4] *Vide* the evidence given by J.C.B. Davis in the Report of the Select Committee on the Law of Partnership, (1851) B.P.P., Vol. XVIII no. 509 Appendix Q. 838-843. Widespread share ownership - an important facet of "popular capitalism" - remains a feature of current socio-economic policy. *Vide* "Capitalism and the saver" *Financial Times*, 6th June 1991.

[5] *Vide* H. Bellenden Ker, Report on the Law of Partnerships, (1837) B.P.P., Vol. XLIV no. 399 p. 22. (The Report however was not in favour of the introduction of the "societe' en commandite" - a partnership with both limited and unlimited partners.) *Vide* also the evidence of G.K. Richards in the First Report, Royal Mercantile Law Commission, (1854) B.P.P. Vol. XXVII no. 1791, Appendix p. 231, and the speech by Lord Stanley on

Others, however, had contended that the separation of ownership and control would lead to higher costs of operation and possibly increased risks as limited liability shifted some of the costs of failure to the creditors.[1] It was also asserted that there was an overabundance of capital[2] and that the limited liability incentive was not necessary for the development of the manufacturing and commercial sectors which had "grown up to their present unexampled state of prosperity"[3] These arguments were however soon swept aside in the surge forward towards limited liability.

However much the investment incentive may justify limited liability in the case of individual investors, it is submitted that the same incentive does not necessarily vindicate the application of limited liability to corporate shareholders. Companies do not require limited liability as an incentive to invest in projects. In other words, they will invest whether or not they are in a position to limit their liability. Unlike the individual investor, a corporate investor is less likely to be risk averse when investing.[4] A holding company is indeed likely to be risk neutral.[5] And given that the primary aim of a firm

*Cont.*
the second reading of the Limited Liability Bill 1855 in Parliamentary Debates (Hansard) 3rd Series Vol. CXXXIX, 7th August 1855, at col. 1919. The "flighting of capital" argument featured prominently in the debate on limited liability in Massachusetts in the 1820's. *Vide* E. Merrick Dodd, "The Evolution of Limited Liability in American Industry : Massachusetts" 61 Harv. L.R. 1351 (1948) p. 1367.

6  *Vide* the Communication from John Coles in H. Bellenden Ker, Report on the Law of Partnerships, (1837) B.P.P., Vol. XLIV no. 399, Appendix p. 81.

1  *Vide* Christine E. Amsler, Robin L. Bartlett and Craig J. Bolton, "Thoughts of some British economists on early limited liability and corporate legislation" 13 Hist. Pol. Econ. 774 (1981) pp. 775-776.

2  *Vide* especially the Communication by Thomas Tooke (a leading economist of the age) in H. Bellenden Ker, Report on the Law of Partnerships, (1837) B.P.P., Vol. XLIV no. 399, Appendix p. 33.

3  "Joint Stock Banks and Companies" LXIII Edinburgh Review (1836) at p. 431. *Vide* further Bishop Carleton Hunt, *The Development of the Business Corporation in England - 1800-1867* (1936) pp. 66-81.

4  Brealey and Myers, *op. cit.* p. 148. A company is less likely to be risk averse than an individual because the shareholders of a company can offset any risks incurred by that company by holding a diversified portfolio of securities. *Vide* Richard A. Posner, "The Right of Creditors of Affiliated Corporations" 43 U. Chic. L. Rev. 499 (1976) p. 502 n. 8; Lawrence D. Schall and Charles W. Haley, *Introduction to Financial Management* (2nd ed. 1980) p. 122.

5  Hansmann and Kraakman enumerate three reasons why a holding company is likely to be so. "First, it may have total assets that are relatively large compared with the potential tort damage exposure of the subsidiary firm. Second, the parent may have a number of

is to maximise its value,[1] companies would, as a rule, even in a world of unlimited liability, invest in all ventures which have a positive "net present value".[2] Naturally, a company will not invest in a venture unless the risks are adequately compensated by increased returns. But unlike a risk-averse individual, a company will not overcompensate for such risks.[3] Nor will a company invest in projects that are deemed "too risky". The availability of the subsidiary mechanism to shield a company from liability in respect of failed ventures will not, therefore, act as an incentive to invest, except in the case of unusually risky ventures. As a rule, companies would invest despite the absence of limited liability.

Another argument previously mentioned in favour of limited liability - that unlimited liability particularly hinders investment where ownership is separated from control[4] - is also inapplicable to a holding company. By definition, a holding company does, or at least can, exercise effective control.

Nor should the risk of exposure to high claims for damages in torts committed by the subsidiary be a disincentive. Liability insurance markets have matured considerably over the last decades and most corporate liabilities in tort are now insurable.

## 4.2.2. Encourages socially desirable high-risk projects

Although corporate investors are not usually as risk averse as individuals and will continue to invest even in a world of unlimited liability, certain projects will be deemed "too risky" even though they may have a positive net present

---

*Cont.*
    other subsidiaries or divisions engaged in projects whose risks are largely uncorrelated so that, as a consequence of diversification, it bears little risk in aggregate. And third, the parent may well be a publicly-traded firm whose tort risk can largely be eliminated by its stockholders through diversification of their shareholdings." *Vide* Henry Hansmann and Reiner Kraakman, "Toward Unlimited Shareholder Liability for Corporate Torts" 100 Yale L.J. 1879 (1991) p. 1882 n. 6.

[1] *Vide* Pinches, *op. cit.* p. 172; Brealey and Myers, *op. cit.* p. 22.

[2] The net present value is determined by discounting the cash inflows back to the present at the required rate of return and then subtracting the initial investment. *Vide* Pinches, *op. cit.* pp. 184, 198-199; Brealey and Myers, *op. cit.* pp. 12-13, 73-75.

[3] *Vide* Note, "Liability of Parent Corporation for Hazardous Waste Cleanup and Damages" 99 Harv. L.R. 986 (1986) pp. 989-990.

[4] *Vide supra* pp. 163-164.

value.[1] Limited liability will however enable a corporate investor to accept high-risk ventures without being exposed to ruin.[2] The investor can then hedge against failure by diversifying his shareholding.[3] Investment in high risk ventures with a positive net present value is socially desirable.[4] Unlimited liability would stultify such investment.

This advantage of limited liability clearly applies even in the context of corporate groups, especially where the group is contemplating an investment in a field - such as the development of new products - unrelated to the existing lines of business. Without limited liability, some socially desirable but risky projects which might be undertaken by large groups would not be undertaken at all.[5]

It is arguable however that limited liability also attracts investment in inefficient projects, that is, investment in projects where the total expected costs exceed the total expected benefits.[6] Limited liability may actually encourage overinvestment in very high risk projects involving the potential for tremendous losses. Because limited liability externalises costs, the company can have positive value for its shareholders even if its net present value to society is negative.[7] This incentive created by limited liability to

---

[1] *Vide* Frank H. Easterbrook and Daniel R. Fischel, "Limited Liability and the Corporation" 52 Univ. of Chicago L.R. 89 (1985) p. 97. The function of limited liability in attracting investment in a hazardous undertaking was clearly identified during the debates preceding the enactment of the Limited Liability Act 1855. *Vide* H. Bellenden Ker's evidence in the Report of the Select Committee on Investments for the Savings of the Middle and Working Classes, (1850) B.P.P., Vol. XIX no. 508, Appendix p. 61, Q. 665; p. 65, Q. 697-703.

[2] *Vide* Frank H. Easterbrook and Daniel R. Fischel, "Limited Liability and the Corporation" 52 Univ. of Chicago L.R. 89 (1985) p. 97.

[3] *Vide post* p. 173.

[4] *Vide* Frank H. Easterbrook and Daniel R. Fischel, "Limited Liability and the Corporation" 52 Univ. of Chicago L.R. 89 (1985) p. 97.

[5] A similar observation was made by Nick Budgen in the House of Commons during the debate on the Companies Bill 1980 in connection with Clinton Davis' proposal for an amendment that would have imposed liability on holding companies for the debts of subsidiaries. *Vide* Parliamentary Debates (Hansard) 5th Series Vol. 979 (House of Commons) 26th February 1980, col. 1254. *Vide* also Tom Hadden, "Inside Corporate Groups" 12 International Journal of the Sociology of Law 271-286 (1984) p. 281.

[6] *Vide* Note, "Liability of Parent Corporation for Hazardous Waste Cleanup and Damages" 99 Harv. L.R. 986 (1986) p. 990; R.S. Nathan, "Controlling the Puppeteers : Reform of Parent-Subsidiary laws in New Zealand" 3 Canterbury L.R. 1 (1986) p. 25.

[7] *Vide* Henry Hansmann and Reiner Kraakman, "Toward Unlimited Shareholder Liability for Corporate Torts" 100 Yale L.J. 1879 (1991) p. 1883.

undertake overly risky projects is probably more severe in the closely-held companies, such as subsidiaries.[1] An enterprise may be especially prompted to engage in high risk ventures - such as hazardous waste disposal - through *undercapitalised* subsidiaries.[2] Companies should not be allowed to create large risks and wield considerable power without a financial responsibility commensurate with those risks and that power.

### 4.2.3. Permits the functioning of an efficient capital market

Limited liability is indispensable to the functioning of an efficient capital market.[3] Efficiency in a capital market requires that information is widely and cheaply available to investors, that share prices quickly adjust to new information about the companies whose shares are being traded and that such share prices provide the best available unbiased estimate of future returns.[4] Limited liability promotes efficient markets because it permits the free transferability of shares by enabling shares to have a single quoted price based on the income stream generated by a company's assets. The free transferability and uniform pricing of shares engender a trading volume which is necessary for an efficient market.[5] Under a rule of unlimited liability, however, the price of shares would vary and would depend, in part, on the identity and wealth of other investors.[6] The greater the investor's wealth in relation to that of other investors, the higher the probability that the investor's wealth would be reached in the event that the company

---

[1] *Vide* Henry Hansmann and Reiner Kraakman, "Toward Unlimited Shareholder Liability for Corporate Torts" 100 Yale L.J. 1879 (1991) p. 1881; Frank H. Easterbrook and Daniel R. Fischel, "Limited Liability and the Corporation" 52 Univ. of Chicago L.R. 89 (1985) p. 110, 111.

[2] *Vide* Note, "Liability of Parent Corporation for Hazardous Waste Cleanup and Damages" 99 Harv. L.R. 986 (1986) p. 991.

[3] P. Halpern, M. Treblicock and S. Turnbull, "Economic Analysis of Limited Liability in Corporation Law" 30 U. Toronto L. J. 117 (1980) pp. 124, 136-137.

[4] *Vide* Eugene F. Fama, "Efficient Capital Markets : A Review of Theory and Empirical Work" 25 J. Fin. 383 (1970) p. 383; Brealey and Myers, *op. cit.* p. 290; Larry E. Ribstein, "Limited Liability and Theories of the Corporation" 50 Maryland L.R. 80 (1991) pp. 99-100.

[5] *Vide* generally, Ronald J. Gilson and Reiner H. Kraakman, "The Mechanisms of Market Efficiency" 70 Virginia L.R. 549 (1984).

[6] Frank H. Easterbrook and Daniel R. Fischel, "Limited Liability and the Corporation" 52 Univ. of Chicago L.R. 89 (1985) pp. 95-96.

defaults. And the greater the risk, the less such investor would pay for the shares. Different prices for a company's shares would result. Unlimited liability would impede the free transferability of shares. An organised liquid market would be impossible.

Quite obviously, an efficient capital market also requires widespread public participation. Investment should be open to all potential investors. If however both substantial investors and small investors were to be made equally liable under a regime of unlimited liability, small investments in companies would tend to come only from investors who were nearly insolvent already. Wealthy investors would not make small investments.[1] Every share would place all of the investor's personal assets at risk. The risk would be too high for the size of their investment. To guard against such risk, the investor would limit the number of companies in which he holds shares and monitor each one closely.

Under a regime of unlimited liability, moreover, an investor's exposure will, as previously noted, be conditioned by the financial position of other investors in the venture. The reason is that creditors would tend to seek recovery from the wealthier investors first. The investor would therefore need to assess the continuing financial condition of other investors. Substantial information and monitoring costs would be involved. The efficiency of the capital market would naturally be impaired.

It is evident however that none of the aforementioned considerations would usually feature in a holding-subsidiary relationship. In the case of wholly-owned subsidiaries, shares are not of course marketed at all. In the case of partly-owned subsidiaries, a market for the publicly held shares may well exist, and the "capital market efficiency" argument of limited liability would clearly apply. In such case, however, limited liability should arguably be restricted to the publicly held shares.

### 4.2.4. Enables the promotion of large projects

A fundamental reason for the introduction of limited liability was that entrepreneurs or promoters needed some device to raise capital from a relatively large number of investors.[2] Large scale ventures generally require

---

[1] Henry G. Manne, " Our Two Corporation System : Law and Economics" 53 Virginia L.R. 259 (1967) p. 124.

[2] *Vide* Henry G. Manne, " Our Two Corporation System : Law and Economics" 53 Virginia L.R. 259 (1967) pp. 260, 262. This advantage of limited liability was recognised at least

many investors and may involve considerable risks. A general rule of unlimited liability would almost certainly hinder large scale projects.[1] The investors' unlimited exposure to risks combined with the loss of participation in management will create disincentives to invest. Limited liability, on the other hand, neutralises such disincentives and permits the promotion of substantial ventures through widely-held companies.[2] In the case of a holding-subsidiary arrangement, however, the question of a widespread allocation of shares is obviously inapplicable.

### 4.2.5. Diminishes agency and social costs - spreads risks efficiently

For an investor, the separation of ownership and control within a company can involve considerable agency costs. These agency costs arise primarily from the need to monitor the activities of management. Undoubtedly, these agency costs on the part of the investor will be experienced both in a limited liability as well as in an unlimited liability regime.[3] In the absence of limited liability, however, agency costs are almost certain to be higher : the activities of the company would not merely affect the wealth of the enterprise (and therefore the value of the investment) but could also expose the investors to the risk of substantial liability. Moreover, in the absence of limited liability, the greater the wealth of the other shareholders, the lower the probability that any one shareholder's assets will be needed to settle the claim. Each shareholder would have to engage in costly monitoring of the other

*Cont.*
as early as 1836. Hunt notes that the point was made in the Circular to Bankers of April 22, 1836. *Vide* Bishop Carleton Hunt, *The Development of the Business Corporation in England - 1800-1867* (1936) p. 73. The increased availability of funds for projects is still recognised as a real benefit of limited liability. *Vide* Frank H. Easterbrook and Daniel R. Fischel, "Limited Liability and the Corporation" 52 Univ. of Chicago L.R. 89 (1985) p. 97.

[1] *Vide* Max Radin, "The Endless Problem of Corporate Personality" 32 Colum. L.R. 643 (1932) p. 654; John Hicks, "Limited Liability : the Pros and Cons" in Tony Orhnial (ed.), *Limited Liability and the Corporation* (1982) pp. 11-12.

[2] In 1926, The Economist remarked that the limited liability company provided "the means by which huge aggregations of capital ... were collected, organized and efficiently administered." *The Economist*, 18th December 1926 (Vol. CIII p. 1053).

[3] *Vide* P. Halpern, M. Treblicock and S. Turnbull, "Economic Analysis of Limited Liability in Corporation Law" 30 U. Toronto L. J. 117 (1980) p. 136; Tony Orhnial, "Liability Laws and Company Finance" in Tony Orhnial (ed.), *Limited Liability and the Corporation* (1982) pp. 181-184.

shareholders in the company to ensure that such other shareholders will neither prejudice their estate nor transfer their shares to investors with less wealth.[1]

Even *creditors'* agency costs would be higher in the case of unlimited liability : creditors may have to monitor the wealth of a constantly shifting body of shareholders.[2] Part of these costs is incurred at the time when credit is extended. Another part of the costs will be of an on-going nature in order to keep the wealth of the shareholders under surveillance.

Clearly, therefore, a rule of unlimited liability would increase agency costs.[3] Limited liability minimises these costs by shifting an easily recognisable risk to the company's creditors.[4] Moreover, by minimising the costs of raising money for investment, an efficient company law reduces the overall social costs of capital.[5] This risk spreading and allocation of costs is of course appropriate where the creditors are better able to monitor the company than the shareholders. It would therefore be desirable for example in the case of publicly-held companies.

It is evident, however, that investors' agency costs would not usually arise in the case of a holding-subsidiary arrangement.[6] In such a case, ownership is not separated from control : a holding company may be directly

---

[1] *Vide* Frank H. Easterbrook and Daniel R. Fischel, "Limited Liability and the Corporation" 52 Univ. of Chicago L.R. 89 (1985) p. 95.

[2] *Vide* generally P. Halpern, M. Treblicock and S. Turnbull, "Economic Analysis of Limited Liability in Corporation Law" 30 U. Toronto L. J. 117 (1980) pp. 133-135.

[3] *Vide* P. Halpern, M. Treblicock and S. Turnbull, "Economic Analysis of Limited Liability in Corporation Law" 30 U. Toronto L. J. 117 (1980) p. 125. Meiners, Mofsky and Tollison, however, argue that regardless of the liability rule, investors will often be unwilling to participate in the management of a company. In their view share prices vary with the investment risk and thus embody all the information, aside from undisclosed inside information, that investors need to make investment decisions. Moreover, they assert that in a world of unlimited liability it is unlikely that creditors would pursue claims against all shareholders because of the high cost of litigation. Creditors will instead only be concerned with those shareholders having the greatest wealth. *Vide* Roger E. Meiners, James S. Mofsky and Robert D. Tollinson, "Piercing the Veil of Limited Liability" 4 Delaware Journal of Corporation Law 351 (1979) p. 363.

[4] *Vide* Henry G. Manne, " Our Two Corporation System : Law and Economics" 53 Virginia L.R. 259 (1967) p. 262; Richard A. Posner, "The Right of Creditors of Affiliated Corporations" 43 U. Chic. L. Rev. 499 (1976) p. 509.

[5] *Vide* Richard A. Posner, "The Right of Creditors of Affiliated Corporations" 43 U. Chic. L. Rev. 499 (1976) pp. 508-509.

[6] *Vide* Tony Orhnial, "Liability Laws and Company Finance" in Tony Orhnial (ed.), *Limited Liability and the Corporation* (1982) p. 182; Blumberg, *Substantive Law* p. 95.

involved in the activities of its subsidiaries and can undoubtedly monitor them better than the creditors can.[1] Because of its controlling interest, a holding company can cheaply and effectively oversee its subsidiaries. Nor would creditors' agency costs be substantial. Creditors need only monitor the wealth of the holding company.[2] In the corporate group context, limited liability will not therefore have the effect of economising on agency costs. Indeed, agency costs will be lower with a rule of unlimited, rather than limited, liability.

### 4.2.6. Encourages diversified portfolios

The holding of a diversified portfolio is widely regarded as a more efficient form of investment : investors can reduce risk by owning a diversified portfolio of assets.[3] A rule of unlimited liability however deters such efficient diversification. The reason is that with unlimited liability diversification increases rather than minimises the risk : if one company becomes insolvent, the investor could lose his entire wealth. Investors would restrict the portfolio down to a minimum and would bear risk that could have been avoided by diversification. The cost to companies of raising capital would rise.[4] Limited liability avoids these inefficiencies.

Yet although the opportunity to diversify is certainly desirable both for individual and even corporate investors generally, it is likely that a holding company would still be able to spread the risk of liability for the debts of an insolvent subsidiary. In any case, the holding company's control of the activities of its subsidiary allows it to assess the risk of insolvency and take appropriate measures to minimise any potential liability.

---

[1] Limited liability moreover does not efficiently allocate risk between shareholders and involuntary creditors, who, by definition, are unable to monitor the company. On the peculiar position of involuntary creditors, *vide post* pp. 176-186.

[2] Halpern et al. concede that unlimited liability might be a more efficient rule in firms which are closely held or small. *Vide* P. Halpern, M. Treblicock and S. Turnbull, "Economic Analysis of Limited Liability in Corporation Law" 30 U. Toronto L. J. 117 (1980) pp. 135, 148-150.

[3] Henry G. Manne, " Our Two Corporation System : Law and Economics" 53 Virginia L.R. 259 (1967) p. 262; Frank H. Easterbrook and Daniel R. Fischel, "Limited Liability and the Corporation" 52 Univ. of Chicago L.R. 89 (1985) pp. 96-97; Brealey and Myers, *op. cit.* pp. 136-139.

[4] Frank H. Easterbrook and Daniel R. Fischel, "Limited Liability and the Corporation" 52 Univ. of Chicago L.R. 89 (1985) p. 97.

## 4.2.7. Reduces costs of contracting around liability

A significant advantage of a rule of limited liability lies in providing a standard, implied contract term, so that a company does not have to stipulate such a term (in favour of its shareholders) every time it transacts business. If the limited liability rule accurately reflects the normal desires of the contracting parties, transaction costs are actually being minimised.[1] The question is whether, in an unlimited liability regime for holding companies, the parties would generally contract out of unlimited liability. It is surmised, that as a rule the parties would not do so. And there appear to be no empirical or theoretical considerations suggesting otherwise.[2] In any event, to support limited liability on the basis that it reduces the costs of contracting around liability ignores the position of involuntary creditors with whom, of course, no negotiation is usually feasible.[3]

## 4.2.8. Avoids litigation and bankruptcy costs

Limited liability is also justified on the basis that it minimises the costs of resolving legal disputes.[4] With a rule of unlimited liability, creditors of an

---

[1] *Vide* Richard A. Posner, "The Right of Creditors of Affiliated Corporations" 43 U. Chic. L. Rev. 499 (1976) p. 506. Easterbrook and Fischel contend that if limited liability were not provided by law, companies would attempt to create it by contract. *Vide* Frank H. Easterbrook and Daniel R. Fischel, "Limited Liability and the Corporation" 52 Univ. of Chicago L.R. 89 (1985) p. 93.

[2] Blumberg would disagree. He implies that contracting parties in a creditor-subsidiary relationship would generally contract for limited liability. *Vide* Blumberg, *Substantive Law* p. 96. Posner would also disagree. He assumes that in the case of large enterprises, creditors normally would have little reason to seek to be able to reach the assets of the holding company and that in the case of small companies, the debtor would normally insist on expressly limiting the liability of the holding company. In his view, therefore, contracting around unlimited liability would occur frequently and would be a source of substantial and avoidable costs. *Vide* Richard A. Posner, "The Right of Creditors of Affiliated Corporations" 43 U. Chic. L. Rev. 499 (1976) p. 515.

[3] *Vide post* pp. 177-178, 182.

[4] *Vide* Richard A. Posner, "The Right of Creditors of Affiliated Corporations" 43 U. Chic. L. Rev. 499 (1976) pp. 525-526; P. Halpern, M. Treblicock and S. Turnbull, "Economic Analysis of Limited Liability in Corporation Law" 30 U. Toronto L. J. 117 (1980) p. 132. The question of litigation costs has attracted elaborate debate on the economic plane. *Vide* Steven Shavell, "The Social versus the Private Incentive to Bring Suit in a Costly

insolvent company would be able to recover from the various shareholders. The volume of litigation and associated costs would be increased, especially if inter-shareholder apportioning claims are also taken into account. These costs may even surpass the gains from internalising the costs of the company's activities. Yet once again, though this argument may well apply in the case of widely-owned companies,[1] it does not justify the extension of limited liability to the holding company. For if the holding company were to be held liable under a rule of unlimited liability, it would be the only additional defendant involved in litigation. Of course the number of potential claims against holding companies would increase.[2] But the increase should not be so substantial as to discourage a rule of unlimited liability on the ground of excessive litigation costs.

### 4.2.9. Socio-economic analysis - conclusion

The foregoing analysis demonstrates beyond question the socio-economic utility of limited liability as a general rule. In the context of corporate groups however, the arguments for limited liability are largely inapplicable. Underlying this observation are some inherent differences between the traditional corporate model and the holding-subsidiary arrangement. A basic difference of course is that in the holding-subsidiary arrangement, limited liability would already have been acquired by the shareholders in the holding company. The fundamental function of limited liability would therefore already have been served. In the second place, a holding-subsidiary arrangement does not typically involve a widespread public participation of shareholders. And yet, several benefits of limited liability presuppose the

*Cont.*

Legal System" 11 J. Legal Stud. 333 (1982); Louis Kaplow, "Private versus Social costs in Bringing Suit" 15 J. Legal Stud. 371 (1986).

[1] A point conceded in P. Halpern, M. Treblicock and S. Turnbull, "Economic Analysis of Limited Liability in Corporation Law" 30 U. Toronto L. J. 117 (1980) p. 132 and "Liability of Parent Corporation for Hazardous Waste Cleanup and Damages" 99 Harv. L.R. 986 (1986) p. 997. But *vide contra* Blumberg, *Substantive Law* p. 72; Henry Hansmann and Reiner Kraakman, "Toward Unlimited Shareholder Liability for Corporate Torts" 100 Yale L.J. 1879 (1991) pp. 1925, 1933. Blumberg and Hansmann and Kraakman argue that even the larger publicly-held companies do not present insurmountable obstacles to the judicial administration of an unlimited liability rule. Blumberg and Hansmann and Kraakman however ignore the question of costs.

[2] A point observed in Richard A. Posner, "The Right of Creditors of Affiliated Corporations" 43 U. Chic. L. Rev. 499 (1976) p. 526.

existence of widespread shareholding.[1] Finally, in a holding-subsidiary arrangement, none of the efficiency based arguments relating to the separation of ownership from control apply. The holding company is either effectively in control or at least has the capability so to be.

## 5.  THE RELEVANCE OF DIFFERENT TYPES OF CREDITORS

### 5.1. The meaning and role of credit

Credit is regarded as the cornerstone of the trading and industrial communities.[2] Credit provides those who possess capital with a market for their capital. In this way considerable resources can be put into circulation for the benefit of society as a whole. Credit is, of course, beneficial also to the debtor who exploits the capital provided by others.

In this context, "credit" refers to the deliberate extension - by a creditor in favour of his debtor - of time for the fulfilment of the obligation. In this sense, credit is extended by banks and lending institutions to entrepreneurs, by trade suppliers to customers, by manufacturers to customers, by customers to manufacturers, by employees and pensioners to employers, by the Government to commercial enterprises, and so on. In each of such cases, the creditor has an element of choice before entering into the transaction.

Sometimes, unfortunately, there is a breakdown of credit. The debtor is unable to fulfil his obligation. Hardship follows. Credit gives rise to a dilemma. On the one hand, there is the fundamental importance of credit; on the other, there is the hardship that could result on the breakdown of credit. A balance must be sought. Notionally, this can perhaps be achieved by giving the creditor confidence to extend credit without encouraging the debtor to behave irresponsibly.

### 5.2. Credit in the corporate world

The dilemma enters a more complex dimension in the corporate world. There the principle of limited liability may add further hardship to creditors.

---

[1] Admittedly, participation by minority shareholders in a partly-owned subsidiary may re-introduce the relevance of some of the benefits of limited liability.

[2] The Cork Report, para. 10, p. 10.

In economic terms, limited liability shifts the costs of entrepreneurship from the shareholders to creditors.[1] Creditors subsidise the owners. The enterprise avoids the costs of fully funding its liabilities.

In defence of the rule of limited liability and the hardship caused to creditors it is often asserted that creditors know that they are dealing with limited liability companies[2] and can either negotiate around the limited liability rule (by demanding appropriate security or a guarantee from the shareholders)[3] or adjust for the risk (by requiring a higher price).[4] Otherwise, they have to assume the risk of business failure. In legal terms, it is said, limited liability is but an implementation of the bargain between the parties.

### 5.3. Existence of "non-consensual" creditors

So far, the discussion has proceeded on the assumption that creditors deliberately consent to the relationship with the corporate debtor. It is plainly obvious, however, that creditors are not all "consensual".[5] Some creditors,

---

[1] *Vide* Tony Orhnial, "Liability Laws and Company Finance" in Tony Orhnial (ed.), *Limited Liability and the Corporation* (1982) pp. 180-181; Henry G. Manne, " Our Two Corporation System : Law and Economics" 53 Virginia L.R. 259 (1967) p. 262; R.A. Posner, *Economic Analysis of Law* (2nd ed. 1977) p. 292.

[2] *Vide* e.g., Lords Watson, Herschell and Macnaghten in *Salomon* v. *A. Salomon and Co. Ltd.* [1897] A.C. 22 (H.L.) at pp. 40, 44-45 and p. 53 respectively. *Vide* also Bernard F. Cataldo, "Limited Liability with One-Man Companies and Subsidiary Corporations" 18 Law and Contemporary Problems 473 (1953) p. 476; Allan G. Gimbel, "Piercing the Corporate Veil" 4 Univ. of Florida L.R. 352 (1951) p. 359; CBI Memorandum (1980) para. 20 p. 7; Note, "Should Shareholders Be Personally Liable For the Torts of Their Corporations" 76 Yale L.J. 1190 (1967) p. 1190; Salmond, *op. cit.* p. 320.

[3] *Vide* Edwin J. Bradley, "A Comparative Evaluation of the Delaware and Maryland Close Corporation Statutes" [1968] Duke L.J. 525, p. 554; Robert W. Hamilton, "The Corporate Entity" 49 Texas L.R. 979 (1971) p. 984; R.A. Posner, *Economic Analysis of Law* (2nd ed. 1977) pp. 292-293; CBI Memorandum (1980) paras. 20, 22, p. 7. Cf. *White* v. *Winchester Land Development Corp.* 584 S.W.2d 56, 62 (Ky. App. 1979).

[4] *Vide* Richard A. Posner, "The Right of Creditors of Affiliated Corporations" 43 U. Chic. L. Rev. 499 (1976) pp. 501-505.

[5] A fact conveniently overlooked by Lord Herschell in *Salomon* v. *A. Salomon and Co. Ltd.* [1897] A.C. 22 (H.L.) when he justified the potential hardship to creditors on the basis that "[t]he creditor has notice that he is dealing with a company the liability of the members of which is limited". *Ibid.* p. 45. A similar *lapsus* was made in *Dollar Cleansers and Dyers, Inc.* v. *MacGregor* 161 A. 159, 161 (1932). The existence of involuntary creditors was also generally ignored by commentators. *Vide* e.g., Henry Thring, *The Joint*

typically accident victims and other tort claimants, simply do not "extend" credit. They do not choose to enter into a transaction. Their claim arises not out of a consensual arrangement with the debtor, but out of the unlawful act of the debtor. Clearly therefore, the argument that creditors know that they deal with limited liability companies and can take appropriate measures is untenable. *Ex hypothesis*, non-consensual creditors do not know that they have dealt with such a company until after the event. In economic terms, limited liability enables the owners of a company to effect uncompensated transfers of the risk of business failure to such creditors.[1] Shifting the cost of entrepreneurship from shareholders to such creditors through the principle of limited liability appears unreasonable.

### 5.4. Corporate liability in tort ignored in the nineteenth century debate

Somewhat surprisingly, the position of tort claimants appears to have been entirely overlooked during the great debate in the earlier part of the nineteenth century on the virtues or otherwise of limited liability. No reference to the lot of tort creditors was ever made in any of the Parliamentary reports commissioned at the time,[2] or in the Parliamentary

---

*Cont.*

*Stock Companies Act 1856* (1856) p. 7 and the Note in the Law Quarterly Review of 1897, 13 L.Q.R. 6 (1897). In an otherwise brilliant article, Radin also neglects the involuntary creditors' position. Defending the principle of limited liability he insists that if the company apprises all those who deal with it of the fact, "it is impossible to see how anyone can be injured". *Vide* Max Radin, "The Endless Problem of Corporate Personality" 32 Colum. L.R. 643 (1932) p. 655. Recent judgments similarly talk of creditors being the "guardians of their own interests" and fail to recognise the unique position of involuntary creditors. *Vide* e.g., *Nicholson* v. *Permakraft (NZ) Ltd.* [1985] 1 NZLR 242, especially at p. 250 per Cooke J. One early commentator did however appear to appreciate the impact that limited liability would have on involuntary creditors. *Vide* Cox, *op. cit.* p. v.

[1] *Vide* P. Halpern, M. Treblicock and S. Turnbull, "Economic Analysis of Limited Liability in Corporation Law" 30 U. Toronto L. J. 117 (1980) p. 145. Many economists acknowledge that some form of unlimited liability may be justified with respect to involuntary creditors. E.g., Halpern *et al. ibid.* p. 145.

[2] H. Bellenden Ker, Report on the Law of Partnerships, (1837) B.P.P., Vol. XLIV no. 399; Report of the Select Committee on Investments for the Savings of the Middle and Working Classes, (1850) B.P.P., Vol. XIX no. 508; Report of the Select Committee on the Law of Partnership, (1851) B.P.P., Vol. XVIII no. 509; First Report, Royal Mercantile Law Commission, (1854) B.P.P. Vol. XXVII no. 1791. In making submissions to the Royal Commission on Mercantile Law, Robert Lowe defended limited liability on the

debates or in any of the writings on the subject.[1] And yet there is no doubt that bodies corporate could during the relative period have been held liable in tort - at least in those actions which did not require the existence of malice.[2] In 1812, for example, it was held that a corporation could be sued in trover.[3] And in 1842 it was held that a corporation could be held liable in trespass.[4] Still, the arguments for and against limited liability seem to have centred exclusively around the contract creditor without any mention of the tort claimant. There may be a possible explanation for the lack of interest in the tort claimants' lot. Liability in tort for negligence - which is of course of paramount importance in the modern corporate scene - only started to be

---

*Cont.*
basis that "if people are willing to contract on the terms of relieving the party embarking his capital from loss beyond a certain amount, there is nothing in natural justice to prevent it." *Vide* First Report, Royal Mercantile Law Commission, (1854) B.P.P. Vol. XXVII no. 1791, Appendix p. 84.

[1] The only exception appears to have been an editorial in the *Law Times*, written three years *after* the enactment of the Limited Liability Act 1855. *The Law Times* had been opposed to the introduction of the "monstrous immorality" of limited liability and in calling for the repeal of "the law which disgraces the statute-book and dishonours the country" remarked that the Limited Liability Act in effect "exempted men from liability to pay their debts, perform their contracts and *make reparation for their wrongs*". *Vide The Law Times*, 27th March, 1858 p. 14 (emphasis added). The comment on making "reparation for his wrongs" is possibly a reference to liability in tort.

[2] Corporate liability for torts involving malice was finally established in the last decade of the 19th century. *Vide Kent* v. *Courage and Co. Ltd. (Croft* v. *Same)* (1890) 55 J.P. 264; *Cornford* v. *Carlton Bank Limited* [(1899] 1 Q.B. 392.

[3] *Yarborough* v. *The Bank of England* (1812) 16 East 6. In this case, Lord Ellenborough stated wherever corporations "can competently do or order any act to be done on their behalf ... they are liable to the consequences of such act, if it be of a tortious nature, and to the prejudice of others." *Ibid.* at p. 7.

[4] *Maund* v. *Monmouthshire Canal Co.* (1842) 4 Man. & G. 452; *Eastern Counties Railway Co.* v. *Broom* (1851) 6 Ex. 314. In the United States it was held, as early as 1818, that a corporation could be liable in trespass. *Vide Chestnut Hill T. Co.* v. *Rutter* 4 Sergeant & Rawle 6 (Penn. March, 1818). By the middle of the nineteenth century it had also been established that a corporation could be indicted for certain criminal offences. *Vide R.* v. *Birmingham and Gloucester Railway Co.* (1842) 3 Q.B. 223; *R.* v. *Great North of England Railway Co.* (1846) 9 Q.B. 315. On the development of corporate liability during the nineteenth century *vide* generally C.T. Carr, *The General Principles of the Law of Corporations* (1905) pp. 72-105; S.J. Stoljar, *Groups and Entities - An Inquiry into Corporate Theory* (1973) pp. 159-161; Frederick Hallis, *Corporate Personality : A Study in Jurisprudence* (1930) pp. xliv-xlvii.

recognised as a separate and independent basis of liability around 1825[1] and it had not yet been well developed by the time of the introduction of general limited liability in the United States in the 1820's and 1830's[2] and in England in 1855.[3] The chances of corporate liability in tort were therefore considerably slimmer when compared with liability in contract.[4] Indeed, torts that could bankrupt a company were apparently unheard of. No one therefore would have expected the principle of limited liability to entail any more than protecting investors from unsatisfied claims of the company's contract creditors. It is this relative insignificance of tort liability in a corporate context which may explain the exclusion of the tort claimants' position from the debate. When, at a later stage in the evolution of the law, considerable advances were being achieved in the law of negligence - and corporate liability for wrongdoing had evolved from the exception to the rule - the notion of limited liability had unfortunately already been entrenched in the law. And yet, the fact that limited liability had been defended on the basis of the creditor's deliberate assumption of the risk without a recognition that different considerations could perhaps have applied in the case of liability in negligence, was never subsequently highlighted or debated. Given that limited liability imperceptibly took on a function not originally intended, it is regrettable that no reassessment of the position has ever been attempted.

## 5.5. Limited liability and tort objectives

Limited liability also conflicts with some fundamental objectives of tort law. The paramount objective of tort law is the provision of adequate compensation for victims.[5] Limited liability can undermine this objective because claimants may receive only a proportionate part, if at all, of what is

---

[1] *Vide* Percy H. Winfield, "The History of Negligence in the Law of Torts" 42 L.Q.R. 184 (1926) especially at pp. 195-199.

[2] *Vide supra* pp. 158-161.

[3] *Vide supra* pp. 155-158.

[4] For a time, the doctrine of *ultra vires* was also to contribute to the difficulties of establishing corporate liability in tort. On the doctrine of *ultra vires* in the context of corporate torts *vide* A.L. Goodhart, "Corporate Liability in Tort and the Doctrine of *Ultra Vires*" 2 C.L.J. 350 (1926); Dafydd Jenkins, "Corporate Liability in Tort and the Doctrine of *Ultra Vires*" [1970] Ir. Jur. 11.

[5] *Vide* B.S. Markensis and S.F. Deakin, *Tort Law* (3rd ed. 1994) p. 38; William L. Prosser, *Handbook of the Law of Torts* (4th ed. 1971) p. 6.

due to them. Another basic objective of tort law is deterrence.[1] Limited liability can thwart this objective because those in control of an enterprise may be tempted to disregard any penalties beyond the company's capacity to pay.[2] An enterprise may, for example, be inclined to externalise the risks of its more hazardous ventures by establishing subsidiaries.[3] Another - more modern - objective of tort law is the allocation of liability to the party involved in the economic process who has the resources available for the satisfaction of costs properly allowable to the product.[4] Tort law seeks to spread the risk of loss to all consumers so that "the product will bear the social and individual costs of its own defects".[5] Limited liability, however, can actually shift the risk onto the consumers themselves by denying them a remedy. Company law appears to use the principle of limited liability for the benefit of a select group of persons (and, to be sure, for the benefit of the economy as a whole) without arguably taking enough heed of another group which the law also deems worthy of protection.

---

[1] *Vide* K.M. Stanton, *The Modern Law of Tort* (1994) p. 11; Prosser, *op. cit.* p. 23. But *vide* Markensis and Deakin, *op. cit.* pp. 36-38. In an incisive and comprehensive article, Professor Schwartz argues that between the economists' claim that tort law systematically deters and the critics' response that tort law rarely deters, there lies an intermediate position : that tort law, while not as effective as economic models suggest, is still useful in achieving stated deterrence goals. *Vide* Gary T. Schwartz, "Reality in the Economic Analysis of Tort Law : Does Tort Law Really Deter?" 42 U.C.L.A. L. Rev. 377 (1994).

[2] Admittedly, the problem of "moral hazard" would exist even under a rule of unlimited liability. Indeed, the incentive to conduct overly risky activities occurs whenever a person or a company has insufficient assets to cover its anticipated liabilities. *Vide* generally Steven Shavell, "Liability for Harm versus Regulation of Safety" 13 J. Legal Stud. 357 (1984) pp. 360-363. Surely, however, the problem must be more acute under a regime of limited liability.

[3] Cf. Note, "Should Shareholders be personally liable for the Torts of their Corporations". 76 Yale L.J. 1190 (1967) p. 1195; Christopher Stone, "Place of Enterprise Liability in the Control of Corporate Conduct" 90 Yale L.J. 1 (1980) pp. 68, 71. The moral hazard problem is probably more serious in the holding-subsidiary situation because subsidiaries have less incentive to insure. *Vide* Frank H. Easterbrook and Daniel R. Fischel, "Limited Liability and the Corporation" 52 Univ. of Chicago L.R. 89 (1985) p. 111.

[4] *Vide* Blumberg, *Substantive Law* p. 163.

[5] *Bonee* v. *L & M Constr. Chemicals* 518 F. Supp. 375 (M.D. Tenn. 1981) at p. 381. *Vide* generally, Guido Calabresi, "Some Thoughts on Risk Distribution and the Law of Torts" 70 Yale L.J. 499 (1961); George L. Priest, "The Invention of Enterprise Liability : A Critical History of the Intellectual Foundations of Modern Tort Law" 14 J. Legal Stud. 461 (1985).

## 5.6. Parameters of voluntary/involuntary creditors' distinction

More fundamentally, it is submitted that the analysis on limited liability should not rest merely on whether or not the parties have given their consent to the relationship out of which the claim arises. The distinction, in other words, is not simply between those creditors who had consented to the relationship and those who did not. Consent is only the threshold question. What counts is whether the creditor really had the practical opportunity and means of assessing the risk of dealing with a corporate debtor. A distinction is therefore drawn in this work between "voluntary" creditors (that is consensual creditors who had the practical opportunity of assessing their debtor) and "involuntary" creditors (that is those creditors, consensual or otherwise, who did not have such opportunity).[1]

The nature of the distinction requires illustration and some further elaboration. To begin with it ought to be clear that among the consensual creditors are (i) those who actually investigate the credit-worthiness of the debtor (typically, such creditors would include banks and other lending institutions); (ii) those who did not investigate but who could have done so (a variety of creditors, such as substantial trade creditors, could fall under this division); and (iii) those who could not have been reasonably expected to conduct the inquiry (such as many trade creditors, consumers, employees, pensioners, and even the Government in respect of VAT and PAYE and national insurance contributions).[2] These categories should not, of course, be viewed exclusively or rigidly, for various factual patterns may arise.

Some of these creditors require further analysis.

## 5.6.1. Trade creditors

Trade creditors present added difficulties. Admittedly, trade creditors would sometimes be expected to investigate the credit standing of their debtors, say where considerable sums are involved, where there is reason to doubt the debtors' solvency, or where long-term credit is extended. In most situations, however, trade creditors are not expected to conduct an investigation or to bargain for a price adjustment to reflect increased risks. Apart from the question whether trade creditors should or should not be expected to conduct

---

[1] Tort victims would obviously also be included as "involuntary" creditors.

[2] *In Re Stanford Services Ltd.* [1987] BCLC 607, the Court considered the Crown as an "involuntary creditor" with respect to VAT, PAYE and National Insurance contributions.

inquiries or bargain for price adjustments, it is evident, even in the absence of empirical data, that trade creditors do *not* normally make any such inquiries[1] or strike any such bargains.[2] To do so would usually involve an inordinately high cost in relation to the value of the transaction.[3] Still, the law ought not perhaps be overly protective. Trade creditors are customarily aware of credit risks and though they might not weigh credit risks on an individual-transaction basis, they generally account for such risk in their overall pricing and budgeting policies and by providing for a reasonable margin of bad debts. Moreover, trade creditors actually pass on a part of the risk to others. Bad debts, for example, are deductible for tax purposes.[4] Part of the loss is therefore absorbed by the Revenue. Consumers too bear part of the loss through increased prices. In reality, therefore, trade creditors ordinarily shift much of the risk rather than absorb it. All told, it is submitted that trade creditors should not qualify as "involuntary" creditors for the purposes of the reform proposals set out in this work.

### 5.6.2. Involuntary claims arising out of contractual relationships

A claim, while traceable to a consensual transaction, may not reasonably have been anticipated at the time of the transaction. A consumer makes a retail purchase. The transaction is concluded on a cash on delivery basis. It would be preposterous to suggest that the consumer conduct a credit investigation. After all, he is not extending credit to the supplier. And yet what happens if the item which has been purchased breaks down within the warranty period and the debtor has in the meantime plunged into insolvency?

---

[1] *Vide* O. Kahn-Freund, "Some Reflections on Company Law Reform" 7 M.L.R. 54 (1944) pp. 58-59. Cf. also Lindley L.J.'s observations in *Broderip* v. *Salomon* [1895] 2 Ch. 323 (C.A.) at p. 339.

[2] *Vide contra* R.C. Downs, "Piercing the Corporate Veil - Do Corporations provide Limited Personal Liability?" 53 UMKC L.R. 174 (1985) where it is asserted that most business relationships are negotiable. *Ibid.* p. 197.

[3] The trade creditor could investigate the financial position of each corporate debtor and pass on the added expense to his own customer by raising the price of his product. Yet the cost of incurring an occasional default due to insolvency of the corporate debtor is generally less than the cost of investigating each corporate debtor. *Vide* Richard A. Posner, "The Right of Creditors of Affiliated Corporations" 43 U. Chic. L. Rev. 499 (1976) pp. 507-508.

[4] *Vide* Income and Corporation Taxes Act 1988, s. 74(j). In the United States, deductions for bad debts are regulated by s. 166 of the Internal Revenue Code (26 U.S.C.).

Surely, the claimant ought not to be considered a voluntary creditor for the purpose of the breach of warranty claim? In other words there should be room for a distinction between a creditor who voluntarily extends credit and one whose claim did not relate at all to the extension of credit. The same should be true even in the case of a claim in tort which arose out of a contractual relationship, such as a passenger injured whilst riding in a taxi, an employee who suffers an accident at his place of work, and the person who has been poisoned by the food in a restaurant. Only if such claimants can reasonably be understood to have contracted in substantial awareness of the risks of injury should they qualify as voluntary creditors in respect of the claim.

### 5.6.3. Employees

The position of employees in relation to the principle of limited liability merits separate consideration. Of all the consensual creditors, employees probably suffer the most severe informational disabilities, are the least able to diversify the risk of business failure and have the least capacity to absorb losses.[1] And yet, some writers persist in placing employees on an equal footing with financial creditors. Posner, for example, surprisingly argues[2] that the employee who is not paid until the end of the week is a creditor (true), and that his estimation of the risk of default will determine the amount of credit extended, the length of time for which it is extended, and the interest rate (false). Posner's views are drowned in unrealistic economic analysis. As a fact, employees do not ask for a set of financial statements from their prospective employers. They do not delve into their employers' financial position. And it would be fatuous to expect them to do so. They should therefore qualify as involuntary creditors. The law, admittedly, does afford employees some measure of protection in so far as wages and salaries are concerned.[3] Employees are also the principal victims of industrial

---

[1] P. Halpern, M. Treblicock and S. Turnbull, "Economic Analysis of Limited Liability in Corporation Law" 30 U. Toronto L. J. 117 (1980) p. 149.

[2] *Vide* Richard A. Posner, "The Right of Creditors of Affiliated Corporations" 43 U. Chic. L. Rev. 499 (1976) p. 505.

[3] Employees of an insolvent employer, for example, may be entitled to a payment under the National Insurance Fund. *Vide* Gwyneth Pitt, *Employment Law* (1992) p. 202; Norman Selwyn, *Law of Employment* (8th ed. 1993) paras. 5.88-5.91, pp. 182-183. In the United States, the bankruptcy laws accord employees a priority on their employer's bankruptcy ahead of most other claimants. *Vide* further Blumberg, *Substantive Law* p. 80.

accidents and as such should, for the purposes of the present discussion, be considered as involuntary creditors even though their cause of action may probably be framed in contract.[1] In this regard, the law does - through compulsory employers' liability insurance - provide such claimants with a remedy.[2] Industrial accidents - at least *vis-a-vis* employees - would appear to put no untoward pressure on the principle of limited liability. The insurance solution shifts the problem out of the corporate arena.

### 5.6.4. Unsophisticated creditors generally

Proponents of the privilege of limited liability argue that a contract involves a bargain in which both the identity and the creditworthiness of the contracting parties represent key elements of the bargain. Moreover, it is claimed, contract creditors can investigate and assess the creditworthiness of their corporate debtor.[3] After all, it is said, financial statements are published precisely for that purpose.[4] This line of argumentation is tenable only to a very limited extent. Certainly, it applies to the sophisticated financial creditor. But what about the unsophisticated creditor? Should it be assumed that a neophyte can readily interpret a company's financial statements, even if an updated set were to be available?[5] Even to merely suggest so sounds absurd.[6] A partial solution may be for the directors'

---

[1] *Vide* Roger W. Rideout, *Principles of Labour Law* (3rd ed. 1979) p. 370.

[2] *Vide* the Employers' Liability (Compulsory Insurance) Act 1969, s. 1. Employers' liability insurance coverage is also compulsory in the United States. *Vide* generally *Corpus Juris Secundum*, Vol. 100, s. 351(1).

[3] *Vide* e.g., CBI Memorandum (1980) paras. 20, 22, p. 7; R.C. Downs, "Piercing the Corporate Veil - Do Corporations provide Limited Personal Liability?" 53 UMKC L.R. 174 (1985) p. 197.

[4] *Vide* e.g., *Dollar Cleansers and Dyers, Inc.* v. *MacGregor* 161 A. 159, 161 (1932); *Obre* v. *Alban Tractor Co.* 179 A.2d 861, 863 (1962).

[5] Audited financial statements are often published well after the close of the relative accounting periods. *Vide* for example, the Department of Trade, The Cornhill Consolidated Group Limited (In Liquidation), Investigation under Section 165(b) of Companies Act 1948, Report by David Calcutt, QC and John Whinney, FCA, (pub. HMSO 1980), para 15.01, p. 285. *Vide* also Gower, p. 87.

[6] A recent study concludes that many City analysts have proved incapable of understanding company accounts and that just a handful can see through the most elementary forms of creative accounting. *Vide* "Accounting tricks fool many City analysts, says study" *Financial Times*, 8th December 1993. *Vide* also P.S. Atiyah, "Thoughts on Company Law Philosophy" 8 Lawyer 15 (1965) p. 17.

report to the financial statements to highlight in clear and unequivocal language whether or not the company is a going concern and whether it is expected to remain so throughout the next accounting period.[1] Admittedly, an unsophisticated creditor is free to engage a credit rating agency to conduct the investigation and report on the corporate debtor's financial status. In many instances, however, this option would simply not be economically feasible.

Adherents of limited liability may also argue that creditors are presumed to rely on the corporate debtor's existing financial position. But if presumptions are to be accommodated, should it not be equally tenable to say that a creditor is entitled to presume that the company had the financial resources to fulfil its obligations?

### 5.6.5. Resources and opportunity to bargain

All told, the issue really boils down to the question whether the claimant had the resources and the practical opportunity to bargain on the credit terms of the transaction, including, for example, a price adjustment or a guarantee.[2] Where a claimant has had neither the resources nor the practical opportunity to bargain on the matter his position is no different from that of an non-consensual creditor.[3] Viewed from this perspective, it is clear that in a corporate insolvency, a large number of involuntary creditors may - in the name of limited liability - absorb the costs of the enterprise. Limited liability is a great stimulant of entrepreneurial activity. But as with all stimulants, an overdose may cause untold plight.

---

[1] The Report of the Committee on The Financial Aspects of Corporate Governance (1992) ("The Cadbury Report") included a recommended Code of Best Practice ("the Code") which provided that the directors of *listed* companies should be required to satisfy themselves that the business is a going concern on the basis that they have a reasonable expectation that it will continue in operation for the time period which the guidelines define. (*Vide* Clause 5.21 at p. 42.) The Auditing Practices Board is discussing the implications of this proposal. *Vide* the Auditing Practices Board, "Disclosures Relating to Corporate Governance" (Bulletin 1993/2, December 1993).

[2] Cf. Blumberg, *Substantive Law* p. 77.

[3] Easterbrook and Fischel would label employees and consumers as voluntary creditors. Somewhat unrealistically, they note that the compensation demanded by employees and consumers will be a function of the risk they face. *Vide* Frank H. Easterbrook and Daniel R. Fischel, "Limited Liability and the Corporation" 52 Univ. of Chicago L.R. 89 (1985) p. 104.

## 5.7. Relevance of the voluntary/involuntary creditor distinction to the holding company liability question

The fundamental issue is whether the voluntary/involuntary creditor distinction should bear any relevance to the question whether the holding company ought, in certain circumstances, to be held liable for the obligations of its subsidiaries. Does one group merit more sympathetic consideration than the other? An affirmative answer seems in order.

### 5.7.1. Different standards required

Designing precise criteria for holding company liability based on the distinction between voluntary and involuntary creditors is no easy task. The interests of the various claimants must be assessed and reconciled in the light both of the policies underlying contract and tort law and of the policies supporting limited liability. The principle of limited liability should not be deemed so sacrosant as to blindfoldedly deny relief in all cases.

In the case of voluntary creditors, the focal point is the bargain struck between the contracting parties. When a plaintiff has deliberately dealt with the subsidiary and bargained or could in practice have bargained over the credit of the subsidiary, then the contracting party should be held to his contract. Account, however, must be taken of the presumed reliance placed by such creditors on the autonomy and integrity of the corporate form with which they have dealt. This means that different considerations should be involved where the defendant company has itself impaired the voluntary creditor's appreciation of the bargain through misrepresentation or confusion as to its financial condition or identity. Different considerations are also involved where the defendant company has breached an implied condition of the bargain by acting, to its own detriment, in the interests of other affiliates as, for example, by allowing its assets to be manipulated.

In the case of involuntary creditors, the factor of choice or of reliance plays only a minor, even insignificant, role. The focus must therefore switch from the claimant to the corporate debtor. Given the overriding importance of limited liability, the principle must still be retained as a general rule. But a higher standard of corporate responsibility must be imposed. This approach will at least minimise the risks to which involuntary creditors are exposed by the corporate mechanism.

Given the different standards involved in the voluntary/involuntary dichotomy and the different types of abuse and unfairness identified in Chapter II, it is now necessary to discuss the distinction in the context of the said abuses and unfairness.

### 5.7.2. The distinction in the subservient subsidiary situation

The subservient subsidiary situation involves a subsidiary which, to its own detriment and at the direction of the holding company, acts in the interest of the holding company or of some other component within the corporate group. It is evident that this form of conduct is not readily recognisable by any person dealing with the subsidiary. The tort claimant is obviously unaware of the abuse. And even the voluntary creditor who has deliberately negotiated credit terms with the subsidiary would not recognise the abuse. The subsidiary would not have put him on notice. The presumed reliance on the subsidiary's autonomy and integrity has therefore been misplaced. The subsidiary has itself impaired the contract creditor's assessment of the bargain and his expectation that there would be no unfair dealings involving the subsidiary. Given that both voluntary and involuntary creditors would be unaware of the subservient nature of the subsidiary, it is clear that any liability to be imposed on the holding company in respect of the subsidiary's obligations should not differentiate between any such creditors.

### 5.7.3. The distinction in the under-capitalised subsidiary

Voluntary creditors of an undercapitalised subsidiary conclude transactions with the subsidiary deliberately. They bargain or can in practice bargain over the credit of the subsidiary. They investigate or at least have the opportunity and means of investigating the subsidiary. Provided there is no element of deception or misrepresentation as to the financial condition of the subsidiary, voluntary creditors should therefore be held to their bargain. They should not benefit from any rule that imposes holding company liability for the debts of an inadequately financed subsidiary. Undercapitalisation should not serve to relieve a creditor of a bargain voluntarily struck.

Entirely different considerations, however, apply to the case of the involuntary creditor, particularly the tort victim. The involuntary creditor stands as an innocent bystander, his rights flouted by the insolvent company. The tort victim never even consented to the relationship. Other types of involuntary creditors may have consented to the transaction, but would not have been reasonably expected or given a practical opportunity to investigate the subsidiary's creditworthiness. Should not such involuntary creditors be able to assume that the subsidiary was adequately capitalised?[1] The unfairness of allowing the holding company to avoid any and all liability through the mechanism of an inadequately capitalised subsidiary is readily apparent. Why should a solvent holding company be entitled to set up a flimsy business which hurts other people?

An inadequately capitalised subsidiary moreover flies in the face of the basic objectives of tort law : compensating the victim and deterrence. The victim receives little or no compensation; and the group, by being permitted to avoid the full costs of the venture performed through the subsidiary, is afforded an incentive for excessive risk-taking.[2] A rule requiring adequate capitalisation would encourage the group to pursue higher standards of care and would provide a satisfactory (though not necessarily complete) fund for compensating involuntary creditors of the subsidiary.

Adequate capitalisation, of course, will not guard the subsidiary against all business risks. Despite adequate capitalisation, the subsidiary may still flounder into insolvency and involuntary creditors remain unsatisfied. This however is a reasonable sacrifice to pay for the overall benefits conferred on society by the principle of limited liability. The ideal solution - given the benefits gained by society through a system of limited liability - would of course be for society itself to provide the subsidy required to compensate involuntary creditors fully. Such a far-reaching compensatory scheme would however involve a most radical deviation from existing notions of liability and remedies. Moreover, its implementation would almost certainly necessitate an excessively expensive and bureaucratic machinery. A less radical but still problematic alternative would be to require each company to take out compulsory insurance covering all involuntary creditors' claims. Such insurance schemes would have the advantage of compensating involuntary creditors without intimidating investors. The major difficulty

---

[1] The position would obviously be different if the involuntary contract creditor is actually informed of the undercapitalisation and is prepared to take the risk.

[2] *Vide* Frank H. Easterbrook and Daniel R. Fischel, "Limited Liability and the Corporation" 52 Univ. of Chicago L.R. 89 (1985) p. 113. Cf. Henry Hansmann and Reiner Kraakman, "Toward Unlimited Shareholder Liability for Corporate Torts" 100 Yale L.J. 1879 (1991) p. 1879.

would lie in the cost of creating and maintaining the regulatory mechanism that would be necessary to implement and oversee such schemes.[1]

### 5.7.4. The distinction in the integrated economic enterprise situation

The abuse inherent in the integrated economic enterprise situation is that one enterprise, one business, is artificially fragmented into several legal units for the sole purpose of insulating the business from any substantial claim, usually in tort. Evidently, the abuse would directly and substantially affect involuntary creditors, especially the tort claimants. Such creditors are either unable to discover the abuse or else do not have the practical opportunity or means of doing so. Enterprise liability should certainly benefit them.

Voluntary creditors present some difficulty. Voluntary creditors bargain, or have the opportunity to bargain, with the subsidiary. By definition, they know, or should know, that the fragmentation device has been utilised. In that event, they have to bear the risk. The position would of course be different where an element of misrepresentation is involved. If a creditor has been misled into believing that the subsidiary he is bargaining with comprises the whole business, then the basis of the bargain has been undermined. Such a creditor would not even qualify as a voluntary creditor for the purposes of the present analysis.

### 5.7.5. The distinction in the group persona situation

The group persona situation involves an element of misrepresentation. The various components within the corporate group are projected to the public as a single enterprise, as a unified persona. Clearly, voluntary creditors who are aware of the reality of the group corporate structure should not be able to assert holding company liability. They have not been misled. Their awareness of reality neutralises their claim.

In so far as involuntary creditors are concerned, a distinction needs to be made. The element of deception inherent in the group persona situation

---

[1] A discussion of the insurance solution is beyond the scope of this work. Useful contributions may be found in David H. Barber, "Piercing the Corporate Veil" 17 Williamette L.R. 371 (1981) pp. 394-395; Frank H. Easterbrook and Daniel R. Fischel, "Limited Liability and the Corporation" 52 Univ. of Chicago L.R. 89 (1985) pp. 114-115; Note, "Should Shareholders be Personally Liable for the Torts of their Corporations" 76 Yale L.J. 1190 (1967) pp. 1201-1204.

would almost certainly affect the "consensual" involuntary creditors, such as consumers. They should clearly benefit from any rule imposing enterprise liability. The element of deception which lulls the consensual involuntary creditors into the misapprehension does not, however, affect tort creditors at all. Tort creditors cannot be deceived by the group persona situation. Nevertheless, it is submitted that a rule imposing enterprise liability should also apply to the benefit of the tort creditors. The imposition of liability, in fact, should be viewed not merely as a means of compensating those who have been misled, but also a means of penalising the wrong and deterring the mischief. Voluntary creditors however, should not benefit from enterprise liability both because their actual knowledge of the situation must be viewed as an overriding consideration and also because they must be held to their bargain.

## 5.8. The judicial approach to the voluntary/involuntary creditor distinction

Notwithstanding the intrinsic differences between voluntary and involuntary creditors and the nature of their claim, the courts generally fail to take such differences into account. In English law, the virtual sanctity of the principles of separate personality and limited liability has of course made the distinction unnecessary and superfluous. Indeed, the distinction has never been discussed (nor has it apparently been raised) in any of the lifting of the veil judgments.[1] In American law, the distinction has received some attention from the courts. Suggestive of the distinction is the fact that American courts sometimes appear more willing to disregard the corporate veil in tort than in contract cases.[2] Fraud, injustice or inequitable conduct must be shown in all types of cases, but in distinguishing contract claims from tort claims, courts sometimes note that a claim of contractual origin presents added difficulties

---

[1] The distinction has however been recognised in at least one Australian case. *Vide Briggs v. James Hardie & Co. Pty. Ltd.* 16 NSWLR 549 (1989) at pp. 578-579 (per Rodgers A-JA).

[2] Undercapitalisation, for example, is an important factor in tort cases (e.g., *Mull v. Colt Co.* 31 F.R.D. 154 (S.D.N.Y. 1962)), but practically irrelevant in contract cases. *Vide* generally, William O. Douglas and Carrol M. Shanks, "Insulation from Liability through Subsidiary Corporations" 39 Yale L.J. 193 (1929); Montgomery E. Pike, "Responsibility of the Parent Corporation for the Acts of its Subsidiary" 4 Ohio State L.J. 311 (1938) pp. 325-326; Charles Rembar, "Claims against Affiliated Companies in Reorganisation" 39 Colum. L.R. 907 (1939) p. 911; Blumberg, *Substantive Law* p. 687.

over a tort claim.[1] Unlike the situation in an action in tort, the plaintiff in an action originating in contract has the burden of justifying a recovery against the holding company when he had willingly contracted with the subsidiary.[2] Stricter standards may be made to apply to contract claims. A contract claim may be considered to require additional compelling facts[3] - although it is recognised that the delineation of such facts in the form of a general rule is difficult.[4] It should however be stressed that the distinction between contract and tort claims is not frequently made by American courts.[5] Often, factors used to disregard entity have been applied indiscriminately to both contract and tort claims without due regard to the policies underlying the decisions.[6]

Although American courts are still more likely to lift the veil and impose liability on a holding company in a tort case than in a contract claim, it is clear that the importance of American lifting the veil jurisprudence in the tort context has somewhat diminished in recent decades. This is due to a number of factors. In the first place, American society has witnessed a vast expansion of product liability law,[7] making the veil-piercing technique to some extent redundant in this field. Strict liability and successor liability in product liability cases (and to a lesser extent in environmental cases) have greatly increased the protection afforded to consumers. Companies within a group which have participated in different stages of the economic process of designing, producing, distributing, selling or installing dangerously defective products, are all made liable.[8] Tort law - rather than company or insolvency law - visits the holding company with liability. Tort law furnishes the solution to the problem of product related injuries. American law is also

---

[1] *Vide* e.g., *Bell Oil & Gas Co.* v. *Allied Chemical Corp.* 431 S.W.2d 336, 339-340 (Tex. 1968); *Edwards Co., Inc.* v. *Monogram Industries, Inc.* 730 F.2d 977, 981-983 (5th. Cir. 1984).

[2] Cf. *Gentry* v. *Credit Plan Corp.* 528 S.W.2d 571, 573 (Tex. 1975); *Hanson* v. *Bradley* 10 N.E.2d 259, 264 (1937).

[3] *Hanson Southwest Corp.* v. *Dal-Mac Construction Co.* 554 S.W.2d 712, 717 (Tex. 1977).

[4] *Bell Oil & Gas Co.* v. *Allied Chemical Corp.* 431 S.W.2d 336, 340 (Tex. 1968).

[5] *Vide* R.C. Downs, "Piercing the Corporate Veil - Do Corporations provide Limited Personal Liability?". 53 UMKC L.R. 174 (1985) p. 195; David H. Barber, "Piercing the Corporate Veil" 17 Williamette L.R. 371 (1981) pp. 385-386.

[6] Robert W. Hamilton, "The Corporate Entity" 49 Texas L.R. 979 (1971) p. 985.

[7] *Vide* The American Law Institute, Enterprise Responsibility for Personal Injury, Reporters' Study, Vol. I - The Institutional Framework (1991) Ch. 9.

[8] *Vide* generally Blumberg, *Substantive Law* Ch. 13.

expanding the traditional notions of direct liability in tort,[1] with the result that where a group involves a high degree of economic integration there is an increased likelihood that the holding company would either be considered a direct participant in the tort or be deemed to have assumed duties towards the victim.

## 6. LIMITED LIABILITY AND CORPORATE GROUPS - SOME CONCLUDING REMARKS

The foregoing analysis of the role of limited liability in the context of corporate groups should have exposed the weakness of the case for the continuing wholesale application of the principle of limited liability to holding companies. Indeed, it would appear that neither the historical record nor the socio-economic benefits of limited liability warrant the spontaneous extension of the principle to groups. Moreover, the case for limited liability in favour of holding companies fizzles out in the context of involuntary creditors. Limited liability is not inherent in the nature of things.

*Quo vadis?* The initial reaction may be to dispense entirely with limited liability in the context of the holding-subsidiary relationship, particularly where involuntary creditors are concerned. Indeed, if the notion of limited liability were being debated for the first time in history, a strong case could arguably be submitted for the denial of limited liability in the context of corporate groups. Yet limited liability has become so ingrained in the legal and economic system that any all-out onslaught is bound to be effectively deflected. More importantly, however, a number of reasons militate against such a revolutionary approach.

To begin with, it is arguable that if a holding company is denied the privilege of limited liability, certain socially desirable but high-risk ventures which might attract investment by corporate groups would not be undertaken at all.[2] The holding company may quite understandably consider that, in the interests of its own shareholders, it should avoid the risk by refraining from the investment. Entrepreneurial activity may be dampened. This would result in a social loss.

In the second place, the imposition of unlimited liability on holding companies would give other companies a competitive advantage. Putting at

---

[1] *Vide* generally Blumberg, *Substantive Law* Ch. 14.

[2] *Vide supra* pp. 167-169.

risk the whole of the assets of the group for claims arising in connection with the activities of each subsidiary, would mean that the group would have to take such risks into account in its costings. Competitive firms in the subsidiary's line of business would clearly have lower costs of operation. Perverse incentives may be created.[1]

Finally, it should be stressed that the goal of the reforms being proposed in this work is to eliminate, as far as practicable, the cases of abuse and unfairness that may arise in the context of corporate groups. That goal can be attained by introducing "limits" on limited liability rather than by jettisoning it altogether. Indeed, the reform proposals are intended to preserve - even for corporate groups - the admitted benefits of limited liability while ensuring higher standards of corporate behaviour and fairer treatment for creditors.

## 7. DISTINCTION BETWEEN THE HOLDING-SUBSIDIARY RELATIONSHIP AND THE ONE-MAN COMPANY

### 7.1. The nature of the distinction

Why, it may be asked, should not the proposals for reform be extended to the one-man company situation? After all, the one-man company is closely analogous to the holding-subsidiary relationship. In both the one-man company and the holding-subsidiary relationship, for example, all - or at least the majority - of shares are held by one person (physical or juridical as the case may be). In both situations, the potential for direct and intrusive control vests in the sole or majority shareholder. Even the risks of subservience and undercapitalisation arise in both situations.[2] Admittedly, therefore, the one-man company bears a close analogy to the holding-subsidiary relationship. Analogous they may be. But certainly not identical. Indeed a fundamental distinction subsists. And the difference is not merely that the holding company is a "juridical" person while the individual

---

[1] *Vide* Frank H. Easterbrook and Daniel R. Fischel, "Limited Liability and the Corporation" 52 Univ. of Chicago L.R. 89 (1985) p. 111.

[2] Since, however, the holding company is more likely to be itself engaged in business, the potential for unfair dealings is higher in a holding-subsidiary relationship than in a one-man company. The risk of undercapitalisation, too, is higher in holding-subsidiary arrangements. *Vide supra* Chapter II p. 86.

shareholder is a "natural" person - a distinction that may be of immense significance to the legal theorist. Rather, the essential difference, at least for the purposes of this study, is that a holding company has already acquired limited liability for its shareholders. In effect, the holding-subsidiary arrangement provides a double layer of immunity. Any rule that imposes liability on the holding company will therefore only be piercing the top layer of immunity. It will not be denying limited liability to the individual shareholders. Consequently, a rule of holding company liability would - in preserving the principle of limited liability *vis-a-vis* the individual owners - effectively safeguard the essential advantages and purposes of that principle. But it is difficult to perceive the social gain of denying - especially to an involuntary creditor of an insolvent subsidiary - a claim against a holding company which itself has been the vehicle of limiting the liability of its own shareholders.

There is another perspective : the need to rank conflicting policies in order of preference. In the case of an individual shareholder, the interests of the company's creditors may have to be sacrificed to the overriding benefits of preserving limited liability. Otherwise, the bastion of limited liability may well crumble at its very foundations. But by "re-incorporating" once over - through the creation of a subsidiary - the individual investors are attempting to escape liability even for their original investment. Liability is being limited not once, but twice or many times over.

## 7.2. The distinction in case-law

The distinction between the one-man company situation and the holding-subsidiary or affiliated company arrangement is, at least implicitly, recognised in a number of American judgments. Some cases, for example, which impose liability on a holding or affiliated company cannot be satisfactorily explained upon principles which would apply to one-man companies generally.[1] Besides, judgments often differentiate between the holding-subsidiary arrangement and the one-man company even when on principle no distinction ought to be made between the two, as in the case of undercapitalisation. Thus, in cases involving undercapitalised subsidiaries - for example, *Joseph R. Foard Co.* v. *State of Maryland*[2] and *Luckenbach*

---

[1] *Vide* e.g., *The Willem Van Driel, Sr.* 252 F. 35, 37-39 (4th Cir. 1918); *Costan* v. *Manila Electric Co.* 24 F.2d 383, 384 (2d Cir. 1928); *Walkovsky* v. *Carlton* 223 N.E.2d 6, 8-9 (1966).

[2] 219 F. 827 (4th Cir. 1914).

*S.S. Co.* v. *W.R. Grace & Co.*[1] - the courts tend to impose holding company liability. In cases involving undercapitalised one-man companies however - such as *J.W. Williams Co.* v. *Leong Sue Ah Quin*[2] and *Hayhurst* v. *Boyd*[3] - the shareholder was kept well insulated from liability. The same observation can be made with regard to the subordination or disallowance cases.[4] Thus, where subordination is ordered or a claim disallowed, a holding-subsidiary set-up is usually present.[5] This greater proclivity to reach holding or affiliated companies as opposed to individual controlling shareholders[6] can only be explained on the basis that the disregard of the entity in the context of the holding-subsidiary or affiliated companies arrangement does not involve additional liability on the individual shareholder. Only rarely, however, have the courts expressly referred to this vital distinction.[7]

For some time, a few English judgments also appeared to perceive a distinction between the holding-subsidiary arrangement and the one-man company. This can be discerned from their propensity to lift the veil in the holding-subsidiary cases (such as *The Roberta*,[8] *Smith, Stone & Knight Ltd.* v. *Birmingham Corporation*[9] and *D.H.N. Food Distributors Ltd.* v. *Tower Hamlets L.B.C.*[10]) but not in analogous one-man company cases (such as *Roberts* v. *Coventry Corporation*[11]). Regrettably however, *Adams* v. *Cape Industries plc*[12] has now probably anaesthetised any inclination on the part

---

[1] 267 F. 676 (4th Cir. 1920).

[2] 186 P. 401 (1919).

[3] 300 P. 895 (1931). *Vide* also *Zubik* v. *Zubik* 384 F.2d, 267, 273 (3d Cir. 1967), *cert. denied*, 390 U.S. 988 (1968).

[4] *Vide* generally *post*, Chapter IX.

[5] E.g., *In re Kentucky Wagon Mfg. Co.* 71 F.2d 802 (6th Cir. 1934).

[6] *Vide* also *Farmers Warehouse of Pelham, Inc.* v. *Collins* 137 S.E.2d 619, 625-626 (1964); *Amsted Industries, Inc.* v. *Pollak Industries, Inc* 382 N.E.2d 393, 397 (1978).

[7] *Vide* e.g., *Pepsi-Cola Metropolitan Bottling Co.* v. *Checkers, Inc.* 754 F.2d 10, 16-17 (1st Cir. 1985); *Laborers Clean-Up Contract Administration Trust Fund* v. *Uriarte Clean-Up Service, Inc.* 736 F.2d 516, 523-525 (9th Cir. 1984). In both these cases the court actually imposed liability on the controlling shareholders as well.

[8] (1937) 58 Ll.L.R. 159, 169.

[9] [1939] 4 All E.R. 116.

[10] [1976] 1 W.L.R. 852 (C.A.).

[11] [1947] 1 All E.R. 308.

[12] [1990] BCLC 479 (C.A.).

of the courts to view the holding-subsidiary relationship any differently from the one-man company situation.

## 8. CONCEPTUAL UNITY TO THE REFORM PROPOSALS

Three general conclusions can, it is submitted, be drawn from the discussion so far conducted in this work. First, that the traditional model of an enterprise on which much of our company law is premised is no longer adequate for tackling the problems arising out of the reality of corporate groups. Second, that the corporate group method of organising and conducting business can lead to situations of potential abuse and unfairness. Third, that the socio-economic arguments supporting limited liability, while generally sound, lose much of their impact in the context of corporate groups. Especially, with regard to involuntary creditors, an erosion of limited liability appears not only compatible with the general objectives of the law, but positively desirable.

The basic thrust of the ensuing Chapters will be (i) to test the efficacy of existing law in controlling or remedying the abuses and unfairness, and (ii) to submit certain proposals for reform where the law fails the test. Before doing so, however, it is pertinent to affirm two underlying propositions that will link together the various reform proposals to be submitted.

### 8.1. The privilege of incorporation

The right of incorporation with limited liability is a privilege. It is a privilege granted by law to those who seek to limit their exposure in any particular investment or undertaking. And although the privilege benefits primarily the investor or entrepreneur, society as a whole is enriched by the collective gain. The corporate privilege can in fact be perceived as a tool, a means by which to attain socially and economically desirable ends. Yet, as often happens, privilege begets power - power which, if abused, can breed hardship. A balance must therefore be struck between promoting the use of the privilege and controlling its abuse. This goal can, it is submitted, be achieved by recognising both that power attracts a corresponding responsibility and that the right to the privilege and its concomitant power depends on satisfying those conditions which are inherent in the grant of the privilege.

Now the fundamental legal consequence of the privilege of incorporation is the creation of a separate juridical person - a person that, for most purposes, is treated by the law as any other person "created by the Almighty".[1] In respect of juridical persons, however, the law by-passes the rule of incapacity associated with the age of minority (the age during which the parents are in general vicariously liable for the acts of minor) and endows such person with practically all the faculties (such as the power to contract obligations and to sue and be sued) that it normally grants only to natural persons who have attained majority. With natural persons, the rights granted on majority are in effect linked to the person's perceived independence. The same notion can, without any undue stretching of the analogy, be applied to corporate persons : once the law is prepared to accord to a corporate person the rights normally associated with majority then it should insist, as a condition of incorporation and its attendant benefits, that the corporate person be truly capable of acting as an independent person. Separate legal personality should rely on the independence of the enterprise. Only in this way can a proper equilibrium be achieved and the interests of the various parties reconciled.

Two factors are essential for a corporate person to achieve this independence. First, that the corporate person is truly organised, operated and promoted in its own self-interest as a separate person. Second, that the corporate person be financially self-sufficient to enable it to conduct its intended functions. In other words, true corporate independence presupposes a good measure both of emancipation and of economic viability. In the context of the holding-subsidiary relationship, a significant departure from any of these two requisites by the holding company should be viewed as an abuse of the privilege of incorporation entailing the total or partial forfeiture of that highly prized asset : the legislative grant of limited liability. The sanctity of separate personality should only be upheld to the extent that the corporate entity adheres to the principles which gave it life. The question whether a holding company ought to be held responsible for the debts of its subsidiary should not be dictated by the abstract nature of corporate personality. Rather it should depend on the social and economic considerations involved. This functional philosophy of corporate personality underlies much of the analysis in the next Chapters.

---

[1] *Exchange Bank of Macon* v. *Macon Co.* 25 S.E. 326 (1895) at p. 328.

## 8.2. Powers in trust

The holding company's relationship with its subsidiary should also be viewed from another perspective. Because of its controlling position, the holding company's powers can be considered as powers in trust for the community of public interests, including shareholders and creditors. The holding company's dealings with its subsidiary should therefore be subject to rigorous scrutiny. Transactions between the holding company and its subsidiary, including the exercise of control by the holding company over the subsidiary must be inherently fair for the subsidiary and those interested therein. Fiduciary standards of conduct should be owed to the entire community of interests in a subsidiary. The reform proposals set out in this work recognise and give effect to this notion.

# 5 The Subservient Subsidiary Situation

## 1. INTRODUCTION

Subsidiary companies are not inherently nefarious. On the contrary, subsidiaries may serve perfectly legitimate functions. In most instances, subsidiaries are indeed legitimately used.

Unfortunately, however, the holding-subsidiary arrangement does increase the risks of abuse and unfairness.[1] These risks are particularly heightened where the subsidiary acts not in the interests of its own corporate enterprise, but in the wider interests of the holding company, or of one or more affiliated companies, or of the group as a whole. In this type of situation, the subsidiary is not allowed to operate as an independent profit-centre. Its interests are submerged, or at least ignored, in the greater interest of the group enterprise. Such subservient behaviour is usually the result of dominating control exercised by the holding company over the subsidiary.

Subservient behaviour on the part of the subsidiary manifests itself in the implementation by the group of a variety of practices. These practices include: various transfer pricing techniques; the diversion of corporate opportunities; the pursuit of a dividend policy influenced by the financial needs of other companies within the group rather than by the best interests of the subsidiary; the commingling and draining of assets; the shuttling of funds and other assets; the provision of financial support by the subsidiary to other components of the group; the operation of the subsidiary without a profit motive; and the use of sham or shell subsidiaries.[2]

In so far as external creditors are concerned, the use of subservient subsidiaries is objectionable on three grounds.[3] In the first place, subservient practices generally lead to a reduction both in profitability and in the net asset value of the subsidiary. The financial backbone of the subsidiary is

---

[1] *Vide* generally, *supra* Chapter II.

[2] *Vide* generally, *supra* Chapter II pp. 65-83.

[3] Minority shareholders also face considerable risks in a subservient subsidiary situation. The subject of minority rights in the corporate group context is however beyond the scope of this work.

thereby weakened. An effect of subservient practices may also be to deprive the subservient subsidiary of sufficient funds to enable it to finance further expansion. Such enterprise-wide strategies may even lead to the subsidiary's insolvency. Especially where the subsidiary is insolvent or becomes insolvent, external creditors are clearly prejudiced by subservient practices. In the second place, the use of a subservient subsidiary reflects a basic disregard by the holding company of the subsidiary's supposedly independent status as a separate juridical person. The conduct of business through a subservient subsidiary can therefore be viewed as an abuse of the privilege of incorporation. Finally, to allow the holding company to milk the subsidiary only to reject it in the event of its insolvency is repugnant to one's sense of justice and fair play.

The purpose of this Chapter is two-fold. Firstly, to assess the extent to which existing law remedies the mischief of the subservient subsidiary company situation. Secondly, to propose the introduction of a rule of holding company liability for the debts of habitually subservient subsidiary companies.

## 2. EXISTING REMEDIES

### 2.1. Introduction

The law is not totally blind to the potential for abuse and unfairness in the subservient subsidiary situation. Indeed, without specifically contemplating the holding-subsidiary relationship, the law does forbid certain forms of subservient practices identified in Chapter II. The law is in fact equipped with a considerable armoury of rules and provisions which can, *prima facie* at least, be called upon to penalise or remedy many such practices. These rules include the *ultra vires* doctrine, the rules on transactions at an undervalue and unlawful preferences, the capital maintenance doctrine, the wrongful trading and fraudulent trading provisions and the whole law of directors' duties. Transfer pricing and the draining of assets, for example, appear to be regulated by the rules of voidable transactions. The provision of financial support by a subservient subsidiary may be regulated by the capital maintenance doctrine as well as by the rules of voidable transactions. The diversion of corporate opportunities is arguably regulated by the law on directors' duties.

Yet despite the wide array of rules at its disposal, the law still fails to adequately remedy the abuse and unfairness that can flow from the subservient subsidiary situation. A number of reasons account for such failure. In the first place, it is evident that certain conduct perceived to be abusive or unfair is simply not prohibited by existing law. Secondly, even where existing rules do regulate particular practices, their field of operation is often too restrictive to be of any effective use. Thirdly, and perhaps most fundamentally, existing remedies as a rule target particular transactions and not a course of conduct generally. The law is far too monotransactional in its approach to be very effective in combating the subservient subsidiary situation. To demonstrate these observations, it is now necessary to identify and examine those rules of law that, *prima facie* at least, could be invoked to regulate the subservient practices.

## 2.2. Holding company liability in tort

A natural consequence of the principle of separate juridical personality is that a holding company is not liable for the torts of its subsidiary. The position does not change in the case of a subservient subsidiary. Certainly, the holding company cannot, as a general rule, be held directly liable in tort for the tortious conduct of its subservient subsidiary. Not even the control typically exercised by a dominating holding company over a subservient subsidiary could saddle the holding company with vicarious liability for the tortious conduct of the subsidiary. The requisites for the imposition of vicarious liability on the basis of a principal-servant or agency relationship would simply not be satisfied. A principal-servant relationship between a dominating holding company and a subservient subsidiary could only exist if the holding company directs not simply the day-to-day affairs of the subsidiary but also goes so far as to control all aspects of its operations, including the activities of its employees.[1] Equally unlikely is the imposition of tort liability on the holding company on the basis of an agency relationship between the holding company and its subservient subsidiary. The essential conditions for the inference of an agency relationship would not usually be present even in the case of a highly intrusive holding company and a submissive subsidiary.[2]

---

[1] *Vide* further *supra* Chapter III p. 130.

[2] *Vide* further *supra* Chapter III pp. 119-125 and *post* pp. 203-205.

Circumstances can of course be envisaged where a holding company would be held liable in tort for acts involving its subservient subsidiary. One situation would be where the holding company has itself assumed certain duties towards third parties in connection with operations carried out by the subsidiary. Another situation is where the holding company's own negligent conduct gives rise to claims by persons dealing with the subsidiary. The holding company can also be jointly liable with its subservient subsidiary for tortious conduct. Joint liability could arise where the holding company is directly involved in the activities of the subsidiary or where domination by the holding company is so intrusive as to make the holding company an actor in the tortious conduct.[1] These however are exceptional circumstances. The general rule remains that a holding company will not usually be liable for the torts of its subservient subsidiary.

## 2.3. Liability based on agency principles

An agency relationship requires that the agent act on behalf of the principal and that both the principal and the agent have consented to the arrangement. The principal effect of an agency relationship in so far as third parties are concerned is that the acts of the agent done within the scope of his authority bind the principal. The essential features of agency in the context of the holding-subsidiary relationship have already been considered in Chapter III.[2] It was there concluded that although an agency relationship between a holding and a subsidiary company is technically feasible, such a relationship is unlikely to be agreed to in practice and certainly cannot be readily inferred.

Now although the agency issues mentioned in Chapter III were discussed in the context of the holding-subsidiary relationship generally, the same analysis and conclusions apply *per equipollens* to the subservient subsidiary situation. Indeed, no matter how submissively the subsidiary may behave and no matter how abusive or unfair the subservient conduct may be, agency cannot and should not be inferred solely on such basis. For even in such circumstances, the essential elements of consent and of authority would still be lacking. The truth is that subservient subsidiaries normally contract on their own behalf and not on behalf of their holding companies. A subservient subsidiary will usually deal with its customers without expressly or

---

[1] *Vide* further *supra* Chapter III pp. 125-129.

[2] *Vide supra* pp. 119-125.

impliedly involving its holding company. Where the extent of domination and subservience is especially acute, the correct analysis may be to consider the holding company as having become the actor in the particular activities. Liability could then be predicated on the holding company's direct intervention.[1] The notion of agency would be irrelevant.

In a broad sense, a subservient subsidiary does of course act on behalf of its holding company.[2] For not only is a subservient subsidiary subject to a large degree of control by its holding company; it actually carries on its business in the exclusive interest of the holding company rather than its own. But to assert that the subsidiary would, in such circumstances, be acting "on behalf of" the holding company in the common law sense of the term is to inaccurately extend the technical notion of agency beyond its well-defined meaning.

The adoption of a wide construction to the agency notion has unfortunately been promoted by a number of authors. Schmitthoff, for example, has suggested that the notion of agency is "a convenient means to escape from the strait-jacket of the rigid interpretation of the rule in Salomon's case ... [and] to give effect in English law to the modern theory of parent and subsidiary as an economic unit."[3] Ottolenghi states that she "cannot agree more" with Schmitthoff's view.[4] And Dobson observes that "[t]he broad scope of agency combined with [the notion of undisclosed principal] make for a most efficient instrument in dealing with lifting the veil problems where the control of a company is in question."[5] Such counsel is somewhat ill-advised. The danger with adopting a wide construction of

---

[1] *Vide supra* Chapter III pp. 125-129.

[2] A wide meaning to the notion of agency in the context of the holding subsidiary relationship has been adopted in many revenue cases. In *Firestone Tyre and Rubber Co. Ltd.* v. *Lewellin* [1957] 1 All E.R. 561 (H.L.), for example, an English subsidiary of an American holding company used to contract on its own behalf. The subsidiary was clearly dominated by the holding company and was financially interdependent on it. It was held that for taxation purposes the subsidiary should be deemed to have acted on behalf of the holding company. The taxation cases however can be distinguished on the ground that serious policy considerations are involved. Kahn-Freund viewed this broader view of agency to be more "realistic". *Vide* O. Kahn-Freund, "Corporate Entity" 3 M.L.R. 226 (1940) at p. 226.

[3] Clive M. Schmitthoff, "Salomon in the Shadow" [1976] J.B.L. 305 at p. 309.

[4] S. Ottolenghi, "From Peeping Behind the Corporate Veil to Ignoring it Completely" 53 M.L.R. 338 (1990) at p. 346 n. 75.

[5] Juan M. Dobson, "'Lifting the Veil' in Four Countries : The Law of Argentina, England, France and the United States" 35 I.C.L.Q. 839 (1986) at p. 848.

agency as a convenient test of liability is to blur an otherwise unambiguous notion and confound the analysis. For once the holding-subsidiary relationship is characterised as one of "agency", the traditional rules of the concept, developed for different circumstances, would necessarily become operative. Would those rules - for example, those relating to undisclosed agency and election - apply to the holding-subsidiary relationship? Would the agency relationship be inferred in respect of all the subsidiary's activities, or in respect of a select few? Clearly, the issues would get considerably complicated. Of course, a wider notion of agency would protect the sanctity of separate juridical personality from being violated. But the price would be too high. Agency should not be strangled to save Salomon.

Fortunately, the Court of Appeal's unequivocal - and commendable - stand on the agency point in *Adams* v. *Cape Industries plc*[1] has now significantly reduced the risk that a wide construction will be afforded to the notion of agency. More than ever, it is now highly unlikely that the courts would use agency to visit the holding company with liability for the debts of a subservient subsidiary.[2]

## 2.4. Fraudulent trading

### 2.4.1. Introduction

A "fraudulent trading" provision was first introduced in the Companies Act 1928[3] and soon consolidated in the Companies Act 1929.[4] A somewhat modified version then appeared in the Companies Act 1948[5] and later in the Companies Act 1985.[6] The current version is found in section 213 of the Insolvency Act 1986. That section essentially provides that if in the course of the winding up of a company it appears that any business of the company has been carried on with intent to defraud creditors of the company or

---

[1] [1990] BCLC 479 (C.A.).

[2] Prior to the *Adams* decision, the position had been somewhat less certain. *Vide* in this connection the understandably more cautious assessment of the agency device by Andrew Beck, "The Two Sides of the Corporate Veil" in J. H. Farrar (ed.), *Contemporary Issues in Company Law* (1987) at p. 75.

[3] s. 75.

[4] s. 275.

[5] s. 332.

[6] s. 630.

creditors of any other person, or for any fraudulent purpose, then the court may declare that any persons who were knowingly parties to the carrying on of the business as aforesaid are to be liable to make such contributions (if any) to the company's assets as the court thinks proper. The provision had originally been introduced in the Companies Act 1928 to combat the case where the person in control of the company held a floating charge, and while knowing that the company was on the verge of liquidation, "filled up" his security by means of goods obtained on credit and then appointed a receiver.[1]

The fraudulent trading provisions, along with other provisions found in the Insolvency Act 1986[2] clearly play a crucial role in persuading those in control of companies to cease business once the company cannot fully pay its debts and when the business is in effect being carried on at the expense of its creditors.[3]

Unfortunately, however, the effectiveness of the fraudulent trading provisions is considerably weakened by the conditions that have to be satisfied for its application. One is that the company must be in the course of winding up. Another - and certainly more crucial - condition is that the business of the company has been carried on "with intent to defraud creditors". In respect of the latter requirement, it has been held that the test of intent will only be satisfied if there is "actual dishonesty involving, according to current notions of fair trading among commercial men, real moral blame."[4] The test will however be satisfied where directors allow a company to incur credit when they have no reason to think that the creditors will ever be paid.[5] It can also be satisfied where the directors obtain credit at a time when they have no good reason to believe that funds will become available to pay the creditors when their debts become due or shortly thereafter.[6] The test of liability is however subjective, so that unreasonable

---

[1] *Vide* the Report of the Company Law Amendment Committee 1925-1926 (the Greene Report), Cmd. 2657 (1926) para. 61, pp. 28-29.

[2] E.g., s. 207 (Transactions in fraud of creditors) and s. 214 (Wrongful trading).

[3] *Vide* Farrar, p. 713.

[4] *In re Patrick & Lyon Ltd.* [1933] Ch. 786 at p. 790 per Maugham J. *Vide* also *In re E.B. Tractors Ltd.* [1987] PCC 313 and *Re a Company (No. 001418 of 1988)* [1991] BCLC 197.

[5] *Re William C. Leitch Bros. Ltd.* [1932] 2 Ch. 71.

[6] *R.* v. *Grantham* [1984] BCLC 270 (C.A.). This case concerned criminal liability for fraudulent trading. In his judgment (*ibid.* at p. 275) Lord Lane C.J. disapproved of the statement in *Re White and Osmond (Parkstone) Ltd.* (unreported, 30 June 1960 Ch.D)

conduct is not in itself sufficient to establish liability. Negligence or incompetence cannot be put on an equal footing with fraud.[1] Moreover, the courts have demanded a strict standard of proof, although *R.* v. *Grantham*[2] has made it somewhat easier to prove the necessary fraudulent intent.[3] It would appear that the difficulty of establishing dishonesty has often deterred the issue of proceedings where a strong case may have otherwise existed for recovering compensation.[4]

In discussing the fraudulent trading remedy in the context of the subservient subsidiary situation, two aspects of the provisions must be highlighted. First, liability can only be imposed on "any persons who were knowingly parties to the carrying on of the business".[5] Second, the business

*Cont.*

that there would be no fraud if the directors genuinely believed "that the clouds will roll away and the sunshine of prosperity will shine upon them again and disperse the fog". *R.* v. *Grantham* was decided at a time when both civil and criminal liability for fraudulent trading were regulated by s. 332 of the Companies Act 1948. Section 332 was split up in the reforms introduced in 1986. The provisions regarding criminal liability are now found in s. 458 of the C.A. 1985, whereas the civil liability provisions are incorporated in s. 213 of the I.A. 1986.

[1] Calls have occasionally been made for "reckless" trading to be brought within the remedy of fraudulent trading. *Vide* e.g., Department of Trade, The Cornhill Consolidated Group Limited (In Liquidation), Investigation under Section 165(b) of Companies Act 1948, Report by David Calcutt, QC and John Whinney, FCA, (pub. HMSO 1980) p. 283. A similar proposal was made by Mr. Stanley Clinton Davis to the House of Commons during the debate on the Companies Bill in 1980. *Vide* Parliamentary Debates (Hansard) 5th Series Vol. 979 (House of Commons) 26th February 1980, cols. 1251-1252. The wrongful trading provisions subsequently introduced in s. 214 of the I.A. 1986 provide a measure of protection against reckless behaviour. *Vide post* pp. 211-218.

[2] [1984] BCLC 270 (C.A.). *Vide* also *R.* v. *Kemp* [1988] QB 645 (C.A.).

[3] The burden of establishing fraudulent intent has often been highlighted even by constituted bodies. *Vide* e.g., CCAB Memorandum (1979) p. 5; CCAB Memorandum (1981) p. 6. The difficulty with proving fraud and thereby establishing liability for fraudulent trading considerably influenced the Cork Committee in recommending the introduction of the remedy of "wrongful trading", now incorporated in s. 214 of the I.A. 1986. *Vide* the Cork Report, paras. 1775-1776, pp. 398-399. On "wrongful trading", *vide post* pp. 211-218.

[4] *Vide* the Cork Report, para. 1776, pp. 398-399. Writing in 1980, Goode termed the fraudulent trading provisions as "almost worthless" for the purposes of protecting creditors. *Vide* Roy M. Goode, "The Death of Insolvency Law" 1 Co. Law. 123 (1980) pp. 127-128. The subsequent decision of the Court of Appeal in *R.* v. *Grantham* [1984] BCLC 270 (C.A.) evidently - and quite rightly - made Goode less sceptical of the remedy. *Vide* R.M. Goode, *Principles of Corporate Insolvency Law* (1990) pp. 201-202.

[5] I.A. 1986, s. 213(2).

of the company must have been "carried on with intent to defraud creditors of the company ... or for any fraudulent purpose".[1] These features raise two questions : (i) could a holding company in a subservient subsidiary company situation qualify as a person who is "knowingly a party to the carrying on of the business"? (ii) does the implementation of subservient practices signify that the business of the subsidiary is being carried on with intent to defraud creditors or for any fraudulent purpose? These questions will now be considered in turn.

### 2.4.2.  Could a holding company qualify as a person who is knowingly a party to the carrying on of the business?

This question should be answered in the affirmative. In the subservient subsidiary situation, the holding company (definitely a "person" in terms of the provisions) would almost certainly - through its exercise of dominating control over the activities of the subsidiary - be knowingly a party "to the carrying on of the business" of the subsidiary. The holding company will usually be the directing mind of the subsidiary. Control is not merely latent. It is quite positively asserted. In the typical subservient subsidiary situation, the holding company would not be able to deny that it was "knowingly" a party to the carrying on of its subsidiary's business.

The question whether a holding company can knowingly be a party to the carrying on of the business of its subsidiary for the purposes of the fraudulent trading provisions was raised in *Re Augustus Barnett & Son Ltd.*[2] Augustus Barnett & Son Ltd. ("Augustus") was a subsidiary of Rumasa S.A. ("Rumasa"). Augustus had for a number of years traded at a loss and its auditors signed its accounts on a going concern basis only because Rumasa had provided letters of comfort that it would continue supporting Augustus. Rumasa also provided Augustus with nearly £4,000,000 by way of subsidies. Augustus's suppliers were reluctant to extend credit, but continued to do so on the basis of reassurances by Rumasa that it would continue to support Augustus. Later, Rumasa withdrew its support and Augustus went into liquidation. The liquidator sought to make Rumasa liable for fraudulent trading. It was not alleged that Rumasa had itself actually carried on the business of Augustus. The liquidator's stand was

---

[1]  I.A. 1986, s.213(1).

[2]  [1986] BCLC 170. For an analysis of this case *vide*, D.D. Prentice, "Fraudulent Trading : Parent Company's Liability for the Debts of its Subsidiary" 103 L.Q.R. 11 (1987).

rather that by (i) giving the auditors letters of comfort and allowing them to be noted in the accounts, (ii) providing subsidies, and (iii) making public statements of intention to continue supporting Augustus, Rumasa had induced creditors to continue to grant credit to Augustus. It was alleged that although the business had been carried on by the directors of Augustus, Rumasa had by its actions been a party to the carrying on of the business. The action failed because the court could find no evidence of any intention by the board of Augustus to defraud. The board had honestly believed that Rumasa would continue to support Augustus. There was therefore no fraud to which Rumasa could be a party. Although the decision could have rested there, the court also considered whether Rumasa could have been carrying on the business with intent to defraud. The court appeared willing to accept as arguable that Rumasa was carrying on the business. The evidence however did not support the contention of an intent to defraud creditors.

The *Augustus Barnett* case is of course distinguishable from the typical subservient subsidiary situation in two important respects. First, *Augustus Barnett* involved a holding company that was supporting a subsidiary rather than a subsidiary that was being subservient to the group. Secondly, and more importantly, there was no evidence in that case that Rumasa was exercising dominating control over the activities of its subsidiary. Indeed, the court acknowledged that the business of Augustus was carried on by its own board without any interference from the holding company. In a subservient subsidiary situation, on the contrary, the holding company would usually exercise significant control over the activities of the subsidiary. Such control, it is submitted, should qualify the holding company as a party to the carrying on of the business of the subservient subsidiary. The *Augustus Barnett* judgment should not therefore be viewed as automatically shielding a holding company from liability for fraudulent trading.

### 2.4.3. Does the implementation of subservient practices signify an intent to defraud creditors?

This question must be answered in the negative. The major difficulty is that subservient practices - no matter how prejudicially they may affect creditors in the long run and no matter how abusive they may be of the privilege of incorporation - will not as a rule satisfy the requirement that the business of the subsidiary be carried on "with intent to defraud creditors" of the subsidiary or "for any fraudulent purpose".

Transfer pricing techniques, the diversion of corporate opportunities, the manipulation of assets, the provision of financial support by the subsidiary and the operation of the subsidiary without a profit motive may all be detrimental to the interests of the creditors. But such practices would usually affect creditors only in the long term. Such practices do not, of themselves, reflect any intent on the part of the holding company (or the subsidiary's directors) to defraud the subsidiary's creditors.[1] Rather, the "intent" on the part of the holding company and of the subsidiary's management in implementing such practices is essentially to pursue a policy of group profit maximisation which may be entirely rational and consistent with good business practice - at least from the group's point of view.[2] Indeed, *Re Augustus Barnett & Son Ltd.*[3] made it clear that the persons involved in the management of a company will not be liable for fraudulent trading even where the company continues to trade at a loss for a considerable period of time as long as steps are taken to ensure that the claims of creditors will be satisfied, even though such steps do not legally guarantee payment. Where, as in the typical case, the subservient subsidiary is not trading at a loss, the risk of liability for fraudulent trading is non-existent. The requisite of dishonesty would simply be lacking. In the case of an insolvent subsidiary or a subsidiary trading at a loss, the risk of liability for fraudulent trading being imposed on the holding company and the subsidiary's directors cannot however be ignored.

Finally, it should be remembered that the difficulties with the fraudulent trading remedy are also clearly compounded by the insistence on the part of the courts of a strict standard of proof. All told, it is evident that the fraudulent trading provisions do not provide an adequate remedy to counter the abuse and unfairness inherent in the subservient subsidiary situation.

---

[1] In *Re Sarflax Ltd.* [1979] 2 W.L.R. 202 a subsidiary ceased trading and then settled a debt due to its holding company in preference to other creditors of the subsidiary. It was held that the mere preference of one creditor over another did not constitute intent to defraud for the purposes of the fraudulent trading provisions. Such a preference may however constitute a voidable preference under s. 239 of the I.A. 1986. On voidable preferences in the context of group trading, *vide post* pp. 218-238.

[2] *Vide supra* Chapter II pp. 66-67.

[3] [1986] BCLC 170.

## 2.5. Wrongful trading

### 2.5.1. The origin of the remedy

The heavy onus of proving fraud to the standard of proof required by the criminal law in order to obtain a remedy under the fraudulent trading provisions discouraged the institution of proceedings and led the Cork Committee to conclude that whilst proof of dishonesty should be required before a person could be convicted of a criminal offence, different considerations should apply to the provision of a civil remedy where foreseeable loss is suffered as a result of unreasonable behaviour.[1] The Committee therefore recommended that the existing civil remedy of fraudulent trading be replaced by a new section under which civil liability could arise without proof of fraud or dishonesty and without requiring the criminal law standard of proof.[2] The Committee's basic proposals were incorporated - with certain modifications[3] - in section 214 of the Insolvency Act 1986.

### 2.5.2. The essential features of wrongful trading

In terms of section 214, directors (including shadow directors)[4] of a company which goes into insolvent liquidation can be ordered to "make such contribution (if any) to the company's assets as the court thinks proper."[5]

---

[1] *Vide* the Cork Report, paras. 1775-1776, pp. 398-399.

[2] *Ibid.* para. 1778, p. 399.

[3] It is beyond the scope of this study to analyse the Committee's recommendations in detail. It should be stated however that that Committee's draft clause is clearer, though more restrictive, than s. 214. The Committee essentially recommended that a company should be deemed to be trading "wrongfully" if at a time when the company is insolvent or unable to pay its debts as they fall due it incurs further debts or other liabilities without a reasonable prospect of meeting them in full. The Committee also proposed that the civil remedy for fraudulent trading be regulated by the same provisions. *Vide* the Cork Report, para. 1806, pp. 404-406.

[4] s. 214(7).

[5] s. 214(1). The liability to make a contribution does not equate with making good the "damages" caused to the company. In *Re Produce Marketing Consortium Ltd. (No. 2)* [1989] BCLC 520 it was held that the measure of the contribution should approximate the amount by which the company's assets were depleted by the wrongful trading. *Vide* also *Re Purpoint Ltd.* [1991] BCLC 491. In the latter case, it was held that the

Such an order can be made where the director, at some time before the commencement of the winding up, knew or ought to have concluded that there was no reasonable prospect that the company could have avoided going into insolvent liquidation[1] and the director failed to take every step which he ought to have taken to minimise the potential loss to the company's creditors.[2] The section does not give any specific guidance as to what steps ought to be taken by a director to avoid liability for wrongful trading.[3] For the purposes of determining (i) whether the director knew or ought to have concluded that there were was no reasonable prospect that the company could have avoided liquidation and (ii) whether he took every step which he ought to have taken, both a subjective and an objective test are involved : the director will be deemed not only to possess the actual skill and knowledge which he has but also to possess the "general knowledge, skill and experience that may reasonably be expected of a person carrying out the same functions".[4]

The wrongful trading provisions contain a number of features which give the remedy an effective bite, especially when compared to the fraudulent trading provisions. First, it is not necessary to establish fraud or dishonesty. Second, the onus is on the director to prove that he has taken every step with

---

*Cont.*

contribution will increase the pool of assets in favour of the creditors generally. It cannot be applied in favour of a particular class of creditors.

[1] For the purposes of s. 214, a company goes into insolvent liquidation if it goes into liquidation at a time when its assets are insufficient for the payment of its debts and other liabilities and the expenses of winding up. s. 214(6).

[2] s. 214 (2). Liability for wrongful trading can be incurred even if the company ceases trading as soon as it is realised that insolvent liquidation is inevitable. Conduct capable of attracting liability for wrongful trading includes the failure to preserve the assets of the company, the conclusion of transactions at an undervalue, the payment of excessive remuneration to the officers of the company and the failure to collect debts due to the company. *Vide* R.M. Goode, *Principles of Corporate Insolvency Law* (1990) p. 205.

[3] Some writers have attempted to list out certain essential measures that should be taken in order to minimise exposure to liability for wrongful trading. *Vide* e.g., Charles D. Drake, "Disqualification of Directors - the Red Card" [1989] J.B.L. 474 p. 489; R.M. Goode, *Principles of Corporate Insolvency Law* (1990) pp. 209-210; Louis G. Doyle, "Anomalies in the Wrongful Trading Provisions" 13 Co. Law. 96 (1992) p. 99.

[4] s. 214 (4). For a discussion on the standard by which the director's conduct is to be judged, *vide Re Produce Marketing Consortium Ltd. (No. 2)* [1989] BCLC 520; D.D. Prentice, "Creditor's Interests and Director's Duties" 10 O.J.L.S. 265 (1990) pp. 269-270; Louis G. Doyle, "Anomalies in the Wrongful Trading Provisions" 13 Co. Law. 96 (1992) pp. 97-98.

a view to minimising the potential loss to creditors.[1] Third, the standard of knowledge, skill and experience is tested by the higher of the objective and the subjective standards. The wrongful trading provisions have in fact been heralded as a potent weapon in the creditor's arsenal against improper conduct.[2]

Whether the wrongful trading remedy can prove effective in controlling the abuse and unfairness inherent in the subservient subsidiary situation is however a different matter altogether.[3] Two questions need to be addressed in this context. First, whether a holding company in a subservient subsidiary situation can qualify as a "shadow director" in terms of the Insolvency Act 1986 and thereby become subject to the duties imposed in section 214. Second, whether the implementation of subservient practices involve a breach of section 214.

### 2.5.3. Could a holding company qualify as a "shadow director"?

An important feature of section 214 is that it applies not only to *de jure* and *de facto* directors,[4] but also to "shadow directors".[5] A "shadow director" is

---

[1] This is evident from the drafting of s. 214 (3). *Vide* also R.M. Goode, *Principles of Corporate Insolvency Law* (1990) p. 207; Charles D. Drake, "Disqualification of Directors - the Red Card" [1989] J.B.L. 474 p. 489.

[2] Prentice, for example, expects that s. 214 will have a significant impact. *Vide* Dan D. Prentice, "A Survey of the Law Relating to Corporate Groups in the United Kingdom" in Eddy Wymeersch (ed.), *Groups of Companies in the EEC* (1993) (hereinafter cited as "Prentice, Survey") p. 314. *Vide* also Fidelis Oditah, "Wrongful Trading" [1990] L.M.C.L.Q. 205 p. 225; Hugh Collins, "Ascription of Legal Responsibility to Groups in Complex Patterns of Economic Integration" 53 M.L.R. 731 (1990) p. 741. Soon after the introduction of the wrongful trading remedy, some writers feared that the provisions might be unfairly applied as they would lead the courts to examine, with the benefit of hindsight, commercial decisions made in good faith but on the basis of inadequate facts. *Vide* e.g., Francis W. Neate, "The Group in Difficulties - a Case Study" in R.M. Goode (ed.), *Group Trading and the Lending Banker* (1988) p. 112. A reading of the wrongful trading judgments reveals such fear to have been unfounded.

[3] A major problem facing any liquidator is that of funding. Creditors of insolvent subsidiaries would be reluctant to contribute money for the expense of litigation unless they are reasonably assured of a successful outcome.

[4] s. 251 of the Insolvency Act 1986 defines a "director" as including "any person occupying the position of director, by whatever name called". *Vide* also *Re Hydrodam (Corby) Ltd.* [1994] 2 BCLC 180 especially at p. 182 per Millett J.

[5] s. 214 (7). In American law, corporations cannot serve as directors. In a holding-subsidiary situation, therefore, the holding company cannot itself be on the board, but

defined as "a person in accordance with whose directions or instructions the directors of the company are accustomed to act".[1]

Whether a holding company qualifies as a shadow director will obviously depend on the particular inter-relationship between the holding company and its subsidiary.[2] Clearly, however, the mere fact that a subsidiary is wholly owned, or that the directors of the holding company also act as the subsidiary's directors should not, as suggested by Prentice,[3] raise a "virtually irrebuttable" inference that the holding company is a shadow director.[4] It is indeed perfectly plausible for wholly owned subsidiaries and even for subsidiaries having common directors with the holding company to retain a sufficient degree of autonomy such that they would not be considered as "accustomed to act" in accordance with the directions or instructions of the

*Cont.*

would be represented by its designee or designees. *Vide* Henn and Alexander, *op. cit.* p. 708.

[1] I.A. 1986, s. 251. In *Re A Company (No 005009 of 1987), ex parte Copp* [1989] BCLC 13 the Court refused to strike out a claim against a bank that it was liable as a shadow director, ruling that the liquidator had raised a triable issue. The bank allegedly used its powers as a secured creditor to intervene in the affairs of the company. On the circumstances in which banks could qualify as shadow directors, *vide* Fidelis Oditah, "Wrongful Trading" [1990] L.M.C.L.Q. 205 pp. 209, 213-214; Weiss, *op. cit.* p. 97; Neate, *op. cit.* p. 126; Denis Keenan, "Banks as Shadow Directors" 17 Accountancy 41 (1991).

[2] Prentice stated that it was "difficult to imagine" that the holding company in *Re Augustus Barnett & Son Ltd.* [1986] BCLC 170 would not be treated as a shadow director. *Vide* Prentice, Group Indebtedness, pp. 78-79. In an earlier contribution, however, Prentice had stated that it was "unclear" whether the holding company could have qualified as a shadow director and went on to return an "open verdict" on the issue. *Vide* D.D. Prentice, "Fraudulent Trading: Parent Company's Liability for the Debts of its Subsidiary" 103 L.Q.R. 11 (1987) pp. 13-14. The judgment - which concerned a claim against a holding company for liability for fraudulent trading - was considered *supra* pp. 208-209. It is submitted that there is in fact no evidence in the judgment to support an inference that the subsidiary was in any way *accustomed* to act on the instructions of the holding company. The financial support provided by the holding company was perfectly compatible with the subsidiary conducting its operations with little interference from the holding company.

[3] Prentice, Survey, p. 313. *Vide* also Hugh Collins, "Ascription of Legal Responsibility to Groups in Complex Patterns of Economic Integration" 53 M.L.R. 731 (1990) where it is stated, at p. 741, that the "concept of shadow director should often encompass parent companies".

[4] Prentice had been more accurate in an earlier contribution when he asserted that a holding company may qualify as a shadow director if it "interferes in the affairs of its subsidiary". *Vide* Prentice, Aspects of British law, p. 78.

holding company. The mere existence (rather than the actual exercise) of latent control by the holding company does not automatically convert the subsidiary into an entity that is accustomed to act as the holding company directs or instructs.[1]

The Cork Committee had recommended that for the purposes of the wrongful trading provisions, the holding company should be presumed, unless the contrary appears, to be party to the decisions of the subsidiary's directors wherever the holding company has been responsible (as is usually the case) for the appointment of the subsidiary's board or a substantial part thereof, or where the boards of the two companies consist of substantially the same persons.[2] This recommendation - which was not eventually incorporated in the Insolvency Act 1986 - was made because the Committee felt that it would often be impossible to determine whether instructions had been given to the board of the subsidiary or whether other means had been used to secure its compliance with the wishes of the holding company.[3] It is submitted however that the Committee somewhat exaggerated the difficulty of proving that instructions are given by the holding company's management. The minutes of meetings and other records (all of which would be accessible to the liquidator) together with other evidence available should quite easily indicate whether or not a holding company had been exerting a substantial influence over its subsidiary. The introduction of a presumption (even though rebuttable) would have had the effect of unjustifiably discriminating against the holding-subsidiary relationship. Parliament sensibly rejected that particular proposal.

There should of course be little doubt that where the relationship involves a *subservient* subsidiary, the inference can usually be drawn that the holding company is acting as a shadow director. In the typical subservient subsidiary situation, the holding company would exercise dominating control over the subsidiary. Such domination would be reflected in various ways. The subsidiary would bow down to direct and specific instructions received from the head office of the holding company. It would abide by both broad and specific policy guidelines established by head office. The subsidiary moreover would seek approval on many issues of varying importance. Typically, therefore, a *habitually* subservient subsidiary would be accustomed to act in accordance with the directions or instructions of the

---

[1] Vide *Re Hydrodam (Corby) Ltd.* [1994] 2 BCLC 180 especially at p. 184 per Millett J.

[2] The Cork Report, para. 1938, p. 437.

[3] *Ibid.* para. 1938, p. 437.

holding company.[1] A subservient subsidiary however need not necessarily be "accustomed to act" in accordance with the directions or instructions of its holding company. A subsidiary may, for example, participate in transfer pricing techniques as part of group tax planning, but otherwise conduct its activities to a large measure independently of the holding company, even though it would remain subject to the holding company's latent control. Such a subsidiary would be subservient, but it would not be "accustomed to act" in accordance with the directions or instructions of the holding company. Probably, however, this type of arrangement is quite unusual.

It should also be observed that the application of the combined objective and subjective tests of knowledge, skill and experience[2] are likely to exact a relatively high standard of conduct from a holding company qualifying as a "shadow director". A holding company is likely to have its own highly skilled and experienced management team providing considerable expertise to other units within the corporate group. Such expertise would no doubt raise the subjective standard of knowledge and skill that would be required of the holding company. And as the level of knowledge, skill and experience in corporate groups generally rises (at least in the large and medium sized groups), so too will the objective standards.[3] Besides, the rule that the knowledge and skill required of a director depends on the nature of the functions entrusted to him[4] effectively broadens the scope of the holding company's liability. For in the normal course, a holding company qualifying as a "shadow director" would be the directing mind behind practically all aspects of the subsidiary's activities. Its position, which could be assimilated to that of a "managing director", is therefore distinguishable from that of a director entrusted with special functions, for example technical or marketing

---

[1] Given that companies are obliged to maintain adequate records of their affairs (e.g., minutes of meetings and accounting records) evidence of subservience would usually be quite readily forthcoming. *Vide* C.A. 1985, s. 382 (duty to make and keep minutes of general meetings and of meetings of directors or managers) and C.A. 1985, s. 221 (duty to keep accounting records sufficient to show and explain the company's transactions). Cf. Prentice, Survey, p. 313.

[2] s. 214(4)(5).

[3] In *Re Produce Marketing Consortium Ltd. (No. 2)* [1989] BCLC 520, Knox J. observed that "the general knowledge, skill and experience postulated will be much less extensive in a small company in a modest way of business, with simple accounting procedures and equipment, than it will be in a large company with sophisticated procedures." *Ibid.* at p. 550. *Vide* also Louis G. Doyle, "Anomalies in the Wrongful Trading Provisions" 13 Co. Law. 96 (1992) p. 97.

[4] s. 214(5).

matters. The latter type of director would not be expected to exercise managerial functions and would not be expected to possess the financial knowledge and skills of the "managing director".

### 2.5.4. Could the holding company in a subservient subsidiary company situation be held liable for wrongful trading?

An essential feature of the wrongful trading provisions is that liability is attracted not by mismanagement leading the company to insolvency, but by the failure - "when the writing is on the wall"[1] - to take appropriate steps to minimise the potential loss to the creditors.[2] This area of the law therefore scrutinises, and penalises, only such conduct as takes place after the time when the director realises or ought to have realised that there was no reasonable prospect of the company avoiding insolvent liquidation.[3] Unfortunately, this particular feature neutralises much of the effectiveness of the wrongful trading provisions as a remedy to combat the abuse and unfairness in the subservient subsidiary situation. For in the typical subservient subsidiary situation, the subservient practices would be conducted during a period when there is no "writing on the wall". The diversion of corporate opportunities, the shuttling of funds and other assets, transfer pricing manipulations and other such subservient conduct would usually be carried out as part of a group profit maximisation policy at a time when no immediate threat to the subsidiary's creditors is occasioned thereby and when there is no reason to conclude that the company was approaching insolvent liquidation. Liability for wrongful trading cannot arise even if the subservient practices play a role in leading a subsidiary to insolvency. For clearly, the wrongful trading remedy does not penalise mismanagement

---

[1] R.M. Goode, *Principles of Corporate Insolvency Law* (1990) pp. 204-205.

[2] This is clearly in line with the Cork Committee's proposals. *Vide* the Cork Report, paras. 1781-1786, pp. 399-400.

[3] In *Re Purpoint Ltd.* [1991] BCLC 491, the company was grossly under-capitalised from its inception and appears to have had a very slim chance of survival. Yet Vinelott J. refused to conclude that the director ought to have known that the company "was doomed to end in an insolvent winding up from the moment it started to trade". To do so, he observed, "would impose too high a test". *Ibid.* at p. 498. The Cork Committee however had expressly considered that "[t]rading when a business is heavily under-capitalised will often come within the concept of 'wrongful trading'." *Vide* the Cork Report, para. 1785, p. 400. The potential use of the remedy of wrongful trading in the context of heavily undercapitalised companies is discussed *post*, Chapter VI pp. 336-340.

leading to insolvency. Nor, as has been suggested by Prentice,[1] does section 214 entail that "holding companies will, in many situations, have to come to the rescue of their failing subsidiaries." Rescue implies some form of financial commitment, such as the payment of debts due by the subsidiary, the subordination of loans due to the holding company or the injection of fresh capital into the subsidiary. Yet section 214 clearly involves no such obligations. The duty is only to take every step to *minimise* the potential loss to creditors. The wording of section 214 cannot be extended to comprise an obligation to make good their losses or to legally ensure that the creditors are protected against loss.[2]

The position would of course be different where the subservient practices occur at a time when the holding company knew or ought to have concluded that there was no reasonable prospect that the company would avoid going into insolvent liquidation. In such circumstances, the subservient practices would directly prejudice the interests of the subsidiary's creditors and would indicate a failure on the part of the holding company, *qua* shadow director, and on the directors of the subsidiary, to take every step they ought to have taken to minimise the potential loss to creditors. Subservient practices would then attract liability for wrongful trading.

## 2.6. Adjustment of prior transactions

### 2.6.1. Introduction

It will have been observed that many of the practices identified as "subservient" in Chapter II[3] involve transactions between a subsidiary and its holding or affiliated companies on terms that the subsidiary receives either no consideration or a consideration which is less than that which would have been received had the transactions been at arm's length. Besides, subservient practices sometimes appear to have the effect of preferring the

---

[1] *Vide* Prentice, Survey, pp. 314-315.

[2] In another contribution, Prentice states that "[i]t might be setting the standard too high to require always that creditors have legal protection *but anything short of this runs the risk of failing to satisfy the standard of taking 'every step'*." (emphasis added). *Vide* D.D. Prentice, "Creditor's Interests and Director's Duties" 10 O.J.L.S. 265 (1990) at p. 269. Prentice makes the same point in Prentice, Aspects of British law, p. 81. It is submitted however that such an interpretation is inconsistent with the clear wording of s. 214 (3). The obligation is to minimise the loss, not to prevent it.

[3] *Vide supra* pp. 65-84.

group (or one member thereof) to the subsidiary's external creditors. Subservient practices bearing such features include transfer pricing manipulations, the shuttling and draining of funds and other assets, the provision of financial support to other members of the group and the operation of a subsidiary without a profit motive. Such practices confer an unfair or improper benefit to the holding company (or to affiliated companies) to the potential prejudice of the subsidiary's creditors.

In these circumstances, it would appear - *prima facie* at least - that there is considerable potential for the application of the statutory remedies of "transactions at an undervalue"[1] and "preferences"[2] in English law[3] and those of "fraudulent transfers"[4] and "voidable preferences"[5] in American law. These remedies, which broadly have the effect of upsetting certain transactions between a company and its creditors in the event of an insolvent winding up of the company,[6] can arm the subsidiary's external creditors with considerable protection against various transactions involving subservient practices. The overall aims of the remedies are essentially threefold : first to inflate the pool of assets available for distribution amongst the creditors;[7] second, to secure parity of treatment as between the creditors;[8] and third, to

---

[1] I.A. 1986, s. 238.

[2] I.A. 1986, s. 239. The provisions on "preferences" represent a significant improvement over the previous position. For a review and criticism of the pre-1986 law *vide* R. Goode, "The Death of Insolvency Law" 1 Co. Law. 123 (1980); Prentice, The English Experience, pp. 107-108; R.M. Goode, *Principles of Corporate Insolvency Law* (1990) pp. 163-164.

[3] The Insolvency Act contains two other "transaction avoidance" remedies, viz., s. 244 (extortionate credit transactions) and s. 245 (avoidance of certain floating charges). These remedies have no particular relevance in the subservient subsidiary situation. Mention should also be made of s. 423 (transactions defrauding creditors). A crucial factor for the application of s. 423 is the transferor's dominant intention to deny assets to creditors (*Chohan* v. *Saggar* [1992] BCC 306). This factor alone renders the remedy virtually inapplicable in the subservient subsidiary context where the element of fraudulent design is usually lacking.

[4] *Vide* the Bankruptcy Code (11 U.S.C. s. 548 (1982)) and the Uniform Fraudulent Conveyance Act (7A U.L.A. 430 (1985)).

[5] *Vide* the Bankruptcy Code (11. U.S.C. s. 547).

[6] In English law the statutory remedies are also available when the company goes into administration.

[7] This is the particular purpose of the provisions on "transactions at an undervalue" and "fraudulent transfers".

[8] This is the particular purpose of the doctrine of "preferences".

deter managerial malpractice.[1] Yet, for the reasons developed later on in this section, the law of voidable transactions - though providing a valuable general remedy - does not offer a comprehensive and adequate solution to the subservient subsidiary situation.

### 2.6.2. Transactions at an undervalue

Of considerable significance in the context of subservient practices are undoubtedly those provisions relating to "transactions at an undervalue" found primarily in section 238 of the Insolvency Act 1986. Section 238 is designed to enable a liquidator to challenge a transaction entered into by a company on significantly unfair terms. Such a transaction is referred to in section 238 as a "transaction at an undervalue". The basic rule is that where a company goes into liquidation or is the subject of an administration order and during the "relevant time"[2] it had entered into a "transaction at an undervalue", the liquidator or administrator can apply to the court for an order to have the position restored to what it would have been had the transaction not been entered into.[3] A transaction is considered to be at an undervalue where the company makes a gift or receives no consideration or where the consideration received by the company "in money or money's worth, is significantly less than the value, in money or money's worth, of the consideration provided by the company."[4] The Court has no jurisdiction to make an order under section 238 if it is satisfied that the company entered into the transaction in good faith for the purpose of carrying on its business and that at the time it did so there were reasonable grounds for believing that the transaction would benefit the company.[5]

The general rule is that only transactions entered into by a company which is insolvent or which render it insolvent can be challenged.[6] In the

---

[1] This is a general aim of this area of the law.

[2] Defined by s. 240(1)(a) as "a time in the period of 2 years ending with the onset of insolvency".

[3] s. 238(3).

[4] s. 238(4)(b). In *Re MC Bacon Ltd.* [1990] BCLC 324, Millet J. stated that s. 238(4)(b) requires "a comparison to be made between the value obtained by the company for the transaction and the value of consideration provided by the company. Both values must be measurable in money or money's worth and both must be considered from the company's point of view." *Ibid.* p. 340.

[5] s. 238(5).

[6] s. 240(2).

case of transactions between a company and a person "connected with the company" however, it is presumed that the company is insolvent or has become insolvent as a result of the transaction, "unless the contrary is shown".[1] The definition of "connected" person is considerably complicated, but clearly comprises transactions between members of a corporate group.[2]

In the context of intra-group transactions, the effectiveness of section 238 is considerably augmented both by the fact that transactions can be challenged if entered into within two years preceding the onset of insolvency and by the provision that the subsidiary entering into such a transaction with a holding or affiliated company is presumed to be insolvent. Undoubtedly, section 238 is a potent repellent that will deter the management of many a holding-subsidiary set-up from concluding transactions that could harm creditors. Head office would indeed be wise to refrain from requiring a subsidiary that is insolvent or of doubtful solvency to participate, for example, in the implementation of excessive transfer pricing arrangements or in the provision of financial support to the group or any member thereof. Unfortunately, however, section 238 cannot - for the reasons to be stated later on in this section - adequately control the mischief inherent in the subservient subsidiary situation.

The American counterpart to the English rules on "transactions at an undervalue" is the set of provisions on "fraudulent conveyances" in the Bankruptcy Code,[3] the Uniform Fraudulent Conveyance Act[4] and similar state statutes. The principal section in the Bankruptcy Code dealing with fraudulent conveyances is section 548, which provides for the avoidance of certain transactions made under particular circumstances. This section is derived largely from section 67d of the Bankruptcy Act, which in its turn substantially incorporated the Uniform Fraudulent Conveyance Act. This Act, together with related state legislation, provides a state law remedy that considerably overlaps (and in certain respects goes beyond) the remedy provided by the bankruptcy law. Given the broad similarity between the statutory provisions in American law, it is proposed, for the sake of

---

[1] s. 240(2).

[2] *Vide* I.A. 1986, ss. 249, 250, 435. Transactions between a company and connected persons are treated more severely because connected persons are more likely to have inside information as to the company's financial dealings and are in a strong position to influence the company's decisions. *Vide* R.M. Goode, *Principles of Corporate Insolvency Law* (1990) p. 139.

[3] 11 U.S.C. s. 548 (1982).

[4] 7A U.L.A. 430 (1985).

conciseness, to deal primarily with the provisions of the Uniform Fraudulent Conveyance Act, which as indicated, is the precursor of the American "fraudulent conveyance" legislation.

The Uniform Fraudulent Conveyances Act ("UFCA") applies to "conveyance[s] made" and "obligation[s] incurred".[1] "Conveyance" is defined as "every payment of money, assignment, release, transfer, lease, mortgage or pledge of tangible or intangible property, and also the creation of any lien or encumbrance."[2] "Obligation" is not defined but its ordinary meaning would clearly include a guarantee. For the purposes of UFCA, therefore, a subsidiary that gives a guarantee incurs an "obligation" and a subsidiary that grants security rights in connection therewith makes a "conveyance". Obligations incurred and transfers made become fraudulent in any one of two situations. The first is where there is an actual intent to hinder creditors.[3] The second is where the corporation does not receive fair consideration[4] and either becomes insolvent,[5] retains an unreasonable small amount of capital,[6] or is about to incur debts which it will be unable to pay.[7] In terms of section 3 of the UFCA, "fair consideration" is given for property or obligation "(a) when in exchange for such property or obligation, as a fair equivalent thereof, and in good faith, property is conveyed or an antecedent debt is satisfied" or "(b) when such property or obligation is received in good faith to secure a present advance or antecedent debt in amount not disproportionately small as compared with the value of the property, or obligation obtained." Paragraph (a) probably covers the granting of a

---

[1] s. 4 UFCA.

[2] s. 1 UFCA.

[3] s. 7 UFCA. s. 7 refers to "actual intent, as distinguished from intent presumed in law". *Vide* also s. 548(a)(1) of the Bankruptcy Code of 1978 (11 U.S.C. ss 101 *et seq*). In English law, s. 423 of the I.A. 1986 would cover a conveyance made with intent to defraud. Transactions involving an actual intent to defraud would be unusual in the corporate group context.

[4] In the Bankruptcy Code, the standard is a "reasonably equivalent value". *Vide* s. 548(a)(2)(A). This standard departs in one significant respect from the standard of "fair consideration" in s. 4 of the UFCA : the reference to "good faith" which appears in the UFCA does not feature in the Bankruptcy Code. Except for this reference to "good faith", the authorities on "fair consideration" under the UFCA are useful in interpreting the "reasonably equivalent value" test in the Bankruptcy Code. *Vide* Blumberg, *Bankruptcy Law* p. 293.

[5] s. 4 UFCA. s. 548(a)(2)(B)(i) of the Bankruptcy Code.

[6] s. 5 UFCA. s. 548(a)(2)(B)(ii) of the Bankruptcy Code.

[7] s. 6 UFCA. s. 548(a)(2)(B)(iii) of the Bankruptcy Code.

guarantee whilst paragraph (b) probably covers the grant of security interests.[1]

It is of course beyond the scope of this study to compare the fraudulent conveyance provisions in American law with the provision in English law on "transactions at an undervalue". For the present purpose, it is enough to highlight two significant differences. In the first place, whereas both the UFCA and the Insolvency Act require a reasonably equivalent *quid pro quo*,[2] the Insolvency Act allows the transaction to stand if the company entered into it in good faith and "there were reasonable grounds for believing that the transaction would benefit the company".[3] This "benefit to the company" defence in English law will save many transactions entered into by a subsidiary, such as the granting of upstream or cross-stream guarantees. No similar defence is available in American law. Secondly, the American provisions appear at once stricter than the corresponding English rules. Under the UFCA, for example, a subsidiary's guarantee and grant of security interests will be deemed fraudulent if the subsidiary (i) is or will thereby be rendered insolvent,[4] or (ii) is engaged or is about to engage in a business or transaction for which the property remaining in his hands is an unreasonably small capital, or (iii) intends or believes that it will incur debts beyond its ability to pay as they mature. These factors can be contrasted with the narrower provisions of section 240(2) of the Insolvency Act which enable a transaction to be challenged only if the company was at the time either (i) unable to pay its debts, or (ii) becomes unable to pay its debts in consequence of the transaction. In particular, the reference to an "unreasonably small capital" clearly enables creditors to impugn transactions under the UFCA which would be unchallengeable under English law.[5]

---

[1] *Vide* William H. Coquillette, "Guaranty of and Security for the Debt of a Parent Corporation by a Subsidiary Corporation" 30 Case Western Reserve Law Review 433 (1980) p. 451.

[2] s. 238 of the I.A. 1986 considers a transaction as vulnerable if the value given is "significantly less" than the value obtained. Section 4 of the UFCA considers the transaction as challengeable if a "fair consideration" is not received. "Fair consideration" is defined in s. 3 of the UFCA.

[3] s. 238(5)(b).

[4] s. 2 of the UFCA adopts a balance sheet test of insolvency. A wider test is utilised by the Insolvency Act 1986 for the purposes of "transactions at an undervalue" and "preferences". *Vide* ss. 240(2) and 123.

[5] It would appear however that American courts have not enforced the capitalisation requirement very rigorously. *Vide* e.g., *Barr & Creelman Mill & Plumbing Supply Co.* v.

## 2.6.3. Preferences

Like the law on transactions at an undervalue in English law and the law on fraudulent transfers in American law, the doctrine of preferences as applied on both sides of the Atlantic is intended to safeguard a debtor's estate against depletion to the detriment of its creditors. Although the remedies overlap to some extent,[1] they are essentially intended to deal with separate issues.

Under section 239 of the Insolvency Act, a court may strike down preferences made during the "relevant time". In the case where the transaction is with a person not "connected"[2] with the company, the "relevant time" is considered to be "the period of 6 months" ending with the onset of insolvency.[3] Where the transaction is with a person "connected" with the company, the "relevant time" is extended to two years.[4] A preference occurs whenever a company has, during the relevant time, put one of the company's creditors or a surety for the company's debts or other liabilities into a better position than he would have been had such thing not been done.[5] The court has no jurisdiction to make an order restoring the position to what it was before the transaction being impugned unless the company was influenced by a desire to put him in that preferential position.[6] In *Re MC Bacon Ltd.*,[7] Millett J. held that the desire to prefer is subjective

---

*Cont.*
   *Zoller* 109 F.2d 924 (2d Cir. 1940). *Vide* generally, Jonathan M. Landers, "A Unified Approach to Parent, Subsidiary, and Affiliate Questions in Bankruptcy" 42 Univ. of Chicago L.R. 589 (1975) p. 595.

[1] *Vide* R.M. Goode, *Principles of Corporate Insolvency Law* (1990) p. 176; Blumberg, *Bankruptcy Law* p. 364.

[2] The definition of "connected" person is the same as in the case of transactions at an undervalue. *Vide* I.A. 1986, ss. 249, 250 and 435. Intra-group transactions are therefore clearly covered.

[3] I.A. 1986, s. 240(1)(b).

[4] s. 240(1)(a).

[5] s. 239(4).

[6] s. 239(5). The previous statutory provision (s. 44(1) of the Bankruptcy Act 1914) required the company to act "with a view" to preferring one creditor over others. The courts interpreted this to mean "the substantial view" (In re *Bird (ex parte Hill)* (1883) 23 Ch.D. 695 C.A.), the "dominant or real motive" (*Sharp* v. *Jackson* [1899] A.C. 419 H.C.) or the "principal or dominant intention" (*In Re Cutts* [1956] 1 W.L.R. 728 (C.A.)

[7] [1990] BCLC 324. *Vide* generally Clare Campbell, "Note on Re MC Bacon Ltd." 11 Co. Law 184 (1990).

and can be demonstrated by examining the evidence and drawing inferences from the facts. The mere presence of the desire to prefer is not in itself sufficient. What is necessary is that the desire influenced the decision to enter into the transaction. The desire to prefer, however, need not be the sole or dominating factor. Where a preference is given to a "connected" person, it is presumed, "unless the contrary is shown" to have been influenced by a desire to put him in such a preferential position.[1]

Given that a transaction with a holding company may be challenged if entered into within a two year period preceding the subsidiary's liquidation, and given also that in such circumstances a presumption arises that the act was entered into with the intent to give an improper preference, a wide range of transactions between the subsidiary and its holding company are potentially open to scrutiny. The presumption and the extension of the "relevant time" in the case of connected persons certainly facilitate efforts at challenging transactions between the subsidiary and its holding company. Despite the general usefulness of such provisions, however, section 239 cannot - for the reasons stated later - adequately control the abuse and unfairness of subservient practices in the holding-subsidiary relationship.

American law on "voidable preferences" is contained primarily in section 547 of the Bankruptcy Code of 1978.[2] In order to be vulnerable as a preference, the transfer must be made while the debtor was insolvent,[3] must violate the policy of "equality amongst creditors" and must enable the creditor to receive more than he would otherwise have received.[4] Moreover, the transfer must have been made during the 90 days immediately preceding the filing of the petition.[5] American law on voidable preferences, like its English counterpart, also deals strictly with persons related to the debtor.

---

[1] s. 239(6).

[2] 11 U.S.C. s. 547. *Vide* generally Blumberg, *Bankruptcy Law* Ch. 9; Richard F. Dole, Jr., "The New Federal Bankruptcy Code : An Overview and Some Observations Concerning Debtors' Exemptions" 17 Hous. L. R. 217 (1980); Michael L. Cook, "Fraudulent Transfer Liability under the Bankruptcy Code" 17 Hous. L. R. 263 (1980); Raymond T. Nimmer, "Security Interests in Bankruptcy : An Overview of Section 547 of the Code" 17 Hous. L. R. 289 (1980).

[3] s. 547(b)(3). Under s. 547(f), insolvency is presumed in the case of transfers made during the 90 day period prior to the filing of the petition of bankruptcy. In the case of transfers made more than 90 days but less than one year prior to the filing, the trustee has the burden of proving the insolvency.

[4] s. 547(b)(5).

[5] s. 547(b)(4)(A).

Section 547 in fact makes voidable certain transfers to "insiders" that occur within one year of the filing of the petition.[1] An "insider" is defined broadly in the Bankruptcy Code to include "a person in control", an "affiliate" or "insider" of an "affiliate".[2] Clearly, the broad definitions of "affiliate" and "insider" include every company within a corporate group. As in English law, the stricter treatment meted out in American law to transactions between a company and its insiders facilitates a close scrutiny of intra-group relationships. Nevertheless, for the reasons developed later on in this section, the American doctrine on voidable preferences is - just like its English twin - also inadequate to remedy the abuse and unfairness of subservient practices between a subsidiary and its holding or affiliated companies.

### 2.6.4. Cross-stream and upstream guarantees

As discussed in Chapter II, the creditworthiness of a subsidiary is sometimes utilised to support borrowing by other weaker affiliates in the group.[3] The support extended by the subsidiary would probably be in the form of guarantees either in respect of the holding company's obligations ("upstream guarantees") or in respect of an affiliate's obligations ("cross-stream guarantees").[4] As a matter of company law, English law requires that the subsidiary has the power in its constitution to enable it to guarantee the debts of a third party.[5] Invariably, subsidiaries will have such a power in their constitution. In the United States, the corporation statutes of the vast majority of states expressly grant to corporations the power to guarantee the obligations of another.[6]

In the context of insolvency, the crucial issue is to determine the extent to which upstream and cross-stream guarantees can be challenged as transactions "at an undervalue" under section 238 of the Insolvency Act or as "fraudulent transfers" under section 4 of the UFCA.[7] In American law,

---

[1] s. 547(b)(4)(B).

[2] *Vide* ss. 101(2) and 101(30)(B) and (E) of the Bankruptcy Code.

[3] *Supra* pp. 79-81.

[4] *Vide supra* Chapter II pp. 80-81.

[5] *Vide* Prentice, Survey, p. 292.

[6] Blumberg, *Bankruptcy Law* pp. 249-251.

[7] It is unlikely for upstream or cross-stream guarantees to be challengeable under the provisions requiring "intent" to defraud (i.e., s. 7 UFCA, s. 548(a)(1) of the Bankruptcy Code of 1978 (11 U.S.C. ss. 101 *et seq*) and s. 423 of the I.A. 1986. With these

upstream and cross-stream guarantees given by a subsidiary company raise similar issues to those raised in English law. In order to escape challenge under American law, the guarantee must be given in consideration of some corporate benefit derived by the subsidiary[1] and must satisfy the tests of the fraudulent conveyancing statutory provisions.[2]

A preliminary point is whether a guarantee can qualify as a transaction within the meaning of section 238 of the Insolvency Act and section 4 of the UFCA. The answer appears to be that it does. Admittedly, most transactions regulated by these sections would involve the transfer of property, the provision of services or the payment of money by the company in exchange for some money or property. Guarantees, by contrast, involve the surety only in a contingent liability which may never materialise and the *quid pro quo* is the loan to a third party, that is the principal debtor. These differences however are relevant only to the question of the valuation of the benefit. The applicability of section 238 of the Insolvency Act and section 4 of the UFCA should not thereby be affected.

Another preliminary observation needs to be made. Neither section 238 of the Insolvency Act nor section 4 of the UFCA specifically indicate to whom the fair consideration is to be made. Given that the purpose of the Insolvency Act and the UFCA is to protect the creditors of the transferor, it follows that the fairness of the consideration should be determined by reference to the transferor's position. For the purposes of section 238 of the Insolvency Act and section 4 of the UFCA, "consideration" therefore clearly refers to the receipt of property or rights by the transferor, or the satisfaction of an antecedent debt of the transferor. Receipt of consideration by a third party is irrelevant.

---

*Cont.*

guarantees the intent is usually to obtain the loan rather than to hinder creditors. *Vide* further William H. Coquillette, "Guaranty of and Security for the Debt of a Parent Corporation by a Subsidiary Corporation" 30 Case Western Reserve Law Review 433 (1980) p. 451.

[1] *Vide Rubin* v. *Manufacturers Hanover Trust Co.* 661 F. 2d 979, 991-992 (2d Cir. 1981).

[2] UFCA (7A U.L.A. 430 (1985)), the Uniform Fraudulent Transfer Act (7A U.L.A. 639 (1985)), and the Bankruptcy Code of 1978 (11 U.S.C. s. 548). *Vide United States of America* v. *Gleneagles Investment Co., Inc.* 565 F. Supp. 556 (1983), *aff'd sub nom. United States of America* v. *Tabor Court Realty Corp.* 803 F. 2d 1288 (3rd Cir. 1986), *cert. denied McClellan Realty Co.* v. *United States* 107 S.Ct. 3229 (1987). The federal bankruptcy provisions incorporate the tests of the UFCA. The discussion will concentrate on the UFCA.

An underlying theme in this area of the law is the broad equality in exchange, that is whether the benefit conferred on the transferee is substantially greater than the value to the transferor. In the context of guarantees given by a subsidiary, say in respect of money lent to its holding company by a bank, the value of the consideration given by the bank is obviously not the amount lent to the holding company, but the value of such loan to the subsidiary, since this is the act exacted by the subsidiary as the price for its guarantee. This is crucial since the purpose of the law is to prevent the depletion of the transferor's assets. The fairness of the consideration should therefore be determined by reference to such transferor's position and not by reference to the primary debtor.[1] The benefit must be to the guarantor.[2]

The crucial question is whether the fact that the guarantor is a subsidiary company within a corporate group makes any difference to the question of the consideration received by the subsidiary. Even where affiliated companies are economically inter-related, an entity analysis would be expected from the English courts and appears to be the prevailing approach adopted by American courts. Occasionally, however, some American courts have refused to recognise the separate entities and have considered them as a single economic enterprise. These courts, utilising an "identity of interest" approach of the lifting the veil doctrine have found "fair consideration" in the transfer by one affiliate that benefited another affiliate within the corporate group.[3]

A serious complication with guarantees is the matter of valuation. It may indeed prove particularly difficult to value the consideration (that is the guarantee) provided by the subsidiary for the purposes of section 238(4)(b) of the Insolvency Act or section 4 of the UFCA. Section 238(4)(b) of the Insolvency Act proscribes transactions if the value obtained by the company is "significantly less than the value, in money or money's worth" of the consideration provided by the company. Section 4 of the UFCA renders impeachable transactions made without "fair consideration".[4] The question is whether a guarantee has a value which is measurable "in money or money's worth" for the purposes of section 238 of the Insolvency Act and

[1] *Vide United States* v. *West* 299 F. Supp. 661 (D. Del. 1969).

[2] *Vide In re Nelsen*, 24 B.R. 701, 702 (Bankr. D. Or. 1982).

[3] Cf. *Klein* v. *Tabatchnick* 610 F. 2d 1043, 1047 (2d Cir. 1979); *Mandel* v. *Scanlon* 426 F. Supp. 519 (W.D. Pa. 1977). *Vide* further *post* pp. 231-232.

[4] "Fair consideration" is defined in s. 3 of the UFCA. *Vide* further *supra* pp. 222-223.

whether it can be measured as a "fair equivalent" for the purposes of the UFCA.

In this matter, it is of course necessary to consider the situation prevailing at the time when the guarantee is extended, rather than the time when payment falls due under the guarantee or the time when payment is actually effected. For clearly, a guarantee is a contingent liability : the amount of the debt or other liability which is covered by the guarantee does not necessarily equate with the actual liability incurred by the guarantor. And the contingency (that is, default by the principal debtor) may never occur. In economic terms, the value of a guarantee provided by a subsidiary depends primarily on the likelihood that the guarantee will be called upon. In fact, the value of a guarantee varies inversely with the financial strength of the principal debtor.[1] The higher the risk, the higher the value of the consideration provided by the subsidiary. Where the principal debtor is financially sound, the creditor's reliance on the guarantee is diminished and with it the value (to the creditor) of the guarantee. On the contrary, where the principal debtor is already insolvent or nearing insolvency, the risk of the guarantee being called increases significantly and its value to the creditor would be much higher, possibly equalling the amount guaranteed.[2] There is of course no scientific method whereby a guarantee can be measured with any degree of accuracy and strictly speaking it would therefore seem that a guarantee cannot be considered to have a value "in money, or money's worth". The danger in such a situation would be that because the transaction is incapable of valuation, it would be treated as a transaction at an undervalue.[3] Goode suggests a "broad brush" approach as a practical solution to the problem. He proposes that, as a working guide, the value of a guarantee to a creditor should be "the amount (if any) for which, at the time of the guarantee, a prudent creditor ... would make provision in his accounts for default, after taking into account what he could reasonably expect to recover from securities taken from the principal debtor and from co-sureties in respect of their proportionate share of the suretyship liabilities."[4] Alternatively, he suggests that the value of the guarantee could be "the

---

[1] R.M. Goode, *Principles of Corporate Insolvency Law* (1990) p. 147.

[2] Another difficulty concerns the extent to which the value of a guarantee to the creditor is reduced by the fact that he already holds some other security. This question is comprehensively dealt with in R.M. Goode, *Principles of Corporate Insolvency Law* (1990) at pp. 148-149.

[3] Cf. Prentice, Group Indebtedness, pp. 69-70.

[4] R.M. Goode, *Principles of Corporate Insolvency Law* (1990) at p. 150.

amount for which a prudent surety ... would make provision in its accounts after allowing for the value of securities taken from the principal debtor and contributions from co-sureties".[1] In making it possible to value guarantees, Goode's pragmatic "broad brush" approach would save many a guarantee from being considered as issued at an undervalue. It is hoped that the courts would adopt the same or a similar approach.

In contrast to English law, the American statutory provisions actually provide guidelines on the valuation of contingent liabilities at least for certain purposes - such as the determination of insolvency and the balance sheet position.[2] Section 2(1) of the UFCA establishes a standard of "probable liability on ... existing debts as they become absolute and matured". In determining "probable liability" on a guarantee, the courts appear to be given a statutory direction to adjust or discount the face value of the guarantee to reflect the likelihood or otherwise of payment by the principal debtor.[3]

The preceding discussion addressed the question of valuation of the guarantee itself. A related issue is the value of the consideration received by the guarantor subsidiary, which in terms of section 238(4) of the Insolvency Act should not be "significantly less" than the value of the guarantee provided by it and which in terms of section 4 of the UFCA should constitute a "fair equivalent". Where the subsidiary does not itself receive a tangible *quid pro quo*, upstream and cross-stream guarantees are, *prima facie* at least, impeachable.[4] This is a crucial issue since in most cases the subsidiary receives no fees or anything tangible in return.[5]

This question has been specifically considered in American law. Where the subsidiary actually receives a portion of the proceeds of the group financing package, such portion is naturally taken into account in determining the question of fair consideration. In the typical situation, however, the aim of the financing is to ameliorate the financial position of an affiliated company and indirectly of the group as a whole. Whether such benefit is too intangible to constitute a "fair consideration" for the purposes of the fraudulent conveyance provisions has been the subject of litigation. In

---

[1] *Ibid.* at p. 150.

[2] s. 502(c) of the Bankruptcy Code requires that contingent obligations be estimated for the purpose of allowance and proof of claims.

[3] *Vide* further Blumberg, *Bankruptcy Law* pp. 303-305.

[4] Even though the liability is admittedly contingent.

[5] *Vide* Blumberg, *Bankruptcy Law* pp. 257-258; Prentice, Aspects of British law, p. 84.

*Rubin* v. *Manufacturers Hanover Trust Company*,[1] subsidiaries gave upstream and cross-stream guarantees in favour of a bank in respect of loans advanced to affiliated companies. The subsidiaries subsequently went into bankruptcy proceedings. The trustee in bankruptcy challenged the guarantees as fraudulent conveyances on the basis that the loans were not given to the subsidiaries but to the affiliates. The bank countered that the guarantor subsidiaries had received an indirect benefit. The first court had found for the bank. The Court of Appeals however held that the lower court was wrong to have found that fair consideration had been given for the guarantees without a finding of economic benefit to each guarantor subsidiary. The Court of Appeals also found that the lower court erred in determining the financial health of the debtor company by reference to its affiliated companies and the solvency of the "enterprise" represented by the group as a whole. The *Rubin* test was applied more recently in the context of a Chapter 11 reorganisation. In the *Matter of the Ohio Corrugating Company*[2] the court considered that it was essential to demonstrate an economic benefit - of a reasonably equivalent value - to the entity within the group which incurs the obligation or makes the transfer. The court rejected the argument that "as long as some entity received a reasonable value for the incurring of the loan obligation or the transferring of the security interest, Plaintiff's case must fail regardless of whether [the guarantor] benefitted from the transaction."[3]

Not all American courts however have been wedded to strict entity law when applying fraudulent transfer law to guarantees extended by subsidiaries. An "enterprise" approach has sometimes been taken, with the result that upstream and cross-stream guarantees are saved from the statutory provisions. In *Telefest, Inc.* v. *VU-TV, Inc.*[4] it was held that an upstream guarantee to assist the holding company in a financing exercise that would be of benefit to the entire group provided sufficient (albeit indirect) benefit to the guarantor subsidiary as to satisfy the "fair consideration" test in the UFCA. The court stated that "the notion that a benefit accrues to a subsidiary only when there is a direct flow of capital to that entity [as] the result of its guarantee ... is inhibitory of contemporary financing practices, which recognize that cross-guarantees are often needed because of the

[1] 661 F. 2d 979 (2d Cir. 1981).

[2] 70 B.R. 920 (B. Ct. N.D. Ohio 1987).

[3] *Ibid.* at p. 927.

[4] 591 F. Supp. 1368 (D.N.J. 1984).

unequal abilities of interrelated corporate entities to collateralize loans."[1] The court observed that contemporary corporate practices "of vertically and horizontally dividing the integrated operations of what is essentially one enterprise among a number of legally distinct entities" made it necessary for financial institutions to frequently seek upstream and cross-stream guarantees.[2] Adopting an unmistakably enterprise approach, the court concluded that in such circumstances a broad view of the "fair consideration" requirement must be taken.[3]

English judgments have not specifically tackled the question of fair consideration in respect of upstream and cross-stream guarantees. Nevertheless, it is arguable that many such guarantees should be saved from the clutches of section 238 on the basis of the defence that at the time of the guarantee, "there were reasonable grounds for believing that the transaction would benefit" the subsidiary.[4] Indeed, guarantees may often be in the interests of the subsidiary as it can plausibly be argued that the welfare of the subsidiary was dependent on the welfare of the group or of the company which received the support.[5] The subsidiary would not receive a direct economic benefit, nor a benefit that is readily quantifiable. But the expectation that the granting of the guarantee would "benefit" the subsidiary company certainly accords with the reality of the intra-corporate relationships within a group. A subsidiary granting a guarantee or security rights may also benefit in other indirect ways. For example, some of the funds obtained by its holding company or affiliate may be re-directed towards the subsidiary. The subsidiary would be also subrogated in the rights of the lender. Besides, it may receive cross-guarantees from other affiliates together with a right of contribution. Moreover, the subsidiary also gains - albeit in an intangible way - by its participation in a financially sound corporate group. All told, an "enterprise" approach should arguably be accepted by the courts for the purpose of a defence under section 238(5)(b).

There is, of course, another limb to the defence under section 238(5) that has to be satisfied to protect the subsidiary's guarantee from challenge in the event that it receives a consideration that is "significantly less" than the

---

[1] *Ibid.* at p. 1379.

[2] *Ibid.* p. 1380.

[3] *Ibid.* p. 1380.

[4] s. 238(5)(b).

[5] *Vide* Prentice, Aspects of British law, p. 84. The position in American law is clearly different. *Vide supra* pp. 230-231.

value of the guarantee. The court must be satisfied that the subsidiary issuing the guarantee "did so in good faith and for the purpose of carrying on its business".[1] Although it is not expected that the element of "good faith" be the cause for any difficulty to arise, it is unlikely that in a typical case, a subsidiary can be considered to have issued the guarantee for the "purpose of carrying on its business" - unless, perhaps, it is the financing division within the group. In the normal course, the guarantee would be issued only because the subsidiary's strong financial position leads the holding company to request the subsidiary to support the extension of banking facilities or some other credit to other affiliates.

Naturally, different considerations would apply where the guarantee is extended in favour of an insolvent subsidiary which stands no chance of recovery. In such a situation, the guarantee is unlikely to be in the interest of the group. Nor, *a fortiori*, will it be in the interest of the subsidiary. The subsidiary would not even be able to satisfy the "reasonable grounds for believing" limb of the defence.

There is perhaps a different argument that could save a guarantee given in respect of the liabilities of a solvent affiliate. Given that the test is whether the guarantor furnished greater consideration than it received, it is arguable that a satisfactory *quid pro quo* is notionally given at the time of the granting of the guarantee, because at that moment, if a call were made, the guarantor subsidiary would become subrogated to the creditor's rights against the then solvent affiliate and would lose nothing. In the case of a solvent principal debtor, a number of American courts have considered that the right of subrogation may offset the liability under the guarantee.[2] The position of course would be completely different where the guarantee is extended in respect of the liabilities of an insolvent affiliate. In such a case, or in the case where the financial position of the principal debtor is poor, the value of the right of subrogation is considerably diminished. Different considerations, moreover, would also obviously apply to a right to a contribution from a co-surety. Even if the co-surety is solvent, the right to a contribution can only partially reduce the liability under the guarantee. The

[1] s. 238(5)(a).

[2] *Vide* e.g., *Telefest, Inc.* v. *VU-TV, Inc.* 591 F. Supp. 1368, 1375 n. 5 (D.N.J. 1984). Cf. *In re Alexander Dispos-Haul Sys., Inc.* 36 Bankr. 612, 616 (Bankr. D. Or. 1983). *Vide* also *In re Ollag Construction Equipment Corp.* 578 F.2d 904 (2d Cir. 1978), a case concerning the solvency or otherwise of a guarantor subsidiary at the time it issued the guarantee. The court held that the actual value of the subsidiary's rights of subrogation and contribution had to be taken into account as assets.

reason is that in the event of the insolvency of the primary debtor the guarantor subsidiary will - notwithstanding the solvency of the co-surety - always bear some liability.

The fact that cross-stream and upstream guarantees may be unchallengeable under the Insolvency Act or the UFCA does not however diminish the inherent unfairness of a group profit maximisation strategy that requires creditworthy subsidiaries to provide financial support by way of such guarantees only for the holding company to abandon them if the interests of the group eventually so demands. Once the interests of the subsidiary are jeopardised for the overall benefit of the group, it should be obligatory on the part of the group, (or at least of the holding company) to come to the rescue of the subservient subsidiary (or at least of its creditors) if and when such subsidiary is itself floundering.

### 2.6.5. Inadequacy of the statutory provisions

As previously suggested, it is evident that the provisions on "preferences" and "transaction at an undervalue" can sometimes play a significant role in redressing a number of abusive practices in the context of the subservient subsidiary situation. Clearly, for example, certain typically subservient practices - such as transfer pricing techniques, the provision of financial support by a subsidiary and the draining of assets from the subsidiary - may be vulnerable as "transactions at an undervalue" or "preferences". The effectiveness of the provisions is especially enhanced both by the fact that transactions can be challenged if entered into within two years preceding the onset of insolvency and by the presumptions laid down in sections 238 and 239 with regard to connected persons.[1] Almost certainly these provisions have the effect of dissuading many a corporate group from concluding certain types of transactions, especially involving subsidiaries that are insolvent or of doubtful solvency. Yet without denying their evident utility, these provisions cannot, for the reasons presently stated, adequately remedy the abuse and unfairness inherent in the subservient subsidiary situation.

A major difficulty is that some forms of subservient practices cannot be characterised either as "transactions at an undervalue" or as "preferences". Thus, typical subservient practices - such as the diversion of corporate opportunities or the commingling of assets - undoubtedly fall outside the ambit of the provisions. Because these provisions focus only on certain types

---

[1] *Vide supra* pp. 220-221.

of transactions, they do not address themselves to the broader subservient practices that make up a subservient subsidiary situation.

A number of "technical" requirements also render the "adjustment of prior transactions" provisions inappropriate as a general remedy to deal with the subservient subsidiary situation. One such requirement is the rule that only transactions entered into during the two year period preceding the onset of insolvency can be impugned. The likelihood of course is that a habitually subservient subsidiary would have been implementing subservient practices ever since its incorporation, possibly several years before the onset of insolvency. The "undervalue" and "preference" provisions would obviously be wholly inapplicable.

The effectiveness of these provisions is also considerably weakened by another technical requirement : that the challenged transactions must take place at a time when the subsidiary is insolvent or becomes insolvent as a consequence of the transaction.[1] Undoubtedly, the insolvency refers to the subsidiary as a separate entity and not to the corporate group. Again it is clear that many transactions qualifying as subservient occur at a time when the subsidiary is not insolvent. And yet, the abuse and unfairness still arise. As a practical matter, therefore, the requirement of insolvency minimises the protection that can otherwise be afforded by the "undervalue" and "preference" provisions.[2] Nothing will stop the dissipation of the subsidiary's resources until it is in dire financial straits. It is true that the English provision on "transactions at an undervalue" raises a presumption of insolvency where the transaction has been entered into between connected persons. The presumption is however rebuttable and it would in most cases be relatively easy to prove the solvency of the subsidiary at the relevant time.

A particular obstacle raised by the "transactions at an undervalue" provision in the Insolvency Act and, to a lesser extent, by the fraudulent conveyance provision in the UFCA concerns the "fair consideration" requirement. In terms of the Insolvency Act, a transaction will be at an undervalue if the value obtained by the subsidiary be "significantly less" than the value given by it.[3] The UFCA uses both a stricter "fair equivalent" test and a wider "not disproportionately small" test depending on the nature

---

[1] s. 240(2) of the I.A. 1986; s. 4 UFCA; s. 548(a)(2)(B)(i) of the Bankruptcy Code.

[2] s. 5 of the UFCA also encompasses transfers that leave the transferor with unreasonably small capital. The capitalisation requirements have not been rigorously enforced. *Vide supra* p. 223 footnote 5.

[3] s. 238(4)(b).

of the transaction.[1] It is beyond the scope of this work to analyse the distinctions between the English test and the American test. For our purposes it is sufficient to note that both the English and American tests will catch only transactions that are substantially imprudent.[2] This effectively means that many subservient transactions - such as those involving transfer pricing manipulations - will escape challenge under the provisions because taken individually the transactions will not reveal a considerable imbalance between the consideration received and that given. It is only when the transactions are examined in their unity (an exercise that is not allowed by the provisions) that an unfair imbalance will be detected in the subservient conduct.

Transactions involving intra-group transfer pricing techniques are also beset with a unique problem related to the determination of a "fair consideration". The problem is to identify the arm's length price. The literature on the tax implications of transfer pricing reveals how difficult it is to determine with any degree of accuracy the arm's length price.[3] One relatively straightforward (and certainly accurate) method is to gauge the arm's length price by reference to comparable transactions between a buyer and a seller who are not associated companies. Unfortunately, such data is very often unavailable, either because there is no open market for the particular products or because there are in fact no comparable products or because it is part of a package whose individual use, and therefore value, will depend on its relation to other parts of the package.[4] Even where comparable prices are available, they may not be appropriate in intra-group

---

[1] *Vide supra* p. 223.

[2] On the English provisions *vide* Prentice, Survey, p. 320. On the UFCA *vide* Note, "Fraudulent Conveyances - Test of 'Fair Consideration'" 42 Mich. L.R. 706 (1944).

[3] *Vide* generally OECD Report on Transfer Pricing (1979) Ch. 1; OECD Report on Transfer Pricing (1984) pp. 11-14; Howard La Mont, "Multinational Enterprise, Transfer Pricing and the 482 Mess" 14 Columbia Journal of Transnational Law 383 (1975); Murray (ed.), *op. cit.* H. Bartlett Brown, "The Specifics of the Section 482 Regulations" in Fordham University School of Law, 1976 Corporate Law Institute - International Taxation and Transfer Pricing (1976) pp. 9-14; J. Roger Mentz, "Sales of Goods under section 482 Regulations" in Fordham University School of Law, 1976 Corporate Law Institute - International Taxation and Transfer Pricing (1976) pp. 15-19; Richard M. Rouse, "The United Kingdom - Practice of the Revenue in Intercompany Pricing" in Fordham University School of Law, 1976 Corporate Law Institute - International Taxation and Transfer Pricing (1976) pp. 109-114.

[4] *Vide* Robin Murray, "Transfer Pricing and its Control : Alternative Approaches" in Murray (ed.), *op. cit.* pp. 159.

trade, where long-term supply of goods may be provided.[1] In any such case, other methods may be used, such as the resale price method, the cost-plus method, or some other equitable measure.[2] The difficulty with establishing an arm's length price is further compounded when the transaction relates not to tangible products but to intangibles such as the provision of services or the grant of licence rights.[3] To determine whether management fees or royalties "agreed to" between a holding and its subsidiary company are essentially at arm's length may prove an impossible task.

A particular difficulty with impugning a transaction as a "preference" under section 239 is the requirement that the subsidiary be "influenced ... by a desire" to put the holding or affiliated company in a preferential position in the event that the subsidiary went into insolvent liquidation.[4] Unfortunately, the effect of this requirement is to put the focus on the motive of the subsidiary rather than on the nature of the inter-corporate relationship. Admittedly, section 239 does raise a presumption in the case of connected persons that the transaction was tainted with the desire to prefer.[5] But the presumption is rebuttable. It would be quite plausible for a subsidiary to contend that the transaction was prompted not by a desire to prefer the holding or affiliated companies, but by a desire to participate in a group profit maximisation policy for the benefit of all the units within the group.

Undoubtedly, however, the major difficulty with the "transfer at an undervalue" and "preference" provisions as a general remedy for subservient practices is that these provisions adopt a "monotransactional" approach. In other words, the "undervalue" or "preference" provisions can only be used to impugn transactions on an individual basis. Transactions therefore have to be scrutinised individually. In the context of subservient practices within corporate groups, this particular requirement will undoubtedly create considerable practical difficulties rendering the provisions virtually unworkable. For in the intricacies of a typical corporate group, hundreds of

---

[1] Frank Wooldridge, *Groups of Companies - The Law and Practice in Britain, France and Germany* (1981) p. 91.

[2] *Vide* Howard La Mont, "Multinational Enterprise, Transfer Pricing and the 482 Mess" 14 Columbia Journal of Transnational Law 383 (1975) pp. 394-405; Frank Wooldridge, *Groups of Companies - The Law and Practice in Britain, France and Germany* (1981) pp. 91-92; Eitmann and Stonehill, *op. cit.* pp. 411-412. On transfer pricing generally, *vide supra* Chapter II pp. 68-73.

[3] *Vide* Joseph Flom, "Tangled skein of tax adjustments" *Financial Times*, 7th May 1992.

[4] s. 239(4)(5).

[5] s. 239(6).

transactions qualifying as subservient can take place even over a short period of time. A court called upon to apply the "undervalue" or "preference" provisions in a corporate group context would find it practically impossible to minutely examine each single transaction in the light of the specific requirements of the said sections. Apart from the practical difficulties, it would also prove extremely costly to analyse separately each transaction, to assess all the related evidence and to then make separate findings as to timing of the transactions, fair consideration, insolvency and the availability or otherwise of applicable defences. The court would of course be able to establish - from behavioural patterns in the holding-subsidiary relationship - that a course of conduct evidencing subservient practices exists. But such a conclusion would clearly not be sufficient to trigger the application of the "undervalue" and "preference" provisions. In the face of such complexity, American courts have sometimes used a "gestalt" approach, thereby avoiding the necessity of applying all of the criteria of "fraudulent conveyance" to a series of transactions.[1] This method of analysis seems to have been used in the cases where a series of non-arm's length transactions were concluded over a period of time and it became impossible as a practical matter to determine with any degree of precision the aggregate amount by which the company had been deprived of fair consideration.[2] In such cases the holding or affiliate companies' claims against the subsidiary may be subordinated to those of *bona fide* outside creditors.[3] Equitable subordination is viewed as a functional substitute for fraudulent conveyance law.[4] In viewing a course of conduct rather than a sequence of snap-shots, American courts have adopted a pragmatic approach which in such complex circumstances is certainly justifiable. Regrettably, English courts have never contemplated adopting a similar attitude.

---

[1] *Vide* R.C. Clark, "The Duties of the Corporate Debtor to its Creditors" 90 Harv. L.R. 505 (1977) p. 531.

[2] *Taylor* v. *Standard Gas & Elec. Co.* 306 U.S. 307 (1939); *Pepper* v. *Litton* 308 U.S. 295 (1939).

[3] On the remedy of subordination, *vide post* Chapter VI pp. 355-360.

[4] *Vide* R.C. Clark, "The Duties of the Corporate Debtor to its Creditors" 90 Harv. L.R. 505 (1977) p. 527.

## 2.7. Common law duties of directors towards creditors

### 2.7.1. Introduction

The 1980s and early 1990s generated considerable academic interest over the question of the judicial extension of directors' common law duties towards creditors.[1] The excitement was originally sparked by remarks made by Mason J. in the Australian case of *Walker* v. *Wimborne*[2] that "the directors of a company in discharging their duty to the company must take account of the interest of its shareholders and its creditors. Any failure by the directors to take into account the interests of the creditors will have adverse consequences for the company as well as for them."[3] Since then, courts appear to have displayed considerable sympathy for the position of creditors. Courts seem to have freed themselves from the shackles of the traditional equation of the company with its shareholders and are beginning to recognise the notion of directors' duties towards the company's creditors.

Although it is beyond the scope of this study to review all aspects of the judicial development, it is pertinent to discuss the role of directors' duties towards creditors in the specific context of the subservient subsidiary situation. Two crucial questions need to be examined. First, do the parameters of the duties of directors towards creditors adequately proscribe

[1] The more important contributions include : M.W. Russell, "A Director's Duty to Creditors" 1 Cantab. L.R. 417 (1982); Francis Dawson, "Acting in the Best Interests of the Company - For Whom are Directors 'Trustees'?" 11 N.Z.U.L.R. 68 (1984); J.H. Farrar, "The obligation of a company's directors to its creditors before liquidation" [1985] J.B.L. 413; R.S. Nathan, "Controlling the Puppeteers : Reform of Parent-Subsidiary laws in New Zealand" 3 Cantab. L.R. 1 (1986); L.S. Sealy, "Directors' 'Wider' Responsibilities - Problems Conceptual, Practical and Procedural" 13 Monash Univ. L.R. 164 (1987); Justin Dabner, "Directors' Duties - The Schizoid Company" 6 Company and Securities Law Journal 105 (1988); L.S. Sealy, "Directors' Duties - An Unnecessary Gloss" [1988] C.L.J. 175; Vanessa Finch, "Directors' duties towards creditors" 10 Co. Law. 23 (1988); Neil Hawke, "Creditors' Interests in Solvent and Insolvent Companies" [1989] J.B.L. 54; John H. Farrar, "The Responsibility of Directors and Shareholders for a Company's Debts" 4 Cantab. L.R. 12 (1989); Dan D. Prentice, "Creditor's Interests and Director's Duties" 10 O.J.L.S. 265 (1990); Ross Grantham, "The Judicial Extension of Directors' Duties to Creditors" [1991] J.B.L. 1; Prentice, Survey, pp. 315-319.

[2] (1976) 50 A.L.J.R. 446.

[3] *Ibid.* at p. 449. Similar observations were made by Street C.J. in another Australian case, *Kinsela* v. *Russell Kinsela Pty. Ltd.* (1986) 10 A.C.L.R. 395 at pp. 401-404. *Vide post* pp. 244-245.

subservient practices in the holding-subsidiary relationship? Second, can a holding company in a subservient subsidiary situation qualify as a "director" for the purposes of directors' duties towards creditors? Before dealing with these questions, a number of preliminary observations need to be made.

### 2.7.2. Directors' fiduciary duties in the group context

A director owes a fiduciary duty to act in the best interests of the company he serves. Given that each company within a group is at law a separate entity, it follows that the directors of a subsidiary are not entitled to sacrifice the interests of that subsidiary in the interests of any other component within the group.[1] The directors of a subsidiary owe, therefore, no fiduciary duties to the holding company, even though they are appointed by the holding company or are directors also of the holding company.[2] Thus in *Scottish Co-Operative Wholesale Society Ltd.* v. *Meyer*,[3] the House of Lords considered that it was a breach of duty for the directors of a subsidiary company (who were also directors of the holding company) to use their position (even by way of omission) to promote the interests of the holding company to the detriment of the subsidiary. It follows that the directors of a subsidiary company should not automatically and without question comply with the instructions of the holding company where to do so would constitute a breach of their duties to the subsidiary.[4] The directors of the subsidiary must ensure that compliance with instructions from the holding company will be for the benefit of the subsidiary as distinct from the group as a whole. Directors, however, would not be held to have abused their powers if they enter into a transaction for the benefit of a holding or affiliated company, provided that the purpose of the transaction is also to confer a real and

---

[1] *Vide Charterbridge Corporation Ltd.* v. *Lloyds Bank Ltd.* [1970] Ch. 62, p. 74. *Vide* also the Cork Report, para. 1969, p. 443. Cf. *Boulting* v. *Association of Cinematograph, Television and Allied Technicians* [1963] 2 Q.B. 606 (C.A.), especially at p. 626 per Lord Denning M.R.; *Kuwait Asia Bank EC* v. *National Mutual Life Nominees Ltd.* [1990] BCLC 868 (P.C.).

[2] E.g., *Scottish Co-Operative Wholesale Society Ltd.* v. *Meyer* [1959] A.C. 324 (H.L.). *Vide* also *Dairy Containers Limited* v. *NZI Bank Limited* [1994] MCLR 465.

[3] [1959] A.C. 324 (H.L.).

[4] *Lonrho Ltd.* v. *Shell Petroleum Co. Ltd.* [1980] 1 W.L.R. 627, 634-635 (H.L.). Cf. *Selangor United Rubber Estates Ltd.* v. *Cradock (No. 3)* [1968] 1 W.L.R. 1555; *Clark* v. *Workman* (1920) 1 I.R. 107.

substantial benefit on the company.[1] Conceivably, for example, a subsidiary threatened by the failure of one of its affiliates will have a real and substantial interest in preserving such an affiliate. Any other view would clearly be too restrictive. In the absence of evidence of what the directors of the subsidiary actually considered, the test of their obligations will depend on what an honest and reasonable director would consider to be in the interests of the company.[2]

So far, the legal position is clear enough. It must however be noted that in practice the law is often ignored and the affairs of the subsidiary systematically conducted in the overall interests of the group and to the potential detriment of the subsidiary.[3] In doing so, directors of a subservient subsidiary would be walking the tightrope of their fiduciary duties. Even where (as frequently happens) the subsidiary is controlled through management links rather than through the subsidiary's directorate - with the subsidiary's board being effectively by-passed[4] - the directors would still be bound by their fiduciary duties.

The director's duty to act in the best interests of the company he serves naturally entails that the directors of a holding company owe no duties to the subsidiary.[5] The directors of a holding company will in fact be guilty of a breach of a fiduciary duty if, let us say, they pledge the assets of the holding company to meet the liabilities of the subsidiary when to do so cannot reasonably be conceived to be of benefit to the holding company. Given however that the property of the holding company comprises the shares

---

[1] *Charterbridge Corporation Ltd.* v. *Lloyds Bank Ltd.* [1970] Ch. 62; Frank Wooldridge, *Groups of Companies - The Law and Practice in Britain, France and Germany* (1981) pp. 12-13. The Bullock Report posed the question whether the directors of a subsidiary should be able to have regard to the interests of the shareholders and employees of the holding and affiliated company. *Vide* the Bullock Report para. 39, p. 84. But the Committee expressed no definite view on the matter.

[2] *Charterbridge Corporation Ltd.* v. *Lloyds Bank Ltd.* [1970] Ch. 62. *Vide* also *Re Horsley & Weight Ltd.* [1982] 3 All E.R. 1045 (C.A.); *Nicholson* v. *Permakraft* [1985] 1 N.Z.L.R. 242.

[3] *Vide supra* Chapter II pp. 65-68. *Vide* also the Cork Report, para. 1926, pp. 434-435 and para. 1951, p. 439; Frank Wooldridge, *Groups of Companies - The Law and Practice in Britain, France and Germany* (1981) p. 108; Department of Trade, The Cornhill Consolidated Group Limited (In Liquidation), Investigation under Section 165(b) of Companies Act 1948, Report by David Calcutt, QC and John Whinney, FCA, (pub. HMSO 1980) para. 17.03, p. 293 and para. 17.14, p. 296.

[4] On this phenomenon, *vide* White, *op. cit.* p. 51 and *supra* Chapter II pp. 58-59.

[5] *Vide Lindgren* v. *L. & P. Estates Ltd.* [1968] Ch. 572 (C.A.) p. 595 and p. 604.

invested in its subsidiary it is arguable that in the normal course directors of the holding company should have the duty to promote the interests of the subsidiaries representing that investment.[1] Whilst this argument may be tenable in cases where the subsidiary is solvent, different considerations will obviously apply where the subsidiary is insolvent or its continuing success in doubt. In such latter cases, the financially sensible approach - from the holding company's point of view - may well be to desist from extending to the subsidiary any financial assistance whatsoever.

*Prima facie*, at least, the duty to act in the interest of the company (and its corollary in the group context - the duty on the part of the directors of a subsidiary not to sacrifice the interests of their company in the interests of any other member in the group) appear to precisely cater for the subservient subsidiary situation, where "by definition" the subsidiary acts not in its own interests, but, to its detriment, in the interests of the holding company or some other member within the group. A director of a subservient subsidiary would indeed be abdicating his responsibilities and be in breach of his duties to the subsidiary. This much is clear. The difficulty is to determine what is meant by the interests of the subsidiary. Where the company is a wholly-owned subsidiary and it remains solvent, there will be no difficulty. There are no minority shareholders or creditors to be prejudiced. Where the company is a partly-owned and solvent subsidiary, minority shareholders (whose expectations may not coincide with those of the group) may undoubtedly be affected,[2] even though, as already indicated, these may face considerable difficulties in practice when attempting to obtain redress.[3] Employees too would clearly be included,[4] even though they appear to have no means of enforcing such interests.[5]

---

[1] This argument was raised by counsel in *Lindgren* v. *L. & P. Estates Ltd.* [1968] Ch. 572 (C.A.) at p. 582. In the Bullock Report it was recommended that the directors of the holding company should be entitled to take into account the interests of the employees and shareholders, present and future, of subsidiaries and sub-subsidiaries within the group. *Ibid.* para. 38, p. 84. In *Nicholas* v. *Soundcraft Electronics Ltd.* [1993] BCLC 360, the Court of Appeal held that the action of a holding company in delaying payments due to its partly-owned subsidiary did not constitute unfairly prejudicial conduct given that the reason for such delay was to try to keep the group, which was in financial difficulties, afloat.

[2] *Scottish Co-Operative Wholesale Society Ltd.* v. *Meyer* [1959] A.C. 324 (H.L.). *Vide* also *Abbey Glen Property Corp.* v. *Stumborg* (1976) 65 D.L.R. (3d) 235 especially at p. 278.

[3] *Vide supra* Chapter I pp. 17-18.

[4] By virtue of s. 309 of the C.A. 1985.

[5] Cf. Gower, pp. 554-555.

The crucial question in our context is whether the interests of the subsidiary can include the interests of the subsidiary's creditors. As long as a subsidiary remains solvent, no difficulties should arise. But where the subsidiary is insolvent, or becomes insolvent in consequence of what has been done, the creditors will be prejudiced. It is on this question that the judicial developments in recent years need to be examined.[1] Until quite recently, it seems to have been assumed that a director owed no duties to the company's creditors. In 1962, for example, the Jenkins Committee noted that *Percival* v. *Wright*[2] provided authority for the proposition "that no fiduciary duty is owed by a director to individual members of his company, but only to the company itself, and *a fortiori* that none is owed to a person who is not a member."[3] Since then, however, the principle has been under considerable strain, with courts being prepared to find that in certain circumstances a director does, through the company,[4] owe "fiduciary" duties to creditors.[5] Most courts seem to use the concept of the "interests of the company" as the medium through which fiduciary duties are owed to the creditors.[6] In *Nicholson* v. *Permakraft (N.Z.) Ltd.*,[7] however, Cooke J. appeared willing to

---

[1] In 1982, the Cork Committee stated that "[a]s the law stands ... the liquidator of a wholly-owned subsidiary cannot complain of anything done at the direction or with the consent of the parent company, the only shareholder of the subsidiary, even if the company was insolvent, unless the act was *ultra vires* the subsidiary. In some cases, it may be possible to escape the conclusion by treating the misapplication [of the subsidiary's assets] as constituting an unlawful dividend or return of capital to shareholders; but in many cases this is not possible, particularly where the act complained of is the assumption of liabilities or the giving of a guarantee." The Cork Report, para. 1971, p. 443. The reforms introduced in the mid-1980s considerably altered the legal position.

[2] [1902] 2 Ch. 421.

[3] The Jenkins Report, para. 89, p. 31.

[4] There are strong reasons for holding that the duty should be exercised through the company. *Vide* Dan D. Prentice, "Creditor's Interests and Director's Duties" 10 O.J.L.S. 265 (1990) pp. 275-276.

[5] There is no doubt that the directors are not, *as such*, liable to creditors. *Kuwait Asia Bank EC* v. *National Mutual Life Nominees Ltd.* [1990] BCLC 868 (P.C.). The position in American law is broadly the same. *Vide* 19 *Corpus Juris Secundum* s. 537.

[6] *Vide Brady* v. *Brady* [1988] BCLC 20 (C.A.); *West Mercia Safetywear Ltd.* v. *Dodd* [1988] BCLC 250 (C.A.); *Winkworth* v. *Edward Baron Development Co. Ltd.* [1987] 1 All E.R. 114 (H.L.).

[7] [1985] 1 N.Z.L.R. 242.

rely on the notion of tort liability in negligence as a route towards securing creditors' interests.[1]

Most judgments draw a distinction. Where a company is solvent, the interests of the company are, normally, taken to be only those of the shareholders. The interests of creditors are not to be factored into the interests of the company.[2] In *Brady* v. *Brady*,[3] Nourse L.J. stated that :

> "The interests of a company, an artificial person, cannot be distinguished from the interests of the persons who are interested in it. Who are those persons? Where a company is both going and solvent, first and foremost come the shareholders, present and no doubt future as well. How material are the interests of the creditors in such a case? Admittedly existing creditors are interested in the assets of the company as the only source for the satisfaction of their debts. But in a case where the assets are enormous and the debts minimal it is reasonable to suppose that the interests of the creditors ought not to count for very much."[4]

Where, on the contrary, the company is insolvent, or perhaps even "doubtfully solvent",[5] the shareholders will cease to have any continued interest in the company. The interests of the company will in reality be the interests of existing creditors alone. This doctrine, clearly stated for the first time in the Australian case of *Kinsela* v. *Russell Kinsela Pty. Ltd.*,[6] has also received recognition by the English courts. In *West Mercia Safetywear Ltd.* v. *Dodd*,[7] a director of an insolvent company was held to have breached the duty he owed to the company's creditors as a class when he used the company's funds to pay the debts owed by the company to its holding company.[8] In delivering judgment for the Court of Appeal, Dillon L.J. cited with approval Street C.J.'s dictum in *Kinsela* v. *Russell Kinsela Pty. Ltd.*[9]

[1] *Ibid.* p. 249.

[2] *Vide Multinational Gas and Petrochemical Co.* v. *Multinational Gas and Petrochemical Services* [1983] 3 W.L.R. 492 (C.A.) especially at p. 519 per Dillon L.J.

[3] [1988] BCLC 20 (C.A.).

[4] *Ibid.* at p. 40. Nourse L.J. also noted that the expression "the interests of the company" might have "slightly different meanings in different contexts." *Ibid.* p. 40.

[5] *Brady* v. *Brady* [1988] BCLC 20 (C.A.) at p. 40 per Nourse L.J.

[6] (1986) 10 A.C.L.R. 395.

[7] [1988] BCLC 250 (C.A.).

[8] The payment would almost certainly now qualify as a "preference" under s. 239 of the I.A. 1986.

[9] (1986) 10 A.C.L.R. 395 at p. 401.

that "[i]n a solvent company the proprietary interests of the shareholders entitle them as a general body to be regarded as the company when questions of the duty of directors arise. ... But where a company is insolvent the interests of the creditors intrude. They become prospectively entitled, through the mechanism of liquidation, to displace the power of the shareholders and directors to deal with the company's assets."[1]

Certain dicta however appear to suggest that the directors owe a duty to the company's creditors even during the company's solvency. Mason J.'s dictum in the Australian case of *Walker* v. *Wimborne*[2] did not in fact suggest that it is insolvency which gives rise to the duty to take account of the interests of creditors.[3] On the contrary, he thought that creditors' interests should always be considered given the theoretical possibility of future insolvency.[4] And in *Ring* v. *Sutton*[5] the New South Wales Court of Appeal, approving of Mason J.'s dicta in *Walker* v. *Wimborne*, held that a loan at less than market value entered into by a company while it was solvent was detrimental to the interests of the creditors. The loan was successfully challenged in a misfeasance summons by the liquidator. There is little doubt, however, that the English version of the doctrine is more restrictive than that suggested by some of the Australian cases.[6] Insolvency, or at least "near" insolvency or "doubtful" insolvency, is clearly established as an essential ingredient for the application of the doctrine in English law.[7]

---

[1] [1988] BCLC 250 (C.A.) at pp. 252-253. Street C.J.'s dictum appears in (1986) 10 A.C.L.R. 395 at p. 401. In the earlier case of *Re Horsley & Weight Ltd.* [1982] 3 All E.R. 1045 (C.A.), Templeman L.J. had stated, *obiter*, that if the company could not afford to make a particular expenditure and was "doubtfully solvent so that the expenditure threatened the continued existence of the company", the directors would have been in breach of duty to the company if such expenditure were effected. Templeman L.J. also doubted whether it was open to the shareholders to ratify such "gross negligence amounting to misfeasance" so as to prejudice creditors. *Ibid.* p. 1056.

[2] (1976) 50 A.L.J.R. 446. *Vide supra* p. 239.

[3] This point was observed by Jacobs J. in *Grove* v. *Flavel* (1986) 11 A.C.L.R. 161 at p. 167.

[4] (1976) 50 A.L.J.R. 446 at p. 449. The company concerned was in fact insolvent at the time of the impugned transactions.

[5] (1980) 5 A.C.L.R. 546 (C.A. N.S.W.).

[6] A number of Australian cases do however clearly require insolvency or financial instability. *Vide* e.g., *Kinsela* v. *Russell Kinsela Pty. Ltd.* (1986) 10 A.C.L.R. 395; *Grove* v. *Flavel* (1986) 11 A.C.L.R. 161.

[7] *Multinational Gas and Petrochemical Co.* v. *Multinational Gas and Petrochemical Services* [1983] 3 W.L.R. 492 (C.A.); *Brady* v. *Brady* [1988] BCLC 20 (C.A.), [1989]

Before looking into the role that the doctrine may play in the specific context of subservient practices, it is essential to make a few general remarks.

### 2.7.2.1. Lack of precise definitions

First, there is as yet no precise definition of the circumstances which trigger the duty towards creditors. The duty will certainly arise if the company is insolvent. But is insolvency determinable by reference to a balance sheet test, by reference to an "inability to pay debts" test, or by reference to either of them? Presumably, the courts would refer to insolvency in the commercial sense, that is the inability to pay debts as they fall due, even though that moment may be difficult to pinpoint precisely. But in *Nicholson* v. *Permakraft (N.Z.) Ltd.*,[1] Richardson J. understood "insolvency" to mean an excess of liabilities over assets[2] while Cooke J. suggested that although balance sheet solvency and the ability to pay capital dividend were important in assessing the transaction proposed, the directors should consider also their company's "practical ability to discharge promptly debts owed to current and likely continuing trade creditors."[3] Apart from the situation of actual insolvency, it has also been stated that creditors are entitled to consideration if the company was "doubtfully solvent"[4] or "near insolvent"[5] or "if a contemplated payment or other course of action would jeopardise its solvency".[6] Unfortunately no attempt is made in the judgments to define such expressions. In *Kinsela* v. *Russell Kinsela Pty. Ltd.*[7] Street C.J.

*Cont.*
>  A.C. 755, 778 (H.L.); *West Mercia Safetywear Ltd.* v. *Dodd* [1988] BCLC 250 (C.A.). This is also the New Zealand approach. *Vide Nicholson* v. *Permakraft (N.Z.) Ltd.* [1985] 1 N.Z.L.R. 242.

[1] [1985] 1 N.Z.L.R. 242.

[2] *Ibid.* at p. 254.

[3] *Ibid.* at p. 249.

[4] E.g., *Brady* v. *Brady* [1988] BCLC 20 (C.A.) at p. 40 per Nourse L.J; *Re Horsley & Weight Ltd.* [1982] 3 All E.R. 1045 (C.A.). at p. 1056 per Templeman L.J. *Vide* also *Nicholson* v. *Permakraft (N.Z.) Ltd* [1985] 1 N.Z.L.R. 242 at p. 249 per Cooke J.

[5] *Nicholson* v. *Permakraft (N.Z.) Ltd* [1985] 1 N.Z.L.R. 242 at p. 249 per Cooke J; *Multinational Gas and Petrochemical Co.* v. *Multinational Gas and Petrochemical Services* [1983] 3 W.L.R. 492 (C.A.).

[6] *Nicholson* v. *Permakraft (N.Z.) Ltd* [1985] 1 N.Z.L.R. 242 at p. 249 per Cooke J. *Vide* also *Brady* v. *Brady* [1988] BCLC 20 (C.A.) p. 41.

[7] (1986) 10 A.C.L.R. 395.

hesitated "to formulate a general test of the degree of financial instability which would impose upon directors an obligation to consider the interests of creditors", believing that this might vary depending on the nature of the business undertaken by the company.[1] In any case, what test is to be applied regarding the directors' appreciation of the company's solvency? Should the matter be determined objectively, as in *Re Horsley & Weight Ltd.*[2] where Templeman J. stated that if the proposed expenditure threatened the continued existence of the company the directors "ought to have known the facts"?[3] Or should the test be more subjective such as that applied when considering the fiduciary duty of the directors to act in good faith in the interests of the company?[4] If the duty to creditors is considered as another facet of the fiduciary duties to the company, then the subjective test should presumably apply. On the other hand, it is arguable that a stricter objective test should be adopted to protect the interests of creditors. Given such difficulties, it is clearly impossible, at this embryonic stage in the development of the doctrine, to define its ambit with any degree of precision.

### 2.7.2.2. Dicta often *obiter*

Secondly, and more fundamentally, it is submitted that if the various dicta are examined in the context of the fact-situations to which they relate, it will be observed that they are often uttered *obiter* and convey little more than a sense of general disapproval towards some wrongdoing by the directors which would in any case probably have been proscribed by some other rule, such as that of fraudulent preference, misfeasance, *ultra vires* or the capital maintenance doctrine. In *West Mercia Safetywear Ltd.* v. *Dodd,*[5] for example, the wrongdoing clearly constituted a fraudulent preference and a misfeasance. And in *Brady* v. *Brady*[6] the ratio of the decision was essentially that the transfer of half of the company's assets for virtually no consideration

---

[1] *Ibid.* p. 404.

[2] [1982] 3 All E.R. 1045 (C.A.).

[3] *Ibid.* at p. 1056. An objective test was applied in *Nicholson* v. *Permakraft (N.Z.) Ltd.* [1985] 1 N.Z.L.R. 242 where Cooke J., at p. 250, expressly adopted Lord Templeman's approach in *Re Horsley & Weight Ltd.* [1982] 3 All E.R. 1045 (C.A.).

[4] *Re Smith & Fawcett Ltd.* [1942] 1 All E.R. 542 (C.A.); *Brady* v. *Brady* [1988] BCLC 20, 40-41 (C.A.).

[5] [1988] BCLC 250 (C.A.).

[6] [1988] BCLC 20 (C.A.).

was *ultra vires* and in breach of sections 151 and 153 of the Companies Act 1985 dealing with the provision of financial assistance. Nourse L.J.'s dictum on directors' duties toward creditors was made in the context of these statutory provisions.[1] And *Winkworth* v. *Edward Baron Development Co. Ltd.*[2] presented such a flagrant case of self-dealing in an insolvency situation that the decision can be distinguished on its particular facts[3] with Lord Templeman's wide ranging remarks - practically requiring guaranteed solvency[4] - viewed as *obiter dicta*. Otherwise, if taken literally, Lord Templeman's approach would produce a veritable revolution in company law. Such an effect could hardly have been intended, given especially that there was no reference whatsoever to any previous authorities on the subject. Even Cooke J.'s statement in *Nicholson* v. *Permakraft (N.Z.) Ltd.*[5] - that the directors' concern for the interests of creditors, though originating "as a matter of business ethics" may be translated into a legal obligation in accordance with "the now pervasive concepts of duty to a neighbour and the linking of power with obligation"[6] - were clearly made *obiter*. The same can be said of *Walker* v. *Wimborne*[7] where directors were held liable in misfeasance after funds had been moved about between companies in a

---

[1] *Ibid.* pp. 40-41.

[2] [1987] 1 All E.R. 114.

[3] The case concerned a claim by a wife, who was a director and shareholder of the company, to be allowed to enforce her equitable interest in the matrimonial home (which was owned by the company) against a mortgagee seeking possession. In the course of dismissing this claim, Lord Templeman referred to the principle that equity would only intervene to uphold a constructive trust where it was conscionable in all the circumstances. In the circumstances, the enforcement of a constructive trust in favour of the director would have defeated the claims of creditors. The greater part of his Lordship's speech is in fact devoted to the trust aspect rather than the question of directors' duties towards creditors.

[4] Lord Templeman stated that " ... a company owes a duty to its creditors, present and future. The company is not bound to pay off every debt as soon as it is incurred and the company is not obliged to avoid all ventures which involve an element of risk, but the company owes a duty to its creditors to keep its property inviolate and available for    the repayment of its debts. ... A duty is owed by the directors to the company and to the creditors of the company to ensure that the affairs of the company are properly administered and that its property is not dissipated or exploited for the benefit of the directors themselves to the prejudice of the creditors." [1987] 1 All E.R. 114 at p. 118. The other Law Lords concurred with Lord Templeman's speech.

[5] [1985] 1 N.Z.L.R. 242.

[6] *Ibid.* at p. 249.

[7] (1976) 50 A.L.J.R. 446.

group as "the exigencies arose" and were used for the payment of the salaries of those other companies. Although the judicial utterances on directors' duties towards creditors cannot be lightly discarded, it is clear therefore that doubts must be cast on whether the judgments can be considered as law in the making.

### 2.7.2.3. Doctrine perhaps stunted by legislative developments

Thirdly, the origins of the doctrine can be traced to the period before the substantial reforms in insolvency law introduced in the mid-1980s. The limited protection that had been afforded to creditors before then may have prompted the courts to attempt to ameliorate their position by judicial creativity.[1] It is now likely, however, that the statutory remedies of "wrongful trading", "transactions at an undervalue" and "preferences" will take centre stage in deterring and penalising objectionable conduct by directors while the doctrine, if it continues to develop, will operate at the margins.[2] Perhaps significantly, no other judgments endorsing the doctrine appear to have been reported - at least in England - since *West Mercia Safetywear Ltd.* v. *Dodd*.[3] The statutory remedies may have stunted the doctrine's further development.

### 2.7.3.  Can a holding company qualify as a director for the purposes of directors' duties towards creditors?

Every single judgment - English and Australasian - promoting the notion of an extension of fiduciary duties towards creditors concerned conduct by directors. The question that now arises is whether this notion can be further

---

[1] It would appear that even the cases decided after the introduction of the reforms concerned situations arising prior to such reforms. E.g., *Winkworth* v. *Edward Baron Development Co. Ltd.* [1987] 1 All E.R. 114; *Brady* v. *Brady* [1988] BCLC 20 (C.A.); *West Mercia Safetywear Ltd.* v. *Dodd* [1988] BCLC 250 (C.A.).

[2] Prentice states that "[t]he primary role of the doctrine will probably be to prevent certain claims being asserted by a director in a winding up where this would be to the prejudice of other creditors". *Vide* Prentice, Survey, p. 317. *Vide* also Dan D. Prentice, "Creditor's Interests and Director's Duties" 10 O.J.L.S. 265 (1990) pp. 276-277.

[3] [1988] BCLC 250 (C.A.). A 1989 Australian case (*Jeffree* v. *National Companies & Securities Commission* (1989) 15 A.C.L.R. 217) has however applied *Winkworth* v. *Edward Baron Development Co. Ltd.* [1987] 1 All E.R. 114.

extended to impose fiduciary duties on a holding company towards the creditors of its subsidiary. In American law, a holding company, qua dominant shareholder, is considered to owe fiduciary duties not only to the minority shareholders,[1] but in certain instances even to the subsidiary's creditors.[2] As we shall see in a later Chapter, American courts have in fact often subordinated the claims of a dominant shareholder to those of ordinary creditors on the basis that the claimant violated the "rules of fair play and good conscience" and breached "the fiduciary standards of conduct which he owes the corporation, its stockholders and creditors."[3] At this stage in the development of English law, it is unlikely however that the courts would be willing to depart so radically from established principle to recognise a duty on the part of a dominant shareholder (including a holding company) towards creditors.

It is submitted, however, that the doctrine of directors' duties towards creditors can, in certain circumstances and without undue strain, be made applicable to the holding company in the subservient subsidiary situation. Such an approach depends on giving the notion of "director" a wide construction. In a subservient subsidiary situation the holding company would generally exercise considerable influence and control - even complete control - over the activities of its subsidiary. The holding company may act, or purport to act, as a director, although not technically appointed as such. In such circumstances, given that a director is defined (in the Companies Act 1985, the Insolvency Act 1986 and the Company Directors Disqualification Act 1986) as including "any person occupying the position of director, by whatever name called"[4] it is arguable that the holding company would be acting as a *de facto* director.[5] Admittedly, the notion of *de facto* directors has

---

[1] *Southern Pacific Co.* v. *Bogert* 250 U.S. 483 (1919); *Pepper* v. *Litton* 308 U.S. 295 (1939). *Vide* generally Henn and Alexander, *op. cit.* pp. 653-656.

[2] Cf. *Pepper* v. *Litton* 308 U.S. 295 (1939).

[3] *Pepper* v. *Litton* 308 U.S. 295 (1939) at p. 310-311. *Vide* further William L. Cary and Melvin Aron Eisenberg, *Cases and Materials on Corporations* (5th ed. 1980) pp. 108-111.

[4] C.A. 1985, s. 741(1); I.A. 1986, s. 251; Company Directors Disqualification Act 1986, s. 22(4). I.A. 1986, s. 251; Company Directors Disqualification Act 1986, s. 22(4).

[5] Cf. *In re Eurostem Maritime Ltd.* [1987] PCC 190; *Re Lo-Line Electric Motors Ltd.* [1988] BCLC 698; *Re Tasbian Ltd. (No. 3)* [1991] BCLC 792; *Re Hydrodam (Corby) Ltd.* [1994] 2 BCLC 180; *Re Moorgate Metals Ltd.* [1995] 1 BCLC 503. Neither Wooldridge nor Pennington would consider a holding company to be a *de facto* director in the subservient subsidiary situation. *Vide* Frank Wooldridge, *Groups of Companies - The Law and Practice in Britain, France and Germany* (1981) p. 21; Robert R.

only received express recognition in the aforesaid statutory context. But there is no reason why the notion should not be afforded the same meaning in a common law context. Once statute itself expands the notion of "director" to include both *de jure* and *de facto* directors, the common law doctrine should similarly be extended to *de facto* directors (and therefore to the holding company in the subservient subsidiary situation).

The extension of the doctrine to a dominating holding company should also be encouraged for two policy reasons: firstly, because the holding company would usually be more closely involved in the subservient practices than the directors of the subsidiary and should therefore bear a heavier responsibility; secondly, because a holding company is normally better able than the directors to absorb the liability and indemnify the creditors (through a contribution to the assets of the subsidiary). The creditors' lot would be considerably ameliorated if the holding company were to be held responsible for breach of fiduciary duties.

A final observation should be made in this context. Where the wrongdoing is attributable to both the holding company and the subsidiary's directors (as in the case of a subservient subsidiary situation) there is another argument for channelling liability more forcefully towards the holding company rather than towards the directors.[1] As a matter of policy, care should be taken not to expose directors too broadly to the risk of personal liability without good and sufficient cause. Not only can the imposition of personal liability lead to individual bankruptcy (with all its personal and social problems), but it could discourage people with the requisite experience and ability from taking up directorships. This would have a

---

*Cont.*

Pennington, *Company Law* (6th ed. 1990) pp. 738-739. Where the directors of the subsidiary are accustomed to act in accordance with the directions or instructions of the holding company, the latter will also qualify as a "shadow director". *Vide* s. 741(2) of the C.A. 1985 and s. 251 of the I.A. 1986. For a full list of those provisions in the C.A. 1985 and the I.A. 1986 that apply to "shadow directors" *vide* Robert R. Pennington, *Company Law* (6th ed. 1990) p. 531. The simple fact that directors are nominees of the holding company does not make the holding company a "shadow director". *Vide Kuwait Asia Bank EC* v. *National Mutual Life Nominees Ltd.* [1990] BCLC 868 (P.C.).

[1] Any provision in the Articles of Association of the subsidiary or in any contract between the holding company and the subsidiary's directors purporting to exempt the subsidiary's directors from, or to indemnify them against, any liability that may be imposed upon them in respect of any breach of duty would be void under s. 310 of the Companies Act 1985.

negative effect both on the market for directorships and on professional corporate rescue operations.

### 2.7.4. Inadequacy of doctrine as a remedy in the subservient subsidiary situation

The doctrine of directors' duties to creditors is still in an early stage of development and it is difficult to surmise the extent to which the courts will expand its field of operation. One matter is clear: that even should one assume that the doctrine of directors' duties to creditors can be extended to a dominating holding company, the doctrine, at least in its present stage of development, cannot adequately remedy the abuse and unfairness inherent in the subservient subsidiary situation. A number of observations need to be made in this regard.

In the first place, although judicial efforts aimed at improving the protection afforded to creditors are certainly commendable, it is essential that the courts provide clearly defined principles on which further developments can be based and accurate advice given. Unfortunately, the judgments so far delivered on the subject are too loosely stated to permit a precise formulation of the doctrine.

Secondly, doubts must be raised as to whether a doctrine is really emerging. As previously stated, the "obiter" flavour of many of the dicta, the fact that many decisions are explicable on other grounds and the absence of further judgments on issues arising after the implementation of the statutory reforms of the mid-1980's inevitably introduce an element of scepticism into the prognosis.

Apart from such reservations however, and even assuming that a doctrine of directors' duties towards creditors is actually developing, there are serious specific difficulties with the doctrine as a remedy to counter the abuse and unfairness of subservient practices.

Firstly, the ambit of operation of the doctrine appears to be quite narrow. The doctrine seems to be concerned with sanctioning conduct which constitutes a wrong to the company and results directly in prejudice to creditors. Preferential payments to the holding company or transactions entered into for no consideration or for very little consideration would obviously qualify as conduct attracting the application of the doctrine. Such wrongdoing may of course also be regulated by statutory rules. The advantage of the doctrine may then be to provide additional relief.[1] But

---

[1] *Vide supra* p. 249.

where the wrongdoing is not so obvious or the harm to creditors not so immediate, the likelihood is that the doctrine will not be invoked. Subtle transfer pricing manipulations, the diversion of corporate assets, the commingling and shuttling of funds and assets, and other such insidious behaviour will almost certainly not be caught within the present confines of the doctrine.

Another serious shortcoming of the doctrine in the context of the subservient subsidiary situation is the requirement that the wrongdoing occurs at a time when the company is insolvent or at least "doubtfully" solvent or "nearly" insolvent.[1] At first sight, this requirement appears justifiable on the ground that where the company is solvent there will be no issue of creditor protection and that therefore the interests of the creditors should not intervene.[2] This however is to take a narrow view of creditor protection. A pattern of conduct involving subservient practices over a period of time may weaken the financial backbone of the subsidiary to the extent that creditors will actually be prejudiced, even though the subservient practices may have taken place mostly at a time when the subsidiary was technically solvent. The requirement of insolvency (or doubtful solvency or near insolvency) does not therefore take into account the fact that subservient practices may have a causal link to the subsidiary's eventual insolvency. Insolvency should not be a decisive factor in any rule attempting to redress the wrongdoing involved in the subservient subsidiary situation. In any case, the difficulty of determining precisely whether a state of insolvency or "doubtful solvency" or "near insolvency" exists can only serve to complicate the investigation into the subservient subsidiary's conduct. The issue is further aggravated by the fact that in the certain cases a subsidiary's financial position may so oscillate that it may regularly move in and out of a condition of "doubtful solvency" or "near insolvency" over a period of time.

Another serious limitation on the usefulness of the doctrine is that it appears to be essentially monotransactional in approach. In each case in which the doctrine was invoked, the claim was to recoup funds or property which allegedly had been diverted from the company, to impugn some particular transaction or to disallow a particular claim. The courts therefore adopt a technique of focusing on specific transactions. The vice with this

---

[1] *Vide supra* pp. 244-245.

[2] Cf. Prentice, Survey, p. 293. Prentice states that where "the various members of a group are solvent ... there will be no issue of creditor protection". *Ibid.* at p. 293. Prentice appears to condone the situation where a member is solvent at the time of the wrongdoing, but declines into insolvency at a later stage in its existence.

monotransactional approach (which as we have seen also affects a number of other potential remedies in the subservient subsidiary situation)[1] is that the court's attention is necessarily drawn away from examining broad patterns of conduct towards investigating specific instances of behaviour which when taken individually may not appear to reflect serious wrongdoing.

## 2.8. Lifting the veil jurisprudence

### 2.8.1. The weakness of English law

In a previous Chapter,[2] it was observed that despite some valiant judicial attempts aimed at forging out broad exceptions to the separate personality rule in the context of the holding-subsidiary relationship, the current attitude, as unequivocally stated by the Court of Appeal in *Adams* v. *Cape Industries plc*,[3] is remarkably narrow and conservative.[4] Following that retrogressive judgment, the courts would now probably be willing to disregard the separate identity of the company and its shareholders for the purposes of imposing liability on the shareholders only in highly abusive or offensive situations, as where corporate personality has been used as a cloak for fraud or improper conduct, where the company is a mere façade concealing the true facts, where the protection of public interests is of paramount importance or where the company has been formed to evade obligations imposed by law.[5]

Given such confining limitations, there is little doubt that the typical subservient subsidiary situation would not qualify for redress. Only one particularly pernicious, though relatively rare, form of subservient practice - the sham or shell situation[6] - is likely to trigger a piercing the veil reflex by the courts. Indeed, in *Adams* v. *Cape Industries plc*, the Court of Appeal conceded that "there is one well-recognised exception to the rule prohibiting the piercing of 'the corporate veil'"[7] and identified it as the situation where

---

[1] E.g., the remedies of avoiding "preferences" and "transactions at an undervalue". *Vide supra* pp. 237-238.

[2] *Supra* Chapter III.

[3] [1990] BCLC 479 (C.A.).

[4] *Vide supra* pp. 109-111.

[5] *Vide supra* Chapter III p. 108.

[6] The features of the sham or shell situation are described *supra* Chapter II pp. 82-83.

[7] [1990] BCLC 479 at p. 515.

there is a "mere façade concealing the true facts".[1] Regrettably, the Court of Appeal expressly declined to "attempt a comprehensive definition" of those features which would determine whether or not a façade arrangement exists,[2] although it would appear that the motive behind the arrangement should be considered as a crucial factor and that only if there is an indication of some behaviour bordering on impropriety or wrongdoing should the arrangement qualify as a "façade".[3] Even within such narrow confines, the sham or shell subsidiary should, it is submitted, qualify as a "façade". The holding company's utter failure to maintain even a minimum level of real and separate existence should lead to an inference of impropriety or wrongdoing. Support for this approach can be derived from *Adams* v. *Cape Industries plc* in which the Court of Appeal was prepared to treat as a "façade" one of the subsidiaries in a group of companies. The subsidiary in question was deemed to be "no more than a corporate name" which "acted through employees or officers" of other affiliated companies.[4]

From the foregoing analysis it is evident that the English piercing the veil doctrine can only play a very limited role in the subservient subsidiary situation. Only in the isolated instances of sham or shell subsidiaries is it likely that the court will pierce the veil to impose liability on the holding company for the debts of its insolvent subsidiary. In the far more common type of subservient practices - where the subsidiary conducts its business in the overall interests of the group as part of a group profit maximisation strategy - the doctrine will clearly be inapplicable.

---

[1] [1990] BCLC 479 at p. 515. The Court of Appeal was quoting from the speech of Lord Keith in *Woolfson* v. *Strathclyde Regional Council* 1978 S.L.T. 159 (H.L. Sc.) at p. 161. Although the Court of Appeal referred to the "façade" situation as the "one well-recognised exception", there can be little doubt that the courts would also pierce the veil in situations where corporate personality has been used as a cloak for fraud or improper conduct, where the protection of public interests is of paramount importance or where the company has been formed to evade obligations imposed by law.

[2] [1990] BCLC 479 at p. 519. In *Woolfson* v. *Strathclyde Regional Council* (1978) S.L.T. 159 (H.L. Sc.) Lord Keith, at p. 161 referring to a passage in the judgment of Ormerod L.J. in *Tunstall* v. *Steigmann* ([1962] 2 Q.B. 593 at p. 602) implied that the corporate veil might be pierced only if the company was a mere "façade". In neither judgment, however, was the meaning of that term explained.

[3] Cf. *Gilford Motor Co. Ltd.* v. *Horne* [1933] 1 Ch. 935 (C.A.); *Jones* v. *Lipman* [1962] 1 All E.R. 442. The latter judgment is referred to with approval in *Adams* v. *Cape Industries plc* [1990] BCLC 479 (C.A.) at p. 518.

[4] [1990] BCLC 479 at p. 519.

## 2.8.2. The position in American law

### 2.8.2.1. The "instrumentality" doctrine

The strictures of the English "piercing the veil" doctrine contrast sharply with the broad ambit of the doctrine in the United States. Although the notion of separate legal personality is a fundamental tenet even of American law, American courts will unhesitatingly pierce the veil where the company is used to evade an existing obligation, to circumvent a statute or to defeat public convenience, justify wrong, protect fraud, or defend crime.[1] But American courts go further and - in stark contrast with the English judicial approach - will avoid a rigid adherence to separate corporate personality when it is necessary to promote justice or to obviate inequitable results.[2]

It should be noted that the equitable power to "pierce the corporate veil" is not exclusive of other legal remedies available under American law. Agency, fraudulent conveyancing, misrepresentation and breach of fiduciary duties, for example, may broadly achieve the same objectives attained by piercing the veil. It is in fact not unusual for a claim to be based both on the piercing the veil doctrine as well as on one or more other theories.[3] The principal advantage of the corporate veil doctrine over such other theories is its wide-ranging ambit. It may also be easier for the plaintiff basing his claim on the doctrine to satisfy his burden of proof.[4]

The liberal approach adopted by American courts since the early years of this century has led to the development of a variation of the "piercing the veil" doctrine, known as the "instrumentality doctrine". The instrumentality doctrine - together with the equitable doctrines of subordination and substantive consolidation in bankruptcy - have to a considerable extent

---

[1] *Vide supra* Chapter III pp. 112-113.

[2] *Vide supra* Chapter III pp. 112-113.

[3] E.g., *Steven* v. *Roscoe Turner Aeronautical Corp.* 324 F.2d 157, 158 (7th Cir. 1963) (agency as an alternative basis for claim); *Puamier* v. *Barge BT 1793*, 395 F. Supp. 1019, 1038-1039 (E.D. Va. 1974) (misrepresentation as alternative basis of liability).

[4] Cathy S. Krendl and James R. Krendl, "Piercing the Corporate Veil : Focusing the Inquiry" 55 Denver L.J. 1 (1978) p. 6.

succeeded in redressing the abuse and unfairness experienced in the subservient subsidiary situation.[1]

The genesis of an "instrumentality" rule can be traced to a dictum in the 1909 case of *In re Watertown Paper Co.*[2] where the court stated that the rule of separate corporate personality may "be disregarded in a case where a corporation is so organized and controlled, and its affairs are so conducted, as to make it merely an instrumentality or adjunct of another corporation."[3] The "rule" then received strong judicial recognition in *Chicago, Milwaukee & St. Paul Railway Co.* v. *Minneapolis Civic & Commerce Association*[4] in which the Supreme Court stated :

"... where stock ownership has been resorted to, not for the purpose of participating in the affairs of a corporation in the normal and usual manner, but for the purpose ... of controlling a subsidiary company so that it may be used as a mere agency or instrumentality ... the courts will not permit themselves to be blinded or deceived by mere forms of law, but, regardless of fictions, will deal with the substance of the transaction involved as if the corporate agency did not exist and as the justice of the case may require."[5]

The systematic formulation of the instrumentality rule, however, owes its origin to a monumental study by Powell published in 1931.[6] Earlier attempts

---

[1] In American law, equitable subordination and substantive consolidation are also relevant to other issues in the holding-subsidiary relationship. *Vide post*, Chapter VI pp. 355-360, Chapter IX pp. 458-460.

[2] 169 F. 252 (2d Cir. 1909).

[3] *Ibid.* at p. 256.

[4] 247 U.S. 490 (1918).

[5] *Ibid.* at p. 501 (references omitted). Two years later, in *United States* v. *Reading* Co. 253 U.S. 26 (1920) the Supreme Court spoke in a similar vein : "... where such ownership of stock is resorted to, not for the purpose of participating in the affairs of the corporation in which it is held in a manner normal and usual with stockholders, but for the purpose of making it a mere agent, or instrumentality, or department of another company, the courts will look through the forms to the realities of the relation between the companies as if the corporate agency did not exist, and will deal with them as the justice of the case may require." *Ibid.* at pp. 62-63. *Vide* also *United States* v. *Lehigh Valley R.R. Co.* 220 U.S. 257 (1911). None of these cases actually involved the principle of limited liability, but the avoidance of statutory provisions by the use of the subsidiary device. *Vide* also *Connectitcut Co.* v. *New York, N. H. & H.R. Co.* 107 A. 646, 651 (1919).

[6] Frederick J. Powell, *Parent and Subsidiary Corporations* (1931).

had already been made to put some order into the decisions,[1] but Powell's work was clearly the most comprehensive and, despite some trenchant criticism,[2] eventually became the most influential.[3] Powell formulated a test for determining whether a subsidiary is so dominated by its holding company that the subsidiary's corporate veil should be pierced to impose liability on the holding company.[4] Although prior to Powell's formulation the term "instrumentality" had already been used, it was used merely to state a legal conclusion rather than as an analytical tool. The instrumentality doctrine has been adopted in various areas of the law including tort,[5] contract,[6] bankruptcy,[7] procedure[8] and property.[9]

The Powell test consisted of three limb: (i) excessive control; (ii) improper use; and (iii) injury or unjust loss proximately caused by the use of such control.[10] Although a strict application of the Powell rule demands the

---

[1] The more important contributions were : I. Maurice Wormser, "Piercing the Veil of the Corporate Entity" 12 Colum. L.R. 496 (1912); Henry W. Ballantine, "Separate Entity of Parent and Subsidiary Corporations" 14 Calif. L. Rev. 12 (1925); William O. Douglas and Carrol M. Shanks, "Insulation from Liability through Subsidiary Corporations" 39 Yale L.J. 193 (1929); Sam Elson, "Legal Liability of Holding Companies for Acts of Subsidiary Companies" 15 St. Louis L. Rev. 333 (1930).

[2] *Vide* e.g., Latty, *op. cit.* pp. 156-163. Latty does not actually mention Powell by name, but it is evident that much of the criticism was levelled at Powell's work.

[3] The Powell analysis has been cited with approval in numerous cases. *Vide* e.g., *Lowendahl* v. *Baltimore & O. Ry.* 287 N.Y.S. 62, 76 *aff'd*, 6 N.E. 2d 56 (1936); *Fisser* v. *International Bank* 282 F.2d 231, 238 (2d Cir. 1960).

[4] The instrumentality doctrine has been used even where the controlling shareholder is an individual. E.g., *Zaist* v. *Olson* 227 A.2d 552 (Conn. 1967).

[5] E.g., *Fidenas AG* v. *Honeywell, Inc.* 501 F.Supp. 1029, 1035-1036 (S.D.N.Y. 1980).

[6] E.g., *Zaist* v. *Olson* 227 A.2d 552 (1967).

[7] *Fish* v. *East* 114 F.2d 177 (10th Cir. 1940).

[8] E.g., *Professional Investors Life Insurance Co.* v. *Roussel* 445 F. Supp. 687, 698 (D. Kan. 1978).

[9] E.g., *Avco Delta Corporation Canada Ltd.* v. *United States* 540 F.2d 258, 264-265 (7th Cir. 1976) *cert. denied*, 429 U.S. 1040 (1977).

[10] This threefold rule has been widely endorsed. *Vide* e.g., *Lowendahl* v. *Baltimore & O. Ry.* 287 N.Y.S. 62 *aff'd*, 6 N.E. 2d 56 (1936); *Zaist* v. *Olson* 227 A.2d 552, 558 (1967); *Worldwide Carriers Ltd.* v. *Aris Steamship Co.* 301 F.Supp. 64, 67 (S.D.N.Y. 1968); *Steven* v. *Roscoe Turner Aeronautical Corp.* 324 F.2d 157, 160-161 (7th Cir. 1963); *Fisser* v. *International Bank* 282 F.2d 231, 238 (2nd Cir. 1960). Judgments following the instrumentality doctrine have tended to apply the formulation in *Lowendahl* v. *Baltimore & O. Ry, supra*, rather the test formulated by Powell. *Vide* Blumberg, *Substantive Law* p. 112.

presence of all three factors, some American courts - by reading the third element into the second and the second into the first - require in effect only one or two of these elements. The result is a largely open-ended test for imposing controlling shareholder liability.[1] The three limbs will now be considered in turn.

### 2.8.2.1.1. Excessive control

Powell concisely stated the rule as follows: "So far as the question of control alone is concerned, the parent corporation will be responsible for the obligations of its subsidiary when its control has been exercised to such a degree that the subsidiary has become its mere instrumentality."[2] This formulation or variations of it have been widely repeated by American courts.[3] In order to satisfy this element, the plaintiff must show that the subsidiary was operated not to serve its own valid objectives and purposes, but that it carried on business under the domination and control and for the purposes of a dominant party, that is the holding company.[4] Ownership alone, even of the entire shareholding, obviously does not give the necessary quantum of control.[5] Indeed, the domination must be significantly more intrusive than the control which is normally exercised by a controlling shareholder.[6] Moreover, the domination must relate to the particular transaction before the court.[7] Evidently, the subservient subsidiary situation described in Chapter II fits neatly into the "instrumentality" limb of the Powell rule. It is true that the domination must relate to the particular

---

[1] Richard S. Kohn, "Alternative Methods of Piercing the Veil in Contract and Tort" 48 Boston Univ. L.R. 123 (1968) p. 129.

[2] Powell, *op. cit.* s. 5, p. 8.

[3] *Vide* William M. Fletcher, *Cyclopedia of the Law of Corporations* (rev. ed. 1990 and supp. 1993) Vol. I, s. 43.10, pp. 758 *et seq.*

[4] *United States* v. *Wood* 366 F. Supp. 1074, 1083 (1973), *rev'd* 505 F.2d 1400 (C.C.P.A. 1974).

[5] *Owl Fumigating Corp.* v. *California Cyanide Co.* 24 Fed. 2d 718 (D. Del. 1928). *Vide* also Warren E. Slagle, "Disregard of Corporate Entity" 6 Univ. of Kansas City L.R. 301 (1938) p. 303; Beatrice J. Handy, "Situations Where Courts will Disregard the Separate Corporate Entities of a Parent and Subsidiary Corporation, even in the Absence of Fraud" 7 Ohio Opinions 143 (1937) p. 144.

[6] E.g., *Davis* v. *Alexander* 269 U.S. 114 (1925). *Vide* William M. Fletcher, *Cyclopedia of the Law of Corporations* (rev. ed. 1990 and supp. 1993) Vol. I, s. 43.10, p. 758.

[7] *Vide* William M. Fletcher, *Cyclopedia of the Law of Corporations* (rev. ed. 1990 and supp. 1993) Vol. I, s. 43.10, p. 758.

transaction, but in the typical subservient subsidiary situation the domination will be so ingrained that it would invariably affect all transactions.

Powell listed eleven circumstances which in various combinations may indicate the subsidiary to be an instrumentality : (i) the holding company owns all or most of the shares in the subsidiary; (ii) the holding and subsidiary companies have common directors or officers; (iii) the holding company finances the subsidiary; (iv) the holding company subscribes to all of the shares of the subsidiary or otherwise causes its incorporation; (v) the subsidiary has grossly inadequate capital; (vi) the holding company pays the salaries and other expenses or losses of the subsidiary; (vii) the subsidiary has substantially no business except with the holding company, or no assets except the ones conveyed to it by the holding company; (viii) in the papers of the holding company or in the statements of the officers, the subsidiary is described as a department or division of the holding company, or its business or financial responsibility is referred to as the holding company's own; (ix) the holding company uses the property of the subsidiary as its own; (x) the directors or executives of the subsidiary do not act independently in the interests of the subsidiary, but take their orders from the holding company in the latter's interest; (xi) the formal legal requirements of the subsidiary are not observed.[1]

A number of comments need to be made regarding Powell's list. First, the existence of instrumentality does not depend on the presence of all eleven circumstances. These circumstances are simply indicative of instrumentality. One circumstance, however - that the directors or executives of the subsidiary do not act independently in the interests of the subsidiary, but take their orders from the holding company in the latter's interest[2] - is particularly significant and most of the other circumstances merely appear to support its existence. Secondly, one circumstance may be decisive even in the absence of a number of the other supporting facts. Subservience, for example, may subsist even in the absence of common directors or officers, even if the

---

[1] Powell, *op. cit.* s. 6, p. 9. In 1936, another author attempted, by reference to the cases, to list the factors that the courts took into account in determining whether one company was the mere "instrument" of another. *Vide* Robert W. Yost, "Liability of a parent corporation for debts of its subsidiary" 21 St. Louis L. Rev. 234 (1936) pp. 240-246. Unfortunately, Yost did not take into consideration what is probably the most significant factor, that is, whether the subsidiary acted independently or in the holding company's interest. Courts too have sometimes recited a list of factors to be taken into account. *Vide* e.g., *DeWitt Truck Brokers* v. *W. Ray Flemming Fruit Co.* 540 F.2d 681, 685-687 (4th Cir. 1976).

[2] E.g., *Connectitcut Co.* v. *New York, N. H. & H.R. Co.* 107 A. 646, 650 (1919).

subsidiary is adequately capitalised, even if it conducts business with third parties and even if the formal legal requirements are observed. Indeed, in some cases a subsidiary has been considered to be an instrumentality where many of Powell's circumstances were not present.[1] Conversely, a subsidiary might not qualify as an instrumentality even if most of the circumstances are present. Only one circumstance - that the subsidiary does not act in its own interests but in the interest of the holding company - is an essential requirement for the instrumentality limb of the Powell test.

Clearly, therefore, Powell's eleven factor list could not provide a scientifically accurate means of testing the existence or otherwise of instrumentality. It did however have the effect of focusing the courts' attention on those aspects of the holding-subsidiary relationship which could be considered unfair. The notion developed that if the holding company dominated the subsidiary to such an extent that the subsidiary has no will of its own or if the holding company treated the subsidiary merely as a department within the business of the holding company, the holding company should not then be able to complain if the courts treated the subsidiary's conduct as virtually that of the holding company.

### 2.8.2.1.2. Improper purpose

The second limb under the Powell rule requires that the holding company's dominant control be used for an improper purpose. The *raison d'etre* underlying this requirement appears to relate to the policy that the corporate entity should not be lightly disregarded given the importance of limited liability. It may also be defensible in view of the somewhat open-ended nature of the instrumentality test. The difficulty is to determine the meaning of improper purpose.

Powell himself gave some examples of improper purpose : actual fraud, violation of a statute, stripping the subsidiary of its assets, misrepresentation, estoppel, torts, and "other cases of wrong or injustice".[2] The last example is of course too widely-stated to be of precise guidance to courts seized of a piercing the veil claim. It does however have the advantage of allowing the courts considerable latitude in determining whether or not an improper purpose existed. In any case, it is clear that while the wrongful conduct is

---

[1] E.g., *Caple v. Raynel Campers, Inc.* 526 P.2d 334 (Nev. 1974).

[2] Powell, *op. cit.* s. 13, p. 54.

sometimes an independently actionable wrong,[1] or an independent ground of relief,[2] the conduct on the part of the controlling shareholder is often less than that.

Courts have adopted two different approaches to the requirement of improper purpose. On the one hand, some courts require specific proof of improper purpose, as in *Pauley Petroleum, Inc.* v. *Continental Oil Co.*[3] where the court, despite a positive finding that the holding company completely controlled and dominated the subsidiary, could not denote any improper purpose in the particular arrangement and declined to pierce the corporate veil. Other courts, however, have so liberally defined "improper purpose" that they have almost automatically found an improper purpose once the excessive control limb is shown to exist. In such cases, an improper purpose appears to be readily inferred from those circumstances which go to make up a finding of instrumentality.[4] In *Consolidated Sun Ray, Inc.* v. *Oppenstein*[5], for example, the court found that an improper purpose was established by the subsidiary's inadequate capitalisation and by the removal of assets from the subsidiary. And in *Parker* v. *Bell Asbestos Mines Ltd.*[6] the court held that the organisation of a subsidiary to insulate the holding company from liability for asbestos injury satisfied the second limb of the test. Such a liberal approach is to be preferred. Subservient practices are essentially abusive and unfair. Such practices prejudice creditors and, because they involve the flagrant disregard of the subsidiary as a separate entity, constitute an abuse of the privilege of incorporation. If a subsidiary is shown to be subservient (in Powell's terms, a "mere instrumentality") it should therefore be considered as inherently offensive, and an improper purpose readily inferred.

---

[1] E.g., *Codomo* v. *Emanuel* 91 So. 2d 653 (Fla. 1956).

[2] E.g., *Henderson* v. *Rounds & Porter Lumber Co.* 99 F. Supp. 376 (W.D. Ark. 1951).

[3] 239 A.2d 629, 632-633 (Del. 1969).

[4] In *Zaist* v. *Olson* 227 A.2d 552 (1967) the Connecticut Supreme Court, in a majority opinion, appeared not to require proof of a "fraudulent or illegal purpose". *Vide* further James F. Farrington, Jr., "Piercing the Connecticut Corporate Veil" U. Bridgeport L. Rev. 109 (1983) pp. 125-135.

[5] 355 F.2d 801 (8th Cir. 1964).

[6] 607 F. Supp. 1397, 1402-1403 (E.D. Pa. 1985).

### 2.8.2.1.3. Injury or injustice to the plaintiff

The third limb of the Powell rule is that the dominating control of the holding company over the subsidiary must result in some damage to the claimant.[1] Again, the rationale underlying this requirement is to restrict - in deference to the policy of limited liability - the types of cases in which the veil can be pierced. In *Schlecht* v. *Equitable Builders, Inc.*[2] the assets of a subsidiary had been improperly used for the benefit of the holding company. The subsidiary, for example, guaranteed loans extended to the holding company and also allowed its own assets to be secured for the purpose. The court however declined to pierce the corporate veil because there was no evidence that the dominating control exercised by the holding company or the subservient activities of the subsidiary prejudiced the rights of creditors.

The requirement of loss to the plaintiff serves not only to support the policy of limited liability but also to restrict the amount of litigation. As long as the subsidiary remains solvent, the third limb of the Powell rule is without doubt desirable. Difficulties arise however where the subservient subsidiary becomes insolvent. In such a situation it may be impossible to prove a causal link between the loss to the plaintiff and the subservient conduct. A strict application of Powell's third requirement would result in the holding company being absolved of liability for conduct that is clearly objectionable. Probably owing to such difficulties, some courts have considered insolvency as an example of the causal link to the unjust loss required by the third element.[3] Given that insolvency is present in most cases,[4] such an approach virtually eliminates the third element.

### 2.8.2.2. Difficulties with the instrumentality doctrine

The instrumentality concept has been subject to considerable criticism. Often the complaint is that the courts use the term "instrumentality" as a

---

[1] Powell, *op. cit.* s. 14, p. 82.

[2] 535 P.2d 86 (Or. 1975).

[3] E.g., *Northern Ill. Gas Co.* v. *Total Energy Leasing Corp.* 502 F.Supp. 412, 420 (N.D. Ill. 1980); *Steven* v. *Roscoe Turner Aeronautical Corp.* 324 F.2d 157, 160 (7th Cir. 1963).

[4] *Vide* Latty, *op. cit.* pp. 207-208; Jules Silk, "One Man Corporations - Scope and Limitations" 100 Univ. of Pennsylavania L.R. 853 (1952) p. 859; Blumberg, *Substantive Law* p. 117.

metaphorical label of convenience to denote a result which the court has reached on the basis of the facts before it. It has, for example, been asserted that "[t]o say that the parent is liable ... because the subsidiary is a mere adjunct or instrumentality adds no substance and gives no real reason for the decision, but merely supplies verbal justification and a metaphorical tag to the conclusion which is predicated on the facts."[1] Similarly, the instrumentality notion has been described as an "alluringly sweeping" formula used as a substitute for reasoned analysis of the real factors behind decisions.[2] This criticism is however somewhat exaggerated and cynical. It is true that American courts have frequently used the term "instrumentality" along with other synonyms[3] to state a legal conclusion in somewhat flowery language. But this does not mean - as seems to be suggested by some commentators[4] - that the judgments have been devoid of analysis. On the contrary, some skilful evaluation can be found in the judgments.[5]

Another criticism levelled at the instrumentality doctrine, and indeed at the piercing the veil jurisprudence generally, is that courts rely on the piercing the veil judgments from different areas of law involving different policy considerations. Thus, courts dealing with an action in tort may follow judgments involving questions of contract, bankruptcy, procedure, or statutory construction.[6] Clearly, the issues of public policy raised by tort

---

[1] *Vide* Bernard F. Cataldo, "Limited Liability with One-Man Companies and Subsidiary Corporations" 18 Law and Contemporary Problems 473 (1953) at pp. 497-498.

[2] Latty, *op. cit.* pp. 157-158.

[3] The piercing the veil doctrine is probably the most fertile doctrine in the law for the propagation of metaphors. Terms used to describe a company over which the controlling shareholder exercises extensive control include "adjunct", "agent", "alias", "alter", "alter ego", "alter idem", "arm", "blind", "branch", "buffer", "bureau", "cloak", "coat", "conduit", "corporate double", "cover", "creature", "curious reminiscence", "delusion", "department", "device", "division", "dry shell", "dummy", "employee", "façade", "fiction", "form", "formality", "idem", "identity", "instrumentality", "little hut", "marionette", "mask", "mere animation", "mere automaton", "mere name", "mere phrase", "mouthpiece", "naked framework", "name", "nominal identity", "paper company", "puppet", "representative", "satellite", "screen", "sham", "simulacrum", "snare", "stooge", "stratagem", "subterfuge" and "tool". Most of these terms appear in American judgments. English judges have been somewhat less effusive in their metaphorical language.

[4] *Vide* e.g., David C. Cummins, "Disregarding the Corporate Entity : Contract Claims" 28 Ohio State L.J. 441 (1967) p. 441.

[5] E.g., *Zaist* v. *Olson* 227 A.2d 552 (1967); *Fidenas AG* v. *Honeywell, Inc.* 501 F. Supp. 1029 (S.D.N.Y. 1980).

[6] Blumberg, *Substantive Law* p. 108.

claims should bear little relationship to the policy issues raised by contract claims.[1] The principal objectives of tort product liability law, for example, include the encouragement of a greater regard for safety precautions and the allocation of risk in such manner as to spread the "risk of loss to all consumers of a product so that the product will bear the social and individual costs of its own defects".[2] By contrast, the principal objective of contract law is the implementation of the contracting parties bargain and expectations. Although the criticism that courts generally fail to distinguish between the policy considerations underlying different areas of law is to a large extent justifiable, the truth remains that in innumerable cases American courts have achieved a fair solution to the issues raised without resort to any conscious distinctions.[3] Moreover, it is submitted that in the context of a subservient subsidiary situation there is little scope for drawing distinctions between tort and contract claims. As already indicated in a previous Chapter,[4] subservient practices prejudice the interests of both voluntary and involuntary creditors without distinction. In any case, the liability of the holding company for the debts of its subservient subsidiary should be promoted not only as a consequence of the prejudice caused to the subsidiary's creditors, but also as a consequence of the wilful disregard of the subsidiary's supposedly independent corporate existence for the holding company's own purposes. For these reasons, the failure of the instrumentality cases to distinguish between the underlying policy considerations does not in itself detract from the usefulness of the doctrine in the context of subservient practices.

Perhaps the major difficulty with the instrumentality test as developed in American law is that it has not been consistently or uniformly applied. Consequently, it has been impossible to formulate the doctrine with an

---

[1] Robert W. Hamilton, "The Corporate Entity" 49 Texas L.R. 979 (1971) p. 985.

[2] *Bonee* v. *L. & M. Construction Chemicals* 518 F. Supp. 375 (M.D. Tenn. 1981) at p. 381. *Vide* also Guido Calbresi, "Some Thoughts on Risk Distribution and the Law of Torts" 70 Yale L.J. 499 (1961).

[3] Some courts relying on the piercing the veil doctrine have in fact recognised that different considerations may apply in different areas, such as bankruptcy, property or statutory construction. *Vide* e.g., *Zubik* v. *Zubik* 384 F. 2d 267, 273 (3d Cir. 1967), *cert. denied*, 390 U.S. 988 (1968); *Queen* v. *Waverley Construction Co. Ltd.* 30 D.L.R. 3d 224, 233 (1972) (vicarious liability); *United States* v. *Firestone Tire & Rubber Co.* 518 F. Supp. 1021, 1039 (N.D. Ohio 1981) (statutory construction). *Vide* generally, Blumberg, *Substantive Law* pp. 109-111.

[4] *Vide supra* Chapter IV, p. 188.

acceptable degree of precision.[1] Some commentators, somewhat overstating the problem, have gone so far as to assert that "[b]eing the vaguest of all tests, it is also the most unsatisfactory upon which judges could base their decision"[2] and that "it does not help to explain the cases but rather tends to interject false issues which becloud the process of disregarding the corporate entity".[3] In defence of the doctrine as it has developed, it must be said that no formula or theory can substitute the need for a careful sifting and weighing of the varied facts bearing on any question concerning the disregard of the entity principle. More importantly, the doctrine has - despite its shortcomings - enabled courts to achieve justice in many situations which would otherwise have remained without a remedy.[4]

## 2.9. The doctrine of *ultra vires*

The classical doctrine of *ultra vires* is related to the notion that companies are incorporated to fulfil the specific limited purposes or objects stated in the

---

[1] *Vide* Robert W. Yost, "Liability of a parent corporation for debts of its subsidiary" 21 St. Louis L. Rev. 234 (1936) p. 239.

[2] Ke Chin Wang, "The Corporate Entity Concept (or Fiction Theory) and the Modern Business Organisation" 28 Minnesota L. R. 341 (1944) at p. 353. *Vide* also Warner Fuller, "The Incorporated Individual : A Study of the One-Man Company" 51 Harv. L.R. 1373 (1938) p. 1378.

[3] David C. Cummins, "Disregarding the Corporate Entity: Contract Claims" 28 Ohio State L.J. 441 (1967) at p. 447. *Vide* also James R. Gillespie, "The Thin Corporate Line: Loss of Limited Liability Protection" 45 North Dakota L. R. 363 (1968) p. 364.

[4] Apart from the instrumentality theory, there have been other attempts to systemise the American "piercing the veil" jurisprudence. Some courts and commentators have used an "alter ego" or "identity" theories. *Vide* e.g., *Marr* v. *Postal Union Life Ins. Co.* 105 P.2d 649 (1940); Denise L. Speer, "Piercing the Corporate Veil in Maryland : An Analysis and Suggested Approach" 14 U. of Baltimore L.R. 311 (1985) pp. 317-318; J. Penn Carolan, "Disregarding the Corporate Fiction in Florida: the Need for Specifics" 27 Univ. of Florida L.R. 175 (1974) pp. 183-183; Patricia Carteaux, "Louisiana adopting a Balancing Test for Piercing the Veil" 58 Tulane L.R. 1089 (1984) pp. 1094-1097. On closer analysis, however, it will be realised that these theories are virtually indistinguishable from the instrumentality doctrine. Many courts regard the theories as interchangeable. *Vide Glazer* v. *Commission on Ethics for Public Employees* 431 So. 2d 752, 757 (La. 1983); *Kamens* v. *Summit Stainless, Inc.* 586 F. Supp. 324, 327-328 (E.D. Pa. 1984). Mention should also be made of Berle's "economic entity" concept. *Vide* Adolf A. Berle, "The Theory of Enterprise Entity" 47 Colum. L.R. 343 (1947). This concept is discussed *post*, Chapter VII.

Memorandum of Association.[1] In its classical form, the doctrine limits the legal capacity of a company to fulfilling those purposes or objects : a company has legal capacity to do only those acts which its memorandum empowers it to do, or which are ancillary to or consequential on the achievement of its express objects or the exercise of its express powers. As a consequence, not only may the company be restrained from engaging in activities which are beyond its objects or powers but any act or transaction which is *ultra vires* is null and of no legal effect.[2] The common law *ultra vires* rule was self-executing in nature, and therefore all acts or transactions which were not relevant to the company's objects,[3] or not authorised by its memorandum or ancillary to or consequential on its objects, were void.[4]

Under the classical *ultra vires* doctrine, it may have been arguable that acts and transactions involving subservient practices by a subsidiary were *ultra vires* - for surely no company could have the capacity to enter into acts or transactions that are potentially detrimental to itself, however beneficial they may be to related third parties.[5] Conceivably, the liquidator of an insolvent subservient subsidiary may have been able to impugn acts and transactions of a subservient nature on the basis that such acts were *ultra vires* the subsidiary. Yet the question whether a given transaction, carried out in purported exercise of any implied or express power in the memorandum of association, was within the capacity of the company depended on the true construction of the memorandum.[6] The same principle applied whether or not the transaction was a gratuitous one.[7] If therefore a subsidiary's memorandum of association was carefully drafted to embody wide ranging

---

[1] Robert R. Pennington, *Company Law* (6th ed. 1990) p. 91. For a historical analysis of the doctrine, *vide* Harry Rajak, "Judicial Control: Corporations and the Decline of Ultra Vires" 26 Cambrian L.R. 9 (1995)

[2] *East Anglian Railway Co.* v. *Eastern Counties Railway Co.* (1851) 11 CB 775; *Taylor* v. *Chichester and Midhurst Railway Co.* (1867) LR 2 Exch 356.

[3] *Ashbury Railway Carriage and Iron Co. Ltd.* v. *Riche* (1875) LR 7 HL 653.

[4] *Attorney General* v. *Great Eastern Railway Co.* (1880) 5 App. Cas. 473.

[5] Cf. *Rolled Steel Products (Holdings) Ltd.* v. *British Steel Corporation* [1986] Ch. 246 (C.A.).

[6] *Rolled Steel Products (Holdings) Ltd.* v. *British Steel Corporation* [1986] Ch. 246 (C.A.); *Re Horsley & Weight Ltd.* [1982] Ch. 442 (C.A.).

[7] *Rolled Steel Products (Holdings) Ltd.* v. *British Steel Corporation* [1986] Ch. 246 (C.A.); *Re Horsley & Weight Ltd.* [1982] Ch. 442 (C.A.).

objects clauses and powers, including an "independent objects" clause[1] and a "subjective objects" clause,[2] the potential application of *ultra vires* in the context of subservient practices would have been virtually nullified.

Quite apart from the protection afforded by the use of wide-ranging objects clauses, it is submitted that the classical *ultra vires* doctrine could only have served a very limited function in controlling the abuse and unfairness inherent in subservient practices. A few observations need to be made in this regard. In the first place, the effect of a successful challenge of an act or transaction on the *ultra vires* ground would have been to completely invalidate the act or transaction. In the case of many intra-group subservient practices the wholesale avoidance of transactions would clearly not have been an appropriate remedy. In many cases, the practical remedy would have been to adjust the effect of the intra-group transactions. Such a solution was obviously not available under the *ultra vires* doctrine. In the second place, it is evident that some types of subservient practices would simply not have been caught within the ambit of the doctrine. The commingling of assets, the operation of subsidiaries without a profit motive and the operation of sham or shell subsidiaries would clearly not have been beyond the "capacity" of the subservient subsidiary. Finally, it is obvious that the *ultra vires* doctrine was basically monotransactional in approach. As already noted on previous occasions, a monotransactional analysis is wholly inappropriate to deal with the vast multitude of complex acts and transactions involved in the subservient subsidiary situation.

Whatever the position under the classical doctrine, the current *ultra vires* rule, originating in legislation dating to 1972[3] and superseded by the provisions of the Companies Act 1989,[4] certainly affords the liquidator of a subservient subsidiary no assistance in impugning acts or transactions involving subservient practices. A closer look at the current position will make this clear.

---

[1] Despite serious reservations, the validity of such a provision was reluctantly upheld by the House of Lords in *Cotman* v. *Brougham* [1918] A.C. 514. *Vide* the observations made by Lord Finlay L.C. at p. 519, Lord Parker at p. 519 and Lord Wrenbury at p. 523.

[2] The Court of Appeal upheld the validity of this type of clause in *Bell Houses Ltd.* v. *City Wall Properties Ltd.* [1966] 1 Q.B. 207 (Mocatta J.), reversed [1966] 2 Q.B. 656 (C.A.).

[3] s. 9(1) of the European Communities Act 1972, re-enacted by s. 35(1) and (2) of the C.A. 1985.

[4] C.A. ss. 35, 35A and 35B, substituted and inserted by the Companies Act 1989, s. 108(1).

The purpose of the provisions introduced by the Companies Act 1989[1] was essentially to validate transactions entered into by the company, even though they are *ultra vires* the company's objects or beyond the powers of the directors. The Companies Act 1985 as amended by the provisions of the Companies Act 1989 now provides that "[t]he validity of an act done by a company shall not be called into question on the ground of lack of capacity by reason of anything in the company's memorandum".[2] The provision effectively confers full and unlimited legal capacity on the company so far as the validity of its acts and transactions are concerned and precludes both the company and the other party to the transaction from disputing its validity on the basis that it is beyond the company's objects or powers. Even assuming that the acts and transactions entered into by a subservient subsidiary are beyond its objects and powers, it is clear that such acts and transactions cannot now be challenged under the *ultra vires* doctrine. Ironically, a statutory development intended primarily to protect third parties dealing with the company from the harshness of the classical *ultra vires* doctrine may have neutralised a potential remedy otherwise available to the liquidator of an insolvent subservient subsidiary.

The statutory developments introduced by the Companies Act 1989 were intended to abolish *ultra vires* in relation to a company's external relations whilst at the same time retaining the status quo in respect of the internal relations between the company and its directors.[3] In the case of acts beyond the capacity of the company, the statutory provisions expressly maintain the "duty of the directors to observe any limitations on their powers flowing from the company's memorandum".[4] Moreover, action by the directors beyond the company's capacity may only be ratified by the company by special resolution and any such ratification shall not affect any liability incurred by the directors.[5] Relief from any such liability must be agreed to

---

[1] ss. 108 and 109.

[2] C.A. 1985, s. 35(1), as substituted by the Companies Act 1989, s. 108(1).

[3] A distinction must be drawn between acts that are beyond the company's capacity and acts which are *intra vires* the company's capacity but beyond the powers of the directors conferred by or under the memorandum or articles of association. The distinction had been clearly expressed in *Rolled Steel Products (Holdings) Ltd.* v. *British Steel Corporation* [1986] Ch. 246 (C.A.) at pp. 286-287. For the legal position regarding acts that are *intra vires* the capacity of the company but beyond the powers of the directors, *vide* Gower, pp. 178-181.

[4] C.A. 1985, s. 35(3).

[5] C.A. 1985, s. 35(3).

separately by special resolution.[1] Ratification is not of course usually necessary to protect the other party to the transaction, for by virtue of section 35(1) the transaction "shall not be called into question on the ground of lack of capacity". Ratification may however be relevant to such party if the transaction took place before any legal obligation to him was incurred. In such an event, ratification would preclude a member from instituting proceedings to restrain the act from being undertaken.[2] Ratification may also be relevant to the other party to the transaction if he can receive no protection from the provisions of section 35A because he had acted in bad faith.

An issue of some concern under the regime existing prior to the reforms introduced in 1989 was the question of the validity of upstream and cross-stream guarantees issued by subsidiary companies. In *Charterbridge Corporation Ltd.* v. *Lloyds Bank Ltd.*[3] a property development company had power by its objects clause to guarantee loans made to other persons and it guaranteed a loan extended to its holding company for the benefit of that company. It was held on the facts that the guarantee could not be *ultra vires*, because upon examination of the company's main objects and the guarantee actually given, it could not be said that the guarantee was necessarily inconsistent with the company's main objects. The guarantee could only be impugned if the directors abused their power in giving it. This, however, was a separate cause of avoidance. To successfully invalidate the guarantee on this basis the company had to prove the creditor's knowledge of the directors' improper motive. In *Rolled Steel Products (Holdings) Ltd.* v. *British Steel Corporation*[4] a company guaranteed the indebtedness of another company in which the first company's controlling shareholder was interested, and charged its assets with amounts payable under the guarantee. The Court of Appeal held that the guarantee and charge were not *ultra vires* because the first company had power by its objects clause to enter into such transactions. The Court did however consider the guarantee to be unenforceable because the motive of the directors of the first company was to benefit its controlling shareholder, and the second company and the

---

[1] C.A. 1985, s. 35(3).

[2] under C.A. 1985, s. 35(2).

[3] [1970] Ch. 62.

[4] [1986] Ch. 246 (C.A.), noted by Clive M. Schmitthoff, "Acts ultra vires the company and acts ultra vires the directors" [1984] J.B.L. 296. *Vide* also Prentice, Group Indebtedness, pp. 60-61; Farrar, pp. 108-109.

creditor "had actual knowledge of facts which showed that the giving of the guarantee and the debenture was an abuse of powers by the directors".[1]

The reforms introduced in 1989 have of course altered the legal position. Under the current regime it is clear that upstream and cross stream guarantees are not challengeable on the ground of a lack of capacity on the part of the subsidiary. As a result, the lack of capacity issues raised in *Charterbridge Corporation Ltd.* v. *Lloyds Bank Ltd.*[2] and *Rolled Steel Products (Holdings) Ltd.* v. *British Steel Corporation*[3] should no longer arise.[4] The question of directors' motives however may still raise difficulties. One approach is to consider the question of motive as irrelevant on the basis that the provisions of section 35 of the Companies Act 1985, as amended, necessarily exclude any enquiry as to the directors' motives in exercising the full and unlimited legal capacity of the company. The result would be that the pursuit of a purpose within the legal capacity of a company must necessarily be *intra vires* and lawful. But the 1989 provisions drew a clear distinction between invalidity caused by lack of capacity on the part of the company and invalidity caused by lack of authority on the part of the directors. It is indeed likely that section 35A of the Companies Act 1985, introduced by the Companies Act 1989 and dealing with the "power of directors to bind the company"[5] may have a bearing on the question of directors' motives and the validity of guarantees. Section 35A provides that in favour of a person dealing with a company in good faith the power of the directors will be deemed to be free of "any limitation under the company's constitution"[6] although a person "shall not be regarded as acting in bad faith by reason only of his knowing that an act is beyond the powers of the directors under the company's constitution".[7] Knowledge of the fact that the guarantee exceeds the directors' authority will not therefore by itself constitute bad faith. Where however, to the knowledge of the creditor, the guarantee exceeds the authority of the directors and in addition involves an improper motive (as where the directors are not acting in the best interests of the company) then the guarantee may be challengeable under the provisions

---

[1] [1986] Ch. 246 at p. 307 per Browne-Wilkinson L.J.

[2] [1970] Ch. 62.

[3] [1986] Ch. 246 (C.A.).

[4] Subject to the provisions of the C.A. 1985, s. 35(2).

[5] This is the marginal note to s. 35A.

[6] s. 35A (1).

[7] s. 35A (2)(b).

of section 35A. In practice of course it is unlikely for a liquidator of a subservient subsidiary to succeed in impugning upstream or cross-stream guarantees on the basis of section 35A both because in the typical case the directors would have been acting within the scope of their authority and also because of the difficulty in proving the requisite of bad faith on the part of the creditor.[1]

The modern American notion of *ultra vires* is broadly similar to the English notion. For a considerable period of time, however, corporate objects and powers had been statutorily limited and strictly construed by the courts. But with the passage of time, corporate statutes and charters became more general, courts construed the notion more liberally and, eventually, the legislatures considerably restricted the assertion of *ultra vires* to a narrowly defined class of cases.[2] Section 3.04 of the Model Business Corporation Act (1984) - on which numerous state statutes are modelled[3] - establishes the general rule that "the validity of corporate action may not be challenged on the ground that the corporation lacks or lacked power to act."[4] Only in three exceptional cases can *ultra vires* be asserted: (i) in a proceeding by a shareholder against the company to enjoin the act;[5] (ii) in a proceeding by the company, directly or derivatively, against the incumbent or former management; or (iii) in a proceeding by the Attorney General.

As state statutes increasingly allowed wider charters, the courts had developed a number of doctrines that effectively restricted the assertion of *ultra vires*. Where, for example, an *ultra vires* contract has been executed by one party, that party could not defeat the contract on the ground that it was *ultra vires*.[6] Nor could *ultra vires* be pleaded where the company had received benefits, where the creditor was aware of the lack of enforceability of the transaction or where there was some other basis for estoppel.[7] The net effect is that the American doctrine of *ultra vires* - as its English counterpart

---

[1] The C.A. 1985, s. 35A (2)(c) provides that "a person shall be presumed to have acted in good faith unless the contrary is proved."

[2] Blumberg, *Bankruptcy Law* p. 248. *Vide* further Arthur Kreidmann, "The Corporate Guaranty" 13 Vand. L. Rev. 229 (1959).

[3] A full list is found in Blumberg, *Bankruptcy Law* pp. 251-252.

[4] s. 3.04(a). This general rule is broadly similar to s. 35 of the C.A. 1985, as amended by the Companies Act 1989.

[5] This exception is also found in English law. *Vide* C.A. 1985, s. 35(2).

[6] In *Re Reliable Manufacturing Corp.* 703 F.2d 996 (7th Cir. 1983).

[7] Blumberg, *Bankruptcy Law* p. 253; Henn and Alexander, *op. cit.* pp. 478-479.

- is today far less significant than it was in the past.[1] And for broadly the same reasons that were given in respect of the English doctrine, the American doctrine is largely irrelevant as a remedy where subservient practices are concerned.[2]

In American law, the doctrine has also received specific attention in the context of corporate guarantees.[3] Modern American corporation statutes today expressly grant to companies the power to give guarantees. Express provisions appear in the vast majority of state legislative enactments[4] and in the Model Business Corporation Act.[5] But the existence of the corporate power does not end the question of validity. Where the guarantee is an accommodation guarantee extended without a fee and the subsidiary company is not wholly owned, its validity depends on a showing that corporate interests are being furthered by the granting of the guarantee. But in such circumstances only the question of minority rights is raised. If the subsidiary is wholly owned, and the holding company has approved the guarantee (as would normally be the case), courts would uphold its enforceability against the subsidiary's defence of *ultra vires* and the assertion that the guarantee was not given for a proper purpose.[6] The notion of *ultra vires* remains irrelevant to the question of creditor protection.

## 2.10. Misfeasance proceedings under section 212 of the Insolvency Act 1986

If only for the sake of completeness, a reference should be made to the statutory action of misfeasance in terms of section 212 of the Insolvency Act 1986. This section enables a liquidator (among others) to bring summary proceedings for the recovery of an insolvent company's property misapplied by its promoters, directors and others involved in its management[7] or for

---

[1] Blumberg, *Bankruptcy Law* p. 253; Henn and Alexander, *op. cit.* pp. 478-479.

[2] *Vide supra* p. 268.

[3] *Vide* William H. Coquillette, "Guaranty of and Security for the Debt of a Parent Corporation by a Subsidiary Corporation" 30 Case Western Reserve Law Review 433 (1980); William Everdell and Bevis Longstreth, "Some Special Problems Raised by Debt Financing of Corporations under Common Control" 17 Bus. Law. 500 (1962); Blumberg, *Bankruptcy Law* pp. 248-256.

[4] A full list is found in Blumberg, *Bankruptcy Law* pp. 249-250.

[5] s. 3.02(7) (1984).

[6] *Re Reliable Manufacturing Corp.* 703 F.2d 996, 1003 (7th Cir. 1983).

[7] *Vide* s. 212(1) I.A. 1986.

compensation for breach of trust or other fiduciary duties. The power to bring such proceedings is purely facultative and enabling. The section, which re-enacts with some modifications a provision which has been a feature of insolvency law for over a century,[1] gives no new rights, "but only provides a summary and efficient remedy in respect of rights which apart from the section might have been vindicated either at law or in equity."[2] Clearly, the procedure contemplated in section 212 can prove a useful aid, in the context of a subservient subsidiary situation, to the collection of assets (from directors and even from the holding company[3]) for distribution amongst the creditors. Where, for example, the subservient practices involve a breach of the directors' - and arguably the holding company's - common law duties towards the subsidiary's creditors, the breach would have caused a loss to the creditors and the liquidator would be able to seek compensation for breach of those duties. The court could then order the directors (or possibly the holding company) to contribute such sum to the company's assets by way of compensation as the court thinks just.[4] Where the subservient practices involve a misapplication of the company's assets, the court is able to order the directors (or possibly the holding company) to repay, restore or account for the money or property or any part of it, with interest as the court thinks just.[5] It should however be emphasised that the procedure can only be utilised to enforce rights derived from wrongs done to the company in terms of some rule of law other than section 212.[6] In other

---

[1] *Vide* Companies Act 1862, s. 165.

[2] Fidelis Oditah, "Misfeasance proceedings against company directors" [1992] L.M.C.L.Q. 207 at p. 208.

[3] A holding company in a subservient subsidiary situation would almost certainly be covered by s. 212(1)(c) ("person concerned ... in the management of the company") and, if it qualifies as a director (*de jure* or *de facto*), also by s. 212(1)(a) ("officer of the company"). Oditah does not consider a *de facto* director to be an "officer" of the company and that therefore a *de facto* director cannot fall under s. 212(1)(a). Fidelis Oditah, "Misfeasance proceedings against company directors" [1992] L.M.C.L.Q. 207 at p. 216. This view would appear to be incorrect. Section 744 of the C.A. 1985 - the interpretation section which applies to the I.A. 1986 by virtue of s. 251 of the latter statute - defines an "officer" to include a "director". Section 251 of the Insolvency Act in its turn defines a "director" as including "any person occupying the position of director, by whatever name called". For the purposes of s. 212(1)(a) of the Insolvency Act, therefore, "officer" appears to include a *de facto* director.

[4] *Vide* s. 212(3)(b).

[5] *Vide* s. 212(3)(a).

[6] *Coventry and Dixon's Case* (1880) 14 Ch. D. 660 (C.A.).

words, the applicant must establish an actionable wrong independently of the misfeasance proceedings being instituted. In effect, section 212 is derivative rather than substantive in nature.

## 3. SPECIAL CASES OF SUBSERVIENT PRACTICES

### 3.1. Diversion of corporate opportunities

#### 3.1.1. The nature of the abuse

One particular form of subservient practice - the diversion of corporate opportunities - raises unique problems and therefore requires special consideration. In the typical "diversion of opportunities" situation, the management of a subsidiary would be approached by a prospective customer inquiring whether the subsidiary can undertake a particular project. The subsidiary's management team - convinced that it would be able to handle the project - informs headquarters of the offer. The subsidiary is however "advised" by headquarters that the project should be performed by an affiliated company. The subsidiary has no option but to comply. A corporate opportunity which had been fairly presented to it is diverted by the holding company not because the subsidiary is unable to profitably and successfully complete the project, but because the group stood to gain some special advantage by such diversion.

The diversion of corporate opportunities away from the subservient subsidiary to the holding company or to some other company within the group may be detrimental to the interests of the subsidiary's creditors and constitutes an abuse of the privilege of incorporation. Where the subsidiary which has been divested of its opportunity remains solvent, the issue should really be of concern only to the minority shareholders in the subsidiary. Where, however, the subsidiary wastes into insolvency, creditors may be directly affected, at least in the situation where, but for the loss of the opportunity, the subsidiary would not have failed. Even where the insolvency of a subsidiary is not causally linked to the diversion of the corporate opportunity, it is at least arguable that the forced submission of the subsidiary to the will of the group creates a corresponding obligation on the part of the holding company to shelter it from any ensuing blizzard.

The discussion on potential remedies in the subservient subsidiary situation would be incomplete without an analysis of the "doctrine of corporate opportunities". This section will assess the extent to which the doctrine controls or redresses the negative effects of the diversion of corporate opportunities in the holding-subsidiary context.

### 3.1.2. The doctrine of corporate opportunities

A "doctrine of corporate opportunities" has enjoyed a long standing in both English and American law.[1] It will however be seen that the American version is considerably more refined and probably more flexible in its application. A few preliminary observations need to be made. First, the rationale of the doctrine is to protect the company from the self-dealing of those persons (usually directors) who, by virtue of their relationship with the company, should act in its best interests.[2] A corporate opportunity is regarded as a corporate asset which such persons cannot appropriate to themselves.[3] Put simply, the doctrine requires such persons to refrain from taking business opportunities that belong to the company. Second, the doctrine has developed in the context of the wider notion of fiduciary duties owed by directors to their companies.[4] The duty inherent in the corporate

---

[1] Early cases include *Cook* v. *Deeks* [1916] 1 A.C. 554 (P.C.); *Am. Circular Loom Co.* v. *Wilson* 84 N.E. 133 (1908). The doctrine is also followed in Canada. *Vide Canadian Aero Service Ltd.* v. *O'Malley* (1974) 40 D.L.R. (3d) 371, noted by Stanley M. Beck, "The Quickening of Fiduciary Obligation : Canadian Aero Services v. O'Malley" 53 Can. Bar Rev. 771 (1975); D. D. Prentice, "The Corporate Opportunity Doctrine" 37 M.L.R. 464 (1974).

[2] Karen McLaughlin, "Corporate Opportunity Doctrine in the Context of Parent-Subsidiary Relations" 8 Northern Kentucky L.R. 121 (1981) p. 121. *Vide* also Adolf A. Berle, "Promoters' Stock in Subsidiary Corporations" 29 Colum. L.R. 35 (1929) p. 37.

[3] *Vide* Victor Brudney and Robert Charles Clark, "A New Look at Corporate Opportunities" 94 Harv. L.R. 998 (1981) p. 999.

[4] *Cook* v. *Deeks* [1916] 1 A.C. 554 (P.C.); *Canadian Aero Service Ltd.* v. *O'Malley* (1974) 40 D.L.R. (3d) 371; *Guth* v. *Loft, Inc.* 5 A.2d 503 (Del. 1939). Thomas W. Walde, "Parent-Subsidiary Relations in the Integrated Corporate System : A Comparison of American and German Law" 9 Journal of International Law and Economics 455 (1974) pp. 462-463, 480-482. In *Mullaney, Wells & Company* v. *Savage* 402 N.E.2d 574 (Ill. 1980) the court considered that an employee of an investment bank who acquired certain shares for himself had breached the fiduciary duty he owed to the company. The court held that "it is a breach of fiduciary obligation for a person to seize for his own advantage a business opportunity which rightfully belongs to the corporation by which he is employed." *Ibid.* at p. 580. The court acknowledged that the cases it referred to involved directors and officers but that "they do not so limit the rule". *Ibid.* at p. 580. English

opportunities doctrine arises because the persons upon whom it is imposed stand in a fiduciary position to the company. This feature (which will be examined more closely at a later stage) considerably restricts the effectiveness of the doctrine as a means of protecting a subservient subsidiary's creditors.

Though relatively easy to state in general terms, the doctrine can give rise to considerable difficulties in its application.[1] One difficulty is to define precisely the meaning of a "corporate opportunity". A workable definition is that contained in the "Principles of Corporate Governance : Analysis and Recommendations" of the American Law Institute.[2] A "corporate opportunity" is there defined as "any opportunity to engage in a business activity that is held out to the shareholders of the corporation as being within the scope of the business in which the corporation is presently engaged or may be reasonably expected to engage, and that is neither developed nor received by the dominating shareholder within the scope and regular course of his own business activities."[3] A "business activity" includes "the acquisition or use of any contract right or other tangible or intangible real or personal property".[4]

Another crucial question is to establish the factors that should be taken into account in determining whether a corporate opportunity exists which should have been offered to the company. The question has been considered both by American and English courts. The American attitude is relatively flexible, but the approach is not entirely consistent. Some courts require that the plaintiff shows that the company had a legal or equitable interest or tangible expectancy growing out of a pre-existing right or relationship.[5]

---

*Cont.*
courts would not go so far, unless perhaps the employee held a managerial post within the company.

[1] *Vide* generally R.P. Austin, "Fiduciary Accountability for Business Opportunities" in P.D. Finn (ed.), *Equity and Commercial Relationships* (1987) pp. 141-185.

[2] Adopted and promulgated on the 13th May 1992 (cited in this work as "ALI Principles of Corporate Governance"). The ALI Principles of Corporate Governance are partly a restatement of American law and partly a set of recommendations addressed to the courts and the legislatures. They are likely to play a significant role in the orderly development of this area of American law.

[3] ALI Principles of Corporate Governance, s. 5.12, pp. 349-350.

[4] *Ibid.* p. 351.

[5] E.g., *Abbott Redmont Thinlite Corp.* v. *Redmont* 475 F.2d 85 (2d Cir. 1973); *Burg* v. *Horn* 380 F.2d 897 (2d Cir. 1967).

Other American courts however have used a more flexible "line of business" test[1] and have taken into account such matters as the relation between the opportunity and the corporate policy,[2] the actual activities of the company[3] and the ability of the company to undertake the opportunity.[4] In so far as the test of ability is concerned, some courts have required proof of financial ability to perform the opportunity,[5] while others consider it sufficient if the company can easily and naturally modify or extend its activities to enable it to undertake the opportunity.[6] If, applying these tests, the company is unable financially or practically, to take advantage of the opportunity, the dominating shareholder would be entitled to fairly divert the opportunity to himself.[7] Others however have adopted a "fairness test" and have held that the inability (for whatever reason) of a solvent company to take an opportunity is no defence.[8] American courts are also influenced by the reaction of the company[9] and the conduct of the defendant.[10]

In its commentary to the Principles of Corporate Governance, the American Law Institute has also attempted to promote a consistent attitude

---

[1] *Guth* v. *Loft, Inc.* 5 A.2d  503, 514 (Del. 1939). The "line of business" test characterises an opportunity as corporate whenever the activity is intimately or closely associated with the existing or prospective activities of the company.  A "line of business" test would ease allocation problems because the opportunity would go to the company which already operates in the field. Such a test would however leave an unacceptably large number of gaps. The opportunity for example may belong to neither the holding company's nor the subsidiary's realm of operations. Or both companies may operate in the same field and the opportunity could be taken by either company. *Vide* Victor Brudney and Robert Charles Clark, "A New Look at Corporate Opportunities" 94 Harv. L.R. 998 (1981) p. 1052.

[2] E.g., *Zidell* v. *Zidell* 560 P.2d 1091, 1092-1094 (1977).

[3] E.g., *Ellzey* v. *Fyr-Pruf, Inc.* 376 So.2d 1328, 1333 (Miss. 1979).

[4] E.g., *Guth* v. *Loft, Inc.* 5 A.2d  503 (Del. 1939).

[5] *Schreiber* v. *Bryan* 396 A.2d 512, 518-519 (Del. Ch. 1978); *Equity Corp.* v. *Milton* 221 A.2d 494, 497 (Del. 1966).

[6] *Vide Miller* v. *Miller* 222 N.W.2d 71, 80-81 (Minn. 1974).

[7] Cf. *Schreiber* v. *Bryan* 396 A.2d 512, 518-519 (Del. Ch. 1978); *Guth* v. *Loft, Inc.* 5 A.2d 503, 514 (Del. 1939); Lawrence P. Kessel, "Trends in the Approach to the Corporate Entity Problem in Civil Litigation" 41 Georgtown L.J. 525 (1953) pp. 539-540.

[8] *Irving Trust Co.* v. *Deutsch* 73 F.2d 121 (2d. Cir. 1934), *cert. denied*, 294 U.S. 708 (1935); *Durfee* v. *Durfee & Canning, Inc.* 80 N.E.2d 522, 529 (Mass. 1948).

[9] E.g., *Kaplan* v. *Fenton* 278 A.2d 834 (Del. 1971).

[10] E.g., *Equity Corp.* v. *Milton* 221 A.2d 494 (Del. 1966); *Schildberg Rock Products Co.* v. *Brooks* 140 N.W.2d 132 (Iowa 1966).

by listing several factors that should be taken into account in determining whether a corporate opportunity exists which must be offered to the company : (1) Has an expectation been created that the company's existing or anticipated scope of operations will include the business activity or geographical area of operation under consideration? (2) If this question is answered in the affirmative, other questions follow : (a) Was it contemplated that the company should exclusively engage in the particular business activity or geographical area or that the dominating shareholder would also engage in such activity or area? (b) How did the dominating shareholder gain access to the opportunity? Was the opportunity developed by the dominating shareholder within the scope and regular course of his own business activities? If it was, then the dominating shareholder should have no duty to allow the company to take the opportunity unless it is an activity that was held out generally to shareholders of the company as being within the company's area of business activity. And if the dominating shareholder is not engaged in the particular activity but the company is, then the fact that the dominating shareholder received the opportunity will not be determinative, since it may be fairly inferred in the absence of other facts that under the circumstances he would not have received the opportunity but for the existing business of the company.[1]

In England, courts have sometimes focused on the capacity of the profiteers : the corporate opportunity must have been acquired by reason of the profiteers' position as directors and the nature of the opportunity itself is not really examined. This approach, which assimilates the "fairness test" sometimes apparent in American judgments, was evident in *Industrial Development Consultants Ltd.* v. *Cooley* decided in 1972.[2] A year later, the Canadian Supreme Court, in *Canadian Aero Service Ltd.* v. *O'Malley*,[3] recognised the limitations of the capacity approach. Laskin J. observed that such an approach stultified the development of the doctrine. He accordingly preferred to consider a number of different factors in order to establish whether or not the defendant was in breach of his fiduciary duties.[4] Factors that should be taken into account include the position or office held by the director, the director's relation to the opportunity, the amount of knowledge possessed, the particular circumstances in which it was obtained and whether

---

[1] *Vide* generally, ALI Principles of Corporate Governance, pp. 350-355.

[2] [1972] 1 W.L.R. 443. Cf. *Regal (Hastings) Ltd.* v. *Gulliver* [1967] 2 A.C. 134.

[3] (1974) 40 D.L.R. (3d) 371.

[4] *Ibid.* at p. 391.

it was "special, or indeed, even private", the nature, "specificness" and "ripeness" of the opportunity.[1]

The different approaches to the corporate opportunities doctrine were more recently considered by Hutchinson J. in *Island Export Finance Ltd.* v. *Umunna*,[2] a case involving a managing director who had resigned and subsequently obtained valuable orders from a client of the company. After considering English and Canadian authorities in this area of the law, Hutchinson J. cited with approval Laskin J.'s key dictum in *Canadian Aero Service Ltd.* v. *O'Malley*[3] and adopted a more flexible doctrine than the previous English judgments. He took into account the lack of maturity of the opportunity as well as the motive for the defendant's resignation from the company and the fact that the company was not actively pursuing further business with the particular client. If Hutchinson J.'s approach were to be followed in subsequent cases, English law would (quite unwittingly) be moving closer to the more flexible doctrine being developed in American law.

### 3.1.3. The doctrine in holding-subsidiary situations

A crucial question is whether the corporate opportunities doctrine can apply in the context of the holding-subsidiary relationship.[4] Two issues need to be

---

[1] *Ibid.* at p. 391.

[2] [1986] BCLC 460.

[3] (1974) 40 D.L.R. (3d) 371 at pp. 390-391. *Vide Island Export Finance Ltd.* v. *Umunna* [1986] BCLC 460 at pp. 481-483.

[4] Writing in 1982, Prentice (presumably referring to the situation in English law) remarked that "[t]he allocation of corporate opportunities between the various companies of a group gives rise to vexing (and as yet relatively unexplored) problems". *Vide* Prentice, The English Experience, p. 125. In English law, the question has remained largely unexplored. In American law, the question had already been considered in a number of judgments and in some valuable academic contributions. *Vide* e.g., *Blaustein* v. *Pan American Petroleum & Transport Co.* 56 N.E. 2d 705 (N.Y. 1944); E. Merrick Dodd, "Liability of a Holding Company for Obtaining for Itself Property Needed by a Subsidiary : the Blaustein Case" 58 Harv. L.R. 125 (1944); Thomas W. Walde, "Parent-Subsidiary Relations in the Integrated Corporate System : A Comparison of American and German Law" 9 Journal of International Law and Economics 455 (1974) pp. 462-463, 480-482; Victor Brudney and Robert Charles Clark, "A New Look at Corporate Opportunities" 94 Harv. L.R. 998 (1981); Karen McLaughlin, "Corporate Opportunity Doctrine in the Context of Parent-Subsidiary Relations" 8 Northern Kentucky L.R. 121 (1981). More recently, the whole issue of corporate opportunities and the duties of

addressed. First, what is the position concerning persons holding common directorships of both the holding company and its subsidiary? Second, does a holding company owe fiduciary duties to the subsidiary such that it would be in breach of such duties if it diverted corporate opportunities that properly belonged to the subsidiary?

Before dealing with these matters in some detail, one general observation needs to be made: the cases show that closely integrated management structures and elaborate divisions of functions within many corporate groups will significantly complicate the question of ownership of corporate opportunities. Frequently, opportunities may not come to a subsidiary as "individualized, identifiable, tangible expectancies".[1] The result will be that the subsidiary may face problems in claiming a right over the opportunity. In a group implementing a group profit maximisation policy, with subsidiaries ceasing to operate as autonomous units, every opportunity may well be considered as an "expectancy" and "in the line of business activity" of the group as a whole, to be allocated as determined by head office in the overall interest of the group. In the face of such difficulties, American courts, at least, have had to take policy decisions concerning the breadth of the doctrine.

### 3.1.3.1. The doctrine and common directorships

A number of cases applying the doctrine of corporate opportunities in the holding-subsidiary context involve the duty of a person who sits on the boards of both a holding and its subsidiary company.[2] Such a situation is evidently a breeding ground for conflicting duties. In the American case of *Weinberger* v. *UOP, Inc.*[3] the court declared :

---

*Cont.*

    controlling shareholders (including holding companies) was considered by the American Law Institute. *Vide* ALI Principles of Corporate Governance, pp. 350-355.

[1] *Vide* Thomas W. Walde, "Parent-Subsidiary Relations in the Integrated Corporate System: A Comparison of American and German Law" 9 Journal of International Law and Economics 455 (1974) p. 484.

[2] A director of a holding company does not, in such capacity, owe any fiduciary duty to the subsidiary. Such a director will be entitled to take into account the interests of other companies within the group only to the extent that this furthers the interest of his company. *Vide* further *supra* p. 240.

[3] 457 A.2d 701 (Del. Supr. 1983).

"The requirement of fairness is unflinching in its demand that where one stands on both sides of the transaction, he has the burden of establishing its entire fairness ... Thus, individuals who act in a dual capacity as directors of two corporations, one of whom is parent and the other subsidiary, owe the same duty of good management to both corporations, and in the absence of an independent negotiating structure, or the directors' total abstention from any participation in the matter, this duty is to be exercised in light of what is best for both companies."[1]

Another American case that highlights the problem of interlocking directorships is *Warshaw* v. *Calhoun*.[2] In that case the plaintiff was a minority shareholder in a holding company. The three defendants were directors and officers of both the holding company and the subsidiary. Due to the subsidiary's need for capital and the desire to spread the ownership of its shares, a stock split was arranged. The holding company declined to subscribe to the offer, but sold its rights to the underwriter concerned in the arrangement.[3] The plaintiff complained that her ownership in the subsidiary was indirectly diluted and alleged that the defendants' conduct involved a breach of their fiduciary duties to the shareholders of the holding company. On the facts, the court found that the defendants had acted in the best interest of both the holding and the subsidiary companies and that there was therefore no breach of fiduciary duties. The court, appearing to play down the possibility of conflicting duties, observed that persons "who act in a dual capacity as directors of two corporations, one of whom is a parent and the other subsidiary, owe the same duty of good management to both corporations. This duty is to be exercised in the light of what is best for both corporations."[4] The court emphasised that the question of subscribing to rights on a stock issue was a matter to be decided in accordance with the "business judgment" of the defendants. As there was no proof of bad faith or gross abuse, the court declined to interfere in the defendants' decision.[5] American courts, however, do not consistently apply a "business judgment"

---

[1] *Ibid.* at pp. 710-711.

[2] 221 A.2d 487 (Del. 1966). The case does not actually involve a question of corporate opportunities. The observations made in the judgment however would also apply in case of corporate opportunities.

[3] *Ibid.* at pp. 489-490.

[4] *Ibid.* at p. 492. *Vide* also *Levien* v. *Sinclair Oil Corp.* 261 A.2d 911, 915 (Del. Ch. 1969).

[5] 221 A.2d 487 (Del. 1966) at pp. 492-493.

test. In *Schreiber* v. *Bryan*,[1] for example, the court expressly rejected the "business judgment" test and appeared to favour an "intrinsic fairness" test.[2]

The American Law Institute's Principles of Corporate Governance also deals with the conflicting duties of loyalty owed by directors who serve both the holding and its subsidiary company.[3] The Principles of Corporate Governance draw a distinction - not generally drawn in the judgments - between transactions in which a director has a pecuniary interest in the transaction and transactions between corporations with common directors who have no such interest.[4] Essentially, the Principles of Corporate Governance provide that a transaction between two corporations is not to be treated as a transaction subject to the general duty of fair dealing as stated in the Principles[5] solely on the ground that the same person is a director of both corporations unless either (a) the director participates personally and substantially in negotiating the transaction for either of the corporations, or (b) the transaction is approved by the board of either corporation and a director on that board who is also a director of the other corporation casts a vote that is necessary to approve the transaction.[6] A director shall not be deemed to have participated "personally and substantially in negotiations" by merely participating in strategy sessions of one corporation in which non-public information concerning the other corporation is not disclosed.[7]

Although there appears to be no judgment specifically on the point, there can be little doubt that English law does impose on the common directors of both the holding company and its subsidiary the duty inherent in the doctrine of corporate opportunity. In *Scottish Co-Operative Wholesale Society Ltd.* v. *Meyer*,[8] a case that touched upon directors' fiduciary duties but not upon the doctrine of corporate opportunities as such, the House of Lords considered that it was a breach of duty for the directors of a subsidiary company, three of whom were also directors of the holding company, to use

---

[1] 396 A.2d 512 (Del. Ch. 1978). This case actually concerned the fiduciary duty of a holding company not to divert a corporate opportunity belonging to its subsidiary.

[2] *Ibid.* at p. 519.

[3] *Vide* ALI Principles of Corporate Governance, s. 5.07, p. 308.

[4] *Ibid.* Commentary p. 308.

[5] *Ibid.* s. 5.02, pp. 209-210.

[6] *Ibid.* s. 5.07, p. 308.

[7] *Ibid.* Commentary at pp. 309-310.

[8] [1959] A.C. 324 (H.L. Sc).

their position to promote the interests of the holding company to the detriment of the subsidiary company. The same attitude would no doubt have been taken had the case involved a question of corporate opportunities. And in contrast to the view expressed by the American court in *Warshaw* v. *Calhoun*,[1] Lord Denning stated that common directors are put in an impossible situation where the interests of the holding and subsidiary companies conflict.[2]

The possibility of conflict was also recognised by the inspectors appointed to investigate and report on the affairs of the Cornhill Consolidated Group Limited.[3] The inspectors observed that where companies within the same group are financially interdependent and have common directors, the common directors need to be especially alert to the need to consider the separate interests of each company.[4] Common directors are not of course always faced with irreconcilable conflict situations. In *Charterbridge Corporation Ltd.* v. *Lloyds Bank Ltd.*,[5] for example, the court held that the common directors of affiliated companies were not guilty of abusing their powers when they caused one company to enter into a transaction for the benefit of another company in the group, provided that the purpose of the transaction was also to confer a real and substantial benefit to the first company.

### 3.1.3.2. The doctrine and holding company liability

In American law, controlling shareholders owe fiduciary duties towards the company and other shareholders.[6] Such fiduciary duties are predicated on two grounds : either on the equitable principle that one who holds a position of superiority and influence over the interests of others is a fiduciary, or on the basis that if the directors and officers owe fiduciary duties, the controlling shareholders who dominate the company through their influence

---

[1] 221 A.2d 487, 492 (Del. 1966). *Vide supra* pp. 282-283.

[2] [1959] A.C. 324 (H.L. Sc.) at p. 366.

[3] Department of Trade, The Cornhill Consolidated Group Limited (In Liquidation), Investigation under Section 165(b) of Companies Act 1948, Report by David Calcutt, QC and John Whinney, FCA, (pub. HMSO 1980).

[4] *Ibid.* at para. 17.02 p. 293.

[5] [1970] Ch. 62.

[6] *Southern Pacific Co.* v. *Bogert* 250 U.S. 483 (1919); *Pepper* v. *Litton* 308 U.S. 295 (1939).

over the directors and officers should be subject to analogous duties.[1] Given this approach, it will come as no surprise to learn that in American law, the doctrine of corporate opportunities applies to impose duties on the holding company. The question of corporate opportunities in the holding-subsidiary context was specifically considered in *David J. Greene & Co.* v. *Dunhill International, Inc.*[2] The plaintiff was a minority shareholder in a subsidiary company whose majority shareholding was held by the defendant holding company. The plaintiff alleged that a proposed merger (which involved the elimination of the subsidiary) was unfair because the proposed exchange ratio failed to take into account a diversion, by the holding company, of a corporate opportunity belonging to the subsidiary. In finding that the holding company had acquired an opportunity owned by the subsidiary, the court expressly extended the notion of directors' fiduciary duties to controlling shareholders and therefore to the holding company in its relationship with a subsidiary. The court observed that while the law "on corporate opportunity has developed around the duty owed by directors and officers ... comparable duties and standards should be imposed when the party whose conduct is in question is a shareholder. In some circumstances a stockholder has opportunities to express and prefer his self-interest to that of the corporation. But we are concerned with circumstances in which a stockholder, by virtue of his control of corporate functions, makes a choice advantageous to himself and against the corporate interest".[3]

A similar question was faced by the court in *Levien* v. *Sinclair Oil Corporation*.[4] The plaintiff was a minority shareholder in a subsidiary of the defendant holding company. The plaintiff alleged *inter alia* that the holding company's development of operations similar to those already undertaken by the subsidiary was a diversion of a corporate opportunity owned by the subsidiary. The Chancery Court of Delaware explained that the holding company "voluntarily took on a fiduciary duty" and that "[t]o meet that obligation it could have installed a truly independent board and had it done so the business judgment test might have been dispositive of most of this

---

[1] Henn and Alexander, *op. cit.* p. 654. *Vide* further Cary and Eisenberg, *op. cit.* pp. 613-637; David Finch and Robert Long, "The Fiduciary Relation of the Dominant Shareholder to the Minority Shareholders" 9 Hastings L.J. 306 (1958).

[2] 249 A.2d 427 (Del. Ch. 1968).

[3] *Ibid.* at p. 434.

[4] 261 A.2d 911 (Del. Ch. 1969).

case."[1] The Court found that the directors of the subsidiary company were not independent of the holding company and were therefore not in a position to make judgements as to what was in the subsidiary's interest without reference to the holding company's position. Accordingly, the test of "intrinsic fairness" ought to apply.[2] On appeal, however, the Supreme Court of Delaware held that the intrinsic fairness standard will be applied only when the fiduciary duty is accompanied by self-dealing - the situation when a holding company is on both sides of a transaction with its subsidiary.[3] "Self-dealing occurs when the parent, by virtue of its domination of the subsidiary, causes the subsidiary to act in such a way that the parent receives something from the subsidiary to the exclusion of, and detriment to, the minority stockholders of the subsidiary."[4] Otherwise the business judgment test ought to be applied. On the facts, the Supreme Court held that as no opportunities actually came to the subsidiary, the holding company had not usurped an opportunity belonging to the subsidiary. And since the holding company received nothing from the subsidiary to the exclusion of and detriment to the minority shareholders, there was no self-dealing. The Supreme Court held that as there was no proof of self-dealing on the part of the holding company the expansion policy of the holding company and the methods used to achieve the desired result must be tested by the standards of the business judgment rule. The Supreme Court did however find the holding company to have breached its fiduciary obligations in other respects[5] and in doing so expressly rejected its plea that it had generally been fair to the subsidiary and that it should not therefore be liable for breach of its fiduciary duty.[6]

---

[1] *Ibid.* at p. 919.

[2] The standard of intrinsic fairness involves both a high degree of fairness and a shift in the burden of proof.

[3] *Sinclair Oil Corp* v. *Levien* 280 A.2d 717, 720 (Del. 1971). *Vide* also *Trans World Airlines, Inc. v. Summa Corp.* 374 A.2d 5, 9, 13 (Del. Ch. 1977).

[4] *Sinclair Oil Corp.* v. *Levien* 280 A.2d 717 (Del. 1971) at p. 720.

[5] *Vide* 280 A.2d 717 (Del. 1971) pp. 722-723. The Chancery Court had also found that the holding company had milked the subsidiary by means of excessive dividends. *Vide* 261 A.2d 911 (Del. Ch. 1969) at pp. 920-921. The Supreme Court however held that because a proportionate part of the dividends was received by the minority shareholder, the dividends were not self-dealing and accordingly that the business judgment test should be applied. *Vide* 280 A.2d 717 (Del. 1971) pp. 721-722.

[6] 280 A.2d 717 (Del. 1971) at p. 723. *Vide* also 261 A.2d 911 (Del. Ch. 1969) at pp. 925-926.

It should also be noted that a holding company in a subservient subsidiary situation is clearly to be considered as a "controlling shareholder" for the purposes of the American Law Institute Principles of Corporate Governance. A "controlling shareholder" is in fact there defined as "a person who, either alone or pursuant to an arrangement or understanding with one or more other persons : (1) owns and has the power to vote more than 50 per cent of the outstanding voting securities of a corporation; or (2) otherwise exercises a controlling influence over the management or policies of the corporation or the transaction in question by virtue of the person's position as a shareholder."[1] A holding company in a subservient subsidiary situation would certainly qualify under the second limb of the definition and would probably also qualify under the first. The "Principles of Corporate Governance : Analysis and Recommendations" stipulate that the controlling shareholder "may not take advantage of a corporate opportunity unless : (1) The taking of the opportunity is fair to the corporation; or (2) The taking of the opportunity is authorised or ratified by disinterested shareholders following disclosure concerning the conflict of interest and the corporate opportunity, and the taking of the corporate opportunity is not equivalent to a waste of corporate assets."[2]

In English law, it is not entirely clear whether the doctrine of corporate opportunities can be applied to involve liability on the holding company itself.[3] Certainly, there is no specific authority on the question. It is submitted however that where a holding company is intrusive in its domination over a subservient subsidiary it would qualify as a *de facto* director and therefore be bound by any fiduciary duty imposed on directors generally.[4] Some support for such an approach can be derived from certain judicial *dicta*. In *Scottish Co-Operative Wholesale Society Ltd.* v. *Meyer*[5] (in which the inaction of the directors appointed to the subsidiary by the holding

---

[1] ALI Principles of Corporate Governance, s. 1.10(a), p. 14.

[2] *Ibid.* s. 5.12(a), p. 349.

[3] Writing in 1982, Prentice seemed uncertain of the position. Referring to two American judgments (*Sinclair Oil Corp.* v. *Levien* 280 A.2d 717 (Del. 1971); *TWA, Inc.* v. *Summa Corp.* 374 A.2d 5 (1977)), Prentice stated that "[a]t the minimum in this situation a parent should be treated as owing a fiduciary duty to its subsidiary and as under an obligation to treat its subsidiary with fairness". *Vide* Prentice, The English Experience, at p. 126.

[4] *Vide supra* pp. 244-245 where this contention was further developed in relation to the notion of directors' duties towards creditors.

[5] [1959] A.C. 324 (H.L.).

company had been intended to allow the taking of business from the subsidiary by the holding company) Viscount Simonds quoted with approval Lord Cooper's words on the first hearing that "whenever a subsidiary is formed ... with an independent minority of shareholders, the parent company must, if it is engaged in the same class of business, accept as a result of having formed such a subsidiary an obligation so to conduct what are in a sense its own affairs as to deal fairly with its subsidiary."[1] And in *Daniels* v. *Daniels*,[2] Templeman J. equated directors and majority shareholders as regards the "duty" which "they owe to the company".[3]

### 3.1.4. The doctrine and creditor protection

A vital question is whether the doctrine of corporate opportunities can play any role in protecting the interests of creditors. In English law, the answer is clearly no. In American law, creditors may possibly be afforded some protection. Clearly, under both American and English law, the doctrine of corporate opportunities is viewed as a subdivision of the wider notion of the fiduciary duty to act in the best interests of the company. Subject to what is stated below with regard to American law, the general rule in both jurisdictions is that fiduciary duties are owed to the company and, through the company, to the shareholders. The doctrine of corporate opportunities adheres to this principle and no action for breach of fiduciary duty would generally be sustainable if the company authorises or ratifies the diversion of the opportunity. Creditors would have no actionable interest. Translating these principles to a holding-subsidiary arrangement, the position would be as follows : (1) In the case of a wholly-owned subsidiary, the diversion of the opportunity by the holding company would not in practice be actionable by the subsidiary because the holding company, *qua* shareholder, would either have expressly or impliedly authorised the diversion or would ratify it if necessary. (2) In the case of a partly-owned subsidiary, the diversion of the opportunity by the holding company would clearly be actionable by the

---

[1] *Ibid.* at p. 343. In *Re A company (No. 002470 of 1988), ex parte Nicholas* [1991] BCLC 480, Harman J. accepted Lord Cooper's dictum as a statement of principle, although he emphasised that "words in judgments are uttered against particular factual backgrounds and are not to be construed as if the judgment were a statute." *Ibid.* at p. 487.

[2] [1978] Ch. 406.

[3] *Ibid.* at pp. 413-414.

minority shareholders under American law,[1] and arguably also under English law (depending in the latter case on whether the courts would be prepared to extend the notion of fiduciary duties to controlling shareholders, including a holding company). Creditors of a partly-owned subsidiary, although having no action (directly or through the subsidiary) against the holding company for breach of the fiduciary duty, do therefore stand to gain by the presence of minority shareholders.

American law, however, has been developing the notion that fiduciary duties can, in certain situations, be owed by a controlling shareholder to the company's creditors. As early as 1939, the Supreme Court had stated, in *Pepper* v. *Litton*,[2] that the "standard of fiduciary obligation is designed for the protection of the entire community of interests in the corporation - creditors as well as stockholders."[3] This notion has, for example, been applied in the bankruptcy cases to justify the subordination of the claims of a controlling shareholder to those of ordinary creditors.[4] Also significant in this regard is the principle stated in the American Law Institute's Principles of Corporate Governance that even the unanimous approval of the disinterested shareholders would not be sufficient if the dominating shareholder's diversion of the corporate opportunity is "equivalent to a waste of corporate assets".[5] In such circumstances, the holding company, qua controlling or dominating shareholder, may also be considered to owe to the subsidiary's creditors the duties inherent in the doctrine of corporate opportunities.

English law appears to be some distance away from the American approach. It is true that for a number of years there has seemed to be developing a judicial willingness to extend the doctrine of directors' fiduciary duties to include duties towards creditors.[6] And it is also true that the holding company's position could arguably be equated with that of

---

[1] Unless of course "the disinterested shareholders, following disclosure concerning the conflict of interest and the corporate opportunity" authorise or ratify the holding company conduct. *Vide* s. 5.12, pp. 349-350, of the ALI Principles of Corporate Governance.

[2] 308 U.S. 295 (1939).

[3] *Ibid.* at p. 307 (references omitted). *Vide* also *McCandless* v. *Furlaud* 296 U.S. 140 (1935); *New York Credit Men's Adjustment Bureau, Inc.* v. *Weiss* 110 N.E.2d 397 (1953).

[4] *Vide* further *post* Chapter VI pp. 355-360.

[5] *Ibid.* s. 5.12(a)(2), p. 349. *Vide* also s. 5.12(c), pp. 349-350 and Commentary p. 354.

[6] *Vide supra* pp. 243-246.

directors for the purposes of such an extension.[1] But as we have seen, not only are there doubts as to whether a notion of directors' duties towards creditors really is emerging, but there is also the question of the scope of the notion.[2] For the notion seems to be concerned with sanctioning conduct which directly prejudices creditors in the context of insolvency or "doubtful" solvency or "near" insolvency.[3] These confining limitations render the notion of directors' duties towards creditors ineffective in remedying the abuse of the unfair diversion of corporate opportunities.

In conclusion, it must be stated that it may make sound economic sense to argue that the allocation of corporate opportunities should be determined on the basis of the promotion of efficiency and economic value and that the subsidiary with the higher potential of increased return should be allowed to develop the opportunity.[4] Such a rule is however workable only if an "enterprise" approach to the phenomenon of corporate groups is taken. This approach would involve sidestepping the entity principle which demands that the management of each company should try to secure and develop the opportunity for the benefit of the company. Such an enterprise approach is nowhere in sight, not even in American law. Nor is such a revolutionary change necessary. An equitable solution lies either in the provision of adequate compensation to the subsidiary for the loss of the corporate opportunity or in the assumption of liability on the part of the holding company for the debts of the subsidiary.

## 3.2. Commingling of assets

### 3.2.1. The nature of the abuse

One other type of subservient practice that deserves special consideration is the "commingling" or "intermingling" of the assets (including properties, stock or funds) of the subsidiary with those of other members within the corporate group.[5] Such commingling - which is more likely to occur in closely integrated groups - is not inherently offensive. Indeed, the

---

[1] *Vide supra* pp. 249-251.

[2] *Vide supra* pp. 246-249.

[3] *Vide supra* pp. 244-245.

[4] *Vide* Victor Brudney and Robert Charles Clark, "A New Look at Corporate Opportunities" 94 Harv. L.R. 998 (1981) p. 1050.

[5] *Vide* further *supra* Chapter II pp. 76-77.

commingling of assets "may be highly desirable in order to maximize overall productive use of the capital and resources of the enterprise."[1] Commingling would however be objectionable if proper records are not kept which would permit an accurate determination to be made of the relative proportions belonging to the various companies within the group. The need for a sharp separation of one corporate estate from another is self-evident : the separate entity principle demands that corporate creditors are to look to the estate of their corporate debtor for payment. Wrongful commingling - that is commingling without proper records - renders the identification of the assets available for the satisfaction of the subsidiary's debts difficult or even impossible.[2] Moreover, wrongful commingling suggests the lack of the subsidiary's financial integrity and heightens the risk that a subsidiary's assets may be utilised to satisfy the creditors of the holding or affiliated companies rather than being available for its own creditors. The holding company's pooling of assets should lead to a pooling of liabilities.

Even where the commingled assets can be traced and recovered, it is arguable that the commingling of assets without accurate record-keeping should still be viewed as abusive because such commingling usually involves the risk that the assets may, from the subsidiary's point of view, be "lost".[3] It is not merely a plain disregard of formalities.[4] The question should however remain one of degree. Liability should not be imposed, for example, where the commingling has been trivial or can be unravelled without undue difficulty.

Cases of wrongful commingling are probably quite rare. Both company and tax legislation require companies to "keep accounting records which are sufficient to show and explain the company's transactions"[5] and which contain "a record of the assets and liabilities of the company".[6] The failure

---

[1] Jonathan M. Landers, "A Unified Approach to Parent, Subsidiary, and Affiliate Questions in Bankruptcy" 42 Univ. of Chicago L.R. 589 (1975) p. 592.

[2] *Vide Chemical Bank N.Y. Trust Co.* v. *Kheel* 369 F.2d 845, 847 (2d Cir. 1966). Cf. *Stone* v. *Marshall Oil Co.* 57 Atl. 183 (1904). *Vide* also Latty, *op. cit.* pp. 184-185.

[3] Blumberg argues that "[t]he imposition of liability because of commingling, even in the few cases where assets can be identified and recovered, introduces salutary deterrence of conduct inherently dangerous to creditors." *Vide* Blumberg, *Substantive Law* at p. 503.

[4] Blumberg, *Substantive Law* p. 503. The mere disregard of corporate formalities is not in itself abusive and should not therefore be afforded any significance.

[5] C.A. 1985, s. 221(1).

[6] C.A. 1985, s. 221(2)(b). In the United States, statutes often impose a similar duty. *Vide*, ABA-ALI Model Business Corporation Act, s. 52.

to comply with these requirements constitutes an offence punishable with imprisonment or a fine, or both.[1] In addition to the obvious desire of avoiding penal sanctions, companies strive to keep adequate records both for reasons of business expediency as well as to be able to furnish shareholders with a "clean" auditor's report to the financial statements.

### 3.2.2. Is a remedy available?

Where wrongful commingling has occurred, it is arguable that the holding company - which has failed in its duty to keep the estates of its subsidiaries separate - should not be able to prevent the creditors of the subsidiary's estate (whose identity has been blurred) from seeking enforcement against the entire estate of such companies whose assets have been commingled. Such a remedy would find an analogy in the law on the confusion of personal property, where the burden of proof is placed on the party responsible for the commingling to show what portion of the commingled assets belongs to him.[2] Applied to a holding-subsidiary arrangement such a remedy would enable an insolvent subsidiary's creditors to seek relief against the holding company. Complications will however arise where the commingling involves not just the holding and one subsidiary company, but also other subsidiaries. Would all the assets have to be consolidated? And what about the liabilities? Creditors of particular subsidiaries are likely to be prejudiced if their debtors' estates had to be consolidated with those of other companies involved in the commingling.

Judgments do not offer precise guidance in this area of the law.[3] Despite considerable judicial disapproval of the practice of commingling, most cases do not actually impose liability on the holding company nor do they order the consolidation of assets merely as a consequence of commingling. Commingling turns out to be only one of the factors leading to liability.[4] There are however cases where the commingling of the assets was considered to be so serious that it destroyed the corporate separateness of the

---

[1] C.A. 1985, s. 221(6).

[2] *Vide* Andrew P. Bell, *Modern Law of Personal Property in England and Ireland* (1989) pp. 71-72; Earl C. Arnold, "Confusion" 23 Col. L.R. 235 (1923).

[3] Not surprisingly, all the cases on the subject are from the United States.

[4] E.g., *Pepsi-Cola Metropolitan Bottling Company, Inc.* v. *Checkers, Inc.* 754 F.2d 10 (1st Cir. 1985); *Worldwide Carriers Ltd.* v. *Aris Steamship Co.* 301 F.Supp. 64 (S.D.N.Y. 1968).

company from its shareholder.[1] Since the holding company rendered the identification of the subsidiary's estate difficult or even impossible, and since the holding company had itself effectively disregarded the separate personality of the subsidiary, the holding company is prevented by the court from pleading the separate existence of the subsidiary. Commingling has also been an important factor in the bankruptcy subordination,[2] consolidation[3] and turnover[4] cases.

A remedy to deal with cases of wrongful commingling was introduced in New Zealand as part of the far-reaching reforms implemented in that country in 1980. New Zealand courts are now empowered, if they consider it just and equitable to do so, to order that the assets and liabilities of two or more insolvent affiliates be pooled for the purpose of the liquidation. In deciding whether to exercise their discretion, the courts are to have regard to a number of matters, including the extent to which the businesses of the companies had been intermingled.[5]

## 4. EXTRA-LEGAL AND INDIRECT CHECKS ON SUBSERVIENT PRACTICES

Apart from the arsenal of statutory and judicial weapons that, to some extent, control and remedy the potentially abusive and unfair subservient subsidiary situation, there exist a number of "extra-legal" and indirect checks on subservient practices that deserve consideration.

### 4.1. Business and managerial expediency

In the first place, there is the strong factor of business and managerial expediency. A subservient subsidiary is a company which, to its own

---

[1] Cf. *Sweet* v. *Watson's Nursery* 92 P.2d 812 (1939); *Long* v. *McGlon* 263 F. Supp. 96 (D.S.C. 1967). *Vide* further Jules Silk, "One man corporations - Scope and limitations" 100 Univ. of Pennsylavania L.R. 853 (1952) p. 859.

[2] *Consolidated Rock Products Co.* v. *DuBois* 312 U.S. 510, 518-519 (1941).

[3] *Chemical Bank N.Y. Trust Co.* v. *Kheel* 369 F.2d 845, 846-847 (2d Cir. 1966).

[4] *Soverio* v. *Franklin National Bank of Long Island* 328 F.2d 446, 448 (2d Cir. 1964).

[5] *Vide* now New Zealand Companies Act 1993, ss. 271(1)(b) and 272(2). Similar provisions had originally been introduced as ss. 315B and 315C of the New Zealand Companies Act 1955 by s. 30 of the Companies Amendment Act 1980. *Vide* further *post* Chapter IX pp. 458-462 where a proposal is submitted that in cases of wrongful commingling a remedy of substantive consolidation should be implemented.

detriment, conducts its activities in the interest of some other component within the corporate group. Unless there are positive and identifiable advantages in pursuing a policy of subservience, such a policy is not very likely to attract much support from the group management team. Indeed, apart from the possible exposure to legal sanctions, the implementation of a policy of subservience may have other disadvantages. The relative profitability between the various companies in the group would for example be artificially distorted leading to inaccurate financial reports and statements and making for faulty strategic planning and performance assessment of the different companies. Appropriate adjustments to the financial and performance records can of course be effected, but such measures may prove to be costly and inefficient and would probably have to be shrouded in secrecy to avert the attention of the revenue authorities' prying eyes. Group headquarters is also sensitive to the attitudes and reactions of the subsidiary's directorate and management team. Directors and managers of a subservient subsidiary may become "attached" to their company and would be less likely to perform at their optimal level if their company appears submissive or if its profitability is being distorted. Headquarters would have to take heed of the disincentive problems that could be created by the related dissatisfaction and resentment, and would need to implant a "group corporate spirit" into the minds of the subservient subsidiary's personnel. Whether such an exercise would yield consistently positive results is another matter. All told, business and managerial expediency does probably act as a forceful limiting check on subservient practices.

### 4.2. Presence of minority shareholders

Another potent check on subservient practices is the presence of minority shareholders in partly-owned subsidiaries. There can be little doubt that subservient practices are potentially detrimental to the interests of minority shareholders and that the implementation of such practices could involve a breach of the fiduciary duty to act in the best interests of the company.[1] The minority has the right to require that the subsidiary be run for his proportionate benefit and to insist that the affairs of the subsidiary be handled as an independent entity. The directors of such a subsidiary must in fact deal with the company's assets on their own independent judgment; the subsidiary must be treated as an independent enterprise. Given these

[1] *Vide supra* pp. 240-241.

principles, it is evident that creditors of a partly-owned subsidiary can gain considerable "vicarious" protection through the presence of minority shareholders. Indeed, the holding company has no choice but to exercise its domination over the subsidiary in such a way as to reflect a more realistic arm's length approach. The holding company has to employ maximum caution in its dealings with the subsidiary.

A different kind of check may exist where the holding company's controlling interest is considerably less than a majority. In such a case, "gross exploitation of the subsidiary might be eschewed simply because it could goad the outsiders into a proxy fight, or alternatively, drive down the price of the subsidiary's stock and make it worthwhile for an outsider to acquire an overmatching control block."[1]

Needless to say, none of these considerations apply in the case of a wholly-owned subsidiary. The salutary presence of minority shareholders is simply missing. Given that the overwhelming majority of subsidiaries are in fact wholly-owned, the minority shareholder factor can only play an insignificant role in limiting the incidence of subservient practices within corporate groups.

## 4.3. Transfer pricing regulation

Mention should also be made of an indirect check on one particular form of subservient practice - transfer pricing manipulation. In a previous Chapter it was pointed out that transfer pricing has long been recognised as offensive by the tax authorities and that arbitrary profit-shifting through transfer pricing and other techniques has therefore been prohibited.[2] Transfer pricing techniques are sometimes used in purely domestic transactions, but the practice is far more widespread in transnational enterprises.[3] Indeed, anti-transfer pricing provisions are particularly aimed at transnational corporate group transactions where the arbitrary allocation of profit is considered particularly reprehensible and certainly more difficult to control.[4] If

---

[1] M.A. Eisenberg, "Megasubsidiaries : The Effect of Corporate Structure on Corporate Control" 84 Harv. L.R. 1577 (1971) at p. 1614.

[2] *Vide supra* Chapter II pp. 70-71.

[3] *Vide* Frank Wooldridge, *Groups of Companies - The Law and Practice in Britain, France and Germany* (1981) p. 83.

[4] Anti-avoidance provisions exist in s. 770 of the Income and Corporation Taxes Act 1988 to prevent artificial prices being placed on trading stock between associated companies

effective, the anti-evasion provisions would considerably reduce the abusive subservient practice of transfer pricing techniques. The subsidiary's creditors (and minority shareholders, if any) would free-ride on the back of the tax man. The available evidence unfortunately suggests that despite the efforts of the tax authorities to control transfer pricing manipulations, abuse is still common.[1] Double taxation treaties do make transfer pricing a far trickier tool to handle than some decades ago. But apart from the obvious obstacle of tax havens (which drive a wedge between investing and host countries) there seems to have been only limited co-operation amongst governments on the control of transfer pricing manipulations, on the exchange of information and on reconciling possible conflicts of interest.[2]

## 5.  INADEQUACY OF EXISTING REMEDIES

There can be no denying that English law appears to be equipped with a veritable armoury of weapons that can, collectively at least, support a sustained assault on abusive and unfair practices. Yet the foregoing sections of this Chapter have shown that on closer analysis, the available remedies - both statutory and common law - do not in fact adequately control or remedy the abuse and unfairness inherent in subservient practices.

This Chapter has identified a number of reasons which explain the inadequacy of existing remedies. The basic difficulty of course is that English law does not consider the subservient subsidiary situation to be inherently objectionable. Admittedly, English law does to some extent control certain forms of subservient practices (such as non-arm's length intra-group transactions) but it simply does not target all forms of subservient practices. The commingling of assets, the allocation of corporate opportunities and the operation of a subsidiary without a profit motive, for example, are practices which cannot really be pigeon-holed under any of the existing remedies.

---

*Cont.*
> unless both are resident in the United Kingdom. *Vide* further Mayson and Blake, *op. cit.* pp. 598-599. In the United States, transfer pricing is regulated by s. 482 of the Internal Revenue Code (26 U.S.C. s. 482). *Vide* further Kahn, *op. cit.* pp. 509-512.

[1]  *Vide supra* Chapter II p. 72.

[2]  *Vide* Stewart, *op. cit.* p. 183. *Vide* further Greenhill and Herbolzheimer, *op. cit.* pp. 185-193; Peter Fitzpatrick, "Transfer Pricing, Company Law and Shareholders' Interests" [1975] J.B.L. 202, p. 205.

Undeniably, some of the remedies - in particular the statutory remedies of wrongful trading and the provisions on transactions at an undervalue and preferences - may have an important role to play in restraining subservient practices. But the effectiveness of these remedies is hamstrung by the difficulty of meeting the statutory conditions needed to activate the application of the remedies.[1]

A particularly confining limitation is the monotransactional approach of most of the remedies. Transactions have to be scrutinised individually. Such an approach may work well in the context of the traditionally independent company for which the remedies were originally devised. But a monotransactional approach renders the applicable remedies (such as the provisions relating to transactions at an undervalue and preferences, the *ultra vires* doctrine and the doctrine of directors' duties towards creditors) virtually unworkable as a means of controlling the abuse and unfairness in the holding-subsidiary relationship. For in the intricacies of a typical corporate group (with a steady flow of goods and services, interactions, instructions and enterprise-wide strategies), hundreds of potentially subservient transactions may occur even over a short period of time. A court will find it practically impossible to minutely examine each single transaction in the light of the specific requirements (and defences) of particular remedies. The exercise would also prove extremely costly and time-consuming.

The use of a monotransactional approach also raises a different type of problem. A particular act or transaction (let us say, the diversion of a corporate opportunity or the sale by the subsidiary of products at an undervalue), if examined on an individual basis, may well appear to be detrimental to the interests of the subsidiary and therefore objectionable. But if examined in the light of a group strategy that confers an overall benefit on the subsidiary, the diversion of the corporate opportunity or the sale at an undervalue may no longer be unacceptable. Indeed, even a whole series of "detrimental" acts or transactions might not be considered offensive at all when the overall direct or indirect benefit gained by the subsidiary is taken into account.

Either way therefore, a monotransactional approach to the analysis of the holding-subsidiary relationship can yield undesirable results. The scrutiny of individual transactions is no longer appropriate. Courts should have

---

[1] *Vide* further *supra* pp. 217-218 (re wrongful trading), pp. 234-239 (re transactions at an undervalue and preferences).

jurisdiction to determine the existence or otherwise of a subservient subsidiary situation from behavioural patterns within a corporate group rather that from a sharpened focus on a limited number of individual transactions. Existing law however does not permit such a *gestalt* approach to the intra-group dealings. The entity principle prevents it.

Some common law notions - such as the piercing the veil doctrine and the doctrine of controlling shareholders' and directors' duties towards creditors - may, it is submitted, offer considerable potential in the control of subservient practices. Yet this potential has either not been perceived by English courts, or if perceived, has not been adequately availed of. In these areas, where judicial law making can have a particularly salutary impact on creditor protection and on safeguarding the privilege of incorporation from abuse, English judicial conservatism stands in marked contrast to the liberal American approach.

It must of course be said that existing remedies combined with certain indirect or extra-legal checks (such as business or managerial expediency and the presence of minority shareholders) *do* have the effect of somewhat limiting the incidence of subservient practices, or of remedying the abuse. Nevertheless, the present web of legal remedies and extra-legal checks still allows many instances of subservient practices to escape control or remedy. There is still a crying need for reform.

## 6. PROPOSAL FOR REFORM

### 6.1. The essence of the reform proposal

The crucial question now is to determine the type of reform that would be appropriate and desirable. Before formulating a proposal for reform, it is essential to re-emphasise a view expressed in an earlier Chapter : that on policy grounds the law should encourage investment and risk-taking and that the principle of limited liability plays a central role in implementing such policies.[1] Where however the privilege of incorporation has been abused, or where the interests of creditors have been unfairly trampled on, inroads into the principle of limited liability are justified. The law has to strike a balance between the strong policy attractions of limited liability and the need to redress abuse and unfairness. It is for these reasons that a blanket form of

---

[1] *Vide supra* Chapter IV pp. 193-194.

liability on the holding company for the debts of its subsidiaries would be singularly inappropriate. The privileges of separate incorporation and limited liability can be abused, but the law should focus on the abuses whilst preserving the principle. An earlier Chapter identified as abusive and unfair the subservient subsidiary situation.[1] The present Chapter proved that existing law does not provide adequate redress. Any proposal for reform must aim only to remedy the abuse and unfairness inherent in the subservient subsidiary situation to the extent that existing law fails to do so. The law should not use dynamite where the rifle will do.

Given the aforesaid underlying principles, it is submitted that the following rule should, as a matter of considerable urgency, be introduced in English law : that a holding company is to be held liable for the debts of its insolvent subservient subsidiaries to such an extent as may be determinable by the court[2].

Several aspects of the reform proposal require elaboration.

---

[1] *Vide supra* Chapter II pp. 65-83.

[2] s. 271(1)(a) of the New Zealand Companies Act 1993 empowers the court "if it is satisfied that it is just and equitable to do so" to order that "a company that is, or has been, related to the company in liquidation must pay to the liquidator the whole or part of any or all of the claims made in the liquidation." The "just and equitable" test is too open-ended to be of much assistance to the practitioner advising on the "safety" of intra-group transactions. Section 272(1) does furnish some guidelines to assist the court in deciding whether it is just and equitable to make an order under s. 271(1)(a). These guidelines however are similarly open-ended. Substantially similar provisions had been incorporated in the New Zealand Companies Act 1955. *Vide* ss 315A and 315C of the 1955 Act which had been inserted by s. 30 of the Companies Amendment Act 1980. A "related" company is defined by s. 2(3) of the Companies Act 1993. The typical subsidiary company would certainly qualify as a "related company". There is very scant authority on the ambit of these provisions. For an informative and critical commentary on the New Zealand position, *vide* R.S. Nathan, "Controlling the Puppeteers : Reform of Parent-Subsidiary laws in New Zealand" 3 Canterbury L.R. 1 (1986). *Vide* also Note, "Liability of Company for Debts of Related Company" 2 Co. Law. 238 (1981); Catherine Watson, "Liability of a company for the debts of an insolvent 'related company'" [1983] J.B.L. 295. In *Home Loans Fund (NZ) Limited* (unreported, M589/78, High Court, Christchurch, 7 December 1982, but cited by Nathan in the aforementioned article at p. 18), Casey J. stated : "I think Parliament intended the Court to have the broadest discretion to effect a result which accords with common notions of fairness in all the circumstances, bearing in mind the cardinal principle underlying insolvency administration, that there should be equality among creditors of the same standing". This attitude bears a striking resemblance to the American doctrines of piercing the veil and subordination in bankruptcy.

## 6.2. Details of the reform proposal

### 6.2.1. Meaning of subservience

Holding company liability should only arise if the subsidiary company has been "subservient" as defined in this work. In other words, liability should be imposed only if the subsidiary, as a result of intrusive domination by the holding company, is made to act, to its own detriment, in the interests of the holding company or some other unit within the corporate group. The holding company is to be held responsible for having manipulated the affairs of its subsidiary in its own interests rather than in the interests of the subsidiary as a separate corporate entity. It follows that group unified management or intrusive domination by the holding company should not alone entail liability. Indeed, neither unified management nor intrusive domination are intrinsically prejudicial to the subsidiary's creditors or abusive of the privilege of incorporation.[1]

### 6.2.2. Subservience must be customary or habitual

The subsidiary should only be deemed to be "subservient" for the purposes of the liability rule if the subservience appears as a customary or habitual course of conduct or pattern of behaviour. Isolated or occasional cases of subservient conduct should not trigger the application of the rule. In such cases, the traditional statutory and common law remedies would probably provide appropriate redress.

### 6.2.3. A *gestalt* approach

In investigating the subsidiary's activities, the court should be allowed, even encouraged, to adopt a *gestalt* approach. The court should not be obliged to focus on individual transactions. It should not have to establish in minute detail the type or number of subservient transactions or to compute with scientific precision the "quantum" of detriment suffered by the subsidiary.

---

[1] *Vide* further supra Chapter II pp. 61-63. A number of commentators however have called for a rule of holding company liability in the case of unified management even though no abuse or unfairness may actually be caused. *Vide* e.g., R.S. Nathan, "Controlling the Puppeteers: Reform of Parent-Subsidiary laws in New Zealand" 3 Canterbury L.R. 1 (1986) p. 19; Avgitidis, *op. cit.* pp. 260-269.

Such monotransactional exercises would be too costly and too time-consuming. Rather, the court would have to search for a course of conduct or a pattern of behaviour.

### 6.2.4. An overall view

Similarly, an overall view of the holding company's conduct and involvement must be taken, balancing the detriment suffered by the subsidiary against the benefits, if any, bestowed upon it. If the detriment caused to the subsidiary by subservient practices is balanced out by benefits otherwise conferred on the subsidiary by the group, no liability should be imposed on the holding company.[1]

### 6.2.5. Recovery conditional upon the subsidiary's insolvent liquidation

The rule should apply only in the event of the subservient subsidiary's demise into insolvent liquidation. Indeed, as long as the subsidiary remains solvent, no benefit will be gained by burdening the holding company with liability. It is only on insolvency that the harm which the reform proposal strives to redress is identifiable and quantifiable. To impose liability on the holding company during the subsidiary's solvency would be premature and would only serve to complicate the liability issues and to encourage unnecessary litigation and increase costs.

Moreover, a balance sheet - rather than a cash flow - test of insolvency should be utilised to determine insolvency for the purpose of the proposed liability rule.[2] Accordingly, the subsidiary should be deemed to go into

---

[1] Given that minority shareholders and external creditors would not usually be in a position to perceive the subservience, it might be useful to oblige the auditors of the subsidiary to certify whether or not the subsidiary's affairs have been conducted in its own interests. Such a statement can then be taken as *prima facie* evidence of the position. The implications of imposing such a duty on the auditors, not least from the point of view of costs, would obviously need to be investigated further.

[2] Under a balance sheet test, a company is insolvent if its assets are insufficient to cover its liabilities and the expenses of the winding up. Under a cash flow test, a company is insolvent when it is unable to pay its debts as they fall due. On the distinction in English law between the balance sheet test and the cash flow tests of insolvency and the relevance thereof in the context of the law of insolvency, *vide* generally R.M. Goode, *Principles of Corporate Insolvency Law* (1990) pp. 26-44; R.M. Goode, "Wrongful Trading and the

insolvent liquidation if it goes into liquidation at a time when its assets are insufficient for the payment of its debts and other liabilities and the expenses of winding up. This definition of insolvent liquidation - identical to the definition of the term as used in the wrongful trading provisions of the Insolvency Act 1986[1] - would be the appropriate test since creditors will only suffer a loss on a winding up if the assets are insufficient to cover the liabilities and the expenses of winding up.[2]

### 6.2.6. Liability to be by way of contribution to the assets of the subsidiary

In line with the provisions on fraudulent and wrongful trading,[3] liability should not be imposed directly towards the subsidiary's creditors. Creditors should not be granted an independent cause of action. Rather, the duty should be mediated through the subsidiary and the relative action vested in the liquidator. Liability should then involve the payment of a contribution to the subsidiary's assets. There are a number of reasons for adopting this approach. In the first place, it will substantially reduce litigation and associated costs. Secondly, such an approach will eliminate entirely the risk of a double recovery. Otherwise, if the holding company's behaviour also constitutes a breach of duty to the creditors, both the creditors and the subsidiary may be able to sue. Thirdly, by pre-empting separate action by individual creditors, the approach will help to maintain that fundamental

---

*Cont.*
Balance Sheet Test of Insolvency" [1989] J.B.L. 436. Broadly the same distinction is made in American law. *Vide* Henn and Alexander, *op. cit.* p. 878.

[1] s. 214(6). The balance sheet test is also one of the tests prescribed for the purpose of the grounds for winding up, administration or the avoidance of transactions (*vide* I.A. 1986, ss 8(1), 123, 240(2) and 245(4)). Additionally, it is the only test for the disqualification of directors under s. 6 of the Company Directors Disqualification Act 1986.

[2] By contrast, the European Union's Draft Ninth Directive proposes that the liability of the controlling company of a group for the debts and liabilities of a dependent company is triggered if a written demand for payment addressed to the dependent subsidiary has failed to obtain satisfaction. *Vide* Art. 29.1 of the Proposal for a Ninth Directive relating to Links between Undertakings, and in particular to Groups. Preliminary drafts were given a limited circulation in 1974/1975, 1981 and 1984. The reference to Art. 29.1 is to the 1984 version.

[3] *Vide* I.A. 1986, s. 213(2) (fraudulent trading); I.A. 1986, s. 214(1) (wrongful trading).

tenet of insolvency law - the principle of *pari passu*[1] - and will preserve the procedural unity of liquidation proceedings and the collective regime of insolvency.

### 6.2.7. Voluntary and involuntary creditors

No distinction ought to be drawn in the subservient subsidiary situation between voluntary and involuntary creditors of the subsidiary. As noted in an earlier chapter,[2] it is evident that subservient activities are not readily recognisable as such by persons dealing with the subsidiary. The *tort* claimant is obviously unaware of the abuse. And even the *contract* claimant who has deliberately negotiated credit terms with the subsidiary would not recognise the abuse. The contract creditors' presumed reliance on the subsidiary's autonomy and integrity would therefore have been misplaced. Given that both voluntary and involuntary creditors would be unaware of the subservient behaviour on the part of the subsidiary, the rule of holding company liability should draw no distinction between such creditors.

### 6.2.8. Courts to exercise discretion in determining extent of liability

The extent of liability to be imposed on the holding company is a matter that should be determined by the court in its discretion. Certainly, liability need not necessarily be co-terminous with the subsidiary's inability to settle its debts. The actual amount ordered to be contributed might in appropriate cases fall considerably short of the balance outstanding to the creditors. The extent of liability should be affected both by the degree of subservience as well as by the causative effect that the subservience has on the financial position of the subsidiary. Liability should be compensatory rather than punitive in nature. And in order to minimise the need for complicated dissections into the causes of insolvency there might be room for a rebuttable presumption that an insolvency is causally attributable to the subservience. But clearly, no *a priori* formulation of the method of

---

[1] I.A. 1986, s.107; (re voluntary winding up); Insolvency Rules 1986, rule 4.181(1) (re compulsory winding up). *Vide* also *Re Gray's Inn Construction Co. Ltd.* [1980] 1 W.L.R. 711 (C.A.) at p. 718.

[2] *Vide supra* Chapter IV p. 188.

assessment or the extent of liability should be attempted.[1] The courts should therefore be given a discretion to order the holding company to make such contribution (if any) to the subsidiary's assets "as it thinks proper".[2] The discretionary nature of the relief should be clearly spelt out.[3]

In order to introduce a desirable degree of predictability and certainty however, it would also be useful if the reforming legislation were to prescribe guidelines in respect of the exercise of the court's discretion.[4] These guidelines could include the following factors : (i) the extent to which the holding company dominated the subservient subsidiary; (ii) the nature and intensity of the subservient practices; (iii) the extent to which the insolvency is attributable to the subservient practices; (iv) the extent to which the detriment caused by the subservient practices were offset by any

[1] American courts exercise a considerable discretion when providing a remedy in the piercing the veil cases. Sometimes the controlling shareholder is made liable for the full amount of the claim. On other occasions he may be held liable for only a portion of the underlying claim. As a general rule, however, the guiding principle is to achieve justice. *Vide* further Thomas V. Harris, "Washington's Doctrine of Corporate Disregard" 56 Washington L.R. 253 (1981) pp. 264-266.

[2] The courts have a similar discretion in imposing liability for fraudulent and wrongful trading. *Vide* I.A. 1986, s. 213(2) (fraudulent trading) and I.A. 1986, s 214(1) (wrongful trading). Company and insolvency law is peppered with statutory provisions allowing the courts a discretion whether, and to what extent, to grant a remedy. Apart from the fraudulent and wrongful trading provisions, *vide* for example, I.A. 1986, s. 112(2) (power of court during voluntary winding up), I.A. 1986 ss. 126(1) and 130(2) (power to stay or restrain proceedings against company), I.A. 1986, s. 183(2)(c) (discretion re execution of judgments), I.A. 1986, s. 213(2) (misfeasance proceedings), C.A. 1985, s. 727 (power to grant relief in certain cases) and C.A. 1985, s. 461 (protection of company's members against unfair prejudice).

[3] s. 271(1)(a) of the New Zealand Companies Act 1993 - which empowers the court to order a company to pay the whole or part of the debts of a related company - contains wording that can, with some adaptation, be utilised for our purposes. Section 271(1)(a) provides, *inter alia*, that "the Court, if satisfied that it is just and equitable to do so, may order that ... a company that is, or has been, related to the company in liquidation must pay to the liquidator the whole or part of any or all of the claims made in liquidation." s. 271(2) provides that "[t]he Court may make such other order or give such directions to facilitate giving effect to [any such order] as it thinks fit."

[4] This is also the approach adopted in s. 272(1) of the New Zealand Companies Act 1993 which provides the court with a number of guidelines "[i]n deciding whether it is just and equitable to make an order under section 271(1)(a)." These include the extent to which the related company took part in the management of the company being wound up, its conduct towards the creditors, and the extent to which the winding up is attributable to the actions of the related company. The court is also empowered to take into account such other matters as it thinks fit.

benefits gained by the subsidiary; (v) the time-scale over which subservience was practised; and (vi) the availability of redress under other statutory or common law principles. It should also be provided that the court should be able to take into account such other matters as it deems appropriate. Similarly, the provisions should also expressly state that any order may be made on such terms and conditions as the court thinks fit.

## 6.2.9. Liability to be complementary to existing remedies

Finally, it should be emphasised that the rule of holding company liability for the debts of its insolvent subservient subsidiaries should be complementary to the other statutory and judicial remedies available. To the extent that the existing rules can provide a remedy, the holding company liability rule should be held in abeyance. In other words, it is only where the existing remedies cannot adequately redress the abuse or unfairness that the holding company rule should be activated and the holding company ordered to contribute to the subsidiary's assets. The holding company liability rule should supplement rather than supplant existing remedies.

# 6 The Undercapitalised Subsidiary Situation

## 1. INTRODUCTION

### 1.1. Different definitions of capital

The term "capital" is understood differently in financial management, accountancy, economics and the law. To a financial manager, capital represents the total of the resources or assets of the firm, over which there may be various creditor and proprietor claims.[1] Accountants treat capital as the proprietor's interest in the enterprise and consider all property rights or contractual claims, whether assets or liabilities, in determining the capital of the firm.[2] In the accounting sense, capital encompasses the entire net worth of the enterprise.[3] It fluctuates with the firm's current operations as the firm earns or loses money.[4] Economists use the term "capital" to describe the total stock of machines and equipment that a society possesses and uses to produce goods and services.[5]

In modern English company law, capital has a variety of meanings.[6] A basic distinction must be drawn between "share capital" and "loan capital". Share capital broadly refers to the funds contributed to the company's resources by the shareholders, *qua* shareholders. Share capital represents rights *in* the company. Unlike share capital, the term "loan capital" is not a legal term of art. It is a commercial expression referring to the funds borrowed by a company otherwise than by short and medium term

---

[1] *Vide* John C. Baker and Deane W. Malott, *Introduction to Corporate Finance* (1936) p. 24.

[2] *Vide* e.g., F.P. Langley and G.S. Hardern, *Introduction to Accounting for Business Studies* (6th ed. 1994) p. 18.

[3] Daniel J. Westerbeck, "The Inadequacy of Stated Capital Requirements" 40 Univ. Cin. L. Rev. 823 (1971) p. 825.

[4] *Ibid.* (1971) pp. 825-826.

[5] Stephen A. Ross et al., *Corporate Finance* (3rd ed. 1993) p. 51. *Vide* also *St. Michael Uranium Mines Ltd.* v. *Rayrock Mines Ltd.* (1958) 15 D.L.R. (2d) 609, 614-615.

[6] Capital also has different meanings in trust law and in revenue law. *Vide* Farrar, p. 150.

borrowing.[1] Loan capital comprises indebtedness secured by mortgages, debentures or debenture stock. In contrast to share capital, loan capital represents rights *against* the company.[2] In the eyes of a lawyer, the phrase "loan capital" is a contradiction in terms.[3]

Share capital has various divisions. The "nominal capital" (or "authorised capital") is the total of the nominal value of the shares which a company may issue. It is the figure which appears in the capital clause of the company's Memorandum of Association.[4] The "issued capital" is the total of the nominal value of the shares which have been allotted to shareholders. The difference between the nominal capital and the issued capital is the "unissued capital". The "paid up capital" is the total amount paid by the shareholders on the shares they have taken. "Called-up capital" is defined statutorily as the company's paid up capital plus unpaid capital which the company has called on its members to pay and any unpaid capital which will fall due for payment on one or more specified future dates under the terms of issue of shares.[5] "Uncalled capital" is that part of the nominal value of the issued shares which the company has not yet called on the shareholders to pay. The members may pass a special resolution converting any part of the company's uncalled capital into "reserve capital". Reserve capital cannot be called up until the company is wound up,[6] and any mortgage of it is void.[7] The purpose of the reserve fund is to provide a fund for the benefit of unsecured creditors in the company's liquidation. Despite these differences in the meaning of share capital, the usage of the term in the Companies Acts and in the cases is rather loose and "it is often difficult to say in which sense the word capital is being used."[8]

The American legal concept of capital differs in a number of respects from the English concept. In American jurisdictions, the Articles of

---

[1] Robert R. Pennington, *Company Law* (6th ed. 1990) pp. 199-200. *Vide* also Farrar, pp. 150, 151. The Court of Appeal in *Atlas Maritime Co. S.A.* v. *Avalon Maritime Ltd. ("The Coral Rose")* [1991] 1 Lloyd's Rep. 563 at p. 569, characterised the financing of the defendant subsidiary by its ultimate holding company as "loan capital".

[2] Farrar, p. 151.

[3] *Palmer's Company Law* (25th ed. 1992) Vol. I para. 4.013.

[4] C.A. 1985, s. 2(5)(a).

[5] C.A. 1985, s. 737(1).

[6] C.A. 1985, s. 120.

[7] *In Re Mayfair Property Co.* [1898] 2 Ch. 28.

[8] Farrar, p. 152.

Incorporation are required to specify the number of authorised shares.[1] And since American law generally allows shares to be with or without a par value, most jurisdictions also require a statement of the par value of any par value shares and, if there are to be shares without a par value, a statement to that effect.[2] The use of shares without par value in American jurisdictions therefore gives the notion of "authorised" capital a different meaning from its English counterpart. Even in American law, however, the authorised shares need not all be issued.

In American law, the terms "unissued capital" and "paid-up capital" have approximately the same meaning attributed to them in English law. In contrast to English law, however, American statutes do not define "called up capital". Nor do they enable the shareholders to convert any part of the company's uncalled capital into "reserve capital" as a fund for the benefit of unsecured creditors in the company's liquidation. It would also appear that American courts and legal commentators do not commonly use the term "loan capital" when referring to the long-term borrowing. The use of the terms "debt financing" or "debt securities" is preferred. Nevertheless, as with loan capital in English law, debt securities in American law create a debtor-creditor relationship[3] - they create rights *against* the company.

Despite such differences, it is evident that the English and American legal notions of capital are broadly similar. And it is also clear that the legal concept as understood in the two jurisdictions is considerably narrower than the concept as understood in finance, accounting and economics. In particular it is much narrower than the accounting definition. A fundamental distinction is that in contrast to the financial, accounting and economic concepts of capital, capital in the legal sense remains unaffected by the company's daily operations.

The diversity in meaning attributed to the term "capital" in finance, accounting, economics and law gives rise to much ambiguity and even confusion,[4] especially amongst laymen. For example, a creditor may, relying on the legal concept of share capital, extend credit to a company only to discover during insolvency proceedings that he should have relied on the accountants' definition of the concept.

---

[1] E.g., California Corporations Code, s. 202(d)(e).

[2] Henn and Alexander, *op. cit.* p. 282.

[3] Henn and Alexander, *op. cit.* p. 380.

[4] *Vide* Farrar, p. 149; Gower, p. 199. *Vide* also *St. Michael Uranium Mines Ltd.* v. *Rayrock Mines Ltd.* (1958) 15 D.L.R. (2d) 609 especially at pp. 614-615.

## 1.2. The need for adequate financing - different forms of financing

If a company is to stand any chance of success it requires adequate financing.[1] The finances necessary to launch and operate the company, at least initially, are obtained principally from "investors" who receive in return "securities" issued by the company evidencing the holders' rights in or against the company.[2] The two main sources of finance, corresponding to the two main types of securities, are the shareholder's equity (evidenced by equity securities) and long-term debt financing (evidenced by debt securities).[3] The initial financial structure of a company usually consists of both equity and debt.[4] For smaller companies, bank borrowing on a short to medium-term basis and trade credit are significant sources of finance.[5]

Shareholder's equity is the simplest and most important source of finance.[6] It is usually raised either by an issue of shares - ordinary or preference - or, at a later stage in the company's existence, by the capitalisation of retained profits.[7] The shareholders' equity constitutes the share capital of the company. Debt, the other important source of finance, comes in many forms.[8] The debt securities constitute the loan capital of the company. As a general rule, debtholders are entitled to a fixed regular payment of interest and eventually the final repayment of principal at a fixed maturity date or serially. By contrast, dividend payments (the "return" on

---

[1] R.P. Brooker, "Company Law Reform : is unlimited liability likely to be effective?" 3 Solicitor Quarterly 239 (1964) p. 249. Ironically, excess capital may also pose certain risks. In the case of banks, for example, excess capital may have "a corrosive effect on prudential discipline" and encourage managers "to overexpand bank loans or engage in injudicious bank loans." *Vide* "Lloyds' capital deployed" *Financial Times*, 22nd April 1994.

[2] Henn and Alexander, *op. cit.* p. 377.

[3] *Vide* Organisation for Economic Co-Operation and Development, Issues in International Taxation No. 2 - Thin Capitalisation (1987) p. 8.

[4] Kathleen Kinney, "Equitable Subordination of Shareholder Debt to Trade Creditors : A Reexamination" 61 Boston Univ. L.R. 433 (1981) p. 433.

[5] *Vide* James Bates and Desmond L. Hally, *The Financing of Small Business* (3rd ed. 1982) pp. 159, 165; Michael Chesterman, *Small Businesses* (2nd ed. 1982) pp. 88-89. *Vide* also the Report of the Committee of Inquiry on Small Firms, Cmnd. 4811 (1971).

[6] *Vide* Brealey and Myers, *op. cit.* p. 334.

[7] Retained profits are a source of "internal" financing.

[8] For a discussion of the various forms of debt, *vide* Brealey and Myers, *op. cit.* Ch. 24.

capital) are largely discretionary and the capital does not usually have a defined compulsory repayment date.[1]

Conceptually, "shareholders place their money 'at the risk of the business' while lenders seek a more reliable return."[2] In fact, a loan is usually made upon the reasonable assumption that it will be repaid no matter whether the business venture is successful or not, while capital is put to the risk of the business.[3] And because the payment of interest is a fixed obligation, debt financing carries a higher degree of risk to the company than equity. But borrowing when the company can earn a return greater than the interest rate increases the corporate profits.

After the company commences its business, corporate funds may be derived from other sources, including provision for depreciation, retention of earnings, trade credits and consumer credit (accounts receivable), accounts payable, short-term borrowing, hire-purchase and other leasing arrangements.[4]

Determining a company's optimum debt-equity ratio (or "financial leverage") is a complex issue that has generated much controversy.[5] Clearly, there are no simple answers.[6] Nevertheless, it is widely recognised by financial managers that the judicious use of debt in the financial structure may - by increasing the value of the firm and lowering its opportunity cost of capital[7] - be beneficial to the company.[8] A few basic observations can be made. Primarily for tax reasons, debt financing tends to be a cheaper source

---

[1] Preference shares (like ordinary shares) may be made redeemable either at the option of the company or of the shareholder. *Vide* C.A. 1985, s. 159(1). In practice, preference shares are made redeemable at the option of the company. Robert W. Hamilton, *Corporation Finance - Cases and Materials* (1984) p. 216.

[2] *Slappey Drive Industrial Park* v. *United States* 561 F.2d 572 (5th Cir. 1977) at p. 581.

[3] *Vide Cuyana Realty Company* v. *United States* 382 F.2d 298, 301 (Ct. Cl. 1967). The observation is of course correct only as a general statement. A purchaser of shares in Royal Dutch Shell bears much less risk than a *bona fide* lender to a small company. Risk therefore depends not just on loan or equity status. Risk is affected by prevailing interest rates, the nature of the industry and other economic variables.

[4] Henn and Alexander, *op. cit.* pp. 377-378; Brealey and Myers, *op. cit.* pp. 724-725.

[5] Pinches, *op. cit.* p. 407.

[6] *Vide* Brealey and Myers, *op. cit.* pp. 447-449.

[7] The opportunity cost of capital is the rate of return offered by other, equivalent-risk investment opportunities. *Vide* Brealey and Myers, *op. cit.* Ch. 2.

[8] *Vide* Pinches, *op. cit.* Ch. 13. *Vide* also Samuel Davis Cheris, "Stockholder Loans and the Debt-Equity Distinction" 22 Stanford L.R. 847 (1970) p. 851.

of financing than shareholders' equity.[1] Debt financing is also attractive because shareholders will generally require a higher rate of return than debtholders as they face a greater risk of loss in the event of a deterioration in the profitability of the company or its insolvency.[2] The advantages of debt financing however can only be carried up to a point. Financial management analysts recommend a multi-pronged approach for making the capital structure decision. The essential factors to be taken into account have been identified as the level of taxes, "risk" and "financial slack".[3] Moreover, if the majority of the company's financing is to be advanced by outside financiers, the shareholders will have to create a capital structure with substantial equity. Outside financiers will not normally advance loans to a company unless the ratio of existing debt to equity is reasonable.[4] They would fear that without a reasonable "cushion", losses might erode the company's assets to the extent that insufficient funds might remain to pay their claims.[5]

## 2. FLEXIBILITY IN CAPITAL STRUCTURE - RESULTING UNFAIRNESS

### 2.1. Introduction

Both English and American law allow the promoters of a business venture considerable flexibility as to the form of capital structure that may be employed. Shareholders may contribute funds in the form of debt as well as equity and thereby acquire both creditor and ownership interests in the company. In particular, the debt-equity composition of the company's capital structure is left entirely to the discretion of the promoters. Moreover, in both English and American law, there is either no minimum paid up capital requirement or the figure is cynically low. In English law, for example, there is no minimum paid up capital requirement except in the case of public

---

[1] *Vide post* pp. 369-374.

[2] *Vide* Royal Commission on the Distribution of Income and Wealth, Report No. 2 - Income from Companies and its Distribution, Cmnd. 6172 (1975) para. 193, p. 73.

[3] *Vide* Pinches, *op. cit.* pp. 430-431. Brealey and Myers add a fourth factor - the "asset type". *Vide* Brealey and Myers, *op. cit.* pp. 447-448. "Financial slack", in the form of cash, marketable securities, or unused debt capacity, reduces the odds that a future stock issue will be necessary. *Ibid.* p. 447.

[4] Detlev F. Vagts, *Basic Corporation Law* (2nd ed. 1979) p. 163.

[5] *Ibid.* p. 163.

companies.[1] In the United States, several jurisdictions require that a company, before doing any business, has a minimum paid-in stated capital. But the amounts prescribed in the statutes[2] are too small to be of any value whatsoever.

The law's flexibility, or (to put it less kindly) the law's indifference, in allowing companies to adopt virtually any form of corporate financial structure, and in particular the law's failure to insist on capital adequacy requirements and on acceptable debt-equity ratios, raises fundamental issues which have largely been ignored. In the context of corporate groups, two quite distinct situations need to be considered. One is the inadequately financed subsidiary (that is, a subsidiary which is provided with only trivial financing). The other is the "thinly capitalised" subsidiary (that is, a subsidiary financed with a "thin" ratio of equity compared to debt so that the holding company will compete as a creditor in the event of the subsidiary's insolvency). Both situations are detrimental to the interests of creditors. Both constitute an abuse of the corporate form. The two situations will now be considered in turn.[3]

## 2.2. The inadequately financed subsidiary

In the case of an inadequately financed subsidiary, the holding company fails to provide the subsidiary with the financing backbone reasonably required to enable it to undertake the business activity for which it was incorporated. The subsidiary is allocated such trivial financing that it will lack the resources necessary to support the minimum effective scale of operations to which it is committed. It stands virtually no chance of successfully undertaking the venture.[4] It is almost certainly doomed to failure.[5] The

---

[1] Public companies have to possess an issued capital of £50,000 (*vide* C.A. 1985, ss. 11 and 118), a figure described as a "derisively small sum for guaranteeing economic viability (assuming that this is theoretically possible)." *Vide* Prentice, The English Experience, p. 107. *Vide* further *post* pp. 325-326.

[2] *Vide post* p. 329 footnote 4.

[3] A preliminary investigation into these two situations was conducted *supra* Chapter II pp. 85-88.

[4] E.g., *Northern Ill. Gas Co.* v. *Total Energy Leasing Corp.* 502 F.Supp. 412 (N.D. Ill. 1980). Two cases involving a non-corporate shareholder are *Henry Browne & Son Ltd.* v. *Smith* [1964] 2 Ll. L.R. 476 and *Re Chartmore Ltd.* [1990] BCLC 673.

[5] Michael Whincup, "'Inequitable Incorporation' - the Abuse of a Privilege" 2 Co. Law. 158 (1981) p. 163.

holding company appreciates the risk. The prejudice to creditors, in particular the involuntary creditors, is self-evident.[1] Creditors should not be regarded as persons to be fleeced. The situation is clearly reprehensible.[2] The law should not tolerate any arrangement whereby all the risks and hazards of a business venture are shifted on to the public. Surely, a holding company should have an obligation to provide its subsidiary with such financing as is reasonably adequate for its needs in the light of the business to be undertaken.[3]

Incorporation with limited liability is a technique enabling the incorporator to conduct business with the benefit of risking not all of his estate but only such a part as he invests in the undertaking. It is in the nature of a compromise between the incorporator who wishes to minimise his liability and the creditors who seek to enlarge it.[4] The incorporator must give as well as take : limited liability must have a price. The provision of sufficient initial financing must be viewed as the consideration for the privilege of doing business with limited liability.[5] Once such a principle is

---

[1] On the distinction between voluntary and involuntary creditors *vide supra* Chapter IV pp. 176-186.

[2] Several writers have considered inadequate financing to be substantially inequitable. *Vide* e.g., Ballantine, *op. cit.* s. 129 p. 302; William O. Douglas and Carrol M. Shanks, "Insulation from Liability through Subsidiary Corporations" 39 Yale L.J. 193 (1929) 203; Latty, *op. cit.* Ch. V; Warner Fuller, "The Incorporated Individual : A Study of the One-Man Company" 51 Harv. L.R. 1373 (1938) p. 1382; Jules Silk, "One man corporations - Scope and limitations" 100 Univ. of Pennsylavania L.R. 853 (1952) p. 861; Bernard F. Cataldo, "Limited Liability with One-Man Companies and Subsidiary Corporations" 18 Law and Contemporary Problems 473 (1953) p. 484; Note, "Liability of a Corporation for Acts of a Subsidiary or Affiliate" 71 Harv. L.R. 1122 (1958) pp. 1126, 1129; J. Penn Carolan, "Disregarding the Corporate Fiction in Florida: the Need for Specifics" 27 Univ. of Florida L.R. 175 (1974) p. 193. Somewhat surprisingly, the problem of inadequate financing has attracted serious debate only amongst American writers. By contrast, English writers appear unperturbed by the problem. Indeed, only fleeting references to undercapitalisation occur in the literature. *Vide* e.g., R.P. Brooker, "Company Law Reform : is unlimited liability likely to be effective?" 3 Solicitor Quarterly 239 (1964) p. 248; Michael Whincup, "'Inequitable Incorporation' - the Abuse of a Privilege" 2 Co. Law. 158 (1981) pp. 162-163; Gower, p. 134.

[3] *Vide In the Matter of Mobile Steel Co.* 563 F.2d 692, 703 (5th Cir. 1977). Cf. *Laborers Clean-Up Contract Administration Trust Fund* v. *Uriarte Clean-Up Service, Inc.* 736 F.2d 516, 524-525 (9th Cir. 1984). *Vide* also William O. Douglas and Carrol M. Shanks, "Insulation from Liability through Subsidiary Corporations" 39 Yale L.J. 193 (1929) p. 196.

[4] Latty, *op. cit.* p. 111.

[5] *Vide* Latty, *op. cit.* p. 121.

recognised, it would follow that to attempt to do business without providing a sufficient basis of financial responsibility to creditors would constitute an abuse of that privilege and attract liability. An alternative approach leading to very much the same result may be to consider the holding company as owing fiduciary duties to the subsidiary's creditors.[1] The fiduciary duties would require the holding company to ensure that the subsidiary is provided with adequate financing.

Without doubt, inadequately financed business ventures exist whatever the organisational medium used. The enterprise need not necessarily be a subsidiary company. Indeed it seems that a number of "ordinary" companies (that is, companies which do not form part of a corporate group) soon run into financial difficulties not because they lack the potential for profitability, but because they are provided with so little resources that the costs of establishing the business are not fully provided for and because little or no cognizance is taken of the time lag involved between the first purchase or manufacture of the goods and the receipt of the proceeds of sale.[2] Subsidiaries however appear to be at a higher risk of being inadequately financed, at least initially, than other companies. This is probably due to the expectation that the group's resources will be made available should the need arise.[3] Ideally, perhaps, the duty to adequately finance a company should be extended to all controlling shareholders, whether individuals or holding companies.[4] But the strong policy of limited liability militates against such an extension to individual controlling shareholders. In the context of corporate groups, however, the arguments for limited liability lose much of their vigour.[5] In particular, the double insulation from liability

---

[1] American law has recognised that a holding company may owe fiduciary duties to creditors. *Vide supra* Chapter V, p. 289. *Vide* also Maurice J. Dix, "Adequate Risk Capital : The Consideration for the Benefits of Separate Incorporation" 53 Northwestern Univ. L.R. 478 (1958) pp. 484-486.

[2] *Vide* R.P. Brooker, "Company Law Reform : is unlimited liability likely to be effective?" 3 Solicitor Quarterly 239 (1964) p. 248.

[3] *Vide* Jonathan M. Landers, "Another Word on Parent, Subsidiaries and Affiliates in Bankruptcy" 43 Univ. of Chicago L.R. 527 (1976) p. 528; Prentice, The English Experience, pp. 104, 106. Cf. Jules Silk, "One man corporations - Scope and limitations" 100 Univ. of Pennsylavania L.R. 853 (1952) p. 861. The risk of undercapitalisation is clearly reduced in the case of multi-shareholder companies. *Vide* Latty, *op. cit.* p. 151.

[4] *Vide* Maurice J. Dix, "Adequate Risk Capital : The Consideration for the Benefits of Separate Incorporation" 53 Northwestern Univ. L.R. 478 (1958) pp. 484-486.

[5] *Vide supra* Chapter IV pp. 161-176.

enjoyed by the shareholders of the holding company justifies the imposition on the holding company of stricter adequate capitalisation requirements for subsidiary companies.

Once the need for the introduction of a rule of adequate financing is acknowledged, a number of specific issues have to be addressed. These issues are identified hereunder, but will be analysed in detail in a later section of this Chapter.[1]

(1) The fundamental question will be to establish a precise definition and test of adequate financing. Should a minimum level of financing apply to all companies across the board, or, as will be suggested, should the measure of financing relate to the specific venture to be undertaken by the company?

(2) Another crucial question is whether the financing must be provided exclusively by way of equity or whether it can be provided by a blend of equity and debt. The principle should be that adequate financing depends essentially on the total funds expended, independently of the equity or debt nature thereof. The debt-equity ratio question is relevant only to the situation where the holding company attempts to compete as a creditor (for debts advanced to the subsidiary) on the insolvency of its subsidiary.

(3) Thirdly, should a distinction be drawn between initial inadequate financing and subsequent inadequacy? Initial inadequacy arises where, from its inception, the company is so financially weak that it is bound, sooner or later, to go into insolvent liquidation. Subsequent inadequacy occurs where the company, though adequately financed on its incorporation for the business venture originally intended, later undertakes operations beyond its financial means either because of previous losses or because the new operations require substantial investment. Should the obligation to provide adequate financing be an on-going obligation? Or should initial adequate financing be sufficient?

(4) Companies may fail for a variety of reasons. These reasons include fraud, management shortcomings,[2] accountancy failings, failure to respond to change (for example, pressures of competition, political change, economic change, social change and technological change), legal and administrative

---

[1] *Vide post* pp. 363-390.

[2] Managerial incompetence is the overwhelming cause of individual firm failures. *Vide* Edward I. Altman, *Corporate Financial Distress* (1983) p. 40.

constraints, the loss of a major customer,[1] a serious slump in the particular market,[2] labour shortage,[3] recession, and possibly creative accounting and excessive gearing.[4] Clearly, inadequate financing is a common cause of business failure.[5] But should liability for inadequate financing depend on a causal link between the inadequacy and the insolvency? What if the cause of the business failure is attributable to some factor independent of inadequate financing? It will be argued that whatever the cause of business failure, liability ought to attach in every case of inadequate financing, independently of the actual cause of insolvency.

(5) Another crucial aspect of a rule of adequate financing relates to the extent of liability in the event that an inadequately financed subsidiary slides into insolvency. Should *unlimited* liability be imposed on the holding company for the debts of the subsidiary? Or should liability be limited to an amount equivalent to the difference between the amount actually invested and the amount which should have been invested by way of adequate financing? Additionally, should a distinction be drawn between voluntary and involuntary creditors on the basis that voluntary creditors were in a position to perceive and assess (and therefore assume) the risk of insolvency?

### 2.3. Holding company competing as creditor

In many instances, a holding company sets up a subsidiary which is, in fact, adequately financed : the subsidiary is provided with sufficient funds to

---

[1] Fidelis Oditah, "Wrongful Trading" [1990] L.M.C.L.Q. 205 p. 210.

[2] *Vide* e.g., *Re Cladrose Ltd.* [1990] BCLC 204.

[3] *Vide* "Japanese bankruptcy debt rises" *Financial Times*, 16th June 1992.

[4] *Vide* generally John Argenti, *Corporate Collapse - The Causes and Symptoms* (1976) pp. 121-147; Harlan D. Platt, *Why Companies Fail - Strategies for Detecting, Avoiding and Profiting from Bankruptcy* (1985) pp. 6-15. Creative accounting and excessive gearing are probably best viewed as symptoms rather than causes of business failure. A new accountancy standard (FRS 5) published in April 1994 by the Accountancy Standard Board clamps down on "off balance sheet" finance, one of the most important elements of creative accounting employed during the 1980's. Under the standard, companies' transactions must reflect their substance and not simply be recorded in accordance with their legal form. *Vide* "Accounts must reveal more" *Financial Times*, 14th April 1994.

[5] Some witnesses before the Jenkins Committee had expressed the view that undercapitalisation was a "major cause of business failures". *Vide* the Jenkins Report, para. 27, p. 7.

enable it to stand a fair chance of success. The financing however may be almost totally debt financing emanating from the holding company itself[1] : the holding company utilises a thin ratio of shares compared to debt. In such a case, the company is said to be "thinly capitalised". There is in principle nothing objectionable in the holding company financing its subsidiary through both equity and debt.[2] But if, despite adequate financing, the subsidiary becomes insolvent, the holding company may claim to be entitled - as creditor for the debt advances - to share in the proceeds with other creditors. Such an arrangement places in sharp relief not just the different legal position of the shareholder and debtholder but also their respective risk. In any corporate commercial undertaking, both the shareholders and the debtholders assume some risk of failure. Yet their risks are different. Put simply, if the venture is successful, the debtholders will receive payment of the principal within a pre-determined period and interest in full at regular intervals; the shareholders will have a right to any dividends that may be declared, but, as a rule, will have no right to a return of capital except on liquidation or by virtue of capital redemption provisions. If the venture fails, the debtholders, *qua* creditors, will have a prior claim on the company's assets over the shareholders' claims, which receive the lowest priority.[3]

A basic objective of the owners of an enterprise is minimisation of risk.[4] Given that the law allows one and the same incorporator to "invest" in the company both by means of equity and by means of debt, and given that the law imposes no restriction on the debt-equity ratio, a shareholder can in fact minimise risks by providing minimal equity and substantial debt. In this way, he would prove in insolvency on a parity with other creditors in respect of his debt. In effect, the shareholder will be in a position of taking all the profits if the venture succeeds and yet will expose himself only to a creditor's risk, if it fails. A thinly capitalised company therefore clearly

---

[1] *Vide* Tom Hadden, "Future Developments" in R.M. Goode (ed.), *Group Trading and the Lending Banker* (1988) p. 101. Cf. Tom Hadden, *The Control of Corporate Groups* (1983) p. 72.

[2] The holding company may for example finance the subsidiary through interest free loans. *Vide* e.g., *B.P. Exploration (Libya) Co. Ltd.* v. *Hunt (No. 2)* [1979] 1 W.L.R. 783, at p. 820.

[3] *Palmer's Company Law* (25th ed. 1992) Vol. I p. 528; Bankruptcy Code (11 U.S.C. s. 726); *Vide* also Learned Hand J.'s dictum in *Re Loewer's Gambrinus Brewery Co.* 167 F.2d 318 (2d Cir. 1948) at p. 320.

[4] *Vide* "Symposium - The Close Corporation - Capitalization" 52 Northwestern Univ. L.R. 345 (1957) p. 365.

reduces the shareholders' risk on their investment.[1] The unfairness to external creditors in the event of insolvency is evident.[2] To the extent that the distribution of corporate assets to the shareholder-creditors reduces payment to external creditors, external creditors absorb the risk of loss ordinarily suffered by the shareholders. Indeed, every creditor "rightly assumes that his risk is measured by the collective claims of other creditors, and by creditors he understands those alone, who like him, have only a stipulated share in the profits."[3] To force a creditor to "divide the assets in insolvency with those who at their option have all along had power to take all the earnings, is to add to the risk which he accepted."[4] And because a thinly capitalised company provides little protection against loss, external creditors have to rely on the company's future earnings to obtain what is due to them. External creditors therefore have to assume part of the risk of entrepreneurship rather than the normal creditors' risks.[5] A holding company which has the power to sweep all the profits should not be allowed to divert the risks and hazards of the business onto the subsidiary's creditors.

There is another perspective meriting examination. Often, especially in the thinly capitalised subsidiaries, the lending appears to amount to the provision of capital on a more or less permanent basis.[6] In this type of situation, it is arguable that what should count is the substance rather than the form. Thus, if the funds have been advanced without any reasonable expectation of payment and are as a matter of substantial economic reality risked on the success of the venture, they may not really be loans but equity.[7]

---

[1] *Ibid.* p. 366.

[2] In *Atlas Maritime Co. S.A.* v. *Avalon Maritime Ltd. ("The Coral Rose")* [1991] 1 Lloyd's Rep. 563 (C.A.), Staughton L.J. stated that "[t]he creation ... of a subsidiary company with minimal liability, which will operate with the parent's funds and on the parent's directions but not expose the parent to liability, *may not seem to some the most honest way of trading.*" (emphasis added). *Ibid.* at p. 571.

[3] *In re Loewer's Gambrinus Brewery Co.* 167 F.2d 318 (2d Cir. 1948) at p. 320.

[4] *Ibid.* at p. 320.

[5] *Vide* Kathleen Kinney, "Equitable Subordination of Shareholder Debt to Trade Creditors: A Reexamination" 61 Boston Univ. L.R. 433 (1981) p. 434.

[6] This was clearly the case in *Atlas Maritime Co. S.A.* v. *Avalon Maritime Ltd. ("The Coral Rose")* [1991] 1 Lloyd's Rep. 563 (C.A.). Cf. Tom Hadden, *The Control of Corporate Groups* (1983) p. 15.

[7] *Vide* Asa S. Herzog and Joel B. Zweibel, "The Equitable Subordination of Claims in Bankruptcy" 15 Vand. L.R. 83 (1961) pp. 94-95; William P. Hackney and Tracey G. Benson, "Shareholder Liability for Inadequate Capital" 43 Univ. of Pittsburgh L.R. 837

In this way, part, or perhaps all, of the debt could properly be characterised as equity investment and therefore be subject to a shareholder's risk.[1] The effect would be that in the event of insolvency, the holding company's claim based on the portion of the financing which it chose to denominate as debt would have to pass the characterisation test before it is accorded a true debt status. If it fails the test, the debt would be treated as an equity investment and therefore be subordinated to the claims of the other creditors.[2] It would then be paid only if such other claims have been paid in full.

At the heart of the matter is the key policy of limited liability. But should the privilege of limited liability be obtainable at absolutely no cost? Should not the contribution of some "risk capital" towards the company's debts be viewed as the consideration for the shareholder's personal immunity? The law should not permit a financial structure which transfers upon external creditors the risks and hazards of the undertaking while at the same time allowing the shareholder to reap all possible gains, safe in the knowledge that his losses can be contained within acceptable limits if the undertaking proves to be unprofitable.

An additional approach may again be suggested by an extension of the doctrine of fiduciary duties. A holding company should arguably be considered to be in the position of a fiduciary *vis-a-vis* the subsidiary's creditors. Such a position would involve the duty not only to provide the subsidiary with adequate financing[3] but to ensure that a reasonable proportion of such financing is risk capital.

Once the need is acknowledged for a rule to remedy the unfairness of the thinly capitalised subsidiary, its precise formulation would require a study of a number of difficult issues and a search for appropriate solutions. At this

---

*Cont.*

(1982) p. 881; Jules S. Cohen, "Shareholder Advances : Capital or Loans?" 52 Am. Bankr. L.J. 259 (1978).

[1] In the United States there is a substantial body of case law dealing with the characterisation issue in the context of tax law. *Vide post* pp. 369-382.

[2] A similar proposal was made in the Cork Report, para. 1963, pp. 441-442. The Cork Committee also recommended that where the holding company's claims are secured, whether by a fixed or floating charge, the security should "be treated as invalid as against the liquidator or administrator or any creditor of the company until all claims to which it is deferred have been met in full." *Ibid.* para. 1963, p. 442. Regrettably, none of these proposals were implemented in the legislation that followed the Report.

[3] *Vide supra* pp. 312-314.

stage it is desirable to identify the issues. Detailed consideration of these issues will have to be postponed to a later section in this Chapter.[1]

(1) The fundamental question is to determine the basis on which the minimum level of *equity* investment is to be calculated. In other words, on which criteria should the categorisation exercise (into debt or equity) be carried out? Should the label attached by the holding company bear any relevance? Should the expectation evidenced by the holding company regarding repayment and interest programmes make any difference? Should the actual history of repayment of principal and interest be taken into account? Should the ratio of debt to equity feature at all in the exercise? Should the financial structure of competitive businesses or industries be used as a guide? Is the subsidiary's inability to borrow from third parties an indication that the holding company's advances are to be treated as capital? Should the subsidiary's subsequent borrowings and earnings history shed any light? And should the question be determined by an entirely objective assessment based on the nature of the business venture and the particular operations actually undertaken?

(2) If the whole or a part of the investment labelled by the holding company as debt is to be characterised by law as equity, should the remedy be merely the subordination of the relative claim or should it be disallowance?

(3) Should the voluntary-involuntary creditor distinction bear any relevance in determining the extent of holding company liability?

(4) Finally, should loans by a holding company to a subsidiary in financial distress be afforded any special consideration?

### 2.4. Creditor-proof subsidiaries

As already stated in a previous Chapter, the strategy of financing on a high debt-equity ratio sometimes assumes particularly obnoxious characteristics through the use of certain "creditor-proof" devices.[2] It is now appropriate to elaborate further on these devices.

---

[1] *Vide post* pp. 363-390.

[2] *Vide supra* Chapter II pp. 88-90.

### 2.4.1. The loan-cum-mortgage device

An incorporator enjoys full freedom under the law to structure the financial organisation of the company in practically any way he chooses. In particular, an incorporator may invest a paltry sum by way of equity and provide for all the company's financial requirements by means of loans. The unfairness of such an arrangement *vis-a-vis* the company's creditors has already been highlighted. But the law's nonchalant attitude towards corporate financial organisation goes even further. For the liberty to invest in the form of debt rather than equity can be combined with the taking of security rights over the debt. A subsidiary may be incorporated with a modicum of share capital. The holding company then lends the subsidiary the substantial funds needed for its business whilst securing the loans on the assets of the subsidiary.[1] Plainly, the intended effect is to enable the holding company to rank first in competition proceedings in the event of the subsidiary's insolvency. The security effectively shields the incorporator from the creditors' claims.

Regrettably, the House of Lords had legitimated this particularly cynical form of skulduggery in *Salomon* v. *Salomon and Co. Ltd.*[2] And more regrettable is the fact that the House of Lords, whilst expressly acknowledging the potential for "great abuse" and "great mischief" of such schemes, deliberately refrained from exercising its judicial creativity to stamp out the abuse and mischief. Indeed, Lord Hershell merely remarked that "as the law at present stands, there is certainly nothing unlawful in the creation of such debentures".[3] But perhaps the most regrettable feature of the loan-cum-mortgage affair following the decision in *Salomon* is the

---

[1] *Vide* e.g., *Erickson* v. *Minnesota and Ontario Power Co.* 158 N.W. 979 (1916).

[2] [1897] A.C. 22 (H.L.). Cf. also Lord Templeman's dictum in *Re Southard & Co. Ltd.* [1979] 1 W.L.R. 1198 (C.A.) at p. 1208.

[3] [1897] A.C. 22 (H.L.) at p. 47. *Vide* also Lord Macnaghten's speech, *ibid.* at p. 53, where he stated that "[e]verybody knows that when there is a winding-up debenture-holders generally step in and sweep off everything; and a great scandal it is." In the Court of Appeal Lindley L.J. had recognised the mischief. He considered such schemes to be "mere devices to enable a man to carry on trade with limited liability ... and to sweep off the company's assets by means of debentures which he has caused to be issued to himself in order to defeat the claims of those who have been incautious enough to trade with the company without perceiving the trap which he has laid for them." *Broderip* v. *Salomon* [1895] 2 Ch. 323 at p. 339. Lindley L.J. considered such a scheme to be "contrary to the true intent and meaning of the Companies Act, 1862". The company had been created for an "illegitimate purpose". *Ibid.* at pp. 337, 340. Lindley L.J.'s analysis was supported by Lopes L.J. *Ibid.* at p. 341.

legislature's inertia and the judiciary's timidity, in dealing with the abuse. Even academic criticism has been remarkably subdued. Indeed, barring a few rare exceptions when the specific vice of the loan-cum-mortgage device has been objected to,[1] academic criticism has centred around the broader issues of holding company liability.[2]

Not surprisingly, traders have long recognised the protective qualities of the device and had employed it even in the nineteenth century.[3] Given the law's blessing, they can hardly be blamed for taking advantage of the facility offered to them.

### 2.4.2. The lease device

In the absence of some basis for direct liability on a shareholder or other third party (for example, by way of a guarantee or joint tort liability),[4] a creditor's ultimate remedy against a company is to its property. If the company owns no property, the creditor is remediless. Such is the natural consequence of separate juridical personality and limited liability.

In many types of business ventures, the enterprise would need tangible property to enable it to carry out its activities. Such tangibles may include land, factories, buildings, machinery, vehicles and raw materials. A holding company wishing to set up a subsidiary for such a type of business venture may be in a position to make such property available to the subsidiary. In other words, rather than supplying the subsidiary with the necessary funds to acquire the tangible property, the holding company may wish to provide the subsidiary with the tangible property itself. There are of course various ways in which property belonging to the holding company may be made available to the subsidiary. The holding company may transfer the property to the subsidiary in full ownership in exchange for shares, debentures or other consideration. In such cases, the property becomes part of the estate of the subsidiary and will usually be available for the satisfaction of creditors'

---

[1] E.g., Gower, p. 87. *Vide* also The Cork Report, paras. 1960, 1963, pp. 441-442.

[2] *Vide supra* Chapter I pp. 35-37. In the United States, the unfairness of the loan-cum-mortgage device attracted sharp criticism at least as early as 1936. *Vide* Latty, *op. cit.* pp. 114-115.

[3] *Vide* Ireland, *op. cit.* p. 50.

[4] For a discussion on these and other instances of direct liability, *vide supra* Chapter III pp. 119-138.

claims in whole or in part. Rather than transferring the property in full ownership, however, the holding company may lease the property to the subsidiary (in consideration for a periodical rent) thereby retaining ownership over the property. In some cases, the holding company has actually leased to the subsidiary all the property that may be needed by the subsidiary in the conduct of its activities.[1] Such an arrangement is easily organised. The lease may be on a short-duration basis or may be terminable at the option of the lessor holding company or on the happening of a specific event such as the insolvency of the subsidiary or the commencement of its winding up.

This lease device has been used by holding companies to protect their investment in the subsidiaries from the creditors' claims. If and when the subsidiary becomes insolvent, the lease is terminated and the property that had appeared to external creditors to belong to the subsidiary is, quite legally, recovered by the holding company. The subsidiary incurs all the risks involved in running the day-to-day business. The holding company, by owning all the assets, assumes none of the risks.[2]

On reflection, it will be realised that the lease device is actually more contemptible than the "loan-cum-mortgage" technique. For in the latter case there is at least the possibility that the value of the property acquired by the loan will be higher than the holding company's claims and the creditors might therefore receive some payment in respect of their claims. When, however, the lease strategy is employed and the subsidiary becomes insolvent there will probably be very little - if anything - left for the creditors.

Again surprisingly, neither Parliament nor the courts have attempted to control the lease device.[3] Even in the face of such a particularly despicable "creditor-proof" scheme, limited liability appears to have been considered too venerable to be poked at.

---

[1] *Vide* e.g., *Oriental Investment Co.* v. *Barclay* 25 Tex. Civ. App. 543, 64 S.W. 80 (1901). Cf. *Luckenbach S.S. Co.* v. *W.R. Grace & Co.* 267 F. 676 (4th Cir. 1920).

[2] Analogous to the lease device is the arrangement whereby a holding company supplies goods to the subsidiary marketing company on "consignment", reserving to itself title to the goods until the goods are actually sold to third parties. *Vide* e.g., *Holland* v. *Joy Candy Manufacturing Corp.* 145 N.E.2d 101, 103 (Ill. App. 1957). *Vide* further James A. Corrigan and James R. Schirott, "Piercing the Corporate Veil : Dispelling the Mists of Metaphor" 17 Trial Lawyer's Guide 121 (1973) pp. 144-145.

[3] By contrast, American courts do not condone such abuse. *Vide post* pp. 348-360.

## 2.5. Creditor-proof devices compounded by "milking" - keeping the subsidiary "dry"

Loan-cum-mortgage and lease devices are occasionally aggravated by "milking". "Milking" involves an arrangement whereby the subsidiary is quite simply not allowed to make a profit.[1] The net income of the subsidiary is creamed off as an operating charge of one sort or another.[2] In the loan-cum-mortgage and lease devices there is at least a possibility that the subsidiary actually becomes profitable and its creditors paid. Where, however, such devices combine with the "milking" of profits, the creditors' chances of recovery are reduced to zero.[3] The subsidiaries have nothing to begin with, they make nothing, and could therefore only end up with nothing.[4] "Milking" is of course also symptomatic of a subservient subsidiary.[5]

## 2.6. Heightened risk of subservience in an inadequately financed subsidiary

Close observation reveals a significant link between an inadequate financial structure and the subservient subsidiary situation discussed in the previous Chapter. The link appears in two ways. In the first place, an inadequate financial structure sometimes leads to an excessive dependence by the subsidiary on its holding company.[6] As in inter-personal relationships, the dependence could be so acute that it naturally begets subservience, impairing the subsidiary's ability to function autonomously and casting doubt on the genuine separation of its activities from those of the holding company.[7] On other occasions, however, an inadequate financial organisation is a symptom, rather than a cause, of subservience. In such cases, undercapitalisation will be one of a number of indicia collectively evidencing subservient conduct.

---

[1] E.g., *Joseph R. Foard Co.* v. *State of Maryland* 219 F. 827 (4th Cir. 1914); *Erickson* v. *Minnesota and Ontario Power Co.* 158 N.W. 979 (1916); *Holbrook, Cabot & Rollins Corp.* v. *Perkins* 147 F. 166 (1st Cir. 1906).

[2] Latty, *op. cit.* p. 138. *Vide* further *supra* Chapter II pp. 90-91.

[3] E.g., *Oriental Investment Co.* v. *Barclay* 64 S.W. 80 (App. Tex. 1901).

[4] Latty, *op. cit.* p. 139.

[5] *Vide supra* Chapter II p. 81.

[6] Cf. Tom Hadden, *The Control of Corporate Groups* (1983) pp. 17-18.

[7] *Vide Garden City Co.* v. *Burden* 186 F.2d 651 (10th Cir. 1951).

## 3. EXISTING REMEDIES AND INADEQUACY THEREOF

### 3.1. Introduction

In contrast to the subservient subsidiary situation - where, as we have seen, the law at least provides external creditors with some remedies[1] - the situation involving an inadequate financial organisation remains virtually without recourse at law. In identifying and assessing existing remedies with regard to the cases involving an inadequate financial organisation, a distinction must be drawn between the three types of inadequate financial organisation previously discussed : the provision of illusory or trifling financing, thin capitalisation and the engagement of creditor-proof strategies.[2] In the cases of thin capitalisation and creditor-proof devices, existing law clearly supplies no remedy. There is no means open to a court to subordinate the holding company's claims for repayment of secured or unsecured loans to the subsidiary. Nor will the court strike down creditor-proof schemes or otherwise require the holding company to accept liability for the debts of its insolvent subsidiary. *Salomon* rules. Entity prevails. In the case of a subsidiary with illusory or trifling financing, existing law, as we shall presently see, does provide a semblance of a remedy, but nothing more.

### 3.2. Lack of statutory minimum capital requirements

Neither English law nor American law link incorporation or limited liability with adequate statutory capital requirements. Generally, the statutes in both systems are merely enabling acts, with no regulatory function designed to provide a cushion of shareholder equity.

In English law there is in fact no minimum paid up capital requirement except in the case of public companies and certain undertakings such as banks and insurance companies.[3] Public companies must have an

---

[1] *Vide* generally *supra* Chapter V.

[2] *Vide supra* pp. 312-324.

[3] Minimum solvency and capital adequacy standards are applied by the regulatory authorities to insurance companies and other financial institutions. The continued solvency of such undertakings is considered crucial to the integrity of the financial system and the protection of the investing public. For banks *vide* the following European Union Directives : Council Directive 89/299 of the 17th April 1989 on the own funds of credit institutions (O.J. L124/89), Council Directive 91/633 of the 3rd December 1991

"authorised minimum" share capital of £50,000 or such other sum as the Secretary of State may specify by statutory instrument.[1] A company formed as a public company cannot commence business or exercise any borrowing powers unless it has satisfied the Registrar (who then issues a certificate to that effect) that it has issued and allotted shares to the nominal value of not less than the authorised minimum,[2] of which at least one quarter and the whole of any premium has been paid up either in cash or (subject to an independent valuation and within certain limits) in kind.[3] The Registrar also has to be satisfied that these conditions are met when a private company re-registers as a public one.[4] If a company does business or exercises borrowing powers without the aforesaid certificate, the company and any of its officers who is in default are liable to a fine, but the validity of any transaction entered into by the company will not be affected.[5] Presumably, the minimum capital requirement is intended as a measure to protect creditors by ensuring that a public company is provided with sufficient funds to secure the successful commencement of operations. But the figure of £50,000 is entirely arbitrary: in no way is it related to the nature of the business to be undertaken by the company or the company's financial structure. Occasionally, the figure may prove to be excessive.More often

*Cont.*
  implementing Council Directive 89/299 (O.J. L339/91), and Council Directive 92/16 of the 16th March 1992 amending Directive 89/299 (O.J. L75/92). *Vide* also Council Directive 89/647 of the 18th December 1989 on a solvency ratio for credit institutions (O.J. L386/89). For insurance companies *vide* Insurance Companies Act 1982, s. 32; E.R. Hardy Ivamy, *General Principles of Insurance Law* (5th ed. 1986) pp. 52-53. For Building Societies *vide* the Building Societies Act 1986, ss. 7-9 and the Building Societies (Supplementary Capital) Order 1988 (S.I. 1988 No. 777).

[1] C.A. 1985, ss. 11 and 118(1).

[2] C.A. 1985, s. 117(1) and (2).

[3] C.A. 1985, s. 101. For a discussion on non-cash issues and transactions in public companies *vide* Gower, pp. 204-207.

[4] C.A. 1985, ss. 43-45.

[5] C.A. 1985, s. 117(7). If, however, the company enters into a transaction without having obtained the certificate from the Registrar and fails to comply with its obligations in that connection within 21 days of being called upon to do so, the directors of the company will be jointly and severally liable to indemnify the other party to the transaction in respect of any loss or damage suffered by him by reason of the company's failure to comply with those obligations. *Vide* C.A. 1985, s. 117(8).

than not, however, the figure will be "derisively small".[1] In any case, the £50,000 minimum limit is almost wholly irrelevant in the context of corporate groups as the overwhelming majority of subsidiaries are private companies.

The notion of a minimum capital requirement is not novel to English company law. Prior to the general incorporation statutes of the first half of the nineteenth century, companies were formed by Act of Parliament or Charter.[2] In such cases, the special legislative Act or Charter would actually specify the business to be done and the amount of capital required. With the coming of general limited liability, however, the previous facility of stipulating on an *ad hoc* basis the capital requirements obviously became inapplicable. Still, when the Limited Liability Bill 1855 was first tabled in Parliament, it had required a minimum nominal capital of £20,000[3] of which three-fourths had to be subscribed.[4] At least one-fifth of each subscribed share had to be paid up prior to the complete registration of the company[5] and each share had to have a minimum value of £25.[6] These proposals met with strong opposition in the House of Commons. At first the Government reduced the amount of the minimum nominal capital from £20,000 to £10,000 and the minimum value of the shares from £25 to £20. And later, fearing a division of the House, the Government dropped the requirement of a minimum capital altogether and reduced the minimum value of the shares to £10.[7] The provisions requiring three-fourths of the nominal capital to be subscribed and one-fifth of the subscribed capital to be paid up were retained.[8] In the House of Lords, an amendment was introduced whereby the Deed of Settlement had to be executed by at least twenty-five shareholders, thus effectively securing a minimum issued capital of £250.[9] A year later, however, all such restrictions were swept

---

[1] *Vide* Prentice, The English Experience, p. 107. In practice, most public companies and all listed companies will have a significantly larger issued share capital than the minimum.

[2] *Vide* Gower, pp. 5-6.

[3] s. 1.

[4] s. 1(4).

[5] s. 1(4).

[6] s. 1.

[7] *Vide* the Limited Liability Bill, as amended in Committee and on Re-Commitment, s. 1.

[8] *Ibid.* s. 1(4).

[9] *Vide* further Walter Horrowitz, "Historical Development of Company Law" 62 L.Q.R. 375 (1946) pp. 379-383.

aside: the Joint Stock Companies Act 1856 no longer required a minimum amount of shares, nor a minimum subscription of a proportion of the nominal capital nor a minimum payment of the subscribed capital. And the minimum number of subscribers was reduced from twenty-five to seven.[1]

Almost a century after the sweeping reforms of the mid-nineteenth century, it was suggested to the Cohen Committee that a minimum paid up capital of around £5000 should be introduced.[2] And later still, the Jenkins Committee declared itself "in principle" in favour of a statutory minimum paid up capital, but having "reluctantly" come to the conclusion that "its purpose would be too easy to evade" recommended against its introduction.[3] Only in 1980 was the present minimum capital requirement in respect of public companies introduced.[4]

In the United States, several jurisdictions require that a corporation, before doing any business, has a minimum paid-in stated capital.[5] The typical statutory provision prohibits the corporation from transacting any business or incurring any indebtedness, except such as shall be incidental to

---

[1] s. 3.

[2] *Vide* The Cohen Report, Report of the Committee on Company Law Amendment, Cmd. 6659 (1945) para. 57, pp. 29-30.

[3] The Jenkins Report, para. 27, p. 7. Surprisingly, the Jenkins Committee was impressed by the observations made by some witnesses that it would be difficult to prevent a company, once formed with a statutory minimum of cash, from returning the cash to the promoters "either in exchange for assets, such as goodwill, or by way of a loan, or in some other way." *Ibid.* para. 27, p. 7. The Committee's endorsement of this view appears to betray a fundamental misunderstanding of the notion of capital. It is an elementary principle that cash received by the company in consideration of an issue of shares may be, and often is, applied for the acquisition of assets and that it makes no difference whether the assets are acquired from the promoters or third parties. The capital would in any such case remain intact, the cash asset being converted into some other form of asset.

[4] The requirement was originally introduced by s. 3(2) and s. 85(1) of the Companies Act 1980 in order to implement the Second Company Law Directive on Company Law Harmonisation issued on December 13, 1976. The rule is now embodied in the C.A. 1985, ss. 11 and 118(1).

[5] *Vide* generally Note, "Statutory Minimum Capitalization Requirements" 5 Williamette L.J. 331 (1969). Before the introduction of general incorporation statutes in the United States, incorporation for business purposes was effected almost entirely by special legislative act with the specific business to be done and the amount of capital required for the specific enterprise. *Vide* William P. Hackney and Tracey G. Benson, "Shareholder Liability for Inadequate Capital" 43 Univ. of Pittsburgh L.R. 837 (1982) pp. 852, 856. The position in the United States therefore corresponded broadly to that in England. *Vide supra* p. 327.

its organisation or to obtaining subscriptions to or payment for its shares, until there has been paid in for the issuance of shares consideration of at least the value prescribed in the statute or in the articles of incorporation.[1] In contrast to the position under English law (where non-compliance with the minimum issued and paid in requirements of a public company merely subjects the company and its officers to a fine),[2] non-compliance with minimum requirements in American jurisdictions will generally subject the designated corporate personnel to joint and several personal liability for the corporate obligations either to the extent of the deficiency in the stated capital or unlimitedly.[3] The problem with the American provisions is simply that the amounts prescribed in the statutes[4] are too small to be of any value whatsoever.

At first glance, the rationale behind the statutory minimum capital requirements may seem to be the protection of creditors.[5] The law appears to presume that the creditors look to the issued capital as a fund for their protection in the event of the company's insolvency.[6] On reflection, however,

---

[1] Henn and Alexander, *op. cit.* pp. 338-339. Previously, the Oklahoma Business Corporation Act had provided the minimum capital was to be paid in as a condition precedent even to corporate existence. *Vide* Okl. Stat. Ann. (1951) s. 18-1.15. The provision was repealed by Laws 1986, c. 292 s. 160. In 1986, Oklahoma also abolished the concept of a minimum capital requirement.

[2] C.A. 1985, s. 117(7).

[3] *Vide* Note, "Statutory Minimum Capitalization Requirements" 5 Williamette L.J. 331 (1969) pp. 335, 341; Henn and Alexander, *op. cit.* pp. 339-340.

[4] For e.g., Texas requires a minimum paid-in capital of $1,000 (Tex. Business Corporation Act, s. 3.02(7)); Georgia $500 (Ga. Code Ann. ss. 22-802(a)(8)(1977)); Arkansas $300 (Ark. Stat. Ann. s. 64-502(G) (1980)). Louisiana and North Carolina prescribe no minimum. In its 1979 revision, the ABA-ALI Model Business Corporation Act dropped its previous $1,000 minimum paid in capital (*vide* Model Bus. Corp. Act Ann. s. 51 para. 4 (1960), Model Bus. Corp. Act Ann. 2d. s. 54 para. 3.03(7) (1971). *Vide* further Henn and Alexander, *op. cit.* p. 339.

[5] West's commentary on the Louisiana Business Corporation Laws prior to the abolition of the minimum capital requirement had stated that "[t]he paid in capital requirements are designed to protect the public against irresponsible use of corporations." West's La. Rev. Stat. Ann. Vol. 5 p. xl. In connection with minimum capital requirements, Hornstein states that "[s]pecific limits were place at one time upon corporate capital - a minimum to protect creditors and a maximum to protect the public against enterprises so large that they might become monopolies." *Vide* George D. Hornstein, *Corporation Law and Practice* (1959) Vol. 1, s. 20 at p. 21.

[6] This "trust fund" is to stand in place of personal liability. The capital maintenance rules is aimed at protecting the fund from dissipation and distribution to shareholders.

it will be realised the such a purpose is nowadays wholly unrealistic. The amount of paid-in capital required by the statutes cannot be such as to offer much (if any) protection to creditors. As pointed out by a Kentucky court, "[o]ne may start business on a shoestring in Kentucky, but if it is a corporate business the shoestring must be worth $1,000."[1] The same criticism can obviously be levelled at other American provisions.[2] Even the £50,000 minimum limit introduced by the Companies Act 1980 in respect of public companies will be trifling for many a business venture. Other factors - and not creditor protection - probably explain the presence of the minimum requirements. In the case of the English requirement, it is clear that the rule was introduced merely to implement Article 6 of the Second Company Law Directive on Company Law Harmonisation issued on December 13, 1976 rather than from a deep-felt domestic belief that the requirement would offer protection to creditors. In the case of the American provisions, it would appear that although the protection of creditors may originally have been the intention of the legislator,[3] the current adherence by a number of jurisdictions to the rule of a minimum capital requirement owes much to tradition. Significantly, the Model Business Corporation Act, in its 1969 revision, actually eliminated the $1,000 minimum[4] and the pattern of statutory amendments has similarly been to abandon statutory minimum capitalisation requirements.[5] The liberalisation of minimum capitalisation requirements in the United States reflected a trend in that country towards the use of enabling acts which place more responsibility on the investor or creditor[6] and less on the state.[7] The recent trend in English law, influenced to an extent by the policies and regulations of the European Union, has

---

[1] *Tri-State Developers, Inc.* v. *Moore* 343 S.W.2d 812 (App. Ky. 1961) at p. 816.

[2] As Hornstein observed, "[m]aking the minimum [capital] nominal or completely eliminating it in most states has substantially undermined one of the props for the 'trust-fund doctrine'." Hornstein, *op. cit.* Vol. 1, s. 20 at p. 21.

[3] *Vide* Note, "Statutory Minimum Capitalization Requirements" 5 Williamette L.J. 331 (1969) p. 339.

[4] The $1,000 minimum was previously contained in ss. 48(g) and 51 of the Act. *Vide* further Ray Garrett, "History, Purpose and Summary of the Model Business Corporation Act" 6 Bus. Law. 1 (1950) p. 3.

[5] William P. Hackney and Tracey G. Benson, "Shareholder Liability for Inadequate Capital" 43 Univ. of Pittsburgh L.R. 837 (1982) p. 853.

[6] *Vide* Wilbur G. Katz, "The Philosophy of Midcentury Corporation Statutes" 23 Law and Contemp. Prob. 177 (1958) pp. 179-181, 187-188.

[7] *Vide* Ray Garrett, "Model Business Corporation Act" 4 Baylor L.R. 412 (1952) p. 416.

probably been somewhat more interventionist and paternalistic, although adequate protection to creditors is still lacking.

The absence of a general statutory requirement for a reasonable level of minimum capitalisation has often been severely criticised.[1] Usually, the commentators' tack is to first highlight the "disturbing" situation where an insolvent company with an issued share capital of say just two pounds ends up with very significant debts[2] and to then argue that the case for a reasonable minimum capital requirement is therefore "virtually unanswerable".[3] For rather obvious reasons, however, reform on the basis of a pre-determined statutory minimum share capital would be entirely unsatisfactory.

In the first place, it is evident that one company's financing requirements may vary immensely from another company's needs. A hotel development project may require several millions of pounds worth of investment while a little stationer may only need a few thousand pounds. It is therefore impossible to pre-determine a "reasonable" amount as a statutory minimum requirement.[4] Indeed, any statutory minimum would be too arbitrary and therefore meaningless : inevitably, it would be too low for some ventures and too high for others. It would be an "empty ritual" fooling no one.[5] Clearly, minimum capitalisation is a problem that goes beyond the capacity of a general statutory provision based on pre-determined limits.

Secondly, calls for a statutory minimum capital requirement appear to ignore the fact that other methods of financing (for example short- and long-term debt) may be beneficial to the company without undermining the interests of creditors and without abusing of the privileges of incorporation and limited liability. The truth is that a company's financing need not all be "risk" capital.

---

[1] *Vide* e.g., Paul Stock, "Case shows why *all* companies need a minimum paid up share capital" 1 Co. Law. 249 (1980); P.S. Atiyah, "Thoughts on Company Law Philosophy" 8 Lawyer 15 (1965); Daniel J. Westerbeck, "The Inadequacy of Stated Capital Requirements" 40 Univ. Cin. L. Rev. 823 (1971) p. 841.

[2] E.g., *In re Camburn Petroleum Products Ltd.* [1980] 1 W.L.R. 86.

[3] Paul Stock, "Case shows why *all* companies need a minimum paid up share capital" 1 Co. Law. 249 (1980).

[4] As Latty bluntly put it, "[o]ne thousand dollars may be adequate capital for a barber shop, but grotesque for a steel mill." Latty, *op. cit.* p. 137.

[5] Ernest L. Folk, "Some Reflections of a Corporation Law Draftsman" 42 Conn. Bar J. 409 (1968) at p. 421.

Finally, the notion of a minimum share capital appears to be based on the wrong economic assumption that the capital will remain unimpaired. In practice, of course, the capital may be diminished or lost through the company's normal trading activities.[1] The law cannot guarantee that this fund will remain intact when the creditors need to have recourse to it, although the doctrine of capital maintenance does reduce the risk of the capital being depleted, say, by improvident dividends.[2] All told, statutory minimum capital requirements do not even qualify as a palliative.

### 3.3. Fraudulent trading

Section 213 of the Insolvency Act 1986 - the fraudulent trading provision - empowers the court to declare that any persons who were knowingly parties to the carrying on of any business of the company with intent to defraud creditors of the company or creditors of any other person, or for any other fraudulent purpose, are to be liable to make such contributions (if any) to the company's assets as it thinks proper. The essential features of the section have already been discussed in connection with the subservient subsidiary situation.[3] In this Chapter it is only necessary to determine the extent to which the provision can provide a remedy in the undercapitalised subsidiary situation.

A distinction must immediately be drawn between (i) the situation where the subsidiary is provided with insufficient funds to enable it to undertake the business venture for which it was set up, and (ii) the situation where the subsidiary has a high debt-equity ratio such that on its insolvency the

---

[1] This was recognised in some of the earliest judgments on company law. *Vide* e.g., *Trevor v. Whitworth* (1877) 12 App. Cas. 409 (H.L.) at p. 423 per Lord Watson.

[2] Moreover, where the net assets of a public company are half or less than half of its called-up capital, the directors are bound to convene an extraordinary general meeting of the company for the purposes of considering whether any, and if so what, steps should be taken to deal with the situation (C.A. 1985, s. 142(1)). The obligation is merely to convene the meeting. There is no duty to wind up the company or to take any remedial measures. This provision contrasts sharply with s. 13 of the Limited Liability Act 1855 which had provided that a company must cease trading and must be wound up if it appeared that three-fourths of the subscribed capital stock of the company had been lost. The following year however the Joint Stock Companies Act 1856, s. 67, changed the "must" to "may".

[3] *Vide supra* Chapter V pp. 205-211.

holding company will compete as a creditor for advances which should, in effect, be treated as "risk" capital.[1]

The fraudulent trading provision clearly supplies no remedy in the case of the financing of a subsidiary on a high debt-equity ratio. Such a "thinly" capitalised subsidiary would have received sufficient funds to enable it to carry out its normal trading activities. Plainly, no intention to defraud the subsidiary's creditors will be present. The subsidiary's directors would not be trading with intent to defraud. Nor can the holding company be held liable for fraudulent trading. There is no fraud to which the holding company can be considered a party.[2] The position does not change even if the holding company is in effective control of the affairs of the subsidiary. The unfairness of such a method of financing will of course surface at a later stage during the company's insolvency when the holding company asserts its claims as a creditor. Clearly, however, the thinly capitalised subsidiary arrangement cannot be equated with fraud. Nor would the fraudulent trading provision be applicable where a thinly capitalised subsidiary situation is combined with a creditor-proof plan (such as the loan-cum-mortgage or lease device). The essential ingredient of a fraudulent intent would usually be lacking even in such case.

Different considerations however apply in the case of a subsidiary which has been provided with illusory or trifling finance. As previously noted, such a subsidiary stands virtually no chance of success.[3] Its failure is written on the wall. Even directors with just a sprinkling of sense will visualise the risks. The directors will know that if the subsidiary obtains credit - as it would have to do in order to commence trading - the likelihood would be that the creditors will not be paid. In effect, the business would be carried on at the expense of its creditors. In such circumstances, the ingredients of fraudulent trading - in particular the "intent to defraud" - would probably exist. The judgments support such a conclusion. In *Re William C. Leitch Brothers Limited*[4] Maugham J. held, in connection with the corresponding provision of the Companies Act 1929,[5] that a proper inference of intent to defraud could be made "if a company continues to carry on business and to incur debts at a time when there is to the knowledge of the directors no

---

[1] *Vide supra* pp. 312-320.

[2] Cf. *Re Augustus Barnett & Son Ltd.* [1986] BCLC 170.

[3] *Vide supra* pp. 312-313.

[4] [1932] 2 Ch. 71.

[5] s. 275 Companies Act 1929.

reasonable prospect of the creditors *ever* receiving payment".[1] In the following year, in *Re Patrick & Lyon, Limited*[2] the same judge explained that the words "defraud" and "fraudulent purpose" connoted "actual dishonesty involving, according to current notions of fair trading among commercial men, real moral blame."[3] More recently, in *R.* v. *Grantham*[4] the Court of Appeal established that the test of fraudulent intent will be satisfied where the directors have no good reason to believe that funds will become available to pay the creditors when their debts become due or shortly thereafter.[5] Two aspects of the Court of Appeal's approach need to be highlighted. First, it is not necessary to show, as Maugham J. had indicated in *William C. Leitch Brothers, Limited*,[6] that there was no reasonable prospect of the creditors *ever* receiving payment. It is sufficient if there is no good reason to believe that payment will be made when the debt becomes due or shortly thereafter. Secondly, the Court of Appeal made it quite clear that a proper inference of fraud could be made if there is no good reason to believe that payment will be made as aforesaid. Dishonesty - an essential ingredient of liability - could be inferred from a reckless disregard of the interests of creditors. In his judgment,[7] Lord Lane C.J. disapproved of the statement in *Re White and Osmond (Parkstone) Ltd.*[8] that there would be no fraud if the directors genuinely believed "that the clouds will roll away and the sunshine of prosperity will shine upon them again and disperse the fog". Although *R.* v. *Grantham* concerned *criminal* liability for fraudulent trading and was decided at a time when both civil and criminal liability for fraudulent trading were regulated by section 332 of the Companies Act 1948,[9] the approach spelt out by the Court of Appeal remains relevant. And the test - formulated in relation to a criminal offence - should apply *a fortiori*

---

[1] [1932] 2 Ch. 71 at p. 77. (Emphasis added).

[2] [1933] 1 Ch. 786.

[3] *Ibid.* at p. 790. *Vide* also *In re E.B. Tractors Ltd.* [1987] PCC 313 and *Re a company (No. 001418 of 1988)* [1991] BCLC 197.

[4] [1984] BCLC 270 (C.A.).

[5] *Vide* also *Re a company (No. 001418 of 1988)* [1991] BCLC 197.

[6] [1932] 2 Ch. 71.

[7] [1984] BCLC 270 (C.A.) at p. 275.

[8] Unreported, 30 June 1960 Ch.D.

[9] The 1986 reforms effectively divided s. 332 : the provisions regarding criminal liability are now found in s. 458 of the C.A. 1985, whereas the civil liability provision are incorporated in s. 213 of the I.A. 1986.

in the case of civil liability. "Dishonesty" and "real moral blame" should be readily inferred whenever the person responsible realises at the time the debts were incurred that there was no reason for thinking that funds would be available to settle the debt when it became due or shortly thereafter.[1]

Liability for fraudulent trading does not however arise merely because the company is trading at a loss, even if for a considerable period of time. *Re Augustus Barnett & Son Ltd.*[2] made it clear that in such circumstances, the management of the company will not be liable for fraudulent trading as long as steps are taken to ensure that the claims of creditors will be satisfied, even though such steps do not legally guarantee payment. The requisite of dishonesty would simply be lacking.

There can be little doubt that apart from the directors, the holding company also faces potential liability for fraudulent trading in the case of a subsidiary with an illusory or trifling financing. Section 213 imposes liability on "... any persons who were knowingly parties to the carrying on of the business".[3] Two situations must be distinguished. One is where the holding company was instrumental in setting up the inadequately financed subsidiary and continues (as is likely) to exercise a degree of control over the activities of the company. In such a situation, the holding company would be "knowingly" a party "to the carrying on" of the subsidiary's business with "intent to defraud". Liability for fraudulent trading should ensue. *Re Augustus Barnett & Son Ltd*[4] lends support to this conclusion. In that case, Hoffmann J. appeared willing to consider the holding company as a party to the carrying on of the business of the subsidiary,[5] but on the facts found that there was no fraud to which the holding company could have been a party.[6]

---

[1] A declaration under s. 213 should specify responsibility for a definite sum and could include a punitive as well as a compensatory element, the latter being limited to the amount of the debts of the creditors proved to have been defrauded. *Vide Re a Company (No. 001418 of 1988)* [1991] BCLC 197, at pp. 204-205.

[2] [1986] BCLC 170.

[3] I.A. 1986, s. 213 (2). A holding company is obviously a "person" in terms of this subsection.

[4] [1986] BCLC 170.

[5] *Ibid.* at p. 173.

[6] The case is of course distinguishable from the situation under consideration. For one thing, the holding company had over a four year period paid the subsidiary considerable subsidies (to the tune of £4m) to help it out of its financial difficulties. Secondly, the holding company did not exert much control over the affairs of its subsidiary. Indeed, the

The other situation occurs where the holding company incorporates a subsidiary with insufficient funds to enable it to stand a fair chance of survival, and proceeds to distance itself from the affairs of the subsidiary, leaving its direction and management entirely in the hands of the subsidiary's own board of directors. However contemptible the holding company's action may be in such a situation, it would, in all likelihood, manage to escape liability for fraudulent trading. Given that the holding company would not be participating in, or at least directing, the affairs of the subsidiary, it would, quite plausibly, be able to plead that it was not "knowingly" a party to the "carrying on of the business" of the subsidiary "with intent to defraud".

The foregoing analysis illustrates that the fraudulent trading provision does at least have a role to play in the undercapitalised subsidiary situation. Unfortunately, the effectiveness of the fraudulent trading provision is considerably weakened by the strict standard of proof required. The result is that in practice proceedings have only been taken in the strongest of cases, although *R. v. Grantham*[1] has probably made it somewhat easier to prove the necessary fraudulent intent.[2]

### 3.4. Wrongful trading

As already stated in a previous Chapter,[3] the heavy onus of proving fraud to the standard of proof required by criminal law in order to obtain a finding of fraudulent trading led the Cork Committee to recommend that the civil remedy of fraudulent trading be replaced by a new section under which civil liability could arise without proof of fraud or dishonesty and without requiring the criminal standard of proof.[4] The Committee's basic proposals were incorporated - with certain modifications - in section 214 (the wrongful trading section) of the Insolvency Act 1986.

*Cont.*
   business of the subsidiary was conducted by its own board of directors without interference from the holding company.

[1] [1984] BCLC 270 (C.A.). *Vide* also *R. v. Kemp* [1988] QB 645 (C.A.).

[2] The difficulties with the strict standard required to prove fraudulent trading has already been discussed in the context of the subservient subsidiary situation. *Vide supra* Chapter V pp. 206-207. The observation made in that context apply *per equipollens* to the undercapitalised subsidiary situation.

[3] *Vide supra* Chapter V pp. 211-212.

[4] The Cork Report, para. 1778, p. 399.

The essential features of the wrongful trading provisions have already been discussed in the context of the subservient subsidiary situation.[1] In this Chapter, it is only necessary to discuss the extent to which section 214 provides a remedy in the undercapitalised subsidiary situation.

As with the fraudulent trading provision, a distinction must be drawn between (i) the situation where the subsidiary is provided with insufficient funds to enable it to undertake the business venture for which it was set up, and (ii) the situation where the subsidiary has an excessive debt-equity ratio such that on its insolvency the holding company will compete as a creditor for advances which should, in effect, be treated as "risk" capital.

The wrongful trading provisions are clearly irrelevant as a means of controlling the unfairness of excessive debt-equity ratio financing. The "thinly" capitalised subsidiary may have received sufficient funds to enable it to carry out its normal trading activities and the insolvency is not likely to be causally linked to that method of financing. The obligation imposed by the wrongful trading provisions is clear : directors who know or ought to conclude that there is no reasonable prospect that the company could avoid going into insolvent liquidation must take every step to minimise the potential loss to the company's creditors. Conduct capable of attracting liability for wrongful trading includes the failure to preserve the assets of the company, the conclusion of transactions at an undervalue, the payment of excessive remuneration to the officers of the company and the failure to collect debts due to the company.[2] But by no stretch of the legal imagination could the duty imposed by section 214 be taken to include an obligation to convert the debt into capital or to otherwise arrange for the subordination of the holding company's loans to the subsidiary. This conclusion is obliquely supported by the rule which empowers a court imposing liability for wrongful trading to direct that the whole or any part of the debt owed by the company to the director (or shadow director) should rank in priority after all other debts owed by the company.[3] In other words, debt may be treated as equity *in consequence* of a finding of wrongful trading. But debt financing cannot in itself be a cause of liability for wrongful trading. Support for this contention may also be derived from the Cork Committee which had - *independently* of its proposals on wrongful trading[4] - specifically

---

[1] *Vide supra* Chapter V pp. 211-213.

[2] *Vide* R.M. Goode, *Principles of Corporate Insolvency Law* (1990) p. 205.

[3] I.A. 1986, s. 215(4). The rule applies also to liability for fraudulent trading.

[4] The Cork Report, Ch. 44.

recommended the deferment of inter-company indebtedness whenever this has for.,ied part of the company's long-term capital structure.[1] Parliament, however, in its infinite wisdom, chose not to implement this proposal.

The case of a subsidiary with illusory or trifling financing presents different considerations. Its directors realise - or at any rate should realise - that if the company is to embark on trading operations (and obtain credit in the process) the likelihood is that the creditors will not be paid. The situation would be no different where the company, though initially set up with adequate financing, runs into severe financial difficulties because of substantial losses and then continues to trade and to incur liabilities. In either situation, the business would be carried on at the expense of creditors.[2] Insolvent liquidation would be inevitable. In any such circumstances, the requisites of wrongful trading would almost certainly be satisfied: (i) the directors would have known, or at least ought to have concluded, that there was no reasonable prospect that the subsidiary could have avoided going into insolvent liquidation; and, (ii) by engaging or continuing to engage in commercial operations the directors actually increased, rather than minimised, the potential loss to the company's creditors.

Unfortunately, this conclusion is not borne out by *Re Purpoint Ltd.*,[3] which is apparently the only reported judgment that has considered the wrongful trading provisions in the context of a company with trivial financing. In that case, the company was grossly under-capitalised from its inception and appears to have had a very slim chance of survival. Yet, somewhat surprisingly, Vinelott J. refused to conclude that the director ought to have known that the company "was doomed to end in an insolvent winding up from the moment it started to trade".[4] To do so, he observed, "would impose too high a test".[5] Vinelott J. in fact thought that the director was justified in his belief that connections in the advertising and publicity fields would enable him to introduce new business.[6]

---

[1] The Cork Report, para. 1963, pp. 441-442.

[2] E.g., *Re Chartmore Ltd.* [1990] BCLC 673; *Re Purpoint Ltd.* [1991] BCLC 491; *Re Austinsuite Furniture Ltd.* [1992] BCLC 1047; *Re Stanford Services Ltd.* [1987] BCLC 607; *Re Lo-Line Electric Motors Ltd.* [1988] BCLC 698.

[3] [1991] BCLC 491.

[4] *Ibid.* at p. 498.

[5] *Ibid.* at p. 498.

[6] *Ibid.* at p. 498.

With respect, however, it is the law which has imposed a strict standard. Once it is acknowledged that pitiful financing renders insolvency unavoidable, the director has the duty not to commence trading at all if to do so would jeopardise the creditors' claims. Significantly, the Cork Committee, in its commentary on the wrongful trading proposals, had expressly considered that "[t]rading when a business is heavily undercapitalised will often come within the concept of 'wrongful trading'" and that "[t]hose responsible for carrying on trading with insufficient share capital and reserves may well find themselves guilty of wrongful trading and accordingly subject to a personal liability in this respect."[1] Moreover, the Committee expected that its proposals would "encourage directors to satisfy themselves that their companies are adequately capitalised when regard is had to the scale of their operations and the level of the commitments into which they are proposing to enter".[2] Hopefully, future judgments will accord the wrongful trading provisions a stricter - and more correct - interpretation than that found in *Re Purpoint Ltd.*

Whether the holding company can itself be liable for wrongful trading depends on whether, in the particular circumstances, it qualifies as a shadow director. A "shadow director" is defined as "a person in accordance with whose directions or instructions the directors of the company are accustomed to act".[3] We have already seen that in appropriate circumstances a holding company may qualify as a shadow director.[4] In the typical subservient subsidiary company situation, for example, the holding company would very probably qualify as such.[5] The position with an undercapitalised subsidiary is not so clear-cut. It is of course possible (perhaps even likely) that the holding company exercises a sufficient degree of control over the directors of the undercapitalised subsidiary to qualify the holding company as a shadow director. Liability would then ensue if the subsidiary conducts business at the expense of its creditors. On the other hand, the holding

---

[1] The Cork Report, para. 1785, p. 400.

[2] *Ibid.* para. 1785 p. 400. The Committee also believed that the new concept would "go a long way to meet the criticisms of those who complain of the absence of a statutory minimum paid-up share capital for all trading companies". *Ibid.* para. 1785 p. 400. The draft wrongful trading clause proposed by the Cork Committee is different in several respects from s. 214 of the I.A. 1986. The modifications do not however affect the relevance of the Committee's observations on capitalisation.

[3] I.A. 1986, s. 251.

[4] *Vide supra* Chapter V pp. 213-214.

[5] *Vide supra* Chapter V pp. 214-217.

company may, after the incorporation of the undercapitalised subsidiary leave its activities in the hands of its own directors. In such a case, the directors of the subsidiary would obviously not become "accustomed" to act in accordance with the directions or instructions of the holding company. No matter how blameworthy the holding company's behaviour had been in incorporating an undercapitalised subsidiary, it would remain immune from liability for wrongful trading. Liability for wrongful trading is attracted not by mismanagement nor by undercapitalised incorporation, but by the failure to take appropriate steps to minimise the potential loss to creditors after insolvency becomes inevitable. Because the remedy penalises only conduct taking place after the time when insolvency is inevitable, the wrongful trading provisions are wholly ineffective to impose liability on the holding company merely for having set up the undercapitalised subsidiary.

### 3.5. Common law duties of directors towards creditors

The preceding chapter examined the judicial extension of directors' common law duties towards creditors in the particular context of the subservient subsidiary situation.[1] Although none of the judgments cited in support of the doctrine specifically consider the question of directors' duties in the context of an undercapitalised company, there should be little doubt that the doctrine can - within the severe confines and subject to the serious reservations identified in that chapter[2] - apply to the undercapitalised company situation.

A distinction must however again be drawn between the company that is supplied with insufficient funds to enable it to conduct commercial operations and the company with a high debt-equity ratio. In the latter case, no breach of the common law duty towards creditors can possibly be involved. But where a company is supplied with trivial financing (and similarly where a company, though initially supplied with adequate financing, runs into financial difficulties following heavy losses) the position is different. In such circumstances the directors would arguably be in breach of their common law duties towards the company's creditors if they fail to take into account their interests, say by commencing to trade or by continuing to trade (as the case may be) when insolvency is inevitable. It is also arguable, as we have seen in the preceding chapter,[3] that the holding

---

[1] *Vide supra* Chapter V pp. 239-252.

[2] *Vide supra* Chapter V pp. 246-249, 252-254.

[3] *Vide supra* Chapter V pp. 249-251.

company can - provided it exercises the requisite degree of control - qualify as a director for the purposes of attributing to it the common law duties towards creditors.

Unfortunately, the notion of directors' duties towards creditors is bedevilled by so many difficulties that its effectiveness as a potential remedy must be seriously questioned. These difficulties were noted and discussed in the preceding chapter[1] and is not necessary to discuss them any further.

One matter should however be stressed. The origins of the doctrine of directors' duties towards creditors can be traced to the period before the introduction of the remedy of wrongful trading in the Insolvency Act 1985[2] - to a time when the protection afforded to creditors was still rudimentary.[3] Given that the wrongful trading provisions can now probably offer some basis for relief in the case of undercapitalised companies, and given the uncertainty surrounding the notion of directors' duties towards creditors, it is likely that judicial attention in tackling the undercapitalisation problem will focus on the statutory provisions. It would be surprising if the common law notion were ever to have an impact on the undercapitalised company situation.

## 3.6. Disqualification of directors

In certain circumstances a director may be disqualified by a court order from acting as a director unless the court grants leave.[4] The statutory provisions are now consolidated in the Company Directors Disqualification Act 1986 which classifies, under three heads, the circumstances in which such an order may be made: (i) disqualification for general misconduct in relation to a company;[5] (ii) disqualification for unfitness;[6] and (iii) other cases of disqualification.[7] An application for a disqualification order may be made by the Secretary of State or the official receiver, or by the liquidator or any past

---

[1] *Vide supra* Chapter V pp. 246-249, 252-254.

[2] The wrongful trading provisions now contained in s. 214 of the I.A. 1986 were derived from ss. 12(9), 15(1)-(5), (7), Sch. 9, para. 4 of the Insolvency Act 1985.

[3] *Vide* further *supra* Chapter V p. 249.

[4] On disqualification of directors generally *vide* Gower, pp. 144-147; Farrar, pp. 349-362.

[5] ss. 2-5.

[6] ss. 6-9.

[7] ss. 10-12.

or present member or creditor of any company in relation to which the person has committed or is alleged to have committed an offence or other default.[1]

Directors involved in companies which are inadequately financed run the risk of being disqualified from acting as directors. Indeed, several cases in which a disqualification order has been made on the ground of "unfitness" involved companies which had suffered from inadequate financing.[2] Many of these "unfitness" cases in fact present surprisingly similar facts : persons who have been directors of a number of inadequately financed and insolvent companies which had continued to trade for a considerable period of time at the expense of creditors, voluntary and involuntary. One of such cases - *Re Chartmore Ltd.*[3] - presents an unusual twist. In that case, Harman J., while holding that a disqualification order was justified on the basis of the director's failure to keep proper accounts and to ensure that the company was adequately capitalised so that it would not trade on the back of creditors, appeared to pay lip service to the importance of adequate capitalisation by granting leave to the same individual to act as a director of another company which was evidently undercapitalised. The court was impressed by the fact that he had a new co-director and that the company appeared "to be trading in a proper and desirable manner".[4] The judgment mists up the importance of adequate capitalisation.

Another question that deserves consideration in the context of corporate groups is whether the holding company itself can be the subject of a disqualification order.[5] A distinction made in the Company Directors Disqualification Act 1986 is relevant to this issue. With regard to certain heads of disqualification (for example, conviction of an indictable offence,[6] persistent breaches of companies legislation,[7] fraud,[8] and summary

---

[1] ss. 16(2).

[2] E.g., *Re Stanford Services Ltd.* [1987] BCLC 607; *Re Lo-Line Electric Motors Ltd.* [1988] BCLC 698; *Re Chartmore Ltd.* [1990] BCLC 673; *Re Austinsuite Furniture Ltd.* [1992] BCLC 1047; *Re City Investment Centres Ltd.* [1992] BCLC 956.

[3] [1990] BCLC 673.

[4] *Ibid.* at p. 676. Leave was only given for one year, subject to renewal. *Ibid.* at p. 676.

[5] In none of the reported judgments on the Company Directors Disqualification Act 1986 was a disqualification order made against a body corporate.

[6] s. 2.

[7] s. 3.

[8] s. 4.

conviction[1]) a disqualification order can be made against *any person* provided of course that the circumstances specified in the relative provisions are satisfied. That person need not have been a director. Accordingly, a holding company can no doubt be disqualified from acting as a director in the aforesaid circumstances. With regard to some of the other heads of disqualification - in particular disqualification on the ground of unfitness to be concerned in the management of a company - the person subject to the order must be or must have been a director of a company which had at some time become insolvent (whether while he was a director or subsequently).[2] Undoubtedly, a holding company can be appointed as a director on the board of its subsidiary and therefore be subject to disqualification for "unfitness". But the term "director" is defined as including "any person occupying the position of director, by whatever name called" and, for the purposes of the provisions on disqualification on the ground of unfitness, "director" also includes a "shadow director".[3] In effect, this means that a holding company exercising dominating control over an undercapitalised subsidiary may well qualify as a *de facto* or shadow director and become the subject of a disqualification order. It should also be noted that whenever a holding company is held liable for fraudulent or wrongful trading, the court may, if it thinks fit, also make a disqualification order against the holding company.[4]

A disqualification order against a holding company can have serious consequences on the practical organisation of a corporate group. In the first place, the holding company would not be able to act as a director (*de jure* or *de facto*)[5] of any company, including of course its subsidiaries. In the second place, it would not be able to be in any way, whether directly or indirectly, concerned or take part "in the promotion, formation or management of a company."[6] The practical effect of the inter-relationship between the various sections in the Company Directors Disqualification Act 1986 is that a holding company disqualified on the basis of "unfitness" (say, in connection

---

[1] s. 5.

[2] s. 6. *Vide* also s. 7(1)(b).

[3] s. 22(4). By s. 22(5) a "shadow director" is attributed the same meaning as that given to a "shadow director" in the C.A. 1985 (s. 741(2)) and the I.A. 1986 (s. 251), that is, "a person in accordance with whose directions or instructions the directors of the company are accustomed to act (but so that a person is not deemed a shadow director by reason only that the directors act on advice given by him in a professional capacity)".

[4] s. 10(1).

[5] ss. 1(1)(a) and 22(4).

[6] s. 1(1)(d).

with its exercise of dominating control over an inadequately financed subsidiary) will be prohibited from incorporating any new subsidiaries and, more seriously, will be unable to participate in any way in the management of its existing subsidiaries. The function of the holding company would have to be limited to that of an "investment" company without the power to promote or form new companies. If a holding company against which a disqualification order is made were to be involved in the management of a subsidiary, it would become liable for all such debts and other liabilities of the subsidiary incurred at a time when the holding company was so involved.[1] And conversely, any director or manager of a subsidiary company who acts or is willing to act on the instructions of the holding company which is subject to a disqualification order will similarly become personally liable for the debts and other liabilities of the subsidiary. Almost certainly, most corporate groups are blissfully unaware of the potential impact of these sections.

Although the disqualification provisions are certainly useful in deterring unconscionable conduct by directors and in protecting the public against the future involvement in companies by persons whose past records as directors of insolvent companies have shown them to be a danger to creditors and others,[2] the provisions do not, of course, offer much comfort to the creditors of an insolvent company managed by such directors. Creditors must look elsewhere for redress.

### 3.7. The doctrine of capital maintenance

If only for the sake of completeness, reference should be made to the doctrine of capital maintenance. The doctrine - originally developed by the courts and later modified by the Companies Acts - regards the company's share capital as a fund to safeguard the interests of creditors.[3] Basically, the doctrine involves two aspects. One concerns the raising of capital - ensuring that appropriate payment is received by the company for the shares issued by it. The other is concerned with ensuring that the capital is not returned to the members ahead of a winding up, that is, that "no part of the capital which has been paid into the coffers of the company has been subsequently paid

---

[1] ss. 15(1)(a) and 15(3)(a).

[2] *Re Lo-Line Electric Motors Ltd.* [1988] BCLC 698 at p. 703 per Browne-Wilkinson V.C.

[3] *Vide Re Exchange Banking Co., Flitcroft's Case* (1882) 21 Ch. D. 519 (C.A.) at p. 533 per Jessel M.R.

out, except in the legitimate course of business."[1] This second aspect seeks to regulate primarily the acquisition by the company of its own shares,[2] the provision of financial assistance in connection with the acquisition of its shares,[3] and the depletion of its assets through improper dividends, funded not out of profits but out of capital.[4] The stringent rules regarding the reduction of the capital fund can also be viewed as part of the capital maintenance doctrine.[5]

A moment's reflection will however convince oneself that the doctrine of capital maintenance, while certainly serving a useful and desirable function, does not in any way remedy or even diminish the problem of undercapitalisation. No aspect of the doctrine in fact seeks to ensure that the company is provided with sufficient funds to enable it to stand a fair chance of success. Even strict dividend rules, for example, can provide only formalistic protection, since a company may usually be formed with no minimum capital or with a trivial amount,[6] and is not obliged to increase its capital as the enterprise grows. Nor is the doctrine of capital maintenance concerned with controlling excessively high debt-equity methods of financing or with the unfairness that may result from the shareholder competing as a creditor on the company's insolvency. Loan capital, being a debt and not equity capital, is obviously not subject to the rules of raising and maintenance of capital. The truth is that doctrine of capital maintenance is designed to deal with entirely different problems. Ideally, the capital maintenance doctrine would fulfil a far more significant function than it presently does if it were to be linked to a legal requirement for a reasonable capital base. Indeed, the "maintenance" of an adequate capital cushion

---

[1] *Trevor* v. *Whitworth* (1877) 12 App. Cas. 409 (H.L.) at p. 424 per Lord Watson.

[2] C.A. 1985, ss. 143-150, 159-181. *Vide* generally Gower, pp. 217-226; Farrar, pp. 178-189; *Palmer's Company Law* (25th ed. 1992) Vol. I paras. 6.401-6.423.

[3] C.A. 1985, ss. 151-158. *Vide* generally Gower, pp. 226-241; Farrar, pp. 189-200; *Palmer's Company Law* (25th ed. 1992) Vol. I paras. 6.501-6.521.

[4] C.A. 1985, s. 263. *Vide* generally Gower, pp. 244-251; Farrar, pp. 20-205; *Palmer's Company Law* (25th ed. 1992) Vol. II paras. 9.801-9.814. For the position in American law *vide* Henn and Alexander, *op. cit.* pp. 890-904.

[5] *Vide* ss. 135-141 of the C.A. 1985. *Vide* generally Gower, pp. 689-692; Farrar, pp. 209-219; *Palmer's Company Law* (25th ed. 1992) Vol. I paras. 4.301-4.324. For the position in American law *vide* Henn and Alexander, *op. cit.* p. 972. The American rules on capital maintenance are generally more liberal than the English rules.

[6] *Vide supra* pp. 325-328.

should be the law's aim. But the development of the capital maintenance doctrine to such a stage appears Utopian.

## 3.8. Lifting the veil jurisprudence

### 3.8.1. The position in English law

It has already been observed that despite some judicial attempts aimed at carving out broad exceptions to the separate personality rule in the context of the holding-subsidiary relationship, the current attitude, as unequivocally stated by the Court of Appeal in *Adams* v. *Cape Industries plc*,[1] is remarkably narrow and conservative.[2] Nowadays, the courts would probably be willing to use the lifting the veiling doctrine to impose liability on the holding company only in highly abusive or offensive situations, as where corporate personality has been used as a cloak for fraud or improper conduct, where the subsidiary is a mere façade concealing the true facts, where the protection of public interests is of paramount importance or where the subsidiary has been formed to evade obligations imposed by law.[3]

Even before the restrictive judgment in *Adams* v. *Cape Industries plc*, however, virtually no significance had been attached to the undercapitalisation factor. In *Re F.G. (Films) Ltd.*[4] the question was whether a film could be deemed a British film in terms of the Cinematograph Films Act 1938. An American film company had incorporated a company in England. The English company had no place of business and did not employ any staff. Its capital was £100, of which the President of the American company, presumably as nominee for the said company, held £90. Financing was made available by the American company. Vaisey J. dismissed as a "mere travesty of the facts" the argument that the film was made by the English company and that it therefore qualified as a British film. In reaching this conclusion, Vaisey J. clearly considered the small amount of issued capital together with the financing of the film by the American company to be significant factors. In an earlier edition of his Principles of Modern Company Law,[5] Gower referred to *Re F.G. (Films) Ltd.* as showing "the first

---

[1] [1990] BCLC 479 (C.A.).

[2] *Vide supra* Chapter III pp. 109-110.

[3] *Vide supra* Chapter III pp. 107-108.

[4] [1953] 1 All E.R. 615.

[5] L.C.B. Gower, *Principles of Modern Company Law* (3rd ed. 1969).

signs of recognition that the under-capitalisation of the subsidiary may be a significant element in deciding whether to treat it as fused with its parent."[1] In the subsequent edition,[2] Gower, again referring to the same judgment, continued to regard undercapitalisation as an important criterion in the lifting the veil jurisprudence.[3] In his latest edition,[4] however, Gower - clearly taking into account the confining limitations of *Adams* v. *Cape Industries plc* - played down the importance of undercapitalisation, stating that undercapitalisation could be "[p]erhaps one factor suggesting that a subsidiary is a mere façade for its parent".[5]

It is submitted, however, that undercapitalisation has never actually had any real impact in the lifting of the veil cases. *F.G. (Films) Ltd.* is in fact probably the only case in the lifting of the veil jurisprudence which attached some importance to the undercapitalisation factor.[6] And that case, it must be remembered, involved an attempt to evade statutory controls - a situation where the courts undoubtedly exhibit a greater willingness to disregard the separate personality of a company from its shareholders. Indeed, *Re F.G. Films Ltd.* can probably be viewed as a case of statutory construction. In any event, there is no doubt that never - before or since *Re F.G. Films Ltd.* - have the courts imposed liability on a shareholder in respect of the debts of an insolvent company on the basis that the company was undercapitalised.

The legislative reforms in insolvency law introduced in the mid-1980's have had, it is suggested, two effects on the doctrine of lifting the veil. First, the reforms have - to the extent that certain abuses have been in fact curtailed - limited the scope for the judicial expansion of the doctrine. Second, the courts may have perceived, subconsciously at least, that the legislature has finally taken the lead in providing appropriate remedies. As a result, the courts may prefer to leave the future development of this area of the law to Parliament. The problem, of course, is that the legislative reforms, while certainly commendable, do not go far enough in protecting the interests of the creditors in abusive holding-subsidiary arrangements.

---

[1] *Ibid.* at p. 203 n. 77.

[2] L.C.B. Gower, *Principles of Modern Company Law* (4th ed. 1979).

[3] *Ibid.* p. 130.

[4] L.C.B. Gower, *Principles of Modern Company Law* (5th ed. 1992).

[5] *Ibid.* p. 134.

[6] In *Littlewoods Mail Order Stores Ltd.* v. *McGregor* [1969] 3 All E.R. 855 (C.A.), Karminski L.J. also appeared to regard the subsidiary's minimal issued capital (£2) as of some significance. *Ibid.* pp. 862-863. The policy considerations underlying the tax cases of course distinguish them from other lifting the veil situations.

Specifically, the legislative reforms do not adequately tackle the whole problem of undercapitalisation. There may therefore still be considerable scope for judicial law-making - although it must be said that legislative, rather than judicial, reform would be far more appropriate and desirable in this highly technical area of the law.

### 3.8.2. The position in American law

### 3.8.2.1. Introduction

The English judicial blinkers in the field of undercapitalisation contrast dramatically with the enlightened attitude adopted by American courts.[1] We have already seen that although the notion of separate legal personality is a fundamental tenet even of American law, American courts will pierce the veil in a variety of circumstances. As a general rule, American courts will avoid a rigid adherence to separate corporate personality when it is necessary to promote justice or to obviate inequitable results.[2] The liberal approach adopted by American courts has led to the development of the "instrumentality doctrine" in which the factor of undercapitalisation can play a significant role. Undercapitalisation also features in a substantial way in the equitable bankruptcy doctrines of subordination and substantive consolidation. It is to the relevance of this factor in American law that the discussion now turns.

### 3.8.2.2. Undercapitalisation and the instrumentality doctrine

It will be recalled that one of the limbs of the Powell formulation of the instrumentality test is the exercise of excessive control by the holding

---

[1] Undercapitalisation has also long been the subject of academic interest in the United States. Significant early contributions include William O. Douglas and Carrol M. Shanks, "Insulation from Liability through Subsidiary Corporations" 39 Yale L.J. 193 (1929) pp. 203-204, 214, 218; Powell, *op. cit.* s. 6(e), p. 14; Note, "Liability of Subsidiary Corporation for Debts Incurred by Parent" 43 Yale L.J. 472 (1934) p. 476; Latty, *op. cit.* Ch. V; Warner Fuller, "The Incorporated Individual : A Study of the One-Man Company" 51 Harv. L.R. 1373 (1938) pp. 1381-1383; Bernard F. Cataldo, "Limited Liability with One-Man Companies and Subsidiary Corporations" 18 Law and Contemporary Problems 473 (1953) pp. 484-485.

[2] *Vide supra* Chapter IV pp. 112-113 and Chapter V pp. 256-263.

company over its subsidiary.[1] Powell listed a number of circumstances which may indicate the subsidiary to be an instrumentality. One of these circumstances is the subsidiary's excessive dependence on the holding company for financing. Another is that the subsidiary has grossly inadequate capital.

Excessive financial dependence on the holding company - often indicative of undercapitalisation - has been deemed a prime factor in piercing the veil. A subsidiary so organised that it has to depend on its holding company's discretion for working capital,[2] or for continuing in business,[3] may be held to be a mere instrumentality of the holding company.[4] Financial dependence is seen to denote the subsidiary's lack of separate, independent existence.

In numerous cases, the failure to adequately capitalise the corporate entity has also been considered as a factor - along with others - that could contribute towards a finding of instrumentality.[5] In *DeWitt Truck Brokers* v. *W. Ray Flemming Fruit Co.*,[6] for example, the court mentioned a long list of factors to be taken into account in piercing the veil[7] but attached considerable importance to undercapitalisation, stating that "[o]ne fact which all the authorities consider significant in the inquiry, and particularly so in the case of the one-man or closely-held corporation, is whether the corporation was grossly undercapitalized for the purposes of the corporate

---

[1] *Vide supra* Chapter V pp. 259-261.

[2] E.g., *Luckenbach S.S. Co.* v. *W.R. Grace & Co.* 267 F. 676, 681 (4th Cir. 1920); *Gentry* v. *Credit Plan Corporation of Houston* 528 S.W.2d 571, 574 (Tex. 1975); *Texas Industries, Inc.* v. *Lucas* 634 S.W.2d 748, 753 (Tex. App. 1982).

[3] E.g., *Clayton Brokerage Co. of St. Louis* v. *Teleswitcher Corp.* 418 F. Supp. 83, 86 (E.D. Mo. 1976), *aff'd*, 555 F.2d 1349, 562 F.2d 1137 (8th Cir. 1977); *United States* v. *Jon-T Chemicals, Inc.* 768 F.2d 686 (5th Cir. 1985, *cert. denied*, 106 S. Ct. 1194 (1986).

[4] Other courts have refused to impose liability on the holding company notwithstanding evidence of financial dependence. *Vide* e.g., *D.L. Auld Co.* v. *Park Electrochemical Corp.* 553 F. Supp. 804, 807 (E.D.N.Y. 1982); *Edwards Company, Inc.* v. *Monogram Industries, Inc.* 730 F.2d 977, 984-985 (5th Cir. 1984).

[5] E.g., *Steven* v. *Roscoe Turner Aeronautical Corp.* 324 F.2d 157, 161 (7th Cir. 1963); *Abraham* v. *Lake Forest, Inc.* 377 So. 2d 465, 468 (La. App. 1979); *Tigrett* v. *Pointer* 580 S.W.2d 375, 382-383 (Tex. Civ. App. 1979); *Harris* v. *Curtis* 87 Cal. Rptr. 614, 619 (App. 1970); *Refco, Inc.* v. *Farm Production Association, Inc.* 844 F.2d 525, 529 (8th Cir. 1988).

[6] 540 F.2d 681 (4th Cir. 1976). The case is discussed at length in Harvey Gelb, "Piercing the Corporate Veil - the Undercapitalization Factor" 59 Chicago-Kent L.R. 1 (1982) pp. 4-15.

[7] 540 F.2d 681 (4th Cir. 1976) at pp. 684-687.

undertaking."[1] Indeed, of the many factors relevant to the holding-subsidiary relationship, "[t]he adequacy or inadequacy of the capital and financial arrangements of the subsidiary weigh heavily in the determination of liability or non-liability of the parent, greatly overshadowing the other so-called indicia of identity between the companies such as common officers, directors, office and lack of separate books."[2] And in *Amsted Industries, Inc.* v. *Pollak Industries, Inc.*[3] the court noted that where there is adequate capitalisation, other evidence as to misuse of the corporate form "pales in significance".[4]

Although the overwhelming majority of cases consider undercapitalisation to be a relevant - even an important[5] - factor, a few courts have refused to attach any relevance to it at all. In *Texas Industries, Inc.* v. *Dupuy & Dupuy Developers, Inc.*,[6] for example, the court dismissed the feature of undercapitalisation on the basis that the amount of paid-in capital was a matter of public record as part of the articles of incorporation and that the plaintiff therefore assumed the risks of the defendant's insolvency by not reviewing the articles.[7]

By contrast, trivial financing has sometimes been considered sufficient in itself to warrant the withdrawal of the protection of limited liability even where none of the other traditional factors were present.[8] Writing almost 50 years ago, Ballantine asserted:

---

[1] *Ibid.* at p. 685.

[2] William O. Douglas and Carrol M. Shanks, "Insulation from Liability through Subsidiary Corporations" 39 Yale L.J. 193 (1929) p. 218. On the relative importance of undercapitalisation, *vide* also *Anderson* v. *Abbott* 321 U.S. 349, 362 (1944); *Carlesimo* v. *Schwebel* 197 P.2d 167, 173-174 (Cal. 1948); *Automotriz Del Golfo de California S.A.* v. *Resnick* 306 P.2d 1, 4 (1957).

[3] 382 N.E.2d 393 (Ill. App. 1978).

[4] *Ibid.* at p. 399.

[5] *Carlesimo* v. *Schwebel* 197 P.2d 167, 174 (1948).

[6] 227 So. 2d 265 (La. Ct. App. 1969).

[7] *Ibid.* at p. 269. *Vide* further Patricia Carteaux, "Louisiana Adopts a Balancing Test for Piercing the Corporate Veil" 58 Tulane L.R. 1089 (1984) pp. 1093-1094 note 21; James F. Farrington Jr., "Piercing the Connecticut Corporate Veil" U. Bridgeport L.R. 109 (1983) p. 122; Note, "Piercing the Corporate Veil in Louisiana" 22 Loyola L.R. 993 (1976) p. 1012.

[8] *Minton* v. *Cavaney* 364 P.2d 473 (Cal. 1961); *Wheeler* v. *Superior Mortgage Co.* 17 Cal. Rptr. 291, 296 (1961); *Automoritz Del Golfo De California S.A.* v. *Resnick* 306 P.2d 1 (1957).

"The attempt to do corporate business without providing any sufficient basis of financial responsibility to creditors is an abuse of the separate entity and will be ineffectual to exempt the shareholders from corporate debts. It is coming to be recognized as the policy of the law that shareholders should in good faith put at the risk of the business unincumbered capital reasonably adequate for its prospective liabilities. If the capital is illusory or trifling compared with the business to be done and the risk of loss, this is a ground for denying the separate entity privilege."[1]

More recently, in *Minton v. Cavaney*,[2] a company was formed for the purpose of leasing and operating a public swimming pool. The plaintiffs' daughter drowned in the pool and the plaintiffs recovered a judgment for $10,000 against the company in a wrongful death action. When the judgment remained unsatisfied, the plaintiffs brought suit personally against the dominant shareholder. No stock was ever issued.[3] It had no assets apart from the lease of the pool. The defendant's personal office was used to keep the company's records and receive its mail. The California Supreme Court stated that "the evidence is undisputed that there was no attempt to provide adequate capitalization. [The company] never had any substantial assets. It leased the pool that it operated and the lease was forfeited for failure to pay the rent. Its capital was 'trifling compared with the business to be done and the risks of loss'".[4] The Court clearly considered this situation to be such an abuse of the privilege of incorporation that the company should be treated as the mere *alter ego* of the defendant and that he should be held personally liable. Although there were probably other grounds on which the veil could have been pierced - such as the blatant disregard of substantial corporate

---

[1] Ballantine, *op. cit.* s. 129 at pp. 302-303 (footnotes omitted).

[2] 364 P.2d 473 (Cal. 1961). This judgment is discussed in several articles. *Vide* e.g., Harvey Gelb, "Piercing the Corporate Veil - the Undercapitalization Factor" 59 Chicago-Kent L.R. 1 (1982) pp. 5, 13-14; Robert C. Downs, "Piercing the Corporate Veil - Do Corporations Provide Limited Personal Liability?" 53 UMKC L.R. 174 (1985) pp. 180-181; Philippe M. Salomon, "Limited Limited Liability : A Definitive Judicial Standard for the Inadequate Capitalisation  Problem" 47 Temple L.Q. 321 (1974) pp. 330-332; Richard S. Kohn, "Alternative Methods of Piercing the Veil in Contract and Tort" 48 Boston Univ. L.R. 123 (1968) pp. 136-138.

[3] At the time, Californian law required every stock corporation to have a stated capital (Cal. Corp. Code s. 1900) but permitted the  directors to organise and transact business prior to issuing shares (Cal. Corp. Code s. 25154). In 1977, California abolished the concept of stated capital entirely.

[4] 364 P.2d 473 (Cal. 1961) at p. 475.

formalities - it is evident that the basis of the decision was inadequate capitalisation.

Some commentators consider *Minton* v. *Cavaney* to have established inadequate capitalisation as an independent ground for shareholder liability.[1] Others, however, view that judgment merely as an "aberration" - an exception rather than the rule.[2] Even Ballantine's comments, quoted above,[3] have not escaped unscathed. One commentator has doubted whether the cases relied on by Ballantine were broad enough to justify his wide-ranging statement.[4] Another has interpreted Ballantine's analysis as being "based on his view of what the law ought to be".[5]

One matter is clear enough - that only rarely has the issue of inadequate capitalisation been afforded the conclusive weight seen in *Minton* v. *Cavaney*.[6] Indeed, some cases decided both before and after *Minton* v. *Cavaney* refute the suggestion that inadequate capitalisation could *per se* render the shareholder liable for the company's debts.[7] Some do so quite explicitly. In *Walkovszky* v. *Carlton*[8] the plaintiff was run down by a taxi owned by the defendant company. The individual defendant, Carlton, owned ten such companies, each of which owned two taxis. The companies did not own any assets, except for the taxis which were encumbered. Each taxi was covered by the minimum ($10,000) liability insurance required by state law. The court denied recovery against Carlton personally, refusing to use

---

[1] *Vide* e.g., Robert E. Dye, "Inadequate Capitalization as a Basis for Shareholder Liability : The California Approach and a Recommendation" 45 S. Cal. L.R. 823 (1972) p. 828.

[2] *Vide* e.g., Philippe M. Salomon, "Limited Limited Liability: A Definitive Judicial Standard for the Inadequate Capitalisation Problem" 47 Temple L.Q. 321 (1974) p. 331.

[3] *Supra* pp. 350-351.

[4] Howard G. Rath Jr., "Disregarding the Corporate Entity - Evidence - Inadequate Capitalisation" 30 S. Cal. L.R. 538 (1957) pp. 540-541.

[5] William P. Hackney and Tracey G. Benson, "Shareholder Liability for Inadequate Capital" 43 Univ. of Pittsburgh L.R. 837 (1982) at p. 884.

[6] E.g., *Segan Construction Corporation* v. *Nor-West Builders, Inc.* 274 F. Supp. 691, 699 (D. Conn. 1967); *Service Iron Foundry, Inc.* v. *M.A. Bell Co.* 588 P.2d 463, 475 (Kan. App. 1978); *Wheeler* v. *Superior Mortgage Co.* 17 Cal. Rptr. 291, 296 (1961); *Automoritz De Golfo De California S.A.* v. *Resnick* 306 P.2d 1 (1957).

[7] E.g., *Berkey* v. *Third Ave. Ry. Co.* 155 N.E. 58 (1926); *Bartle* v. *Home Owners Cooperative, Inc.* 127 N.E.2d 832 (App. N.Y. 1955); *Fisser* v. *International Bank* 282 F.2d 231, 240 (2d Cir. 1960); *Tigrett* v. *Pointer* 580 S.W.2d 375, 382 (Tex. Civ. App. 1979); *Harris* v. *Curtis* 87 Cal. Rptr. 614, 618-619 (App. 1970).

[8] 223 N.E.2d 6 (1966).

undercapitalisation as the sole factor justifying corporate disregard.[1] *Walkovszky* v. *Carlton* of course involved a particular issue - that of minimum insurance requirements - which perhaps enabled the court to avoid tackling the undercapitalisation argument directly. In fact, the court concentrated on the insurance aspect and, apparently impressed by the legislative requirement of liability insurance cover to a minimum level of $10,000, observed that if the insurance cover required by statute was inadequate for the protection of the public, the remedy would lie not with the courts but with the legislature.[2]

*Harris* v. *Curtis*[3] probably represents a stronger rejection of any suggestion that inadequate capitalisation alone could lead to liability. In that case, the court conceded that the company was inadequately capitalised, but bluntly remarked: "Appellants would have us declare that, per se, inadequate capitalization renders the shareholders, officers and directors liable for the obligations of the corporation. They cite no case so holding, and we know of none."[4]

An open verdict should probably be returned on the question whether inadequate capitalisation alone is sufficient to pierce the corporate veil. Courts may continue to experiment with the issue and developments can go either way. On balance, however, it must be said that most courts have insisted that inadequate capitalisation is but one of a number of factors to be taken into account.

Where the undercapitalisation has been combined with some creditor-proof plan,[5] courts have appeared more willing to impose liability on the shareholder. In *Mull* v. *Colt Co.*[6] a trivial amount of capital was provided to the company and necessary expenses were advanced through secured devices. The court considered that "it would be a gross inequity to allow

---

[1] *Ibid.* at p. 9.

[2] *Ibid.* at p. 9. In *Teller* v. *Clear Service Co., Inc.* 173 N.Y.S. 2d 183 (Sup. Ct. 1958) the court expressly stated that the filing of a bond (guaranteeing payment of any judgment up to $5,000 for injury to one person and up to $10,000 for injuries to more than one person) did not offer sufficient protection to tort victims and concluded that "true owners of most of the large fleets of taxicabs [were] using a corporate device to defraud the public". *Ibid.* at p. 190.

[3] 87 Cal. Rptr. 614 (App. 1970).

[4] *Ibid.* at pp. 617-618. Curiously, *Minton* v. *Cavaney* was not cited to the court. *Vide* also *Gartner* v. *Snyder* 607 F.2d 582, 588 (2d Cir. 1979).

[5] On the unfairness of creditor-proof plans, *vide supra* pp. 320-324.

[6] 31 F.R.D. 154 (S.D.N.Y. 1962).

such a flimsy organization to provide a shield for personal liability. Courts will not tolerate arrangements which throw all the risk on the public and which enable stockholders to reap profits while being insulated against losses."[1]

Undercapitalisation has featured both in contract[2] and tort cases.[3] A number of cases, however, have distinguished between tort and contract creditors on the basis that certain contract claimants have a choice whether or not to extend credit, whereas tort claimants are invariably involuntary creditors.[4] Undercapitalisation is of course considered irrelevant if the corporate financial position is actually known to the contract creditor at the time of contracting or if the holding company had informed the creditor that it would not be liable for the subsidiary's debts.[5]

Occasionally, the courts have stressed that the question of adequate capitalisation does not relate merely to the moment of the formation of the enterprise, but that the obligation to provide adequate capital begins with incorporation and remains a continuing obligation during the company's operations.[6] And where the scale of business operations has altered by a very substantial degree, initial adequate capitalisation may be considered irrelevant.[7] Most courts, however, have viewed the measurement date for the adequacy of capitalisation as the time of incorporation.[8]

---

[1] *Ibid.* at p. 165. *Vide* also *Dixie Coal Min. & Mfg. Co.* v. *Williams* 128 So. 799, 800 (Ala. 1930); *Wallace* v. *Tusla Yellow Cab Taxi & Baggage Co.* 61 P.2d 645, 648-649 (Okl. 1936).

[2] E.g., *Laborers Clean-Up Contract Administration Trust Fund* v. *Uriarte Clean-Up Service, Inc.* 736 F.2d 516 (9th Cir. 1984); *DeWitt Truck Brokers* v. *W. Ray Flemming Fruit Co.* 540 F.2d 681 (4th Cir. 1976); *National Marine Service, Inc.* v. *C.J. Thibodeaux & Co.* 501 F.2d 940 (5th Cir. 1974).

[3] E.g., *Mull* v. *Colt Co.* 31 F.R.D. 154 (S.D.N.Y. 1962); *Minton* v. *Caveney* 364 P.2d 473 (1961).

[4] *Vide* e.g., *Weisser* v. *Mursam Shoe Corp.* 127 F.2d 344, 347 n. 6 (2d Cir. 1942); *Gentry* v. *Credit Plan Corporation of Houston* 528 S.W.2d 571 (Tex. 1975).

[5] *Vide Abraham* v. *Lake Forest, Inc.* 377 So. 2d 465, 469 (La. Ct. App. 1980); *Bell Oil & Gas Co.* v. *Allied Chemical Corp.* 431 S.W.2d 336, 340-341 (Tex. 1968).

[6] *DeWitt Truck Brokers* v. *W. Ray Flemming Fruit Co.* 540 F.2d 681, 686 (4th Cir. 1976). Cf. *United Rubber, Cork, Linoleum & Plastic Workers of America, AFL-CIO* v. *Great American Industries, Inc.* 479 F. Supp. 216, 244 (S.D.N.Y. 1979).

[7] *In re Mader's Store for Men, Inc.* 254 N.W.2d 171, 187 (Wis. 1977).

[8] E.g., *In the Matter of Mobile Steel Co.* 563 F.2d 692, 694, 703 (5th Cir. 1977); *Laborers Clean-Up Contract Administration Trust Fund* v. *Uriarte Clean-Up Service, Inc.* 736 F.2d 516, 524 (9th Cir. 1984). *Vide* also Maurice J. Dix, "Adequate Risk Capital : The

### 3.8.2.3. Undercapitalisation and the doctrine of subordination

American bankruptcy courts are equity courts with power to examine the fairness of each claim against the estate (in particular the claims of "insiders" such as directors, officers and controlling or dominating shareholders)[1] and with power to subordinate claims or adjudicate equities arising out of the relationship between the several creditors.[2]

---

*Cont.*
Consideration for the Benefits of Separate Incorporation" 53 Northwestern Univ. L.R. 478 (1958) p. 491; Robert W. Hamilton, "The Corporate Entity" 49 Texas L.R. 979 (1971) p. 986; Harvey Gelb, "Piercing the Corporate Veil - The Undercapitalization Factor" 59 Chicago-Kent L.R. 1 (1982) pp. 17-18.

[1] *Pepper* v. *Litton* 308 U.S. 295, 307-308 (1939).

[2] *Vide Sampsell* v. *Imperial Paper & Color Corp.* 313 U.S. 215 (1941) where it was stated that "[t]he power of the bankruptcy court to adjudicate equities arising out of the relationship between the several creditors is complete." *Ibid.* at p. 219. The American courts' equitable jurisdiction to subordinate claims is expressly preserved by the Bankruptcy Code of 1978 (11 U.S.C. s. 510(c)). In England, the principle of *pari passu* distribution has statutory force (I.A. 1986, s. 107) and the court's jurisdiction to subordinate particular claims is thereby excluded. The I.A. 1986 does however make some exceptions. By s. 215(4), for example, a court making a declaration under the fraudulent and wrongful trading provisions in relation to a creditor may direct that the whole or any part of any debt owed by the company to that person be subordinated to all other debts owed by the company. Similarly, by s. 74(2)(f) a sum due to any member of the company (in his capacity as member) by way of dividends, profits or otherwise is not deemed to be a debt of the company payable to that member in a case of competition between himself and any other creditor not a member of the company. If, however, unpaid dividends have been converted into a loan, such loan will escape subordination. *Vide Re L.B. Holliday & Co. Ltd.* [1986] BCLC 227. At times, English and American law have also appeared to adopt contrasting positions with regard to *contractual* subordination. In the United States, the Bankruptcy Code of 1978 (11 U.S.C. s. 510(a)) expressly allows the enforcement of subordination agreements in bankruptcy. The English position was for a long time somewhat uncertain. Because contractual subordination arrangements purport to contract out of the statutory *pari passu* principle of distribution, they have sometimes been considered contrary to public policy. The Cork Committee clearly thought that subordination agreements were invalid, but it saw "no reason why a creditor who wished to do so should not be permitted to subordinate his claim to those of all other creditors, or all other creditors except those of a like degree." The Cork Report, para. 1449, p. 328. The Cork Committee had therefore recommended the inclusion of an appropriate proviso to the *pari passu* provisions allowing effect to be given to subordination agreements. *Ibid.* para. 1448, p. 328. (The proposal has not however been implemented.) Goode, too, concluded that debt subordination was unlawful. *Vide* R. M. Goode, *Legal Problems of Credit and Security* (2nd ed. 1988)

To allow the holding company to claim as a creditor for advances which should have been contributed as capital would be unjust to the other creditors. By postponing payment of the shareholder's claims until the claims of the other creditors are satisfied, equitable subordination effectively requires the shareholder to make such loans available for other creditors.[1] The shareholder's loans are treated as capital, elevating economic substance over legal form. Subordination operates on the assumption that the loans advanced by the shareholder are roughly equivalent to the extent of capital inadequacy, often placing outside creditors in the position they would have been had the company been adequately capitalised. Although both subordination and piercing the veil can be viewed as exceptions to the limited liability rule, the piercing the veil remedy can of course erode much deeper into the rock of limited liability. With subordination, the extent of the erosion is at least bounded by the total amount of the investment. It is understandable, therefore, that the courts have required lesser evidence of misuse of the corporate form when subordinating the shareholder's claim than when piercing the veil.[2] For this reason, undercapitalisation is possibly of greater significance in the subordination cases than it is in the piercing the veil cases.

---

*Cont.*

p. 96. Cf. Bruce Johnston, "Contractual Debt Subordination and Legislative Reform" [1991] J.B.L. 225 pp. 234-235 and 244. Another view was that the validity of a subordination depended primarily on the way the documents were drawn up. *Vide In Re British & Commonwealth Holdings plc (No 3)* [1992] BCLC 322; the Law Society Memorandum (1981) para. 4.01, p. 9; J.H. Farrar, "Negative Pledges, Debt Defeasance and Subordination of Debt" in J.H. Farrar (ed.), *Contemporary Issues in Company Law* (1987) pp. 135-158; Philip R. Wood, *The Law of Subordinated Debt* (1990); Fidelis Oditah, *Legal Aspects of Receivables Financing* (1991) pp. 172-176. John R. Powell, "Rethinking Subordinated Debt" [1993] L.M.C.L.Q. 357. More recently, in *Re Maxwell Communications Corp plc (No 2)* [1994] BCLC 1, Vinelott J., after a thorough review of the authorities, unequivocally stated that there was no principle of insolvency law or of public policy which invalidated subordination agreements. *Vide* also *Stotter* v. *Arimaru Holdings Ltd.* [1994] 2 N.Z.L.R. 655 (C.A.). For a critical appraisal of *Re Maxwell Communications Corp plc (No 2) vide* R. C. Nolan, "Less Equal Than Others - Maxwell and Subordinated Unsecured Obligations" [1995] J.B.L. 485.

[1] On subordination generally *vide Collier on Bankruptcy* (15th ed. 1994) Vol. 3, s. 510.05; Asa S. Herzog and Joel B. Zweibel, "The Equitable Subordination of Claims in Bankruptcy" 15 Vand. L.R. 83 (1961); Henn and Alexander, *op. cit.* pp. 369-372; Blumberg, *Bankruptcy Law* Ch. 4-5; Cashel, *op. cit.* pp. 35-36.

[2] William P. Hackney and Tracey G. Benson, "Shareholder Liability for Inadequate Capital" 43 Univ. of Pittsburgh L.R. 837 (1982) p. 882.

The landmark case on the status of a holding company's position as a creditor in the bankruptcy or reorganisation of its subsidiary is *Taylor* v. *Standard Gas & Electric Corporation*[1] - the so-called *Deep Rock* case.[2] The Deep Rock Oil Corporation was organised by Standard Gas & Electric Corporation. It was inadequately capitalised from its inception. Throughout its existence, Deep Rock was heavily indebted to Standard on open account. On the date of its bankruptcy the amount stood at around $9,000,000 of which about $5,000,000 represented the principal of cash advanced by Standard to Deep Rock over the years. Standard owned all of Deep Rock's common stock. Officers of Standard completely controlled Deep Rock's management. The Supreme Court disregarded the previous practice of the federal courts of allowing the holding company's claim when the subsidiary was a separate legal entity[3] and rejecting them when the subsidiary was an instrumentality.[4] Instead, the Supreme Court recognised the separate personality of the subsidiary but established a new test for subordination based on considerations of "fairness". In effect, the basis for the decision shifted from instrumentality to one of fairness. The Supreme Court held that Standard's claim should be subordinated to the claims of other creditors and preferred shareholders because it had not provided its subsidiary with adequate capital and had not allowed the subsidiary's affairs to be conducted "with an eye single to its own interests."[5] The Supreme Court appeared to have been particularly disturbed by the fact that "[f]rom the outset Deep Rock was insufficiently capitalized, was topheavy with debt and was in parlous financial condition".[6] *Deep Rock* clearly established that where a subsidiary was inadequately capitalised from the outset and was managed substantially in the interests of its holding company, rather than in its own

---

[1] 306 U.S. 307 (1939).

[2] The case has attracted much academic attention. *Vide* e.g., Carlos L. Israels, "The Implications and Limitations of the 'Deep Rock' Doctrine" 42 Colum. L.R. 376 (1942); Note, "Parent Corporation's Claims in Bankruptcy of a Subsidiary: Effect of a Fiduciary Relationship" 54 Harv. L.R. 1045 (1941).

[3] E.g., *In re Watertown Paper Co.* 169 F. 252 (2d Cir. 1909); *Duffy* v. *Treide* 75 F.2d 17 (C.C.A. 4th 1935).

[4] E.g., *In re Kentucky Wagon Mfg. Co.* 71 F.2d 802, 804 (C.C.A. 6th 1934); *Baker Motor Vehicle Co.* v. *Hunter* 238 Fed. 894, 899 (C.C.A. 2d 1916); *In re Ostego Waxed Paper Co.* 14 F. Supp. 15, 16 (W.D. Mich. 1935).

[5] 306 U.S. 307 (1939) at p. 323.

[6] *Ibid.* at p. 315. The remedy of subordination is now codified in the Bankruptcy Code (11 U.S.C. s. 510(c)).

interests, the holding company's claims will be subordinated to the claims of outside creditors and preferred stockholders.[1]

Just nine months after *Deep Rock*, the Supreme Court delivered another landmark judgment involving subordination. In *Pepper* v. *Litton*,[2] the Court enunciated in broad terms the fiduciary duties of a controlling shareholder, violation of which would result in his claims being subordinated.[3] On the question of undercapitalisation, the Court emphatically stated that "so-called loans or advances by the dominant or controlling stockholder will be subordinated to claims of other creditors and thus treated as in effect as capital contributions ... where the paid-in capital is purely nominal, the capital necessary for the scope and magnitude of the operations of the company being furnished by the stockholder as a loan."[4]

Whether - as seems to be suggested by the aforesaid dictum in *Pepper* v. *Litton* - undercapitalisation alone will involve the remedy of subordination is uncertain.[5] Only a few cases actually tackle the issue. And those that do adopt conflicting approaches and reach different conclusions. In most cases where undercapitalisation was present and subordination ordered, fraud or mismanagement were also involved and the courts did not have to decide whether undercapitalisation alone was enough to support subordination.[6] In some cases, however, both fraud and mismanagement were absent. The factor of capitalisation stood alone. In such circumstances, the courts' reaction has varied. In *Re Branding Iron Steak House*[7] a company which owned a restaurant had two shareholders. Both were directors, but only one managed the business. The other provided virtually all the required financing

---

[1] Inadequate capitalisation is only one form of misconduct that will support subordination. It is not essential for subordination. *Vide In the Matter of Mobile Steel Co.* 563 F.2d 692 (5th Cir. 1977).

[2] 308 U.S. 295 (1939).

[3] The fiduciary duties are owed to "the corporation, its stockholders and creditors." *Pepper* v. *Litton* 308 U.S. 295 (1939) at p. 311.

[4] *Ibid.* at pp. 309-310. The statement was made *obiter*, as the company in question was not in fact undercapitalised.

[5] *Vide* generally Kathleen Kinney, "Equitable Subordination of Shareholder Debt to Trade Creditors : A Reexamination" 61 Boston Univ. L.R. 433 (1981) pp. 438-441; Robert Charles Clark, "The Duties of the Corporate Debtor to its Creditors" 90 Harv. L.R. 505 (1977) pp. 534-536.

[6] E.g., *Taylor* v. *Standard Gas & Elec. Co.* 306 U.S. 307, 323 (1939); *Costello* v. *Fazio* 256 F.2d 903, 909-910 (9th Cir. 1958); *Braddy* v. *Randolph* 352 F.2d 80, 84 (4th Cir. 1965).

[7] 536 F.2d 299 (9th Cir. 1976).

through loans. The court acknowledged that the company was undercapitalised, but held that undercapitalisation alone did not amount to inequitable conduct justifying subordination of the loans. In so holding, the court implied that the fact that the creditor-shareholder did not participate in the actual management of the business precluded a finding of an inequitable exercise of control.[1] The same approach was adopted in *Re Brunner Air Compressor Corp.*[2] where the court, conceding that the company was undercapitalised[3] remanded the case to the lower court to determine whether the shareholders had made their loans in good faith. The court, emphasising the policy of encouraging investment by allowing entrepreneurs to choose how to finance their ventures, expressly stated that undercapitalisation was not *per se* indicative of the requisite inequitable exercise of control.[4]

In some cases, however, there is language suggesting that inadequate capitalisation alone is sufficient to subordinate the claims of the controlling shareholder. In *Re Fett Roofing & Sheet Metal Co.*[5] the company was undercapitalised throughout its existence and terminated its business with a debt-equity ratio of eighty-to-one.[6] It was owned and operated by a sole shareholder. The court subordinated the shareholder's claim upon a finding of undercapitalisation alone, citing *Pepper* v. *Litton* in support of its approach.[7] Undercapitalisation in itself constituted the inequitable conduct necessary for the application of subordination.[8]

The different effects of piercing the veil and subordination on the shareholder, and the greater readiness on the part of the bankruptcy court to order subordination rather than to pierce the veil are illustrated by *Arnold* v. *Phillips.*[9] In that case the original financing consisted of $50,000 in equity and $75,500 in shareholders' loans. Two years after incorporation further

---

[1] *Ibid.* at p. 302.

[2] 287 F. Supp. 256 (N.D.N.Y. 1968).

[3] *Ibid.* at p. 264.

[4] *Ibid.* at p. 264.

[5] 438 F. Supp. 726 (E.D. Va. 1977), *aff'd*, 605 F.2d 1201 (4th Cir. 1979).

[6] *Ibid.* at p. 730.

[7] *Ibid.* at pp. 729-731.

[8] Cf. also *In the Matter of Mobile Steel Co.* 563 F.2d 692 (5th Cir. 1977); *International Telephone & Tel. Corp.* v. *Holton* 247 F.2d 178 (4th Cir. 1957); *Vide* also *In re Rego Crescent Corp.* 23 Bankr. 958 (Bank. E.D.N.Y. 1982) where it was held that loans would not be subordinated unless it were shown that the debtor corporation was undercapitalised at the time the loans were made or that there was inequitable conduct.

[9] 117 F.2d 497 (5th Cir. 1941).

substantial loans were advanced. The original loan of $75,500 was later subordinated to the general creditors in the bankruptcy proceedings, the court concluding that the sum actually represented capital investment. The subsequent advances were held to be *bona fide* debt which the shareholder could claim as a corporate creditor. Moreover, the court refused to consider the company to be undercapitalised for the purposes of piercing the veil.[1]

The difference between piercing the veil and equitable subordination can also be seen by comparing two related cases : *Marsch* v. *Southern New England R. Corp.*[2] and *Centmont Corp.* v. *Marsch.*[3] In the former case, a creditor of the subsidiary was denied recovery against the holding company - the veil was not pierced. In the latter case, however, the same holding company was not allowed, on the objection of the same creditor, to share *pari passu* with that creditor in the insolvent estate of the subsidiary.

### 3.8.3. Inconsistency and imprecision in American position

Although the importance of adequate capitalisation in American jurisprudence is beyond question, considerable difficulties unfortunately arise in connection therewith. The principal difficulty, no doubt, is the lack of a consistent doctrinal pattern, with some judgments viewing undercapitalisation as *per se* sufficient to remove the shield of limited liability,[4] while many others regarding undercapitalisation as but one factor to be taken into account.[5] Confusion reigns even amongst textwriters, with some insisting that courts condition the recognition of corporateness on the establishment of an adequate financial basis,[6] and others maintaining that inadequate capitalisation remains but one factor - albeit an important one - to

---

[1] *Ibid.* at p. 502.

[2] 120 N.E. 120 (Mass. 1918).

[3] 68 F.2d 460 (C.C.A. 1st 1933), *cert. denied* 291 U.S. 680 (1934).

[4] E.g., *Minton* v. *Cavaney* 364 P.2d 473 (App. 1961). *Vide* further *supra* pp. 351-353.

[5] E.g., *Steven* v. *Roscoe Turner Aeronautical Corp.* 324 F.2d 157, 161 (7th Cir. 1963); *Abraham* v. *Lake Forest, Inc.* 377 So. 2d 465, 468 (La. App. 1979); *Tigrett* v. *Pointer* 580 S.W.2d 375, 382-383 (Tex. Civ. App. 1979). *Vide* further *supra* pp. 349-353.

[6] E.g., Norman D. Lattin, *The Law of Corporations* (1959) p. 68; Harry G. Henn, *Handbook of the Law of Corporations* (2d. ed. 1970) ss. 146-148 pp. 250-261; Ballantine, *op. cit.* s. 129 pp. 302-303; Andrew J. Natale, "Expansion of Parent Corporate Shareholder Liability Through the Good Samaritan Doctrine - a Parent Corporation's Duty to Provide a Safe Workplace for Employees of Its Subsidiary" 57 Univ. of Cin. L.R. 717 (1988) pp. 721-722.

be taken into account.[1] Clearly, veil piercing remains an uncertain prospect. Even the equitable subordination cases present similar uncertainties.[2]

Another problem is that the courts have not succeeded in establishing a definite legal standard of adequate capitalisation. In particular, the courts have been unable to define the meaning of inadequate capitalisation for different types of businesses or the level of capitalisation at which (whether alone or with other factors) the courts will intervene.[3] Although courts have made it quite clear that adequate capitalisation means capital sufficient to meet the reasonable requirements of the business[4] and that the adequacy or otherwise is to be measured by the nature and magnitude of the corporate undertaking,[5] no practical formulation has been offered by the courts.[6] Where the level of capitalisation is so low as to be virtually non-existent, there will of course be no real difficulty. But the courts have not yet convincingly dealt with the situation where significant but insufficient capital has been invested. Indeed, courts often appear to require "gross" or "obvious"[7] undercapitalisation and in so doing lessen the impact of that

---

[1] E.g., Warner Fuller, "The Incorporated Individual : A Study of the One-Man Company" 51 Harv. L.R. 1373 (1938) p. 1382; Note, "Should Shareholders Be Personally Liable for the Torts of Their Corporations" 76 Yale L.J. 1190 (1967) pp. 1193-1194; Alfred F. Conard, *Corporations in Perspective* (1976) s. 277 at p. 431; William P. Hackney and Tracey G. Benson, "Shareholder Liability for Inadequate Capital" 43 Univ. of Pittsburgh L.R. 837 (1982) p. 885.

[2] *Vide supra* pp. 358-359.

[3] *Vide* James R. Gillespie, "The Thin Corporate Line: Loss of Limited Liability Protection" 45 North Dakota L.R. 363 (1968) p. 386; Philippe M. Salomon, "Limited Limited Liability : A Definitive Judicial Standard for the Inadequate Capitalisation Problem" 47 Temple L.Q. 321 (1974) p. 321.

[4] *Vide Arnold* v. *Phillips* 117 F.2d 497 (5th Cir. 1941), *cert. denied*, 313 U.S. 583 (1941); *Ohio Edison Co.* v. *Warner Coal Corp.* 72 N.E.2d 487, 488 (App. Ohio 1946).

[5] E.g., *Anderson* v. *Abbott* 321 U.S. 349, 362 (1944); *Francis O. Day Co.* v. *Shapiro* 267 F.2d 669, 673 (1959).

[6] Commentators have suggested a number of methods by which adequate capitalisation can be measured, including financial analysis of comparable businesses and debt-equity ratios. *Vide* e.g., David H. Barber, "Piercing the Corporate Veil" 17 Williamette L.R. 371 (1981) pp. 392-394 (discussing a comparable financial analysis approach); Robert E. Dye, "Inadequate Capitalization as a Basis for Shareholder Liability : The California Approach and a Recommendation" 45 S. Cal. L.R. 823 (1972) at pp. 842-843 (suggesting debt-equity ratios as a guideline).

[7] E.g., *Anderson* v. *Abbott* 321 U.S. 349, 362 (1974); *Fisser* v. *International Bank* 282 F.2d 231, 240 (2d Cir. 1960).

factor. Nor have the courts given suitable guidance with regard to those situations where sufficient capital had once been injected but was lost or diminished by the time the claim was made.[1] The truth is that most cases that have come before the courts have involved relatively easy circumstances where the company had trifling or no capital and continued in that condition throughout its existence. Such cases may explain the zealous remarks in the judgments but do not provide guidance for the less severe cases.

Moreover, the courts sometimes appear to confuse a low equity capital with inadequate financing. In *Harris* v. *Curtis*,[2] for example, a company was organised with a stated capital of $1,000 of which $811 were used for the expenses of incorporation. With funds borrowed principally from banks but partly guaranteed by the shareholders, the company proceeded to construct a motel and to purchase an adjacent restaurant and other property. A third party then took an option to purchase the shares of the company and loaned to it a sum of $19,000. When the company defaulted on the loan, the third party claimed against the company and its shareholders for the outstanding balance. The court conceded that the company was underfinanced, but, noting that corporate formalities had been complied with and that there was no evidence that the company had been used for the private affairs of the shareholders, concluded that the undercapitalisation factor alone was not sufficient to render the shareholders, officers and directors *per se* liable for the debts of the company.[3] The third party obtained judgment against the company but not against the individual shareholders. Unfortunately, in its assessment on the adequacy or otherwise of corporate capitalisation the court seemed to place too much emphasis on the issued capital and too little on the other methods of financing that were utilised.

A final criticism that may be levelled at the American position is that despite the significant differences between voluntary and involuntary claimants,[4] undercapitalisation has featured almost indiscriminately in both contract and tort cases.[5]

---

[1] Contrast for e.g., *Pierson* v. *Jones* 625 P.2d 1085, 1087 (1981) with *United States* v. *Healthwin-Midtown Convalescent Hospital and Rehabilitation Center, Inc.* 511 F. Supp. 416, 419 (C.D. Cal. 1981).

[2] 87 Cal. Rptr. 614 (App. 1970).

[3] *Ibid.* pp. 617-619.

[4] *Vide supra* Chapter IV pp. 176-186.

[5] *Vide supra* p. 354.

## 4. PROPOSAL FOR REFORM

So far, this chapter has revealed (i) the abuse and unfairness involved in the undercapitalised subsidiary situation, and (ii) the inadequacy of English law in dealing with such abuse and unfairness. The need for reform is self-evident.[1] This last section of the chapter will set out a proposal for reform. The proposal will first be expressed briefly. Its various aspects will then be discussed in turn.

### 4.1. Statement of principle

Concisely stated, the basic proposal comprises the following propositions:

(i) When setting up a subsidiary, the holding company should be obliged to provide it with sufficient funds to enable it to meet the reasonable requirements of the business.

(ii) Such funds need not be advanced by way of share capital but could be supplied as debt.

(iii) A reasonable portion of the financing supplied by the holding company should be treated as "risk" capital.

(iv) On the subsidiary's insolvency, the holding company's claim to such portion of the financing qualifying as "risk" capital should be subordinated to the claims of outside creditors.

---

[1] Calls for reform to deal specifically with the problem of undercapitalisation have only rarely been made. Over 30 years, however, Wedderburn had suggested that "[e]xperience in the United States ought surely to encourage us ... to experiment with the removal of the corporate mask in cases of undercapitalisation. A statute could empower the court in any case where it seemed that inadequate capital had been put into the enterprise to ignore the 'personality' of the company to the extent needed to produce a just result." K.W. Wedderburn, "A Corporations Ombudsman?" 23 M.L.R. 663 (1960) at p. 667 (footnote omitted). More recently, the Cork Report recognised the abuse of undercapitalisation and recommended the deferment of intercompany indebtedness on the subsidiary's insolvency (the Cork Report, Ch. 51).

(v) If the holding company fails to supply the subsidiary with adequate financing as aforesaid, the holding company should, on the subsidiary's insolvency, become liable for the debts of its subsidiary, up to an amount determinable by the court in its discretion, provided that the holding company shall always be liable at least to an amount equivalent to the "risk" capital reasonably required.[1]

The above proposal will, it is submitted, effectively remedy the abuse and unfairness inherent in all the three forms of inadequate financial organisation identified earlier in this chapter, that is: the provision of inadequate financing in whatever form, the use of excessive debt in proportion to equity, and the engagement of creditor-proof strategies. The implementation of the reform proposal will not, it is submitted, negative the social and economic virtues of limited liability.

## 4.2. Various aspects of the proposal

Several aspects of the proposal require elaboration and discussion. This exercise will be conducted in the remaining pages of this chapter.

### 4.2.1. Requirement of insolvency

An essential feature of the proposal is that the remedy of subordination and the imposition of liability on the holding company will only be activated once the subsidiary has gone into insolvent liquidation. It is only at that stage that the harm to creditors, which the proposal seeks to redress, can actually be determined and quantified. As long as the subsidiary continues to honour its commitments and to settle its debts, the need for redress does not arise. Indeed, to trigger the remedy during the subsidiary's insolvency would also encourage litigation and increase costs without any corresponding benefit. In addition, the requirement of insolvency would ensure consistency and

---

[1] While subordination alone may compensate for the inadequate capitalisation when a holding company has substantial claims against its subsidiary, the holding company may never have had such claims or may have reduced them during the subsidiary's pre-insolvency existence. Where subordination is insufficient to make up for the inadequacy, a contribution from the holding company would be required.

harmonisation not just with the other "veil piercing" remedies of the Insolvency Act 1986 (such as the fraudulent and wrongful trading provisions[1] and the provisions on transactions at an undervalue and preferences[2]) but also with the proposal for reform set out in an earlier chapter to deal with the subservient subsidiary problem.[3] Finally, and again in line with the recommendations made in respect of the subservient subsidiary problem, a balance sheet - rather than a cash flow - test of insolvency should be utilised to determine insolvency.[4]

### 4.2.2. Complementary remedies

The proposed remedies will naturally be complementary to the other remedies potentially applicable on insolvency. It may of course happen that a particular holding-subsidiary relationship triggers off three different remedies, say, the subservient subsidiary remedy, the undercapitalised subsidiary remedy and even the wrongful trading provisions. In the event of such overlapping remedies, the court should have a discretion to determine the holding company's overall exposure to liability.

### 4.2.3. Measuring adequate capitalisation

Undoubtedly, the most difficult aspect of the proposal is the measurement of adequate financing and "risk" capital. Two questions arise. First, how is the holding company to determine what amount of financing will be sufficient to enable the subsidiary company to meet the reasonable requirements of the business? Second, on what basis is the holding company to determine what portion of the financing supplied is to be treated as "risk" capital?[5] These are admittedly perplexing questions. In view of the difficulties involved, some institutions and commentators have in fact argued against the

---

[1] ss. 213 and 214 respectively.

[2] ss. 238 and 239 respectively.

[3] *Vide supra* Chapter V pp. 301-302.

[4] *Vide* further *supra* Chapter V pp. 301-302.

[5] In any eventual litigation on liability or subordination, these questions would of course have to be determined by the courts.

imposition of liability for undercapitalisation.[1] Moreover, fears have been expressed that the vagueness of the concept could have a chilling effect on corporate investment.[2] But to allow the complexity of the issues to dishearten the search for a solution is to enable abuse and unfairness to endure. Workable solutions must - and can - be found. Of course, care must be taken to prevent the "benefit of hindsight" from playing too dominant a role in determining the adequacy of financing arrangements. But the law should not be deterred or discouraged from drawing lines.

### 4.2.3.1. Adequate financing

It would not be realistic to impose upon a holding company the obligation to provide the subsidiary with adequate financing unless the holding company can, in practice, determine the type and level of financing required. There is in fact no doubt that such an exercise can be effected without any undue difficulty. Whenever a business is to be set up, the promoters (in our case, the holding company) can, and often do, carry out a study to assess the short- and long-term financing requirements of the proposed business. The aim of the exercise would be to determine the amount of financing required to enable the subsidiary to generate sufficient cash flow from revenues and other sources to cover the reasonably anticipated costs and expenses of the business. The study would take into account several factors that would usually have a bearing on the financial requirements of the business, including start-up costs, estimates of income and expenditure, turnover, cash-flow, interest payments, foreseeable hazards and business risks. Few businesses are unique. Financial managers can in fact often examine the financial structures of similar organisations to arrive at a realistic assessment of adequate financing for their particular business.[3] Such an analysis will provide a reasonably accurate indication of whether the contractual obligations of the company will be covered.

---

[1] *Vide* e.g., The Law Society Memorandum (1981) para. 2.02 pp. 5-6; David C. Cummins, "Disregarding the Corporate Entity : Contract Claims" 28 Ohio State L.J. 441 (1967) p. 459-460; Robert C. Downs, "Piercing the Corporate Veil - Do Corporations Provide Limited Personal Liability?" 53 UMKC L.R. 174 (1985) pp. 185-189.

[2] E.g., *In re Brunner Air Compressor Corp.* 287 F. Supp. 256, 265-266 (N.D.N.Y. 1968). The difficulty of measuring adequate capitalisation and the possible negative effect on investment may explain the American courts' willingness to pierce the corporate veil only in cases of *gross* undercapitalisation.

[3] Cf. *In re Lumber, Inc.* 124 F. Supp. 302, 307 (D. Or. 1954).

In practice many holding companies do actually carry out such studies.[1] Most holding companies are probably able to engage "in-house" expertise to prepare the study. If such expertise is not available, the holding company can engage professional personnel to carry out the assignment. Expert advice is both available and reliable, although it may, admittedly, be costly. A properly conducted study would clearly identify the type and level of financing required in order to secure a fair chance of success for the venture.

The carrying out of such studies should be viewed not merely as a matter of financial prudence but also as a legal obligation.[2] Once the question of financing has been determined, it would then be incumbent upon the holding company to ensure that such financing is made available to the subsidiary. Otherwise, the project should be aborted. Obliging promoters to undertake such a study will have the positive effect of applying the brakes on some overly sanguine dream projects. On the other hand, of course, due allowance will have to be made for a reasonable degree of optimism that often spurs promoters into pursuing a business venture. In determining the adequacy of financing, comparison could properly be made with other business of a similar size and nature.[3]

It should be stressed that the holding company's obligation to provide the subsidiary with adequate financing does not involve an obligation to provide the subsidiary with a pool of assets sufficiently large to meet *all* claims, tort and contract, which might arise. The obligation is only to furnish such funds as would enable the subsidiary to meet the reasonable and predictable requirements of the business.[4] If the subsidiary has been provided with such a level of financing, then the risk that certain claims may not be satisfied (or at least not be satisfied in full) can justifiably be shifted onto the creditors. Tort creditors, in particular, would remain at risk. Thus, despite a rule of adequate financing, tort creditors - whose claims may well exceed the net asset value of an adequately financed company - may still be left without adequate compensation. The solution to the tort creditors' plight in such

---

[1] Such planning would be customary for the large and medium sized corporate groups. The likelihood of such planning probably diminishes progressively with the size of the group.

[2] For a broadly similar proposal *vide* R.P. Brooker, "Company Law Reform : Is Unlimited Liability Likely to be Effective?" 3 Solicitor Quarterly 239 (1964) pp. 248-249.

[3] Charles Rembar, "Claims against Affiliated Companies in Reorganisation" 39 Colum. L.R. 907 (1939) p. 915.

[4] *Vide In Re Mader's Store for Men, Inc.* 254 N.W.2d 171, 188 (Wis. 1977).

circumstances may lie in some other arrangement, such as compulsory liability insurance or a national accident-compensation scheme.

Some commentators, it should be noted, have argued that a company should not be considered to be adequately capitalised if its financing does not bear any relation to the actual risks (usually of accident-related claims) that it poses to the public.[1] Such commentators would argue that the ability of the company to provide compensation for such injuries should be an important factor in determining the adequacy of financing. A major difficulty with such an approach is that it is often practically impossible to assess the extent of the risk to the public. Besides, such an approach would involve funds being tied up unproductively. Again, compulsory insurance or accident-compensation schemes would offer a more realistic protection to most tort victims while preserving the policy advantages of limited liability especially in the context of high risk activities.

In assessing the adequacy or otherwise of financing, the company's performance history should offer persuasive evidence. Thus, the successful operation of the business for a number of years would be persuasive evidence that the subsidiary was adequately financed.[2] On the other hand, insolvency within a year or two is evidence that the financing may have been inadequate.[3] There may even be a role in the legislative reform for the introduction of rebuttable presumptions.

### 4.2.3.2. "Risk" capital

While it is essential that the subsidiary be provided with adequate funds to conduct its business,[4] the financing need not all be considered as "risk" capital. The difficulty is to establish a test which can, within reasonably accurate limits, be used to determine the level of "risk" capital required. For if the contribution of adequate "risk" capital is to be made obligatory, it is essential that the law provide a workable standard that will allow the holding company to make a reasonably precise judgement on its exposure to liability.

---

[1] *Vide* e.g., Richard S. Kohn, "Alternative Methods of Piercing the Veil in Contract and Tort" 48 Boston Univ. L.R. 123 (1968) pp. 138-139.

[2] *Vide In re Branding Iron Steak House* 536 F.2d 299, 302 (9th Cir. 1976); *In re Lumber, Inc.* 124 F. Supp. 302, 307-308 (D. Or. 1954).

[3] *Vide* e.g., *Costello* v. *Fazio* 256 F.2d 903 (9th Cir. 1958); *Baker Motor Vehicle Co.* v. *Hunter* 238 F. 894 (2d Cir. 1916).

[4] *Vide supra* p. 309.

There can, of course, be no mathematically exact formula for determining adequate "risk" capital. But a principle can, it is submitted, be evolved to provide sufficient guidance to holding companies and the courts. In principle, the "risk" capital should correspond to the long-term capital requirements of the subsidiary. Various criteria can be used to distinguish capital contributions from other advances. If the funds are advanced with a reasonable expectation of repayment, they should be treated as a loan. If, on the other hand the funds are risked upon the success of the venture, they should be considered as capital contributions.[1] To require that much risk investment does not appear unreasonable. When the law replaces a general fund (that is unlimited responsibility) with a special fund (that is the company's capital), as a source from which creditors are to be paid, it should expect not only that such a fund exists, but that such fund normally answers the capital requirements of the business.[2] The holding company must, to achieve limited liability, assume a reasonable proportion of the business risk. It must provide the subsidiary with a permanent capital reasonable for its needs in the light of the business to be undertaken. The alternative is to throw the risk of doing business entirely on third parties.

Several factors may be relevant to the determination of the question whether funds are advanced as loan or as "risk" capital. These include: (i) the expectation of payment; (ii) the debt-equity ratio; (iii) the use made of the loan; (iv) the nomenclature chosen by the parties, the terms on which the advance was made and the length of time for which it has been outstanding; (v) the existence of proportionality of advances with equity holdings; (vi) whether outsiders would make such advances; (vii) the subsidiary's borrowing and earnings history; and (viii) the motive of the parties. A court would have to weigh these factors in the light of the particular circumstances before it.

Before elaborating on these factors, it should be noted that the issue of characterising debt as equity plays a significant role in taxation, both at the

---

[1] Cf. *Nassau Lens Co.* v. *Commissioner* 308 F.2d 39, 47 (2d Cir. 1962); *Affiliated Research, Inc.* v. *United States* 351 F.2d 646, 648 (Ct. Cl. 1965). No distinction should be made between contributions in money and contributions in property.

[2] Latty, *op. cit.* p. 120. *Vide* also Maurice J. Dix, "The Economic Entity" 22 Fordham L.R. 254 (1953) p. 269; Philippe M. Salomon, "Limited Limited Liability : A Definitive Judicial Standard for the Inadequate Capitalisation  Problem" 47 Temple L.Q. 321 (1974) p. 339.

domestic as well as at the international level.[1] A brief explanation of the tax implications is called for. As a general rule, the tax treatment of interest-bearing debt often differs from that of equity capital. Interest-bearing debt normally yields a particular tax advantage : the interest on the debt will be an allowable deduction for corporate tax purposes in the borrowing company's hands. Dividend payments, on the other hand, will not usually qualify for a deduction against the profits of the borrowing company. The advantages to a corporate group are plain. If the holding company decides to provide funds to a subsidiary almost entirely by way of debt, the subsidiary's tax liability may be substantially reduced compared with the situation where the same funds are provided as equity capital. In an international context, tax authorities are concerned about the loss of tax revenue through the repatriation of profits to other countries by means of interest on debt rather than dividends on equity capital. As a result, the tax legislation of many countries includes "thin capitalisation" provisions in their tax laws empowering the tax authorities to scrutinise the financing arrangements and allowing debt to be recharacterised as equity in appropriate circumstances.[2] The difference in tax treatment between debt and equity may be of considerable relevance even in a purely domestic context.

Some jurisdictions tackle the issue of thin capitalisation by specifically providing for fixed debt-equity ratios beyond which a company will be treated as thinly capitalised.[3] This approach has the merit of certainty. Other jurisdictions, preferring flexibility over certainty, have no fixed ratios but have adopted thin capitalisation provisions which treat as distributions (broadly similar to dividends) "interest payments which exceed those which would have been made between parties acting at arm's length either by reference to the amount of interest due on the debt itself or by reference to

---

[1] *Vide* generally Organisation for Economic Co-Operation and Development, Issues in International Taxation No. 2 - Thin Capitalisation (1987) (hereinafter cited as "OECD Report on Thin Capitalisation (1987)").

[2] *Vide* generally, the OECD Report on Thin Capitalisation (1987) pp. 14-16. The OECD Report deals extensively with the tax implications of equity or debt financing, the tax policy aspects related to equity or debt financing, the main alternative approaches to the thin capitalisation provisions and the interaction between the thin capitalisation provisions in domestic tax law and double tax treaties that are patterned on the OECD Model Convention. The OECD Report also makes some broad policy recommendations on the nature of the thin capitalisation provisions in domestic tax legislation.

[3] *Vide* Amanda K. Rowland, "Thin Capitalization in the United Kingdom" 49 Bulletin for International Fiscal Documentation" 554 (1995).

the fact that the loan would never have been granted by an independent lender."[1] Payments qualifying as distributions are not deductible in computing the paying company's taxable income for corporation tax purposes.

The principal provisions on thin capitalisation in the United Kingdom are found in the Income and Corporation Taxes Act 1988, as substantially modified by the Finance Act of 1995. Prior to the changes introduced by the Finance Act 1995 certain interest payments on loans and securities were treated as distributions for tax purposes. Section 209 of the Income and Corporation Taxes Act 1988 in fact used to treat interest paid on securities issued by a company as a distribution  if the securities were held by a company not resident in the United Kingdom and if either of the following conditions are satisfied: (i) the issuing company is a 75% subsidiary of the non-resident company or both are 75% subsidiaries of a third company that is not resident in the United Kingdom; or (ii) both the issuing company and the non-resident company are 75% subsidiaries of a third company that is resident in the United Kingdom, but less than 90% of the share capital of the issuing company is directly owned by a company resident in the United Kingdom.[2]

These provisions have now been replaced by a rule[3] treating as distributions interest payments made between companies in specific circumstances. The rule will apply where the issuer and holder of the security are 75% subsidiaries of a third company or where the issuer is a 75% subsidiary of the holder.[4] If that relationship exists and "the whole or any part of the distribution represents an amount which would not have fallen to be paid to the other company if the companies had been companies between whom there was ... no relationship, arrangement or other connection (whether formal or informal)"[5] the interest payment, to the extent only that it

---

[1] *Ibid.* at p. 554.

[2] s. 209(2)(e)(iv) and (v). Many double taxation treaties contain a provision that rules of domestic law which treat as a distribution only interest paid to a non-resident company should not apply to interest payments to which the treaty applies. In such cases, the provisions of s. 209(2)(e)(iv) and (v) would be inapplicable. *Vide* e.g., Article 11(7) of the United Kingdom - United States Double Taxation Treaty. *Vide* further Amanda K. Rowland, "Thin Capitalization in the United Kingdom" 49 Bulletin for International Fiscal Documentation" 554 (1995) pp. 554-555.

[3] s. 209(2)(*da*) of the Income and Corporation Taxes Act 1988, introduced by s. 87 of the Finance Act 1995.

[4] s. 209(2)(*da*)(i) of the Income and Corporation Taxes Act 1988.

[5] s. 209(2)(*da*)(ii) of the Income and Corporation Taxes Act 1988.

is such an amount, will be treated as a distribution.[1] United Kingdom tax law has therefore maintained a flexible approach and no definite debt-equity ratio or other precise test has been introduced.

Unfortunately, the new provisions furnish no guidelines as to what constitutes a "relationship, arrangement or other connection". The notion is so widely drafted that its limits can only start to be delineated either when the Inland Revenue publishes practice statements or correspondence or when there is case-law on the matter.[2]

In order to determine whether the amount of interest exceeds that which would have been paid in the absence of the "relationship", reference could be made to section 808A of the Income and Corporation Taxes Act 1988 which had been introduced in 1992 to provide guidance on the interpretation of the "special relationship" provisions commonly found in double tax treaties. Section 808A provides that in determining the amount of interest which would have been paid in respect of the security in the absence of the "relationship" all factors are to be taken into account, including (i) whether the loan would have been made or the security issued; (ii) the amount, if any, of the loan; and (iii) the rate of interest and other terms that would have been agreed upon. In considering all the factors, no account is however to be taken in respect of certain specified matters (noted below), of any other relationship, connection or arrangements between the issuer and any person except where the other person: (i) is not "connected" with the issuer; or (ii) is a member of the same United Kingdom group as the issuer. The specified matters which, in such circumstances, could be taken into account are: (i) the appropriate level of overall indebtedness for the issuer; (ii) whether it might have been expected that the issuer and another person would enter into a transaction involving the issue of a security, the making of a loan or a loan of a particular amount; and (iii) the rate of interest and other terms which might be expected to be applicable.[3]

---

[1] Where a double tax treaty applies in relation to interest payments, the treaty provisions will take precedence over the provisions of the Income and Corporation Taxes Act 1988.

[2] Amanda K. Rowland, "Thin Capitalization in the United Kingdom" 49 Bulletin for International Fiscal Documentation" 554 (1995) p. 556. *Vide* also Amanda K. Rowland, "Impenetrable Drafting" Taxation, 6th April 1995 pp. 9-12.

[3] For a detailed discussion on these provisions *vide* Amanda K. Rowland, "Thin Capitalization in the United Kingdom" 49 Bulletin for International Fiscal Documentation" 554 (1995) p. 556 and Amanda K. Rowland, "Impenetrable Drafting" Taxation, 6th April 1995 p. 10.

In the United States, debt financing may attract favourable tax treatment. First, the company obtains a deduction for interest paid on indebtedness[1] whereas dividends come out of after-tax earnings.[2] Second, repayment of debt principal is a tax-free recovery of capital to the creditor, whereas the redemption of shares is often taxed as dividend rather than as recovery of capital.[3] Thirdly, the allowable deduction for losses sustained on stock investment in any one year is limited,[4] whereas bad debts are fully deductible if incurred in the taxpayer's trade or business.[5] The Internal Revenue Code however seeks to ensure that taxpayers cannot, by choosing a particular form of transaction, in effect choose the type of tax for which they are liable.[6] If a company is too thinly capitalised, the purported loans may be treated as capital contributions for tax purposes. The company, for example, will not then be able to deduct the interest payments. In addition, repayments of principal may be treated as dividends to the shareholders. In line with this approach, a new section 385 of the Code, adopted in 1969,[7] attempted to distinguish between debt and equity instruments and authorised the Secretary to the Treasury to prescribe rules for distinguishing debt from equity.[8]

---

[1] Internal Revenue Code, s. 163(a).

[2] Internal Revenue Code, ss. 11(a), 301 and 316.

[3] Internal Revenue Code, s. 302.

[4] Internal Revenue Code, ss. 165(f)-(g), 1211 and 1212.

[5] Internal Revenue Code, s. 166.

[6] H.R. Rep. No. 1337, 83d Cong., 2d Sess. 39 (1954).

[7] By the Tax Reform Act 1969, Pub. L. No. 91-172, Title IV, s. 415(a), 83 Stat. 613.

[8] s. 385 provides :

(a) The Secretary [of the Treasury] is authorized to prescribe such regulations as may be necessary or appropriate to determine whether an interest in a corporation is to be treated for purposes of this title as stock or indebtedness (or as in part stock and in part indebtedness).

(b) The regulations prescribed under this section shall set forth factors which are to be taken into account in determining with respect to a particular factual situation whether a debtor-creditor relationship exists or a corporation-shareholder relationship exists. The factors so set forth in the regulations may include among other factors :

(1) whether there is a written unconditional promise to pay on demand or on a specified date a sum certain in money in return for an adequate consideration in money or money's worth, and to pay a fixed rate of interest,

(2) whether there is subordination to or preference over any indebtedness of the corporation,

(3) the ratio of debt to equity of the corporation,

(4) whether there is convertibility into the stock of the corporation, and

Efforts by the Treasury or Congress to identify exclusive criteria have not however proved very successful.[1] In the absence of an acceptable regulatory scheme, courts have attempted to formulate their own standards and have done so primarily by resorting to the pre-section 385 standards.[2]  A substantial body of American case law (both pre- and post-section 385) has in fact developed dealing with the recharacterisation of debt into equity capital for tax purposes. Unfortunately, the federal courts have failed to establish a consistent, uniform test on the matter.[3] Despite such shortcomings, it is submitted that the tax materials *do* provide some useful guidance in formulating the criteria suggested in this work for characterising debt as "risk" capital. This is so even though the legislative provisions and the tax cases obviously deal with policy issues inherently distinct from the liability question with which this work is concerned. Significantly, the sophisticated analysis developed in the tax cases has, to some extent (and usually in the context of "close corporations"), been adopted in the American subordination cases.

The factors that should be taken into account in determining whether funds are advanced as loan or as "risk" capital are now considered in turn.

*Cont.*

(5) the relationship between holdings of stock in the corporation and holdings of the interest in question.

[1] *Vide* Paul R. Erickson, "Capitalization of Close Corporations After 1980" 17 Idaho L.R. 139 (1980).

[2] *Vide* generally Margaret A. Gibson, "The Intractable Debt/Equity Problem : A New Structure for Analyzing Shareholder Advances" 81 Northwestern U.L.R. 452 (1987) pp. 452-453. For the pre-section 385 position (which is still largely relevant) *vide* Martin J. Kurzer, "Thin Incorporation : A Continuing Problem" 51 Marquette L.R. 158 (1968); James H. McLean, "Thin Corporations - Advantages and Pitfalls" 14 The Practical Lawyer 81 (1968); Eli Gerver, "De-emphasis of debt-equity test for thin corporations requires new defense tactics" 23 Journal of Taxation 28 (1965); Lehman C. Aarons, "Debt vs Equity - special hazards in setting up the corporate capital structure" 23 Journal of Taxation 194 (1965).

[3] *Vide* Margaret A. Gibson, "The Intractable Debt/Equity Problem : A New Structure for Analyzing Shareholder Advances" 81 Northwestern U.L.R. 452 (1987) pp. 453, 461-465; Martin J. Kurzer, "Thin Incorporation : A Continuing Problem" 51 Marquette L.R. 158 (1968) pp. 160-161, 168; Stuart M. Weis, "The Labyrinth of the Thin Corporation" 40 Taxes 568 (1962) p. 589; Frederic W. Hickman, "The Thin Corporation : Another Look at an Old Disease" 44 Taxes 883 (1966) p. 885; Samuel Davis Cheris, "Stockholder Loans and the Debt-Equity Distinction" 22 Stanford L.R. 847 (1970) pp. 847, 850-851.

## (i) Reasonable expectation of payment

Given that an essential conceptual difference between loan and equity is that normally a loan is made upon the reasonable assumption that it will be repaid no matter whether the business venture is successful or not, while capital is put to the risk of the business,[1] a reasonable expectation of payment should be required if the advance is to qualify as a loan. If funds are advanced without a reasonable expectation of payment but are, in "substantial economic reality"[2] risked upon the success of the venture, the advance should actually be viewed as capital.[3] In the United States, this factor has been considered relevant in both the tax[4] and the bankruptcy subordination cases.[5] Objective criteria can be utilised to test the reasonableness of the expectation, including the adequacy of the capital structure (and in particular the debt-equity ratio),[6] the existence of a fixed maturity date for the repayment,[7] and the willingness of third parties to advance loans to the company.[8]

## (ii) Debt-equity ratio

An important factor in identifying an adequate level of risk capital within the total funds advanced to a subsidiary is its debt-equity ratio.[9] Where the debtor company is too thinly capitalised, the likelihood is that a business loss would result in an inability to repay advances made to the company.[10] An advance made to such a thinly capitalised company savours of risk capital rather than loan.[11] By contrast, a debt-holder's position is obviously more

[1] *Vide supra* p. 310.

[2] *Gilbert* v. *Commissioner* 248 F.2d 399, 407 (2d Cir. 1957).

[3] *Vide* Asa S. Herzog and Joel B. Zweibel, "The Equitable Subordination of Claims in Bankruptcy" 15 Vand. L.R. 83 (1961) p. 94.

[4] E.g., *Gilbert* v. *Commissioner* 248 F.2d 399, 406-407 (2d Cir. 1957).

[5] E.g., *In re Transystems, Inc.* 569 F.2d 1364, 1370 (5th Cir. 1978); *L & M Realty Corp.* v. *Leo* 249 F.2d 668, 670 (4th Cir. 1957).

[6] *Vide post* pp. 375-378.

[7] *Vide post* pp. 378-379.

[8] *Vide post* pp. 380-381.

[9] The debt-equity ratio has certainly been an important element in the tax cases. *Vide* e.g., *Bruce* v. *Knox* 180 F. Supp. 907, 912 (D. Minn. 1960); *Liflans Corp.* v. *United States* 390 F.2d 965, 969-970 (Ct. Cl. 1968).

[10] *Bauer* v. *Commissioner* 748 F.2d 1365, 1369 (9th Cir. 1984).

[11] *Bauer* v. *Commissioner* 748 F.2d 1365, 1369 (9th Cir. 1984).

secure if there is a cushion at the equity level. As a rule, more assets will be available to support additional loans if the company has a low debt-equity ratio. Indeed, banks and other institutional creditors routinely examine the debt-equity ratio to determine whether the debtor-company is too thinly capitalised.[1]

In computing the subsidiary's debt-equity ratio all outstanding debt should be included even though only insider debt is being tested.[2] Moreover, the equity should include not just issued capital but also retained earnings.[3]

The difficulty, of course, is to establish what constitutes an excessive debt-equity ratio. In the American tax cases, a ratio of 5:1 or less does not usually result in equity characterisation.[4] Indeed, in the many cases where debt was reclassified as equity, the debt-equity ratio was inordinately high.[5] Sometimes, however, even a considerably high debt-to-equity ratio did not, in the circumstances, lead to equity characterisation.[6] Yet there have been cases where debt was treated as equity even when the ratio was 10:1 or less.[7] And occasionally it has been held that the debt-equity ratio is not relevant to the question of classification.[8] The point is that the courts will view the debt-equity ratio as only one of the factors to be taken into account.

The debt-equity ratio has been considered relevant even in a number of American bankruptcy cases. In *Re Fett Roofing & Sheet Metal Co.,*[9] for

[1] Samuel Davis Cheris, "Stockholder Loans and the Debt-Equity Distinction" 22 Stanford L.R. 847 (1970) p. 852.

[2] *Vide The Motel Co.* v. *Commissioner* 340 F.2d 445, 446 (2d Cir. 1965).

[3] *Vide Bauer* v. *Commissioner* 748 F.2d 1365, 1368 (9th Cir. 1984).

[4] E.g., *John Kelley Co.* v. *Commissioner* 326 U.S. 521, 524 (1946) (4:1); *Bauer* v. *Commissioner* 748 F.2d 1365 (9th Cir. 1985) (2.15:1).

[5] E.g., *Pocatello Coca-Cola Bottling Co.* v. *United States* 139 F. Supp. 912, 916 (D. Idaho 1956) (24:1); *Affiliated Research, Inc.* v. *United States* 351 F.2d 646, 650 (Ct. Cl 1965) (131:1); *In re Indian Lake Estates, Inc.* 448 F.2d 574, 579 (5th Cir. 1971) (35:1).

[6] E.g., *Liflans Corp.* v. *United States* 390 F.2d 965 (Ct. Cl. 1968) (17:1 - 2:1); *Sun Properties, Inc.* v. *United States* 220 F.2d 171, 172, 175 (5th Cir. 1955) (310:1). An extreme case is *Byerlite Corp.* v. *Williams* 286 F.2d 285, 287, 290 (6th Cir. 1960) where the court held a ratio of 18,800:1 acceptable.

[7] E.g., *Beaver Pipe Tools, Inc.* v. *Carey* 240 F.2d 843 (6th Cir. 1957) (10:1); *Vide* also *Gooding Amusement Co.* v. *Commissioner* 236 F.2d 159 (6th Cir. 1956). And in *Brake & Electric Sales Corp.* v. *United States* 287 F.2d 426 (1st Cir. 1961) it was acknowledged that the absence of a disproportionate debt-equity ratio was not controlling.

[8] E.g., *Rowan* v. *United States* 219 F.2d 51, 55 (5th Cir. 1955); *Sun Properties, Inc.* v. *United States* 220 F.2d 171, 175 (5th Cir. 1955).

[9] 438 F. Supp. 726, 730 (E.D. Va. 1977) *aff'd* 605 F.2d 1201 (4th Cir. 1979).

example, a debt-equity ratio of 80:1 helped the court to conclude that the capital was inadequate.[1] And in *Tigrett* v. *Pointer*[2] evidence that the controlling shareholder had advanced loans totalling more than 400 times the initial capitalisation was taken by the court to be conclusive proof that the initial capitalisation was inadequate.[3] There have however also been cases where the courts have refused to subordinate the holding company's claim where the ratio was 10 to 1.[4]

A company's debt-equity ratio should be examined both in relation to the industry-wide standard and in relation to the particular characteristics of the individual subsidiary.[5] A debt-equity ratio considerably higher than the average for the particular type of business would be strong evidence of undercapitalisation. An obvious difficulty with using an industry-wide standard is that companies vary in their financial requirements even within the same industry.[6] Another problem is that it may be difficult to find an enterprise which is really comparable.

Where the subsidiary's ratio deviates from the average for the particular type of business, the financial characteristics of the subsidiary should be scrutinised. A number of factors need to be taken into account to determine the standard debt-equity ratio for the particular subsidiary. Thus, a subsidiary guaranteed of a relatively stable demand can afford heavier debt-financing. A subsidiary engaged in more speculative activities will however require greater equity to withstand possible downward fluctuations in demand.

The lack of consistency and precision prevalent in the American cases does not of course promote the cause of using financial ratios as a test for undercapitalisation in the liability issue. "Safe harbour" guidelines could however be developed by financial analysts indicating which ratios would in principle be considered adequate. Such guidelines could then be introduced in the reforming legislation. Moreover, since a financial ratio cannot present

---

[1] *Vide* also *In re Brunner Air Compressor Corp.* 287 F. Supp. 256 (N.D.N.Y. 1968) (9 to 12:1).

[2] 580 S.W.2d 375 (Tex. Civ. App. 1978).

[3] *Ibid.* pp. 383-385.

[4] *In re Branding Iron Steak House* 536 F.2d 299 (9th Cir. 1976). A similar refusal to subordinate appeared in the *Matter of Mobile Steel Co.* 563 F.2d 692 (5th Cir. 1977) (7:1).

[5] *In the Matter of Mobile Steel Co.* 563 F.2d 692, 702-703 (5th Cir. 1977).

[6] *Vide* Boris I. Bittker and James S. Eustice, *Federal Income Taxation of Corporations and Shareholders* (4th ed. 1979) s. 4.04, at 4-13.

a complete "financial picture" of the company, the legislative provision would have to stipulate that financial ratio analysis should only be one of the factors to be taken into account by the court in determining the adequacy of the capital structure. In all cases, moreover, the court would have to be allowed considerable discretion and flexibility in applying the guidelines.

### (iii) Use made of the loan

The purpose for which the loan was made may be a significant factor. Thus, a loan used to purchase basic assets of the business is probably intended as a permanent part of capital structure of the company.[1] Clearly, an advance made in respect of capital assets involves a greater inherent risk because it represents a long term commitment dependent on the success of the business.[2] By contrast, an advance used "to provide working capital for the day-to-day operations" is "in no way connected to any acquisition of capital assets".[3] Such an advance would be more akin to a loan supporting the short-term cash requirements of the company. Similarly, where the debt represents trading balances arising from intercompany trading, the holding company should obviously be entitled to prove in the subsidiary's insolvency *pari passu* with external creditors.

Admittedly, it may sometimes be difficult to determine precisely the purpose of the loan.[4] In such cases, the "purposes of the loan" test will prove to be unsatisfactory.

### (iv) Terms of the loan and nomenclature

The terms on which the advance was made may provide additional evidence of an equity investment. An arm's length loan transaction usually provides

---

[1] *Vide Boyum* v. *Johnson* 127 F.2d 491, 494 (8th Cir. 1942); *Arnold* v. *Phillips* 117 F.2d 497, 501 (5th Cir. 1941). This factor is used even in the tax cases. *Vide* e.g., *Texas Farm Bureau* v. *United States* 725 F.2d 307, 314 (5th Cir. 1984), *cert. denied*, 469 U.S. 1106 (1985); *Gilbert* v. *Commissioner* 248 F.2d 399, 406 (2d Cir. 1957); *Plantation Patterns, Inc.* v. *Commissioner* 462 F.2d 712, 722 (5th Cir. 1972), *cert. denied*, 409 U.S. 1076 (1972).

[2] *Fin Hay Realty Co.* v. *United States* 398 F.2d 694, 698 (3d. Cir. 1968).

[3] *Estate of Mixon* v. *United States* 464 F.2d 394, 410 (5th Cir. 1972).

[4] *Vide* "Symposium - The Close Corporation - Capitalization" 52 Northwestern Univ. L.R. 345 (1957) p. 370.

for a fixed rate of interest and a fixed or determinable maturity date.[1] Thus, the absence of a maturity date "would indicate that repayment was in some way tied to the fortunes of the business, indicative of an equity advance."[2] So too would the absence of an interest rate.[3] Significant too, is the actual performance of the stated terms. No genuine debt will probably exist where, despite continued solvency, the principal or interest payments are not made, or the maturity date is considerably extended.[4] Naturally, the extension of a maturity date for a reasonable period should not of itself transform a loan into equity.

Moreover, although the creation of a formal debt instrument should not constitute a necessary condition for debt characterisation, the absence of a formal document may suggest a capital contribution rather than a *bona fide* debt.[5] The nomenclature chosen by the parties is relevant, but should be far from conclusive on the question of characterisation.[6]

### (v) Proportionality of advances with equity holdings

"Proportionality" or "proportionate holding" refers to the situation where advances are made in proportion to the equity investments of the parties. In the context of corporate groups "proportionality" could of course only be relevant where minority shareholders are present. In a number of American tax cases proportionality has been considered as indicative of the loans being

---

[1] *Vide Pocatello Coca-Cola Bottling Co.* v. *United States* 139 F. Supp. 912, 915 (D. Idaho 1956); *John Kelley Co.* v. *Commissioner* 326 U.S. 521, 526 (1946). For an example of a bona fide debt in the context of a claim for its subordination, *vide Obre* v. *Alban Tractor Co.* 179 A.2d 861 (1962). *Vide* further Robert W. Baker, "Subordination Of Stockholder Loans On The Ground Of Corporate Undercapitalization" 23 Maryland L.R. 260 (1963).

[2] *Estate of Mixon* v. *United States* 464 F.2d 394, 404 (5th Cir. 1972). *Vide* also *Beaver Pipe Tools, Inc.* v. *Carey* 240 F.2d 843 (6th Cir. 1957); *Nassau Lens Co.* v. *Commissioner* 308 F.2d 39, 47 (2d. Cir. 1962); *Arlington Park Jockey Club* v. *Sauber* 262 F.2d 902, 906 (7th Cir. 1959).

[3] *Jones* v. *Commissioner* 357 F.2d 644, 645 (6th Cir. 1966).

[4] *Vide L & M Realty Corp.* v. *Leo* 249 F.2d 668, 670 (4th Cir. 1957).

[5] *Vide Stinnett's Pontiac Service, Inc.* v. *Commissioner* 730 F.2d 634, 638 (11th Cir. 1984).

[6] *Vide In re Lane* 742 F.2d 1311, 1315 (11th Cir. 1984); *Estate of Mixon* v. *United States* 464 F.2d 394, 403 (5th Cir. 1972); *Byerlite Corp.* v. *Williams* 286 F.2d 285, 290 (6th Cir. 1960).

capital contributions.[1] The same factor has featured in the bankruptcy cases, but to a more limited extent.[2] The rationale of the factor is that when shareholders expressly agree to maintain their loans in proportion to their shareholding interests in a situation where they do not expect timely repayment of their loan, they probably view their advances as risk capital and do not intend to enforce their creditors' rights.[3]

## (vi) Whether outsiders would make such advances

Further indication that an advance involved a capital contribution may be suggested by the fact that at the time the advance was made, the company could not have borrowed a similar amount from an informed outside source.[4] If an outside creditor was not prepared to lend, but the holding company advances the funds anyway, such an advance could be considered as an attempt to keep the business going in circumstances when the capital was inadequate. The holding company could not therefore really have had the intention of a lender and the advance could not be considered a *bona fide* loan. If on the other hand, a bank or other financial institution would lend, the holding company should itself be allowed to advance funds by way of loan. This is the attitude adopted in American cases. Where the company

---

[1] E.g., *Arlington Park Jockey Club* v. *Sauber* 262 F.2d 902, 906 (7th Cir. 1959); *Stinnett's Pontiac Service, Inc.* v *Commissioner* 730 F.2d 634, 639-640 (11th Cir. 1984); *Gilbert* v. *Commissioner* 248 F.2d 399, 406 (2d Cir. 1957).

[2] E.g., *In re Loewer's Gambrinus Brewery Co.* 167 F.2d 318 (2d Cir. 1948); *L & M Realty Corp.* v. *Leo* 249 F.2d 668, 670 (4th Cir. 1957).

[3] *Gilbert* v. *Commissioner* 248 F.2d 399, 407 (2d Cir. 1957). *Vide* further Margaret A. Gibson, "The Intractable Debt/Equity Problem: A New Structure for Analyzing Shareholder Advances" 81 Northwestern U.L.R. 452 (1987) pp. 475-478.

[4] Charles Rembar, "Claims against Affiliated Companies in Reorganisation" 39 Colum. L.R. 907 (1939) p. 916; Note, "Parent Corporation's Claims in Bankruptcy of Subsidiary: Effect of Fiduciary Relationship" 54 Harv. L.R. 1045 (1941) p. 1047. This factor is sometimes used by American courts as evidence of undercapitalisation. *Vide In the Matter of Mobile Steel Co.* 563 F.2d 692, 703 (5th Cir. 1977); *In re Trimble Co.* 479 F.2d 103, 116 (3d Cir. 1973). It is also a significant factor in the tax cases. *Vide* e.g., *Stinnett's Pontiac Service, Inc.* v. *Commissioner* 730 F.2d 634, 640 (11th Cir. 1984); *Austin Village, Inc.* v. *United States* 432 F.2d 741, 745 (6th Cir. 1970); *Affiliated Research, Inc.* v. *United States* 351 F.2d 646, 649-650 (Ct. Cl. 1965). One commentator had previously considered this factor to be impracticable in tax issues. *Vide* Myron Semmel, "Tax Consequences of Inadequate Capitalization" 48 Colum. L.R. 202 (1948).

shows an ability to obtain external financing, the funds advanced by the shareholder have in fact generally been viewed as debt.[1]

The test is not however always reliable. External financing may be unavailable not because of the financial condition of the company, but because of factors in the money market which make loans difficult to procure.[2] As a practical matter, moreover, difficulties with the matter of proof may arise years later when the question falls to be determined.[3]

Naturally, the possibility of borrowing from an informed third party must be tested on the strength of the subsidiary's creditworthiness alone. If a bank was prepared to advance funds on the basis of the holding company's security, the holding company's advances would more closely resemble a capital contribution.

### (vii) Borrowing and earnings history

An analysis of the subsidiary's borrowing and earnings history will provide a useful insight into the adequacy of the subsidiary's capital structure.[4] Thus, regular borrowing by the subsidiary from its holding company is strongly indicative of inadequate capitalisation.[5] Conversely, where a subsidiary which has been profitable for some time and has been honouring its interest-on-debt obligations, the indications are that the company has been adequately capitalised.[6]

### (viii) Motive of the parties

The motive of the parties may also be relevant. If, for example, an advance is not intended to be repaid in the ordinary course of business (despite "agreed" terms to the contrary), but is expected to remain outstanding - as long as needed - as part of the company's financial structure, an inference

---

[1] *Vide Estate of Mixon* v. *United States* 464 F.2d 394, 410 (5th Cir. 1972); *Bauer* v. *Commissioner* 748 F.2d 1365, 1370 (9th Cir. 1984).

[2] "Symposium - The Close Corporation - Capitalization" 52 Northwestern Univ. L.R. 345 (1957) p. 369.

[3] *Ibid.* p. 369.

[4] *Vide* Blumberg, *Bankruptcy Law* pp. 93-94.

[5] *Vide Taylor* v. *Standard Gas & Electric Co.* 306 U.S. 307, 315-316 (1939); *Boyum* v. *Johnson* 127 F.2d 491, 494 (8th Cir. 1942).

[6] Cf. *In the Matter of Mobile Steel Co.* 563 F.2d 692 (5th Cir. 1977); *Arnold* v. *Phillips* 117 F.2d 497, 501 (5th Cir. 1941), *cert. denied* 313 U.S. 583 (1941).

could properly be drawn to treat it as part of the capital.[1] In such a case, the "right to enforce payment [is] only a mirage".[2] The "motive" factor, however, being essentially subjective, should only be used sparingly. For the same reason, moreover, it should not be accorded independent significance. It could however be used to interpret the other more objective factors.[3]

### 4.2.3.3. Concluding remarks on adequate financing and "risk" capital

A number of concluding remarks on the questions of adequate financing and "risk" capital need to be made.

First, since it is impossible to measure with mathematical certainty the level of adequate financing and the quantum of risk capital, the legislative reform should only provide broad guidelines. It would have to be made clear that such guidelines are only intended as helpful factors to be considered and not *fiats* binding the courts. Each case will have to be assessed upon its own factual flavour.

Second, and again given the impossibility of using mathematically precise tests in questions of capitalisation, the holding company should perhaps be given "the benefit of the doubt" in an evenly-balanced situation. However, in view of the holding company's "inside" knowledge of the subsidiary's affairs and financial structure, it may be desirable to place on such company the onus of proving that the subsidiary had an adequate level of financing.

Third, it should not be necessary to rigidly treat particular advances as either debt or equity. The courts should be allowed to take an overall view of the subsidiary's financing and to determine the element of risk capital as a global figure. Moreover, no particular factor should be considered decisive

---

[1] This point is often made in the tax cases. E.g., *Nassau Lens Co.* v. *Commissioner* 308 F.2d 39, 47 (2d Cir. 1962). It also appears in the bankruptcy subordination cases. *Vide* e.g., *In re Mader's Store for Men, Inc.* 254 N.W.2d 171, 185-186 (Wis. 1977).

[2] *Texas Farm Bureau* v. *United States* 725 F.2d 307, 313 (5th Cir. 1984), *cert. denied*, 469 U.S. 1106 (1985).

[3] The tax cases present a conflicting picture. Some cases consider intent independently from the objective nature of the advance (e.g., *Texas Farm Bureau* v. *United States* 725 F.2d 307, 311 (5th Cir. 1984), *cert. denied*, 469 U.S. 1106 (1985)). Others view intent as it appears through other factors (e.g., *Sarkes Tarzian, Inc.* v. *United States* 240 F.2d 467, 470-471 (7th Cir. 1957)). *Vide* further Margaret A. Gibson, "The Intractable Debt/Equity Problem : A New Structure for Analyzing Shareholder Advances" 81 Northwestern U.L.R. 452 (1987) pp. 465-466.

in the risk capital rule. The relevant factors should be evaluated and balanced against one another. Each factor should carry an unspecified weight and no particular combination of factors should necessitate equity or debt characterisation of the advances. Courts would have to evaluate the subsidiary's ability to repay its loan obligations as they would have fallen due. To do so, courts would need to take into account the overall financial structure, history and performance of the company. Such flexibility would ensure a fairer and more realistic application of the risk capital rule. It would also deter artificial manipulation.

One other matter should be clarified. A basic principle of the reform proposal put forward in this chapter is that on the insolvency of the subsidiary that part of debt which should be treated as "risk" capital will have to be subordinated to the claims of external creditors. This principle can, of course, apply only as long as the debt is still outstanding. Sometimes, however, the holding company may be tempted, before the onset of insolvency, to "repay itself" with the subsidiary's assets before the subsidiary's creditors can reach them. If the debt has actually been repaid then provision should be made for the avoidance of such payment to the extent that it represented a "return" of "risk" capital.[1]

### 4.2.4. The voluntary-involuntary creditor distinction

A previous chapter highlighted the distinction between voluntary and involuntary creditors.[2] The distinction is relevant to the proposals for reform put forward in the present chapter.

By definition, voluntary creditors deal deliberately with the subsidiary. They investigate or at least have a realistic opportunity (and means) of investigating the subsidiary. The investigation should accurately reveal the deficiencies in the subsidiary's financial structure. The voluntary creditors can assess the risks. And they bargain - or could in practice bargain - over the credit of the subsidiary.[3] Provided there is no element of deception or

---

[1] Such a payment may possibly be impugned under s. 239 of the I.A. 1986.

[2] *Vide supra* Chapter IV pp. 176-186.

[3] Banks or other sophisticated lenders have both the opportunity to assess the financial condition of the borrower as well as the bargaining power to insist on an interest rate commensurate with the risk and/or on appropriate security.

misrepresentation, they should be held to their bargain : they have voluntarily assumed the risk of loss. Voluntary creditors should not therefore benefit from any rule that imposes on the holding company liability for failing to adequately finance its subsidiaries or for failing to contribute a reasonable amount of risk capital. Even where creditor-proof strategies have been engaged by the holding company, voluntary creditors should not be relieved of their bargain. A proper investigation would expose such strategies. The law should not disturb the voluntary allocation of risk exercised through the parties' relative bargaining power.[1]

Entirely different considerations, however, apply to the case of the involuntary creditor, particularly the tort victim. An involuntary creditor is not aware of the risks inherent in the various forms of inadequate financial organisation. With one type of involuntary creditor - the tort victim - there is usually no element of prior dealing. The tort victim does not ordinarily consent to the relationship. Other involuntary creditors (such as employees and consumers) may have consented, but they would not have had the practical opportunity of measuring the financial pulse of the subsidiary or of determining its financial organisation.[2] It is submitted that involuntary creditors should be entitled to assume that the subsidiary was organised on a fair and reasonable financial basis : that the holding company provided the subsidiary with adequate financing; that the holding company contributed a reasonable amount of risk capital; and that no creditor-proof devices were employed. The law cannot guarantee successful ventures. But it can, and it should, insist on fair dealing.

The reform proposals set out in this chapter would also serve two basic objectives of tort law : compensation of the victim and deterrence. For a rule requiring a fair and reasonable financial organisation would provide a deeper pocket for the satisfaction of the claims of involuntary creditors and would foster higher standards of care.

The reform proposals will not of course immunise the subsidiary against business risks. Insolvency will remain a commercial reality. There will therefore still be several instances when involuntary creditors of insolvent subsidiaries will not receive full compensation. That is the sacrifice that has

---

[1] One commentator has suggested that because inadequate capitalisation is an abuse of the corporate privilege, the shareholders of an undercapitalised company should be held personally liable *vis-à-vis* all creditors indiscriminately. *Vide* Philippe M. Salomon, "Limited Limited Liability: A Definitive Judicial Standard for the Inadequate Capitalisation Problem" 47 Temple L.Q. 321 (1974) p. 344.

[2] These issues were discussed *supra* Chapter IV pp. 182-186.

to be paid for retaining the virtues of limited liability. As previously mentioned,[1] the uncompensated claims of involuntary creditors - in particular those of tort victims - should ideally be settled through some other arrangement, such as compulsory liability insurance or a national accident-compensation scheme.

The practical implementation of the foregoing distinction between voluntary and involuntary creditors in an insolvency context would require two separate calculations in the liquidation process. In the first place, the respective claims of the various creditors (voluntary, involuntary and holding company) would be taken into account as in a normal liquidation. The *voluntary* creditors' share of the estate will be calculated on such a basis. In the second place, a further calculation would have to be made to take into account (i) any contribution to be made by the holding company to the assets of the subsidiary and/or (ii) any subordination of the holding company's claims to those of the involuntary creditors. The *involuntary* creditors' share would be calculated on the basis of this "inflated" fund.

### 4.2.5. Is the provision of an adequate financial structure a continuing obligation?

Should the holding company's obligation to provide the subsidiary with an adequate financial structure be a continuing one? The question is not answerable by a simple yes or no. The answer depends on which aspect of the rule is being considered. The rule, it will be remembered, has three facets: (i) the obligation to supply the subsidiary with adequate funds to enable it to have a reasonable chance of success; (ii) the obligation to provide a reasonable proportion of such funds by way of "risk" capital; and (iii) the obligation to abstain from creditor-proof strategies. Certainly, the rule that a reasonable proportion of funds should be deemed to have been provided by way of "risk" capital should apply both to funds advanced on inception as well as to funds advanced during the subsidiary's lifetime. Likewise, the duty to refrain from the use of creditor-proof devices should endure throughout the subsidiary's existence.

Insofar as the holding company's obligation to furnish the subsidiary with sufficient funds to enable it to stand a reasonable chance of success, a distinction must be drawn. On the one hand, there is the situation where the

[1] *Supra* pp. 367-368 and Chapter IV pp. 189-190.

subsidiary, though adequately financed on inception, suffers a deterioration in its financial condition through business adversity. In such a situation the holding company should not be bound to pour further funds into the subsidiary. To saddle the holding company with such an obligation would convert the holding company from an investor to a guarantor. Such an obligation would act as a significant disincentive to the creation of new companies. Indeed limited liability would become meaningless. Where the subsidiary's financial position has deteriorated, the holding company's obligations should merely be to minimise the potential loss to the subsidiary's creditors[1] and, if insolvency has set in, to place it in liquidation.[2]

If on the other hand the subsidiary is adequately financed for its current operations but plans to embark on a project requiring considerable additional financing, then - provided that the holding company is aware of the project and has the means of imposing its will on the subsidiary - the holding company's obligation to adequately finance its subsidiary should be viewed as a continuing one. Where the scale of the business has significantly altered, the issue of adequate financing should not be frozen arbitrarily by reference to the time of incorporation. To allow the subsidiary to proceed with a substantial project without ensuring adequate financing would be as scornful as the setting up of an inadequately financed subsidiary.

### 4.2.6. Intrusive domination - a *sine qua non* condition?

Should the holding company's liability in terms of the proposed reforms be dependent on the holding company's exercise of intrusive domination over its inadequately capitalised subsidiary? Clearly not. The mischief exists in the deliberate organisation of a subsidiary under any of the forms of

---

[1] Cf. s. 214 of the I.A. 1986.

[2] s. 13 of the Limited Liability Act 1855 had provided that a company must cease trading and must be wound up if it appeared that three-fourths of the subscribed capital stock of the company had been lost. Section 142(1) of the C.A. 1985 provides where the net assets of a public company are half or less than half of its called-up capital, the directors are bound to convene an extraordinary general meeting of the company for the purposes of considering whether any, and if so what, steps should be taken to deal with the situation. There is no duty to wind up the company or to take any remedial measures. A company's inability to pay its debts is, in terms of s. 122(1)(f) of the I.A. 1986, a ground for its compulsory winding up. Inability to pay debts is defined in s. 123 of the I.A. 1986.

financial structure which have been identified as abusive or unfair.[1] Any such arrangement is obviously implemented by the holding company. It must therefore bear corresponding responsibility. Whether or not the holding company subsequently exercises intrusive domination is irrelevant to the issue of financial organisation.[2]

Even where the financial structure is initially adequate, but becomes inadequate at a later stage, the holding company must still bear responsibility independently of intrusive domination. In all likelihood, the holding company would be directly responsible for such inadequacy independently of whether it exercises intrusive domination. The holding company may, for example, have advanced funds by way of debt rather than equity (in a situation where risk capital ought to have been provided) or has attempted to entrench its position by means of creditor-proof devices. In any case, of course, the holding company always retains a latent power of control. That latent control could, and should, be exercised to prevent the subsidiary from adopting any of the forms of inadequate financial organisation. The holding company should however be able to escape responsibility in the unlikely event that the management of an autonomously run subsidiary expands its operations without raising the necessary financing and without referring the matter back to the holding company.

### 4.2.7. Is a causal link necessary?

We have already seen that the causes of business failure are varied.[3] A subsidiary founded on an inadequate financial structure may sink into insolvency for a reason wholly unrelated to such inadequacy. Should the proposed reforms come into play even where the insolvency is causally unrelated to the inadequacy of the financial structure? The answer is clearly yes. The holding company's obligation to provide the subsidiary with an adequate financial structure stands as an independent obligation. It is the price that should be paid for obtaining limited liability. That price must be paid whatever the cause of the insolvency. Indeed, it is arguable that where the insolvency *is* brought about by the inadequacy of the financial structure,

---

[1] *Vide supra* pp. 312-324.

[2] Intrusive domination may of course be relevant to the question whether the holding company is to be liable on the basis that the subsidiary is "subservient". *Vide supra* Chapter IV.

[3] *Vide supra* pp. 315-316.

then the liability of the holding company should not be limited to the amount of adequate capitalisation but should, at the court's discretion, be expanded to compensate creditors fully for harm proximately caused by the inadequacy. Such an approach - analogous to the notion of liability in tort for negligence - would clearly constitute a serious erosion into the principle of limited liability and may lead to enormous liability on the part of the holding company for claims which might have remain unpaid even if an adequate financial structure had been in place. To adopt such an approach may be going too far.

### 4.2.8. The problem of shareholder-guaranteed loans

Throughout the discussion on the financing of subsidiaries by means of a high debt-to-equity ratio, it was assumed that the relative advances are made by the holding company. It was argued that in such a situation a reasonable proportion of the financing ought to be considered as risk capital. Sometimes, however, the debt financing is effected directly by a third party (a bank or institutional lender) against a guarantee provided by the holding company.[1] Given that in such a situation the holding company would not be a creditor in respect of these loans, it would appear that this method of financing could circumvent the application of the reform proposals set out in this chapter. For rather than advancing the necessary funds directly to the subsidiary, the holding company would be able to defeat the purpose of the proposed rules by the simple expedient of arranging for the funds to be loaned by a bank coupled with the holding company's guarantee. A solution must - and can - be found.

The solution, it is submitted, is to consider the holding company as the constructive borrower of the loans and the constructive lender of the proceeds to the subsidiary.[2] Whether or not the loans are to be considered as risk capital will then be determined on the basis of the general rules

---

[1] In financial management, these advances are referred to as "fronting loans" or "link financing". *Vide* David K. Eiteman and Arthur I. Stonehill, *Multinational Business Finance* (5th ed. 1989) p. 562.

[2] A similar approach has sometimes been adopted in the United States tax cases. *Vide* e.g., *Plantation Patterns, Inc.* v. *Commissioner* 462 F.2d 712, 723-724 (5th Cir. 1972), *cert. denied*, 409 U.S. 1076 (1972). *Vide* also Lehman C. Aarons, "Debt vs Equity - special hazards in setting up the corporate capital structure" 23 Journal of Taxation 194 (1965) p. 195; Paul R. Erickson, "Capitalization of Close Corporations After 1980" 17 Idaho L.R. 139 (1980) pp. 146-147.

discussed earlier on in this chapter. This approach would of course apply only for the purposes of the proposed rules. It would not affect the contractual relationship between the bank, the holding company and its subsidiary.

### 4.2.9. Duty owed to the subsidiary and not directly to creditors

In line with the provisions on fraudulent and wrongful trading,[1] and with the proposals made in the previous chapter on the subservient subsidiary situation,[2] the holding company's duty to adequately capitalise its subsidiary should notionally be owed to the subsidiary itself rather that to the subsidiary's creditors. The relative proceedings would be commenced during the course of the subsidiary's winding up at the instance of the liquidator by means of an application. Where the court finds the holding company to have breached its duty, the court would be entitled either to order the holding company to make such contributions (if any) to the subsidiary's assets as it thinks proper or to direct that the whole or any part of any debt owed by the subsidiary to the holding company be subordinated to other debts owed by the subsidiary.

### 4.2.10. Extent of contribution or subordination in court's discretion

Given the general complexity of the adequate capitalisation issue and the impossibility of determining with scientific precision the required levels of adequate financing and risk capital, it is evident that the court must be allowed considerable latitude in establishing the quantum of the contribution to be made by the holding company or the extent to which the holding company's claims are to be subordinated to other debts due to other creditors. No *a priori* definitive formulation can be attempted. But in exercising its discretion, the court would of course be obliged to take into account the proposed legislative guidelines previously discussed. And certainly, the extent of contribution or subordination should be related both

---

[1] *Vide* I.A. 1986, s. 213(2) (fraudulent trading); I.A. 1986, s. 214(1) (wrongful trading).

[2] *Vide supra* Chapter V pp. 302-303.

to the degree of inadequate capitalisation as well as to the causative effect that the inadequacy may have on the creditors of the subsidiary. Liability should be compensatory rather than punitive in nature.

# 7 The Integrated Economic Enterprise Situation

## 1. TYPES OF ECONOMIC INTEGRATION

### 1.1. Introduction

A striking feature of many corporate groups with affiliates engaged in related businesses is the centralised control or co-ordination of the activities of the various affiliates.[1] In some groups with affiliates engaged in related businesses a deeper form of integration actually occurs - deeper than the mere centralisation or co-ordination of the group's activities. In such groups, the separate legal units operate as closely inter-related fragments of a single unitary business. The legal personality does not correspond to the actual enterprise, but merely to a fragment of it.[2] Economically, however, the various companies constitute a "firm". No law limits the freedom of an entrepreneur to organise the enterprise through a number of economically integrated legal units.[3] Apart from the obvious protection of the "limited liability" factor, such fragmentation may be dictated by tax, political, accountancy or administrative considerations. The law's *laissez faire* attitude to such fragmentation contributes to the perpetuation of the great divide between the legal organisation of the enterprise and economic reality.

As has been pointed out in a previous chapter,[4] economic integration can be of two types : vertical or horizontal.

### 1.2. Vertical integration

In a vertically integrated group, the various companies within the group enterprise perform industrial or commercial functions that are geared to the

---

[1] Centralised control and co-ordination is naturally much less common in the highly diversified groups.

[2] Adolf A. Berle, "The Theory of Enterprise Entity" 47 Colum. L.R. 343 (1947) p. 348.

[3] Cf. *Adams* v. *Cape Industries plc* [1990] BCLC 479 (C.A.) p. 513.

[4] *Supra* Chapter II pp. 92-93.

activities of one another. If a particular function is not exercised by one subsidiary, it would have to be performed either by some other unit in the group or by some third party. In all likelihood, a subsidiary in a vertically integrated group would provide its services only to some other company within the group. Sometimes, however, the subsidiary may "sell" its services even to third parties outside the group.

Vertically integrated groups are found in many sectors of the economy. Vertical integration, for example, is often resorted to in the development and construction of large housing or apartments projects, shopping centres, industrial parks or similar enterprises. In such projects, one company may be used to acquire and own land, another company to undertake actual construction and a third to acquire the materials and services required for construction.[1] A typical vertically integrated group in a manufacturing or chemicals industry may comprise several subsidiaries : one performing research and development functions, others involved in different stages of manufacture or production, and others carrying out activities related to marketing, selling, distribution, transportation and financing. Judgments provide numerous examples of vertically integrated groups : a subsidiary owning property occupied by the holding company as licensee;[2] a hotel operating company conducting the business of the affiliated hotel owning company;[3] a fish-catching subsidiary and a fish-selling holding company;[4] a company operating a number of vessels leased to it by a vessel-owning affiliate;[5] a pulp company supplying a paper manufacturing affiliate;[6] a management services company for a railway-owning affiliate;[7] a credit insurance company serving a finance affiliate;[8] a company providing stevedoring services for a holding company operating as a ship broker and

---

[1] *Vide* George Ashe, "Lifting the Corporate Veil: Corporate Entity in the Modern Day Court" 73 Commercial L.J. 121 (1973) p. 121.

[2] E.g., *D.H.N. Food Distributors Ltd.* v. *Tower Hamlets L.B.C.* [1976] 1 W.L.R. 852 (C.A.). The vehicles used in the business were owned by another subsidiary. *Vide* also *Baker* v. *Caravan Moving Corp.* 561 F. Supp. 337, 341 (N.D. Ill. 1983).

[3] *Glenn* v. *Wagner* 313 S.E.2d 832 (N.C. Ct. App. 1984).

[4] *Friedman* v. *Snelling* 389 F. Supp. 684, 686-687 (D. Mass. 1975).

[5] *Luckenbach S.S. Co.* v. *W.R. Grace & Co* 267 F. 676 (4th Cir. 1920).

[6] *In re Watertown Paper Co.* 169 F. 252, 254-255 (2d Cir. 1909).

[7] E.g., *Costan* v. *Manila Electric Co.* 24 F.2d 383 (2d Cir. 1928).

[8] *Houston-American Life Ins. Co.* v. *Tate* 358 S.W. 2d 645 (Tex. Civ. App. 1962).

freight agent;[1] a retail car distribution company for a holding company wholesaler;[2] a distribution company selling its holding company's products;[3] a company mining raw materials for the sale, or the use by, affiliated companies;[4] a transportation subsidiary serving a stevedoring holding company;[5] a sales subsidiary selling products manufactured by affiliated companies;[6] and a group of six companies conducting the purchasing, slaughtering, processing, and selling of meat in an integrated meat business at the same location.[7]

## 1.3. Horizontal integration

In horizontally integrated groups, each subsidiary operates a business that is virtually identical to the business undertaken by its affiliates. The businesses would normally be operated from different localities. Hotel chains, retail stores, car park services, department stores, catering businesses and ship owning and ship chartering organisations, for example, are often organised as horizontally integrated groups comprising a number of subsidiaries each operating one garage, one hotel, one shop, one car park, one restaurant, one department store or one ship.[8] *Berkey* v. *Third Avenue Railway Co.*[9] - the celebrated case in which Cardozo J. expressed his oft-quoted "mists of metaphor" warning on the piercing the veil jurisprudence[10] - involved a fine example of horizontal integration. In that case, all the railway cars on the

---

[1] *Joseph R. Foard Co.* v. *State of Maryland* 219 F. 827 (4th Cir. 1914).

[2] *Edgar* v. *Fred Jones Lincoln-Mercury of Oklahoma City, Inc.* 524 F.2d 162 (10th Cir. 1975).

[3] *Bathory* v. *Procter & Gamble Distributing Co.* 306 F.2d 22, 23 (6th Cir. 1962).

[4] E.g., *Adams* v. *Cape Industries plc* [1990] BCLC 479 (C.A.); *United States* v. *Reserve Mining Co.* 380 F.Supp. 11 (D. Minn. 1974) *modified*, 514 F.2d 492 (8th Cir. 1975).

[5] E.g., *New Zealand Shipping Co. Ltd.* v. *A. M. Satterthwaite & Co. Ltd. ("The Eurymedon")* [1975] A.C. 154, 164 (P.C.).

[6] E.g., *George Fischer (Great Britain) Ltd.* v. *Multi Construction Ltd, Dexion Ltd. (third party)* [1995] 1 BCLC 260 (C.A.).

[7] *In re Snider Bros., Inc.* 18 B.R. 230, 232 (Bankr. D. Mass. 1982).

[8] *Vide* e.g., *Creasey* v. *Breachwood Motors Ltd.* [1992] BCC 638 (garages); *Allright Texas, Inc.* v. *Simons* 501 S.W.2d 145 (Tex. Civ. App. 1973) (parking lots); *Geletucha v. 222 Delaware Corp.* 7 A.D.2d 315, 182 N.Y.S.2d 893 (4th Dept. 1959) (retail cleaning establishments).

[9] 155 N.E. 58 (1926).

[10] *Ibid.* p. 61.

"Third Avenue System" were owned by the holding company (the Third Avenue Railway Company) but leased to several subsidiaries whose interconnecting lines provided an integrated railway service.[1]

## 1.4. Various combinations possible

In practice, of course, various permutations and degrees of integration are likely to arise. Thus, a group may be partly diversified and partly integrated.[2] A group may comprise both vertical and horizontal integration.[3] And it is also plausible for one and the same subsidiary to be both vertically and horizontally integrated with other affiliates within the group.

## 2. SHOULD ECONOMIC INTEGRATION LEAD TO ENTERPRISE LIABILITY?

### 2.1. Arguments for enterprise liability

A number of commentators have asserted that economic integration within a corporate group should lead to enterprise liability - that is, the law should ignore the separate personality of the various legal units within the group and impose liability on the assets of economic enterprise constituted by the various units collectively.[4] The earliest and most influential exponents of this view were Latty and Berle. Writing in 1936, Latty, while noting that

---

[1] *Vide* also *Miles* v. *American Telephone and Telegraph Co.* 703 F.2d 193, 194-196 (5th Cir. 1983).

[2] *Vide* e.g., *Tigrett* v. *Pointer* 580 S.W.2d 375 (Tex. Civ. App. 1979); *In re Interstate Stores, Inc.* 15 Collier Bankr. Cas. 634, 640-641 (Bankr. S.D.N.Y. 1978).

[3] E.g., *Revlon, Inc.* v. *Cripps & Lee Ltd.* [1980] F.S.R. 85 (C.A.); *Pennsylvania Railroad Co.* v. *Jones* 155 U.S. 333 (1894).

[4] Latty, *op. cit.* pp. 212-220; Adolf A. Berle, "The Theory of Enterprise Entity" 47 Colum. L.R. 343 (1947); David Aronofsky, "Piercing the Transnational Corporate Veil : Trends, Developments and the Need for Widespread Adoption of Enterprise Analysis" 10 North Carolina Journal of International Law & Commercial Regulation 31 (1985); Neil C. Sargent, "Corporate Groups and the Corporate Veil in Canada : a Penetrating Look at Parent - Subsidiary relations in the Modern Corporate Enterprise" 17 Manitoba L.J. 156 (1988) pp. 157-158. For the only English contribution advocating a wide-ranging enterprise approach to the liability problem *vide* Hugh Collins, "Ascription of Legal Responsibility to Groups in Complex Patterns of Economic Integration" 53 M.L.R. 731 (1990).

"[h]istorically the legal unit did coincide with the economic unit" argued that once the ultimate shareholder is insulated from liability the "[t]reatment of the economic unit as a legal unit satisfies the need which limited liability was devised to meet."[1] And in 1947, Berle, observing that "[t]he corporation is emerging as an enterprise bounded by economics, rather than as an artificial mystic personality bounded by forms of words in a charter, minute books, and books of account"[2] and noting that "[t]he change seems to be for the better",[3] called for the corporate fiction to be disregarded where it does not reflect the reality of the enterprise-fact.[4]

There is certainly much to be said for an "enterprise approach" to liability in the case of economically integrated corporate groups. *Vertically* integrated subsidiaries exist solely, or almost solely, to serve the operational functions of the group. The economic autonomy of the individual subsidiaries may be effectively destroyed. Group profit maximisation will be the goal. Economic autonomy may also be lacking in *horizontal* integration, although in this type of integration there is a greater likelihood that each subsidiary will be operated as a separate profit centre. Both in the public's perception - as well as in economic terms - integration means that the same business is involved.[5] The insulation of the group's assets from liability therefore appears hard to justify. In particular, insulation would appear especially unjustifiable - even offensive - in certain situations, such as disasters involving massive personal injury or environmental claims.[6] Indeed, it is arguable that once the group

---

[1] Latty, *op. cit.* p. 199. Latty's enterprise entity approach has only rarely been expressly endorsed. *Vide*, for an example, *Glenn* v. *Wagner* 313 S.E.2d 832, 844 (N.C. Ct. App. 1984). In one of the concluding remarks in his treatise, Latty asserted that companies within a group may still form an economic unit even if their business functions differ considerably. To him, the two significant factors were "substantial identity of ownership" and "unified administrative control" (which, he contended, "follows almost automatically from such ownership"). *Ibid.* p. 218. Latty conceded that if the activities of the various units were similar or complementary the case would be so much the stronger. He stressed however that the presence of an identity of ownership and unified administrative control seemed to outweigh the absence of similar or complementary business. *Ibid.* pp. 218-219. Latty's overall approach, it is submitted, goes too far. *Vide post* pp. 397-399.

[2] Adolf A. Berle, "The Theory of Enterprise Entity" 47 Colum. L.R. 343 (1947) p. 345.

[3] *Ibid.* p. 345.

[4] *Ibid.* p. 348.

[5] *Vide* Blumberg, *Substantive Law* p. 691.

[6] An enterprise analysis had been suggested as an alternative approach that could be adopted by the Indian courts in the Bhopal proceedings. *Vide* P.T. Muchlinski, "The

enjoys the benefits of integration, so also should it assume the corresponding burdens.

Adherents of the enterprise approach contend that the systematic fragmentation of an enterprise can be viewed as an abuse of the corporate privilege.[1] They argue that the law should not allow the owners of capital to avoid responsibility by artificially scattering an economic enterprise amongst a number of legal units.[2] In effect, the law should disregard the corporate "fiction" where it has broken away from the enterprise-fact for whose furtherance incorporation was created.[3] Once the corporate fiction is disregarded - that is, once it is recognised that although there are two or more personalities, there is but one enterprise - the law should attach to the actual enterprise the consequences of the acts of the separate personalities to the extent that the economic situation warrants or requires.[4] The enterprise as a whole should respond to the debts of the several legal components.[5] Economic reality should rip through the fabric of incorporation. Substance should prevail over form.

---

*Cont.*

Bhopal Case : Controlling Ultrahazardous Industrial Activities undertaken by Foreign Investors" 50 M.L.R. 545 (1987) pp. 572-573.

[1] *Vide* J. Penn Carolan, "Disregarding the Corporate Fiction in Florida: the Need for Specifics" 27 Univ. of Florida L.R. 175 (1974) p. 184 note 57.

[2] *Vide* e.g., Hugh Collins, "Ascription of Legal Responsibility to Groups in Complex Patterns of Economic Integration" 53 M.L.R. 731 (1990) p. 744. Collins recognises that to overcome this problem "requires extremely subtle legal principles." *Ibid.* p. 774. He does not however propose any specific solution.

[3] Adolf A. Berle, "The Theory of Enterprise Entity" 47 Colum. L.R. 343 (1947) p. 348.

[4] Adolf A. Berle, "The Theory of Enterprise Entity" 47 Colum. L.R. 343 (1947) p. 348. Berle believed that the American "agency", "identity", "instrumentality" and even the "undercapitalisation" and "subordination" cases could be explained on an enterprise theory. *Ibid.* pp. 348-350, 354. It is submitted, however, that the enterprise theory does not in fact adequately explain the aforesaid cases. *Vide* further *post* pp. 406-413.

[5] Most commentators favouring an enterprise approach to the liability issue would advocate a similar analysis to other problem areas of the law, such as jurisdiction and competition. *Vide* e.g., David Aronofsky, "Piercing the Transnational Corporate Veil : Trends, Developments and the Need for Widespread Adoption of Enterprise Analysis" 10 North Carolina Journal of International Law & Commercial Regulation 31 (1985) p. 32; Neil C. Sargent, "Corporate Groups and the Corporate Veil in Canada : a Penetrating Look at Parent-Subsidiary relations in the Modern Corporate Enterprise" 17 Manitoba L.J. 156 (1988) p. 157.

## 2.2. Enterprise liability unwarranted

It is submitted however that neither form of integration - vertical or horizontal - should, *per se*, lead to the imposition of holding company or group liability. A number of observations need to be made in this regard.

Firstly, it must be emphasised that when a common business is collectively conducted by a number of separate legal units within a corporate group, there is often some organisational, commercial or technical benefit to be gained out of such arrangement. Moreover, each unit is often operated as a separate profit centre. In some enterprises, for example, subsidiaries may perform specialised functions - such as research and development, marketing, financing or distribution. Separate incorporation - with consequent vertical integration - may make organisational or economic sense.[1] Moreover, the affiliates' activities may be carried out from different localities. In such a situation, separate incorporation may be useful both in cases of vertical integration (for example, a subsidiary producing a limited range of components or sub-assemblies for sale both on the market and also to other members of the group)[2] and in cases of horizontal integration (for example, catering establishments in different towns or even in different districts within the same town).

More fundamentally, however, it is submitted that mere economic integration - horizontal or vertical - does not necessarily result in unfairness or prejudice to creditors. Normally, it would be other factors - such as subservience, inadequate capitalisation or the abuse of a group persona - that are the root cause of the unfairness or prejudice to creditors. Such factors, rather than economic integration, would constitute the mischief. And it is those abuses which should attract a remedy. To be sure, economic integration does set the stage for and probably increases the likelihood of abuse. But economic integration, *per se*, should not be perceived as inherently abusive or unfair. Put another way, as long as an economically integrated group ensures that its subsidiaries are operated with an eye single to their own interests, as long as subsidiaries are provided with an adequate financial structure and as long as the public is not misled by an abuse of the group persona, the group should be entitled to take advantage of the

---

[1] E.g., *Vaughn* v. *Chrysler Corp.* 442 F.2d 619 (10th Cir.), *cert. denied*, 404 U.S. 857 (1971).

[2] *Vide* Brooke and Remmers, *op. cit.* p. 70.

privileges of separate juridical personality and limited liability and organise its structure on the basis of economically inter-related but legally separate components. There is no compelling reason why a group's economic organisation should correspond with its formal legal structure. It would be perverse to penalise a group for its superior efficiency in the absence of specific elements of abuse.

It must of course be admitted that there is something distasteful about allowing an economically integrated group to bloom into prosperity whilst one of its subsidiaries decays into insolvency to the obvious distress of its creditors. Yet unless we are prepared to sanction the virtual elimination of limited liability in the context of groups such unfortunate consequences are inevitable. The policy of limited liability, though much abused of, is still worthy of protection.[1] The economic benefits inherent in a system of limited liability - even within the context of corporate groups - outweigh the unfortunate consequences that occasionally result from its implementation. Certainly, it is imperative to control and remedy abuses and unfair practices. But organisation of an enterprise into legally separate but economically inter-dependent units should not in itself be perceived as an abuse warranting the removal of limited liability.

A practical difficulty also militates against the equation of economic integration with holding company or group liability. The difficulty is one of definition. Economists themselves have no formulation of what constitutes a single economic unit.[2] And even if they did, there may in practice be so many permutations and degrees of economic integration that a reasonably accurate and consistent determination of the issue may be impossible to achieve.

All told, it is submitted that the division of an enterprise into separate legal units ought to be permitted whenever some organisational, commercial or technical advantage stands to be gained by the conduct of the enterprise through a number of subsidiaries. Horizontal economic integration, for example, ought to be allowed where the separate legal units, can, at least notionally, be viewed as economically self-supporting - as is the case with different hotels in a hotel chain, various car-parks in a car-park organisation, a string of retail stores in a retailing chain or a fleet of vessels in the shipping industry. Vertical economic integration within a corporate group should be accepted whenever the separate legal units realistically perform functionally

---

[1] *Vide supra* Chapter IV pp. 193-194.

[2] Latty, *op. cit.* p. 213.

different activities - as in the case of a group with separate legal units involved in the different processes of production, marketing, distribution, research and development, transportation and financing.

## 3. ABUSIVE ECONOMIC INTEGRATION

One particular form of economic integration, however, is clearly abusive and requires control. "Abusive" economic integration occurs where the unitary enterprise, for no functional reason whatsoever, is artificially fragmented into several legal units with the sole aim of insulating the enterprise from potential claims. In effect, this dispersal of a single enterprise into a horde of separate legal persons amounts to a cynical manipulation of the privilege of incorporation. Both vertical and horizontal integration may be involved.

Abusive vertical integration will be illustrated first. An entrepreneur intends to operate in the construction business. In a crude and shameless attempt to lower the exposure virtually down to zero, he causes the incorporation of a holding company and a series of subsidiaries. The construction business will be conducted through the subsidiaries: one to purchase the raw materials, one to own the plant, one to execute the actual building works, another to execute the "wet" trades, one or more to employ personnel, one or more to enter into the contracts of work, and so on. The execution of the contracts of work would naturally have to be co-ordinated and integrated between the various affiliates.[1] One of the subsidiaries or possibly the holding company itself might take overall managerial charge of the execution of the works. The business would no doubt be centrally conducted from one office. There would almost certainly be just one directing mind. Corporate formalities may be retained. But the various affiliates would remain mere automatons devoid of any realistic functional existence.[2]

The use of abusive horizontal integration has already been illustrated by the taxi-cab situation[3] in which an enterprise consisting of a fleet of vehicles for hire incorporates a separate subsidiary for every one or two of the

---

[1] *Vide* e.g., *Mangan* v. *Terminal Transportation System, Inc.* 284 N.Y.S. 183, 187 (Sup. Ct. 1935), *aff'd per curiam*, 286 N.Y.S. 666 (3d. Dept. 1936); *Teller* v. *Clear Service Co.* 173 N.Y.S. 2d 183, 186 (Sup. Ct. 1958).

[2] *Vide*, for another example of abusive vertical integration, *supra* Chapter II pp. 94-95.

[3] *Vide supra* Chapter II p. 95.

vehicles.[1] This type of integration can be attempted in many types of business. A hotel business may, for example, be operated through a separate subsidiary for each floor (or even for each room), a separate subsidiary for the breakfast room and even separate subsidiaries for the car park, the cloak room and so on.[2] A railway enterprise may incorporate a separate company in respect of each of its trains. A car park business may incorporate a separate company for each parking floor. And a cinema complex may do the same for each one of its theatres. In all such cases the businesses would be centrally managed either by the holding company or by one of the subsidiaries.

Invariably, the intention underlying the strategy of excessive vertical and horizontal integration as illustrated above is quite simply to painlessly sacrifice the particular subsidiary in the event of a substantial claim, usually in tort, whilst leaving the enterprise (comprised in the other affiliates) virtually intact.[3] It has already been argued that economic integration is not *per se* objectionable. But there has to be a reasonable limit on the extent to which an enterprise can be allowed to partition itself. The privileges of incorporation and limited liability should be bounded by realistic limits. After all, the holding company is already an insulating device for its shareholders. Does not the multiple and artificial sub-division of one integrated economic enterprise into several subsidiaries for no reason other than to obtain for the enterprise virtual immunisation against liability extend beyond the purposes of the privilege of incorporation? To deny a remedy would be to unduly exalt sterile technical doctrine.

"Abusive" economic integration does not, of course, occur very frequently in practice. The entrepreneur himself would acknowledge the unfairness of the strategy. He would realise that third parties would despise the arrangement and possibly snub the business altogether. Moreover the costs involved in setting up, maintaining and monitoring such an artificial structure may be prohibitive.

Nevertheless, for the cases when it does occur, "abusive" economic integration needs to be proscribed. Given that English law does not provide a

---

[1] *Vide* e.g., *Mull* v. *Colt Co.* 31 F.R.D. 154 (S.D.N.Y. 1962); *Teller* v. *Clear Service Co.* 173 N.Y.S. 2d 183 (Sup. Ct. 1958); *Robinson* v. *Chase Maintenance Corp.* 190 N.Y.S.2d 773 (Sup. Ct. 1959); *Walkovszky* v. *Carlton* 223 N.E.2d 6 (1966).

[2] *Vide* Latty, *op. cit.* p. 197.

[3] Cf. Note "Should Shareholders be personally liable for the Torts of their Corporations" 76 Yale L.J. 1190 (1967) p. 1191.

clear and effective remedy to redress "abusive" economic integration,[1] legislative reform seems desirable. A proposal in this regard is set out later on in this chapter.[2]

## 4. LIMITED LEGAL RECOGNITION OF THE GROUP AS AN ECONOMIC UNIT

### 4.1. Position under English law

#### 4.1.1. Economic integration generally

There is, of course, no general principle under English law that the companies in a corporate group are to be regarded as one.[3] On the contrary, it is axiomatic that "each company in a group of companies ... is a separate legal entity possessed of separate legal rights and liabilities".[4] The law does not fetter the entrepreneur's freedom to organise the enterprise through a number of economically integrated legal units.

Occasionally, however, the courts have appeared willing to recognise the economic unity of an integrated group of companies and to grant legal effect to such unity. A handful of judgments illustrate the judicial recognition of this reality : *D.H.N. Food Distributors Ltd.* v. *Tower Hamlets L.B.C.*,[5] *Harold Holdsworth & Co. (Wakefield) Ltd.* v. *Caddies*,[6] *Scottish Co-Operative Wholesale Society Ltd.* v. *Meyer*,[7] *The Roberta*,[8] *Merchandise Transport Ltd.* v. *British Transport Commission*,[9] *Commercial Solvents Corporation* v. *E.C. Commission (Nos. 6-7/74)*,[10] *Re Southard & Co.*

---

[1] *Vide post* pp. 404-406.

[2] *Vide post* pp. 413-415.

[3] *Adams* v. *Cape Industries plc* [1990] BCLC 479 (C.A.) p. 508.

[4] *The Albazero* [1977] A.C. 774 at p. 807, per Roskill L.J. Roskill L.J.'s statement was quoted with approval in *Adams* v. *Cape Industries plc* [1990] BCLC 479 (C.A.) p. 508.

[5] [1976] 1 W.L.R. 852 (C.A.).

[6] [1955] 1 W.L.R. 352 (H.L.).

[7] [1959] A.C. 324 (H.L.).

[8] (1937) 58 Ll.L.R. 159.

[9] [1962] 2 Q.B. 173.

[10] [1974] 1 ECR 223.

*Ltd.*,[1] *Revlon, Inc.* v. *Cripps & Lee Ltd.*, [2] and *Atlas Maritime Co. S.A.* v. *Avalon Maritime Ltd. (No. 3).*[3] These cases have already been considered elsewhere in this work[4] and it is not here necessary to deal with them at length. It suffices to make just two points. First, that in these cases economic unity was discerned from a number of factors (such as complete or almost complete ownership of the subsidiary's shares, the exercise of managerial control by the holding company over the subsidiary and the lack of financial independence of the subsidiary) and not merely from the integration of operations. Secondly, and more significantly, the courts have given legal effect to economic reality only in rather exceptional circumstances and certainly never in the context of holding company or group liability. Most of the aforementioned cases are in fact explicable either as cases on statutory interpretation[5] or as cases on contractual interpretation.[6] Admittedly, the *D.H.N. Food Distributors* case - in which Lord Denning made his wide-ranging call for the recognition in certain circumstances of the group as an "economic unit"[7] - cannot be so narrowly interpreted. But given especially the negative reception it later received,[8] the judgment can hardly be regarded as authoritative. In any case, of course, *D.H.N. Food Distributors* was not concerned with the imposition of holding company liability for the debts of a subsidiary. Another case which cannot be considered as one of statutory or contractual interpretation is *Atlas Maritime Co. S.A.* v. *Avalon Maritime Ltd. (No. 3).*[9] But that case involved more than mere economic integration. Indeed the subsidiary was completely dominated by the holding company and seemed "not to have exercised any mind of its own, even in the

---

[1] [1979] 1 W.L.R. 1198 (C.A.).

[2] [1980] F.S.R. 85 (C.A.).

[3] [1991] 1 W.L.R. 917.

[4] *Vide supra* Chapter III pp. 107-112.

[5] *Scottish Co-Operative Wholesale Society Ltd.* v. *Meyer* [1959] A.C. 324 (H.L.); *Revlon, Inc.* v. *Cripps & Lee Ltd.* [1980] F.S.R. 85 (C.A.); *Merchandise Transport Ltd.* v. *British Transport Commission* [1962] 2 Q.B. 173; *Commercial Solvents Corporation* v. *E.C. Commission (Nos. 6-7/74)* [1974] 1 ECR 223.

[6] *The Roberta* (1937) 58 Ll.L.R. 159; *Harold Holdsworth & Co. (Wakefield) Ltd.* v. *Caddies* [1955] 1 W.L.R. 352 (H.L.).

[7] [1976] 1 W.L.R. 852 (C.A.) at p. 860.

[8] *Vide Woolfson* v. *Strathclyde Regional Council* 1978 S.L.T. 159 (H.L. Sc.); *Adams* v. *Cape Industries plc* [1990] BCLC 479 (C.A.). *Vide* also *Re Securitibank Ltd. (No. 2)* [1978] 2 NZLR 136, 158-159.

[9] [1991] 1 W.L.R. 917.

attenuated sense in which that frequently is the case with wholly-owned subsidiary companies."[1] The holding company had "controlled the purse-strings, on an item-by-item basis."[2] And significantly, the Court of Appeal, whilst remarking that in granting injunctive relief it was willing to look behind the corporate veil to achieve justice, emphasised that it was not prepared to treat the subsidiary's liabilities as the liabilities of its ultimate holding company.[3]

The death knell of the "economic unit" concept as a potential general therapeutic remedy was of course clearly sounded in *Adams* v. *Cape Industries plc*.[4] In that case, the Court of Appeal, stressing that it had no discretion to reject the distinction between the members of the group "as a technical point",[5] approved of Goff L.J.'s observations in *Bank of Tokyo Ltd.* v. *Karoon*[6] that the courts "are concerned not with economics but with law" and that "[t]he distinction between the two is, in law, fundamental and cannot here be bridged."[7] Moreover the Court of Appeal bluntly asserted that "[n]either in this class of case nor in any other class of case is it open to this court to disregard the principle of Salomon ... merely because it considers it just so to do."[8] The current position therefore appears to be that the courts might only be willing to have regard to the economic realities either as an aid to the interpretation of a particular statute or document[9] or in the granting of injunctive relief.[10]

---

[1] *Ibid.* at p. 929 per Nicholls L.J.

[2] *Ibid.* at p. 929 per Nicholls L.J.

[3] *Ibid.* at pp. 924-927 per Lord Donaldson. *Vide* also *Atlas Maritime Co. S.A.* v. *Avalon Maritime Ltd. ("The Coral Rose") (No. 1)* [1991] 1 Lloyd's Rep. 563 especially at p. 571 per Staughton L.J.

[4] [1990] BCLC 479 (C.A.). *Vide* also the earlier judgment of the House of Lords in *The Albazero* [1976] 3 W.L.R. 419, [1976] 3 All E.R. 129 reversing the judgment of the Court of Appeal [1975] 3 W.L.R. 491 (C.A.).

[5] *Ibid.* at p. 514.

[6] [1987] 1 A.C. 45 (C.A.).

[7] *Ibid.* at p. 64.

[8] *Adams* v. *Cape Industries plc* [1990] BCLC 479 (C.A.) at p. 513.

[9] *Adams* v. *Cape Industries plc* [1990] BCLC 479 (C.A.) at p. 512.

[10] *Vide Atlas Maritime Co. S.A.* v. *Avalon Maritime Ltd. (No. 3)* [1991] 1 W.L.R. 917 (C.A.) especially at p. 924 per Lord Donaldson; *Atlas Maritime Co. S.A.* v. *Avalon Maritime Ltd. ("The Coral Rose") (No. 1)* [1991] 1 Lloyd's Rep. 563 especially at p. 569 per Neill L.J.

Finally, it should be noted that a partnership notion has occasionally crept into the analysis of the group as an economic unit. The notion of a partnership in the context of groups owes its origin to Lord Denning's judgment in *D.H.N. Food Distributors Ltd.* v. *Tower Hamlets L.B.C.*[1] when he observed that the group in that case was "virtually the same as a partnership in which all the three companies are partners."[2] There can be little doubt that Lord Denning was referring not to a partnership in the technical legal sense but to a partnership as loosely understood in commercial terms. Although a true legal partnership between the various companies in a corporate group is not a legal impossibility, it is very unlikely to be established in practice. Caution must therefore be exercised so as not to read too much into Lord Denning's dictum. Unfortunately, such caution is not always practised.[3]

### 4.1.2. Abusive economic integration

Is the legal position any different in the case of "abusive" economic integration? In *Adams* v. *Cape Industries plc* the Court of Appeal considered that "there is one well-recognised exception to the rule prohibiting the piercing of 'the corporate veil'".[4] That exception was identified as the case of "a mere façade concealing the true facts".[5] Can the "abusive" economic enterprise situation qualify as a "façade"? There is no clear-cut answer. In its judgment, the Court of Appeal unfortunately declined to "attempt a comprehensive definition" of those principles which should guide the court in determining whether or not a particular arrangement involves a façade.[6] It

---

[1] [1976] 1 W.L.R. 852 (C.A.).

[2] *Ibid.* at p. 860.

[3] *Vide* for e.g., *Pioneer Concrete Services Ltd.* v. *Yelnah Pty. Ltd.* (1986) 11 ACLR 108 at p. 119. In *Adams* v. *Cape Industries plc* [1990] BCLC 479, the Court of Appeal saw the "attraction" of Lord Denning's partnership approach but maintained that "it had no discretion to reject the distinction between the members of the group as a technical point." *Ibid.* at p. 514. Very rarely, a partnership analysis has also appeared in the American cases. *Vide* e.g., *Lehigh Valley R. Co.* v. *Dupont* 128 F. 840, 845-846 (2d Cir. 1904).

[4] [1990] BCLC 479 at p. 515.

[5] [1990] BCLC 479 at 515. The Court of Appeal was quoting from the speech of Lord Keith in *Woolfson* v. *Strathclyde Regional Council* (1978) S.L.T. 159 (H.L. Sc.) at p. 161.

[6] [1990] BCLC 479 at p. 519.

would appear, however, that the motive behind the arrangement should be considered as a crucial factor and that only if there is an indication of some behaviour bordering on impropriety or wrongdoing should the arrangement be regarded as a "façade".[1]

Notwithstanding such stringent limitations it is arguable that each one of the companies involve in "abusive" economic integration constitutes a "façade". Indeed, each of the companies in such a group, though formally existing as a legal entity, would probably lack significant indicia of a separate corporate existence. This lack of separate existence would be evidenced by several factors. In all likelihood, for example, there would be common directors and common offices. It is unlikely that they would employ separate personnel. And it is unlikely that they would operate separate bank accounts. The companies might have assets, but would not really be running any business (except, of course, on a collective basis). Separate books of account may be kept and separate board and general meetings may be held - but the books or proceedings, as the case may be, would be mere formalities distorting the reality of the situation. The group's failure to maintain a modicum of reality for each one of the legally separate units introduces an element of impropriety or wrongdoing. Each company could then be considered as a "façade concealing the true facts".[2]

Some support for such an analysis may be derived from *Adams* v. *Cape Industries plc* in which the Court of Appeal was prepared to treat as a "façade" one of the subsidiaries in the Cape Industries group. The Court of Appeal agreed with Scott J.'s view in the court of first instance that the subsidiary in question was "no more than a corporate name" which "acted through employees or officers" of two affiliated companies within the group.[3] Further support for a façade analysis of abusive economic integration may be drawn from a dictum in the Australian case of *Pioneer Concrete Services Ltd.* v. *Yelnah Pty. Ltd.*[4] In that case, Young J. observed that "only if the court can see that there is in fact or in law a partnership between companies in a group, or alternatively where there is a mere sham

---

[1] Cf. *Gilford Motor Co. Ltd.* v. *Horne* [1933] 1 Ch. 935 (C.A.) especially at pp. 955-956; *Jones* v. *Lipman* [1962] 1 All E.R. 442 at p. 445. The latter judgment is referred to with approval in *Adams* v. *Cape Industries plc* [1990] BCLC 479 (C.A.) at p. 518.

[2] [1990] BCLC 479 at p. 515.

[3] [1990] BCLC 479 at p. 519.

[4] (1986) 11 ACLR 108.

or façade that one lifts the veil."[1] In Young J.'s view, the said principle was inapplicable in the particular circumstances as "there was a good commercial purpose for having separate companies in the group performing different functions".[2] The implication appears to be that if no realistic commercial purpose existed for having separate companies, the arrangement could be considered as a sham or façade.

In the absence of clearer guidance from the courts as to the precise meaning and ambit of the façade exception, the potential role of the exception in the context of abusive economic integration will remain shrouded in uncertainty. A clear legislative statement on the issue - preferably on the basis recommended later on in this chapter[3] - would be welcome.

## 4.2. Position under American law

### 4.2.1. Economic integration generally

As in English law, there is in American law no general principle that companies in a corporate group are to be regarded as one. On the contrary, American law, like English law, abides by the notion that each company in a group is a separate legal entity possessed of separate legal rights and liabilities.[4]

In contrast to the position in English law, however, the element of economic integration has featured quite frequently in the American lifting the veil cases. Certainly, many of the cases imposing intragroup *tort* liability have involved corporate groups with a high degree of vertical[5] or horizontal[6] integration. Economic integration has also played a prominent role in some of the cases imposing intragroup *contract* liability.[7] On the whole, however,

---

[1] *Ibid.* at p. 119.

[2] *Ibid.* at p. 119.

[3] *Vide post* pp. 413-415.

[4] *Exchange Bank of Macon* v. *Macon Construction Co.* 25 S.E. 326 (Ga. 1895).

[5] E.g., *Joseph R. Foard Co.* v. *State of Maryland* 219 F. 827 (4th Cir. 1914). Cf. *Geletucha* v. *222 Delaware Corp.* 182 N.Y.S. 2d 893 (4th Dept. 1959).

[6] E.g., *Allright Texas, Inc.* v. *Simons* 501 S.W.2d 145, 149-150 (Tex. Civ. App. 1973).

[7] *Vide* e.g., *Mississippi River Grain Elevator, Inc.* v. *Bartlett & Co.* 659 F.2d 1314 (5th Cir. 1981); *Laborers Clean-Up Contract Administration Trust Fund* v. *Uriarte Clean-Up*

economic integration seems to have had little effect in the intra-group contract cases.[1] Economic integration has also played an insignificant part in the bankruptcy subordination cases, where the remedy of subordination rests mainly on equitable considerations.[2] By contrast, economic integration appears to be playing an increasingly important role in the bankruptcy substantive consolidation cases.[3]

In the lifting of the veil jurisprudence - especially in the intra-group tort cases - the close economic interdependence of the various companies within the group has often contributed to a finding that the subsidiary existed primarily to serve the operational business of the holding company or of the group. The conclusion would then be drawn that the subsidiary was therefore a "mere instrumentality" for which the holding company was to be held liable. Economic integration, however, although relevant to the piercing the veil question, is not *per se* decisive. It is merely one of the factors that the courts take into account in determining whether to impose intra-group tort or contract liability. Indeed several cases have declined to impose such liability notwithstanding a high level of economic integration.[4] Significantly, however, a number of cases refusing to impose such liability acknowledge the relevance of economic integration by noting, for example, that the subsidiary in question did little or no business with the holding company[5] or that the subsidiary was not exclusively engaged in the business of the

*Cont.*
   *Service, Inc.* 736 F.2d 516 (9th Cir. 1984); *Worldwide Carriers Ltd.* v. *Aris Steamship Co.* 301 F.Supp. 64 (S.D.N.Y. 1968).

[1] E.g., *Kashfi* v. *Phibro-Salomon, Inc.* 628 F. Supp. 727, 733-735 (S.D.N.Y. 1986); *Bendix Home Systems, Inc.* v. *Hurston Enterprises, Inc.* 566 F.2d 1039 (5th Cir. 1978); *Penick* v. *Frank E. Basil, Inc.* 579 F.Supp. 160 (D.D.C. 1984). *Vide* further Blumberg, *Substantive Law* pp. 508-510.

[2] Blumberg, *Bankruptcy Law* p. 126.

[3] *In re Interstate Stores, Inc.* 15 Collier Bankr. Cas. 634 (Bankr. S.D.N.Y. 1978); *In re Vecco Const. Indus., Inc.* 4 B.R. 407, 409 (Bankr. E.D. Va. 1980); *In re Continental Vending Machine Corp.* 517 F.2d 997 (2d. Cir. 1975), *cert. denied sub. nom. James Talcott, Inc.* v. *Wharton* 424 U.S. 913 (1976). *Vide* further Blumberg, *Bankruptcy Law* pp. 419-420.

[4] E.g., *Garrett* v. *Southern Railway Co.* 173 F.Supp. 915 (E.D. Tenn. 1959), *aff'd*, 278 F.2d 424 (6th Cir.), *cert. denied*, 364 U.S. 833 (1960); *Fidenas AG* v. *Honeywell, Inc.* 501 F.Supp. 1029, 1037 (S.D.N.Y. 1980). *Vide* further Blumberg, *Substantive Law* pp. 195, 218, 440.

[5] E.g., *Allegheny Airlines, Inc.* v. *United States* 504 F.2d 104, 113 (7th Cir. 1974), *cert. denied*, 421 U.S. 978 (1975); *American Trading & Production Corp.* v. *Fischbach & Moore, Inc.* 311 F.Supp. 412, 414 (N.D. Ill. 1970).

holding company.[1] The lack of economic integration is seen as demonstrating the separate existence of the companies within the group. Even in the substantive consolidation cases, economic integration is not necessarily decisive, although it will be one of the important factors to be taken into account.[2]

There are however a limited number of cases where the integrated nature of the group's operations appears to have been decisive in imposing intragroup tort liability. The early railroad cases provide the clearest examples. In *Pennsylvania Railroad Co. v. Jones*,[3] a railroad system involved a holding company and a number of subsidiaries operating on an integrated basis. The Supreme Court imposed liability on the subsidiary companies on the basis of their joint operations, but maintained that there was insufficient evidence to establish liability on the part of the holding company. The significance of integrated operations was also stressed in *Lehigh Valley R. Co. v. Dupont*[4] and *Lehigh Valley R. Co. v. Delachesa*[5] which based liability on the notion that the joint operations gave rise to a partnership arrangement.[6] The landmark judgment is *Davis v. Alexander*.[7] In that case the Supreme Court held that where "one railroad company actually controls another and operates both as a single system, the dominant company will be liable for the injuries due to the negligence of the subsidiary company."[8]

The integrated economic approach exemplified by the early railroad cases[9] was not destined to last. The turning point came with *Berkey v. Third Avenue Railway Co.*[10] The case concerned an integrated street railway

---

[1] *Schmid v. Roehm GmbH* 544 F.Supp. 272, 276 (D. Kan. 1982); *Carl Zeiss Stiftung* v. *V.E.B. Carl Zeiss, Jena* 298 F. Supp. 1309, 1317 (S.D.N.Y. 1969). *Vide* further Blumberg, *Substantive Law* p. 218.

[2] *Vide* Blumberg, *Bankruptcy Law* p. 420.

[3] 155 U.S. 333 (1894).

[4] 128 F. 840 (2d Cir. 1904).

[5] 145 F. 617 (2d. Cir. 1906).

[6] *Vide Lehigh Valley R. Co. v. Dupont* 128 F. 840, 845-846 (2d Cir. 1904).

[7] 269 U.S. 114 (1925).

[8] *Ibid.* at p. 117.

[9] *Vide* also e.g., *Pennsylvania R.R. v. Anoka Nat. Bank* 108 F. 482 (8th Cir. 1901); *Specht* v. *Missouri Pac. R. Co.* 191 N.W. 905, 907 (1923).

[10] 155 N.E. 58 (1926). Even before this landmark judgment, a number of state decisions had relied on the principle of separate juridical personality to insulate the holding company from liability for the torts of their subsidiaries. *Vide* e.g., *Atchison, T. & S.F.R.*

system comprising several affiliated companies. The boards of the various companies were almost identical. The executives, president, treasurer, general manager and paymaster were common to the companies. The repairs department, the legal, accounting and claims department, the printing plant and the employment bureau were all single departments operated for the entire system and under the direct control of the holding company. The street cars were owned by the holding company and leased to the various subsidiaries at a substantial rent. The subsidiaries' expenses were first settled by the holding company and then charged to the subsidiaries. Despite this evidence of a closely interwoven system, the New York Court of Appeals found a number of indicia pointing to the "separate existence"[1] of the particular subsidiary, including a surplus of assets over liabilities, the keeping of separate records and accounts and the employment of its own motormen and conductors. Also considered significant was the fact that the subsidiaries' cars, motormen and conductors never ran beyond their own lines. The holding company was held not responsible to the plaintiff who had been injured through the negligence of a motorman of one of the subsidiaries. In adopting this approach, the court was clearly rejecting an economic enterprise basis of liability and approving the more traditional piercing the veil doctrine. The court also distinguished *Davis* v. *Alexander*[2] on its facts, emphasising especially the fact that the subsidiaries had used locomotives, cars and employees indiscriminately and that the proceeds from the integrated business had been commingled into a single fund.[3]

Following the *Berkey* case, the notion of economic integration as a basis for liability virtually evaporated.[4] Only in the taxi-cab cases, and in a few

---

*Cont.*

   Co. v. *Cochran* 23 P. 151, 154-155 (Kan. 1890); *Stone* v. *Cleveland, C.C. & St. L. Ry. Co.* 95 N.E. 816 (1911).

[1] *Ibid.* p. 61.

[2] 269 U.S. 114 (1925).

[3] 155 N.E. 58, 61 (1926).

[4] Courts have however continued to use enterprise analysis in other areas of law, such as taxation (*vide* e.g., *Mobil Oil Corp.* v. *Commissioner of Taxes of Vermont* 445 U.S. 425, 438-441 (1980)) and federal collective bargaining litigation (vide *Radio and Television Broadcast Technicians Local Union* v. *Broadcast Service of Mobile, Inc.* 380 U.S. 255, 256 (1965)). *Vide* further David Aronofsky, "Piercing the Transnational Corporate Veil : Trends, Developments and the Need for Widespread Adoption of Enterprise Analysis" 10 North Carolina Journal of International Law & Commercial Regulation 31 (1985) pp. 42-44.

isolated cases,[1] did the feature of economic integration continue to exert a decisive influence.[2] Generally, the instrumentality doctrine of the piercing the veil jurisprudence[3] prevailed. This happened even in the railway cases.[4] As a result, the existence of a corporate group comprising an economically integrated enterprise is not considered to be irreconcilable with the notion of separate personality and the protection that that notion affords to the enterprise as a whole. Berle's enterprise entity theory[5] - in which he observed that "[t]he corporation is emerging as an enterprise bounded by economics, rather than as an artificial mystic personality bounded by forms of words in a charter, minute books, and books of account"[6] - appears therefore to have been somewhat misguided.[7] Other earlier commentators also seem to have overestimated the influence of the enterprise concept.[8]

---

[1] E.g., *Sisco-Hamilton Co.* v. *Lennon* 240 F.2d 68, 69 (7th Cir. 1957); *Glenn* v. *Wagner* 313 S.E.2d 832, 844-845 (N.C. Ct. App. 1984); *St. Paul Fire & Marine Insurance Co.* v. *Arkla Chemical Corp.* 435 F.2d 857, 858-859 (8th Cir. 1971) (wholly owned subsidiary liable for the negligent act of employees of its holding company).

[2] It is submitted however that the taxi-cab cases involve "abusive" economic integration and are therefore distinguishable from the more general economic integration situations. *Vide post* pp. 411-413.

[3] *Vide supra* Chapter V pp. 256-263.

[4] *Vide* e.g., *Lowendahl* v. *Baltimore & O. Ry.* 247 A.D. 144, *aff'd*, 6 N.E. 2d 56 (1936); *Soanes* v. *Baltimore & O. R. Co., Inc.* 89 F.R.D. 430, 431-432 (E.D.N.Y. 1981). But cf. *Overstreet* v. *Southern Railway Co.* 371 F.2d 411, 412 (5th Cir. 1967), *cert. denied*, 387 U.S. 912 (1967).

[5] Adolf A. Berle, "The Theory of Enterprise Entity" 47 Colum. L.R. 343 (1947). *Vide supra* pp. 394-396.

[6] *Ibid.* at p. 345. *Vide* also generally *ibid.* pp. 348-350.

[7] Berle had also over-confidently asserted that "[i]f it be shown that the enterprise is not reflected and comprehended by the corporate papers, books and operation, the court may reconstruct the actual enterprise, giving entity to it, based on the economic facts." *Ibid.* at p. 354. Clearly, the courts have not adopted Berle's wide-ranging enterprise theory.

[8] *Vide* e.g., Note, "'Merger' or Agency of Subsidiary Corporations as Grounds of the Liability of the Liability of the Parent Corporation for Acts of its Subsidiary" 27 Colum. L.R. 702 (1927); pp. 704-705, 708; Burt Franklin, "Parent and Subsidiary - Parent Not Liable for Tort of Subsidiary" 12 Cornell L.Q. 504 (1927) p. 507; Note, "Disregarding Corporate Fiction, Liability of Parent Corporation for Acts of Subsidiary" 43 Harv. L.R. 1154 (1930).

## 4.2.2. Abusive economic integration

In American law, "abusive" economic integration is, however, likely to attract enterprise liability on the basis of the traditional veil piercing doctrine. The New York taxi-cab cases, it is submitted, provide clear and specific authority. The typical taxi-cab case involved a sizeable, fully-integrated and centralised operation conducted from common terminals.[1] The taxis were usually garaged in a common garage, maintained and repaired by the same mechanics, and dispatched from a centralised group dispatch centre. Spare parts, servicing supplies and fuel would be purchased and stored centrally. The accounting, claims and administrative departments were generally run by the same personnel serving the entire fleet. Moreover, the taxis were operated under a common name, common logos and a common identity. With the aim of insulating the enterprise from tort liability however, the enterprise was apportioned into several affiliated companies, with each company owning one, or perhaps a handful, of vehicles.[2] Although the subsidiaries would also take out the compulsory minimum liability insurance cover, each subsidiary was usually devoid of any assets except for the particular vehicle or vehicles operated by it.

In these circumstances, the courts imposed liability for the negligence of one company within the "fleet" upon its affiliated companies.[3] Traditional piercing the veil analysis was used, with subsidiaries being characterised as "instrumentalities", "agencies" and "conduits"[4] through which the taxi-cab business was operated. In the celebrated case of *Mull* v. *Colt Co.*,[5] the court concluded that if there was such a unity of interest and ownership that the independence of the separate subsidiaries had "in effect ceased or had never

---

[1] *Vide* e.g., *Mangan* v. *Terminal Transportation System, Inc.* 284 N.Y.S. 183, 187 (Sup. Ct. 1935), *aff'd per curiam*, 286 N.Y.S. 666 (3d. Dept. 1936); *Teller* v. *Clear Service Co.* 173 N.Y.S. 2d 183 (Sup. Ct. 1958).

[2] E.g., *Mull* v. *Colt Co.* 31 F.R.D. 154 (S.D.N.Y. 1962).

[3] *Mull* v. *Colt Co.* 31 F.R.D. 154 (S.D.N.Y. 1962); *Robinson* v. *Chase Maintenance Corp.* 190 N.Y.S.2d 773 (Sup. Ct. 1959); *Mangan* v. *Terminal Transportation System, Inc.* 284 N.Y.S. 183 (Sup. Ct. 1935), *aff'd per curiam* 286 N.Y.S. 666 (3d Dept. 1936). The New York approach has been adopted in other jurisdictions. *Vide* e.g., *Black & White, Inc.* v. *Love* 367 S.W.2d 427, 432 (Ark. 1963).

[4] *Vide Mull* v. *Colt Co.* 31 F.R.D. 154, 162 (S.D.N.Y. 1962); *Robinson* v. *Chase Maintenance Corp.* 190 N.Y.S.2d 773, 775 (Sup. Ct. 1959); *Mangan* v. *Terminal Transportation System, Inc.* 284 N.Y.S. 183, 191 (Sup. Ct. 1935), *aff'd per curiam* 286 N.Y.S. 666, 667 (3d Dept. 1936).

[5] 31 F.R.D. 154 (S.D.N.Y. 1962).

begun" then "an adherence to the fiction of separate identity would serve only to defeat justice and equity by permitting the economic entity to escape liability arising out of an operation conducted by one corporation for the benefit of the whole enterprise."[1] The courts have evidently been impressed by the economic unity of the business organisation and its artificial fragmentation into several subsidiaries.[2] Such fragmentation, resulting in a yawning gulf between the financial position of the subsidiary and that of the enterprise, was clearly perceived as abusive and unfair,[3] even "morally" reprehensible.[4]

So far, we have discussed the imposition of enterprise or "fleet" liability on all the subsidiaries within the group. What, however, is the position of the ultimate shareholder or shareholders? American courts have, quite rightly, been very careful to distinguish between enterprise or "fleet" liability and liability on the ultimate shareholder or shareholders. In *Robinson* v. *Chase Maintenance Corp.*,[5] the court - evidently mindful of the strong policy considerations especially with regard to individual investors - found that the complaint did not warrant the imposition of liability on the individual shareholder.[6] "To pursue the theories of recovery to that extent" said the court, "would destroy completely the efficacy of the corporate structure".[7] A few years later, the question of personal liability was again specifically considered in *Walkovszky* v. *Carlton*.[8] That case involved ten companies (each owning two taxi-cabs) conducting a closely integrated taxi-cab operation. A pedestrian injured by one of the taxis sued all ten companies and their shareholders.[9] The New York Court of Appeals drew a sharp distinction between the economic entity involved in the corporate group and

---

[1] *Ibid.* at p. 163.

[2] Two other factors were relevant in these cases : undercapitalisation and the conduct of the business under a "group persona". Neither factor, however, appears to have been decisive.

[3] *Vide Robinson* v. *Chase Maintenance Corp.* 190 N.Y.S.2d 773, 775 (Sup. Ct. 1959); *Teller* v. *Clear Service Co.* 173 N.Y.S. 2d 183, 190 (Sup. Ct. 1958).

[4] *Mull* v. *Colt Co.* 31 F.R.D. 154, 158, 164-165 (S.D.N.Y. 1962).

[5] 190 N.Y.S.2d 773 (Sup. Ct. 1959).

[6] *Ibid.* p. 776.

[7] *Ibid.* p. 776. *Vide* also *Glenn* v. *Wagner* 313 S.E.2d 832, 844 (N.C. Ct. App. 1984).

[8] 223 N.E.2d 6 (1966).

[9] The plaintiff also sued the taxi-cab driver, two other companies and three individuals involved in the accident.

the ultimate shareholders. In a simply-stated, yet incisive analysis, the court remarked :

> "It is one thing to assert that a corporation is a fragment of a larger corporate combine which actually conducts the business. It is quite another to claim that the corporation is a 'dummy' for its individual stockholders who are in reality carrying on the business in their personal capacities for purely personal rather than corporate ends. Either circumstance would justify treating the corporation as an agent and piercing the corporate veil to reach the principal but a different result would follow in each case. In the first, only a larger *corporate* entity would be held financially responsible ... while, in the other the stockholder would be personally liable."[1]

The distinction is neatly drawn. If the various companies function as "dummies" for each other but not for the individual shareholders then only the enterprise (that is the various companies within the group) will be responsible, but not the individual investors. If, on the other hand, the various companies operate as "dummies" for the individual investors, then liability will be also saddled on such investors.

## 5. ABUSIVE ECONOMIC INTEGRATION - PROPOSAL FOR REFORM

Given the inherent unfairness of "abusive" economic integration[2] and the uncertainty of the position in English law, a clear legislative statement on the issue would appear desirable.

### 5.1. Statement of principle - holding company or group liability

The law should expressly provide for a rule of enterprise liability in cases of "abusive" economic integration. Where the group corporate organisation involves a holding company with various subsidiaries, liability could be imposed upon the holding company for the debts of the insolvent subsidiary.

In two situations however, a modified form of enterprise liability should attach. The first situation is where the group does not actually comprise a holding company - in other words, where the various affiliates constituting

---

[1] *Ibid.* at pp. 8-9 (references omitted).

[2] *Vide supra* pp. 399-401.

the enterprise are owned by one or more individual shareholders. Considering the paramount importance of preserving the effectiveness of limited liability for individual investors, no liability should attach to the ultimate individual shareholders of the enterprise. The law should therefore carefully distinguish between the enterprise conducting the business and the owners of the enterprise. Only the internal subdivision of the unitary enterprise should be pulled down. The separate personality should be horizontally, but not vertically, disregarded. In this manner, the ultimate shareholders would retain their own shield of limited liability while liability would be imposed on the affiliated companies. The second situation where a modified form of enterprise liability is indicated occurs when all the various affiliates slide into insolvency - in other words, when the enterprise itself has become insolvent. In such an eventuality, the appropriate remedy would probably be substantive consolidation - that is the pooling of the assets *and* liabilities of the various affiliates within the group.[1] Substantive consolidation would almost certainly accord with the expectations of the creditors who would probably have perceived the various affiliates as one enterprise.

## 5.2. Voluntary and involuntary creditors

In so far as the distinction between voluntary and involuntary creditors is concerned, it is evident that abusive economic integration would directly and substantially affect involuntary creditors, especially the tort claimants. Such creditors are either literally unaware of the abusive practice or else do not have the practical opportunity or means of discovering it. The remedy of enterprise liability should clearly benefit them. Voluntary creditors require a different analysis. By definition, voluntary creditors bargain, or at least have the opportunity to bargain, with the subsidiary with which they contract.

---

[1] On the remedy of substantive consolidation, *vide post* Chapter IX pp. 458-462. A New Zealand court may, if it considers it just and equitable to do so, order that the assets and liabilities of two or more insolvent affiliates be pooled for the purpose of the liquidation. In deciding whether to exercise its discretion, the court is to have regard to a number of matters, including "[t]he extent to which any of the companies took part in the management of any of the other companies" and "[s]uch other matters as the Court thinks fit." *Vide* ss. 271(1)(b) and 272(2) of the New Zealand Companies Act 1993. Similar provisions had been previously incorporated in ss. 315B and 315C of the New Zealand Companies Act 1955. Sections 315B and 315C had been inserted by s. 30 of the Companies Amendment Act 1980.

They know, or at any rate should know, that the fragmentation strategy has been deployed. Voluntary creditors therefore assume the risk and cannot later complain. Different considerations would naturally apply in the event of a misrepresentation. Thus, if a voluntary creditor is misled into believing that the subsidiary he is bargaining with comprises the whole enterprise, then the basis of the bargain has been undermined. Such a creditor would qualify as an involuntary creditor for the purposes of the application of the proposed remedy.

## 5.3. Other aspects of the reform proposal

In line with the proposals for reform made in this work in connection with the subservient subsidiary situation[1] and the undercapitalised subsidiary situation,[2] the following additional rules should apply in the case of the remedy for "abusive" economic integration: (i) the remedy should only operate on the insolvent liquidation of the particular subsidiary or subsidiaries; (ii) the courts should be granted a discretion to allocate liability as they deem expedient in the circumstances; (iii) except where substantive consolidation is ordered, the remedy should involve a contribution to be made by the holding company to the assets of the insolvent subsidiary.

---

[1] *Vide supra* Chapter V pp. 298-305.
[2] *Vide supra* Chapter VI pp. 363-3364.

# 8    The Group Persona Situation

## 1. INTRODUCTION

Many corporate groups employ a "group persona" policy. Through the use of a group persona, the various components within the corporate group are held out to the public as a single enterprise, as a unified persona. Undoubtedly, the group persona policy is a marketing strategy intended to benefit the entire group.

### 1.1. The means of promoting a group persona

Several techniques may be used in the implementation of a group persona policy. These methods include the adoption of a common group name or title, the use of common trade marks, trade names, logos, emblems and symbols, the publication of statements that a company is a member of a particular group, the adoption of integrated advertising campaigns, the promotion of a group slogan, the use of a distinctive colour scheme, the use of common letterheads, and the depiction in the corporate literature - such as stationery, newsletters, promotional pamphlets and annual reports - of each company as part of one whole corporate family.[1] Moreover, companies in a group often have a common element in their names which suggests that they are parts of a greater whole.[2] Sometimes, there is even a conspicuous lack of identification of the separate subsidiaries.[3] The extent to which such methods are used varies from one group to another.

[1] *Vide* generally, The Law Society Memorandum (1981) para. 2.02(3), pp. 4-5; CBI Memorandum (1980) para. 11, p. 3; CCAB Memorandum (1979) paras. 6-7, p. 4; CCAB Memorandum (1981) para. 8, p. 4; The Cork Report, para. 1932, p. 435. *Vide* also *Revlon, Inc.* v. *Cripps & Lee Ltd.* [1980] F.S.R. 85; *FMC Finance Corp.* v. *Murphree* 632 F.2d 413 (5th Cir. 1980); *Texas Industries, Inc.* v. *Lucas* 634 S.W.2d 748 (Tex. Ct. App. 1982).

[2] E.g., *Soverio* v. *Franklin National Bank* 328 F.2d 446 (2d Cir. 1964); *Sagebrush Sales Co.* v. *Strauss* 605 S.W.2d 857 (Tex. 1980); *Revlon, Inc.* v. *Cripps & Lee Ltd.* [1980] F.S.R. 85; *Allright Texas, Inc.* v. *Simons* 501 S.W.2d 145 (Tex. Civ. App. 1973). *Vide* also CBI Memorandum (1980) p. 33; "Banker named as Prudential Chief" *Financial Times*, 21st October 1994.

[3] *Vide Mangan* v. *Terminal Transportation System, Inc.* 284 N.Y.S. 183, 191 (Sup. Ct. 1935), *aff'd per curiam*, 286 N.Y.S. 666 (3d. Dept. 1936).

The use of a group persona is of course possible in any type of group. It is however more typical in the highly integrated groups[1] where the promotion of an overall group image or reputation can naturally be of considerable mutual benefit to the various affiliates.

## 1.2. The nature of the abuse

Where the use of group persona techniques is particularly vigorous, the risk arises that creditors dealing with a particular subsidiary may be confused into believing that they are actually doing business either with the group as a separate trading entity in its own right, or with the holding company, or perhaps even with some other, financially stronger, subsidiary within the group.[2] Unsophisticated creditors are particularly at risk. Take, for example, a scenario where a holding company with an insurance subsidiary desires to enter into the real estate business. The holding company sets up a real estate subsidiary and gives it a name that is either confusingly similar to, or at least suggests an association with, that of its already established insurance subsidiary. Moreover, the real estate subsidiary will use a common logo and stationery, and will share premises with the insurance subsidiary. Unsophisticated third parties dealing with the real estate subsidiary are likely to automatically assume that they are contracting either with the insurance subsidiary or with the holding company itself. The dangers associated with such arrangements are widely acknowledged. Even the Confederation of British Industry - itself strongly opposed to the introduction of holding company liability - conceded in 1980 that unsophisticated creditors were particularly at risk from such techniques : "The CBI recognises ... that the practice of companies holding themselves out as subsidiaries of other companies or as a group or members of a group may tend to obscure the true identity or status of a company for others. It may be used as a device for, or

---

[1] *Vide* Blumberg, *Substantive Law* p. 296; Richard A. Posner, "The Right of Creditors of Affiliated Corporations" 43 U. Chic. L. Rev. 499 (1976) p. 514.

[2] Cf. *Revlon, , v. Cripps & Lee Ltd.* [1980] F.S.R. 85; *Darling Stores Corp.* v. *Young Realty Co.* 121 F.2d 112 (8th Cir.), *cert. denied*, 314 U.S. 658 (1941); R.A. Posner, *Economic Analysis of Law* (2nd ed. 1977) p. 300; Frank H. Easterbrook and Daniel R. Fischel, "Limited Liability and the Corporation" 52 Univ. of Chicago L.R. 89 (1985) p. 112; Frank Wooldridge, *Groups of Companies - The Law and Practice in Britain, France and Germany* (1981) p. 126. The risk of confusion has long been perceived in the United States. *Vide* Montgomery E. Pike, "Responsibility of the Parent Corporation for the Acts of Its Subsidiary" 4 Ohio State L.J. 311 (1938) p. 330.

have the effect of, mustering confidence in a business among people who cannot be expected to make proper enquiries to ascertain its credibility or are deterred from so doing."[1]

The policy of a common group persona may affect creditors in a different way. Creditors may, while recognising the individuality of the subsidiary they are contracting with, be led to believe that the group or the holding company will financially support the subsidiary in the event it encounters financial problems. In September 1979, the Consultative Committee of Accountancy Bodies - referring to "[t]he growing practice of companies within groups to refer to that group in all but formal documentation" - lamented that such practice "could create the impression, particularly to the uninitiated, that the resources of that group were available to meet the liabilities of all companies within the group."[2] A few months later, these misgivings were echoed in Parliament. During the Parliamentary debate on the Companies Bill 1980, Clinton Davis (who had proposed the introduction of a rule of holding company liability)[3] stated that "[s]mall firms become impressed by the connection of a subsidiary with a substantial, highly prestigious holding company, a connection that is often mercilessly exploited by the subsidiary for its own commercial purposes to give the impression that it has backing from the parent company."[4] And in a similar vein during the same debate, Ernie Roberts noted that "[s]ome subsidiary companies build their businesses on the well-known name of their parent companies. In fact, they would not obtain the business that they do if it had not been that they were able to use, by association, the names of their parent companies, which refuse in times of financial difficulty to accept any responsibility for the debts incurred".[5]  Though these observations are perhaps too cynically

---

[1] *Vide* CBI Memorandum (1980) para. 23, p. 7. The Confederation of British Industry considered that that was scope "both for considerable improvement in company practice and for tightening up of existing law in this respect." *Ibid.* para. 23, p. 7. Cf. also The Law Society Memorandum (1981) para. 2.01, p. 3.

[2] CCAB Memorandum (1979) para. 6, p. 4.

[3] *Vide post* Chapter X p. 468.

[4] *Vide* Parliamentary Debates (Hansard) 5th Series Vol. 979 (House of Commons) 26th February 1980 at col. 1253. *Vide* also Mr. Davis' comments in Parliamentary Debates, Standing Committee A, Session 1979-1980 Vol. I, 11th December 1979 cols. 717-718, 724.

[5] *Vide* Parliamentary Debates, Standing Committee A, Session 1979-1980 Vol. I, 11th December 1979 at col. 723. *Vide* also Mr. Roberts' comments in Parliamentary Debates (Hansard) 5th Series Vol. 979 (House of Commons) 26th February 1980, at col. 1258.

stated (a shortcoming probably induced by the highly contentious nature of the debate), they broadly represent what does sometimes happen in practice. Similar views were in fact soon being expressed by the Cork Committee.[1] In highlighting the need for reform, the Committee referred to the situation where an undercapitalised subsidiary "obtains credit by relying on its membership of the group of companies headed by the parent."[2] Such a subsidiary would indicate its membership of the group "on its letter heading" and would advertise "its membership on all documents and billings by showing a device or logo distinctive of the group."[3]

It is by no means easy to decide whether the use of the group persona techniques to promote the group image or to "sell" a subsidiary's product or service is so abusive that it justifies a legal sanction. One matter is clear enough. Many people do not clearly perceive the legal distinction between a holding and its subsidiary companies. Indeed, in *Adams* v. *Cape Industries plc*,[4] the Court of Appeal realistically acknowledged that the distinction between a holding and a subsidiary company may "[t]o the layman at least ... seem a slender one."[5] And the potential for confusion affects not just ordinary mortals. It apparently affects parliamentarians too - or at any rate some of them. During the debate in the House of Commons on the Bill that was eventually to become the Companies Act 1980, Martin Stevens frankly admitted that "to many members of the public, including me, it came as something of a surprise that this [holding company liability for debts of insolvent subsidiaries] was not automatically the case; I had supposed that the holding company would be responsible for the burdens and the benefits of its subsidiary, howsoever caused."[6] Nicholas Baker, on the other hand, suggested that in ordinary negotiations people understand the differences between holding and subsidiary companies.[7] Unless Mr. Baker was referring

---

[1] *Vide* the Cork Report, para. 1932, p. 435. *Vide* also Juan M. Dobson, "'Lifting the Veil' in Four Countries : The Law of Argentina, England, France and the United States" 35 I.C.L.Q. 839 (1986) p. 840.

[2] The Cork Report, para. 1932, p. 435.

[3] *Ibid.* para. 1932, p. 435.

[4] [1990] BCLC 479.

[5] *Ibid.* at p. 512.

[6] *Vide* Parliamentary Debates, Standing Committee A, Session 1979-1980 Vol. I, 11th December 1979 at col. 720.

[7] *Ibid.* at col. 722.

to negotiations conducted between sophisticated parties, his views would appear to be somewhat out of touch with reality.[1]

Even if the legal distinction between the holding and subsidiary companies were to be appreciated (let it be conceded that the layman is presumed to know the law), there can be little doubt that many would still be quite easily impressed by tactfully designed corporate identification strategies.[2] Where a unitary image of the group is ingeniously promoted, confusion may very well cloud the creditor's mind and the distinction between the holding company and its subsidiaries completely missed. This particular aspect had also been discussed in the House of Commons during the aforementioned debate on the Companies Bill. During the debate, Clinton Davis spoke of the "common practice ... to create a group image".[3] And Martin Stevens pertinently observed that "the growing practice of establishing corporate identification strategies across a whole range of companies manifestly implies to the public at large that they are part of the same family, that they are interdependent and that those who enter into business arrangements with the one may expect to benefit from its involvement with the others."[4] It may of course be possible - even for the unsophisticated creditors - to see through the promotional techniques and appreciate that a separate legal entity is involved. But to do so may well require more than just a moment's reflection. Unsophisticated creditors cannot be expected to pause and reflect on the complex legal structure of the organisation he is dealing with.

The conduct of a business under a common group image may cause another form of prejudice to creditors : occasionally, it may be difficult, if not impossible, for a claimant to identify which of the various companies

---

[1] In *Qintex Australia Finance Limited* v. *Schroders Australia Limited* (1990) 3 A.C.S.R. 267, Rodgers C.J. observed that "[i]n the every day rush and bustle of commercial life in the last decade it was seldom that participants to transactions involving conglomerates with a large number of subsidiaries paused to consider which of the subsidiaries should become the contracting party." *Ibid.* at p. 268.   Though the analogy may not be too precise, it is also eye-opening that a survey of 517 company *directors* conducted in 1993 showed that nearly 60 per cent of the directors did not even know of the existence of the Directors' Disqualification Act, 1986. *Vide* "Call to bar more unfit directors" *Financial Times*, 20th October 1993.

[2] *Vide* e.g., *Hertz International Ltd.* v. *Richardson* 317 So.2d 824 (Fla. Dist. Ct. App. 1975).

[3] *Vide* Parliamentary Debates, Standing Committee A, Session 1979-1980 Vol. I, 11th December 1979 at col. 717.

[4] *Ibid.* at col. 720.

within a group is answerable for the claim.[1] The problem can be especially acute in tort claims. The increasing complexity of a technologically advanced business world leads to increasing difficulty in establishing which company within the group is actually at fault. Sophisticated and integrated technical processes utilised within groups combined with elaborate and co-ordinated management systems make the accurate dissection of the decision-making process (necessary to establish the tortfeasor) an arduous task.[2] Indeed, the group's management may *itself* find it difficult to "unravel the baffling network of corporate relations" and it would then be "a sheer impossibility for those on the outside to locate the party directly responsible".[3] The task will be made all the more onerous where group persona techniques have been used.[4] Of course, it cannot be alleged that the tort victim had been misled by the group persona policy. He will however certainly encounter the problem raised by that policy at the time he attempts to identify the proper defendant. Clearly, he should not be thwarted in his attempt to do so. The issue is a question of fact within the particular knowledge of the group.

### 1.3. Should a group persona strategy lead to liability?

The crucial question is : should the use of a group persona strategy automatically saddle the holding company with liability for the debts of its subsidiaries? Some have argued that it should. Their argument basically is that once the group benefits from its promotion as a unitary enterprise, then

---

[1] In *Qintex Australia Finance Limited* v. *Schroders Australia Limited* (1990) 3 A.C.S.R. 267, Rodgers C.J. noted that "creditors of failed companies encounter difficulty when they have to select from among the moving targets the company with which they consider they concluded a contract." *Ibid.* p. 269.

[2] Cf. Sigmund Timberg, "Corporate Fiction - Logical, Social and International Implications" 46 Colum. L.R. 533 (1946) pp. 576-578; Ghertman and Allen, *op. cit.* pp. 41-43. This was also the plaintiffs' contention in the proceedings against Union Carbide Corporation arising out of the Bhopal tragedy. The plaintiffs argued that enterprise liability should be imposed. *Vide* Karl Hofstetter, "Multinational Enterprise Parent Liability : Efficient Legal Regimes in a World Market Environment" 15 North Carolina J. of Int. Law and Comm. Reg. 299 (1990) pp. 299-300; P.T. Muchlinski, "The Bhopal Case : Controlling Ultrahazardous Industrial Activities undertaken by Foreign Investors" 50 M.L.R. 545 (1987) pp. 556-557.

[3] Latty, *op. cit.* p. 99.

[4] *Vide Merriman* v. *Standard Grocery Co.* 242 N.E.2d 128, 130 (Ind. App. Ct. 1968).

it should accept the corresponding burdens.[1] Enterprise liability, they would argue, should therefore be imposed on the holding company. It is submitted, however, that such an approach goes too far. Certainly, the group as a whole benefits from a group marketing strategy. Even the individual companies themselves may stand to gain from such promotional techniques. But the mere fact that the various companies within the group gain some goodwill or advantage - perhaps even considerable goodwill or advantage - out of their mutual association is not inherently prejudicial to creditors dealing with them. Indeed, as long as the subsidiary is not subservient or undercapitalised, the participation of the subsidiary in a group persona policy can only strengthen its financial position. In effect, therefore, creditors are more likely to gain rather than to suffer as a result of a group persona strategy.

The position however changes if group persona techniques involve an element of misrepresentation. The use of a group persona strategy becomes unacceptable in two situations: (i) where creditors are given the impression that they are actually doing business either with the group as a separate person or with the holding company;[2] and (ii) where creditors are led to believe that the group, the holding company, or some other subsidiary will financially support the subsidiary in the event it encounters financial problems.[3]

In both such cases, an element of misrepresentation would be involved. In both cases, the employment of group persona tactics is abusive. The group would have implemented a strategy intended to instil in the creditor a belief that he is extending credit to an economic entity larger than the subsidiary he actually contracted with[4] or that the group is financially backing the subsidiary. At least where the creditors have relied on such misrepresentation, the piercing of the corporate veil is clearly warranted.[5] Holding company liability should be imposed.

---

[1] *Vide* comments made by Ernie Roberts Parliamentary Debates (Hansard) 5th Series Vol. 979 (House of Commons) 26th February 1980, at col. 1258. *Vide* also the observations made by Clinton Davis in Parliamentary Debates, Standing Committee A, Session 1979-1980 Vol. I, 11th December 1979 at cols. 717-718.

[2] *Vide supra* p. 417.

[3] *Vide supra* pp. 418-419.

[4] *Vide FMC Finance Corp.* v. *Murphree* 632 F.2d 413 (5th Cir. 1980).

[5] Even commentators who generally extol the virtues of limited liability for holding companies, concede that liability should be imposed on the holding company in cases of misrepresentation. *Vide* e.g., P. Halpern, M. Treblicock and S. Turnbull, "Economic

Economic analysis also supports the granting of a remedy in the case of misrepresentation. If companies are allowed to represent that they have greater assets than they actually possess, the result will be to increase the costs that creditors must incur to ascertain the true creditworthiness of the companies with which they deal.[1] To permit misrepresentation would therefore increase creditors' information costs. Any such costs are clearly wasted to the extent that misrepresentation could be prevented at a lower cost by adequate legal controls.[2]

## 2. GROUP PERSONA AND EXISTING REMEDIES

### 2.1. Position under English law

#### 2.1.1. Liability as a contracting party

In appropriate circumstances, a holding company implementing an abusive group persona policy may be held directly liable as a contracting party. Such a situation would arise, for example, where the representations made by a holding company amount to the granting of a guarantee in favour of the creditors of the subsidiary.[3] In the typical abusive group persona situation, however, such circumstances would not usually exist.

#### 2.1.2. Misrepresentation

Where the promotion of a group persona policy is abusive, a remedy may, in principle at least, be available under English law. Thus if the holding company has itself blatantly promoted a group persona policy which conceals the separate identity of its subsidiaries or which induces the subsidiaries' creditors to believe that the holding company or the group as a

---

*Cont.*
Analysis of Limited Liability in Corporation Law" 30 U. Toronto L. J. 117 (1980) at pp. 149-150; Frank H. Easterbrook and Daniel R. Fischel, "Limited Liability and the Corporation" 52 Univ. of Chicago L.R. 89 (1985) p. 112; Richard A. Posner, "The Right of Creditors of Affiliated Corporations" 43 U. Chic. L. Rev. 499 (1976) pp. 520-524.

[1] Richard A. Posner, "The Right of Creditors of Affiliated Corporations" 43 U. Chic. L. Rev. 499 (1976) p. 520.

[2] *Ibid.* pp. 520-521.

[3] *Vide supra* Chapter III pp. 131-132.

separate trading entity are responsible for the debts of the subsidiary, then the holding company may well be held liable in damages if the creditors relied on such statements. The appropriate remedy would be an action in tort for deceit or for negligent misstatement. It should of course be appreciated that in practice the representor is more likely to be the subsidiary itself rather than the holding company - it would be the subsidiary that would promote itself as forming part of a unitary enterprise and as having the financial backing of the group. To be sure, the subsidiary would be towing the group strategy line dictated by head office. But the representation would still be emanating from the subsidiary. The action would therefore lie against the subsidiary. The creditor may be able to claim damages or to rescind the contract or to avail himself of both remedies.[1] In practice, however, the strict conditions for an action based on misrepresentation will not easily be satisfied.[2]

Apart from the difficulty of complying with the technical requirements for an action based on misrepresentation, three other considerations point to the inadequacy of existing remedies as an antidote to the abusive group persona situation. In the first place, it is clear that any such action would have to be instituted against the representor. As already noted, in the typical case the representor would be the subsidiary. Where the subsidiary is insolvent, the successful outcome of any such action is unlikely to offer much comfort to the representee. The second reason for the inadequacy of existing remedies is that they are evidently monotransactional in nature.[3] The court would have to examine each creditor's claims on an individual basis to determine whether the requisite conditions have been satisfied. Hundreds or even thousands of claims may be involved. Litigation costs would be exorbitant. The third consideration is that the existing remedies, based as they are on the concept of detrimental reliance, are inapplicable to the subsidiary's involuntary creditors. As argued later on in this Chapter, however, involuntary creditors should also benefit by any rule that introduces enterprise liability in cases where abusive group persona strategies are deployed.

---

[1] *Vide* generally Treitel, *op. cit.* pp. 307-345.

[2] On the actions in tort for deceit and negligent misstatements, *vide* generally W.V.H. Rogers, *Winfield and Jolowicz on Tort* (13th ed. 1989) Ch. 11. On liability for misleading statements in a contractual context *vide* generally Treitel, *op. cit.* Ch. 9.

[3] On the problems associated with a monotransactional analysis, *vide* generally *supra* Chapter V pp. 237-238.

## 2.1.3. Sections 216 and 217 Insolvency Act 1986

As previously observed,[1] one common method of promoting a group persona is for the group to christen the various affiliates with names that suggest an association with one another. No law actually prohibits this practice. But the insolvency of any such company may trigger the application of sections 216 and 217 of the Insolvency Act 1986. In essence, these sections provide that when a company ("the liquidating company") has gone into insolvent liquidation, any name by which such company was known in the previous 12 months, or which is so similar as to suggest an association with it, becomes a "prohibited name" in relation to a person who was a director or shadow director[2] of it at any time in those twelve months.[3] Any such person must not, without leave of the court or in such circumstances as may be prescribed,[4] for five years, be a director of or be concerned in the promotion, formation or management of a company using a prohibited name.[5] Breach of these provisions amounts to a criminal offence and in addition will result in such person being personally liable (jointly and severally with the company and with any other person who is so liable) for the debts incurred during the period of the breach.[6] In the vast majority of cases, however, companies having a name similar to that of a liquidating company will not need to apply to the court for leave to continue using their existing name. The reason is that regulations made under section 216 dispense with the need for such application in the case where the solvent company has been known by the prohibited name for the whole of the period of 12 months ending with the

---

[1] *Supra* p. 416.

[2] A holding company may well qualify as a "shadow director". *Vide* I.A. 1986, s. 251 and *supra* Chapter V pp. 213-217.

[3] s. 216(1)(2).

[4] Insolvency Rules 1986, SI 1986/1925, rr 4.226-4.230.

[5] s. 216(3).

[6] s. 217. The mischief sought to be controlled by ss. 216 and 217 was probably the eradication of the "Phoenix syndrome", that is the practice whereby a person trading through the medium of one or more companies can allow such company to become insolvent, form a new company with an identical or a similar name, trades with assets purchased at a discount from the liquidator of the old company, and then carry on trading much as before, leaving a trail of unpaid creditors. *Vide* the Cork Report, para. 1813, p. 408; Ian F. Fletcher, *The Law of Insolvency* (1990) p. 402; It is clear however that the sections as enacted apply to a wider arena than the case of a person exploiting the goodwill of a previous insolvent company. *Vide Thorne* v. *Silverleaf* [1994] 1 BCLC 637 (C.A.) at p. 642 per Peter Gibson L.J.

day before the liquidating company went into liquidation and has not at any time in those 12 months been "dormant".[1] These conditions are likely to be satisfied in practice. The vast majority of groups comprising companies with similar names should not therefore be affected by the provisions of section 216 and 217 if one or more of the subsidiaries had to go into insolvent liquidation.

## 2.2. Position under American law

As in other areas of the law examined in this work, English and American law react differently to the use of group persona strategies. Especially through the medium of the piercing the veil jurisprudence and the equitable doctrines in bankruptcy, American courts have traditionally striven to control the abuse sometimes resulting from the implementation of group persona techniques.[2] More recently, the element of group persona has also left a significant impact in the area of product liability.[3]

### 2.2.1. Liability as a contracting party

In American law, as in English law,[4] a holding company implementing an abusive group persona policy may, in appropriate circumstances, be held directly liable as a contracting party, for example as a guarantor. But as already mentioned,[5] such circumstances are not likely to arise in the typical abusive group persona situation.

### 2.2.2. Group persona sometimes actionable *per se*

In a number of American cases in which the group was held out as a unified persona, the element of misrepresentation to the public appears to have been a significant factor in the imposition of liability on the holding company for

---

[1] Insolvency Rules 1986, SI 1986/1925, rr 4.230.

[2] *Vide post* pp. 427-430.

[3] *Vide post* pp. 431-433.

[4] *Vide supra* p. 423.

[5] *Supra* p. 423.

the debts of its subsidiary.[1] Where the misrepresentation is clear and has induced reliance, liability is imposed on the basis of familiar principles of misrepresentation. In *FMC Finance Corporation* v. *Murphree*,[2] for example, a number of group persona features were involved : similar names, common offices and joint negotiations by the affiliates of the contract in question. The court held that when an affiliate "engages in conduct likely to create in the creditor the reasonable expectation that he is extending credit to an economic entity larger than the corporation he actually contracted with, and the creditor reasonably relies to his detriment on his reasonable belief concerning who or what he was dealing with, then the corporate veil can be pierced."[3] And in *Dunn Appraisal Company* v. *Honeywell Information Systems, Inc.*,[4] the plaintiff sued both a holding company and its subsidiary for fraud and breach of contract. There was evidence of group persona techniques.[5] The court, finding that the plaintiff had been misled into thinking that he was dealing with just one company, allowed the plaintiff to recover against the holding company on the grounds of misrepresentation.[6]

### 2.2.3. A factor in the piercing the veil jurisprudence

Even where the promotion of the group persona is not *per se* actionable as a misrepresentation, it may still be considered as an important factor to be taken into account in establishing liability on the basis of the piercing the veil jurisprudence. In the taxi-cab cases, for example, the marketing of the fleet as a unitary business had clearly contributed to the imposition of a "fleet liability".[7] It should be stressed however that the group persona

---

[1] E.g., *My Bread Baking Co.* v. *Cumberland Farms, Inc.* 233 N.E.2d 748 (Mass. 1968); *Orlando Executive Park, Inc.* v. *P.D.R.* 402 So.2d 442, 449-450 (Fla. Dis. Ct. App. 1981); *Dunn Appraisal Co.* v. *Honeywell Information Systems, Inc.* 687 F.2d 877 (6th Cir. 1982).

[2] 632 F.2d 413 (5th Cir. 1980).

[3] *Ibid.* at p. 423. This case actually concerned the liability of a subsidiary for the acts of its holding company.

[4] 687 F.2d 877 (6th Cir. 1982).

[5] *Ibid.* at p. 881.

[6] *Vide* also *Dare To Be Great, Inc.* v. *Commonwealth ex rel. Hancock* 511 S.W.2d 224 (Ky. 1974).

[7] *Vide* e.g., *Mull* v. *Colt Co.* 31 F.R.D. 154 (S.D.N.Y. 1962); *Robinson* v. *Chase Maintenance Corp.* 190 N.Y.S.2d 773 (Sup. Ct. 1959); *Mangan* v. *Terminal*

strategy is not in itself an essential factor for the imposition of liability on the piercing the veil grounds. In other words, the corporate veil may be pierced to impose liability on the holding company even where the element of group persona is missing. Nor is element of group persona *per se* a decisive factor. There are indeed many cases where the courts refused to impose liability on the holding company despite the use of group persona techniques.[1] In effect, the element of group persona is merely one of the factors that may be taken into account, along with many others, in determining the question of liability.[2] Thus, in *My Bread Baking Co.* v. *Cumberland Farms, Inc.*[3] the plaintiff in an action for conversion proved that a number of affiliated companies used a common trade name, operated out of the same premises and confused creditors as to the identity of the company responsible. The affiliates shared common officers and directors. There was also agency-like interference - such as direct instructions given to personnel of the affiliates - by the shareholder-manager of the dominant affiliate. The court held the dominant affiliate could be found liable for the claim against the various affiliates.[4] The group persona factor had added support to the other elements making for liability.

As we have already seen,[5] the vice with the group persona strategy lies in its strong propensity to mislead creditors dealing with the subsidiary. Consequently, the abuse of a group persona should in principle affect only

---

*Cont.*

*Transportation System, Inc.* 284 N.Y.S. 183 (Sup. Ct. 1935), *aff'd per curiam*, 247 A.D. 853 (3d Dept. 1936). *Vide* further *supra* Chapter VII pp. 411-412.

[1] *Vide* e.g., *Nelson* v. *International Paint Co., Inc.* 734 F.2d 1084 (5th Cir. 1984); *D.L. Auld Co.* v. *Park Electrochemical Corp.* 553 F. Supp. 804 (E.D.N.Y. 1982); *Owl Fumigating Corp.* v. *California Cyanide Co.* 24 F. 2d 718 (D. Del. 1928); *Berkey* v. *Third Ave. Ry. Co.* 155 N.E. 58 (1926); *Japan Petroleum Co. (Nigeria) Ltd.* v. *Ashland Oil, Inc.* 456 F.Supp. 831 (D.Del. 1978); *Hanson Southwest Corp.* v. *Dal-Mac Construction Co.* 554 S.W.2d 712, 716-717 (Tex. Civ. App. 1977).

[2] *Vide* e.g., *Handlos* v. *Litton Industries, Inc.* 326 F.Supp. 965 (E.D. Wis. 1971).

[3] 233 N.E.2d 748 (Mass. 1968).

[4] The inter-play between the various factors emerges clearly from the following dictum : "Where there is common control of a group of separate corporations engaged in a single enterprise, failure (a) to make it clear which corporation is taking action in a particular situation and the nature and extent of that action, or (b) to observe with care the formal barriers between the corporations with a proper segregation of their separate businesses ... records and finances, may warrant some disregard of the separate entities in rare particular situations in order to prevent gross inequity." *Ibid.* at p. 752.

[5] *Supra* p. 417.

the consensual creditors. Yet the American piercing the veil cases have considered the abuse of a group persona to be relevant in both contract and tort cases. The taxi-cab cases again provide unequivocal confirmation of this approach. Those cases allowed recovery even to pedestrians who could not have relied on the unitary business image projected by the fleet.[1] The same reluctance to distinguish between tort and contract situations had appeared also in the railway cases.[2] Indeed, the abuse of the group persona continues to be a relevant factor in other contract and tort cases where liability is imposed on traditional piercing the veil grounds.

In situations involving a corporate group promoted as a unified enterprise, the courts have occasionally used the agency notion of "apparent authority" to impose liability on the holding company.[3] In *Hertz International Ltd.* v. *Richardson*,[4] the plaintiff had hired a car from a Hertz subsidiary and was injured in an accident allegedly caused by defective brakes. The group was steeped in group persona features : the car was hired from a "Hertz" outlet bearing the "Hertz" emblems and colours, the subsidiary used "Hertz" stationery and the employees wore "Hertz" uniforms. The court held that the subsidiary had been acting as the "agent" of the holding company with "apparent authority". The "apparent authority" basis of the decision has been sharply criticised by Blumberg on the ground that that doctrine is "employed to impose liability upon a principal for *unauthorized* acts of an *agent* because the principal's representations made it reasonable for a third party to assume that the agent was authorized to perform the acts, although in fact it was not."[5] In *Hertz*, of course, the issue was "whether the subsidiary had been acting as the parent's agent, not whether a party conceded to be an agent was authorized to perform the acts in question."[6] As Blumberg points out, however, another closely related agency doctrine may in fact be relevant : the doctrine of "apparent agency".[7] Under this doctrine, a "principal" is liable for the torts of persons who are

---

[1] *Vide* e.g., *Walkovszky v. Carlton* 223 N.E.2d 6 (1966).

[2] *Vide* e.g., *Lehigh Valley R. Co.* v. *Dupont* 128 F. 840 (2d Cir. 1904); *Conry* v. *Baltimore & O. R. Co.* 112 F. Supp. 252 (W.D. Pa. 1953).

[3] Under the law of agency, a principal is liable for the torts of an agent acting with apparent authority. *Vide* Restatement (Second) of Agency, section 27 (1958).

[4] 317 So.2d 824 (Fla. Dist. Ct. App. 1975).

[5] Blumberg, *Substantive Law* p. 313.

[6] Blumberg, *Substantive Law* pp. 313-314.

[7] Blumberg, *Substantive Law* p. 314.

not agents if he led third parties to believe that those persons were his agents.[1] The doctrine however requires that the "apparent agent" must have acted for the immediate benefit of the "principal" - a condition that will not usually be fulfilled in corporate group situations.[2]

### 2.2.4. A factor in the bankruptcy cases

The conduct of the business of affiliated companies under a unified group persona has also been considered a relevant factor in the bankruptcy cases,[3] with substantive consolidation (involving the pooling of all the group assets and all the group liabilities) sometimes being ordered. The rationale is reliance. The use of a group persona is not, however, an essential factor for substantive consolidation.[4] Nor is it *per se* decisive. Where substantive consolidation is ordered, it would usually affect the totality of the creditors. If, however, individual creditors prove reliance on particular affiliates, the courts have sometimes ordered partial consolidation.[5] The effect of partial consolidation is that the claims of those creditors proving reliance on the credit of particular affiliates would be preserved against the assets of such affiliates and the claims of other creditors would be subject to the procedure of substantive consolidation. After an inclination to allow partial consolidation in earlier years,[6] the process now seems to have fallen into desuetude.[7]

In a bankruptcy setting, the misleading use of group persona techniques has also enabled a creditor to set off his claim against one affiliate against his indebtedness to another affiliate.[8] Even if the separate personality of the various companies within the group was apparent, setoff may still be allowed

---

[1] Two cases have applied this doctrine. *Vide Dania Jai-Alai Palace, Inc.* v. *Sykes* 425 So.2d 594, 598 (Fla. Dis. Ct. App. 1983), *rev'd*, 450 So.2d 1114 (Fla 1984); *Orlando Executive Park, Inc.* v. *P.D.R.* 402 So.2d 442, 449-450 (Fla. App. 1981).

[2] *Vide* further Blumberg, *Substantive Law* pp. 314-315.

[3] *Vide Soverio* v. *Franklin National Bank* 328 F.2d 446 (2d Cir. 1964).

[4] *Chemical Bank New York Trust Co.* v. *Kheel* 369 F.2d 845, 847 (2d Cir. 1966).

[5] *In re Food Fair, Inc.* 10 Bankr. 123, 127 (Bankr. S.D.N.Y. 1981); *In re Lewellyn* 26 Bankr. 246, 251-252 (Bankr. S.D. Iowa 1982).

[6] *Stone* v. *Eacho* 127 F.2d 284, 290 *reh'g denied*, 128 F.2d 16 (4th Cir.), *cert. denied*, 317 U.S. 635 (1942).

[7] *Vide* Blumberg, *Bankruptcy Law* p. 408.

[8] *Lucey Mfg. Corp.* v. *Oil City Iron Works* 131 So. 57 (La. Ct. App. 1930).

if the contracting parties intended to consider the separate companies as a single enterprise.[1]

## 2.2.5. Impact in the area of product liability

The element of group persona has also had a significant impact in the area of product liability.[2] Thus, in cases where products were sold under a group name, a number of courts have imposed liability on the holding company notwithstanding that it had not been involved in the manufacturing process or had not been responsible for the defect in the products. In *Vaughn* v. *Chrysler Corporation*,[3] a vehicle - free of any defects - had been manufactured by the holding company and then sold to a first-tier subsidiary, which in its turn sold it to a second-tier subsidiary. The second-tier subsidiary then defectively modified the vehicle and sold it to a dealer who in his turn sold it to a consumer. The consumer was subsequently injured as a result of the modification carried out by the second-tier subsidiary. The court was impressed by the reliance placed by the consumer on the reputation of the product which was promoted and sold under the group name. The court stated that "[t]he imposed liability on Chrysler Corporation [the holding company] is ... strict to the extent that the reliance of a consumer on the integrity of manufacturer is not defeated by a complicated corporate structure in which the consumer has no interest nor knowledge that his confidence in the product has been legally thwarted through the mysteries of business technicalities and complications".[4] A similar approach was adopted in *Kasel* v. *Remington Arms Co.*[5] where a consumer was injured by a product manufactured by a 40% owned subsidiary. The group was operated on an integrated basis and the products were traded under the Remington name. The court held that the group was a "composite business enterprise"[6] and that the consumer had relied on the group name. Liability was imposed on the holding company.

---

[1] *Vide Piedmont Print Works, Inc.* v. *Receivers of People's State Bank* 68 F.2d 110 (4th Cir. 1934); *Black & Decker Mfg. Co.* v. *Union Trust Co.* 4 N.E.2d 929 (1936).

[2] *Vide* generally Blumberg, *Substantive Law* pp. 267-273.

[3] 442 F.2d 619 (10th Cir.), *cert. denied*, 404 U.S. 857 (1971).

[4] *Ibid.* at pp. 621-622.

[5] 101 Cal. Rptr. 314 (App. 1972).

[6] *Ibid.* at p. 322.

A stronger case is *Connelly* v. *Uniroyal, Inc.*[1] in which a subsidiary of Uniroyal, Inc. manufactured tyres and distributed them under the group trademark "Uniroyal". The subsidiary conducted its business with considerable autonomy from its holding company and had been in business long before the acquisition of its shareholding by the holding company.[2] The plaintiff's father purchased an Opel vehicle fitted with a defective "Uniroyal" tyre manufactured and sold to Opel by the subsidiary. Subsequently, the plaintiff was injured in an accident caused by the tyre. The Appellate Court of Illinois held that the use of the holding company's trademark could not expose the holding company to liability as it had neither been involved in the design, manufacture or distribution of the defective tyre nor had it dominated the subsidiary to make it its instrumentality.[3] The Appellate Court was also impressed by the fact that the plaintiff was not even aware that the vehicle had been fitted with "Uniroyal" tyres.[4] The Supreme Court adopted a fundamentally different approach. It held that the societal purposes underlying the imposition of strict liability on one who holds himself out as a manufacturer requires that "the doctrine be applicable to one who, for a consideration, authorizes the use of his trademark, particularly when, as here, the product bears no indication that it was manufactured by any other entity."[5] The Supreme Court's judgment in *Connelly* furnishes a more forceful approach than the *Vaughn* and *Kasel* decisions both because the subsidiary in *Connelly* was in a large measure autonomously operated - and more importantly - because the injured plaintiff was not even aware that the vehicle had been fitted with "Uniroyal" tyres. The element of reliance - a significant factor in *Vaughn* and *Kasel* - was patently missing from Connelly.

It should be stressed that other American courts dealing with product liability cases have not afforded any particular importance to the group persona element and have refused to impose liability on the holding company on such grounds. *Nelson* v. *International Paint Co.*,[6] for example, involved

---

[1] 370 N.E.2d 1189 (Ill. App. 1977) *rev'd* 389 N.E.2d 155 (Sup. Ct. 1979).

[2] 370 N.E.2d 1189 (Ill. App. 1977) pp. 1196-1197.

[3] 370 N.E.2d 1189 (Ill. App. 1977) p. 1196.

[4] 370 N.E.2d 1189 (Ill. App. 1977) pp. 1195, 1198.

[5] 389 N.E.2d 155 (Sup. Ct. 1979) at p. 163.

[6] 734 F.2d 1084 (5th Cir. 1984).

a first-tier and a second-tier subsidiary, both using the group trademark and name. The court, stating that no ground for piercing the veil had been proved,[1] declined to impose liability on the first-tier subsidiary for damages resulting from a defective product manufactured and sold by the second-tier subsidiary.[2]

## 3. PROPOSAL FOR REFORM

### 3.1. Holding company liability

As we have already seen,[3] the mischief inherent in the abusive form of the group persona situation is misrepresentation : the various affiliated companies are projected to the public as a single enterprise, as a unified persona, with the result that creditors are misled as to the true worth of the subsidiary or are given a false impression that the group is either a separate trading entity in its own right or is financially backing the subsidiary. Given that English law does not adequately remedy the mischief,[4] the introduction of a rule imposing holding company liability in such circumstances appears desirable.[5]

---

[1] *Ibid.* at pp. 1092-1093.

[2] *Vide* also *Califf* v. *Coca Cola Co.* 326 F. Supp. 540 (N.D. Ill. 1971).

[3] *Supra* pp. 417-419.

[4] *Vide supra* pp. 423-426.

[5] In 1980 the Confederation of British Industry, recognising the potential abuse of the group persona situation proposed that personal liability should attach to the case where a "company fails to make apparent or obscures its true identity to a third party with whom it is contracting." It also suggested that "[w]here such confusion is caused by a wholly-owned UK subsidiary of a UK company holding itself out as a subsidiary or member of a group the authorisation of the parent company for the behaviour of the subsidiary may be presumed." *Vide* CBI Memorandum (1980) para. 25, p. 8. Though not very clearly stated, it would appear that the Confederation of British Industry was in favour of imposing liability both on the directors personally and on the holding company. In 1981, the Consultative Committee of Accountancy Bodies proposed that "the law should be strengthened where a company can be said to have held itself out as being underwritten by its parent". *Vide* CCAB Memorandum (1981) para 9, pp. 4-5. In apparently excluding the holding company from potential liability, the proposal of the Consultative Committee of Accountancy Bodies was narrower than that submitted by the Confederation of British Industry.

## 3.2. Voluntary and involuntary creditors

Should a distinction be drawn between voluntary and involuntary creditors for the purposes of allowing them recovery against any contribution to be made by the holding company to the assets of the subsidiary? Clearly, voluntary creditors who are aware of the reality of the group corporate structure should not be able to assert holding company liability. They have not been misled. They must be held to their bargain. Their awareness of the actual position should therefore estop them from pursuing their claims against the holding company. Admittedly, such a "misrepresentation basis" of liability will require the court to examine each particular creditor's claim and the surrounding circumstances in order to determine whether the creditor was aware of the reality of the group structure and, if he was not so aware, whether the unawareness was reasonable. Such a test would in practice be fraught with considerable difficulties : clearly the litigation may have to involve numerous creditors. Creditors are not a monolithic group. Considerable variations may occur on the extent of reliance. Litigation costs would be excessive. A solution may be to introduce an objective test with regard to voluntary creditors : the court would determine, for the voluntary creditors as a class, whether - in the light of the overall picture presented by the group persona - a reasonable person voluntarily contracting with the subsidiary would have been misled. In this manner, voluntary creditors would be treated on an aggregated basis.

In so far as involuntary creditors are concerned, a distinction needs to be drawn. The element of misrepresentation in an abusive group persona situation would almost certainly affect the "consensual" involuntary creditors, such as consumers. They should clearly benefit from any rule imposing liability on the holding company. The misrepresentation which entraps the consensual involuntary creditors, however, does not ordinarily affect. For tort does not generally involve reliance by the creditor.[1] In his case, therefore the element of abusive group persona is usually fortuitous. Nevertheless, it is submitted that a rule imposing holding company liability for abusive group persona tactics should also benefit tort creditors. The imposition of liability in these circumstances would serve not merely as a

---

[1] It is of course possible, though unlikely, that the tort creditor had initially been induced to enter into a contractual relationship with the company in reliance on the group image. The original contractual relationship (e.g., a stay in a hotel or a ride in a taxi) may then have given way to a tort claim.

means of compensating those who have been misled, but also a means of penalising the abuse and deterring such unconscionable conduct.

## 3.3. Substantive consolidation

Where the creditors of the various companies within a group have generally believed that they have been dealing with one trading enterprise rather than with the individual components and the various subsidiaries have declined into insolvency, substantive consolidation - rather than holding company liability - would appear more appropriate. Substantive consolidation, in making the entire assets of the group available for the satisfaction of all the creditors' claims, would accord with the creditors' reasonable expectations.[1] To avoid unfairness, the rule of substantive consolidation would have to be modified where certain creditors have relied specifically on the credit of particular subsidiaries. Partial, rather than complete, consolidation may then be proper.

## 3.4. Other aspects of the reform proposal

As with the other proposals for reform suggested in this work,[2] holding company liability should only arise on the insolvent liquidation of the subsidiary and should then be by way of a contribution to the assets of the subsidiary.[3] The action will lie in the hands of the liquidator. Subject to what is stated above regarding voluntary creditors, any contribution to the assets of the subsidiary should enure to the benefit of the creditors of the subsidiary. Also in line with the other proposals for reform,[4] the extent of

---

[1] The company law reforms introduced in New Zealand to the New Zealand Companies Act 1955 by the Companies Amendment Act 1980 enabled a court in certain circumstances and if the court considered it just and equitable to do so, to order the pooling of the assets and liabilities of "related companies". The term "related companies" encompassed those companies which have carried on business in such a way that the separate business of each company, or a substantial part thereof "is not readily identifiable." *Vide* now ss. 2(3) 271(1)(b) and 272(2) of the New Zealand Act 1993. Abusive group persona techniques would arguably render the separate businesses not "readily identifiable".

[2] *Vide supra* Chapter V pp. 301-302; Chapter VI pp. 364-365; Chapter VII p. 415.

[3] The proposed remedy would not of course exclude the right of creditors from seeking redress under the existing law of misrepresentation.

[4] *Vide supra* Chapter V pp. 303-305; Chapter VI pp. 389-390; Chapter VII p. 415

holding company liability should be determined by the court in its discretion. In exercising its discretion, the court should take into account the seriousness of the misrepresentation, the length of time over which the misrepresentation was practised, and the extent to which the holding company itself directed the implementation of the group persona strategy.

### 3.5. Identifying the proper defendant

Finally, to deal with those cases where the difficulty lies in identifying which group component is the proper defendant,[1] the law should, independently of whether or not group persona techniques have been used, impose upon the holding company a duty to furnish to the claimant satisfactory evidence of the intra-group network of relationships as would enable him to pinpoint the responsible affiliate. Alternatively, the onus can be shifted onto the holding company to demonstrate which affiliate was responsible. As long as the identification of the appropriate defendant by one of such means is feasible, then the imposition of enterprise liability would clearly be unwarranted. Where, however, such an identification has not been made, it would be proper to impose liability either on the holding company or collectively on those affiliates who may have participated in the process giving rise to the claim.

---

[1] *Vide supra* pp. 420-421.

# 9  Common Issues

## 1. INTRODUCTION

This chapter deals with a number of issues that are common to the reform proposals set out in this work. Other common issues of a "preliminary" nature were tackled in an earlier chapter.[1]

## 2. THE MEANING OF "HOLDING COMPANY" AND "GROUP OF COMPANIES" FOR PURPOSES OF REFORM PROPOSALS

### 2.1. The need for definitions

In terms of the reform proposals, "enterprise" liability should, depending on the circumstances, take the form either of holding company liability or of substantive consolidation (that is, the pooling of the assets and liabilities of the whole group). So far, the terms "holding company" and "group" have been used quite generically and without actually having been defined. Without intending to make a fetish of definitions, it must be acknowledged that a precise and practicable definition of the terms is essential to the implementation of the proposed rules. Having examined, in the previous chapters, various aspects of the inter-relationship between companies in the closely-knit arrangements we have called groups, we are now in a better position to attempt the task of definition. Before doing so, however, it would be pertinent to glance at existing judicial and legislative definitions.

### 2.2. Current definitions of the holding-subsidiary relationship

No judicial definition of the holding-subsidiary relationship exists in English law. Indeed, there has been no need for one. The reason, of course, is that no particular issue has come up before the courts requiring such an exercise. And probably for the same reason, writers on English company law have quite rightly declined to propose a general definition of the holding-subsidiary relationship, preferring instead to focus their discussion on the

---

[1] *Vide supra* Chapter IV.

definitions contained in the Companies Acts.[1] In the United States, however - where the holding-subsidiary relationship has had a significant impact on the law, especially in the piercing the veil[2] and equitable subordination doctrines[3] - cases and writers have attempted to define the relationship. Although no "standard" definition of the holding-subsidiary has been formulated, the cases and writers appear to agree that a holding company embraces a company which is in a position to control the management of another company ("the subsidiary") by virtue of its ownership.[4] So defined, the term "holding company" will include companies whose ownership of the shares of other companies is less than one hundred per cent and even less than fifty one per cent.[5]

Existing United Kingdom legislation does not define the holding-subsidiary or group relationship in a uniform manner. Indeed, different definitions may be contained in the same statute. In tax legislation, for example, various definitions are given for different purposes.[6] The Companies Act 1985 itself contains two sets of definitions. Sections 736[7] and 736A[8] define the holding-subsidiary relationship for general non-accounting purposes.[9] By section 736(1) a company is treated as a "subsidiary" of another company (its "holding company") if that other company (i) holds a majority of the voting rights in it, or (ii) is a member of it and has the right to appoint or remove a majority of its board of directors, or (iii) is a member of it and controls alone, pursuant to an agreement with

---

[1] *Vide* e.g., Gower, pp. 118-122; *Palmer's Company Law* (25th ed. 1992) Vol. I, pp. 1066-1068.

[2] *Vide supra* Chapter V pp. 256-263; Chapter VI pp. 348-354.

[3] *Vide supra* Chapter VI pp. 355-360.

[4] *Vide* Latty, *op. cit.* p. 3; William T. Walker, "Some Comments on the Liability of a Parent Corporation for the Torts or Contracts of its Subsidiary" 18 Ohio State Bar Association Report 198 (1945) p. 199.

[5] *Vide* e.g., *Kohn* v. *American Metal Climax, Inc.* 322 F.Supp. 1331, 1355 (E.D. Pa. 1971).

[6] *Vide* Income and Corporation Taxes Act 1988, ss. 218(1), 229(1), 413(3)(b). Cf. also s. 838 (subsidiaries) and s. 839(5) (connected companies).

[7] Substituted by s. 144(1) of the Companies Act 1989.

[8] Inserted by s. 144(1) of the Companies Act 1989.

[9] Non-accounting provisions in the C.A. 1985 in respect of which the holding-subsidiary issue may be relevant include s. 151 (prohibition on financial assistance for purchase of shares), s. 319 (employment contracts for more than five years), ss. 320-322 (substantial property transactions), s. 323 (dealings in share options), ss. 324-329 (disclosure of shareholdings) and ss. 330-342 (loans and quasi-loans).

other shareholders or members, a majority of the voting rights in it, or (iv) if it is a subsidiary of a company which is itself a subsidiary of that other company.[1] Section 736A amplifies and explains this definition.[2]

As a result of the implementation of the Seventh Company Law Directive,[3] a wider and more flexible definition of the holding-subsidiary relationship is then contained in section 258[4] and Schedule 10A[5] for the purposes of determining when consolidated financial statements have to be prepared. The Seventh Directive provided for mandatory implementation of tests based on legal control[6] and for optional implementation of tests based on factual control.[7] The definition - which refers to "parent undertakings" and "subsidiary undertakings"[8] rather than holding and subsidiary companies - establishes six ways in which an undertaking may be a parent undertaking in relation to a subsidiary undertaking. Four of them[9] - the ones based on legal control - substantially mirror the tests found in section 736. The other

---

[1] The previous s. 736 (which was substituted by s. 144 of the Companies Act 1989) had provided that a holding-subsidiary relationship existed where one company was a member of and controlled the composition of the board of the other company, or held more than one-half of the nominal value of its equity share capital. The difficulty with the latter test was that in terms of s. 744 "equity share capital" was defined not in terms of voting rights but in terms of capital and dividends. Control, therefore, played no role. As early as 1962, the Jenkins Committee had already recommended that the majority holding criterion be dropped "so that the definition of a subsidiary is in future based solely on membership and control." The Jenkins Report, para. 156(a), p. 56. For the Report's criticism of the position then obtaining, *vide ibid.* paras. 149-150, pp. 53-54. For a similar criticism, *vide* also Frank Wooldridge, *Groups of Companies - The Law and Practice in Britain, France and Germany* (1981) pp. 17-18.

[2] By s. 736B (inserted by s. 144 of the Companies Act 1989) the Secretary of State is empowered by regulations to amend ss. 736 and 736A so as to alter the meaning of the expressions "holding company", "subsidiary" or "wholly-owned subsidiary". The regulations may also make different provisions for different cases or different classes of cases.

[3] EEC Council Directive 83/349 of June 13, 1983.

[4] Inserted by s. 21(1) of the Companies Act 1989.

[5] Inserted by Sched. 9 of the Companies Act 1989.

[6] EEC Council Directive 83/349, Art. 1(1)(a), (b) and (d).

[7] EEC Council Directive 83/349, Art. 1(1)(c).

[8] An "undertaking" means (i) a body corporate or partnership, or (ii) an unincorporated association carrying on a trade or business, with or without a view to profit. *Vide* C.A. 1985, s. 259 (inserted by s. 22 of the Companies Act 1989).

[9] *Vide* C.A. 1985, ss. 258(2)(a),(b),(d) and 258(5).

two - those based on factual control[1] - are: (i) where one undertaking (the "parent") has the right to exercise a "dominant influence" over another undertaking (the "subsidiary") by virtue of a provision in the subsidiary's memorandum or articles of association or by virtue of a control contract,[2] and (ii) where one undertaking (the "parent") holds a "participating interest" over another undertaking (the "subsidiary") and either actually exercises a dominant influence over it or the two undertakings are managed on a "unified basis".[3]

It is of course beyond the scope of this work to discuss in detail the highly technical provisions of the Companies Act 1985.[4] One point should however be emphasised. The four tests of the holding-subsidiary relationship for general non-accounting purposes are based on legal control and are capable of relatively precise application. By contrast, the two additional tests for accounting purposes based on factual control depend to a large extent on

[1] The optional tests based on factual control were implemented in the United Kingdom in the hope that they would curb the use of "off-balance sheet financing" whereby assets or liabilities are acquired by controlled non-subsidiaries with the aim of keeping them off the consolidated financial statements. *Vide* Farrar, p. 487. A further clamp-down on "off-balance sheet financing" was recently provided by FRS 5 from the Accounting Standards Board. *Vide* "Accounts must reveal more" *Financial Times*, 14th April 1994.

[2] C.A. 1985, s. 258(2)(c). The "right to exercise a dominant influence" is not defined. It is however provided that "[f]or the purposes of s. 258(2)(c) an undertaking shall not be regarded as having the right to exercise a dominant influence over another undertaking unless it has a right to give directions with respect to the operating and financial policies of that other undertaking which its directors are obliged to comply with such directions whether or not they are for the benefit of that other undertaking." Para. 4(1) of Sched. 10A of the C.A. 1985.

[3] C.A. 1985, s. 258(4). A "participating interest" means "an interest held by an undertaking in the shares of another undertaking which it holds on a long-term basis for the purpose of securing a contribution to its activities by the exercise of control or influence arising from or related to that interest." (C.A. 1985, s. 260(1) inserted by s. 22 of the Companies Act 1989). Neither "dominant influence" nor "managed on a unified basis" is defined. The definition of "dominant influence" found in para. 4(1) of Sched. 10A with reference to s. 258(2)(c) is expressly stated not to affect the meaning of the expression "actually exercises a dominant influence" in s. 258(4)(a). *Vide* para. 4(3) of Sched. 10A. A statutory definition would probably encourage evasion. The terms were therefore deliberately left undefined.

[4] For a general discussion on the definitions found in the Companies Act 1985 *vide* Gower, pp. 119-122; Farrar, pp. 486-489; *Palmer's Company Law* (25th ed. 1992) Vol. 2, pp. 9072-9075. On the meaning of parent and subsidiary undertakings and on the implications of the amendments introduced by the Companies Act 1989 to implement the Seventh Directive, *vide* John Kitching and Marco Compagnoni, "Subsidiary undertakings in the U.K." International Corporate Law, February 1991, pp. 27-32.

an element of judgement on the relationship between the undertakings. As a result, they are less capable of precise application. The looser tests based on factual control were not made applicable to non-accounting contexts primarily because of the need for greater precision and certainty in such cases.

## 2.3. Definition for the purposes of this study

The question now is: what criteria should determine whether a company qualifies as a holding company for the purposes of the reform proposals? It will be recalled that the aim of the proposed remedies is primarily to compensate creditors in cases where the privilege of separate juridical personality has been abused by the corporate shareholder. Such aim is achieved by withholding the benefit of limited liability. It is clear that the loss of limited liability should affect only those in control - those who have actively caused, or who could have at least prevented, the abuse. Control is therefore a natural pre-condition to the loss of limited liability. It should not however be necessary for control to be positively exercised : the failure to exercise control should in itself provide the causal link with the abuse.[1] Latent control, in other words, should be sufficient.[2] Policy considerations militate in favour of the requisite of control as a condition for the loss of limited liability. In the first place, it provides an incentive for those in control to ensure that situations of abuse do not develop. Secondly, it encourages investment by shielding passive investors from liability.[3]

The difficulty is to ascertain the existence - and even the true meaning - of control. Clearly, a company is in a position of control if it has the means of making another company comply with its wishes. Control is the power to determine the fundamental features of corporate behaviour. But control is an ambiguous concept. A principal ambiguity is between control in the sense of the ability to impose one's will by coercion despite resistance and control in the sense of the probability that an order will be obeyed. Control, moreover, comes in infinite shades and gradations and can be exercised in different

---

[1] Such a failure may be especially relevant in the undercapitalisation cases.

[2] On factual and latent control by the holding company *vide supra* Chapter II pp. 49-51.

[3] Where American courts have saddled a controlling shareholder with liability they have refused to impose liability on the passive shareholders. *Vide* e.g., *Jefferson Pilot Broadcasting Co.* v. *Hilary & Hogan, Inc.* 617 F.2d 133 (5th Cir. 1980).

ways.[1] Berle and Means, for example, had identified five species of control : (i) control through almost complete ownership, (ii) majority control, (iii) control through legal devices without majority ownership, (iv) minority control, and (v) management control.[2] Clearly, quantitative tests based on levels of shareholding should not necessarily be conclusive, for control can be exercised by the possession of a number of shares which falls well below *de jure* control.[3] The phenomenon is particularly noticeable in the case of large public companies with widely dispersed shareholding.

In determining what relationship should carry with it financial responsibility and what should not, the employment of precise and detailed legal criteria is essential. Otherwise a fair measure of certainty and predictability - so desirable in liability matters - would be lacking. In this regard, it is submitted that the "general purpose" definition of the holding-subsidiary relationship contained in section 736[4] of the Companies Act 1985 satisfies both the underlying requirement of control and the need for precision and certainty in matters of definition. The more elastic "accounting purposes" tests of section 258 and Schedule 10A of the Act, being less capable of precise and predictable application, are inappropriate for defining the holding-subsidiary relationship for the purposes of substantive liability. Admittedly, a strict definition of control will mean that marginal cases may escape the liability rules. This would however be preferable to allowing uncertainty to exist.

## 2.4. Definition of a "group of companies"

The Companies Act 1985 does not contain any *general* definition of a group of companies. A definition is however given for the purposes of certain provisions of the Act. Thus, for the purposes of section 319 (dealing with certain directors' contracts of employment for more than five years), a "group" is defined as a holding company together with its subsidiaries.[5] This definition broadly tallies with the common understanding of the term. It is

---

[1] *Vide* generally, Herman, *op. cit.*; Wallace, *op. cit.* pp. 11-15; Richard B. Miner, *Associated Corporations* (1983) pp. 14-59; John Scott, *Corporations, Classes and Capitalism* (2nd ed. 1985) pp. 43-56.

[2] Berle and Means, *op. cit.* Ch. V.

[3] *Vide* Berle and Means, *op. cit.* Ch. V; Scott, *op. cit.* p. 46.

[4] As supplemented by s. 736A.

[5] s. 319(7)(b).

also appropriate for the purposes of the analysis conducted in this work. In this study, therefore, a group should, as a general rule, be taken to mean a holding company and its subsidiaries (including, of course, any sub-subsidiaries). Occasionally, however, the term "group of companies" is also used in this work to refer to an organisation composed of a number of companies sharing a common individual shareholder or a number of individual shareholders.[1] Such affiliated companies would together constitute a group.

## 2.5. Should liability be on the immediate holding company or on the ultimate holding company?

Sometimes, a group consists of several tiers of companies with the "ultimate" holding company at the apex. At a level below the ultimate holding company there would be companies which qualify both as subsidiaries (of the ultimate holding company) and as "immediate" holding companies of other companies. A sub-subsidiary of the ultimate holding company would be a subsidiary of its immediate holding company.

In the event of the insolvency of a sub-subsidiary, should liability attach to the immediate holding company or to the ultimate holding company?[2] Various considerations suggest that in such a case, liability ought to be directed to the immediate holding company. In the first place, such an approach would fit in with the underlying "control" basis of liability. Indeed, in multi-tiered corporate structures, it is likely that actual or latent control will be exercised by the immediate holding company, rather than by the ultimate holding company, although it has to be acknowledged that the ultimate holding company can always dictate matters in the end. Secondly, since the nature of the relationship between the subsidiary and its immediate holding company is probably easier to unravel than the relationship (if any) between the subsidiary and its ultimate holding company, judicial proceedings are likely to be less complicated if the immediate holding company were to be involved as a party rather than the ultimate holding company. Thirdly, the imposition of liability on the immediate holding company is more likely to reflect the realities of the commercial division

---

[1] *Vide* e.g., *post* pp. 464-465.

[2] The question was raised, but left unanswered, both by the Cork Committee and by the Law Society. *Vide* The Cork Report, para. 1943, p. 438; The Law Society Memorandum (1981) para. 3.05(2), p. 8.

within the group and the enterprise notion of liability. In fact, multi-tiered structures are usually used in the context of diversification: a number of subsidiaries, together with their immediate holding company would constitute one enterprise in one sector; other subsidiaries with their own immediate holding company would constitute another enterprise in a different sector. Liability should, as far as possible, be restricted within an enterprise context.

### 2.6. Qualification as a holding company - only the threshold question

It should of course be emphasised that the qualification of a company as a "holding company" for the purposes of the liability rules set out in this work represents only a threshold question. For liability to attach, one or more of the abusive situations discussed in this study must exist and the specific requirements thereof satisfied.

## 3.  IRRELEVANT FACTORS TO THE QUESTION OF HOLDING COMPANY LIABILITY

In discussing the question of holding company liability for the debts of its insolvent subsidiaries, it is essential to ignore as irrelevant certain factors relating to organisation, control and formalities which may *prima facie* appear to play a role in the analysis. That these factors are not "liability-imposing" is implied by the investigation conducted in the previous chapters. For the sake of completeness, a brief discussion of those "irrelevant" factors appears appropriate.

### 3.1. One hundred per cent share ownership

Two observations need to be made in connection with wholly owned subsidiaries. In the first place, it bears underlining that a holding company should be held liable under the proposed rules independently of whether the subsidiary is wholly or partly owned. Liability on the holding company is imposed because it has exercised its control over the subsidiary in an abusive manner detrimental to the interests of the subsidiary's external creditors. The fact that the subsidiary is only partly-owned by the holding company is plainly irrelevant to the liability question.[1] Conversely, it is evident that even a one hundred per cent ownership of the shares in a subsidiary does not necessarily lead to abusive behaviour.[2] The same observation of course applies to the cases of an identity of interest in affiliated companies - that is, where an individual shareholder holds the entire shareholding in a string of companies. Admittedly, complete ownership of a subsidiary does heighten the risk of abusive control - simply because there will be no minority to exercise a "look-out" function.[3] Clearly, however, the complete ownership of a subsidiary should not in itself lead to holding company liability.

## 3.2. Incorporation by the holding company

Liability should not depend on whether the holding company had itself set up the subsidiary. Holding company liability should still attach (in the circumstances defined in this work) even though the subsidiary had been acquired by the holding company rather than having been originally set up by it.[4] The history of the subsidiary's ownership may however have a bearing on the measure of liability to be imposed on the holding company. And in extreme cases, the fact that the subsidiary was acquired from third parties may immunise the holding company from liability that would otherwise have arisen. Thus, if a newly acquired subsidiary is clearly undercapitalised, the holding company should not be held liable for such

---

[1] In the American piercing the veil cases, the absence of one hundred per cent ownership does not impede the imposition of holding company liability. *Vide Henderson* v. *Rounds & Porter Lumber Co.* 99 F.Supp. 376 (W.D. Ark. 1951). Nor is complete ownership an essential condition for the application of equitable subordination in bankruptcy. *Vide* e.g., *Taylor* v. *Standard Gas & Elec. Co.* 306 U.S. 307 (1939).

[2] American courts have repeatedly asserted that one hundred per cent ownership is not in itself sufficient for piercing the corporate veil. *Vide* e.g., *Miles* v. *American Tel. & Tel. Co.* 703 F.2d 193, 195 (5th Cir. 1983); *United States* v. *Jon-T Chemicals, Inc.* 768 F.2d 686, 691 (5th Cir. 1985), *cert. denied*, 106 S. Ct. 1194 (1986).

[3] *Vide* further *supra* Chapter V, pp. 294-295.

[4] The organisation of the subsidiary by the holding company appears to be a requirement for imposition of liability under the instrumentality doctrine. *Vide* Powell, *op. cit.* pp. 9, 12-14; Charles Rembar, "Claims against Affiliated Companies in Reorganisation" 39 Colum. L.R. 907 (1939) p. 929. There is clearly no such requirement in the equitable subordination cases. *Vide Consolidated Rock Products Corp.* v. *DuBois* 312 U.S. 510 (1941).

undercapitalisation. The holding company would however be bound either to provide the subsidiary with adequate financing or else to put it into liquidation. Similarly, a holding company should not be responsible for the debts of a newly acquired subsidiary which was subservient to its previous owners. In any such cases, liability would more appropriately be channelled towards the previous owners.

### 3.3. Domination and unified management

Intrusive domination by the holding company over the affairs of its subsidiaries does not *per se* involve abusive or unfair conduct that could prejudice the interests of external creditors. Nor is the management of a group on a unified basis necessarily abusive or prejudicial to the interests of such creditors. The prejudice occurs only in the forms of abusive behaviour identified in this work. Owing to their very nature, however, the cases of abusive behaviour are of course likely to involve intrusive domination or unified management. But the vice would still lie in the abusive behaviour itself and not in the fact of intrusive domination or unified management.[1] Accordingly, neither intrusive domination nor group unified management should of themselves provoke liability.[2]

---

[1] *Vide* further on this issue *supra* Chapter II pp. 61-63.

[2] Some American judgments have considered intrusive domination as a decisive factor in the imposition of holding company liability. *Vide Costan* v. *Manila Electric Co.* 24 F.2d 383, 384 (2d Cir. 1928); *The Willem Van Driel, Sr.* 252 F. 35, 37-39 (4th Cir. 1918). A number of commentators however have called for a rule of holding company liability in the case of unified management even though no abuse or unfairness may actually be caused. *Vide* e.g., R.S. Nathan, "Controlling the Puppeteers : Reform of Parent-Subsidiary laws in New Zealand" 3 Canterbury L.R. 1 (1986) p. 19; Avgitidis, *op. cit.* 1993 pp. 264-265. In his comprehensive study of corporate groups, Antunes argues that, in deciding whether the holding company should be made liable for the debts of a group affiliate, the decisive question should be "whether the particular business decision(s) from which the concrete liabilities in dispute arose was (were) taken under the autonomous decision-making authority of the subsidiary corporation or under the control exercised by the parent." *Vide* José Engracia Antunes, *Liability of Corporate Groups* (1994) p. 495.

## 3.4. Common directors

Clearly, the use of common directors[1] - though giving rise to conflict of interest questions - is not in itself abusive and should not therefore lead to liability.[2] In certain circumstances, however, such as in the case of intentional or joint torts, the existence of common directors may prove to be of crucial importance.[3]

## 3.5. Lack of compliance with corporate formalities

The element of compliance with corporate formalities - such as the holding of board and general meetings, the keeping of minute books, the keeping of separate records and the filing of statutory returns and financial statements - should be neutral to the holding company liability question.[4] Clearly, the mere disregard of corporate formalities is not in itself prejudicial to the interests of external creditors and should not therefore be afforded any significance.[5] Indeed, except in the case of the failure to keep proper records

---

[1] *Vide supra* Chapter V pp. 281-284.

[2] The American piercing the veil jurisprudence clearly adopts this approach. *Vide* e.g., *Nelson* v. *International Paint Co., Inc.* 734 F.2d 1084 (5th Cir. 1984); *United States* v. *Jon-T Chemicals, Inc.* 768 F.2d 686, 691 (5th Cir. 1985), *cert. denied*, 106 S. Ct. 1194 (1986). Rarely, however, the existence of common directorships is a significant factor in the "alter ego" or instrumentality doctrines. *Vide* e.g., *American Pioneer Life Ins. Co.* v. *Sandlin* 470 So. 2d 657, 668 (Ala. 1985).

[3] *Vide* Latty, *op. cit.* pp. 82-87.

[4] Various commentators take this view. *Vide* e.g., Philippe M. Salomon, "Limited Limited Liability : A Definitive Judicial Standard for the Inadequate Capitalisation Problem" 47 Temple L.Q. 321 (1974) pp. 341-342; Robert C. Downs, "Piercing the Corporate Veil - Do Corporations provide Limited Personal Liability?" 53 UMKC L.R. 174 (1985) pp. 176-177; John F. Dobbyn,"A practical approach to consistency in Veil piercing Cases" 19 Kansas L.R. 185 (1971) p. 189; Robert W. Hamilton, "The Corporate Entity" 49 Texas L.R. 979 (1971) p. 990; Harvey Gelb, "Piercing the Corporate Veil - the Undercapitalization Factor" 59 Chicago-Kent L.R. 1 (1982) pp. 7-8; James R. Gillespie, "The Thin Corporate Line: Loss of Limited Liability Protection" 45 North Dakota L. R. 363 (1968) pp. 391-392.

[5] In some American cases (both in tort and contract), the lack of compliance with corporate formalities has been considered as one of the relevant factors making for liability. *Vide* e.g., *Dudley* v. *Smith* 504 F.2d 979 (5th Cir. 1974); *Pepsi-Cola Metropolitan Bottling Co.* v. *Checkers, Inc.* 754 F.2d 10, 16 (1st Cir. 1985). The element of corporate formalities, however, is neither decisive nor essential. *Vide United States* v. *Jon-T Chemicals, Inc.* 768 F.2d 686 (5th Cir. 1985, *cert. denied*, 106 S. Ct. 1194 (1986). In other cases,

(dealt with presently), there can be no causal connection between the lack of compliance with corporate formalities and the claims of voluntary or involuntary creditors. A judgment against the holding company based on the lack of compliance with corporate formalities would simply represent a windfall. On the other hand, of course, even the most ritualistic observance of corporate formalities should not screen the holding company from liability for behaviour which is otherwise abusive.[1] Were it not so, the legitimate claims of creditors could be thwarted merely by the expedient of keeping a watchful eye on the details of corporate form.

The situation is of course entirely different where the failure to comply with corporate formalities leads to the wrongful commingling of assets. The wrongful commingling of assets, it will be recalled, involves the intermingling of the assets of the subsidiary with those of other affiliates combined with the failure to keep proper records of ownership. Such a failure renders difficult or even impossible the identification of the assets available for the satisfaction of the subsidiary's debts.[2] In such cases, the failure to keep proper records is a significant abuse of the corporate form and should lead to a remedy.

## 3.6. The size of the group

As we have seen in a previous chapter,[3] corporate groups come in widely varying dimensions : from having just one beneficial shareholder to literally thousands, from comprising just two companies to several hundreds, and

---

*Cont.*

compliance with formalities is ignored as being virtually irrelevant. *Vide* e.g., *Schmid* v. *Roehm GmbH* 544 F. Supp. 272, 276-277 (D. Kan. 1982). Vide further Blumberg, Substantive *Law* pp. 204-206, 216-217, 459-465, 526-534.

[1] American courts have expressed a similar attitude. *Vide Hayes* v. *Sanitary & Improvement District No. 194*, 244 N.W.2d 505, 511 (Neb. 1976); *Tigrett* v. *Pointer* 580 S.W.2d 375, 382 (Tex. Civ. App. 1979). But *vide* contra *Fisser* v. *International Bank* 282 F.2d 231, 240 (2d Cir. 1960). In the American cases, compliance with corporate formalities is often a contributing factor supporting a refusal to impose intragroup liability. The observance of corporate formalities is seen as reinforcing the separate existence of the affiliates. *Vide* e.g., *Advocat* v. *Nexus Industries, Inc.* 497 F. Supp. 328, 334 (D. Del. 1980); *Carl Zeiss Stiftung* v. *V.E.B. Carl Zeiss Jena* 298 F. Supp. 1309, 1317-1318 (S.D.N.Y. 1969).

[2] *Vide supra* Chapter V pp. 290-291.

[3] *Supra* Chapter I p. 15.

from owning hardly any assets to billions of pounds worth. Undoubtedly, the majority of groups comprise medium sized and small enterprises. Should the liability rules proposed in this study be applicable to all groups independently of the size factor? Or should liability attach solely to the larger enterprises? It is submitted that there is no sound basis for drawing any such distinction. The proposals made in this work seek to remedy certain abusive practices within corporate groups that are of potential detriment to external creditors. Abusive practices may occur within any group, irrespective of size. Indeed, it is probable that creditors are exposed to greater danger in their dealings with the smaller sized groups. Larger groups, being often protective of, and dependent on, their group image, are less likely to indulge in abusive practices or to abandon an insolvent subsidiary's creditors to their fate. Smaller groups, however, are not likely to be influenced by such factors. There must be no doubt the liability regime suggested in this work ought to apply to all groups, independently of size.

## 3.7. Public and private companies

The liability rules proposed in this work do not distinguish between holding companies that are public and those that are private.[1] Indeed, given the closely-knit familial nature of many private companies, the risk of abusive behavioural practices is probably heightened in the case of such companies.[2] To exclude private companies from a holding company liability regime - as proposed by the Draft Ninth Directive[3] - would leave many cases of abuse without an adequate remedy.

---

[1] For the differences between public and private companies in English law, *vide* Gower, pp. 12-13; Farrar, pp. 43-46. For the differences between publicly-held and closely-held corporations in American law, *vide* Henn and Alexander, *op. cit.* pp. 694-697, 785-786; Henry G. Manne, " Our Two Corporation System : Law and Economics" 53 Virg. L.R. 259 (1967).

[2] *Vide* B.J. Tennery, "The Potential of the Close Corporation: A Question of Economic Viability" 14 How. L.J. 241 (1968) p. 256. In the United States, the piercing the veil jurisprudence draws no theoretical distinction between a publicly held and a "closely held" corporation.

[3] Art. 1 of the "Proposal for a Ninth Directive relating to Links between Undertakings and in particular to Groups" expressly limits its scope to public companies.

## 4. SHOULD A FLOATING CHARGE ATTACH TO THE SUMS RECOVERED FROM THE HOLDING COMPANY?

Should the holders of a floating charge benefit from the monies recovered by the liquidator of an insolvent subsidiary from the holding company in terms of the recommendations set out in this work? For the reasons presently stated, this question is, at one level, linked to the voluntary-involuntary creditor distinction that lies at the heart of the reform proposals.[1] It will be recalled that of the four situations of abusive behaviour discussed in this work - the subservient subsidiary situation, the undercapitalised subsidiary situation, the integrated economic enterprise situation and the group persona situation - it is only in respect of the subservient subsidiary situation that this study has proposed that both voluntary and involuntary creditors should benefit from a rule of holding company liability.[2] In the other three situations, holding company liability should favour only the involuntary creditors.[3] Given that the holders of a floating charge would almost certainly qualify as voluntary creditors for the purposes of the reform proposals, it is clear that the floating charge question is primarily relevant only to the subservient subsidiary situation. The question should not arise in the other three situations because the holders of the floating charge - being voluntary creditors - would not benefit from the implementation of reform proposals.

The essential question therefore is whether a floating charge should attach to the proceeds of any sums recovered by the liquidator in the subservient subsidiary situation. This question raises both legal and policy considerations.

The question whether a floating charge should attach to proceeds recovered by a liquidator has arisen in somewhat analogous contexts. In *Re Yagerphone Limited*,[4] the court held that monies recovered from a creditor on the ground that they had been paid out as a fraudulent preference were not subject to a floating charge over the company's assets. The court reasoned that those monies did not, at the time of the crystallisation of the charge, constitute property of the company. In addition, the court was of the

---

[1] *Vide supra* Chapter IV pp. 176-197.

[2] *Vide supra* Chapter V p. 303.

[3] *Vide supra* Chapter VI pp. 383-385; Chapter VII pp. 414-415; Chapter VIII pp. 434-435.

[4] [1935] Ch. 392. *Vide* also *Willmott* v. *London Celluloid Co.* [1886] 31 Ch. D. 425; *Ex p. Cooper, Re Zucco* (1875) L.R. 10 Ch. App. 510 at p. 511.

opinion that the right to recover assets paid out as a preference existed for the benefit of the general body of creditors and should therefore inflate the general assets available to such creditors.[1]

On the other hand, where monies are recovered in pursuance of an order made in misfeasance proceedings under section 212 of the Insolvency Act 1986 there has been no doubt that the proceeds are subject to a floating charge.[2] Misfeasance proceedings create no new right. They merely establish a summary procedure for compelling officers of the company to account for any breach of duties.[3] The right would have inhered in the company at the time the offending officers breached their duties.[4]

The same question regarding floating charges also arises in the context of contribution orders made under the wrongful trading provisions of the Insolvency Act 1986.[5] In *Re Produce Marketing Consortium Ltd. (No. 2)*,[6] Knox J. had to identify which factors were relevant to the quantification of the amount that the directors should contribute to the assets of the company. Although the question of the floating charge does not appear to have been argued, Knox J. considered as relevant the fact that the bank as a secured creditor would be the first to take advantage of any contribution. Knox J. accordingly thought that the court should exercise its jurisdiction "in a way which will benefit unsecured creditors."[7] Implicit in Knox J.'s dictum is the assumption that the bank's floating charge would attach to any proceeds

---

[1] These grounds of the decision have been criticised by Prentice. *Vide* Dan D. Prentice, "Creditor's Interests and Director's Duties" 10 O.J.L.S. 265 (1990) pp. 271-272. *Vide* also Sally Wheeler, "Swelling the Assets for Distribution in Corporate Insolvency" [1993] J.B.L. 256 pp. 261-262.

[2] *Re Anglo-Austrian Printing and Publishing Union* [1985] 2 Ch. 891. The case concerned moneys recovered in a winding-up in misfeasance proceedings under s. 10 of the Companies (Winding-up) Act of 1890.

[3] *Re Etic Ltd.* [1928] Ch. 861; *Re B. Johnson & Co. (Builders) Ltd.* [1955] Ch. 634. *Vide* further Fidelis Oditah, "Misfeasance proceedings against company directors" [1992] L.M.C.L.Q. 207 at p. 208.

[4] *Vide Re Park Gate Waggon Works Co.* (1881) 17 Ch. D. 234 (C.A.); *Re Asiatic Electric Co. Pty. Ltd.* (1970) 92 W.N. (N.S.W.) 361. *Vide* further Fidelis Oditah, "Misfeasance proceedings against company directors" [1992] L.M.C.L.Q. 205 p. 217; Sally Wheeler, "Swelling the Assets for Distribution in Corporate Insolvency" [1993] J.B.L. 256 pp. 259-260.

[5] s. 214.

[6] [1989] BCLC 520.

[7] *Ibid.* at p. 554.

recovered under the contribution order.[1] Knox J.'s assumption has been strongly challenged by Prentice who, though acknowledging that that matter is not free from doubt, has argued[2] that recovery under section 214 is more appropriately governed by the reasoning in *Re Yagerphone Ltd*.[3] Prentice rightly observes that it is difficult to see how a right of action which may arise in the future but which is not connected with any existing right could be caught by a charge.[4]

Given the somewhat technical arguments affecting the whole question of the attachment of floating charges over the proceeds recovered by the liquidator and in particular the uncertainty of the exact legal position, it is submitted that any reform introducing holding company liability should expressly stipulate whether or not a floating charge should attach to the proceeds recovered. On balance, it is suggested that a floating charge should *not* attach to a recovery made under the holding company liability rule. The reforming legislation should expressly state that the claim against the holding company should be treated as a right vested in the liquidator and not as a chose in action vesting in the company which it could charge. Such an approach would go some way towards ameliorating the lot of the unsecured creditors in insolvency.[5]

Also with a view to improving the position of unsecured creditors, it is suggested that any sums recovered by the liquidator in an action against the

---

[1] Oditah reports that following this lead and in order to avoid any ambiguity arising on account of construction of the debenture, "bank charge documents are now being altered to include, in terms, the proceeds of wrongful trading." Fidelis Oditah, "Wrongful Trading" [1990] LMCLQ 205 at p. 216.

[2] *Vide* Dan D. Prentice, "Creditor's Interests and Director's Duties" 10 O.J.L.S. 265 (1990) p. 272.

[3] [1935] Ch. 392.

[4] Dan D. Prentice, "Creditor's Interests and Director's Duties" 10 O.J.L.S. 265 (1990) p. 272. *Vide* also Fidelis Oditah, "Wrongful Trading" [1990] LMCLQ 205 pp. 218-220; Sally Wheeler, "Swelling the Assets for Distribution in Corporate Insolvency" [1993] J.B.L. 256 p. 266. More recently, in *Re Esal Commodities* [1993] BCLC 872 the question arose whether the court could, in an action for fraudulent trading, order recovery in favour of an individual shareholder. Lindsay J. referred with approval to *Re Yagerphone Ltd.* [1935] Ch. 392 and stated that sums recovered under the fraudulent trading provisions should be treated in the same way. *Ibid.* at p. 883.

[5] The predicament of unsecured creditors *vis-à-vis* secured creditors was highlighted by the Cork Committee in 1982. *Vide* the Cork Report, Ch. 32. The reforms introduced in the mid-1980s, though commendable in several respects, did precious little to improve the position of unsecured creditors relative to the secured creditors.

holding company on the basis of the reform proposals should enure solely to the benefit of unsecured creditors.[1] Within the arena of unsecured creditors, the distribution would be determined in accordance with the voluntary-involuntary creditor distinction underlying the reform proposals.

## 5. LIABILITY IN RESPECT OF AN "ACQUIRED" COMPANY

Complex liability issues arise where a subsidiary which was not originally organised by the holding company is acquired by the holding company some time after its organisation by a third party, possibly another holding company.[2] One matter is clear enough : the acquiring holding company should not be able to claim exemption from the liability rules proposed in this work merely because the subsidiary had not been organised by it. Significant problems however arise concerning the allocation and apportionment of liabilities as between the acquiring holding company and the previous holding company, if any. Each case will have to be analysed on its own merits and a decision on the liability question taken accordingly. Clearly, the courts must be afforded a broad discretion in determining the questions of allocation and apportionment.

---

[1] In its 1988 proposals for the introduction of legislation imposing on directors a duty to prevent the company from engaging in "insolvent trading" the Australian Law Reform Commission similarly recommended that the sums recovered should be applied for the benefit of all unsecured creditors. *Vide* The Law Reform Commission of Australia, General Insolvency Inquiry Report No. 45, Vol. 1, Ch. 7, para. 283 P. 127. Calls for the abolition of the floating charge in English law were recently made in the financial press. *Vide* letter by Sir Michael Grylls, "Case for abolishing banks' floating charge", Letters to the Editor, *Financial Times*, 28th June 1994 and letter by William G. Poeton, "'Sword of Damocles' must be removed", Letters to the Editor, *Financial Times*, 5th July 1994.

[2] The Cork Committee recognised the complexity of the problems arising out of this scenario and considered such complexity as one of the major difficulties facing any reform in the area of group liability. *Vide* the Cork Report, para. 1944, p. 438. Wooldridge had expressed a similar preoccupation. *Vide* Frank Wooldridge, *Groups of Companies - The Law and Practice in Britain, France and Germany* (1981) p. 111. Both the Cork Committee and Wooldridge appear to have been assuming that a rule of holding company liability would involve full and unqualified liability for the debts of the subsidiary. The same assumption was also made by the Law Society in its memorandum on group liability. *Vide* The Law Society Memorandum (1981) para. 3.05(3), p. 8. This work of course proposes the imposition of holding company liability only in a restricted number of abusive situations.

It is appropriate to suggest how some possibly typical situations should be tackled. If a subsidiary has, for example, become subservient under the acquiring holding company, it is evident that liability should be imposed upon it in accordance with the principles suggested in this work. Naturally, the court would, when exercising its discretion to determine the extent of liability, take into account the ownership history of the subsidiary and in particular the length during which the subservience under the acquiring holding company was practised. In the event that the subsidiary was subservient also under the previous holding company, then the latter holding company should also be held liable to make a contribution to the assets of the insolvent subsidiary (provided of course that a causal link can be established between the subservience and the detriment suffered by the subsidiary's creditors). The court would then have to use its discretion to apportion liability between the two holding companies. In the event that the subsidiary was subservient only under the previous holding company, liability should attach solely to such holding company (provided once again that a causal link can be established between the subservience and the prejudice to the creditors). To impose liability on the acquiring holding company would be to unjustly penalise it for abusive behaviour committed by a third party.[1]

The case of an undercapitalised subsidiary requires a slightly different analysis. A holding company that acquires an undercapitalised subsidiary from a previous holding company will be bound either to adequately finance the subsidiary soon after acquisition or else put it into liquidation. The obligation to adequately finance a newly acquired undercapitalised subsidiary follows from the recommendation made in a previous chapter that the obligation to adequately finance a subsidiary is a continuing one.[2] A court faced with an insolvent subsidiary should also be able to visit the previous holding company with liability in the event that the subsidiary had been undercapitalised under its ownership. Such a holding company should not be permitted to exonerate itself from liability by the simple expedient of

---

[1] A similar observation was made by Douglas Hogg during the debate in Parliament on the Companies Bill 1980 in response to the Opposition proposal for a wide-ranging rule of holding company liability. He remarked that it would be "highly offensive" if the "liability of the holding company could be a liability in respect of judgment debts arising from debts that pre-dated the time when it entered into a relationship with a defaulting company." *Vide* Parliamentary Debates (Hansard) 5th Series Vol. 979 (House of Commons) 26th February 1980 at col. 1257.

[2] *Vide supra* Chapter VI pp. 385-386.

selling the subsidiary. Where both holding companies are to be held liable, the court should use its discretion to apportion liability amongst them taking into account all relevant factors, including any agreement reached between the holding companies on the sale of the subsidiary.

The problems associated with a change in ownership of the subsidiary are hardly likely to arise in the case of "abusive" economic integration. The reason is that sales of such subsidiaries (which by definition form an integral part of, and are entirely dependent upon, the enterprise) are simply not feasible. To take the example of abusive economic integration in the hotel industry : who would be interested in purchasing a one-room subsidiary that merely constitutes a wholly artificial division of a large enterprise? Still, if such a sale does, for whatever reason, actually take place then the rule of enterprise liability suggested in this work to deal with the cases of abusive economic integration should still be operative.[1] The mischief in this type of integration consists in the artificial fragmentation of a unitary enterprise into several parts. The fact that one or some of the subsidiaries have been "sold" should not prevent a "collective" or "enterprise" treatment of the various components.

The group persona situation presents an easier case for analysis. Indeed, the vice inherent in abusive group persona practices will be quite easily identifiable with one or another holding company. Clearly, in those cases where an abusive group persona strategy calls for a remedy, liability can only attach to the holding company whose group image has been promoted by or through the subsidiary.

The above proposals to deal with the sale of subsidiaries find an analogy in the wrongful trading provisions.[2] Under the said provisions, a director or shadow director (including, where applicable, a holding company qualifying as a shadow director[3]) will not be absolved of liability simply because the company is sold prior to its insolvent winding up. Thus, where a holding company qualifies as a shadow director it may no doubt remain liable for wrongful trading even if it has disposed of the subsidiary. Where the disposal has been made to another holding company, the latter company may similarly be liable for wrongful trading if it qualifies as a shadow director. If both holding companies are liable for wrongful trading, the court is able to

---

[1] *Vide supra* Chapter VII pp. 413-415.

[2] I.A. 1986, s. 214.

[3] *Vide supra* Chapter V pp. 213-217.

apportion liability between them.[1] Finally, it should be noted that the courts have also been given a very broad discretion in deciding matters relating to wrongful trading.[2]

## 6.  INSOLVENCY OF HOLDING COMPANY AND OF VARIOUS AFFILIATES

So far, the discussion in this work has proceeded on the assumption that only the subsidiary is insolvent. If only for the sake of completeness, three other scenarios should be considered. First, what should happen if the holding company becomes insolvent while the subsidiary remains solvent? Second, what should happen if both the subsidiary and the holding company are insolvent? Finally, what should happen if several companies within the group, including the holding company, are insolvent?

Where the holding company is insolvent while the subsidiary remains solvent, the reverse of the problem of inter-corporate vicarious liability dealt with in this work is presented. In such a reverse situation, however, an essential condition for the imposition of holding company liability - that is, the insolvency of the subsidiary - would obviously be lacking. Accordingly, no question of holding company liability will arise. But should the assets of the solvent subsidiary contribute in some way towards the debts of the holding company? The answer is clearly no. The shares that the holding company holds in the subsidiary represent its assets. As such, they can be dealt with in the same manner as any other asset of the holding company and can be disposed of for the benefit of the holding company's creditors. Alternatively, the subsidiary may be liquidated, its creditors paid and the surplus combined with the other assets of the holding company. There would however be no justification in treating the debts of the holding company as the debts of the subsidiary or in consolidating the assets and liabilities of the companies into one common pool. To do so may unfairly prejudice the creditors of the subsidiary and would constitute an unwarranted erosion of the separate juridical personality of the companies. Nor would the elimination of inter-company claims between an insolvent holding company and a solvent subsidiary be justifiable, except of course in the case of abusive practices.

---

[1] Cf. *Re Produce Marketing Consortium Ltd. (No. 2)* [1989] BCLC 520. In this case, liability was imposed on a joint and several basis. *Ibid.* at p. 554.

[2] *Vide Re Produce Marketing Consortium Ltd. (No. 2)* [1989] BCLC 520 p. 553.

Assuming that none of the abusive practices identified in this work exist, the separate personality of the holding and subsidiary companies should in principle continue to be respected even where both the holding company and the subsidiary are insolvent.[1] Separate estates should therefore be retained for the separate groups of creditors. To do otherwise - by for example consolidating the assets and liabilities of the companies - would unjustifiably prejudice the interests of some creditors while providing a windfall for others. Where abusive practices do exist and holding company liability arises, the insolvency of the holding company should make no theoretical difference to the liability rule. The liquidator of the subsidiary would still be entitled to institute the relative action and the court should make the appropriate contribution order. The subsidiary would then compete in the liquidation of the holding company as a creditor for the amount awarded by the court. Admittedly, such an approach would in effect penalise not the holding company (which is anyway insolvent) but its own "innocent" creditors.[2] On balance, however, it appears more reasonable to prefer the equally "innocent" creditors of an abused subsidiary rather than the creditors of the defaulting holding company.[3]

Even in the case of the insolvency of several affiliates, it is submitted that the separate identity rule should be preserved. Otherwise, some of the creditors may be unjustly enriched while others may find their portion of the recovery further eroded.

There may however be certain exceptional circumstances where substantive consolidation is desirable or necessary. It is to this remedy that the discussion now turns.

---

[1] *Vide* contra Latty, *op. cit.* p. 154. Latty had suggested that "[p]erhaps the fairest way of dealing with the situation when both the parent and subsidiary corporations are insolvent is to let all the creditors of each share pro rata in the pooled assets of both." *Ibid.* at p. 154. A similar suggestion was made by Rodgers C.J. in *Qintex Australia Finance Limited* v. *Schroders Australia Limited* (1990) 3 A.C.S.R. 267 at p. 269.

[2] Blumberg makes a similar point when discussing the doctrine of equitable subordination. *Vide* Blumberg, *Bankruptcy Law* p. 142.

[3] The position in American law is that the existence of competing innocent creditors will not prevent the subordination of the insolvent holding company's claims against an insolvent subsidiary. *Vide In re Commonwealth Light & Power Co.* 141 F.2d 734 (7th Cir.), *appeal dismissed*, 322 U.S. 766 (1944); *In re Inland Gas Corp.* 187 F.2d 813 (6th Cir. 1951). For an early contribution on this question *vide* Charles Rembar, "Claims against Affiliated Companies in Reorganisation" 39 Colum. L.R. 907 (1939) pp. 919-920.

## 7. SUBSTANTIVE CONSOLIDATION

### 7.1. The remedy of substantive consolidation in American law

American bankruptcy courts have developed doctrines that deal with the issues of fairness arising out of the bankruptcy of affiliated companies. One remedy - that of equitable subordination - has already been discussed.[1] Another doctrine developed by the courts in proceedings involving groups of companies[2] or controlled companies and controlling shareholders,[3] is that of substantive consolidation.[4] As with the doctrine of equitable subordination, the doctrine of substantive consolidation rests on the bankruptcy courts' equity jurisdiction to achieve equality of distribution and fairness amongst creditors.[5] Without affecting the rights of secured creditors,[6] substantive consolidation involves the pooling of the assets and liabilities of the various companies within the group and the elimination of intercompany claims and guarantees.[7] The pooled assets of the group are distributed amongst the unsecured creditors on a *pari passu* basis. In effect, the unsecured creditors of the various affiliates are treated as creditors of the pooled resources.[8] For a few years, the bankruptcy courts had occasionally ordered "partial" substantive consolidation: this involved substantive consolidation, with the difference that certain claims are settled out of the assets of particular

---

[1] *Vide supra* Chapter VI pp. 355-360.

[2] *Vide In re Interstate Stores, Inc.* 15 Collier Bankr. Cas. 634 (Bankr. S.D.N.Y. 1978); *In re Vecco Const. Indus., Inc.* 4 B.R. 407 (Bankr. E.D. Va. 1980).

[3] *Vide Chemical Bank N.Y. Trust Co.* v. *Kheel* 369 F.2d 845 (2d Cir. 1966).

[4] In 1980, New Zealand introduced a similar remedy as part of its wide-ranging reforms on groups of companies. *Vide* ss. 315B and 315C of the Companies Act 1955. These sections were inserted by s. 30 of the Companies Amendment Act 1980. Broadly similar provisions are now incorporated in ss. 271(1)(b) and 272(2) of the New Zealand Companies Act 1993. *Vide* R.S. Nathan, "Controlling the Puppeteers : Reform of Parent-Subsidiary laws in New Zealand" 3 Canterbury L.R. 1 (1986) pp. 16-19.

[5] *In re Flora Mir Candy Corp.* 432 F.2d 1060, 1062 (2d Cir. 1970); *In re DRW Property Co.* 54 B.R. 489, 494 (Bankr. N.D. Tex. 1985).

[6] *Vide In re Gulfco Inv. Corp.* 593 F.2d 921 (10th Cir. 1979). The New Zealand provisions expressly provide that the pooling of assets shall not affect the rights of secured creditors of any of the companies. *Vide* s. 315B(3)(c) of the Companies Act 1955.

[7] *Vide In Re T.E. Mercer Trucking Co.* 16 B.R. 176, 188 (Bankr. N.D. Tex. 1981); *In re DRW Property Co.* 54 B.R. 489, 494 (Bankr. N.D. Tex. 1985). *Vide* further Blumberg, *Bankruptcy Law* pp. 26, 402.

[8] *In re Gulfco Inv. Corp.* 593 F.2d 921 (10th Cir. 1979).

affiliates.[1] Partial consolidation seems however to have fallen into desuetude.

Substantive consolidation should be contrasted with *procedural* consolidation. Procedural consolidation involves only the joint administration of the separate proceedings of the various affiliated companies without affecting substantive rights and liabilities.[2] Indeed, in many respects it resembles the joinder of civil actions.[3]

Clearly, substantive consolidation is an extraordinary remedy.[4] Since substantive consolidation may affect the substantive rights of creditors of the individual affiliates and since creditors may have dealt with one corporate debtor without knowledge of the interrelationship with others, substantive consolidation should, and is in fact, used only sparingly.[5] The courts sift through and weigh the facts to determine whether circumstances exist which justify equitable consolidation. The courts need to assess whether the prejudice caused by consolidation is outweighed by the prejudice that would follow from a failure to consolidate.[6] The remedy is considered appropriate only where the overall fairness to the creditors as a whole outweighs the negative effect on particular creditors.[7]

The American bankruptcy courts have considered a number of factors to be relevant to the question whether substantive consolidation is appropriate.

---

[1] *Vide* further Blumberg, *Bankruptcy Law* pp. 406-408.

[2] For an identification and analysis of the applicable statutory provisions, *vide* Blumberg, *Bankruptcy Law* pp. 402-405.

[3] The joinder of civil actions is regulated by R.S.C., Ord. 15 in England and by s. 42(a) of the Federal Rules of Civil Procedure in the Federal Courts of the United States.

[4] Cashel, *op. cit.* p. 37.

[5] *Vide In re Flora Mir Candy Corp.* 432 F.2d 1060, 1062 (2d Cir. 1970), especially Judge Friendly's opinion at p. 1062. *Vide* also *Chemical Bank N.Y. Trust Co.* v. *Kheel* 369 F.2d 845, 847 (2d Cir. 1966); *In re Snider, Bros., Inc.* 18 B.R. 230, 234 (Bankr. D. Mass. 1982). Landers, who had proposed a wide-ranging rule of substantive consolidation, acknowledged that the fact that creditors may not know of the interrelationship between affiliates posed the most serious challenge to his proposal. *Vide* Jonathan M. Landers, "A Unified Approach to Parent, Subsidiary, and Affiliate Questions in Bankruptcy" 42 Univ. of Chicago L.R. 589 (1975) p. 638. Landers however asserts that "knowledge of the interrelationship is likely to be the rule rather than the exception." *Ibid.* pp. 638-639.

[6] *In re Snider Bros., Inc.* 18 B.R. 230, 234 (Bankr. D. Mass. 1982). *Vide* also Cashel, *op. cit.* p. 38.

[7] *Chemical Bank N.Y. Trust Co.* v. *Kheel* 369 F.2d 845, 847 (2d Cir. 1966).

In the earlier cases,[1] two factors were deemed pertinent: (i) the cost and time involved in unravelling a complex interrelationship and (ii) the reasonable expectations of the external creditors dealing with the group as an "enterprise".[2] More recently, other factors have been considered relevant. These include (i) the operation of the group as an integrated enterprise; (ii) the contribution that consolidation would make to the increased feasibility of reorganisation; (iii) the use of consolidated financial statements (iv) the existence of commingled operations, including both commingling and shuttling of assets; (v) the existence of intragroup loans and guarantees; (vi) lack of observance of corporate formalities on the intragroup transfer of assets and (vii) the creditors' difficulties in establishing proof of prejudice from consolidation.[3] Of these factors, the most common and probably the most significant is the integrated nature of the enterprise. Clearly, however, the integrated nature of the enterprise is not necessarily decisive.

The doctrine of substantive consolidation, though increasingly influential and undergoing extensive development, is not yet fully accepted. At least where separate records are available or can be devised, some courts still refuse to apply the doctrine. Such courts may use the doctrine to control fraud or injustice in the "sham" situation, but will not use it as a general bankruptcy remedy to achieve equitable distribution amongst creditors.[4]

### 7.2. The role of substantive consolidation in the reform proposals

To counter the mischief of abusive practices within corporate groups, this work has proposed a rule that in such cases the holding company should be obliged to contribute such amount to the assets of the insolvent subsidiary as may be determined by the court. In particular instances, however, this study has suggested that a remedy of substantive consolidation may be more appropriate than holding company liability. The American doctrine of substantive consolidation certainly offers considerable guidance in this

---

[1] *Soverio v. Franklin National Bank* 328 F.2d 446 (2d Cir. 1964); *Chemical Bank N.Y. Trust Co.* v. *Kheel* 369 F.2d 845 (2d Cir. 1966); *In re Flora Mir Candy Corp.* 432 F.2d 1060 (2d. Cir. 1970); *In re Continental Vending Machine Corp.* 517 F.2d 997 (2d. Cir. 1975), *cert. denied sub. nom James Talcott, Inc.* v. *Wharton* 424 U.S. 913 (1976).

[2] *Vide* Blumberg, *Bankruptcy Law* p. 27.

[3] *Vide* generally the extensive discussion in Blumberg, *Bankruptcy Law* at pp. 27-28, 416-432 and the various judgments cited therein.

[4] *Vide* Blumberg, *Bankruptcy Law* pp. 28, 432-434.

regard. But the American doctrine raises one particular concern. Its scope seems to be expanding without any clear and precise definition of its boundaries. Admittedly, American courts have emphasised that the doctrine is only to be used sparingly and then only to balance the equities of the parties involved in bankruptcies of affiliated companies.[1] Yet its parameters still appear somewhat amorphous. It is therefore submitted that although a remedy of substantive consolidation for corporate groups be introduced as part of English insolvency law, clear statutory guidelines should be provided to ensure an element of certainty and ease of application.[2]

Typical cases where substantive consolidation may be warranted are certain situations involving (i) abusive commingling of assets,[3] (ii) abusive economic integration,[4] and (iii) abusive group persona techniques.[5] The justification for substantive consolidation varies from one situation to another.[6] In the case of abusive commingling of assets of insolvent subsidiaries, substantive consolidation may be necessary because of the

---

[1] *Vide supra* p. 459.

[2] s. 272(2) of the New Zealand Companies Act 1993 includes statutory guidelines which the court should have regard to in deciding whether it is "just and equitable" to make an order for the pooling of the assets of related companies. Unfortunately, the guidelines are rather widely and vaguely stated and are unlikely to offer a court much assistance. The guidelines also enable the court to take into account "[s]uch other matters as the Court thinks fit." *Vide* s. 272(2)(e).

[3] *Supra* Chapter V, pp. 290-293.

[4] *Supra* Chapter VII, especially at pp. 413-414.

[5] *Supra* Chapter VIII, especially at p. 435.

[6] Landers has proposed a far wider-ranging regime of substantive consolidation. He asserts that where no creditors have relied on the credit of a particular constituent company, the enterprise factors typically present in a group situation "suggest the need for a consolidation approach to multiple bankruptcies." He argues that "[i]f the owners of the enterprise treat it as a single entity and seek to maximize its overall profitability, it is necessarily artificial for the law to treat the companies as separate entities simply because bankruptcy has intervened." Jonathan M. Landers, "A Unified Approach to Parent, Subsidiary, and Affiliate Questions in Bankruptcy" 42 Univ. of Chicago L.R. 589 (1975) pp. 630-632, 640-641. Landers' broad enterprise solution goes well beyond the reform proposals suggested in this work. It is extreme. By tearing down the veil of separate incorporations in most groups, it would effectively nullify the advantages of limited liability within such corporate groups. Moreover, Landers' approach is not essential either for the control of abusive practices or for the protection of the legitimate interests of external creditors. *Vide* also Posner's critique of Landers' proposals in Richard A. Posner, "The Right of Creditors of Affiliated Corporations" 43 U. Chic. L. Rev. 499 (1976). The main features of the Landers-Posner debate have been considered *supra* Chapter II pp. 99-100.

impossibility of identifying the assets available for the satisfaction of the various claims.[1] Even where the task of identifying the assets is technically possible, the administrative costs of disentangling the commingled assets may be so high that without substantive consolidation, the costs may significantly diminish the value of the separate estates. Substantive consolidation would then be justified. The potential injustice to a few creditors may be justified by the overwhelming advantage to the creditors generally. In the case of abusive economic integration, substantive consolidation would be appropriate where the various affiliates in the integrated chain all slide into insolvency. In such cases the pooling of the assets and liabilities of one artificially fragmented enterprise would almost certainly accord with the expectations of the creditors who would probably have failed to distinguish between the various affiliates. Similar considerations apply in the case of insolvent affiliates tainted by an abusive group persona stratagem. Where the creditors generally believe that they are dealing with one trading enterprise rather than with the individual components, substantive consolidation would more accurately reflect the creditors' reasonable expectations. In all such cases, substantive consolidation would be proper only in the event of the insolvency of the holding company and should then only affect those affiliates which have become insolvent. As long as the holding company remains solvent, a rule of holding company liability should provide an adequate remedy.

In cases where some creditors have relied specifically on the credit of particular subsidiaries, the rule of substantive consolidation may, in order to avoid unfairness, have to be modified by allowing partial consolidation. Otherwise, such creditors may find themselves in a predicament for which they had not bargained. Partial consolidation may also be appropriate where certain creditors have dealt with one company without knowing that it was part of a group.

## 8.  LIABILITY IN RESPECT OF PARTLY OWNED SUBSIDIARIES

It has already been said that one hundred per cent ownership of the shares by the holding company is not an essential condition for the imposition of

---

[1] *Vide* e.g., *Chemical Bank N.Y. Trust Co.* v. *Kheel* 369 F.2d 845, 847 (2d Cir. 1966); *In re Evans Temple Church of God in Christ and Communication Center, Inc.* 55 B.R. 976, 981 (Bankr. N.D. Ohio 1986).

liability under the rules being proposed in this work.[1] Liability may arise even in respect of partly owned subsidiaries. But should the fact that the subsidiary is partly owned mean that the holding company's liability ought to be reduced, say in proportion to its shareholding interest in the subsidiary? Or should such fact be irrelevant to the liability issue? It is submitted that the latter approach should be adopted. The liability regime proposed in this work is - like the fraudulent and wrongful trading remedies in the Insolvency Act 1986 - essentially "fault" based. The liability of a holding company rests on the element of control and on the exercise of such control in an abusive manner detrimental to the interests of external creditors. Once such conditions are satisfied, the holding company should, in principle, be liable irrespective of the percentage of shares it holds in the subsidiary.[2] In the unlikely event that the application of such a rule would cause an unfair prejudice to the holding company or an unjustified benefit to the external creditors, the courts would of course be able to use their discretion to adjust the level of the contribution payable by the holding company.[3]

At first glance, the imposition of liability on the holding company of a partly owned subsidiary may appear to provide the outside shareholders with a windfall, particularly in the case where holding company liability results from the inadequate capitalisation of the subsidiary. For together with the holding company, the outside shareholders would also have risked too little in proportion to their shareholding interest. A rule of holding company liability may even appear to place these outside shareholders in a position to recover some of their capital investment on the subsidiary's insolvency. Under the proposed liability regime however, such a result will not occur.

---

[1] *Vide supra* pp. 444-445.

[2] American piercing the veil cases have generally imposed "full" liability on a holding company notwithstanding less than one hundred per cent ownership of the subsidiary. *Vide* e.g., *Henderson* v. *Rounds & Porter Lumber Co.* 99 F.Supp. 376 (W.D. Ark. 1951).

[3] During the debate on the question of holding company liability in the early 1980s, the Law Society had expressed the view that should holding company liability apply to partly owned subsidiaries, the majority shareholder should "in some cases at least" have the right to obtain contribution from other shareholders. *Vide* the Law Society Memorandum (1981) para. 3.05(7), p. 9. Unfortunately, the Law Society did not identify the type of situation in which the holding company would have the right to obtain a contribution from the minority shareholders. A year later, the Cork Committee identified the same issue as one of the difficulties with a rule of holding company liability. *Vide* the Cork Report, para. 1942, pp. 437-438. Being clearly beyond the scope of its terms of reference, the Cork Committee did not discuss the matter any further.

The purpose of the reform proposals is to protect and benefit external creditors and not the passive shareholders. Accordingly, the proposed rules have consistently emphasised that any contribution payable by the holding company should only enure to the benefit of the subsidiary's creditors. Passive shareholders will not be obliged to make any contribution on the subsidiary's insolvency;[1] nor, however, will they be entitled to benefit in any way out of the holding company's liability.

## 9. LIABILITY OF AFFILIATED COMPANIES IN THE ABSENCE OF A HOLDING COMPANY

Throughout this work, we have primarily discussed the typical situation where a group of companies consists of a holding company with one or more subsidiaries. Occasionally however, a group may consist of a number of affiliated companies which are owned not by a holding company but by an individual or a number of individuals.[2] Assuming the presence of the abusive practices described in this work, should anybody be saddled with liability in this form of arrangement? Owing to the fundamental importance of limited liability *vis-a-vis* individuals,[3] the individual shareholders (even if controlling) should certainly be shielded from liability. This policy consideration however would not be undermined if liability were to be directed at the various affiliated companies. In such an eventuality, the affiliated companies, though themselves liable, would continue to furnish a ring of insulation around the shareholders whose immunity from liability would remain untouched. But should liability attach to the affiliated companies? In some, though certainly not in all cases, the answer is yes. Where abusive behavioural practices occur within a group of affiliated companies having common shareholders, the various companies may constitute together one integrated enterprise under a common unified control. The integrated nature of the enterprise combined with a common unified control should be considered decisive. To shelter the affiliates from liability in such circumstances would undermine the essence of enterprise liability promoted in this work and would provide easy route for the evasion of the liability rules being proposed. Where only some of the affiliated

---

[1] *Vide supra* pp. 441-442.

[2] E.g., *Chemical Bank N.Y. Trust Co.* v. *Kheel* 369 F.2d 845 (2d Cir. 1966).

[3] *Vide supra* Chapter IV pp. 161-175.

companies form an integrated enterprise under a common unified control, then only such affiliates should bear enterprise liability.

Whenever liability is to be imposed on affiliated companies (or on such of them as constitute an integrated enterprise) it should, in line with the reform proposals, be by way of a contribution to the assets of the insolvent affiliate. Moreover, liability on the various affiliates should attach on a joint and several basis. As far as possible however the separate personality of such other affiliates should be respected and the creditors of those affiliates should continue to be separately treated. Otherwise prejudice may be suffered by such creditors who may have known or may have relied on the separate existence of the affiliate they dealt with. But the substantive consolidation of the estates of the affiliates should be avoided, unless of course there exist specific reasons for such consolidation.[1]

[1] *Vide supra* pp. 460-462.

# 10 Conclusion

## 1. VARIOUS RECOMMENDATIONS FOR REFORM MADE OVER A NUMBER OF YEARS

This study will not be the first to have raised the issue of holding company liability. Nor will this study be the only one to have submitted concrete proposals for the reform of English law. Indeed, various recommendations for reform in this area of the law have been put forward over a number of years.[1] Some of the recommendations have been rather wide-ranging. Others have been more narrowly circumscribed. The principal ideas which have been developed are the following :

(1) Each company in a corporate group should be jointly and severally liable for the debts due to external creditors of insolvent affiliates.[2]

(2) The holding company should be liable for the debts due to external creditors of a subsidiary whenever "unified management" is practised irrespective of whether unified management results in a detriment to the subsidiary.[3]

(3) Liability should be imposed on the holding company on the basis of the distinction drawn in German law - and imported with modifications into the European Union draft Ninth Company Law Directive - between contractual and *de facto* groups.[4] In contractual groups, the controlling enterprise is bound to make good for the losses of the subsidiaries at the end of the year. The controlling enterprise is however expressly allowed to induce the subsidiary to act against its own interest. In the *de facto* group, the

---

[1] *Vide supra* Chapter I pp. 35-38.

[2] This idea was floated by the Consultative Committee of Accountancy Bodies in 1979 but abandoned as "too drastic". *Vide* CCAB Memorandum (1979) paras. 13(a) and 14, pp. 5-6.

[3] Avgitidis, *op. cit.* pp. 260-269. According to this proposal, a subsidiary should be rebuttably presumed to be under the unified management of its holding company. *Ibid.* p. 265. Moreover, the creditor must first proceed against the subsidiary and only if he fails to obtain satisfaction, should he be able to proceed against the holding company. *Ibid.* p. 268.

[4] This appears to be Hopt's preferred solution. *Vide* Hopt, Regulating Groups, pp. 96, 102-105.

controlling enterprise may not use its influence to induce the subsidiary to enter into transactions disadvantageous to it or to take or to refrain from taking measures to its disadvantage unless the subsidiary is adequately compensated usually within the same financial year. If compensation is not paid, the controlling enterprise becomes liable to the subsidiary for the damages incurred.[1]

(4) Holding company or group liability should attach following an optional "contracting-in procedure". Such a proposal was made by the Law Society's Standing Committee on Company Law in 1985. The Standing Committee suggested that it might be desirable to allow companies to choose whether or not to declare themselves as groups.[2] The Standing Committee was of the opinion that if the companies decided to act as a group (or if the holding company declares that they would act as a group) then the holding company (or the group jointly and severally) should "perhaps" become liable for all the group obligations. If, on the other hand, it is decided not to declare group status, then neither the holding company nor any of the subsidiary companies would be liable for each other's obligations and they would be treated as independent bodies. According to the Standing Committee's proposals, groups would be obliged to declare which alternative applied. This would enable investors and creditors to act as they thought appropriate.[3]

(5) Holding company liability should arise in the absence of a "contracting-out procedure", that is the registration of a disclaimer of liability which should also be published on all business documents.[4]

---

[1] *Vide* generally Frank Wooldridge, *Groups of Companies - The Law and Practice in Britain, France and Germany* (1981) pp. 125-132; Hopt, Regulating Groups, pp. 94-96, 103-105; Avgitidis, *op. cit.* pp. 214-232; 246-252; José Engracia Antunes, *Liability of Corporate Groups* (1994) pp. 277-287.

[2] The Law Society, European Communities Draft Ninth Company Law Directive on the Conduct of Groups Containing a Public Limited Company as a Subsidiary, Memorandum by the Society's Standing Committee on Company Law, October 1985, Part II, para. 2.7.

[3] *Ibid.* Part II para. 2.7(c). For a comment on the Law Society's proposals *vide* Frank Wooldridge, "Aspects of the Regulation of Groups of Companies in European Laws" in Drury and Xuereb (ed.), *op. cit.* pp. 128-129.

[4] *Vide* the CCAB Memorandum (1979) paras. 13-20, pp. 5-7. Following a strong reaction to its 1979 proposal, the Consultative Committee of Accountancy Bodies changed its mind and in 1981 conceded that "legislation should not attempt to deal, by way of a guarantee system" with the problems of group liability. *Vide* CCAB Memorandum (1981) para. 14, p. 6.

(6) Each company within a group should be held liable for the debts of an insolvent affiliate unless specific notice had been given to the affiliate's creditors excluding such liability.[1]

(7) The holding company should always be liable for the debts of its wholly owned insolvent subsidiaries. In the case of a non-wholly owned subsidiary, there should be a presumption of such liability which is rebuttable if it is shown that the interests of the holding company and the subsidiary are not substantially identical.[2]

(8) Such part of an affiliate's intercompany indebtedness which appears to represent the long-term capital structure of the affiliate should, on its insolvent winding-up, be subordinated to the claims of its external creditors.[3]

It is obviously beyond the scope of this study to consider in detail the above recommendations. A few general observations however need to be made.

In the first place, some of the recommendations impose too sweeping a liability regime. As argued in this work, the principle of limited liability is of considerable socio-economic importance, even in the context of enterprises organising themselves as corporate groups.[4] Accordingly, it has been submitted that the benefits of limited liability should in principle continue to be extended to holding companies. Only where the twin privileges of incorporation and limited liability are abused and creditors unfairly prejudiced should such privileges be denied. Unfortunately, some of the recommendations for reform listed above apply a blanket form of liability - with liability being imposed independently of abuse or prejudice to creditors.

---

[1] This proposal was put forward by Mr. Clinton Davis during the debates on the Companies Act 1980. Mr. Davis had also tabled draft clauses. *Vide* Parliamentary Debates (Hansard) 5th Series Vol. 979 (House of Commons) 26th February 1980, cols. 1249-1272. A leader in the *Financial Times* recently expressed the view that "[a]t the very least, all subsidiary companies should be required to state clearly on their notepaper whether the parent stands behind them." *Vide* "Make them liable" *Financial Times* 5th January 1995.

[2] These were Schmitthoff's proposals. *Vide* Clive M. Schmitthoff, "Lifting the Corporate Veil" [1980] J.B.L. 156 p. 160. *Vide* also for his earlier recommendations, Clive M. Schmitthoff, "The Wholly owned and Controlled Subsidiary" [1978] J.B.L. 218 pp. 226, 229.

[3] The Cork Report, para. 1963, pp. 441-442.

[4] *Vide supra* Chapter IV pp. 193-194.

In suggesting the use of dynamite where a bullet would do, such proposals would reduce the scope for the beneficial effects of limited liability and would almost certainly trigger a "flighting of capital" reflex.[1] The proposals that would produce such negative effects are : the proposal that each company in a group should be jointly and severally bound for the debts of an insolvent subsidiary;[2] the proposal that the holding company should be bound whenever "unified management" is practised;[3] the proposal that each company should be held liable for the debts of an insolvent affiliate unless specific notice to creditors is otherwise given;[4] and the proposal that a holding company should always be liable in respect of wholly owned subsidiaries and presumed liable in the case of non-wholly owned subsidiaries.[5]

Secondly, some of the proposals are too narrowly drawn to be effective at curbing the cases of abuses or unfairness in corporate group operations. The proposal for the subordination of intercompany loans to the extent that the loans represent the long-term capital structure of the affiliate,[6] for example, while certainly a step in the right direction does not go far enough. Other proposals, such as those involving a "contracting-in" procedure[7] or a "contracting-out" procedure[8] would have an even more limited impact as the liability rule can in their case be quite easily circumvented.

Perhaps the liability regime which, in part at least, comes close to the reform proposals set out in this work is the one based on the German concept of *de facto* groups.[9] In such groups, the controlling enterprise is bound to compensate any subsidiary which has been induced to enter into transactions disadvantageous to it or to take or to refrain from taking measures to its disadvantage. This principle is broadly analogous to the liability rule proposed in an earlier chapter in connection with the subservient subsidiary situation. The German provisions on *de facto* groups do not however appear to cater for the other situations of abuse identified in this study, that is the

---

[1] *Vide post* pp. 475-478.

[2] *Supra* p. 466 para. (1).

[3] *Supra* p. 466 para. (2).

[4] *Supra* p. 468 para. (6).

[5] *Supra* p. 468 para. (7).

[6] *Supra* p. 468 para. (8).

[7] *Supra* p. 467 para. (4).

[8] *Supra* p. 467 para. (5).

[9] *Supra* p. 466 para. (3).

inadequately financed subsidiary, the abusive economic enterprise situation and the abusive group persona situation.

Finally, it should be observed that none of the recommendations give any serious consideration to the crucial distinction drawn in this work between voluntary and involuntary creditors. Admittedly, three of the proposals - the ones involving the contracting-in and contracting-out procedures[1] and the one providing for liability unless specific notice to creditors is otherwise given[2] - do seem to be linked to the voluntary-involuntary creditor distinction. It is not at all clear however whether the distinction was actually being contemplated when those proposals were drawn up. Nor is the ambit of the proposals easily determinable. In the case of the "contracting-out" proposal,[3] for example, would the relative disclaimer affect involuntary creditors? And in the case of a "contracting-in" proposal,[4] would involuntary creditors be entitled to claim the benefit of a declaration to which they were oblivious?

## 2. EFFECT ON OTHER AREAS OF THE LAW

The introduction of holding company liability in the limited circumstances outlined in this work will obviously have some repercussions on other areas of company and insolvency law, involving the need for some adjustment in such areas. In the field of company law, for example, the notion of directors' duties will clearly require some modification. Thus, if the holding company is to become liable to contribute to the assets of a subservient or undercapitalised subsidiary, the directors of the holding company would, in the interests of their company and its shareholders, be bound to take into account the interests of the various subsidiaries and their financial structure. This may involve an adjustment to the present rule - a corollary of the entity doctrine - that the directors of a holding company owe their fiduciary duties to the holding company and not to the subsidiary.[5] An effect of the reform

---

[1] *Supra* p. 467 paras. (4) and (5).

[2] *Supra* p. 468 para. (6).

[3] *Supra* p. 467 para. (5).

[4] *Supra* p. 467 para. (4).

[5] Strictly speaking, these directors should only take the interests of the subsidiary into account in so far as this contributes to the economic well-being of the holding company. *Vide supra* Chapter V pp. 240-242.

proposals would be to oblige holding company directors to consider the interests of subsidiaries, something which they already do anyway as a matter of practice. Similarly, the fundamental distinction between voluntary and involuntary creditors will necessitate a re-definition of the rules regarding the priority of claims on a winding up. To ensure consistency, the implementation of the reform proposals would need to be preceded by a thorough assessment of their possible impact on other rules of company and insolvency law.

## 3. CALL FOR AN INTERNATIONAL AND COMPREHENSIVE SYSTEM GOVERNING CORPORATE GROUPS

As we have seen in an earlier chapter, the group phenomenon breeds a wide range of complex and inter-related issues.[1] Unfortunately, English law, still essentially based on the 19th century notion of the "one-company" enterprise, has not adapted well to the challenge of dealing with the various issues raised by the group phenomenon.[2] This study has been concerned with one of those issues : the liability of the holding company for debts of insolvent subsidiaries. Preferably, of course, a comprehensive system of law governing all aspects of corporate groups should be introduced. Ideally, such a comprehensive system would be on an international - or at least on a European - basis.[3] Realistically, however, there appears to be little chance of comprehensive reforms being introduced on a national level in the near future. On an international, and even on a European level, the chances drop down to zero.

This admittedly negative view of the prospects for the introduction of a comprehensive regime governing corporate groups should not however discourage the continuing study of the various issues. For even if the introduction of a comprehensive system remains a pious hope, it should still be possible to introduce reforms on an issue-by-issue basis. The issues can be clearly identified, the underlying policies examined, present law critically analysed and proposals for reform at both the domestic and the international

---

[1] *Vide supra* Chapter I pp. 15-24.

[2] *Vide supra* Chapter I pp. 27-28.

[3] On the desirability of regional or international uniformity *vide supra* Chapter IV pp. 151-152.

level put forward and vigorously debated. Only by such efforts can progress be achieved.

## 4. POSSIBLE OBJECTIONS TO THE REFORM PROPOSALS

### 4.1. Objections to the proposals as a whole

Any proposal to burden companies with additional responsibilities is bound to attract considerable criticism and opposition, especially from the commercial sectors. The reforms being proposed in this work will be no exception. The criticism will come at two levels. On a broad level, opponents of the reform proposals will extol the socio-economic virtues of limited liability and decry any erosion of that principle. These arguments have already been dealt with in an earlier chapter[1] and require no further elaboration at this stage. It is worth emphasising, however, that the goal of the reform proposals is only to curb the abuse and unfairness that may arise in the context of corporate groups. Effectively, the proposals would only introduce "limits" on limited liability. They would not jettison the notion altogether.

Apart from the broad arguments in favour of limited liability, opponents of the reform proposals may also raise objections on a more specific level. In an effort to head off criticism at such a level, an attempt is now made to identify and assess specific objections that are likely to be raised.

### 4.1.1. "Bailing out"

It is sometimes asserted that a solvent holding company will usually come to the rescue of its insolvent subsidiary : the holding company will not allow its own reputation in the market to be tarnished by abandoning the subsidiary and its creditors to the dogs. It is not therefore necessary - so the argument goes - to impose on the holding company a legal obligation to comply with a standard of behaviour which it would follow anyway.

There is, to be sure, an element of truth in the "bailing out" argument. Some holding companies do - because it is in their best interest - launch a salvage operation to save an insolvent subsidiary from shipwreck.[2] The

---

[1] *Vide supra* Chapter IV pp. 161-176.

[2] *Cf.* the observations made by Nicholls L.J. in *Atlas Maritime Co. S.A.* v. *Avalon Maritime Ltd. (No. 3)* [1991] 1 W.L.R. 917 (C.A.) at p. 928.

"image factor" may be too precious to forfeit.[1] Besides, to permit an insolvent subsidiary to fail could also damage the financial credibility of the group.[2] These factors however are only likely to arise in the case of the larger groups which exude a strong public image of unity[3] or which rely on bank financing.[4] In the case of the smaller or the lesser known groups these credibility factors are likely to be either irrelevant or insignificant. And even in the case of the larger groups with strong credibility factors, an insolvent subsidiary and its creditors may still be left to their fate if to do so were to be in the greater overall interests of the group. The truth is that parent companies of whatever size do periodically refuse to honour the debts of their subsidiary companies.[5] Recent experience proves the point. Union Carbide Corporation, for example, would clearly not contemplate any form of direct compensation to the victims of the Bhopal disaster and it was only after the Indian High Court, in an intermediate judgment,[6] held the holding

---

[1] This point was made during the debate in the House of Commons on the Companies Bill 1980 in connection with the Opposition's proposed amendment for imposing liability on the holding company for the debts of insolvent subsidiaries. *Vide* Mr. Budgen's comments in Parliamentary Debates (Hansard) 5th Series Vol. 979 (House of Commons) 26th February 1980, col. 1260. *Vide* also "Euro Disney shares plunge as $930m loss is announced" *Financial Times*, 11th November 1993.

[2] In *Lawson (HM Inspector of Taxes)* v. *Johnson Matthey PLC* (*Financial Times*, 19th April 1991) a lump sum injected into an insolvent subsidiary by the holding company was considered by the Court of Appeal to have been done by way of a rescue operation to which the only alternative would have been a disaster for the holding company. The holding company had come to the conclusion that the cessation of the subsidiary's business and resulting damage to confidence in the holding company was likely to lead to repayment demands by lending institutions which the company would be unable to meet.

[3] *Vide* "Suppliers left holding the baby" *Financial Times*, 17th January 1995.

[4] Hadden reports that the senior executives of large commercial groups were unanimously of the opinion that no large group could afford to "walk away" from the debts of a subsidiary if it wished to retain its credit in the financial and commercial world. *Vide* Tom Hadden, *The Control of Corporate Groups* (1983) p. 18. A similar observation has been made with regard to banking groups. *Vide* A.C. Page, "The State and Corporate Groups in the United Kingdom" in Clive M. Schmitthoff and Frank Wooldridge (ed.), *Groups of Companies* (1991) p. 118. Large groups often commit themselves to help out a subsidiary in financial distress. For some examples *vide* "What parents are for" *Financial Times*, 17th June 1994.

[5] *Vide* "Make them liable" *Financial Times* 5th January 1995.

[6] Order of Judge Deo, Dist. Judge of Bhopal, Dec. 17, 1987, *aff'd and modified*, High Court of Madhya Pradesh, Apr. 4, 1988, Civil Revision 26/88.

company tentatively liable for US$190 million that an out-of-court settlement was reached.[1] And Pentos, the holding company whose operations included Dillons and Ryman, withdrew support from Athena Holdings (its poster and card retailing subsidiary) causing widespread anger among creditors, some of whom alleged that they had received orders for new stock only days before the collapse.[2] Even decided cases suggest that holding companies would not hesitate to take cover behind the screen of limited liability.[3] Sometimes, large groups show an initial reluctance to rescuing a subsidiary only to come to its aid at a later stage. Thus, in 1993 the Volkswagen Group did not, at first, appear very keen on rescuing one of its ailing subsidiaries.[4] Nor did the Walt Disney Corporation initially appear willing to rescue Euro Disney, its troubled European theme park subsidiary,[5] although it did eventually participate in a rescue package.[6] Clearly, it is the overall interest of the group which will determine whether or not a holding company will save a subsidiary or, at least, compensate its creditors.

In any case, the "bailing out" approach may be difficult to reconcile with the fiduciary duty of directors to act in the best interests of their company.[7] The directors of a holding company are of course required to act in the best interests of that company and they would be guilty of a breach of the

---

[1] *Vide* generally Karl Hofstetter, "Multinational Enterprise Parent Liability : Efficient Legal Regimes in a World Market Environment" 15 North Carolina J. of Int. Law and Comm. Reg. 299 (1990) pp. 299-300; P.T. Muchlinski, "The Bhopal Case : Controlling Ultrahazardous Industrial Activities undertaken by Foreign Investors" 50 M.L.R. 545 (1987).

[2] *Vide* "Receivers close most Athena shops" *Financial Times*, 11th January 1995; "Make them liable" *Financial Times*, 5th January 1995.

[3] *Vide* e.g., *Re Augustus Barnett & Son Ltd.* [1986] BCLC 170; *Adams* v. *Cape Industries plc* [1990] BCLC 479 (C.A.).

[4] *Vide* "VW agrees rescue package for Seat" *Financial Times*, 15th September 1993; "Tensions grow over threat to VW jobs" *Financial Times*, 2nd-3rd October 1993.

[5] *Vide* "Euro Disney shares plunge as $930m loss is announced" *Financial Times*, 11th November 1993; "Euro Disney shares fall after threat of closure" *Financial Times*, 1st-2nd January 1994.

[6] The rescue deal struck with the banks involved a rights issue and a five-year waiver of Disney's royalty entitlements and management fees. *Vide* "Disney plans $2bn rescue for theme park" *Financial Times*, 15th March 1994; "Walt Disney prepares to share the pain" *Financial Times*, 15th March 1994.

[7] *Vide supra* Chapter V pp. 240-242.

fiduciary duty if they commit the assets of the holding company to settle the debts of an insolvent subsidiary when to do so cannot reasonably be conceived to be in the interest of the holding company.

Clearly, the "bailing out" duty cannot rest on anything assimilating a voluntary code of conduct.[1] It must be statutorily imposed.

## 4.1.2. "Flighting of capital"

Most countries, including the United Kingdom, are highly sensitive about the effect that their laws and policies may have on investment.[2] As far as is reasonable and consonant with other policies, countries in fact seek to maximise inward investment and to minimise outward investment.[3] Given

---

[1] Voluntary codes of conduct are not likely to be very efficacious in practice. As stated by a leading article in the *Financial Times*, a "voluntary code of conduct is hardly the most effective tool for holding dominant entrepreneurs in check." *Vide* "Tilting at Cadbury" *Financial Times*, 4th August 1992. The *Financial Times* was commenting on the proposals submitted by the Report of the Committee on The Financial Aspects of Corporate Governance (1992) ("The Cadbury Report"). For an incisive criticism of voluntary codes of conduct, *vide* "Cadbury Committee draft offers mixed news for stakeholders" *Financial Times*, 2nd June 1992.

[2] In 1992, disagreement within the British administration led to the failure to freeze Libyan assets in connection with the alleged bombing by two Libyan nationals of a Pan-Am airliner in 1988. Stiff opposition to Foreign Office support for a freezing of assets had been mounted by the Treasury which feared that freezing Libya's assets could damage London's position as a financial centre. The Treasury argued that a unilateral freezing of another state's assets without any backing in international law could prompt other countries to shift their funds to rival financial centres such as Switzerland, Paris, Frankfurt or Amsterdam. London's importance to the UK economy could not be overlooked. *Vide* "Whitehall row foils freezing of Libyan assets" *Financial Times*, 6th March 1992. United Nations sanctions involving the freezing of Libyan assets were actually imposed in November 1993. *Vide* Resolution 883 (1993) adopted by the Security Council at its 3212th meeting on the 11th November 1993.

[3] In June 1994, the Confederation of British Industry had observed that weaknesses in the way London is governed were damaging its reputation as a centre of world business. *Vide* "London's world role 'under threat'" *Financial Times*, 21st June 1994. In July 1994, the Corporation of London commissioned consultants to draw up the first economic development strategy for the capital's financial district. The aim was to identify opportunities for attracting new businesses to the City while maintaining its position as one of the world's three leading financial centres. *Vide* "The City calls for economic strategy" *Financial Times*, 4th July 1994. *Vide* also "City ready to combat 'usurpers'" *Financial Times*, 2nd February 1995. The final report was published early in 1995. *Vide* "Still growing after all these years" *Financial Times*, 13th March 1995.

the huge volume of funds invested in the United Kingdom, it must be acknowledged that even a subtle shift in investment will have far reaching implications for the financial markets.[1] Undoubtedly, any proposal for reform in the law that will involve a significant "flighting of capital" or that will undermine London's position as a leading international financial centre is bound to be rejected by the competent authorities. Excessive regulation of the holding company may kill the goose that lays the golden egg.

At first sight, it might appear that the introduction in English law of any rule imposing liability on a holding company for the debts of its subsidiary would result in a considerable export of capital from the country. Given that the established principle in private international law is that the liability of members of a corporate body for the debts of the corporation is determined by the law of the place of incorporation,[2] companies contemplating setting up a subsidiary in England may decide to incorporate the subsidiary in other countries where less stringent liability rules apply. For the same reason, corporate groups might actually consider re-allocating their existing subsidiaries to other countries.[3] Investors may be attracted by elaborate schemes involving outward investment. Investor activity in the United Kingdom may be chilled.

The "flighting of capital" factor has actually featured in a somewhat analogous context both in England and in the United States. In England, the proponents of limited liability in the nineteenth century had vigorously argued that the rule of unlimited liability was encouraging investors to

---

*Cont.*

[1] *Vide* Lex Column, *Financial Times*, 1st October 1993. The comment in the *Financial Times* was made in connection with the minimum solvency requirements for pension funds proposed by the Pensions Law Review Committee on Pension Law Reform chaired by Professor Roy Goode, Cm 2342 (1993). For the Review Committee's recommendations on minimum solvency requirements *vide* Vol. I (Report) paras. 4.4.9-4.4.16 pp. 232-234, paras. 4.4.20-4.4.26 pp. 236-237.

[2] *J.H. Rayner Ltd.* v. *Dept of Trade and Industry* [1989] 3 W.L.R. 969, 1010; [1990] BCLC 102, 137 (H.L.). *Vide* also Dicey and Morris, *The Conflict of Laws*, Vol. 2 (12th ed. 1993) p. 1113.

[3] *Vide* also The Law Society Memorandum (1981) p. 6. The Memorandum however assumes that the concept of holding company liability could only affect U.K. holding companies and contends that there might be elaborate schemes for the formation of foreign holding companies and the removal of assets abroad. The risk of re-allocating assets to countries which do not impose holding company liability was also mentioned by Jay Lawrence Westbrook in "Theories of Parent Company Liability and the Prospects for an International Settlement" 20 Texas Int. L.J. 321 (1985) p. 325.

speculate abroad.[1] Although the evidence on the point of flighting of capital may be inconclusive, it is undeniable that the effect of the radical reforms introduced by the Limited Liability Act 1855 and the Joint Stock Companies Act 1862 were immediate and substantial. Between 1856 and 1868, 7056 companies were registered involving an aggregate nominal investment of £893,000,000. Of these, 6960 - with a capital of £883,000,000 - were limited liability companies, while 96 - with a capital of £10,000,000 - were with unlimited liability.[2]

In the United States, where the market for company registrations is keenly competitive amongst a number of states,[3] the separate states have, ever since the early days of the enactment of the general incorporation statutes, recognised that strict regulation - including of course a rule of unlimited liability - involved the risk of putting companies "to flight" and keeping new incorporators away.[4] The effect of a rule of unlimited liability on flighting of capital was studied by Dodd in the context of Massachusetts.[5] He came to the conclusion that the early industrial history of that state furnished persuasive evidence that, granted otherwise favourable conditions, industrial organisation could survive and thrive under an unlimited liability regime.[6] He conceded however that the development of American industry would eventually have been seriously retarded if the states had failed to encourage investment by limiting the investor's risk.[7] Competition amongst

---

[1] In giving evidence to the Royal Mercantile Commission in 1854, R.C. Fane, Commissioner of Bankruptcy, stated that he was "convinced that English law of unlimited liability [had] done more to send English capital to be lost in Pennsylvania and Mississippi bonds, South American bonds, Spanish bonds, Greek bonds, and an endless number of other foreign delusions, than all other causes put together". First Report, Royal Mercantile Law Commission, (1854) B.P.P. Vol. XXVII no. 1791, Appendix, p. 228. *Vide* also A.B. Levy, *Private Corporations and their Control*, Volume I, (1950) p. 74.

[2] *Vide* Cooke, *op. cit.* p. 175.

[3] *Vide* Jonathan R. Macey and Geoffrey P. Miller, "Towards an Interest-Group Theory of Delaware Corporate Law" 65 Tex. L. Rev. 469 (1987) pp. 484-485, 490. Incorporation statutes are a matter of state legislatures.

[4] *Vide* E. Merrick Dodd, "The Evolution of Limited Liability in American Industry: Massachusetts" 61 Harv. L.R. 1351 (1948) p. 1366; Levy, *op. cit.* p. 154.

[5] E. Merrick Dodd, "The Evolution of Limited Liability in American Industry: Massachusetts" 61 Harv. L.R. 1351 (1948).

[6] *Ibid.* at p. 1378.

[7] *Ibid.* pp. 1378-1379.

states has clearly had the effect of a relatively lenient regulation of the creation and management of companies.[1]

The "flighting of capital" fear, however, should not apply to any of the reforms being suggested in this work. The reform proposals do not involve the introduction of a general rule of liability on the holding company for the debts of an insolvent subsidiary. Rather, liability would be imposed only in certain situations which have been identified as abusive or unfair. The aim is to redress the abuse and unfairness, thereby strengthening the professional standards of corporate behaviour. London's status as a financial centre should be enhanced.

### 4.1.3. Creditors of the holding company adversely affected

It has to be acknowledged that a rule imposing liability on the holding company for the debts of its insolvent subsidiaries may adversely affect the creditors of the holding company.[2] The reason is clear : a holding company which has to settle the debts of its insolvent subsidiary out of its own assets may end up with insufficient assets to pay its own creditors. The result would be that one company's creditors are being preferred to another company's creditors.[3] This observation is of course valid - but only in the event either that the holding company is itself insolvent or that the payment of the subsidiary's debts will render the holding company insolvent. In the more usual case - where the holding company will remain solvent despite settlement of the subsidiary's debts - the position of the holding company's

---

[1] *Vide* Levy, *op. cit.* p. 155. State incorporation statutes are strongly influenced by political and economic considerations, including inward investments and especially franchise-tax revenues. The Florida Limited Liability Company Act of 1982, for example, was motivated by the desire to provide a business vehicle to accommodate international investments from Central and South America. *Vide* Richard Johnson, "The Limited Liability Company Act" 11 Flor. State Univ. L.R. 387 (1973) p. 387. Commentators have sometimes strongly rebuked states for their passion to focus on considerations of franchise-tax revenue rather than fairness and efficiency. *Vide* e.g., M.A. Eisenberg, *The Structure of the Corporation : A Legal Analysis* (1976) pp. 319-320.

[2] The point was advanced by the Law Society in 1981 as one of its objections to the imposition of liability on the holding company. *Vide* the Law Society Memorandum (1981) para. 2.02(2), p. 4.

[3] *Vide* R. A. Posner, *Economic Analysis of Law* (2nd ed. 1977) p. 300. Posner also argues that the information costs borne by the holding company's creditors would be higher. *Ibid.* p. 300. Cf. also Clive M. Schmitthoff, "The Wholly Owned and Controlled Subsidiary" [1978] J.B.L. 218 pp. 220-221.

creditors will not be adversely affected. Even where the holding company is insolvent or will be rendered insolvent if it had to settle the subsidiary's debts it is arguable that the holding company still ought to be saddled with liability.

### 4.1.4. Fear of frequent insolvencies

In a somewhat cautious assessment of the problem of group liability, it has been stated that "a genuine fear may well exist that the imposition of increased liabilities on parent companies might discourage innovation and perhaps lead to frequent insolvencies and the collapse of groups".[1] The spectre of frequent insolvencies and the collapse of groups following the imposition of holding company liability is quite unlikely to materialise. Indeed, the likelihood is that fewer insolvencies would result, if only because holding companies would be obliged to salvage insolvent subsidiaries. Only rarely - say in the case of tort claims arising out of catastrophic incidents - would the insolvency of particular subsidiaries lead to the insolvency of an otherwise financially sound holding company.

### 4.1.5. Elaborate schemes to avoid liability

The introduction of any stringent rule of holding company liability may well prompt corporate groups to devise simple or elaborate schemes in order to remove, or at least to minimise, the risk of exposure to liability. The corporate instinct not just to survive but also to flourish would certainly cultivate some thoughtful strategies.[2] Some arrangements - such as the re-allocation of subsidiaries to other parent-friendly jurisdictions - will involve "flighting of capital" and would not really represent schemes to evade the law. Other arrangements, however, may indicate an attempt to evade the proposed statutory provisions. Such schemes may include the use of offshore companies or trusts and the use of nominee shareholdings to conceal the

---

[1] Frank Wooldridge, "Aspects of the Regulation of Groups of Companies in European Laws" in Drury and Xuereb (ed.), *op. cit.* p. 127.

[2] When the Bullock Report had proposed reforms in the field of employee participation, there was evidence that "plans were being prepared in some British groups to create separate holding or operating companies for their British activities ... to lessen the impact of the Bullock proposals should they be enacted". *Vide* Tom Hadden, *The Control of Corporate Groups* (1983) p. 41.

identity of the holding company,[1] and the disposal of high-risk subsidiaries. Given that the reforms being proposed in this work will only burden a holding company with liability in specific cases of abuse and unfairness, it is not likely that many such schemes will be set in motion. But the law will have to grapple with attempts at evasion and a number of anti-evasion provisions may have to be included. Thus, in order to enable a liquidator to identify the beneficial shareholder in the case where he suspects that a holding company is involved, "right to know" provisions analogous to the ones found in the Companies Act 1985[2] may be necessary. The existence of secretive tax havens will of course complicate investigations and occasionally render enforcement of the liability provisions impossible.[3] But these difficulties - which can only be solved by international agreement - should not in themselves deter the implementation of the necessary reforms. And to curb the sidestepping of liability by the disposal of subsidiaries nearing insolvency, the law should provide that any such disposal will not in itself exempt the holding company from liability which would otherwise have arisen.[4] Precise and comprehensive legislative drafting - backed, where necessary, by adequate investigative powers exercisable by the Department of Trade and Industry - can thwart any but the most ingenious evasion schemes.

### 4.2. Specific objections to an "adequate capitalisation" rule

In addition to the foregoing objections that may be raised against the reform proposals generally, it is anticipated that specific arguments will be levelled

---

[1] *Vide Re a Company* [1985] BCLC 333 (C.A.).

[2] *Vide* Parts VI, XIV and XV.

[3] Secretive tax havens can create acute problems, especially in taxation or where fraud is involved. *Vide* Organisation for Economic Co-Operation and Development, Issues in International Taxation No. 1 - International Tax Avoidance and Evasion (1987) pp. 20-57. In the Maxwell empire saga, Members of Parliament had called for an official investigation, and pensioners had expressed outrage, on the disclosure that some of the companies involved in the group were controlled from Liechtenstein, were still trading and were apparently beyond the reach of administrators and creditors. *Vide* "Probe of Maxwell links urged by MPs" *Financial Times*, 3rd June 1992; "Maxwell millions hunt speeded up" *The Observer*, 14th June 1992.

[4] *Vide supra* Chapter IX pp. 453-456.

at the proposals for the introduction of an adequate capitalisation rule.[1] These arguments merit consideration. They are dealt with hereunder.

### 4.2.1. Courts lack requisite expertise

Some commentators have argued that courts are not properly qualified to deal with the complex issues involved in implementing tests of adequate capitalisation.[2] Such commentators contend that judges - who would typically have little or no prior business experience - are unable to make an appropriate analysis of the underlying financial considerations.[3] But such reservations seriously underestimate judicial talent. Both in the United States as well as in England, a reading of commercial and company law reports reveals that judges are capable of tackling highly complex issues of law and of fact with very considerable expertise.[4] In any case, of course, courts can always engage expert assistance - in the form of skilled financial analysts - to serve the court in evaluating the corporate financial structure.

---

[1] *Supra* Chapter VI pp. 363-364.

[2] E.g., Cathy S. Krendl and James R. Krendl, "Piercing the Corporate Veil : Focusing the Inquiry" 55 Denver L.J. 1 (1978) pp. 37-38; Robert C. Downs, "Piercing the Corporate Veil - Do Corporations provide Limited Personal Liability?" 53 UMKC L.R. 174 (1985) p. 186 n. 62.

[3] E.g., Robert C. Downs, "Piercing the Corporate Veil - Do Corporations provide Limited Personal Liability?" 53 UMKC L.R. 174 (1985) p. 186 n. 62. Courts have never attracted much faith in their understanding of intricate financial matters. Reflecting the opinion of a number of other witnesses submitting evidence to H. Bellenden Ker's Committee on the Law of Partnerships in 1837, Lord Ashburton bluntly observed: "Intricate commercial accounts are seldom understood by lawyers, and can never be made clear to the Judges who hear the case; and such questions [settlement of partnership disputes] in my opinion are generally very imperfectly decided; the decision generally turning on some legal technicalities, and very seldom on the merits of the case." *Vide* H. Bellenden Ker, Report on the Law of Partnerships, (1837) B.P.P., Vol. XLIV no. 399 p. 13. *Vide* generally *ibid.* pp. 12-17.

[4] In the United States, expert evidence is admitted on questions of adequate capitalisation. *Vide J-R Grain Co.* v. *FAC, Inc.* 627 F.2d 129, 135 (8th Cir. 1980); *Costello* v. *Fazio* 256 F.2d 903, 906 (9th Cir. 1958); *In re Mobile Steel Co.* 563 F.2d 692, 703 (5th Cir. 1977). Although, adequacy of capital is essentially a triable issue of fact, many American courts are willing to make that decision as a matter of law. William P. Hackney and Tracey G. Benson, "Shareholder Liability for Inadequate Capital" 43 Univ. of Pittsburgh L.R. 837 (1982) p. 893.

### 4.2.2.  Holding company would not advance funds to enable the subsidiary to weather the storm

A subsidiary which has sustained serious losses sometimes survives on the strength of financial assistance from its holding company. Such assistance would almost certainly not have been obtainable from external sources. Undeniably, an injection of funds by the holding company to enable the subsidiary to weather the storm may secure payment to the subsidiary's creditors who would otherwise not have been paid.[1]

It has been argued that any rule which seeks to treat such advances as risk capital would dissuade the holding company from providing the necessary assistance. And if the holding company turns the tap off, the subsidiary's creditors (and the economic order generally) would suffer.[2] Accordingly, it is argued that any such advances should continue to be treated as debt. This line of argument, however, somewhat oversimplifies the situation. A holding company faced with a subsidiary which requires immediate financial assistance to enable it to survive has to take a calculated decision - based on a number of factors - whether to go to its rescue. Certainly, the holding company would take into account whether the necessary advances are, in any subsequent insolvency, to be treated as debt or capital. But this is only one of the factors that will be considered by the holding company. The holding company will invariably consider the overall interests of the group : the likelihood of the subsidiary making a sustained recovery in the long term and the beneficial effects of such a recovery on the group; the negative publicity effects of failing to "bail out" the subsidiary; and the costs to the holding company were the subsidiary to be allowed to slide into insolvency. It is evident the holding company's decision whether or not to embark on a salvage operation will be dictated primarily by its own self-interest or that of the group. The question whether the funds will, on a subsequent insolvency, be treated as debt or equity will feature in the holding company's arithmetics, but it would not be determining.

It is submitted that funds advanced by the holding company to enable the subsidiary to weather the storm should not automatically be treated as debt.

---

[1] *Vide* CBI Memorandum (1980) para. 26 p. 8.

[2] *Vide* Richard A. Posner, "The Right of Creditors of Affiliated Corporations" 43 U. Chic. L. Rev. 499 (1976) p. 518; Blumberg, *Bankruptcy Law* p. 101; CBI Memorandum (1980) para. 26 p. 8. American courts also appear unwilling to subordinate claims based on such advances. *Vide* e.g., *Barlow* v. *Budge* 127 F.2d 440, 444 (8th Cir.), *cert. denied*, 317 U.S. 647 (1942); *Small* v. *Williams* 313 F.2d 39, 42-43 (4th Cir. 1963).

The nature of the advance should still be examined. If, for example, the loans are advanced with a reasonable expectation of repayment, they should be treated as a loan. If, on the other hand the funds are risked upon the success of the venture, they should be considered as capital contributions. For the purposes of characterisation, therefore, no distinction ought to be drawn between funds advanced in inclement weather and other funds advanced during the subsidiary's lifetime. The courts will have to assess the overall financial organisation of the subsidiary to decide what proportion of the holding company's funding should be treated as risk capital.

Another consideration militates against the mandatory treatment of advances "in extremis" as debt. If the holding company is assured that its advances are to be treated as debt, then it may be tempted to continue extending financial assistance when to do so would only prolong the inevitable insolvency of the subsidiary.[1] The effect may actually be to place the subsidiary's creditors in a worse position in its eventual liquidation than if liquidation occurred earlier.

## 5. CONCLUDING THOUGHT

This study does not purport to offer a definitive solution to the question of holding company liability for the debts of insolvent subsidiaries. The subject involves such profound socio-economic policy considerations that legislative reform can only be implemented after a thorough multi-disciplinary investigation into the various ramifications of the proposed changes in the law. The hope is that this study will kindle the debate and constitute a modest contribution thereto.

---

[1] *Vide* CCAB Memorandum (1979) para. p. 4; CCAB Memorandum (1981) para. 10. p. 5.

# Bibliography of Works Cited

## TREATISES

Altman, Edward I., *Corporate Financial Distress* (1983)

American Law Institute, *Enterprise Responsibility for Personal Injury, Reporters' Study, Vol. I - The Institutional Framework* (1991)

Antunes, José Engracia, *Liability of Corporate Groups - Autonomy and Control in Parent-Subsidiary Relationships in US, German and EU Law : An International and Comparative Perspective* (1994)

Argenti, John, *Corporate Collapse - The Causes and Symptoms* (1976)

Ashton, R. K., *Anti-Avoidance Legislation* (1981)

Austin, R.P., "Fiduciary Accountability for Business Opportunities" in P.D. Finn (ed.), *Equity and Commercial Relationships* (1987)

Avgitidis, Dimitris, *Groups of Companies : The Liability of the Parent Company for the Debts of Its Subsidiary* Ph.D. thesis, University of London (1993)

Baker, John C., and Malott, Deane W., *Introduction to Corporate Finance* (1936)

Ballantine, Henry W., *Ballantine on Corporations* (rev. ed. 1946)

Bates, James, and Hally, Desmond L., *The Financing of Small Business* (3rd ed. 1982)

Beck, Andrew, "The Two Sides of the Corporate Veil" in J.H. Farrar (ed.), *Contemporary Issues in Company Law* (1987)

Bell, Andrew P., *Modern Law of Personal Property in England and Ireland* (1989)

Berle, Adolf A., and Means, Gardiner C., *The Modern Corporation and Private Property* (rev. ed. 1968)

Bittker, Boris I., and Eustice, James S., *Federal Income Taxation of Corporations and Shareholders* (4th ed. 1979)

Blackstone, William, *Commentaries on the Laws of England*, Vol. I

Blanpain, R., *The Badger Case and the OECD Guidelines on Multinational Enterprises* (1977)

Blumberg, Phillip I., *The Law of Corporate Groups - Bankruptcy Law* (1985)

Blumberg, Phillip I., *The Law of Corporate Groups - Substantive Law* (1987)

Bowstead on Agency (15th ed. 1985)

Brealey, Richard A., and Myers, Stewart C., *Principles of Corporate Finance* (4th ed. 1991)

Brooke, Michael Z., and Remmers, H. Lee, *The Strategy of Multinational Enterprise* (1978)

Buckland, W.W. and McNair, Arnold D., *Roman Law and Common Law - A Comparison in Outline* (1952)

Carr, C.T., *The General Principles of the Law of Corporations* (1905)

Cary, William L., and Eisenberg, Melvin Aron, *Cases and Materials on Corporations* (5th ed. 1980)

Cashel, T.W., "Groups of Companies - Some US Aspects" in Clive M. Schmitthoff and Frank Wooldridge (ed.), *Groups of Companies* (1991)

Caves, Richard E., *Multinational Enterprise and Economic Analysis* (1982)

Chesterman, Michael, *Small Businesses* (2nd ed. 1982)

Collier on Bankruptcy (15th ed. 1994)

Conard, Alfred F., *Corporations in Perspective* (1976)

Cooke, C.A., Corporation, *Trust and Company - An Essay in Legal History* (1950)

Coopers & Lybrand, *Accounting Comparisons - UK/USA* (1990)

Cox, Edward W., *The New Law and Practice of Joint Stock Companies with and without Limited Liability* (3rd ed. 1856)

Cressey, Peter, "Employee Participation" in Michael Gold (ed.), *The Social Dimension - Employment Policy in the European Community* (1993)

Dewing, Arthur S., *The Financial Policy of Corporations* (5th ed. 1953)

Dias, R.W.M., *A Bibliography of Jurisprudence* (3rd ed. 1979)

Dine, Janet, *Company Law* (2nd ed. 1994)

Drury, Robert, and Xuereb, Peter G., (ed.), *European Company Laws : A Comparative Approach* (1991)

DuBois, Armand Budington, *The English Business Company after the Bubble Act, 1720-1800* (1938)

Dunning, John H., *Economic Analysis and the Multinational Enterprise* (1974)

Dunning, John H., *Multinational Enterprises and the Global Economy* (1993)

Eisenberg, M.A., *The Structure of the Corporation : A Legal Analysis* (1976)

Eitmann, David K., and Stonehill, Arthur I., *Multinational Business Finance* (2nd ed. 1979)

Elias, Sian, "Company Law in the 1990s" in J.H. Farrar (ed.), *Contemporary Issues in Company Law* (1987)

Elliott, William F., *A Treatise on the Law of Bailments and Carriers* (1914)

Farrar, J.H., "Negative Pledges, Debt Defeasance and Subordination of Debt" in J.H. Farrar (ed.), *Contemporary Issues in Company Law* (1987)

Farrar J.H., et al., *Company Law* (3rd ed. 1991)

Fletcher, Ian F., *The Law of Insolvency* (1990)

Fletcher, William M., *Cyclopedia of the Law of Private Corporations* (1917)

Fletcher, William M., *Cyclopedia of the Law of Corporations* (rev. perm. ed. 1983 and Supp. 1987)

Franko, Lawrence G., *The European Multinationals* (1976)

Fridman, G.H.L., *The Law of Agency* (6th ed. 1990)

Friedmann, *Legal Theory* (5th ed. 1967)

Ghertman, M., and Allen, M., *An Introduction to the Multinationals* (1984)

Goode, R.M., *Legal Problems of Credit and Security* (2nd ed. 1988)

Goode, R.M., (ed.), *Group Trading and the Lending Banker* (1988)

Goode, R.M., *Principles of Corporate Insolvency Law* (1990)

Goold, Michael, Campbell, Andrew, and Alexander, Marcus, *Corporate-Level Strategy* (1994)

Gower, L.C.B., *Principles of Modern Company Law* (2nd ed. 1957)

Gower, L.C.B., *Principles of Modern Company Law* (3rd ed. 1969)

Gower, L.C.B., *Principles of Modern Company Law* (5th ed. 1992)

Grant, James, *A Practical Treatise on the Law of Corporations* (1850)

Greenhill, C.R., and Herbolzheimer, E.O., "Control of Transfer Prices in International Transactions : The Restrictive Business Practices Approach" in Robin Murray (ed.), *Multinationals beyond the Market - Intra-Firm Trade and the Control of Transfer Pricing* (1981)

Hadden, Tom, *Company Law and Capitalism* (1972)

Hadden, Tom, *Company Law and Capitalism* (2nd ed. 1977)

Hadden, Tom, *The Control of Corporate Groups* (1983)

Hadden, Tom, "Problems with integrated financing" in R.M. Goode (ed.), *Group Trading and the Lending Banker* (1988)

Hadden, Tom, "Future Developments" in R.M. Goode (ed.), *Group Trading and the Lending Banker* (1988)

Hall, Maximillian J.B., "BCCI and the Lessons for Bank Supervisors" in Joseph J. Norton (ed.), *Banks : Fraud and Crime* (1994)

Halsbury's *Laws of England* (4th ed., reissue, 1993) Vol. 5

Hayton, D.J., *The Law of Trusts* (1989)

Henn, Harry G., and Alexander, John R., *Laws of Corporations and other Business Enterprises* (3rd ed. 1983)

Herman, Edward S., *Corporate Control, Corporate Power* (1981)

Hicks, John, "Limited Liability : the Pros and Cons" in Tony Orhnial (ed.), *Limited Liability and the Corporation* (1982)

Hallis, Frederick, Corporate Personality : *A Study in Jurisprudence* (1930)

Hamilton, Robert W., *Corporation Finance - Cases and Materials* (1984)

Hadden, Tom, "Future Developments" in R.M. Goode (ed.), *Group Trading and the Lending Banker* (1988)

Hertner, Peter, and Jones, Geoffrey, (ed.), *Multinationals : Theory and History* (1986)

Holdsworth, W.S., *A History of English Law*, Vol. VIII (1925)

Hopt, Klaus J., "Self-Dealing and the Use of Corporate Opportunity and Information : Regulating Directors' Conflicts of Interests" in Klaus J. Hopt and Gunther Teubner (ed.), *Corporate Governance and Directors' Liabilities* (1985)

Hopt, Klaus J., "Legal Elements and Policy Decisions in Regulating Groups of Companies" in Clive M. Schmitthoff and Frank Wooldridge (ed.), *Groups of Companies* (1991)

Hornstein, George D., *Corporation Law and Practice* (1959)

Hurst, James W., *The Legitimacy of the Business Corporation in the Law of the United States, 1780-1970* (1970)

Husband, William H., and Dockeray, James C., *Modern Corporation Finance* (1947)

Ireland, Paddy, "The Triumph of the Company Legal Form, 1856-1914" in John Adams (ed.), *Essays for Clive Schmitthoff* (1983)

Jenks, C. Wilfred, "Multinational Entities in the Law of Nations" in Wolfgang Friedmann et al. (ed.), *Transnational Law in a Changing Society, Essays in Honor of Philip C. Jessup* (1972)

Kahn, Douglas A., *Basic Corporate Taxation* (3rd ed. 1981)

Keir, James, "Legal Problems in the Management of a Group of Companies" in Clive M. Schmitthoff and Frank Wooldridge (ed.), *Groups of Companies* (1991)

Lalor, John, *Money and Morals : A Book for the Times* (1852)

Langley F.P., and Hardern, G.S., *Introduction to Accounting for Business Studies* (6th ed. 1994)

Lattin, Norman D., *The Law of Corporations* (1959)

Latty, Elvin R., *Subsidiaries and Affiliated Corporations : A Study in Stockholders' Liability* (1936)

Levy, A.B., *Private Corporations and their Control*, Volume I (1950)

Markensis, B.S., and Deakin, S.F., *Tort Law* (3rd ed. 1994)

Matthews, M.R., and Perera, M.H.B., *Accounting Theory and Development* (1991)

Mayson, Stephen W., and Blake, Susan, *Mayson on Revenue Law* (13th ed. 1992-1993)

Millett, Sir Peter, (ed.), *The Encyclopaedia of Forms and Precedents* (5th ed. 1990)

Miner, Richard B., *Associated Corporations* (1983)

Mocatta, Alan Abraham, et al. (ed.), *Scrutton On Charterparties and Bills of Lading* (19th ed. 1984)

Muller, Welf, "Group Accounts under the Proposed Seventh EEC Directive : A Practitioner's View" in Klaus J. Hopt (ed.), *Groups of Companies in Europe* (1982)

Murray, Robin, (ed.), *Multinationals beyond the Market - Intra-Firm Trade and the Control of Transfer Pricing* (1981)

Murray, Robin, "Transfer Pricing and its Control : Alternative Approaches" in Robin Murray (ed.), *Multinationals beyond the Market - Intra-Firm Trade and the Control of Transfer Pricing* (1981)

Muscat, Andrew, *The Liability of Carriers engaged in Through Carriage and Combined Transport of Goods* (M.Litt. thesis, Oxford University, 1983)

Neate, Francis W., "The Group in Difficulties - a Case Study" in R.M. Goode (ed.), *Group Trading and the Lending Banker* (1988)

Oditah, Fidelis, *Legal Aspects of Receivables Financing* (1991)

Orhnial, Tony, "Liability Laws and Company Finance" in Tony Orhnial (ed.), *Limited Liability and the Corporation* (1982)

Page, A.C., "The State and Corporate Groups in the United Kingdom" in Clive M. Schmitthoff and Frank Wooldridge (ed.), *Groups of Companies* (1991)

Palmer, Francis B., *Company Precedents* (6th ed. 1895)

Paillusseau, Jean, "The Nature of the Company" in Robert Drury and Peter G. Xuereb (ed.), *European Company Laws : A Comparative Approach* (1991)

Palmer's Company Law (25th ed. 1992)

Pennington, Robert, "Personal and real security for group lending" in R.M. Goode (ed.), *Group Trading and the Lending Banker* (1988)

Pennington, Robert. R., *Company Law* (6th ed. 1990)

Pinches, George E., *Essentials of Financial Management* (4th. ed., 1992)

Pitt, Gwyneth, *Employment Law* (1992)

Platt, Harlan D., *Why Companies Fail - Strategies for Detecting, Avoiding and Profiting from Bankruptcy* (1985)

Posner, R.A., *Economic Analysis of Law* (2nd ed. 1977)

Powell, Frederick J., *Parent and Subsidiary Corporations* (1931)

Prentice, D.D., "Groups of Companies : The English Experience" in Klaus J. Hopt (ed.), *Groups of Companies in Europe* (1982)

Prentice, D.D., "Some aspects of current British law" in R.M. Goode (ed.), *Group Trading and the Lending Banker* (1988)

Prentice, D.D., "Group Indebtedness" in Clive M. Schmitthoff and Frank Wooldridge (ed.), *Groups of Companies* (1991)

Prentice, Dan D., "A Survey of the Law Relating to Corporate Groups in the United Kingdom" in Eddy Wymeersch (ed.), *Groups of Companies in the EEC* (1993)

Prosser, William L., *Handbook of the Law of Torts* (4th ed. 1971)

Robbins, Sidney M., and Stobaugh, Robert B., *Money in the Multinational Enterprise : A Study of Financial Policy* (1975)

Rodriguez, Rita M., and Carter, E. Eugene, *International Financial Management* (1976)

Rogers, W.V.H., *Winfield and Jolowicz on Tort* (13th ed. 1989)

Ross, Stephen A., et al., *Corporate Finance* (3rd ed. 1993)

Salmond, J.W., *Jurisprudence* (12th ed. P.J. Fitzgerald, 1966)

Schall, Lawrence D., and Haley, Charles W., *Introduction to Financial Management* (2nd ed. 1980)

Schmitthoff, Clive M., and Wooldridge, Frank, (ed.), *Groups of Companies* (1991)

Scott, John, *Corporations, Classes and Capitalism* (2nd ed. 1985)

Selwyn, Norman, *Law of Employment* (8th ed. 1993)

Smith and Keenan's *Company Law* (7th ed. 1987)

Spero, Joan Edelman, *The Politics of International Economic Relations* (4th ed. 1990)

Squires, Michael B., *Tax Planning for Groups of Companies* (2nd ed. 1990)

Stanton, K.M., *The Modern Law of Tort* (1994)

Stein, Eric, Harmonisation of European Company Laws - *National Reform and Transnational Coordination* (1971)

Stewart, Frances, "Taxation and the Control of Transfer Pricing" in Robin Murray (ed.), *Multinationals beyond the Market - Intra-Firm Trade and the Control of Transfer Pricing* (1981)

Stokes, Mary, "The Problem of the Legitimacy of Corporate Managerial Power" in William Twining (ed.), *Legal Theory and Common Law* (1986)

Stoljar, S.J., *Groups and Entities - An Inquiry into Corporate Theory* (1973)

Stopford, J.M., et al., *Managing the Multinational Enterprise* (1972)

Thring, Henry, *The Joint Stock Companies Act 1856* (1856)

Thring, Henry, *The Law and Practice of Joint Stock and Other Companies* (4th ed., edited by G.A.R. Fitzgerald, 1880)

Thring, Henry, *The Law and Practice of Joint Stock and Other Companies* (5th ed., 1889)

Treitel, G.H., *The Law of Contract* (8th ed. 1991)

Tricker, Robert Ian, *Corporate Governance* (1984)

Tugendhat, Christopher, *The Multinationals* (1971)

Tunc, André, "The Fiduciary Duties of a Dominant Shareholder" in Clive M. Schmitthoff and Frank Wooldridge (ed.), *Groups of Companies* (1991)

Vagts, Detlev F., *Basic Corporation Law* (2nd ed. 1979)

Wallace, Cynthia Day, *Legal Control of the Multinational Enterprise* (1982)

Wedderburn, Lord, "The Legal Development of Corporate Responsibility : For Whom Will Corporate Managers Be Trustees?" in Klaus J. Hopt and Gunther Teubner (ed.), *Corporate Governance and Directors' Liabilities* (1985)

Weiss, Gerry, "The Collapse of a Single Company in the Group" in R.M. Goode (ed.), *Group Trading and the Lending Banker* (1988)

White, T.H., *Power or Pawns : Boards of Directors in Canadian Corporations* (1978)

Wilberforce, Lord, "Law and Economics" Presidential Address to the Holdsworth Club on the 25th February 1966, published by the Holdsworth Club of the University of Birmingham in 1966

Wilkins, Mira, *The Emergence of Multinational Enterprise : American Business Abroad from the Colonial Era to 1914* (1970)

Wilkins, Mira, *The Maturing of Multinational Enterprise : American Business Abroad from 1914 to 1970* (1974)

Wilson, Charles, *Unilever 1945-1965 - Challenge and Response in the Post-War Industrial Revolution* (1968)

Wood, Philip R., *The Law of Subordinated Debt* (1990)

Wooldridge, Frank, *Groups of Companies - The Law and Practice in Britain, France and Germany* (1981)

Wooldridge, Frank, "The Treatment of Groups of Companies in Germany and Brazil" in John Adams (ed.), *Essays for Clive Schmitthoff* (1983)

Wooldridge, Frank, "Aspects of the Regulation of Groups of Companies in European Laws" in Robert Drury and Peter G. Xuereb (ed.), *European Company Laws : A Comparative Approach* (1991)

Zweigert, Konrad, and Kotz, Hein, *Introduction to Comparative Law* (2nd rev. ed. 1992)

## PERIODICAL LITERATURE

Aarons, Lehman C., "Debt vs Equity - special hazards in setting up the corporate capital structure" 23 Journal of Taxation 194 (1965)

Amsler, Christine E., Bartlett, Robin L. and Bolton, Craig J., "Thoughts of some British economists on early limited liability and corporate legislation" 13 Hist. Pol. Econ. 774 (1981)

Arnold, Earl C., "Confusion" 23 Col. L.R. 235 (1923)

Ashe, George, "Lifting the Corporate Veil: Corporate Entity in the Modern Day Court" 73 Commercial L.J. 121 (1973)

Aronofsky, David, "Piercing the Transnational Corporate Veil : Trends, Developments and the Need for Widespread Adoption of Enterprise Analysis" 10 N.C.J. Int'l L. & Com. Reg. 31 (1985)

Atiyah, P.S., "Thoughts on Company Law Philosophy" 8 Lawyer 15 (1965)

Baker, Robert W., "Subordination Of Stockholder Loans On The Ground Of Corporate Undercapitalization" 23 Maryland L.R. 260 (1963).

Ballantine, Henry W., "Separate Entity of Parent and Subsidiary Corporations" 14 Calif. L. Rev. 12 (1925)

Barber, David H., "Piercing the Corporate Veil" 17 Williamette L.R. 371 (1981)

Beck, Stanley M., "The Quickening of Fiduciary Obligation : Canadian Aero Services v. O'Malley" 53 Can. Bar Rev. 771 (1975)

Berle, Adolf A., "Subsidiary corporations and credit manipulation" 41 Harv. L.R. 874 (1928)

Berle, Adolf A., "Promoters' Stock in Subsidiary Corporations" 29 Colum. L.R. 35 (1929)

Berle, Adolf. A., "For whom Corporate Managers *are* Trustees : A Note" 45 Harv. L.R. 1365 (1932)

Berle, Adolf A., "The Theory of Enterprise Entity" 47 Colum. L.R. 343 (1947)

Boyle, A.J., "Draft Fifth Directive : Implications for Directors' Duties, Board Structure and Employee Participation" 13 The Company Lawyer 6 (1992)

Boyle, Stanley E., "The Joint Subsidiary : An Economic Appraisal" 5 Antitrust Bulletin 303 (1960)

Brassard, Rene A., "Parent and Subsidiary" 22 Boston Univ. L.R. 127 (1942)

Brooker, R.P., "Company Law Reform : is unlimited liability likely to be effective?" 3 Solicitor Quarterly 239 (1964)

Brooks, C.E., "Parent and Subsidiary, right of parent or subsidiary to share with other creditors in assets of associated corporation on the latter's insolvency" 37 Michigan L.R. 440 (1939)

Brudney, Victor, and Clark, Robert Charles, "A New Look at Corporate Opportunities" 94 Harv. L.R. 997 (1981)

Butler, Henry N., "General Incorporation in Nineteenth Century England : Interaction of Common Law and Legislative Processes" 6 International Review of Law and Economics 169 (1986)

Calabresi, Guido, "Some Thoughts on Risk Distribution and the Law of Torts" 70 Yale L.J. 499 (1961)

Calnan, R.J., "Corporate Gifts and Creditors' Rights" 11 Co. Law. 91 (1990)

Campbell, Clare, "Note on Re MC Bacon Ltd." 11 Co. Law 184 (1990)

Campbell, John, "Hong Kong Companies on the Bermuda Trail" International Corporate Law, March 1991

Canfield, G.F., "Scope and limits of the corporate entity theory" 17 Colum. L.R. 128 (1917)

Carteaux, Patricia, "Louisiana adopting a Balancing Test for Piercing the Veil" 58 Tulane L.R. 1089 (1984)

Cataldo, Bernard F., "Limited Liability with One-Man Companies and Subsidiary Corporations" 18 Law and Contemporary Problems 473 (1953)

Cheris, Samuel Davis, "Stockholder Loans and the Debt-Equity Distinction" 22 Stanford L.R. 847 (1970)

Wang, Ke Chin, "The Corporate Entity Concept (or Fiction Theory) and the Modern Business Organisation" 28 Minnesota L. R. 341 (1944)

Clark, Robert Charles, "The Duties of the Corporate Debtor to its Creditors" 90 Harv. L.R. 505 (1977)

Clough, Mark, "Trying to make the Fifth Directive Palatable" 3 The Company Lawyer 109 (1982)

Cohen, Jules S., "Shareholder Advances : Capital or Loans?" 52 Am. Bankr. L.J. 259 (1978)

Collins, Hugh, "Ascription of Legal Responsibility to Groups in Complex Patterns of Economic Integration" 53 M.L.R. 731 (1990)

Columbia Law Review, Note, "Merger" or Agency of Subsidiary Corporations as Grounds of the Liability of the Parent Corporation for Acts of its Subsidiary" 27 Colum. L.R. 702 (1927)

Company Lawyer, Note, "Liability of Company for Debts of Related Company" 2 Co. Law. 238 (1981)

Company Lawyer, Note, "Is Company Law Still in a Muddle?", 12 Co. Law. 42 (1991)

Compton, William Randall, "Early History of Stock Ownership by Corporations" 9 Geo. Wash. L.R. 125 (1940)

Connell, Rupert M.A., "Chapter 11 - the United Kingdom Dimension" (1990) 6 Ins. L. & P. 90

Cook, Michael L., "Fraudulent Transfer Liability under the Bankruptcy Code" 17 Hous. L. R. 263 (1980)

Cook, William W., "Watered Stock" - Commissions - "Blue Sky Laws" - "Stock Without Par Value" 19 Mich. L.R. 583 (1921)

Coquillette, William H., "Guaranty of and Security for the Debt of a Parent Corporation by a Subsidiary Corporation" 30 Case Western Reserve Law Review 433 (1980)

Corrigan James A., and Schirott, James R., "Piercing the Corporate Veil : Dispelling the Mists of Metaphor" 17 Trial Lawyer's Guide 121 (1973)

Cummins, David C., "Disregarding the Corporate Entity : Contract Claims" 28 Ohio State L.J. 441 (1967)

Dabner, Justin, "Directors' Duties - The Schizoid Company" 6 Company and Securities Law Journal 105 (1988)

Davies, John, and Goodlife, Jonathan, "Parent liability for subsidiaries - The right move for effective redress" 4 Practical Law for Companies 17 (1993)

Dawson, Francis, "Acting in the Best Interests of the Company - For Whom are Directors 'Trustees'?" 11 N.Z.U.L.R. 68 (1984)

Derom, P., "The EEC Approach to Groups of Companies" 16 Va. J. Int. L. 565 (1976)

Dine, Janet, "The Draft Fifth EEC Directive on Company Law" 10 The Company Lawyer 10 (1989)

Dix, Maurice, "Adequate Risk Capital : The Consideration for the Benefits of Separate Incorporation" 53 N.W.U.L. Rev. 478 (1958)

Dobbyn, John F., "A Practical Approach to Consistency in Veil Piercing Cases" 19 Kansas L.R. 185 (1971)

Dobson, Juan M., "'Lifting the Veil' in Four Countries : The Law of Argentina, England, France and the United States" 35 I.C.L.Q. 839 (1986)

Dodd Jr., E. Merrick, "For whom are Corporate Managers Trustees?" 45 Harv. L.R. 1145 (1932)

Dodd, E. Merrick, "Liability of a Holding Company for Obtaining for Itself Property Needed by a Subsidiary : the *Blaustein* Case" 58 Harv. L.R. 125 (1944)

Dodd, E. Merrick, "The Evolution of Limited Liability in American Industry : Massachusetts" 61 Harv. L.R. 1351 (1948)

Dole, Jr., Richard F., "The New Federal Bankruptcy Code : An Overview and Some Observations Concerning Debtors' Exemptions" 17 Hous. L. R. 217 (1980)

Douglas William O., and Shanks, Carrol M., "Insulation from Liability through Subsidiary Corporations" 39 Yale L.J. 193 (1929)

Downs, Robert C., "Piercing the Corporate Veil - Do Corporations provide Limited Personal Liability?" 53 UMKC L.R. 174 (1985)

Doyle, Louis G., "Anomalies in the Wrongful Trading Provisions" 13 Co. Law. 96 (1992)

Drake, Charles D., "Disqualification of Directors - the Red Card" [1989] J.B.L. 474

Dye, Robert E., "Inadequate Capitalization as a Basis for Shareholder Liability : The California Approach and a Recommendation" 45 S. Cal. L.R. 823 (1972)

Easterbrook Frank H., and Fischel, Daniel R., "Limited Liability and the Corporation" 52 Univ. of Chicago L.R. 89 (1985)

Edinburgh Review, Article V.1 XCV Edinburgh Review 405 (1852)

Edinburgh Review, "Joint Stock Banks and Companies" LXIII 431 Edinburgh Review (1836)

Eisenberg, M.A., "Megasubsidiaries : The Effect of Corporate Structure on Corporate Control" 84 Harv. L.R. 1577 (1971)

Ellinger, E.P., "Letters of comfort" [1989] J.B.L. 259

Elson, Sam, "Legal Liability of Holding Companies for Acts of Subsidiary Companies" 15 St. Louis L. Rev. 333 (1930)

Erickson, Paul R., "Capitalization of Close Corporations After 1980" 17 Idaho L.R. 139 (1980)

Everdell, William, and Longstreth, Bevis, "Some Special Problems Raised by Debt Financing of Corporations under Common Control" 17 Bus. Law. 500 (1962)

Fama, Eugene F., "Efficient Capital Markets : A Review of Theory and Empirical Work" 25 J. Fin. 383 (1970)

Farrar, J.H., "The obligation of a company's directors to its creditors before liquidation" [1985] J.B.L. 413

Farrar, John H., "The Responsibility of Directors and Shareholders for a Company's Debts" 4 Cantab. L.R. 12 (1989)

Farrington, Jr., James F., "Piercing the Connecticut Corporate Veil" U. Bridgeport L. Rev. 109 (1983)

Fawcett, J.J., "Jurisdiction and Subsidiaries" [1985] J.B.L. 16

Finch, Vanessa, "Directors' duties towards creditors" 10 Co. Law. 23 (1988)

Finch, David, and Long, Robert, "The Fiduciary Relation of the Dominant Shareholder to the Minority Shareholders" 9 Hastings L.J. 306 (1958)

Fitzpatrick, Peter, "Transfer Pricing, Company Law and Shareholders' Interests" [1975] J.B.L. 202

Franklin, Burt, "Parent and Subsidiary " Parent Not Liable for Tort of Subsidiary" 12 Cornell L.Q. 504 (1927) p. 507

Fuller, Warner, "The Incorporated Individual : A Study of the One-Man Company" 51 Harv. L.R. 1373 (1938)

Garrett, Ray, "History, Purpose and Summary of the Model Business Corporation Act" 6 Bus. Law. 1 (1950)

Gelb, Harvey, "Piercing the Corporate Veil  - the Undercapitalization Factor" 59 Chicago-Kent L.R. 1 (1982)

Gerver, Eli, "De-emphasis of debt-equity test for thin corporations requires new defense tactics" 23 Journal of Taxation 28 (1965)

Gibson, Margaret A., "The Intractable Debt/Equity Problem : A New Structure for Analyzing Shareholder Advances" 81 Northwestern U.L.R. 452 (1987)

Gillespie, James R., "The Thin Corporate Line: Loss of Limited Liability Protection" 45 North Dakota L. R. 363 (1968)

Gilson, Ronald J., and Kraakman, Reiner H., "The Mechanisms of Market Efficiency" 70 Virginia. L.R. 549 (1984)

Gimbel, Allan G., "Piercing the Corporate Veil" 4 Univ. of Florida L.R. 352 (1951)

Goode, Roy. M.,"The Death of Insolvency Law" 1 Co. Law. 123 (1980)

Goode, R.M., "Wrongful Trading and the Balance Sheet Test of Insolvency" [1989] J.B.L. 436

Goode, Roy, "Relections on the Harmonisation of Commercial Law" in [1991] Vol. I Uniform Law Review 54 (pub. International Institute for the Unification of Private Law)

Goodhart, A.L., "Corporate Liability in Tort and the Doctrine of *Ultra Vires*" 2 C.L.J. 350 (1926);

Gower, L.C.B., "Some contrasts between British and American Corporation Law" 69 Harv. L.R. 1369 (1956)

Gower, L.C.B., "Reforming Company Law" 14 L. Teach. 111 (1980)

Grantham, Ross, "The Judicial Extension of Directors' Duties to Creditors" [1991] J.B.L. 1

Griffin, Joseph P., "The Power of Host Countries over the Multinational : Lifting the Veil in the European Economic Community and the United States" 6 Law and Policy in International Business 375 (1974)

Hackney William P., and Benson, Tracey G., "Shareholder Liability for Inadequate Capital" 43 Univ. of Pittsburgh L.R. 837 (1982)

Hadden, Tom, "Inside Corporate Groups" 12 International Journal of the Sociology of Law 271 (1984)

Hale, William B., "Holding Companies in Illinois Law" 7 Illinois L.R. 529 (1913)

Halpern, P., Treblicock, M., and Turnbull, S., "Economic Analysis of Limited Liability in Corporation Law" 30 U. Toronto L. J. 117 (1980)

Hamilton, Robert W., "The Corporate Entity" 49 Texas L.R. 979 (1971)

Handlin, Oscar, and Handlin, Mary F., "Origins of the American Business Corporation" 5 J. Econ. Hist. 1 (1945)

Handy, Beatrice J., "Situations Where Courts will Disregard the Separate Corporate Entities of a Parent and Subsidiary Corporation, even in the Absence of Fraud" 7 Ohio Opinions 143 (1937)

Hansmann, Henry, and Kraakman, Reiner, "Toward Unlimited Shareholder Liability for Corporate Torts" 100 Yale L.J. 1879 (1991)

Harris, Thomas V., "Washington's Doctrine of Corporate Disregard" 56 Washington L.R. 253 (1981)

Harvard Law Review, Note, "Disregarding Corporate Fiction, Liability of Parent Corporation for Acts of Subsidiary" 43 Harv. L.R. 1154 (1930)

Harvard Law Review, Note, "Parent Corporation's Claims in Bankruptcy of a Subsidiary : Effect of a Fiduciary Relationship" 54 Harv. L.R. 1045 (1941)

Harvard Law Review, "Liability of a Corporation for Acts of a Subsidiary or Affiliate" 71 Harv. L.R. 1122 (1958)

Harvard Law Review, Note, "Piercing the Corporate Veil : the Alter Ego Doctrine under Federal Common Law" 95 Harv. L.R. 853 (1982)

Harvard Law Review, "Liability of Parent Corporation for Hazardous Waste Cleanup and Damages" 99 Harv. L.R. 986 (1986)

Hausman, Daniel M., and McPherson, Michael S., "Taking Ethics Seriously : Economics and Contemporary Moral Philosophy" 31 J. of Econ. Lit. 671 (1993)

Hawke, Neil, "Creditors' Interests in Solvent and Insolvent Companies" [1989] J.B.L. 54

Heller, Albert C., "Corporate Entity" 9 Wisconsin L.R. 286 (1934)

Herzog, Asa S., and Zweibel, Joel B., "The Equitable Subordination of Claims in Bankruptcy" 15 Vand. L.R. 83 (1961)

Hickman, "The Thin Corporation : Another Look at an Old Disease" 44 Taxes 883 (1966)

Hofstetter, Karl, "Parent Responsibility for Subsidiary Corporations : Evaluating European Trends" 39 I.C.L.Q. 576 (1990)

Hofstetter, Karl, "Multinational Enterprise Parent Liability : Efficient Legal Regimes in a World Market Environment" North Carolina J. of Int. Law and Comm. Reg. 299 (1990)

Horrowitz, Walter, "Historical Development of Company Law" 62 L.Q.R. 375 (1946)

Huddleston, John, "Can Subsidiaries be Purchasers from their Parents under the Robinson-Patman Act? A Plea for a Consistent Approach" 63 Wash. L.R. 957 (1988)

Iowa Law Review, Note, "Efficacy of the Corporate Entity in evasion of statutes" 26 Iowa L.R. 350 (1941)

Israel, Abner M., "The Legal Fiction of Corporate Entity and Modern Law" 3 Georgia Bar Journal 46 (1940)

Israels, Carlos L., "The Implications and Limitations of the 'Deep Rock' Doctrine" 42 Colum. L.R. 376 (1942)

Jenkins, Dafydd, "Corporate Liability in Tort and the Doctrine of *Ultra Vires*" [1970] Ir. Jur. 11

Johnson, Richard, "The Limited Liability Company Act" 11 Flor. State Univ. L.R. 387 (1973)

Johnston, Bruce, "Contractual Debt Subordination and Legislative Reform" [1991] J.B.L. 225

Journal of Business Law, Editorial, "Employee participation" [1984] J.B.L. 7

Journal of Business Law, Editorial, "Amendments to the Fifth Draft Directive and to Vredeling" [1983] J.B.L. 456

Journal of Business Law, Editorial, "Further comments on the Draft Fifth Directive and Vredeling" [1984] J.B.L. 100

Journal of Business Law, Editorial, "Vredeling" [1984] J.B.L. 103

Kahn-Freund, O., "Corporate Entity" 3 M.L.R. 226 (1940)

Kahn-Freund, O., "Some Reflections on Company Law Reform" 7 M.L.R. 54 (1944)

Kahn-Freund, O., "On Uses and Misuses of Comparative Law" 37 M.L.R. 1 (1974)

Kaplow, Louis, "Private versus Social costs in Bringing Suit" 15 J. Legal Stud. 371 (1986)

Katz, Wilbur G., "The Philosophy of Midcentury Corporation Statutes" 23 Law and Contemp. Prob. 177 (1958)

Keenan, Denis, "Banks as Shadow Directors" 17 Accountancy 41 (1991)

Kessel, Lawrence P., "Trends in the Approach to the Corporate Entity Problem in Civil Litigation" 41 Georgtown L.J. 525 (1953)

Kinney, Kathleen, "Equitable Subordination of Shareholder Debt to Trade Creditors : A Reexamination" 61 Boston Univ. L.R. 433 (1981)

Kitching, John, and Compagnoni, Marco, "Subsidiary undertakings in the U.K." International Corporate Law, February 1991

Kohn, Richard S., "Alternative Methods of Piercing the Veil in Contract and Tort" 48 Boston Univ. L.R. 123 (1968)

Kreidmann, Arthur, "The Corporate Guaranty" 13 Vand. L. Rev. 229 (1959)

Krendl, Cathy S., and Krendl, James R., "Piercing the Corporate Veil : Focusing the Inquiry" 55 Denver L.J. 1 (1978)

Kurzer, Martin J., "Thin Incorporation : A Continuing Problem" 51 Marquette L.R. 158 (1968)

La Mont, Howard, "Multinational Enterprise, Transfer Pricing and the 482 Mess" 14 Columbia Journal of Transnational Law 383 (1975)

Landers, Jonathan M., "A Unified Approach to Parent, Subsidiary, and Affiliate Questions in Bankruptcy" 42 Univ. of Chicago L.R. 589 (1975)

Landers, Jonathan M., "Another Word on  Parent, Subsidiaries and Affiliates in Bankruptcy"  43 Univ. of Chicago L.R. 527 (1976)

Latty, Elvin R., "Corporate Entity as a solvent of legal problems" 34 Michigan L.R. 597 (1936)

Latty, Elvin R., "Corporation Statutes as the Answer to Parent-Subsidiary Liability" 35 Michigan L.R. 794 (1937)

Law Review, "Limited Liability in Partnership" 9 Law Review 74 (1848-1849)

Law Times, 27th March 1858

Law Quarterly Review, Note, 13 L.Q.R. 6 (1897)

Macey, Jonathan R., and Miller, Geoffrey P., "Towards an Interest-Group Theory of Delaware Corporate Law" 65 Tex. L. Rev. 469 (1987)

Machen Jr., A.W., "Corporate personality" 24 Harv. L.R. 253-267, 347-365 (1911);

Manne, Henry G., "Our Two Corporation System : Law and Economics" 53 Virginia. L.R. 259 (1967)

Markson, Henry E., "Corporate Unveiling : Judicial Attitudes" 123 Solictors' Journal 831

McCoy, Henry D., "The United States Parent Corporation - European Subsidiary Relationship under the European Antitrust Regulations" 3 Virginia Journal of International Law 46 (1963)

McLaughlin, Karen, "Corporate Opportunity Doctrine in the Context of Parent - Subsidiary Relations" 8 Northern Kentucky L.R. 121 (1981)

McLean, James H., "Thin Corporations - Advantages and Pitfalls" 14 The Practical Lawyer 81 (1968)

McWilliams, Robert L., "Limitations of the Theory of Corporate Entity in California" 4 Calif. L.R. 465 (1916)

Meiners, Roger E., Mofsky, James S., and Tollinson, Robert D., "Piercing the Veil of Limited Liability" 4 Delaware Journal of Corporation Law 351 (1979)

Milman, David, "Insolvency Act 1986 : how not to legislate" 7 Co. Law. 178 (1986)

Milman, David, "The Courts and the Companies Acts : the Judicial Contribution to Company Law" [1990] LMCLQ 402

Minnesota Law Review, Note, "Right of parent corporation to set off deposit of subsidary against parent's indebtedness to insolvent bank" 21 Minnesota L.R. 851 (1937)

Muchlinski, P.T., "The Bhopal Case : Controlling Ultrahazardous Industrial Activities undertaken by Foreign Investors" 50 M.L.R. 545 (1987)

Murphy, Robert W., "Corporate Divisions vs Subsidiaries" 34 Harv. Bus. Rev. 83 (1956)

Natale, Andrew J., "Expansion of Parent Corporate Shareholder Liability through the Good Samaritan Doctrine - a Parent Corporation's duty to provide a safe workplace for employees of its subsidiary" 57 Univ. of Cin. L.R. 717 (1988)

Nathan, R.S., "Controlling the Puppeteers : Reform of Parent-Subsidiary laws in New Zealand" 3 Canterbury L.R. 1 (1986)

Nimmer, Raymond T., "Security Interests in Bankruptcy : An Overview of Section 547 of the Code" 17 Hous. L. R. 289 (1980)

Northwestern University Law Review, "Symposium - The Close Corporation - Capitalization" 52 Northwestern Univ. L.R. 345 (1957)

Oditah, Fidelis, "Wrongful Trading" [1990] LMCLQ 205

Oditah, Fidelis, "Misfeasance proceedings against company directors" [1992] L.M.C.L.Q. 207

Oditah, Fidelis, "Assets and the Treatment of Claims in Insolvency" 108 L.Q.R. 459 (1992)

Ottolenghi, S., "From Peeping Behind the Corporate Veil, to Ignoring it Completely" 53 M.L.R. 338 (1990)

Palmer's In Company, Issue 10/93, October 20, 1993

Palmer's In Company, Issue 10/94, November 16, 1994

Parliamentary History and Review, "Joint Stock Companies", Parliamentary History and Review, 1825 Part II, 709

Penn Carolan, J., "Disregarding the Corporate Fiction in Florida: the Need for Specifics" 27 Univ. of Florida L.R. 175 (1974)

Pickering, Murray A., "The Company as a Separate Legal Entity" 31 M.L.R. 481 (1968)

Pike, Montgomery E., "Responsibility of the Parent Corporation for the Acts of its Subsidiary" 4 Ohio State L.J. 311 (1938)

Posner, Richard A., "The Right of Creditors of Affiliated Corporations" 43 U. Chic. L. Rev. 499 (1976)

Powell, John R., "Rethinking Subordinated Debt" [1993] L.M.C.L.Q. 357.

Prentice, D.D., "The Corporate Opportunity Doctrine" 37 M.L.R. 464 (1974)

Prentice, D.D., "Fraudulent Trading : Parent Company's Liability for the Debts of its Subsidiary" 103 L.Q.R. 11 (1987)

Prentice, Dan D., "Creditor's Interests and Director's Duties" 10 O.J.L.S. 265 (1990)

Priest, George L., "The Invention of Enterprise Liability : A Critical History of the Intellectual Foundations of Modern Tort Law" 14 J. Legal Stud. 461 (1985)

Radin, Max, "The Endless Problem of Corporate Personality" 32 Colum. L.R. 643 (1932)

Rajak, Harry, "Judicial Control : Corporations and the Decline of Ultra Vires" 26 Cambrian L.R. 9 (1995)

Rath Jr., Howard G., "Disregarding the Corporate Entity - Evidence - Inadequate Capitalisation" 30 S. Cal. L.R. 538 (1957)

Rembar, Charles, "Claims against Affiliated Companies in Reorganisation" 39 Colum. L.R. 907 (1939)

Ribstein, Larry E., "Limited Liability and Theories of the Corporation" 50 Maryland L.R. 80 (1991)

Rice, D.G., in "One man" Company or one man "Company" [1964] J.B.L. 36

Rider, B.A.K., "Report Shows How Insolvent Companies are Kept at the Creditors' Cost" 2 Co. Law. 274 (1981)

Rixon, F.G., "Lifting the Veil between Holding and Subsidiary Companies" 102 L.Q.R. 415 (1986)

Rothpletz, John K., "Ownership of a subsidiary as a Basis for Jurisdiction" 20 New York University Intramural Law Review 127 (1965)

Rowland, Amanda K., "Thin Capitalization in the United Kingdom" 49 Bulletin for International Fiscal Documentation (1995) 554

Rowland, Amanda K., "Impenetrable Drafting" Taxation, 6th April 1995, 9

Russell, M.W., "A Director's Duty to Creditors" 1 Cantab. L.R. 417 (1982)

Salomon, Philippe M., "Limited Limited Liability : A Definitive Judicial Standard for the Inadequate Capitalisation Problem" 47 Temple L.Q. 321 (1974)

Sargent, N.C., "Corporate Groups and the Corporate Veil in Canada : a penetrating look at Parent-Subsidiary relations in the modern Corporate Enterprise" 17 Manitoba L.J. 156 (1988)

Sargent, N.C., "Beyond the legal entity doctrine : Parent-Subsidiary relations under the West German Konzernrecht" 10 Can. Bus. L.J. 327

Sarker, Rinita, "Pyramid selling" 16 The Company Lawyer 278 (1995)

Schmitthoff, Clive M., "Multinationals in Court" [1972] J.B.L. 103

Schmitthoff, Clive M., "Salomon in the Shadow" [1976] J.B.L. 305

Schmitthoff, Clive M., "The Wholly Owned and Controlled Subsidiary" [1978] J.B.L. 218

Schmitthoff, Clive M., "Lifting the Corporate Veil" [1980] J.B.L. 156

Schmitthoff, Clive M., "Banco Ambrosiano and modern company law" [1982] J.B.L. 361

Schmitthoff, Clive M., "Multinationals and the antiquity of company law" [1984] J.B.L. 194

Schmitthoff, Clive M., "Acts ultra vires the company and acts ultra vires the directors" [1984] J.B.L. 296

Schwartz, Gary T., "Reality in the Economic Analysis of Tort Law : Does Tort Law Really Deter?" 42 U.C.L.A. L.Rev. 377 (1994)

Sealy, Leonard, "A Company Law for Tomorrow's World" 2 Co. Law. 195 (1981)

Sealy, L.S., "Directors' 'Wider' Responsibilities - Problems Conceptual, Practical and Procedural" 13 Monash Univ. L.R. 164 (1987)

Sealy, L.S., "Directors' Duties - An Unnecessary Gloss" [1988] C.L.J. 175

Semmel, Myron, "Tax Consequences of Inadequate Capitalization" 48 Colum. L.R. 202 (1948)

Shannon, H.A., "The Coming of General Limited Liability" (1931-1932) 11 Economic History 267

Shavell, Steven, "The Social versus the Private Incentive to Bring Suit in a Costly Legal System" 11 J. Legal Stud. 333 (1982)

Shavell, Steven, "Liability for Harm versus Regulation of Safety" 13 J. Legal Stud. 357 (1984)

Silk, Jules, "One Man Corporations - Scope and Limitations" 100 Univ. of Pennsylavania L.R. 853 (1952)

Slagle, Warren E., "Disregard of Corporate Entity" 6 Univ. of Kansas City L.R. 301 (1938)

Speer, Denise L., "Piercing the Corporate Veil in Maryland: An analysis and Suggested Approach" 14 U. of Baltimore L.R. 311 (1985)

Stock, Paul, "Case shows why *all* companies need a minimum paid up share capital" 1 Co. Law. 249 (1980)

Stone, Christopher, "Place of Enterprise Liability in the Control of Corporate Conduct" 90 Yale L.J. 1 (1980)

Stopford, John M., "The Origins of British-Based Multinational Manufacturing Enterprises" Business History Review, Vol. XLVIII 303 (1974)

Sykes, Charles Scott, "Corporate Control through Holding Companies" 3 Mississippi L.J. 151 (1930)

Tennery, B.J., "The Potential of the Close Corporation : A Question of Economic Viability" 14 How. L.J. 241 (1968)

Timberg, Sigmund, "Corporate Fiction - Logical, Social and International Implications" 46 Colum. L.R. 533 (1946)

University of Chicago Law Review, Note, "Set-off of Subsidiary's Claims against Parent's Indebtedness" 5 Univ. of Chic. L.R. 682 (1938)

University of Cinncinnati Law Review, Note, "Disregarding the Separate Entity" 8 Univ. of Cinn. L.R. 348 (1934)

University of Pennysylvania Law Review, Note, 78 Univ. of Pennsylvania L.R. 908-9 (1930)

University of Pittsburgh Law Review, Note, "Disregard of the Corporate Entity in an Intra-Corporate Dispute" 6 Univ. Pitt. L.R. 38 (1939)

Vagts, Detlev F., "The Multinational Enterprise : A New Challenge for Transnational Law" 83 Harv. L.R. 739 (1970)

Vanderbilt Law Review, Note, "Parent and Subsidiary - subsidiary as instrumentality of parent when used to carry on unfair trade practices" 5 Vanderbilt L.R. 637 (1952)

Vernon, Raymond, "The Role of U.S. Enterprises Abroad" 98 Daedalus 113 (1969)

Walde, Thomas W., "Parent-Subsidiary Relations in the Integrated Corporate System: A Comparison of American and German Law" 9 Journal of International Law and Economics 455 (1974)

Walker, William T., "Some Comments on the Liability of a Parent Corporation for the Torts or Contracts of its Subsidiary" 18 Ohio State Bar Association Report 198 (1945)

Watson, Catherine, "Liability of a company for the debts of an insolvent 'related company'" [1983] J.B.L. 295I.

Wedderburn, K.W., "A Corporations Ombudsman?" 23 M.L.R. 663 (1960)

Wedderburn, K.W., "Corporate Personality and Social Policy: the Problem of the Quasi-Corporation" 28 M.L.R. 62 (1965)

Wedderburn, K.W., "Multinationals and the Antiquities of Company Law" 47 M.L.R. 87 (1984)

Weis, "The Labyrinth of the Thin Corporation" 40 Taxes 568 (1962)

Westbrook, Jay Lawrence, "Theories of Parent Company Liability and the Prospects for an International Settlement" 20 Texas Int. L.J. 321 (1985)

Westbrook, Jay Lawrence, "A Comparison of Bankruptcy Reorganisation in the US with the Administration Procedure in the UK" 6 Ins. L. & P. 86 (1990)

Westerbeck, Daniel J., "The Inadequacy of Stated Capital Requirements" 40 Univ. Cin. L. Rev. 823 (1971)

Westminister Review, "Partnerships with Limited Liability" LX Westminister Review 375 (1853)

Westminister Review, "The Limited Liability Act of 1855" LXV Westminister Review 34 (1856)

Wheeler, Sally, "Swelling the Assets for Distribution in Corporate Insolvency" [1993] J.B.L. 256

Whincup, Michael, "'Inequitable Incorporation' - the Abuse of a Privilege" 2 Co. Law. 158 (1981)

Wilkins, Mira, "Modern European Economic History and the Multinationals", [1977] Journal of European Economic History 575

Williamette Law Journal, Note, "Statutory Minimum Capitalization Requirements" 5 Williamette L.J. 331 (1969)

Winfield, Percy H., "The History of Negligence in the Law of Torts" 42 L.Q.R. 184 (1926)

Wolff, Martin, "Nature of Legal Persons" 54 L.Q.R. 494 (1988).

Wormser, I. Maurice, "Piercing the Veil of the Corporate Entity" 12 Colum. L.R. 496 (1912)

Wormser, I. Maurice, "Letter to the Editor" 5 Calif. L.R. 65 (1916)

Yale Law Journal, Note, "Liability of Subsidiary Corporation for Debts Incurred by Parent" 43 Yale L.J. 472 (1934)

Yale Law Journal, Note, "Should Shareholders Be Personally Liable For the Torts of Their Corporations" 76 Yale L.J. 1190 (1967)

Yost, Robert W., "Liability of a parent corporation for debts of its subsidiary" 21 St. Louis L. Rev. 234 (1936)

## PARLIAMENTARY DEBATES, OFFICIAL REPORTS, NEWSPAPER LITERATURE AND OTHER MISCELLANEOUS DOCUMENTATION

American Law Institute, Principles of Corporate Governance and Structure : Analysis and Recommendations (Proposed Final Draft, March 31, 1992)

Auditing Practices Board, "Disclosures Relating to Corporate Governance" (Bulletin 1993/2, December 1993) Auditing Practices Board, "Disclosures Relating to Corporate Governance" (Bulletin 1993/2, December 1993).

Bellenden Ker, H., Report on the Law of Partnerships, (1837) B.P.P., Vol. XLIV no. 399

Bingham Report, Foreign and Commonwealth Office, Report on the Supply of Petroleum and Petroleum Products to Rhodesia (1978)

The Bullock Report, Report of the Committee of Inquiry on Industrial Democracy, (1977) Cmnd. 6706

Report of the Committee of Inquiry on Small Firms, Cmnd. 4811 (1971)

Cadbury Report, Report of the Committee on The Financial Aspects of Corporate Governance (1992)

Confederation of British Industry, Responsibility for the Liabilities of Group Companies - Memorandum by the Confederation of British Industry, October 1980

Consultative Committee of Accountancy Bodies, External Liabilities of Groups of Companies - Memorandum submitted in September 1979 to the Companies Division of the Department of Trade and to the Insolvency Law Review Committee of the Department of Trade on behalf of the Consultative Committee of Accountancy Bodies

Consultative Committee of Accountancy Bodies, External Liabilities of Groups of Companies - Memorandum submitted in January 1981 to the Companies Division of the Department of Trade and to the Insolvency Law Review Committee of the Department of Trade on behalf of the Consultative Committee of Accountancy Bodies

Cork Report, Report of the Review Committee, Insolvency Law and Practice, Cmnd. 8558 (1982)

Report of the Committee on the Law of Partnership of the Law Society for Promoting the Amendment of the Law" in 10 Law Review 123 (1849)

Department of Trade, The Cornhill Consolidated Group Limited (In Liquidation), Investigation under Section 165(b) of Companies Act 1948, Report by David Calcutt, QC and John Whinney, FCA, (pub. HMSO 1980)

Department of Trade, Report by R.A. Morritt, QC and P.L. Ainger, FCA into the affairs of Gilgate Holdings Ltd., Raybourne Group Ltd., Calomefern Ltd. and Desadean Properties Ltd., Investigation under Section 165(b) of the Companies Act 1948 (pub. HMSO 1981)

Department of Trade and Industry, The Single Market - Company Law Harmonisation (1989)

"Draft European Communities Directive on Procedures for Informing and Consulting Employees - A Consultative Document" published jointly by the Department of Employment and the Department of Trade and Industry (November, 1993)

*Economist*, 1st July 1854, Vol. XII pp. 698-700

*Economist*, 13th February 1858 (Vol. XVI pp. 166-167)

*Economist*, 18th December 1926 (Vol. CIII p. 1053)

*Economist*, "Does it matter where you are?", 30th July 1994 (Vol. 332, no. 7874)

*Financial Times*, "Capitalism and the saver", 6th June 1991

*Financial Times*, "Whitehall row foils freezing of Libyan assets", 6th March 1992

*Financial Times*, "DPP chief suggests safeguards for companies", 29th April 1992

*Financial Times*, "Time comes to mind corporate Ps and Qs", 8th May 1992

*Financial Times*, "Cadbury Committee draft offers mixed news for stakeholders", 2nd June 1992

*Financial Times*, "Investigators unravel more of Maxwell web", 2nd June 1992

*Financial Times*, "Probe of Maxwell links urged by MPs", 3rd June 1992

*Financial Times*, "Japanese bankruptcy debt rises", 16th June 1992

*Financial Times*, "Ethics and worse", 31st July 1992

*Financial Times*, "Dixons' £1m to aid study into ethics of business", 31st July 1992

*Financial Times*, "Tilting at Cadbury", 4th August 1992

*Financial Times*, "High cost of failure to carry out reforms", 16th March 1993

*Financial Times*, "Head of US arm of O&Y threatens to resign", 7th June 1993

*Financial Times*, "Multinationals take lead as world economic force", 21st July 1993

*Financial Times*, Letter from Mr. Alastair Bruce to the Editor, 14th September 1993

*Financial Times*, "Letters to the Editor", 14th September 1993

*Financial Times*, "VW agrees rescue package for Seat", 15th September 1993

*Financial Times*, "Keeping ahead of the game", 21st September 1993

*Financial Times*, "LUI brokers diverted millions to Liechtenstein accounts", 24th September 1993

*Financial Times*, Lex Column, 1st October 1993

*Financial Times*, "Tensions grow over threat to VW jobs", 2nd-3rd October 1993

*Financial Times*, "Towards a rescue culture", 5th October 1993

*Financial Times*, "Call to bar more unfit directors", 20th October 1993

*Financial Times*, "Euro Disney shares plunge as $930m loss is announced", 11th November 1993

*Financial Times*, "Levitt Group was 'riddled with fraud'", 12th November 1993

*Financial Times*, "Levitt trial ends with guilty plea", 24th November 1993

*Financial Times*, "Accounting tricks fool many City analysts, says study", 8th December 1993

*Financial Times*, "Maxwell ruled a fraudster", 11th-12th December 1993

*Financial Times*, "Euro Disney shares fall after threat of closure", 1st-2nd January 1994

*Financial Times*, "Disney plans $2bn rescue for theme park", 15th March 1994

*Financial Times*, "Walt Disney prepares to share the pain", 15th March 1994

*Financial Times*, "UK company law faces widespread reform", 7th April 1994

*Financial Times*, "Accounts must reveal more", 14th April 1994

*Financial Times*, "Fake Kidder trading profits date back to 1991", 20th April 1994

*Financial Times*, "EU plans rules on bankruptcy", 21st April 1994

*Financial Times*, "Lloyds' capital deployed", 22nd April 1994

*Financial Times*, "Foreign companies angered by Japanese tax increases", 16th May 1994

*Financial Times*, "The Schneider imbroglio", 6th June 1994

*Financial Times*, "Telecommunications in Business" *Financial Times* Survey, 15th June 1994

*Financial Times*, "What parents are for", 17th June 1994

*Financial Times*, "London's world role 'under threat'", 21st June 1994

*Financial Times*, "The City calls for economic strategy", 4th July 1994

*Financial Times*, "'Sword of Damocles' must be removed", Letters to the Editor, 5th July 1994

*Financial Times*, "US allows more flexible transfer pricing", 6th July 1994

*Financial Times*, "Alchemy turns to dust under DTI spell", 5th August 1994

*Financial Times*, "DTI pulls another company into pyramid selling probe", 6th-7th August 1994

*Financial Times*, "Japanese investors hit by the curse of the pyramids", 10th August 1994

*Financial Times*, "Banker named as Prudential Chief", 21st October 1994

*Financial Times*, "Make them liable", 5th January 1995

*Financial Times*, "Receivers close most Athena shops", 11th January 1995

*Financial Times*, "Suppliers left holding the baby", 17th January 1995

*Financial Times*, "City ready to combat 'usurpers'", 2nd February 1995

*Financial Times*, "Still growing after all these years", 13th March 1995

Flom, Joseph, "Tangled skein of tax adjustments", *Financial Times*, 7th May 1992

Grylls, Sir Michael, "Case for abolishing banks' floating charge", Letters to the Editor, *Financial Times*, 28th June 1994

Greene Report, Report of the Company Law Amendment Committee 1925-1926, Cmd. 2657 (1926)

Jenkins Report, Report of the Company Law Committee, Cmnd. 1749 (1962)

Law Reform Commission of Papua New Guinea, Transfer Pricing Manipulation Report no. 12, November 1981

Law Society, External Liabilities of Groups of Companies - Memorandum by the Standing Committee on Company Law of the Law Society, January 1981

Law Society, European Communities Draft Ninth Company Law Directive on the Conduct of Groups containing a Public Limited Company as a Subsidiary, Memorandum by the Society's Standing Committee on Company Law, October 1985

Law Society, The Reform of Company Law - Memorandum of the Company Law Committee of the Law Society, July 1991

Memorandum of the Committee of Merchants and Traders for the Amendment of the Law of Debtor and Creditor - Appendix to the First Report, Royal Mercantile Law Commission, (1854) B.P.P. Vol. XXVII no. 1791

Model Double Taxation Agreement on Income and on Capital, Report of the OECD Committee on Fiscal Affairs (1977)

*The Observer*, "Maxwell millions hunt speeded up", 14th June 1992

Organisation for Economic Co-operation and Development (OECD), Transfer Pricing and Multinational Enterprises (1979)

Organisation for Economic Co-operation and Development (OECD), Report on Transfer Pricing and Multinational Enterprises - Three Taxation Issues (1984)

Organisation for Economic Co-Operation and Development, Issues in International Taxation No. 1 - International Tax Avoidance and Evasion (1987)

Parliamentary Debates (Hansard) 3rd Series Vol. XXXIII, 12th May 1836

Parliamentary Debates (Hansard) 3rd Series Vol. CXIX, 17th February 1852

Parliamentary Debates (Hansard) 3rd Series Vol. CXXXIX, 26th July 1855

Parliamentary Debates (Hansard) 3rd Series Vol. CXXXIX, 7th August 1855

Parliamentary Debates (Hansard) 3rd Series Vol. CXL, 1st February 1856

Parliamentary Debates (Hansard) New Series Vol. XII, 29th March 1856

Parliamentary Debates (Hansard) 3rd Series Vol. CXLII, 26th May 1856

Parliamentary Debates (Hansard) 5th Series Vol. 979 (House of Commons) 26th February 1980, cols. 1249-1272

Parliamentary Debates, Standing Committee A, Session 1979-1980 Vol. I, 11th December 1979 cols. 715-729

Pensions Law Review Committee on Pension Law Reform chaired by Professor Roy Goode, Cm 2342 (1993)

First Report, Royal Mercantile Law Commission, (1854) B.P.P. Vol. XXVII no. 1791

Report of the Select Committee on Joint Stock Companies, (1843) B.P.P. Vol. XI no. 215

Report of the Select Committee on Investments for the Savings of the Middle and Working Classes, (1850) B.P.P., Vol. XIX no. 508

Report of the Select Committee on the Law of Partnership, (1851) B.P.P., Vol. XVIII no. 509

Royal Commission on the Distribution of Income and Wealth, Report No. 2 - Income from Companies and its Distribution, Cmnd. 6172 (1975)

*The Times*, 17th April 1854

*The Times*, 25th July 1855

UNCITRAL, Note by the Secretariat of the United Nations Commission on International Trade Law (UNCITRAL), ref. A/CN.9/378/Add.4, 23 June 1993

UNCITRAL, Note by the Secretariat of the United Nations Commission on International Trade Law (UNCITRAL), ref. A/CN.9/398, 31 May - 17 June 1994

United Nation Conference on Trade and Development (UNCTAD), World Investment Report 1993, Transnational Corporations and Integrated International Production, ref. ST/CTC/156 (1993)

University of Warwick, School of Industrial & Business Studies, Industrial Research Unit, "The Control of Industrial Relations in Large Companies : An Initial Analysis of the Second Company Level Industrial Relations Survey" (Warwick Papers in Industrial Relations, Paper no. 45, December 1993)

# Index

Adequate capitalisation rule 99, 189,
    342, 361, 366
    company, obligation of, 354
    insolvent subsidiary, 317
    instrumentality doctrine, 350
    judicial latitude, 389
    objections for reform to, 480
    subsidiary companies, 315
Affiliated companies
Agency, 23, 45, 119, 120, 121, 122,
    123, 124, 125, 150, 171, 172, 173,
    186, 203, 204, 205, 429
    liability of holding company, 429
    holding subsidiary relationship
        and, 1, 2, 32, 49, 108, 111, 116,
        120, 121, 158, 194, 203, 205,
        215, 261
    liability of, 464
    tort liability and, 202
American law
    agency, 122
    comparison with, 43
    comparisons with, 117
    corporate opportunity, 74
    corporate personality, 112
    entity principle, 42
    lifting the veil, 39, 114, 192
    limited liability, 158
    product liability, 192
    statutory reform, 149
    substantive consolidation doctrine,
        458
    tort law, 130
Assets
    commingling of, See Commingling
        of assets
    draining of, 76, 78, 200

manipulation of, 76, 114
    shuttling of, 62, 76, 99
Asset-stripping, 78
Autonomous subsidiaries, 52

Bailing out, 472 et seq.
Bankruptcy
    substantive consolidation doctrine,
        458 et seq.
Bullock Report, 19, 51, 52, 58, 146,
    241, 242
Business enterprises
    transformation into corporate
        groups, 47

Capital
    meaning
        English law, 306
        US law, 307
    minimum capital requirements
        English law, 325
        US law, 328
    structure, 38, 84, 311, 374, 375,
        389
Capital maintenance doctrine, 344
    undercapitalisation, 345
Capitalisation
    adequate, 86, 99, 189, 315, 361,
        366
    inadequate, 86
Commercial law, 146
Commercial morality, 140, 141
Commingling of assets 68, 76, 77, 83,
    200, 290, 291, 448
    transactions at an undervalue
        234
    wrongful commingling , 292

Companies
  adequate financing, 309, 321, 366
  corporate formalities, 447
  inadequate financing , 325
  thinly capitalised, 317
Company law
  harmonisation, 151
  objectives, 141
  reform, 34, 40, 150
Competition, 16, 22, 89,142, 146,
  355
Consultative Committee of
  Accountancy Bodies, 37, 38, 42,
  418, 433, 466, 467
Contract creditors, 34, 180, 185
Control of corporate groups, 49
  factual control, 51
  latent control, 49, 128, 216, 387
Co-ordinated subsidiaries, 51, 55
Cork Committee, 38, 39, 207, 217,
  243, 355, 419, 452, 463
  wrongful trading, 211, 215, 337
Corporate governance, 19, 20, 49
Corporate groups, 3, 4, 5, 7, 8, 29, 41,
  45, 47, 63, 68, 75, 92, 97, 98, 99,
  100, 101, 134, 135, 139, 141, 151,
  193, 194, 367, 468
  abusive and unfair practices,
    categories of, 33, 62, 63, 64
  benefits of, 11
  competing interests in, 25
  competition policy, 16
  composition, 3
  control of affiliates, 391
  creditor interest groups, 33
  creditor protection, 18
  directors, accountability of, 19
  disclosure of information, 19
  diversification in, 6
  domination, 58
  enterprise liability, 394

  employee representation, 19
  enforcement problems, 22
  enterprise organisation, 3, 11, 13,
    47, 290
    separate legal units, 398
  entity principle, 39
  financing, 312
  fraud, 63, 64
  group persona situation, 31, 95,
    416
  group profit maximisation, 61, 65,
    66, 67, 68, 75, 81, 82, 210, 217,
    281
  historical development of,
    in England, 1
    in the United States, 1
  holding company liability, 471
  horizontally economically
    integrated, 393
  judicial attitude to, 108
  legal problems raised by, 16, 22
  management structure, 50
  meaning, 437, 442
  medium sized and smaller
    enterprises, 3, 15
  minority shareholders and, 17
  single company enterprise, 63
  single economic enterprise, 16, 17
  substantive consolidation doctrine,
    458
  taxation, 17
  transnational, See Transnational
    corporate groups
  vertically economically integrated,
    391
Corporate insolvency, 143, 186
  objectives, 143
Corporate investors, 166-168, 173
Corporate liability
  tort, 178, 180
Corporate membership, 155, 158, 161

Corporate opportunities doctrine, 62, 68, 73, 74, 75, 83, 276, 280
  creditor protection, 288
  different approaches to, 280
  diversion of, 275
  holding company liability, 285, 287
  holding subsidiary company relationship, 280
  meaning, 74
  ownership of, 75
  transactions at an undervalue, 234
Corporate personality, 45
  evolution of notion, 104
  instrumentality test, 114
  judicial and statutory exceptions, 107
  limited liability, 30, 103
  position in American law, 112
  position in English law, 107, 108
  Roman Law, 104
Corporate responsibility, 146, 187
Corporate shareholder, 156, 158, 161, 441
Credit 176
Creditor protection, 19, 30, 141, 298
  corporate groups, 141
  corporate opportunities doctrine, 288
  duties of directors, 253
Creditor-proof devices, 62, 89, 90, 91, 325, 384
  types of, 88
Creditors
  contract, 34, 180, 185
  exploitation of, 78
  external, 18, 29, 32, 36, 38, 42, 48, 49, 62, 64, 75, 81, 200, 446
    interests of, 42, 64, 75, 446
    protection for, 34

  insolvent subsidiary creditors, 34, 134
  interest groups, 33
  involuntary, 34, 154, 182, 183, 316, 383
  outside, 35
  tort, 33, 34, 178, 191
  trade, 91, 182, 183
  types of, 33, 139
  voluntary, 182, 316, 383
Cross-border acquisitions, 23
Cross-border insolvency, 23
Cross-border mergers, 23

Debt securities, 309
Directors
  accountability of, 19, 30
  definition, 343
  disqualification, 341
  duties
    company, owed to, 240
    creditors' interests, regard to 239, 252
      subservient subsidiary, 250, 253
    fiduciary duties in group context, 240
    holding company, not owed to, 240
  holding companies, directors of, 241
  notion of director
    expansion of, 251
  personal liability 251
  subservient subsidiaries, directors of, 241
  subsidiary companies, directors of, 240
  wrongful trading, 249

Disqualification of directors, 341
  application for disqualification
    order, 341
  grounds for, 341
  inadequately financed companies,
    342
  leave to act after order made, 341
Dominated subsidiaries, 51, 53, 57,
  58, 61, 62, 65, 204, 446

Economic integration, 92, 391
  abusive, 94, 397, 399, 455
    substantive consolidation
      doctrine, 462
    voluntary/involuntary creditors,
      414
  horizontal, 93, 393
  lifting the veil and,
      English law position, 404
      US law position, 406, 411
  position in American law, 406
  position in English law, 401
  vertical, 93, 391
Employee participation, 19, 20
Employee representation, 19
Employees
  corporate governance, 19
  corporate groups, 47
  limited liability concept, 184
  subsidiary companies, 48
Enterprise liability, 394
  corporate groups, 394
Entity law, 28, 32, 103, 137
Entity principle, 23, 33, 39, 111, 112,
  290, 298
  commingling of assets, 291
  English courts' attitude to, 42
  instrumentality doctrine, 266
  judicial inroads to, 116
Equity securities, 309
Estoppel, 133
European Directives on company law

5th. draft, 19, 21
7th, 439
9th. draft, 36, 302, 449
subject matters of -
  employee participation and the
    company structure, 19
External creditors, 18, 447
  insolvent companies, 318
  inter-corporate liability towards,
    18, 29
  interests of, 42, 62, 64, 75, 446,
    463
  meaning, 18
  protection to, 34
  subservient subsidiary, 201

Financial investors, 25
Financial structure, 84
Floating charge, 450
  wrongful trading, 451
Fraud
  corporate groups, 63
Fraudulent conveyances, 221
Fraudulent trading, 205
  liability, determination of, 206
  meaning, 205
  persons liable, 208
  subservient subsidiary, 207

Group persona situation, 416
  abusive practices, 455
    remedies in English law, 423
    US law, 426
  bankruptcy, 430
  creditors, prejudice to, 418
  holding company liability, 421,
    423
  lifting of the veil, 427
  product liability, 431
Guarantees, 80, 132, 226, 227, 232,
  234
  cross-stream, 80

fraudulent transfer law, 231
holding company, 131
liability of subsidiary company, 80
subsidiary companies, 223, 228
*ultra vires* doctrine, 270
upstream, 80
US law, 227
valuation of, 228, 230

Holding companies
degrees of control, 51, 52, 126
direct liability, 134
director, qualification as
    wrongful trading, 455
disqualification order, 342
domination, 60, 67, 446
guarantees, 131, 132
immediate companies, 443
insolvent, 456
liability 30, 174
    Cork Committee, 38
    creditor distinction, 187
    instrumentality doctrine, 265
    legal implications, 41
    partly owned subsidiaries, 463
    wholly owned subsidiaries, 444
liability for debts of insolvent
    subsidiaries, 2, 29, 32
    company and insolvency law,
        effect on, 470
    creditors of holding company,
        478
    creditors of subsidiary, 302
    group persona situation, 421
    insolvent liquidation, 301
    public/private companies, 449
    reform proposals, 466
    schemes to avoid liability, 479
liability for debts of insolvent sub-
    subsidiaries, 443
liability for torts of subsidiary, 125

liability for wrongful trading, 217,
    339
liability in tort, 125, 202
liability on agency principles, 203
liquidation, 457
meaning, 437
obligation to adequately finance
    subsidiaries, 366, 385, 389
public/private companies, 449
shadow director, 339
wholly owned subsidiaries, 444
Holding subsidiary company
relationship, 1
agency, 1, 121
corporate opportunities doctrine,
    280
definition, 437
estoppel, 133
inadequately financed subsidiary,
    312
insolvent holding companies, 456
insolvent subsidiary, 456
liability for torts of subsidiary, 125
one-man company, 194
principal-servant relationship, 130,
    202
risks of abuse and unfairness, 200
US courts' approach, 117

Incorporation
abuse of, 49, 83, 94, 262
limited liability, 106
limits to, 95
nature of, 197
subsidiary company and, 86
US position, 106
Insolvency
holding companies, 456
objectives, 141
reduction of risk of, 11
reforms on, 36, 347

subsidiary companies, 456
voluntary/involuntary creditors,
    385
Instrumentality doctrine, 256, 263
    undercapitalisation and, 348
Integrated economic enterprise
    situation, 65, 190, 400, 450
Inter-corporate liability, 102
    external creditors of insolvent
        companies and, 18, 29
    protection to external creditors, 34
    separate juridical personality and
        limited liability notions, 30
International tax regulation, 71
Involuntary creditors, 34, 41, 91, 173,
    174, 177, 178, 182, 184, 185, 186,
    187, 188, 189, 190, 191, 193, 197
    inadequately financed subsidiary,
        313, 384
    subservient subsidiary, 303

Joint-venture subsidiaries, 53

Lifting the veil, 109
    abusive economic integration
        English law position, 404
        US law position, 406
    American Courts' approach, 256
    American law, 149
    holding company, 39
    identity of interest approach,
        228
    insolvency law reforms, 347
    intra-group tort liability, 407
    group persona objectives, 427
    sham/shell subsidiaries, 254
    subordination doctrine, 359
    subservient subsidiary, 255
    undercapitalisation
        English Courts' approach, 346
        US Courts' approach, 348
Limited liability

abuse of, 99
history
    American law, 106, 158
    English law, 103, 155
legal personality, 103
notion, 30
re-examination of, 154
reforms, 35
role of, 34
Loan capital
    capital maintenance doctrine,
        345
    meaning, 307

Minority shareholder
    position in subsidiary company, 17
    check on subservient practices, 294
Misrepresentation
    action on, 424
Multi-corporate organisation, 29

One-man company, 35, 113, 114, 139,
    157, 158, 194, 195, 196, 197

Par value shares, 308
Patent, 127
    infringement, 127
Phantom subsidiaries, 62
Preferences doctrine, 224, 297
    voidable preferences, 225
Product liability, 431
Public interest, 142, 143
Pyramiding
    meaning, 9
    problems, 9
Reform proposals
    adequate financing, 384
    aims of, 472
    company and insolvency law, 147
    conceptual unity, 197
    economic integration
        abusive, 413, 415

enterprise liability, 437
group persona situation, 433
holding company, qualifications
    for, 441
holding company liability
    debts of insolvent subservient
        subsidiaries, 298
    objections to, 472
    implementation of, 148
    insolvent subsidiary 383
    substantive consolidation doctrine,
        460
    undercapitalised subsidiary
        situation, 363
        adequate financing
            measurement, 365
        insolvency requirement, 364
    voluntary and involuntary
        creditors, 450
Risk capital, 368, 382, 483
    debt-equity ratio, 375
    judicial latitude, 389
    loan purpose, 378
    proportionate holding, 379
Roman Law
    notion of separate personality, 104

Shadow director, 339
    holding company, 216
    subservient subsidiary, 213
Share capital
    called-up, 307
    issued, 307
    meaning, 306
    nominal, 307
    paid up, 307
    reserve, 307
    uncalled, 307
Shareholder-guaranteed loans, 388
Shareholders
    liability on, 254

Shares
    acquisition, 1
    issued shares, 107
    preference shares, 84
    transferable, 169
Shuttling of funds, 77, 200
Single system analysis, 137
Subordination doctrine
    lifting the veil, 359
    undercapitalisation, 355
Subsidiary companies
    adequate capitalisation, 86
    agency, 121
    autonomous, 52
    co-ordinated, 55
    directors
        breach of duty, 283
        liability to creditors, 19
        liability to minority
            shareholders, 19
    dominated, 51
    employees of, 48
    financing, 388
    inadequately financed
        fraudulent trading provision,
            332
    insolvent, 15, 456
    joint-venture subsidiaries, 53
    Lifting the veil, 111
    phantom, 62
    sham/shell subsidiaries, 82, 200
        lifting the veil, 255
    subservient subsidiary, 64, 65, 68,
        69, 73, 82, 83, 188, 200, 201,
        203, 219, 234, 251, 287, 293,
        296, 450
        abusive and unfair practices,
            201, 202, 217
        directors' duties to creditors of
            subsidiary, 250
        floating charges, 450

fraudulent trading, 207
inadequate financing, 324
instrumentality doctrine, 260,
     265
misfeasance proceedings, 274
reform proposals, 299
subservient practices, 68, 200
     commingling of assets, 290
     diversion of corporate
          opportunities, 275
     extra-legal/indirect checks,
          293
     tortious conduct, 202
     voluntary/involuntary creditors,
          303
     wrongful trading, 213
thinly capitalised, 318
"through carriage" operations, 135
undercapitalised
     wrongful trading provision, 337
Substantive consolidation doctrine,
     458
abusive economic integration, 462
procedural consolidation, 459
US bankruptcy courts, 459

Tax avoidance, 24, 70
Tax planning
     corporate groups, 216
     transnational corporate groups, 12
Tax relief, 12
Taxation, 17
     debt as equity, 369
     double taxation treaties, 72, 296
     group relief provisions, 39
     OECD Model Double Taxation
          Convention, 71
     separate personality, 12
Thin capitalisation, 371
Tort
     intra-group liability, 406

joint tort liability, 127 322
liability in enterprise situation, 411
liability of holding company in,
     125, 180, 202, 244
Tort creditors, 33, 34, 178, 191
adequate financing and, 367
Tort law, 130
limited liability, 180
objectives, 181, 189, 384
product liability, 192
Trade creditors, 91, 182, 183
Transactions at an undervalue, 220,
     297
fair consideration requirement, 235
fraudulent conveyances, 221
guarantees, 226
insolvency, presumption of,
     235
intra-group transactions, 221
subservient practices, 234
subservient subsidiary, 221, 234
Transfer pricing, 68
check on subservient practices, 295
group tax planning, 216
regulation, 295
Transnational corporate groups
complexities, 22
dominance, 5, 7
foreign subsidiary of, 53
tax planning, 13

*Ultra Vires* doctrine, 266
company capacity, 269
developments of doctrine, 269
guarantees issued by subsidiary
     companies, 270
notion in US law, 272
     corporate guarantees, 273
objects and powers of company,
     266
reforms of 1989, 271

subservient practices by subsidiary, 267
transactions in excess of authority
   subservient subsidiary, 269
Undercapitalisation, 41, 46, 114, 115, 189, 194, 195, 324, 350, 363, 366, 412
   contract/tort creditors, 354
   creditor-proof plan, 353
   debt-equity ratio, 377
   insolvency law reforms, 348
   instrumentality doctrine, 349
   lifting of the veil
      English approach, 347
      US approach, 348
   subordination doctrine, 356
   US courts' approach, 360
Undercapitalised company
   duties of directors, 340
Undercapitalised subsidiary, 64, 188, 450
   acquiring holding companies, 454
   fraudulent trading provision, 336
   holding company liability
      wrongful trading, 340

remedy, 332
   wrongful trading provision, 337

Veil of incorporation, 36
Vicarious liability
   holding company, 202
   insolvent holding companies, 456
   inter-corporate, 136
Voluntary creditors, 184, 187, 191
   holding company liability, 384
   integrated economic enterprise, 190
   subservient subsidiary, 303
   undercapitalised subsidiary, 188

Wrongful trading, 31, 88, 112, 134, 148, 207, 211, 212, 213, 217, 297, 302, 355, 389, 452
   contribution order
      floating charge, 451
   directors' liability, 212
   fraudulent trading, compared with, 212
   holding company as director, 455